TAXATION LAWS

Direct and Indirect Taxes

TAXATION LAWS

Direct and Indirect Taxes

Nitin Dewan

MD PUBLICATIONS PVT LTD
NEW DELHI
www.mdppl.com

Published by :

MD Publications Pvt Ltd
"MD House", 11, Darya Ganj,
New Delhi - 110002
Phone : +91-11-45355555
E-mail : contact@mdppl.com
Website: www.mdppl.com

ISBN: 978-81-7533-452-6

Published and Printed by Mr. Pranav Gupta on behalf of **MD Publications Pvt Ltd** at Mohit Enterprises, Delhi.

PREFACE

Taxation is a governmental assessment upon property value, transactions, estates of the deceased, licenses granting a right and/or income, and duties on imports from foreign countries. It includes all contributions imposed by the government upon individuals for the service of the state. Taxes are usually divided into two main classes: direct and indirect. Generally speaking, direct taxes are those assessed against income, land or real property, and personal property, which are paid directly to the government; whereas indirect taxes are assessed against articles of consumption, such as products or services, but collected by an intermediary, such as a retailer.

It covers the rules, policies and laws that oversee the tax process, which involves charges on estates, transactions, property, income, licenses and more by the government. Taxation also includes duties on imports from foreign countries and all compulsory levies imposed by the government upon individuals for benefit of the state.

The intricate body of tax law covers payment of taxes to a minimum of four levels of government, either directly or indirectly. Indirect taxes are assessed against products and services that are meant to be consumed, but are paid to an intermediary. Direct taxes are those you pay directly to the government and are imposed against things like land or real property, personal property and income. There is a seemingly endless list of entities that create and enforce tax laws and collect tax revenues. They range from the local government level, such as cities and other municipalities, townships, districts and counties to regional, state and federal levels.

The area of tax law is exceedingly complex and in constant flux largely due to two reasons. The first is that the tax code has been used increasingly more often for objectives other than raising revenue, such as meeting political, economic and social agendas. The second reason is the manner in which the tax code is amended.

Tax law for state and local government is also contained in codes sections, regulations, administrative codes, procedures and statements issued by the respective government authorities, as well as state court decisions.

In preparation of this book, I am thankful to my family, friends and colleagues for their constant support and guidance. I am grateful to Mr Pranav Gupta, Director of MD Publications Pvt Ltd, for his encouragement in preparation of this book.

Nitin Dewan

CONTENTS

1

Additional Duties of Excise (Textiles and Textile Articles) Act, 1978

AN ACT to provide for the levy and collection of additional duties of excise on certain textiles and textile articles.

Be it enacted by Parliament in the Twenty-ninth Year of the Republic of India as follows:-

1. Short title and commencement.

(1) This Act may be called the Additional Duties of Excise (Textiles and Textile Articles) Act, 1978.

(2) It shall be deemed to have come into force on the 4th day of October, 1978.

2. Omitted.

3. Levy and collection of additional duties of excise on certain textiles and textile articles.

(1) When goods of the description mentioned in the Schedule chargeable with a duty of excise under the Central Excise Act, 1944 (1 of 1944), read with any notification for the time being in force issued by the Central Government in relation to the duty so chargeable (not being a notification providing for any exemption for giving credit with respect to, or reduction of duty of excise under the said Act on such goods equal to, any duty of excise under the said Act, or the additional duty under Section 3 of the Customs Tariff Act,1975 (51 of 1975), already paid on the raw material used in the production or manufacture of such goods), are assessed to duty, there shall be levied and collected a duty of excise equal to fifteen per cent of the total amount so chargeable on such goods.

(2) The duties of excise referred to in sub-section (1) in respect of the goods specified in the Schedule shall be in addition to the duties of excise chargeable on such goods under the Central Excise Act, 1944 (1 of 1944), or any other law for the time being in force and shall be levied for the purpose of Union and the proceeds thereof shall not be distributed among the States.

(3) The provisions of the Central Excise Act, 1944 (1 of 1944), and the rules made thereunder, including those relating to refunds and exemptions from duties, all, so far as may be, apply in relation to the levy and collection of the duties of excise leviable under this section in respect of any goods as they apply in relation the levy and collection of the duties of excise on such goods under that Act or those rules.

4. Repeal and saving.

(1) The Additional Duties of Excise (Textiles and Textile Articles) Ordinance, 1978 (4 of 1978), is hereby repealed.

(2) Notwithstanding such repeal, anything done or any action taken under the Ordinance so repealed shall be deemed to have been done or taken under the corresponding provisions of this Act.

THE SCHEDULE

[*See* Section 3]

NOTES

1. In this Schedule "Chapter" and "heading" mean a Chapter or heading in the Schedule to the Central Excise Tariff Act, 1985.
2. The rules for the interpretation of the Schedule to the Central Excise Tariff Act, 1985, and the Section and Chapter Notes of the said Schedule shall apply for the purposes of classification of goods specified in this Schedule.

Sl. No. (1)	**Description of goods** (2)
1.	Silk, that is to say, all goods falling within Chapter 50.
2.	Wool, that is to say, all goods falling within Chapter 51 other than fabrics of heading Nos. 51.10, 51.11 and 51.12
3.	Cotton, that is to say, all goods falling within Chapter 52.
4.	Man-made filaments; strip and the like of man-made textile materials, that is to say, all goods falling within Chapter 54. (Description of goods at Sl. No. 4 has been substituted vide Union Budget 2006-2007 - Finance Bill) [**OLD-** Man-made filaments, that is to say, all goods falling within Chapter 54.]
5.	Man-made staple fibres, that is to say, all goods falling within Chapter 55.
6.	Terry towelling and similar woven terry fabrics, falling within heading No. 58.02.
7.	Tulles and other net fabrics, not including woven, knitted or crocheted fabrics; lace in the piece, in strips or in motifs, other than fabrics of heading No. 60.02.
8.	Knitted or crocheted fabrics, that is to say, all goods falling within Chapter 60.
9.	Metallised yarn, falling within heading No. 56.05.
10.	Embroidery in the piece, in strips or in motifs, falling within heading No. 58.05.

❑❑❑

2

Collection of Statistics Act, 2008

Act No. 7 of 2009 (7th January, 2009)

Preamble

AN ACT to facilitate the collection of statistics on economic, demographic, social, scientific and environmental aspects, and for matters connected therewith or incidental thereto.

Be it enacted by Parliament in the Fifty-ninth Year of the Republic of India as follows:-

CHAPTER - I : PRELIMINARY

1. Short title, extent and commencement.

(1) This Act may be called the Collection of Statistics Act, 2008.

(2) It extends to the whole of India except the State of Jammu and Kashmir.

(3) It shall come into force on such date as the Central Government may, by notification in the Official Gazette, appoint.

2. Definitions. In this Act, unless the context otherwise requires,-

(a) "agency" includes a person or persons engaged by the appropriate Government, directly or by outsourcing, for collection of statistics;

(b) "appropriate Government" means-

(i) any Ministry or Department in the Central Government; or

(ii) any Ministry or Department in a State Government or Union territory Administration; or

(iii) any local government that is to say, Panchayats or Municipalities, as the case may be, in relation to the collection of statistics under a direction issued by it under Section 3;

(c) "informant" means any person, who supplies or is required to supply statistical information and includes a owner or occupier or person in-charge or his authorised representative in respect of persons or a firm registered under the Indian Partnership Act, 1932 or a co-operative society registered under any Co-operative Societies Act or a company registered under the Companies Act, 1956 or a society registered under the Societies Registration Act, 1860 or any association recognised or registered under any law for the time being in force;

(d) "information schedule" means any book, document, form, card, tape, disc or any storage media on which information required is entered or recorded or is required to be entered or recorded for statistical purposes under this Act;

(e) "prescribed" means prescribed by rules made under this Act;

(f) "sampling" means a statistical procedure by which information relating to a particular field of inquiry is derived by applying statistical techniques to information obtained in respect of a proportion of the total number of persons or units concerned relevant to the field of inquiry;

(g) "statistical survey" means a census or a survey, whereby information is collected from all the informants in the field of inquiry or from a sample thereof, by an appropriate Government under this Act or any other relevant Act, wholly or primarily for the purposes of processing and summarising by appropriate statistical procedures;

(h) "statistics" means statistics derived by collecting, classifying and using statistics, specially in or for large quantities or numbers by appropriate Government from statistical surveys, administrative and registration records, and other forms and papers, the statistical analysis of which are, whether in a published or unpublished form;

(i) "statistics officer" means any officer appointed under Section 4 for the purposes of any direction issued under Section 3 of this Act.

CHAPTER - II : COLLECTION OF STATISTICS

3. Collection of statistics. The appropriate Government may, by notification in the Official Gazette, direct that the statistics on economic, demographic, social, scientific and environmental aspects shall be collected through a statistical survey or otherwise, and thereupon the provisions of this Act shall apply in relation to those statistics:

PROVIDED that-

(a) nothing contained in this Section shall be deemed to authorise a State Government or Union territory Administration or any local government to issue any direction with respect to the collection of statistics relating to any matter falling under any of the entries specified in List I (Union List) in the Seventh Schedule to the Constitution; or

(b) where the Central Government has issued any direction under this Section for the collection of statistics relating to any matter, no State Government or Union territory Administration or any local government shall, except with the previous approval of the Central Government, issue any similar direction for so long as the collection of

such statistics by the Central Government remain to be completed; or

(c) *where a State Government or Union territory Administration or any local government has issued a direction under this Section for the collection of statistics relating to any matter, the Central Government shall not issue any similar direction for so long as the collection of such statistics by the State Government remain to be completed, except in cases where such statistics have to be collected with reference to two or more States or Union territories.*

4. Powers of appropriate Government to appoint statistics officer, etc.

(1) The appropriate Government may appoint or cause to appoint an officer to be the statistics officer for any geographical unit for the purpose of collecting any statistics directed by it.

(2) The appropriate Government may appoint any agency or persons working in such agencies to take, or aid in, or supervise the collection of the statistics within any specified geographical unit and such agencies or persons, when so appointed, shall be bound to serve accordingly.

(3) The appropriate Government may employ on contract basis any agency or company or organisation or association or person, on such terms and conditions and on such safeguards as may be prescribed, for the purpose of collecting the statistics directed by it.

(4) The appropriate Government may delegate to any statistics officer, as it thinks fit, the power of appointing agencies or persons working in such agencies or employing on contract basis any agency or company or organisation or association of persons, conferred on it by sub-sections (2) and (3) within the geographical unit for which such statistics officer is appointed.

(5) The appropriate Government may, by order specify the form, the particulars required or the interval within which, and the statistics officer to whom, the statistical information by the informants shall be furnished.

(6) The appropriate Government may, by order published in the Official Gazette, delegate to any statistics officer, as it thinks fit, any power conferred under sub-section (5) for the purpose of the collection of statistics under a direction issued by it under Section 3.

5. Power of statistics officer to call for information. The statistics officer may, for the purpose of collection of statistics on any specified subject in any geographical unit for which the said officer was appointed-

(a) serve or cause to be served on any informant a notice in writing asking him to furnish the information specified under sub-section (5) of Section 4 or cause a information schedule to be given to any informant for the purpose of its being filled up; or

(b) cause all questions relating to the subject to be asked from any informant; or

(c) seek information through tele fax or telephone or e-mail or in any other electronic mode or in a combination of different modes for different sets of information so specified.

6. Duty of informants. The informants who are asked to furnish any information under the provisions of this Act shall be bound to furnish the information so asked in the prescribed manner to the best of knowledge or belief; and in cases where only a portion of a particular class or group of persons or units is asked to furnish information because of any sampling procedure, it shall not be a defence in failure on the part of any informant to furnish that information, if so asked.

7. All agencies to assist. Every agency shall render such help and assistance and furnish such information to the statistics officer or a person or an agency authorised by him in writing, as he may require for the discharge of his functions, and shall make available for inspection and examination of such records, plans and other documents, as may be necessary.

8. Right of access to records or documents. The statistics officer or any person authorised by him in writing in this behalf shall, for the purposes of collection of any statistics under this Act, have access to any relevant record or document in the possession of any informant required to furnish any information under this Act, and may enter at any reasonable time any premises where he believes such record or document is kept and may inspect or take copies of relevant records or documents or ask any question necessary for obtaining any information required to be furnished under this Act.

CHAPTER - III : DISCLOSURE OF INFORMATION IN CERTAIN CASES AND RESTRICTIONS OF THEIR USE

9. Security of information.

(1) Any information furnished to the statistics officer or to any person or agencies authorised under this Act shall only be used for statistical purposes.

(2) No person other than a person engaged in the work of collection of statistics under this Act or preparation of statistics resultant to such collection shall be permitted to see any information schedule or any answer to a question asked, except for the purposes of a prosecution under this Act.

(3) No information contained in any information schedule and no answer to any question asked shall, except for the purposes of a prosecution under this Act, be separately published, or disclosed without suppressing the identification of informants to any agency.

(4) All statistical information published by any agency shall be arranged in such a manner so as to prevent any particulars becoming identifiable by any person (other than the informant by whom those particulars were supplied) as the particulars relating to the informant who supplied it, even through the process of elimination, unless-

(a) that informant has consented to their publication in that manner; or

(b) their publication in that manner could not reasonably have been foreseen by the concerned agency or any employee thereof.

(5) For the purposes of sub-section (4), the Central Government may make such rules or make such arrangement, as it may consider necessary.

10. Appropriate Government authorised to disclose certain information. Notwithstanding the provisions contained in Section 9 of this Act, the appropriate Government may disclose the following information, namely:-

(a) information supplied by informant in respect of which disclosure is consented to in writing by the informant or by any person authorised by the said informant;

(b) information otherwise available to the public under any Act or as a public document;

(c) information in the form of an index or list of the names and addresses of informants together with the classification, if any, allotted to them and the number of persons engaged.

11. Disclosure of information schedules for bona fide research or statistical purposes.

(1) Notwithstanding the provisions contained in Section 9 of this Act, the appropriate Government may disclose individual returns or formats or information schedules to other agency or person or institutions or universities solely for bona fide research or statistical purposes pursuant to their functions and duties.

(2) No individual return or information schedule shall be disclosed pursuant to this Section unless–

  (a) the name and address of the informant by whom the schedule or related information was supplied is deleted;

  (b) every agency or person or institutions or Universities involved in the research or statistical project makes a declaration to use the schedules disclosed to them only for bona fide research or statistical purposes; and

  (c) the appropriate Government, making such disclosure is satisfied that the security of the schedules and any information contained therein shall not be impaired.

(3) The published results of any research or statistical project shall not divulge any more information than what the agency authorised for collection of statistics could publish under this Act.

(4) Every agency or person or institutions or universities to whom any individual return or information schedule is disclosed under this Section shall comply with directions given by the agency authorised for collection of statistics making the disclosure relating to the schedules and any information contained therein.

12. Disclosure of historical documents. Notwithstanding anything contained in Section 9 of this Act, the appropriate Government may release such documents relating to information schedules, which in its opinion have attained historical importance.

13. Security of recorded information. The statistics officer or any person or agency authorised for collection of statistics shall, while copying or recording any statistical information collected pursuant to this Act from individual returns, information schedules, worksheets or any other confidential source by means of cards, tapes, discs, film or any other method, whether using encoded or plain language symbols for processing, storage or reproduction of particulars, take and cause to take such steps as are necessary to ensure that the security provisions of this Act are complied with.

14. Restrictions on use of information. Save as otherwise provided under this Act,-

(a) no information obtained pursuant to this Act and no copy of the information in the possession of any informant shall be disclosed or used as evidence in any proceedings whatsoever; and

(b) no person who has access to any information because of his official position in the collection of any statistics shall be compelled in any proceedings whatsoever to give oral testimony regarding the information or to produce any schedule, document, or record with respect to any information obtained in the course of administering this Act, except in the manner provided under this Act.

CHAPTER - IV : OFFENCES AND PENALTIES

15. Penalty for neglect or refusal to supply particulars.

(1) Whoever, fails to produce any books of accounts, vouchers, documents or other business records or whoever neglects or refuses to fill in and supply the particulars required in any information schedule or return given or sent to him or whoever neglects or refuses to answer any question or inquiry addressed to him as may be required under or for the purposes of any provision of this Act and the rules made thereunder, shall be punishable with a fine which may extend to one thousand rupees or, in the case of a company, with a fine which may extend to five thousand rupees.

(2) The conviction of a person or company for an offence shall not relieve him or it of the obligations under sub-section (1) and if after the expiry of fourteen days from the date of conviction, he or it still fails to give the required particulars or continues to neglect or refuses to fill in and supply the particulars or to answer the question or inquiry, then he or it shall be punishable with a further fine which may extend to one thousand rupees or, in the case of a company, with a fine which may extend to five thousand rupees, for each day after the first during which the failure continues.

16. Penalty for making false statement. Whoever, wilfully makes any false or misleading statement or material omission in any information schedule or return filled in or supplied, or in answer to any question asked to him under this Act or the rules made thereunder, shall be punishable with simple imprisonment for a term which may extend to six months or with a fine which may extend to one thousand rupees or, in the case of a company, with a fine which may extend to five thousand rupees or with both.

17. Penalty for mutilation or defacement of information schedule. Whoever, destroys, defaces, removes, or mutilates any information schedule, form, or other document containing particulars collected under this Act or requesting any such particulars, shall be punishable with simple imprisonment for a term which may extend to six months or with a fine which may extend to two thousand rupees or, in the case of a company with a fine which may extend to ten thousand rupees or with both.

18. Penalty for obstruction of employees. Whoever, interferes with, hinders, or obstructs any employee in the exercise of any power or duty conferred by this Act, shall be punishable with simple imprisonment for a term which may extend to six months or with a fine which may extend to two thousand rupees or, in the case of a company with a fine which may extend to ten thousand rupees or with both.

19. Penalty for other offences. Whoever-

(a) acts in contravention of or fails to comply with any provision of this Act or any requirement imposed under this Act; or

(b) wilfully deceives or attempts to deceive any statistics officer or any agency or any employee thereof, shall be punishable with simple imprisonment for a term which may extend to six months or with a fine which may extend to two thousand rupees or, in the case of a company, with a fine which may extend to ten thousand rupees or with both.

20. Penalty for failure to carry out duties and functions by employees. If any person employed in the execution of any duty or functions under this Act,-

(a) omits without lawful excuse to carry out his duty, or knowingly makes any false declaration, statement or return; or

(b) pretends performance of his duties or obtains or seeks to obtain information which he is not authorised to obtain; or

(c) fails to keep inviolate the secrecy of the information gathered or entered in the information schedules collected pursuant to this Act and, except as permitted under this Act, divulges the contents of any schedule filled in or any information furnished by any informant under this Act, shall be punishable with simple imprisonment for a term which may extend to six months or with a fine which may extend to two thousand rupees or, in the case of a company, with a fine which may extend to ten thousand rupees or with both.

21. Penalty for impersonation of employee. Whoever, not being authorised to collect statistics under the provisions of this Act, by words, conduct or demeanor pretends that he is authorised to do so, shall be punishable with simple imprisonment for a term which may extend to six months or with a fine which may extend to two thousand rupees or, in the case of a company, with a fine which may extend to ten thousand rupees or with both.

22. General penalty. Whoever, commits an offence under this Act for which no penalty is prescribed elsewhere than in this Section, shall be punishable with simple imprisonment for a term which may extend to six months or with a fine which may extend to two thousand rupees or, in the case of a company, with a fine which may extend to ten thousand rupees or with both.

23. Offences by companies.

(1) Where an offence under this Act has been committed by a company, every person who at the time the offence was committed was in charge of, and was responsible to, the company for the conduct of the business of the company, as well as the company, shall be deemed to be guilty of the offence and shall be liable to be proceeded against and punished accordingly:

PROVIDED that nothing contained in this sub-section shall render any such person liable to any punishment provided in this Act, if he proves that the offence was committed without his knowledge or that he had exercised all due diligence to prevent the commission of such offence.

(2) Notwithstanding anything contained in sub-section (1), where an offence under this Act has been committed by a company and it is proved that the offence has been committed with the consent or connivance of, or is attributable to, any neglect on the part of any director, manager, secretary or other officer of the company, such director, manager, secretary or other officer shall also be deemed to be guilty of the offence and shall be liable to be proceeded against and punished accordingly.

EXPLANATION: For the purpose of this Section-

(a) "company" means any body corporate and includes a firm or other association of individuals; and

(b) "Director", in relation to a firm, means a partner in the firm may be, the statistics officer, and no court inferior to that of a Metropolitan Magistrate or a Judicial Magistrate of the first class shall try any offence punishable under this Act.

24. Cognizance of offences. No court shall take cognizance of any offence under this Act except on a complaint made by the appropriate Government or an officer authorised in this behalf by such appropriate Government or, as the case may be, the statistics officer, and no court inferior to that of a Metropolitan Magistrate or a Judicial Magistrate of the first class shall try any offence punishable under this Act.

25. Sanction for prosecution for offence. No prosecution for an offence committed by any informant shall be instituted except by or with the sanction of the statistics officer, and no prosecution for an offence committed by persons other than informants shall be instituted except by or with the consent of the appropriate Government.

26. Power of court to try cases summarily. Notwithstanding anything contained in the Code of Criminal Procedure, 1973, all offences under this Act shall be tried in a summary way by a Judicial Magistrate of the first class or by a Metropolitan Magistrate and the provisions of Sections 262 to 265 (both inclusive) of the said Code shall, as far as may be, apply to such trial:

PROVIDED that when in the course of, a summary trial under this Section it appears to the Magistrate that the nature of the case is such that it is, for any reason, undesirable to try the case summarily, the Magistrate shall after hearing the parties, record an order to that effect and thereafter recall any witness who may have been examined and proceed to hear or rehear the case in the manner provided by the said Code.

CHAPTER - V : POWER IN RESPECT OF CORE STATISTICS

27. Power in respect of core statistics. Without prejudice to the provisions contained in this Act, the Central Government may, by notification in the Official Gazette, declare from time to time any subject for the collection of statistics of national importance as 'core statistics' and make such arrangement, as it may consider necessary, for regulating the collection and dissemination of statistics on the subject so declared.

CHAPTER - VI : MISCELLANEOUS

28. Power to give directions. The Central Government may give directions to any State Government or Union territory Administration or to any local government that is to say Panchayats or Municipalities, as to the carrying into execution of this Act in the State or Union territory or Panchayats or Municipalities, as the case may be.

29. Public servants. Any statistics officer and any person authorised for the collection of statistics or preparation of official statistics under the provisions of this Act shall be deemed to be a public servant within the meaning of Section 21 of the Indian Penal Code, 1860.

30. Bar of jurisdiction. No civil court shall have jurisdiction to entertain any suit or proceeding in respect of any matter which the appropriate Government or the statistics officer or the agency is empowered by or under this Act to determine, and no injunction shall be granted by any court or other authority in respect of any action taken or to be taken in pursuance of any power conferred by or under this Act.

31. Protection of action taken in good faith. No suit or other legal proceedings shall lie against the appropriate Government or agency or any statistics officer or other officers or employees in respect of anything which is in good faith done or intended to be done in pursuance of this Act or the rules or directions issued there under.

32. Overriding effect. The provisions of this Act shall have effect notwithstanding anything inconsistent therewith contained in any other law for the time being in force except in relation to the conduct of human population census as per the directions, if any, issued under the Census Act, 1948.

33. Power to make rules.

(1) The Central Government may, by notification in the Official Gazette, make rules for carrying out the provisions of this Act.

(2) In particular, and without prejudice to the generality of the foregoing power, the Central Government may make rules under this Section for all or any of the following matters, namely:-

   (a) principles for coordinating as effectively as possible to achieve the objectives of Section 3 including nomination and registration of statistics officers by the Central Government and also to avoid unnecessary duplication in the collection of statistics;

   (b) the terms, conditions and safeguards under which any person or agency or company or organisation or association may be engaged by the appropriate Government for the purpose of collection of statistics under sub-section (3) of Section 4;

   (c) principles for prescribing the form and manner in which the information may be required to be furnished;

(d) principles for prescribing the manner in which the right of access to documents and the right of entry conferred by Section 8 may be exercised; and

(e) any other matter which is to be or may be prescribed under this Act.

(3) Every rule made by the Central Government under this Act shall be laid, as soon as may be after it is made, before each House of Parliament, while it is in session, for a total period of thirty days which may be comprised in one session or in two or more successive sessions, and if, before the expiry of the session immediately following the session or the successive sessions aforesaid, both Houses agree in making any modification in the rule or both Houses agree that the rule should not be made, the rule shall thereafter have effect only in such modified form or be of no effect, as the case may be; so, however, that any such modification or annulment shall be without prejudice to the validity of anything previously done under that rule.

34. Repeal and savings.

(1) The Collection of Statistics Act, 1953 is hereby repealed.

(2) Notwithstanding such repeal, anything done or any action taken under the said Act shall be deemed to have been done or taken under the corresponding provisions of this Act.

(3) All rules made under the said Act shall continue to be in force and operate till new rules are made under this Act.

❑❑❑

3

Customs Act, 1962

[Act No. 52 of Year 1962 Dated 13th December, 1962]

AN ACT to consolidate and amend the law relating to customs.

Be it enacted by Parliament in the Thirteenth Year of the Republic of India as follows: -

CHAPTER - I : PRELIMINARY

1. Short title, extent and commencement.

(1) This Act may be called the Customs Act, 1962.

[1][(2) It extends to the whole of India.]

(3) It shall come into force on such date[2] as the Central Government may, by notification in the Official Gazette, appoint.

2. Definitions. In this Act, unless the context otherwise requires-

[3][(1) "**adjudicating authority**" means any authority competent to pass any order or decision under this Act, but does not include the Board, Commissioner (Appeals) or Appellate Tribunal;

(1A) "**aircraft**" has the same meaning as in the Aircraft Act, 1934 (22 of 1934);

(1B) "**Appellate Tribunal**" means the Customs, Excise and Gold (Control) Appellate Tribunal constituted under Section 129;

(2) "**assessment**" includes provisional assessment, reassessment and any order of assessment in which the duty assessed is nil;

(3) "**baggage**" includes unaccompanied baggage but does not include motor vehicles;

(4) "**bill of entry**" means a bill of entry referred to in Section 46;

(5) "**bill of export**" means a bill of export referred to in Section 50;

(6) "**Board**" means the Central Board of Excise and Customs constituted under the Central Boards of Revenue Act, 1963 (54 of 1963);

(7) "**coastal goods**" means goods, other than imported goods, transported in a vessel from one port in India to another;

[5][(7A) "**Commissioner (Appeals)** "means a person appointed to be a Commissioner of Customs (Appeals) under sub-section (1) of Section 4;

(8) "**Commissioner of Customs**", except for the purposes of Chapter XV, includes an Additional Commissioner of Customs;

(9) "**conveyance**" includes a vessel, an aircraft and a vehicle;

(10) "**customs airport**" means any airport appointed under clause (a) of Section 7 to be a customs airport;

(11) "**customs area**" means the area of a customs station and includes any area in which imported goods or export goods are ordinarily kept before clearance by customs authorities;

(12) "**customs port**" means any port appointed under clause (a) of Section 7 to be a customs port [6][and includes a place appointed under clause (aa) of that Section to be an inland container depot;

(13) "**customs station**" means any customs port, customs airport or land customs station;

(14) "**dutiable goods**" means any goods which are chargeable to duty and on which duty has not been paid;

(15) "**duty**" means a duty of customs leviable under this Act;

(16) "**entry**" in relation to goods means an entry made in a bill of entry, shipping bill or bill of export and includes in the case of goods imported or to be exported by post, the entry referred to in Section 82 or the entry made under the regulations made under Section 84;

(17) "**examination**", in relation to any goods, includes measurement and weighment thereof;

(18) "**export**", with its grammatical variations and cognate expressions, means taking out of India to a place outside India;

(19) "**export goods**".means any goods which are to be taken out of India to a place outside India;

(20) "**exporter**", in relation to any goods at any time between their entry for export and the time when they are exported, includes any owner or any person holding himself out to be the exporter;

(21) "**foreign-going vessel or aircraft**" means any vessel or aircraft for the time being engaged in the carriage of goods or passengers between any port or airport in India and any port or airport outside India, whether touching any intermediate port or airport in India or not, and includes-

(i) any naval vessel of a foreign government taking part in any naval exercises;

(ii) any vessel engaged in fishing or any other operations outside the territorial waters of India;

(iii) any vessel or aircraft proceeding to a place outside India for any purpose whatsoever;

[7][(21A) "**Fund**" means the Consumer Welfare Fund established under Section 12C of the Central Excises and Salt Act, 1944 (1 of 1944);

(22) "**goods**" includes-

(a) vessels, aircraft and vehicles;

(b) stores;

(c) baggage;

(d) currency and negotiable instruments; and

(e) any other kind of movable property;

(23) "**import**", with its grammatical variations and cognate expressions, means bringing into India from a place outside India;

(24) "**import manifest**" or "**import report**" means the manifest or report required to be delivered under Section 30;

(25) "**imported goods**" means any goods brought into India from a place outside India but does not include goods which have been cleared for home consumption;

(26) "**importer**", in relation to any goods at any time between their importation and the time when they are cleared for home consumption, includes any owner or any person holding himself out to be the importer;

(27) "**India**" includes the territorial waters of India;

(28) "**Indian customs waters** " means the [8][waters extending into the sea up to the limit of contiguous zone of India under Section 5 of the Territorial Waters, Continental Shelf, Exclusive Economic Zone and other Maritime Zones Act, 1976 (80 of 1976)] and includes any bay, gulf, harbour, creek, or tidal river;

(29) "**land customs station**" means any place appointed under clause (b) of Section 7 to be a land customs station;

(30) "**market price**", in relation to any goods, means the wholesale price of the goods in the ordinary course of trade in India;

(31) "**person-in-charge**" means-

(a) in relation to a vessel, the master of the vessel;

(b) in relation to an aircraft, the commander or pilot-in-charge of the aircraft;

(c) in relation to a railway train, the conductor, guard or other person having the chief direction of the train;

(d) in relation to any other conveyance, the driver or other person-in-charge of the conveyance;

(32) "**prescribed**" means prescribed by regulations made under this Act;

(33) "**prohibited goods**" means any goods the import or export of which is subject to any prohibition under this Act or any other law for the time being in force but

does not include any such goods in respect of which the conditions subject to which the goods are permitted to be imported or exnorted have been complied with;

(34) "**proper officer**", in relation to any functions to be performed under this Act, means the officer of customs who is assigned those functions by the Board or the [5][Commissioner of Customs;]

(35) "**regulations**" means the regulations made by the Board under any provision of this Act;

(36) "**rules**" means the rules made by the Central Government under any provision of this Act;

(37) "**shipping bill**" means a shipping bill referred to in Section 50;

(38) "**stores**" means goods for use in a vessel or aircraft and includes fuel and spare parts and other articles of equipment, whether or not for immediate fitting;

(39) "**smuggling**", in relation to any goods, means any act or omission which will render such goods liable to confiscation under Section 111 or Section 113;

(40) "**tariff value**", in relation to any goods, means the tariff value fixed in respect thereof under sub-section (2) of Section 14;

(41) "**value**", means relation to any goods, means the value thereof determined in accordance with the provisions of sub-section (1) of Section 14;

(42) "**vehicle**" means conveyance of any kind used on land and includes a railway vehicle;

(43) "**warehouse**" means a public warehouse appointed under Section 57 or private ware house licensed under Section 58;

(44) "**warehoused goods**" means goods deposited in a warehouse;

(45) "**warehousing station** "means a place declared as a warehousing station under Section 9.

CHAPTER - II : OFFICERS OF CUSTOMS

[5][3.Classes of officers of customs. There shall be the following classes of officers of customs, namely:

(a) Chief Commissioners of Customs;

(b) Commissioner of Customs;

(c) Commissioners of Customs (Appeals);

[9][(cc) Joint Commissioners of Customs;]

(d) Deputy Commissioners of Customs;

(e) Assistant Commissioners of Customs; and

(f) such other class of officers of customs as may be appointed for the purposes of this Act.]

[5][4. Appointment of officers of customs.

(1) The Central Government may appoint such persons as it thinks fit to be officers of customs.

(2) Without prejudice to the provisions of sub-section (1), the Central Government may authorise the Board, a Commissioner of Customs or a Deputy or Assistant Commissioner of Customs [9][or Deputy Commissioner of Customs] to appoint officers of customs below the rank of Assistant Commissioner of Customs 9[or Deputy Commissioner of Customs.

5. Powers of officers of customs.

(1) Subject to such conditions and limitations as the Board may impose, an officer of customs may exercise the powers and discharge the duties conferred or imposed on him under this Act.

(2) An officer of customs may exercise the powers and discharge the duties conferred or imposed under this Act on any other officer of customs who is subordinate to him.

(3) Notwithstanding anything contained in this Section [5][a Commissioner (Appeals)] shall not exercise the powers and discharge the duties conferred or imposed on an officer of customs other than those specified in Chapter XV and Section 108.

6. Entrustment of functions of Board and Customs Officers on certain other officers. The Central Government may, by notification in the Official Gazette, entrust either conditionally or unconditionally to any officer of the Central or the State Government or a local authority any functions of the Board or any officer of customs under this Act.

CHAPTER - III : APPOINTMENT OF CUSTOMS PORTS, AIRPORTS, WAREHOUSING STATIONS, ETC.

7. Appointment of customs ports, airports, etc. The Central Government may, by notification in the Official Gazette, appoint-

(a) the ports and airports which alone shall be customs ports or customs airports for the unloading of imported goods and the loading of export goods or any class of such goods;

[6][(aa) the places which alone shall be inland container depots for the unloading of imported goods and the loading of export goods or any class of such goods;]

(b) the places which alone shall be land customs stations for the clearance of goods imported or to be exported by land or inland water or any class of such goods.

(c) the routes by which alone goods or any class of goods specified in the notification may pass by land or inland waters into or out of India, or to or from any land customs station from or to any land frontier;

(d) the ports which alone shall be coastal ports for the carrying on of trade in coastal goods or any class of such goods with all or any specified ports in India.

8. Power to approve landing places and specify limits of customs area. The Commissioner of Customs] may-

(a) approve proper places in any customs port or customs airport or coastal port for the unloading and loading of goods or for any class of goods;

(b) specify the limits of any customs area.

9. Power to declare places to be warehousing stations. The Board may, by notification in the Official Gazette, declare places to be warehousing stations at which alone public warehouses may be appointed and private warehouses may be licensed.

10. Appointment of boarding stations. The [5][Commissioner of Customs] may, by notification in the Official Gazette, appoint, in or near any customs port, a boarding station for the purpose of boarding of, or disembarkation from, vessels by officers of customs.

CHAPTER - IV : PROHIBITIONS ON IMPORTATION AND EXPORTATION OF GOODS

11. Power to prohibit importation or exportation of goods.

(1) If the Central Government is satisfied that it is necessary so to do for any of the purposes specified in sub-section (2), it may, by notification in the Official Gazette, prohibit either absolutely or subject to such conditions (to be fulfilled before or after clearance) as may be specified in the notification, the import or export of goods of any specified description.

(2) The purposes referred to in sub-section (1) are the following:-

(a) the maintenance of the security of India;

(b) the maintenance of public order and standards of decency or morality;

(c) the prevention of smuggling;

(d) the prevention of shortage of goods of any description;

(e) the conservation of foreign exchange and the safeguarding of balance of payments;

(f) the prevention of injury to the economy of the country by the uncontrolled import or export of gold or silver;

(g) the prevention of surplus of any agricultural product or the product of fisheries;

(h) the maintenance of standards for the classification, grading or marketing of goods in international trade;

(i) the establishment of any industry;

(j) the prevention of serious injury to domestic production of goods of any description;

(k) the protection of human, animal or plant life or health;

(l) the protection of national treasures of artistic, historic or archaeological value;

(m) the conservation of exhaustible natural resources;

(n) the protection of patents, trademarks and copyrights;

(o) the prevention of deceptive practices;

(p) the carrying on of foreign trade in any goods by the State, or by a corporation owned or controlled by the State to the exclusion, complete or partial, of citizens of India.

(q) the fulfilment of obligations under the Charter of the United Nations for the maintenance of international peace and security;

(r) the implementation of any treaty, agreement or convention with any country;

(s) the compliance of imported goods with any laws which are applicable to similar goods produced or manufactured in India;

(t) the prevention of dissemination of documents containing any matter which is likely to prejudicially affect friendly relations with any foreign State or is derogatory to national prestige;

(u) the prevention of the contravention of any law for the time being in force; and

(v) any other purpose conducive to the interests of the general public.

CHAPTER - IVA : DETECTION OF ILLEGALLY IMPORTED GOODS AND PREVENTION OF THE DISPOSAL THEREOF

11A. Definitions. In this Chapter, unless the context otherwise requires,-

(a) "**illegal import**" means the import of any goods in contravention of the provisions of this Act or any other law for the time being in force;

(b) "**intimated place**" means a place intimated under sub-section (1), sub-section (2) or sub-section (3), as the case may be, of Section 11C;

(c) "**notified date**", in relation to goods of any description, means the date on which the notification in relation to such goods is issued under Section 11B;

(d) "**notified goods**" means goods specified in the notification issued under Section 11B.

11B. Power of Central Government to notify goods. If, having regard to the magnitude of the illegal import of goods of any class or description, the Central Government is satisfied that it is expedient in the public interest to take special measures for the purpose of checking the illegal import, circulation or disposal of such goods, or facilitating the detection of such goods, it may, by notification in the Official Gazette, specify goods of such class or description.

11C. Persons possessing notified goods to intimate the place of storage, etc.

(1) Every person who owns, possesses or controls, on the notified date, any notified goods, shall, within seven days from that date, delivery to the proper officer a statement (in such form, in such manner and containing such particulars as may be specified by rules made in this behalf) in relation to the notified goods owned, possessed or controlled by him and the place where such goods are kept or stored.

(2) Every person who acquires, after the notified date, any notified goods, shall, before making such acquisition, deliver to the proper officer an intimation containing the particulars of the place where such goods are proposed to be kept or stored after such acquisition and shall, immediately on such acquisition,

deliver to the proper officer a statement (in such form, in such manner and containing such particulars as may be specified by the rules made in this behalf, in relation to the notified goods acquired by him:

PROVIDED that a person who has delivered a statement, whether under sub-section (1) or sub-section (2) in relation to any notified goods, owned, possessed, controlled or acquired by him, shall not be required to deliver any further statement in relation to any notified goods acquired by him, after the date of delivery of the said statement, so long as the notified goods so acquired are kept or stored at the intimated place.

(3) If any person intends to shift any notified goods to any place other than the intimated place, he shall, before taking out such goods from the intimated place, deliver to the proper officer an intimation containing the particulars of the place to which such goods are proposed to be shifted.

(4) No person shall, after the expiry of seven days from the notified date, keep or store any notified goods at any place other than the intimated place.

(5) Where any notified goods have been sold or transferred, such goods shall not be taken from one place to another unless they are accompanied by the voucher referred to in Section 11F.

(6) No notified goods (other than those which have been sold or transferred) shall be taken from one place to another unless they are accompanied by a transport voucher (in such form and containing such particulars as may be specified by the rules made in this behalf) prepared by the persons owning, possessing or controlling such goods.

11D. Precautions to be taken by persons acquiring notified goods. No person shall acquire (except by gift or succession, from any other individual in India), after the notified date, any notified goods-

(i) unless such goods are accompanied by,-

(a) the voucher referred to in Section 11F or the memorandum referred to in sub-section (2) of Section 11G, as the case may be; or

(b) in the case of a person who has himself imported any goods, any evidence showing clearance of such goods by the customs authorities; and

(ii) unless he has taken, before acquiring such goods from a person other than a dealer having a fixed place of business, such reasonable steps as may be specified by rules made in this behalf, to ensure that the goods so acquired by him are not goods which have been illegally imported.

11E. Persons possessing notified goods to maintain accounts

(1) Every person who, on or after the notified date, owns, possesses, controls or acquires any notified goods shall maintain (in such form and in such manner as may be specified by rules made in this behalf) a true and complete account of such goods and shall, as often as he acquires or parts with any notified goods, made an entry in the said account in relation to such acquisition or parting with, and shall also state therein the particulars of the persons from whom such goods have been acquired or in whose favour such goods have been

parted with, as the case may be, and such account shall be kept, along with the goods, at the place of storage of the notified goods to which such accounts relate:

PROVIDED that it shall not be necessary to maintain separately accounts in the form and manner specified by the rules made in this behalf in the case of a person who is already maintaining accounts which contain the particulars specified by the said rules.

(2) Every person who owns, possesses or controls any notified goods and who uses any such goods for the manufacture of any other goods, shall maintain (in such form, in such manner and containing such particulars as may be specified by rules made in this behalf) a true and complete account of the notified goods so used by him and shall keep such account at the intimated place.

11F. Sale, etc, of notified goods to be evidenced by vouchers. On and from the notified date, no person shall sell or otherwise transfer any notified goods, unless every transaction in relation to the sale or transfer of such goods is evidenced by a voucher in such form and containing such particulars as may be specified by rules made in this behalf.

11G. Sections 11C, 11E, and 11F not to apply to goods in personal use.

(1) Nothing in Sections 11C, 11E and 11F shall apply to any notified goods which are -

(a) in personal use of the person by whom they are owned, possessed or controlled, or

(b) kept in the residential premises of a person for his personal use.

(2) If any person, who is in possession of any notified goods referred to in sub-section (1), sells, or otherwise transfers for a valuable consideration, any such goods, he shall issue to the purchaser or transferee, as the case may be, a memorandum containing such particulars as may be specified by the rules made in this behalf and no such goods shall be taken from one place to another unless they are accompanied by the said memorandum.

CHAPTER - IVB : PREVENTION OR DETECTION OF ILLEGAL EXPORT OF GOODS

11H. Definitions. In this Chapter, unless the context otherwise requires,-

(a) **"illegal export"** means the export of any goods in contravention of the provisions of this Act or any other law for the time being in force;

(b) **"intimated place"** means a place intimated under sub-section (1), sub-section (2) or sub-section (3), as the case may be, of Section 11J;

(c) **"specified area"** includes the Indian customs waters, and such inland area, not exceeding one hundred kilometres in width from any coast or other border of India, as the Central Government may, having regard to the vulnerability of that area to smuggling, by notification in the Official Gazette, specify in this behalf:

PROVIDED that where a part of any village, town or city falls within a specified area, the whole of such village, town or city shall, notwithstanding that the whole of it is not within one hundred kilometres from any coast or other border of India, be deemed to be included in such specified area;

(d) "**specified date**", in relation to specified goods, means the date on which any notification is issued under Section 11-I in relation to those goods in any specified area;

(e) "**specified goods**" means goods of any description specified in the notification issued under Section 11-I in relation to a specified area.

11-I. Power of Central Government to specify goods. If, having regard to the magnitude of the illegal export of goods of any class or description, the Central Government is satisfied that it is expedient in the public interest to take special measures for the purpose of checking the illegal export or facilitating the detection of goods which are likely to be illegally exported, it may, by notification in the Official Gazette, specify goods of such class or description.

11J. Persons possessing specified goods to intimate the place of storage, etc.

(1) Every person who owns, possesses or controls, on the specified date, any specified goods, the market price of which exceeds fifteen thousand rupees shall, within seven days from that date, deliver to the proper officer an intimation containing the particulars of the place where such goods are kept or stored within the specified area.

(2) Every person who acquires (within the specified area), after the specified date, any specified goods,-

(i) the market price of which, or

(ii) the market price of which together with the market price of any specified goods of the same class or description, if any, owned, possessed or controlled by him on the date of such acquisition, exceeds fifteen thousand rupees shall, before making such acquisition, deliver to the proper officer an intimation containing the particulars of the place where such goods are proposed to be kept or stored after such acquisition:

PROVIDED that a person who has delivered an intimation, whether under sub-section (1) or sub-section (2), in relation to any specified goods, owned, possessed, controlled or acquired by him, shall not be required to deliver any further intimation so long as the specified goods are kept or stored at the intimated place.

(3) If any person intends to shift any specified goods to which sub-section (1) or sub-section (2) applies, to any place other than the intimated place, he shall, before taking out such goods from the intimated place, deliver to the proper officer an intimation containing the particulars of the place to which such goods are proposed to be shifted.

(4) No person shall, after the expiry of seven days from the specified date, keep or store any specified goods to which sub-section (1) or sub-section (2) applies, at any place other than the intimated place.

11K. Transport of specified goods to be covered by vouchers.

(1) No specified goods shall be transported from, into or within any specified area or loaded on any animal or conveyance in such area, unless they are

accompanied by a transport voucher (in such form and containing such particulars as may be specified by rules made in this behalf) prepared by the person owning, possessing, controlling or selling such goods:

PROVIDED that no transport voucher shall be necessary for the transport, within a village, town or city, of any specified goods the market price of which, on the date of transport, does not exceed one thousand rupees.

(2) Notwithstanding anything contained in sub-section (1), where the Central Government, after considering the nature of any specified goods, the time, mode, route and the market price of the goods intended to be transported, the purpose of the transportation and the vulnerability of the specified area with regard to the illegal export of such goods, is satisfied that it is expedient in the public interest so to do, it may-

(i) by notification in the Official Gazette, specify goods of such class or description and of a market price exceeding such sum as that government may notify; and different sums in relation to the specified goods of the same class or description, or different classes or descriptions, may be notified for the same specified area or for different specified areas, and

(ii) direct that no person shall transport any goods so specified unless the transport voucher in relation to them has been countersigned by the proper officer.

11L. Persons possessing specified goods to maintain accounts.

(1) Every person who, on or after the specified date, owns, possesses or controls, within a specified area, any specified goods of a market price exceeding fifteen thousand rupees, shall maintain (in such form and in such manner as may be specified by rules made in this behalf) a true and complete account of such goods and shall, as often as he acquires or parts with any specified goods, make an entry in the said account in relation to such acquisition or parting with, and shall also state therein the particulars of the person from whom such goods have been acquired or in whose favour such goods have been parted with, as the case may be, and such account shall be kept, along with the goods, at the place of storage of the specified goods to which such accounts relate:

PROVIDED that it shall not be necessary to maintain separately accounts in the form and manner specified by rules made in this behalf in the case of a person who is already maintaining accounts which contain the particulars specified by the said rules.

(2) Every person who owns, possesses or controls any specified goods to which the provisions of sub-section (1) apply, and who uses any such goods for the manufacture of any other goods, shall maintain (in such form, in such manner and containing such particulars as may be specified by rules made in this behalf) a true and complete account of the specified goods so used by him and shall keep such account at the intimated place.

(3) If at any time, on a verification made by a proper officer, it is found that any specified goods owned, possessed or controlled by a person are less in quantity

than the stock of such goods as shown, at the time of such verification, in the account referred to in sub-section (1), read with the accounts referred to in sub-section (2), it shall be presumed, unless the contrary is proved, that such goods, to the extent that they are less than the stock shown in the said accounts, have been illegally exported and that the person owning, possessing or controlling such goods has been concerned with the illegal export thereof.

11M. Steps to be taken by persons selling or transferring any specified goods. Except where he receives payment by cheque drawn by the purchaser, every person who sells or otherwise transfers within any specified area, any specified goods, shall obtain, on his copy of the sale or transfer voucher, the signature and full postal address of the person to whom such a sale or transfer is made and shall also take such other reasonable steps as may be specified by rules made in this behalf to satisfy himself as to the identity of the purchaser or the transferee, as the case may be, and if after an inquiry made by a proper officer, it is found that the purchaser or the transferee, as the case may be, is not either readily traceable or is a fictitious person, it shall be presumed, unless the contrary is proved, that such goods have been illegally exported and the person who had sold or otherwise transferred such goods had been concerned in such illegal export:

PROVIDED that nothing in this Section shall apply to petty sales of any specified goods if the aggregate market price obtained by such petty sales, made in the course of a day, does not exceed two thousand and five hundred rupees.

EXPLANATION: In this Section "petty sale" means a sale at a price which does not exceed one thousand rupees.

CHAPTER - IVC : POWER TO EXEMPT FROM THE PROVISIONS OF CHAPTERS IV-A AND IV-B

1IN. Power to exempt. If the Central Government is satisfied that it is necessary in the public interest so to do, it may, by notification in the Official Gazette, exempt generally, either absolutely or subject to such conditions as may be specified in the notification, goods of any class or description from all or any of the provisions of Chapter IVA or Chapter IVB.1

CHAPTER - V : LEVY OF, AND EXEMPTION FROM, CUSTOMS DUTIES

12. Dutiable goods.

(1) Except as otherwise provided in this Act or any other law for the time being in force, duties of customs shall be levied at such rates as may be specified under [11][the Customs Tariff Act, 1975 (51 of 1975),] or any other law for the time being in force, on goods imported into, or exported from, India.

[12][(2) The provisions of sub-section (1) shall apply in respect of all goods belonging to government as they apply in respect of goods not belonging to Government.]

13. Duty on pilfered goods. If any imported goods are pilfered after the unloading thereof and before the proper officer has made an order for clearance for home consumption or deposit in a warehouse, the importer shall not be liable to pay the duty leviable on such goods except where such goods are restored to the importer after pilferage.

14. Valuation of goods for purposes of assessment.

(1) For the purposes of [11][the Customs Tariff Act, 1975 (51 of 1975)], or any other law for the time being in force where-under a duty of customs is chargeable on any goods by reference to their value, the value of such goods shall be deemed to be[13] the price at which such or like goods are ordinarily sold, or offered for sale, for delivery at the time and place of importation or exportation, as the case may be, in the course of international trade, where the seller and the buyer have no interest in the business of each other and the price is the sole consideration for the sale or offer for sale:

[14][PROVIDED that such price shall be calculated with reference to the rate of exchange as in force on the date on which a bill of entry is presented under Section 46, or a shipping bill or bill of export, as the case may be, is presented under Section 50;]

[15][(1A) Subject to the provisions of sub-section (1), the price referred to in that sub-section in respect of imported goods shall be determined in accordance with the rules made in this behalf.]

(2) Notwithstanding anything contained in sub-section (1) [14][or sub-section (1A)], if the Central Government is satisfied that it is necessary or expedient so to do it may, by notification in the Official Gazette, fix tariff values for any class of imported goods or export goods, having regard to the trend of value of such or like goods, and where any such tariff values are fixed, the duty shall be chargeable with reference to such tariff value.

(3) For the purposes of this Section-

- (a) "rate of exchange" means the rate of exchange-
  - (i) determined by the Central Government, or
  - (ii) ascertained in such manner as the Central Government may direct, for the conversion of Indian currency into foreign currency or foreign currency into Indian currency.
- (b) "foreign currency" and "Indian currency" have the meanings respectively assigned to them in the Foreign Exchange Regulation Act, 1973 (46 of 1973)

15. Date for determination of rate of duty and tariff valuation of imported goods.

(1) [16][The rate of duty [17][***]] and tariff valuation, if any, applicable to any imported goods, shall be the rate and valuation in force -

- (a) in the case of goods entered for home consumption under Section 46, on the date on which a bill of entry in respect of such goods is presented under that Section;
- (b) in the case of goods cleared from a warehouse under Section 68, on the date on which the goods are actually removed from the warehouse;
- (c) in the case of any other goods, on the date of payment of duty:

[18]*[PROVIDED that if a bill of entry has been presented before the date of entry inwards of the vessel or the arrival of the aircraft by which the goods are imported, the bill of entry shall be deemed to have been presented or the date of such entry inwards or the arrival, as the case may be.]*

(2) The provisions of this Section shall not apply to baggage and goods imported by post.

16. Date for determination of rate of duty and tariff valuation of export goods.

[19][(1) The rate of duty and tariff valuation, if any, applicable to any export goods, shall be the rate and valuation in force-

(a) in the case of goods entered for export under Section 50, on the date on which the proper officer makes an order permitting clearance and loading of the goods for exportation under Section 51;

(b) in the case of any other goods,on the date of payment of duty.]

(2) The provisions of this Section shall not apply to baggage and goods exported by post.

17. Assessment of duty

(1) After an importer has entered any imported goods under Section 46, or an exporter has entered any export goods under Section 50 the imported goods or the export goods, as the case may be, or such part thereof as may be necessary may, without undue delay, be examined and tested by the proper officer.

(2) After such examination and testing, the duty, if any, leviable on such goods shall, save as otherwise provided in Section 85, be assessed.

(3) For the purpose of assessing duty under sub-section (2), the proper officer may require the importer, exporter or any other person to produce any contract, broker's note, policy insurance, catalogue or other document whereby the duty leviable on the imported goods or export goods, as the case may be, can be ascertained, and to furnish any information required for such ascertainment which it is in his power to produce or furnish, and thereupon the importer, exporter or such other person shall produce such document and furnish such information.

(4) Notwithstanding anything in this Section, imported goods or export goods may, prior to the examination or testing thereof, be permitted by the proper officer to be assessed to duty on the basis of the statements made in the entry relating thereto and the documents produced and the information furnished under sub-section (3); but if it is found subsequently on examination or testing of the goods or otherwise that any statement in such entry or document or any information so furnished is not true in respect of any matter relevant to the assessment, the goods may, without prejudice to any other action which may be taken under this Act, be re-assessed to duty.

18. Provisional assessment of duty.

(1) Notwithstanding anything contained in this Act but without prejudice to the provisions contained in Section 46-

(a) where the proper officer is satisfied that an importer or exporter is unable to produce any document or furnish .any information necessary for the assessment of duty on the imported goods or the export goods, as tie case may be; or

(b) where the proper officer deems it necessary to subject any imported goods or export goods to any chemical or other test for the purpose of assessment of duty thereon ; or

(c) where the importer or the exporter has produced all the necessary documents and furnished full information for the assessment of duty but the proper officer deems it necessary to make further enquiry for assessing the duty, the proper officer may direct that the duty leviable on such goods may, pending the production of such documents or furnishing of such information or completion of such test or enquiry, be assessed provisionally if the importer or the exporter, as the case may be, furnishes such security as the proper officer deems fit for the payment of the deficiency, if any, between the duty finally assessed and the duty provisionally assessed.

(2) When the duty leviable on such goods is assessed finally in accordance with the provisions of this Act, then-

(a) in the case of goods cleared for home consumption or exportation, the amount paid shall be adjusted against the duty finally assessed and if the amount so paid falls short of, or is in excess of 20[the duty finally assessed,] the importer or the exporter of the goods shall pay the deficiency or be entitled to a refund, as the case may be;

(b) in the case of warehoused goods, the proper officer may, where the duty finally assessed is in excess of the duty provisionally assessed, require the importer to execute a bond, binding himself in a sum equal to twice the amount of the excess duty.

19. Determination of duty where goods consist of articles liable to different rates of duty. Except as otherwise provided in any law for the time being in force, where goods consist of a set of articles, duty shall be calculated as follows:-

(a) articles to duty with reference to quantity shall be chargeable to that duty;

(b) articles liable to duty with reference to value shall, if they are liable to duty at the same rate, be chargeable to duty at that rate, and if they are liable to duty at different rates, be chargeable to duty at the highest of such rates;

(c) articles not liable to duty shall be chargea'ole to duty at the rate at which articles liable to duty with reference to value are liable under clause (b):

PROVIDED that-

(a) accessories of, and spare parts or maintenance and repairing implements for any article which satisfies the conditions specified in the rules made in this behalf shall be chargeable at the same rate of duty as that article;

(b) *if the importer produces evidence to the satisfaction of the proper officer regarding the value of any of the articles liable to different rates of duty, such article shall be chargeable to duty separately at the rate applicable to it.*

[21][20. Re-importation of goods produced or manufactured in India.

(1) If goods are imported into India after exportation therefrom, such goods shall be liable to duty and be subject to all the conditions and restrictions, if any, to which goods of the like kind and value are liable or subject, on the importation thereof.]

21. Goods derelict, wreck, etc. All goods, derelict, jetsam, flotsam, and wreck brought or coming into India shall be dealt with as if they were imported into India, unless it be shown to the satisfaction of the proper officer that they are entitled to be admitted duty-free under this Act.

[22][* * *]

22. Abatement of duty on damaged or deteriorated goods.

(1) Where it is shown to the satisfaction of the [23][Assistant Commissioner of Customs or Deputy Commissioner of Customs]-

(a) that any imported goods had been damaged or had deteriorated at any time before or during the unloading of the goods in India; or

(b) that any imported goods, other than warehoused goods, had been damaged at any time after the unloading thereof in India but before their examination under Section 17, on account of any accident not due to any wilful act, negligence or default of the importer, his employee or agent; or

(c) that any warehoused goods had been damaged at any time before clearance for home consumption on account of any accident not due to any wilful act, negligence or default of the owner, his employee or agent, such goods shall be chargeable to duty in accordance with the provisions of sub-section (2).

(2) The duty to be charged on the goods referred to in sub-section (1) shall bear the same proportion to the duty chargeable on the goods before the damage or deterioration which the value of the damaged or deteriorated goods bears to the value of the goods before the damage or deterioration.

(3) For the purposes of this Section, the value of damaged or deteriorated goods may be ascertained by either of the following methods at the option of the owner:-

(a) the value of such goods may be ascertained by the proper officer, or

(b) such goods may be sold by the proper officer by public auction or by tender, or with the consent of the owner in any other manner, and the gross sale proceeds shall be deemed to be the value of such goods.

23. Remission of duty on lost, destroyed or abandoned goods.

(1) [24][Without prejudice to the provisions of Section 13, Where it is shown] to the satisfaction of the [23][Assistant Commissioner of Customs or Deputy

Commissioner of Customs] that any imported goods have been lost [6][(otherwise than as a result of pilferage)] or destroyed, at any time before clearance for home consumption, the [23][Assistant Commissioner of Custom or Deputy Commissioner of Customs] shall remit the duty on such goods.

[21][(2) The owner of any imported goods may at any time before an order for clearance of the goods for home consumption under Section 47 or an order for permitting the deposit of goods in a warehouse under Section 60 has been made, relinquish his title to the goods and thereupon he shall not be liable to pay the duty thereon.]

24. Power to make rules for denaturing or mutilation of goods. The Central Government may make rules for permitting at the request of the owner the denaturing or mutilation of imported goods which are ordinarily used for more than one purpose so as to render them unfit for one or more of such purposes; and where any goods are so denatured or mutilated they shall be chargeable to duty at such rate as would be applicable if the goods had been imported in the denatured or mutilated form.

25. Power to grant exemption from duty.

(1) If the Central Government is satisfied that it is necessary in the public interest so to do, it may, by notification in the Official Gazette, exempt generally either absolutely or subject to such conditions (to be fulfilled before or after clearance) as may be specified in the notification goods of any specified description from the whole or any part of duty of customs leviable thereon.

[25][(2) If the Central Government is satisfied that it is necessary in the public interest so to do, it may, by special order in each case, exempt from payment of duty, for reasons to be stated in such order, any goods, of strategic or secret nature, or for charitable purpose, on which duty is leviable.]

[6][(3) An exemption under sub-section (1) or sub-section (2) in respect of any goods from any part of the duty of customs leviable thereon (the duty of customs, leviable thereon being hereinafter referred to as the statutory duty) may be granted by providing for the levy of a duty on such goods at a rate expressed in a form or method different from the form or method in which the statutory duty is leviable and any exemption granted in relation to any goods in the manner provided in this sub-section shall have effect subject to the condition that the duty of customs chargeable on such goods shall in no case exceed the statutory duty.

EXPLANATION: "Form or method", in relation to a rate of duty of customs, means the basis, namely, valuation, weight, number, length, area, volume or other measure with reference to which the duty is leviable.]

[26][(4) Every notification issued under sub-section (1) shall-

(a) unless otherwise provided, come into force on the date of its issue by the Central Government for publication in the Official Gazette;

(b) also be published and offered for sale on the date of its issue by the Directorate of Publicity and Public Relations of the Board, New Delhi.

(5) Notwithstanding anything contained in sub-section (4), where a notification comes into force on a date later than the date of its issue, the same shall be published and offered for sale by the said Directorate of Publicity and Public Relations on a date on or before the date on which the said notification comes into force.]

26. Refund of export duty in certain cases. Where on the exportation of any goods any duty has been paid, such duty shall be refunded to the person by whom or on whose behalf it was paid, if-

(a) the goods are returned to such person otherwise than by way of re-sale;

(b) the goods are re-imported within one year from the date of exportation; and

(c) an application for refund of such duty is made before the expiry of six months from the date on which the proper officer makes an order for the clearance of the goods.

[27][**27. Claim for refund of duty.**

(1) Any person claiming refund of any [28][duty and interest, if any, paid on such duty]-

(a) paid by him in pursuance of an order of assessment; or

(b) borne by him, may make an application for refund of such [28][duty and interest, if any, paid on such duty] to the [23][Assistant Commissioner of Customs or Deputy Commissioner of Customs]-

(a) in the case of any import made by any individual for his personal use or by government or by any educational, research or charitable institution or hospital, before the expiry of one year;

(b) in any other case, before the expiry of six months from the date of payment of duty and interest, if any, paid on such duty, in such form and manner as may be specified in the regulations made in this behalf and the application shall be accompanied by such documentary or other evidence (including the documents referred to in Section 28 (C) as the applicant may furnish to establish that the amount of [28][duty and interest, if any, paid on such duty] in relation to which such refund is claimed was collected from, or paid by, him and the incidence of such [28][duty and interest, if any, paid on such duty] had not been passed on by him to any other person:

PROVIDED that where an application for refund has been made before the commencement of the Central Excise and Customs Laws (Amendment) Act, 1991, such applications shall be deemed to have been made under this sub-section and the same shall be dealt with in accordance with the provisions of sub-section (2).

PROVIDED FURTHER that the limitation of one year or six months, as the case may be, shall not apply where any duty and interest, if any, paid on such duty has been paid under protest.

PROVIDED ALSO that in the case of goods which are exempt from payment of duty by a special order issued under sub-section (2) of Section 25, the limitation of one year or six months, as the case may be, shall be computed from the date of issue of such order.

EXPLANATION I: For the purposes of this sub-section, the date of payment of [28][duty and interest, if any, paid on such duty], in relation to a person, other than the importer, shall be construed as "the date of purchase of goods" by such person.

EXPLANATION II : Where any duty is paid provisionally under Section 18, the limitation of one year or six months, as the case may be, shall be computed from the date of adjustment of duty after the final assessment thereof.

(2) If, on receipt of any such application, the [23][Assistant Commissioner of Customs or Deputy Commissioner of Customs] is satisfied that the whole or any part of the[29][duty and interest, if any, paid on such duty] paid by the applicant is refundable, he may make an order accordingly and the amount so determined shall be credited to the Fund:

PROVIDED that the amount of [28][duty and interest, if any, paid on such duty] as determined by the Assistant Commissioner of Customs or Deputy Commissioner of Customs under the foregoing provisions of this sub-section shall, instead of being credited to the Fund, be paid to the applicant, if such amount is relatable to-

(a) the [28][duty and interest, if any, paid on such duty] paid by the importer, if he had not passed on the incidence of such duty and interest, if any, paid on such duty to any other person;

(b) the duty and interest, if any, paid on such duty] on imports made by an individual for his personal use;

(c) the duty and interest, if any, paid on such duty borne by the buyer, if he had not passed on the incidence of such duty and interest, if any, paid on such duty to any other person;

(d) the export duty as specified in Section 26;

(e) drawback of duty payable under Sections 74 and 75;

(f) the duty and interest, if any, paid on such duty borne by any other such class of applicants as the Central Government may, by notification in the Official Gazette specify:

PROVIDED FURTHER that no notification under clause (f) of the first proviso shall be issued unless in the opinion of the Central Government the incidence of [28][duty and interest, if any, paid on such duty] has not been passed on by the persons concerned to any other person.

(3) Notwithstanding anything to the contrary contained in any judgement, decree, order or direction of the Appellate Tribunal or any court or in any other provision of this Act or the regulations made thereunder or any other law for the time being in force, no refund shall be made except as provided in sub-section (2).

(4) Every notification under clause (f) of the first proviso to sub-section (2) shall be laid before each House of Parliament, if it is sitting, as soon as may be after the issue of the notification, and, if it is not sitting, within seven days of its re-assembly, and the Central Government shall seek the approval of Parliament to the notification by a resolution moved within a period of fifteen days beginning with the day on which the notification is so laid before the House of the People and if Parliament makes any modification in the notification, or directs that the notification should cease to have effect, the notification shall thereafter have effect only in such modified form or be of no effect, as the case may be, but without prejudice to the validity of anything previously done thereunder.

(5) For the removal of doubts, it is hereby declared that any notification issued under clause (f) of the first proviso to sub-section (2), including any such notification approved or modified under sub-section (4), may be rescinded by the Central Government at any time by notification in the Official Gazette.

CHAPTER - V : LEVY OF, AND EXEMPTION FROM, CUSTOMS DUTIES

27A. Interest on delayed refunds. If any duty ordered to be refunded under sub-section (2) of Section 27 to an applicant is not refunded with three months from the date of receipt of application under sub-section (1) of that Section, there shall be paid to that applicant interest at such rate, not below ten per cent and not exceeding thirty per cent per annum as is for the time being fixed by the Board, on such duty from the date immediately after the expiry of three months from the date of receipt of such application till the date of refund of such duty:

PROVIDED that where any duty, ordered to be refunded under sub-section (2) of Section 27 in respect of an application under sub-section (1) of that Section made before the date on which the Finance Bill, 1995 receives the assent of the President, is not refunded within three months from such date, there shall be paid to the applicant interest under this Section from the date immediately after three months from such date, till the date of refund of such duty.

EXPLANATION: Where any order of refund is made by the Commissioner (Appeals), Appellate Tribunal or any court against an order of the Assistant Commissioner of Customs or Deputy Commissioner of Customs] under sub-section (2) of Section 27, the order passed by the Commissioner (Appeals), Appellate Tribunal or, as the case may be, by the court shall be deemed to be an order passed under that sub-section for the purposes of this Section.

28. Notice for payment of duties, interest, etc.

(1) When any duty has not been levied or has been short-levied or erroneously refunded, or when any interest payable has not been paid, part paid or erroneously refunded, the proper officer may,-

(a) in the case of any import made by any individual for his personal use or by government or by any educational, research or charitable institution or hospital, within one year;

(b) in any other case, within six months, from the relevant date, serve notice on the person chargeable with the duty or interest which has not been levied or charged or which has been short-levied or part paid or to whom the refund has erroneously been made, requiring him to show cause why he should not pay the amount specified in the notice:

PROVIDED that where any duty has been levied or has been short-levied or the interest has not been charged or has been part paid or the duty or interest has been erroneously refunded by reason of collusion or any willful mis-statement or suppression of facts by the importer or the exporter or the agent or employee of the importer or exporter, the provisions of this sub-section shall have effect as if for the words "one year" and "six months", the words "five years" were substituted.

EXPLANATION: Where the service of the notice is stayed by an order of a court, the period of such stay shall be excluded in computing the aforesaid period of one year or six months or five years, as the case may be.

(2) The proper officer, after considering the representation, if any, made by the person on whom notice is served under sub-section (1), shall determine the amount of duty or interest due from such person (not being in excess of the amount specified in the notice) and thereupon such person shall pay the amount so determined.

(3) For the purposes of sub-section (1), the expression "relevant date" means,-

(a) in a case where duty is not levied, or interest is not charged, the date on which the proper officer makes an order for the clearance of the goods;

(b) in a case where duty is provisionally assessed under Section 18, the date of adjustment of duty after the final assessment thereof;

(c) in a case where duty or interest has been erroneously refunded, the date of refund;

(d) in any other case, the date of payment of duty or interest.]

28A. Power not to recover duties not levied or short-levied as a result of general practice.

(1) Notwithstanding anything contained in this Act, if the Central Government is satisfied-

(a) that a practice was, or is, generally prevalent regarding levy of duty (including non-levy thereof) on any goods imported into, or exported from India; and

(b) that such goods were, or are, liable-

(i) to duty, in cases where according to the said practice the duty was not, or is not being, levied, or

(ii) to a higher amount of duty than what was, or is being, levied, according to the said practice, then the Central Government may, by notification in the Official Gazette, direct that the whole of the duty payable on such goods, or, as the case may be, the duty in excess of that payable on such goods, but for the said practice, shall not be required to be paid in respect of the goods on which the duty was not, or is not being, levied, or was, or is being, short-levied, in accordance with the said practice.

(2) Where any notification under sub-section (1) in respect of any goods has been issued, the whole of the duty paid on such goods, or, as the case may be, the duty paid in excess of that payable on such goods, which would not have been paid if the said notification had been in force, shall be dealt with in accordance with the provisions of sub-section (2) of Section 27:

PROVIDED that the person claiming the refund of such duty, or, as the case may be, excess duty, makes an application in this behalf to the [23][Assistant Commissioner of Customs or Deputy Commissioner of Custom], in the form referred to in sub-section (1) of Section 27, before the expiry of six months from the date of issue of the said notification.

28AA. Interest on delayed payment of duty. Subject to the provisions contained in Section 28AB, where a person, chargeable with the duty determined under sub-section (2) of Section 28, fails to pay such duty within three month from the date of such determination, he shall pay, in addition to the duty, interest at such rate not below ten per cent and not exceeding thirty per cent per annum, as is for the time being fixed by the Board, on such duty from the date immediately after the expiry of the said period of three months till the date of payment of such duty:

PROVIDED that where a person chargeable with duty determined under sub-section (2) of Section 28 before the date on which the Finance Bill, 1995 received the assent of the President, fails to pay such duty within three months from such date, then, such person shall be liable to pay interest under this Section from the date immediately after three months from such date, till the date of payment of such duty.

EXPLANATION 1: Where the duty determined to be payable is reduced by the Commissioner (Appeals), Appellate Tribunal or, as the case may be, the court, the date of such determination shall be the date on which an amount of duty is first determined to be payable.

EXPLANATION 2: Where the duty determined to be payable is increased or further increased by the Commissioner (Appeals), Appellate Tribunal or, as the case may be, the court, the date of such determination shall be,-

(a) for the amount of duty first determined to be payable, the date on which the duty is so determined;

(b) for the amount of increased duty, the date of order by which the increased amount of duty is first determined to be payable;

(c) for the amount of further increase of duty, the date of order on which the duty is so further increased.

28AB. Interest on delayed payment of duty in special cases.

(1) Where any duty has not been levied or has been short levied or erroneously refunded by reason of collusion or any wilful mis-statement or suppression of facts, the person who is liable to pay the duty as determined under sub-section (2) of Section 28, shall, in addition to the duty, be liable to pay interest at such rate not below ten per cent and not exceeding thirty per cent per annum, as is for the time being fixed by the Board, from the first day of the month succeeding the month in which the duty ought to have been paid under this Act, but for

the provisions contained in sub-section (2) of Section 28, till the date of payment of such duty.

(2) For the removal of doubts, it is hereby declared that the provisions of sub-section (1) shall not apply to cases where the duty became payable before the date on which the Finance (No. 2) Act, 1996 receives the assent of President.

EXPLANATION 1: Where the duty determined to be payable is reduced by the Commissioner (Appeals), the Appellate Tribunal or, as the case may be, the court, the interest shall be payable on such reduced amount of duty.

EXPLANATION 2: Where the duty determined to be payable is increased or further increased by the Commissioner (Appeals), the Appellate Tribunal or, as the case may be, the court, the interest shall be payable on such increased or further increased amount of duty.

28B. Duties collected from the buyer to be deposited with the Central Government.

(1) Notwithstanding anything to the contrary contained in any order or direction of the Appellate Tribunal or any court or in any other provision of this Act or the regulations made thereunder, every person who has collected any amount from the buyer of any goods in any manner as representing duty of customs, shall forthwith pay the amount so collected to the credit of the Central Government.

(2) The amount paid to the credit of the Central Government under sub-section (1) shall be adjusted against the duty payable by the person on finalisation of assessment and where any surplus is left after such adjustment, the amount of such surplus shall either be credited to the Fund or, as the case may be, refunded to the person who has borne the incidence of such amount, in accordance with the provisions of Section 27 and the application under that Section in such cases shall be made before the expiry of six months from the date of the public notice to be issued by the [23][Assistant Commissioner of Customs or Deputy Commissioner of Customs].

CHAPTER - V-A : INDICATING AMOUNT OF DUTY IN PRICE OF GOODS, ETC., FOR PURPOSE OF REFUND

28C. Price of goods to indicate the amount of duty paid thereon. Notwithstanding anything contained in this Act or any other law for the time being in force, every person who is liable to pay duty on any goods shall, at the time of clearance of the goods, prominently indicate in all the documents relating to assessment, sales invoice, and other like documents, the amount of such duty which will form part of the price at which such goods are to be sold.

28D. Presumption that incidence of duty has been passed on to the buyer. Every person who has paid the duty on any goods under this Act shall, unless the contrary is proved by him, be deemed to have passed on the full incidence of such duty to the buyer of such goods.

28E. Definitions. In this Chapter, unless the context otherwise requires,-

(a) "**activity**" means import or export;

(b) "**advance ruling**" means the determination, by the authority, of a question of law or fact specified in the application regarding the liability to pay duty in relation to an activity which is proposed to be undertaken, by the applicant;

(c) "**applicant**" means a non-resident setting up a joint venture in India in collaboration with a non-resident or resident, or a resident setting up a joint venture in India in collaboration with a non-resident, making application;

(d) "**application**" means an application made to the authority under sub-section (1) of Section 28H;

(e) "**authority**" means the authority for advance ruling constituted under Section 28F;

(f) "**chairperson**" means the Chairperson of the authority;

(g) "**member**" means a member of the authority and includes the chairperson; and

(h) "**non-resident**" shall have the meaning assigned to it in clause (30) of Section 2 of the Income Tax Act, 1961 (43 of 1961).

28F. Authority for advance rulings.

(1) The Central Government shall, by notification in the Official Gazette, constitute an authority for giving advance rulings, to be called as "the authority for advance rulings".

(2) The authority shall consist of the following members appointed by the Central Government, namely:-

  (a) a Chairperson, who is a retired Judge of the Supreme Court;

  (b) an officer of the Indian Customs and Central Excise Service who is qualified to be a member of the Board;

  (c) an officer of the Indian legal service who is, or is qualified, to be, an Additional Secretary to the Government of India.

(3) The salaries and allowances payable to, and the terms and conditions of service of, the members shall be such as the Central Government may by rules determine.

(4) The Central Government shall provide the authority with such officers and staff as may be necessary for the efficient exercise of the powers of the authority under this Act.

(5) The office of the authority shall be located in Delhi.

28G. Vacancies, etc. not to invalidate proceedings. No proceeding before, or pronouncement of advance ruling by, the authority under this Chapter shall be questioned or shall be invalid on the ground merely of the existence of any vacancy or defect in the constitution of the authority.

28H. Application for advance ruling.

(1) An applicant desirous of obtaining an advance ruling under this Chapter may make an application in such form and in such manner as may be prescribed, stating the question on which the advance ruling is sought.

(2) The question on which the advance ruling is sought shall be in respect of,-

(a) classification of goods under the Customs Tariff Act, 1975;

(b) applicability of a notification issued under sub-section (1) of Section 25, having a bearing on the rate of duty;

(c) the principles to be adopted for the purposes of determination of value of the goods under the provisions of this Act.

(3) The application shall be made in quadruplicate and be accompanied by a fee of two thousand five hundred rupees.

(4) An applicant may withdraw his application within thirty days from the date of the application.

28-I. Procedure on receipt of application.

(1) On receipt of an application, the authority shall cause a copy thereof to be forwarded to the Commissioner of Customs and, if necessary, call upon him to furnish the relevant records:

PROVIDED that where any records have been called for by the authority in any case, such records shall, as soon as possible, be returned to the Commissioner of Customs.

(2) The authority may, after examining the application and the records called for, by order, either allow or reject the application:

PROVIDED that the authority shall not allow the application except in the case of a resident applicant where the question raised in the application is,-

(a) already pending in the applicant's case before any officer of customs, the Appellate Tribunal or any court;

(b) the same as in a matter already decided by the Appellate Tribunal or any court:

PROVIDED FURTHER that no application shall be rejected under this sub-section unless an opportunity has been given to the applicant of being heard:

PROVIDED ALSO that where the application is rejected, reasons for such rejection shall be given in the order.

(3) A copy of every order made under sub-section (2) shall be sent to the applicant and to the Commissioner of Customs.

(4) Where an application is allowed under sub-section (2), the authority shall, after examining such further material as may be placed before it by the applicant or obtained by the authority, pronounce its advance ruling on the question specified in the application.

(5) One a request received from the applicant, the authority shall, before pronouncing its advance ruling, provide an opportunity to the applicant of being heard, either in person or through a duly authorised representative.

EXPLANATION: For the purposes of this sub-section, "authorised representative" shall have the meaning assigned to it in sub-section (2) of Section 146A.

(6) The authority shall pronounce its advance ruling in writing within ninety days of the receipt of application.

(7) A copy of the advance ruling pronounced by the authority, duly signed by the members and certified in the prescribed manner shall be sent to the applicant and to the Commissioner of Customs, as soon as may be, after such pronouncement.

28J. Applicability of advance ruling.

(1) The advance ruling pronounced by the authority under Section 28-I shall be binding only,-

(a) on the applicant who had sought it;

(b) in respect of any matter referred to in sub-section (2) of Section 28H;

(c) on the Commissioner of Customs, and the customs authorities subordinate to him, in respect of the applicant.

(2) The advance ruling referred to in sub-section (1) shall be binding as aforesaid unless there is a change in law or facts on the basis of which the advance ruling has been pronounced.

28K. Advance ruling to be void in certain circumstances.

(1) Where the authority finds, on a representation made to it by the Commissioner of Customs or otherwise, that an advance ruling pronounced by it under sub-section (6) of Section 28-I has been obtained by the applicant by fraud or misrepresentation of facts, it may, by order, declare such ruling to be void *ab initio* and thereupon all the provisions of this Act shall apply (after excluding the period beginning with the date of such advance ruling and ending with the date of order under this sub-section) to the applicant as if such advance ruling had never been made.

(2) A copy of the order made under sub-section (1) shall be sent to the applicant and the Commissioner of Customs.

28L. Powers of authority.

(1) The authority shall, for the purpose of exercising its powers regarding discovery and inspection, enforcing the attendance of any person and examining him on oath, issuing commissions and compelling production of books of account and other records, have all the powers of a civil court under the Code of Civil Procedure, 1908 (5 of 1908).

(2) The authority shall be deemed to be a civil court for the purposes of Section 195, but not for the purposes of Chapter XXVI of the Code of Criminal Procedure, 1973 (2 of 1974), and every proceeding before the authority shall be deemed to be a judicial proceeding within the meaning of Sections 193 and 228, and for the purpose of Section 196, of the Indian Penal Code (45 of 1860).

28M. Procedure of authority. The authority shall, subject to the provisions of this Chapter, have power to regulate its own procedure in all matters arising out of the exercise of its powers under this Act.]

CHAPTER - VI : PROVISIONS RELATING TO CONVEYANCES CARRYING IMPORTED OR EXPORTED GOODS

29. Arrival of vessels and aircraft in India.

(1) The person-in-charge of a vessel or an aircraft entering India from any place outside India shall not cause or permit the vessel or aircraft to call or land-

(a) for the first time after arrival in India; or

(b) at any time while it is carrying passengers or cargo brought in that vessel or aircraft; at any place other than a customs port or a customs airport, as the case may be.

(2) The provisions of sub-section (1) shall not apply in relation to any vessel or aircraft which is compelled by accident, stress of weather or other unavoidable cause to call or land at a place other than a customs port or customs airport but the person-in-charge of any such vessel or aircraft-

(a) shall immediately report the arrival of the vessel or the landing of the aircraft to the nearest customs officer or the officer-in-charge of a police station and shall on demand produce to him the log book belonging to the vessel or the aircraft;

(b) shall not without the consent of any such officer permit any goods carried in the vessel or the aircraft to be unloaded from, or any of the crew or passengers to depart from the vicinity of, the vessel or the aircraft; and

(c) shall comply with any directions given by any such officer with respect to any such goods, and no passenger or member of the crew shall, without the consent of any such officer, leave the immediate vicinity of the vessel or the aircraft:

PROVIDED that nothing in this Section shall prohibit the departure of any crew or passengers from the vicinity of, or the removal of goods from, the vessel or aircraft where the departure or removal is necessary for reasons of health, safety or the preservation of life or property.

30. Delivery of import manifest or import report.

(1) The person in charge of a vessel or an aircraft carrying imported goods shall, deliver to the proper officer, an import manifest, and in the case of a vehicle, an import report, within twenty-four hours after arrival thereof at a customs station in the case of a vessel and twelve hours after arrival in the case of an aircraft or a vehicle, in the prescribed form:

PROVIDED that,-

(a) in the case of a vessel or an aircraft, any such manifest may be delivered to the proper officer before the arrival of the vessel or aircraft;

(b) if the proper officer is satisfied that there was sufficient cause for not delivering the import manifest or import report or any part thereof within the time specified in this sub-section, he may accept it at any time thereafter.

(2) The person delivering the import manifest or import report shall at the foot thereof make and subscribe to a declaration as to the truth of its contents.

(3) If the proper officer is satisfied that the import manifest or import report is in any way incorrect or incomplete, and that there was no fraudulent intention, he may permit it to be amended or supplemented.

31. Imported goods not to be unloaded from vessel until entry inwards granted.

(1) The master of a vessel shall not permit the unloading of any imported goods until an order has been given by the proper officer granting entry inwards to such vessel.

(2) No order under sub-section (1) shall be given until an import manifest has been delivered or the proper officer is satisfied that there was sufficient cause for not delivering it.

(3) Nothing in this Section shall apply to the unloading of baggage accompanying a passenger or a member of the crew, mail bags, animals, perishable goods and hazardous goods.

32. Imported goods not to be unloaded unless mentioned in import manifest or import report. No imported goods required to be mentioned under the regulations in an import manifest or import report shall, except with the permission of the proper officer, be unloaded at any customs station unless they are specified in such manifest or report for being unloaded at that customs station.

33. Unloading and loading of goods at approved places only. Except with the permission of the proper officer, no imported goods shall be unloaded, and no export goods shall be loaded, at any place other than a place approved under clause (a) of Section 8 for the unloading or loading of such goods.

34. Goods not to be unloaded or loaded except under supervision of customs officer. Imported goods shall not be unloaded from, and export goods shall not be loaded on, any conveyance except under the supervision of the proper officer:

PROVIDED that the Board may, by notification in the Official Gazette, give general permission and the proper officer may in any particular case give special permission, for any goods or class of goods to be unloaded or loaded without the supervision of the proper officer.

35. Restrictions on goods being water-borne. No imported goods shall be water-borne for being landed from any vessel, and no export goods which are not accompanied by a shipping bill, shall be water-borne for being shipped, unless the goods are accompanied by a boat-note in the prescribed form:

PROVIDED that the Board may, by notification in the Official Gazette, give general permission, and the proper officer may in any particular case give special permission, for any goods or any class of goods to be water-borne without being accompanied by a boat-note.

36. Restrictions on unloading and loading of goods on holidays, etc. No imported goods shall be unloaded from, and no export goods shall be loaded on, any conveyance on any Sunday or on any holiday observed by the Customs Department or on any other day after the working hours, except after giving the prescribed notice and on payment of the prescribed fees, if any:

PROVIDED that no fees shall be levied for the unloading and loading of baggage accompanying a passenger or a member of the crew, and mail bags.

37. Power to board conveyances. The proper officer may, at any time, board any conveyance carrying imported goods or export goods and may remain on such conveyance for such period as he considers necessary.

38. Power to require production of documents and ask questions. For the purposes of carrying out the provisions of this Act, the proper officer may require the person-in-charge of any conveyance or animal carrying imported goods or export goods to produce any document and to answer any questions and thereupon such person shall produce such documents and answer such questions.

39. Export goods not to be loaded on vessel until entry-outwards granted. The master of a vessel shall not permit the loading of any export goods, other than baggage and mail bags, until an order has been given by the proper officer granting entry-outwards to such vessel.

40. Export goods not be loaded unless duly passed by proper officer. The person-in-charge of a conveyance shall not permit the loading at a customs station-

(a) of export goods, other than baggage and mail bags, unless a shipping bill or bill of export or a bill of transhipment, as the case may be, duly passed by the proper officer, has been handed over to him by the exporter;

(b) of baggage and mail bags, unless their export has been duly permitted by the proper officer.

41. Delivery of export manifest or export report.

(1) The person-in-charge of a conveyance carrying export goods shall, before departure of the conveyance from a customs station, deliver to the proper officer in the case of a vessel or aircraft, an export manifest, and in the case of a vehicle, an export report, in the prescribed form:

PROVIDED that if the agent of the person-in-charge of the conveyance furnishes such security as the proper officer deems sufficient for duly delivering within seven days from the date of departure of the conveyance the export manifest or the export report, as the case may be, the proper officer may (subject to such rules as the Central Government may make in this behalf) accept such manifest or report within the aforesaid period.

(2) The person delivering the export manifest or export report shall at the foot thereof make and subscribe to a declaration as to the truth of its contents.

(3) If the proper officer is satisfied that the export manifest or export report is in any way incorrect or incomplete and that there was no fraudulent intention, he may permit such manifest or report to be amended or supplemented.

42. No conveyance to leave without written order.

(1) The person-in-charge of a conveyance which has brought any imported goods or has loaded any export goods at a customs station shall not cause or permit the conveyance to depart from that customs station until a written order to that effect has been given by the proper officer.

(2) No such order shall be given until-

(a) the person-in-charge of the conveyance has answered the questions put to him under Section 38;

(b) the provisions of Section 41 have been complied with;

(c) the shipping bills or bills of export, the bills of transhipment, if any, and such other documents, as the proper officer may require have been delivered to him;

(d) all duties leviable on any stores consumed in such conveyance, and all charges and penalties due in respect of such conveyance or from the person-in-charge thereof have been paid or the payment secured by such guarantee or deposit of such amount as the proper officer may direct;

(e) the person-in-charge of the conveyance has satisfied the proper officer that no penalty is leviable on him under Section 116 or the payment of any penalty that may be levied upon him under that Section has been secured by such guarantee or deposit of such amount as the proper officer may direct;

(f) in any case where any export goods have been loaded without payment of export duty or in contravention of any provision of this Act or any other law for the time being in force relating to export of goods -

(i) such goods have been unloaded, or

(ii) where the Assistant Commissioner of Customs or Deputy Commissioner of Customs is satisfied that it is not practible to unload such goods, the person-in-charge of the conveyance has given an undertaking, secured by such guarantee or deposit of such amount as the proper officer may direct, for bringing back the goods to India.

43. Exemption of certain classes of conveyances from certain provisions of this Chapter.

(1) The provisions of Sections 30, 41 and 42 shall not apply to a vehicle which carries no goods other than the luggage of its occupants.

(2) The Central Government may, by notification in the Official Gazette, exempt the following classes of conveyances from all or any of the provisions of this Chapter-

(a) conveyances belonging to the government or any foreign government;

(b) vessels and aircraft which temporarily enter India by reason of any emergency.

CHAPTER - VII : CLEARANCE OF IMPORTED GOODS AND EXPORT GOODS

44. Chapter not to apply to baggage and postal articles. The provisions of this Chapter shall not apply to (a) baggage, and (b) goods imported or to be exported by post.

CLEARANCE OF IMPORTED GOODS

45. Restrictions on custody and removal of imported goods.

(1) Save as otherwise provided in any law for the time being in force, all imported goods, unloaded in a customs area shall remain in the custody of such person as may be approved by the [5][Commissioner of Customs] until they are cleared for home consumption or are warehoused or are transhipped in accordance with the provisions of Chapter VIII.

(2) The person having custody of any imported goods in a customs area, whether under the provisions of sub-section (1) or under any law for the time being in force -

(a) shall keep a record of such goods and send a copy thereof to the proper officer;

(b) shall not permit such goods to be removed from the customs area or otherwise dealt with, except under and in accordance with the permission in writing of the proper officer.

(3) Notwithstanding anything contained in any law for the time being in force, if any imported goods are pilfered after unloading thereof in a customs area while in the custody of a person referred to in sub-section (1), that person shall be liable to pay duty on such goods at the rate prevailing on the date of delivery of an import manifest or, as the case may be, an import report to the proper officer under Section 30 for the arrival of convenience in which the said goods were carried.

46. Entry of goods on importation.

(1) The importer of any goods, other than goods intended for transit or transhipment, shall make entry thereof by presenting to the proper officer a bill of entry for home consumption or warehousing in the prescribed form:

PROVIDED that if the importer makes and subscribes to a declaration before the proper officer to the effect that he is unable for want of full information to furnish all the particulars of the goods required under this sub-section, the proper officer may, pending the production of such information, permit him, previous to the entry thereof (a) to examine the goods in the presence of an officer of customs, or (b) to deposit the goods in a public warehouse appointed under Section 57 without warehousing the same.

(2) Save as otherwise permitted by the proper officer, a bill of entry shall include all the goods mentioned in the bill of lading or other receipt given by the carrier to the consignor.

(3) A bill of entry under sub-section (1) may be presented at any time after the delivery of the import manifest or import report, as the case may be:

PROVIDED that the Commissioner of Customs may in any special circumstance permit a bill of entry to be presented before the delivery of such report:

PROVIDED FURTHER that a bill of entry may be presented even before the delivery of such manifest if the vessel or the aircraft by which the goods have been shipped for importation into India is expected to arrive within thirty days from the date of such presentation.

(4) The importer while presenting a bill of entry shall at the foot thereof make and subscribe to a declaration as to the truth of the contents of such bill of entry and shall, in support of such declaration, produce to the proper officer the invoice, if any, relating to the imported goods.

(5) If the proper officer is satisfied that the interests of revenue are not prejudicially affected and that there was no fraudulent intention, he may permit substitution of a bill of entry for home consumption for a bill of entry for warehousing or vice versa.

47. Clearance of goods for home consumption.

(1) Where the proper officer is satisfied that any goods entered for home consumption are not prohibited goods and the importer has paid the import duty, if any, assessed thereon and any charges payable under this Act in respect of the same, the proper officer may make an order permitting clearance of the goods for home consumption.

(2) Where the importer fails to pay the import duty under sub-section (1) within two days, excluding holidays [from the date on which the bill of entry is returned to him for payment of duty, he shall pay interest at such rate not below ten percent] and not exceeding thirty per cent per annum, as is for the time being fixed by the Board on such duty till the date of payment of the said duty:

PROVIDED that where the bill of entry is returned for payment of duty before the commencement of the Customs (Amendment) Act, 1991, and the importer has not paid such duty before such commencement, the date of return of such bill of entry to him shall be deemed to be the date of such commencement for the purpose of this Section.

PROVIDED FURTHER that if the Board is satisfied that it is necessary in the public interest so to do, it may, by order for reasons to be recorded, waive the whole or part of any interest payable under this Section.

48. Procedure in case of goods not cleared, warehoused or transhipped within thirty days after unloading. If any goods brought into India from a place outside India are not cleared for home consumption or warehoused or transhipped within 41[thirty days] from the date of the unloading thereof at a customs station or within such further time as the proper officer may allow or if the title to any imported goods is relinquished, such goods may, after notice to the importer and with the permission of the proper officer, be sold by the person having the custody thereof:

PROVIDED that-

(a) *animals, perishable goods and hazardous goods, may, with the permission of the proper officer, be sold at any time;*

(b) *arms and ammunition may be sold at such time and place and in such manner as the Central Government may direct.*

EXPLANATION: In this Section, "arms" and "ammunition" have the meanings respectively assigned to them in the Arms Act, 1959 (54 of 1959).

49. Storage of imported goods in warehouse pending clearance. Where in the case of any imported goods, whether dutiable or not, entered for home consumption, the [23][Assistant Commissioner of Customs or Deputy Commissioner of Customs] is satisfied on the application of the imported that the goods cannot be cleared within a reasonable time, the goods may, pending clearance, be permitted to be stored in a public warehouse, or in a private warehouse if facilities for deposit in a public warehouse are not available; but such goods shall not be deemed to be warehoused goods for the purposes of this Act, and accordingly the provisions of Chapter IX shall not apply to such goods.

CLEARANCE OF EXPORT GOODS

50. Entry of goods for exportation.

(1) The exporter of any goods shall make entry there of by presenting to the proper officer in the case of goods to be exported in a vessel or aircraft, a shipping bill, and in the case of goods to be exported by land, a bill of export in the prescribed form.

(2) The exporter of any goods, while presenting a shipping bill or bill of export, shall at the foot thereof make and subscribe to a declaration as to the truth of its contents.

51. Clearance of goods for exportation. Where the proper officer is satisfied that any goods entered for export are not prohibited goods and the exporter has paid the duty, if any, assessed thereon and any charges payable under this Act in respect of the same, the proper officer may make an order permitting clearance and loading of the goods for exportation

CHAPTER VIII : GOODS IN TRANSIT

52. Chapter not to apply to baggage, postal articles and stores. The provisions of this Chapter shall not apply to (a) baggage, (b) goods imported by post, and (c) stores.

53. Transit of certain goods without payment of duty. Subject to the provisions of Section 11, any goods imported in a conveyance and mentioned in the import manifest or the import report, as the case may be, as for transit in the same conveyance to any place outside India or any customs station may be allowed to be so transited without payment of duty.

54. Transhipment of certain goods without payment of duty.

(1) Where any goods imported into a customs station are intended for transhipment, a bill of transhipment shall be presented to the proper officer in the prescribed form:

PROVIDED that where the goods are being transhipped under an international treaty or bilateral agreement between the Government of India and Government of a foreign country, a declaration for transhipment instead of a bill of transhipment shall be presented to the proper officer in the prescribed form.

(2) Subject to the provisions of Section 11, where any goods imported into a customs station are mentioned in the import manifest or the import report, as the case may be, as for transhipment to any place outside India, such goods may be allowed to be so transhipped without payment of duty.

(3) Where any goods imported into a customs station are mentioned in the import manifest or the import report, as the case may be, as for transhipment-

(a) to any major port as defined in the Indian Ports Act, 1908 (15 of 1908), or the customs airport at Mumbai, Calcutta, Delhi or Chennai or any other customs port or customs airport which the Board may, by notification in the Official Gazette, specify in this behalf, or

(b) to any other customs station and the proper officer is satisfied that the goods are *bonafide* intended for transhipment to such customs station, the proper officer may allow the goods to be transhipped, without payment of duty, subject to such conditions as may be prescribed for the due arrival of such goods at the customs station to which transhipment is allowed.

55. Liability of duty on goods transited under Section S3 or transhipped under Section 54. Where any goods are allowed to be transited under Section 53 or transhipped under sub-section (3) of Section 54 to any customs station, they shall, on their arrival at such station, be liable to duty and shall be entered in like manner as goods are entered on the first importation thereof and the provisions of this Act and any rules and regulations shall, so far as may be, apply in relation to such goods.]

56. Transport of certain classes of goods subject to prescribed conditions. Imported goods may be transported without payment of duty from one land customs station to another, and any goods may be transported from one part of India to another part through any foreign territory, subject to such conditions as may be prescribed for the due arrival of such goods at the place of destination.

CHAPTER - IX : WAREHOUSING

57. Appointing of public warehouses. At any warehousing station, the Assistant Commissioner of Customs or Deputy Commissioner of Customs may appoint public warehoused wherein dutiable goods may be deposited.

58. Licensing of private warehouses.

(1) At any warehousing station, the [23][Assistant Commissioner of Customs or Deputy Commissioner of Customs] may license private warehouses wherein dutiable goods imported by or on behalf of the licensee, or any other imported goods in respect of which facilities for deposit in a public warehouse are not available, may be deposited [42][* * *].

(2) The [23][Assistant Commissioner of Customs or Deputy Commissioner of Customs] may cancel a licence granted under sub-section (1)-

(a) by giving one month's notice in writing to the licensee; or

(b) if the licensee has contravened any provisions of this Act or the rules or regulations or committed breach of any of the conditions of the licence:

PROVIDED that before any licence is cancelled under clause (b), the licensee shall be given a reasonable opportunity of being heard.

(3) Pending an enquiry whether a licence granted under sub-section (1) should be cancelled under clause (b) of sub-section (2), the Assistant Commissioner of Customs or Deputy Commissioner of Customs] may suspend the licence.

59. Warehousing bond.

43[(1) The importer of any goods specified in [44][***] sub-section (1) of Section 61, which have been entered for warehousing and assessed to duty under Section 17 or Section 18 shall execute a bond binding himself in a sum equal to twice the amount of the duty assessed on such goods,-

(a) to observe all the provisions of this Act and the rules and regulations in respect of such goods;

(b) to pay on or before a date specified in a notice of demand,-

(i) all duties, and interest, if any, payable under sub-section (2) of Section 61,

(ii) rent and charges claimable on account of such goods under this Act, together with interest on the same from the date so specified at the rate of six per cent per annum or such other rate as is for the time being fixed by the Board; and

(c) to discharge all penalties incurred for violation of the provisions of this Act and the rules and regulations in respect of such goods.

(2) For the purposes of sub-section (1), the Assistant Commissioner of Customs or Deputy Commissioner of Customs may permit an importer to enter into a general bond in such amount as [the Assistant Commissioner of Customs or Deputy Commissioner of Customs] may approve in respect of the warehousing of goods to be imported by him within a specified period.

(3) A bond executed under this Section by an importer in respect of any goods shall continue in force notwithstanding the transfer of the goods to any other person or the removal of the goods to another warehouse:

PROVIDED that where the whole of the goods or any part thereof are transferred to another person, the proper officer may accept a fresh bond from the transferee in a sum equal to twice the amount of duty assessed on the goods transferred and thereupon the bond executed by the transferor shall be enforceable only for a sum mentioned therein less the amount for which a fresh bond is accepted from the transferee.

59A. Conditions for warehousing of certain goods]

60. Permission for deposit of goods in a warehouse. When the provisions of [28][Section 59 [46][* * *]] have been complied with in respect of any goods, the proper officer may make an order permitting the deposit of the goods in a warehouse [42][* * *].

61. Period for which goods may remain warehoused.

(1) Any warehoused goods may be left in the warehouse in which they are deposited or in any warehouse to which they may be removed,-

(a) in the case of capital goods intended for use in any hundred per cent export oriented undertaking, till the expiry of five years; and

(b) in the case of any other goods, till the expiry of one year, and the date on which the proper officer has made an order under Section 60 permitting the deposit of the goods in a warehouse:

PROVIDED that-

(i) in the case of any goods which are not likely to deteriorate, the period specified in sub-section (1) may, on sufficient cause being shown, be extended by the 5[Commissioner of Customs] for a period not exceeding six months and by the 5[Chief Commissioner of Customs] for such further period as he may deem fit;

(ii) in the case of any goods referred to in clause (b), if they are likely to deteriorate, the aforesaid period of one year may be reduced by the [Commissioner of Customs] to such shorter period as he may deem fit:

PROVIDED FURTHER that when the licence for any private warehouse is cancelled, the owner of any goods warehoused therein shall, within seven days from the date on which notice of such cancellation is given or within such extended period as the proper officer may allow, remove the goods from such warehouse to another warehouse or clear them for home consumption or exportation.

(2) Where any warehoused goods-

(i) specified in sub-clause (a) of sub-section (1), remain in a warehouse beyond the period specified in that sub-section by reason of extension of the aforesaid period or otherwise, interest at such rate as is specified in Section 47 shall be payable, on the amount of duty payable at the time of clearance of the goods in accordance with the provisions of Section 15 on the warehoused goods, for the period from the expiry of the said warehousing period till the date of payment of duty on the warehoused goods;

(ii) specified in sub-clause (b) of sub-section (1), remain in a warehouse beyond a period of six months, interest shall be payable at such rate or rates not exceeding the rate specified in Section 47, as may be fixed by the Board, on the amount of duty payable at the time of clearance of the goods in accordance with the provisions of Section 15 on the warehoused goods, for the period from the expiry of the said six months till the date of payment of duty on the warehoused goods:]

PROVIDED that the Board may, if it considers it necessary so to do in the public interest, by order and under circumstances of an exceptional nature, to be specified in such order, waive the whole or part of any interest payable under this Section in respect of any warehoused goods:

PROVIDED FURTHER that the Board may, if it is satisfied that it is necessary so to do in the public interest, by notification in the Official Gazette, specify the class of goods in respect of which no interest shall be charged under this Section.

EXPLANATION: For the purposes of this Section, "hundred per cent export oriented undertaking" has the same meaning as in Explanation 2 to sub-section (1) of Section 3 of the Central Excises and Salt Act, 1944 (1 of 1944).]

62. Control over warehoused goods.

(1) All warehoused goods shall be subject to the control of the proper officer.

(2) No person shall enter a warehouse or remove any goods therefrom without the permission of the proper officer.

(3) The proper officer may cause any warehouse to be locked with the lock of the Customs Department and no person shall remove or break such lock.

(4) The proper officer shall have access to every part of a warehouse and power to examine the goods therein.

63. Payment of rent and warehouse charges.

(1) The owner of any warehoused goods shall pay to the warehouse keeper rent and warehouse charges at the rates fixed under any law for the time being in force or where no rates are so fixed,at such rates as may be fixed by the 5[Commissioner of Customs].

(2) If any rent or warehouse charges are not paid within ten days from the date when they became due, the warehouse-keeper may, after notice to the owner of the warehoused goods and with the permission of the proper officer cause to be sold (any transfer of the warehoused goods notwithstanding) such sufficient portion of the goods as the warehouse-keeper may select.

64. Owner's right to deal with warehoused goods. With the sanction of the proper officer and on payment of the prescribed fees, the owner of any goods may either before or after warehousing the same-

(a) inspect the goods;

(b) separate damaged or deteriorated goods from the rest;

(c) sort the goods or change their containers for the purpose of preservation, sale, export or disposal of the goods;

(d) deal with the goods and their containers in such manner as may be necessary to prevent loss or deterioration or damage to the goods;

(e) show the goods for sale; or

(f) take samples of goods without entry for home consumption, and if the proper officer so permits, without payment of duty on such samples.

65. Manufacture and other operations in relation to goods in a warehouse.

(1) With the sanction of the 23[Assistant Commissioner of Customs or Deputy Commissioner of Customs] and subject to such conditions and on payment of such as may be prescribed, the owner of any warehoused goods may carry on any manufacturing process or other operations in the warehouse in relation to such goods.

(2) Where in the course of any operations permissible in relation to any warehoused goods under sub-section (1) there is any waste or refuse, the following provisions shall apply:

(a) if the whole or any part of the goods resulting from such operations are exported, import duty shall be remitted on the quantity of the warehoused goods contained in so much of the waste or refuse as has arisen from the operation carried on in relation to the goods exported:

PROVIDED that such waste or refuse is either destroyed or duty is paid on such waste or refuse as if it has been imported into India in that form;

(b) if the whole or any part of the goods resulting from such operation are cleared from the warehouse for home consumption, import duty shall be charged on the quantity of the warehoused goods contained in so much of the waste or refuse as has arisen from the operations carried on in relation to the goods cleared for home consumption.

66. Power to exempt imported materials used in the manufacture of goods in warehouse. If any imported materials are used in accordance with the provisions of Section 65 for the manufacture of any goods and the rate of duty leviable on the imported materials exceeds the rate of duty leviable on such goods, the Central Government, if satisfied that in the interests of the establishment or development of any domestic industry it is necessary so to do, may, by notification in the Official Gazette, exempt the imported materials from the whole or part of the excess rate of duty.

67. Removal of goods from one warehouse to another. The owner of any warehoused goods may, with the permission of the proper officer, remove them from one warehouse to another, [42][***] subject to such conditions as may be prescribed for the due arrival of the warehoused goods at the warehouse to which removal is permitted.

68. Clearance of warehoused goods for home consumption. The importer of any warehoused goods may clear them for home consumption of-

(a) a bill of entry for home consumption in respect of such goods has been presented in the prescribed form;

(b) the import duty leviable on such goods and all penalties, rent, interest and other charges payable in respect of such goods have been paid; and

(c) an order for clearance of such goods for home consumption has been made by the proper officer.

69. Clearance of warehoused goods for exportation.

(1) Any warehoused goods may be exported to a place outside India without payment of import duty if-

(a) a shipping bill or a bill of export has been presented in respect of such goods in the prescribed form;

(b) the export duty, penalties, rent, interest and other charges payable in respect of such goods have been paid; and

(c) an order for clearance of such goods for exportation has been made by the proper officer.

(2) Notwithstanding anything contained in sub-section (1), if the Central Government is of opinion that warehoused goods of any specified description are likely to be smuggled back into India, it may, by notification in the Official Gazette, direct that such goods, shall not be exported to any place outside India without payment of duty or may be allowed to be so exported subject to such restrictions and conditions as may be specified in the notification.

70. Allowance in case of volatile goods.

(1) When any warehoused goods to which this Section applies are at the time of delivery from a warehouse found to be deficient in quantity on account of natural loss, the Assistant Commissioner of Customs or Deputy Commissioner of Customs may remit the duty on such deficiency.

(2) This Section applies to such warehoused goods as the Central Government, having regard to the volatility of the goods and the manner of their storage, may, by notification in the Official Gazette, specify.

71. Goods not to be taken out of warehouse except as provided by this Act. No warehoused goods shall be taken out of a warehouse except on clearance for home consumption or re-exportation, or for removal to another warehouse, or as otherwise provided by this Act.

72. Goods improperly removed from warehouse, etc.

(1) In any of the following cases, that is to say,-

(a) where any warehoused goods are removed from a warehouse in contravention of Section 71;

(b) where any warehoused goods have not been removed from a warehouse at the expiration of the period during which such goods are permitted under Section 61 to remain in a warehouse;

(c) where any warehoused goods have been taken under Section 64 as samples without payment of duty;

(d) where any goods in respect of which a bond has been executed under [28][Section 59 [47][***]] and which have not been cleared for home consumption or exportation are not duly accounted for to the satisfaction of the proper officer;

the proper officer may demand, and the owner of such goods shall forth with pay, the full amount of duty charge able on account of such goods together with all penalties, rent, interest and other charges payable in respect of such goods.

(2) If any owner fails to pay any amount demanded under sub-section (1), the proper officer may, without prejudice to any other remedy, cause to be detained and sold, after notice to the owner (any transfer of the goods notwithstanding) such sufficient portion of his goods, if any, in the warehouse, as the said officer may select.

73. Cancellation and return of warehousing bond. When the whole of the goods covered by any bond executed under [28][section 59 [46][***]] have been cleared for home consumption or exported or are otherwise duly accounted for, and when all amounts due on account of such goods have been paid, the proper officer shall cancel the bond as discharged in full, and shall on demand deliver it, so cancelled, to the person who has executed or is entitled to receive it.

CHAPTER - X : DRAWBACK

74. Drawback allowable on re-export of duty-paid goods.

(1) When any goods capable of being easily identified which have been imported into India and upon which any duty has been paid on importation,-

(i) are entered for export and the proper officer makes an order permitting clearance and loading of the goods for exportation under Section 51; or

(ii) are to be exported as baggage and the owner of such baggage, for the purpose of clearing it, makes a declaration of its contents to the proper officer under Section 77 (which declaration shall be deemed to be an entry for export for the purposes of this Section) and such officer makes an order permitting clearance of the goods for exportation; or

(iii) are entered for export by post under Section 82 and the proper officer makes an order permitting clearance of the goods for exportation, ninety-eight per cent, of such duty shall, except as otherwise here in after provided, the re-paid as drawback, if]-

(a) the goods are identified to the satisfaction of the [23][Assistant Commissioner of Customs or Deputy Commissioner of Customs] as the goods which were imported; and

(b) the goods are entered for export within two years from the date of payment of duty on the importation thereof :

PROVIDED that in any particular case the aforesaid period of two years may, on sufficient cause being shown, be extended by the Board by such further period as it may deem fit.

(2) Notwithstanding anything contained in sub-section (1), the rate of drawback in the case of goods which have been used after the importation thereof shall be such as the Central Government, having regard to the duration of use, depreciation in value and other relevant circumstances, may, by notification in the Official Gazette, fix.

(3) The Central Government may make rules for the purpose of carrying out the provisions of this Section and, in particular, such regulations may-

(a) provide for the manner in which the identity of goods imported in different consignments which are ordinarily stored together in bulk, may be established;

(b) specify the goods which shall be deemed to be not capable of being easily identified; and

(c) provide for the manner and the time within which a claim for payment of drawback is to be filed.]

(4) For the purposes of this Section-

(a) goods shall be deemed to have been entered for export on the date with reference to which the rate of duty is calculated under Section 16;

(b) in the case of goods assessed to duty provisionally under Section 18, the date of payment of the provisional duty shall be deemed to be the date of payment of duty.

75. Drawback on imported materials used in the manufacture of goods which are exported.

(1) Where it appears to the Central Government that in respect of goods of any class or description manufactured, processed or on which any operation has been carried out in India [6][being goods which have been entered for export and in respect of which an order permitting the clearance and loading thereof for exportation has been made under Section 51 by the proper officer or being goods entered for export by post under Section 82 and in respect of which an order permitting clearance for exportation has been made by the proper officer] a drawback should be allowed of duties of customs chargeable under this Act on any imported materials of a class or description used in the [50][manufacture or processing of such goods or carrying out any operation on such goods, the Central Government may, by notification in the Official Gazette, direct that drawback shall be allowed in respect of such goods in accordance with, and subject to, the rules made under sub-section (2):

PROVIDED that no drawback shall be allowed under this sub-section in respect of any of the aforesaid goods which the Central Government may, by rules made under sub-section (2), specify, if the export value of such goods or class of goods is less than the value of imported materials used in the [50][manufacture or processing of such goods or carrying out any operation on such goods or class of goods, or is not more than such percentage of the value of the imported materials used in the [50][manufacture or processing of such goods or carrying any operation on such goods] or class of goods as the Central Government may, by notification in the Official Gazette, specify in this behalf:

PROVIDED FURTHER that where any drawback has been allowed on any goods under this sub-section and the sale proceeds in respect of such goods are not received by or on behalf of the exporter in India within the time allowed under the Foreign Exchange Regulation Act, 1973 (46 of 1973), such drawback shall be deemed never to have been allowed and the Central Government may, by rules made under sub-section (2), specify the procedure for the recovery or adjustment of the amount of such drawback;

(1A) Where it appears to the Central Government that the quantity of a particular material imported into India is more than the total quantity of like material that has been used in the goods manufactured, processed or on which any operation has been carried out in India] and exported outside India, then, the Central Government may, by notification in the Official

Gazette, declare that so much of the material as is contained in the goods exported shall, for the purpose of sub-section (1), be deemed to be imported material.

(2) The Central Government may make rules for the purpose of carrying out the provisions of sub-section (1) and, in particular, such rules may provide -

(a) for the payment of drawback equal to the amount of duty actually paid on the imported materials used in the manufacture or processing of the goods or carrying out any operation on the goods or as is specified in the rules as the average amount of duty paid on the materials of that class or description used in the manufacture or processing of export goods or carrying out any operation on export goods of that class or description either by manufacturers generally or by persons processing or carrying on any operation generally or by any particular manufacturer or particular person carrying on any process or other operation, and interest, if any, payable thereon ;]

(aa) for specifying the goods in respect of which no drawback shall be allowed;

(ab) for specifying the procedure for recovery or adjustment of the amount of any drawback which had been allowed under sub-section (1) or interest chargeable thereon];

(b) for the production of such certificates, documents and other evidence in support of each claim of drawback as may be necessary;

(c) for requiring the [5][manufacturer or the person carrying out any process or other operation] to give access to every part of his manufactory to any officer of customs specially authorised in this behalf by the [23][Assistant Commissioner of Customs or Deputy Commissioner of Customs] to enable such authorised officer to inspect the processes of [5][manufacture, process or any other operation carried out] and to verify by actual check or otherwise the statements made in support of the claim for drawback.

(d) for the manner and the time within which the claim for payment drawback may be filed;

(3) The power to make rules conferred by sub-section (2) include the power to give drawback with retrospective effect from a date not earlier than the date of changes in the rates of duty on inputs used in the export goods.]

75A. Interest on drawback.

(1) Where any drawback payable to a claimant under Section 74 or Section 75 is not paid within a period of one month from the date of filing a claim for payment of such drawback, there shall be paid to that claimant in addition to the amount of drawback, interest at the rate fixed under Section 27A from the date after the expiry of the said period of one month till the date of payment of such drawback:

(2) Where any drawback has been paid to the claimant erroneously or it becomes otherwise recoverable under this Act or the rules madethereunder, the claimant shall, within a period of two months from the date of demand, pay in addition to the said amount of drawback, interest at the rate fixed under Section 28AB and the amount of interest shall be calculated for the period beginning from the date of payment of such drawback to the claimant till the date of recovery of such drawback.

76. Prohibition and regulation of drawback in certain cases. –

(1) Notwithstanding anything hereinbefore contained, no drawback shall be allowed –

(a) omitted;

(b) in respect of any goods the market-price of which is less than the amount of drawback due thereon;

(c) where the drawback due in respect of any goods is less than fifty rupees.

(2) Without prejudice to the provisions of sub-section (1), if the Central Government is of opinion that goods of any specified description in respect of which drawback may be claimed under this Chapter are likely to be smuggled back into India, it may, by notification in the Official Gazette, direct that drawback shall not be allowed in respect of such goods or may be allowed subject to such restrictions and conditions as may be specified in the notification.

CHAPTER - XA: SPECIAL PROVISIONS RELATING TO SPECIAL ECONOMIC ZONE

[**76A to 76N.** *Omitted vide by Section 99 of Finance Act, 2007 (22 of 2007) w.e.f. 11.5.2007*]

CHAPTER - XI : SPECIAL PROVISIONS REGARDING BAGGAGE, GOODS IMPORTED OR EXPORTED BY POST, AND STORES BAGGAGE

77. Declaration by owner of baggage. The owner of any baggage shall, for the purpose of clearing it, make a declaration of its contents to the proper officer.

78. Determination of rate of duty and tariff valuation in respect of baggage. The rate of duty and tariff valuation, if any, applicable to baggage shall be the rate and valuation in force on the date on which a declaration is made in respect of such baggage under Section 77.

79. Bona fide baggage exempted from duty.

(1) The proper officer may, subject to any rules made under sub-section (2), pass free of duty -

(a) any article in the baggage of a passenger or a member of the crew in respect of which the said officer is satisfied that it has been in his use for such minimum period as may be specified in the rules;

(b) any article in the baggage of a passenger in respect of which the said officer is satisfied that it is for the use of the passenger or his family or is a *bona fide* gift or souvenir; provided that the value of each such article and the total value of all such articles does not exceed such limits as may be specified in the rules.

(2) the Central Government may make rules for the purpose of carrying out the provisions of this Section and, in particular, such rules may specify -

(a) the minimum period for which any article has been used by a passenger or a member of the crew for the purpose of clause (a) of sub-section (1);

(b) the maximum value of any individual article and the maximum total value of all the articles which may be passed free of duty under clause (b) of sub-section (1);

(c) the conditions (to be fulfilled before or after clearance) subject to which any baggage may be passed free of duty.

(3) Different rules may be made under sub-section (2) for different classes of persons.

80. Temporary detention of baggage. Where the baggage of a passenger contains any article which is dutiable or the import of which is prohibited and in respect of which a true declaration has been made under Section 77, the proper officer may, at the request of the passenger, detain such article for the purpose of being returned to him on his leaving India and if for any reason, the passenger is not able to collect the article at the time of his leaving India, the article may be returned to him through any other passenger authorised by him and leaving India or as cargo consigned in his name.

81. Regulations in respect of baggage. The Board may make regulations, -

(a) providing for the manner of declaring the contents of any baggage;

(b) providing for the custody, examination, assessment to duty and clearance of baggage;

(c) providing for the transit or transhipment of baggage from one customs station to another or to a place outside India.

GOODS IMPORTED OR EXPORTED BY POST

82. Label or declaration accompanying goods to be treated as entry. In the case of goods imported or exported by post, any label or declaration accompanying the goods, which contains the description, quantity and value thereof, shall be deemed to be an entry for import or export, as the case may be, for the purposes of this Act.

83. Rate of duty and tariff valuation in respect of goods imported or exported by post.

(1) The rate of duty and tariff value, if any, applicable to any goods imported by post shall be the rate and valuation in force on the date on which the postal authorities present to the proper officer a list containing the particulars of such goods for the purpose of assessing the duty thereon:

PROVIDED that if such goods are imported by a vessel and the list of the goods containing the particulars was presented before the date of the arrival of the vessel, it shall be deemed to have been presented on the date of such arrival.

(2) The rate of duty and tariff value, if any, applicable to any goods exported by post shall be the rate and valuation in force on the date on which the exporter delivers such goods to the postal authorities for exportation.

84. Regulations regarding goods imported or to be exported by post. The Board may make regulations providing for -

(a) the form and manner in which an entry may be made in respect of any specified class of goods imported or to be exported by post, other than goods which are accompanied by a label or declaration containing the description, quantity and value thereof;

(b) the examination, assessment to duty, and clearance of goods imported or to be exported by post;

(c) the transit or transhipment of goods imported by post, from one customs station to another or to a place outside India.

STORES

85. Stores may be allowed to be warehoused without assessment to duty. Where any imported goods are entered for warehousing and the importer makes and subscribes to a declaration that the goods are to be supplied as stores to vessels or aircrafts without payment of import duty under this Chapter, the proper officer may permit the goods to be warehoused without the goods being assessed to duty.

86. Transit and transhipment of stores.

(1) Any stores imported in a vessel or aircraft may, without payment of duty, remain on board such vessel or aircraft while it is in India.

(2) Any stores imported in a vessel or aircraft may, with the permission of the proper officer, be transferred to any vessel or aircraft as stores for consumption therein as provided in Section 87 or Section 90.

87. Imported stores may be consumed on board a foreign-going vessel or aircraft. Any imported stores on board a vessel or aircraft (other than stores to which Section 90 applies) may, without payment of duty, be consumed thereon as stores during the period such vessel or aircraft is a foreign-going vessel or aircraft.

88. Application of Section 69 and Chapter X to stores. The provisions of Section 69 and Chapter X shall apply to stores (other than those to which Section 90 applies) as they apply to other goods, subject to the modifications that -

(a) for the words "exported to any place outside India" or the word "exported", wherever they occur, the words "taken on board any foreign-going vessel or aircraft as stores" shall be substituted;

(b) in the case of drawback on fuel and lubricating oil taken on board any foreign-going aircraft as stores, sub-section (1) of Section 74 shall have effect as if for the words "ninety-eight per cent", the words "the whole" were substituted.

89. Stores to be free of export duty. Goods produced or manufactured in India and required as stores on any foreign-going vessel or aircraft may be exported free of duty in such quantities as the proper officer may determine, having regard to the size of the vessel or aircraft, the number of passengers and crew and the length of the voyage or journey on which the vessel or aircraft is about to depart.

90. Concessions in respect of imported stores for the Navy.

(1) Imported stores specified in sub-section (3) may without payment of duty be consumed on board a ship of the Indian Navy.

(2) The provisions of Section 69 and Chapter X shall apply to stores specified in sub-section (3) as they apply to other goods, subject to the modifications that -

(a) for the words "exported to any place outside India" or the word "exported" wherever they occur, the words "taken on board a ship of the Indian Navy" shall be substituted;

(b) or the words "ninety-eight per cent" in sub-section (1) of Section 74, the words "the whole" shall be substituted.

(3) The stores referred to in sub-sections (1) and (2) are the following : –

(a) stores for the use of a ship of the Indian Navy;

(b) stores supplied free by the Government for the use of the crew of a ship of the Indian Navy in accordance with their conditions of service.

CHAPTER - XII : PROVISIONS RELATING TO COASTAL GOODS AND VESSELS CARRYING COASTAL GOODS

91. Chapter not to apply to baggage and stores. The provisions of this Chapter shall not apply to baggage and stores.

92. Entry of coastal goods.

(1) The consignor of any coastal goods shall make an entry thereof by presenting to the proper officer a bill of coastal goods in the prescribed form.

(2) Every such consignor while presenting a bill of coastal goods shall, at the foot thereof, make and subscribe to a declaration as to the truth of the contents of such bill.

93. Coastal goods not to be loaded until bill relating thereto is passed, etc. The master of a vessel shall not permit the loading of any coastal goods on the vessel until a bill relating to such goods presented under Section 92 has been passed by the proper officer and has been delivered to the master by the consignor.

94. Clearance of coastal goods at destination.

(1) The master of a vessel carrying any coastal goods shall carry on board the vessel all bills relating to such goods delivered to him under Section 93 and shall, immediately on arrival of the vessel at any customs or coastal port, deliver to the proper officer of that port all bills relating to the goods which are to be unloaded at that port.

(2) Where any coastal goods are unloaded at any port, the proper officer shall permit clearance thereof if he is satisfied that they are entered in a bill of coastal goods delivered to him under sub-section (1).

95. Master of a coasting vessel to carry an advice book.

(1) The master of every vessel carrying coastal goods shall be supplied by the Customs authorities with a book to be called the "advice book".

(2) The proper officer at each port of call by such vessel shall make such entries in the advice book as he deems fit, relating to the goods loaded on the vessel at that port.

(3) The master of every such vessel shall carry the advice book on board the vessel and shall on arrival at each port of call deliver it to the proper officer at that port for his inspection.

96. Loading and unloading of coastal goods at customs port or coastal port only. No coastal goods shall be loaded on, or unloaded from, any vessel at any port other than a customs port or a coastal port appointed under Section 7 for the loading or unloading of such goods.

97. No coasting vessel to leave without written order.

(1) The master of a vessel which has brought or loaded any coastal goods at a customs or coastal port shall not cause or permit the vessel to depart from such port until a written order to that effect has been given by the proper officer.

(2) No such order shall be given until –

(a) the master of the vessel has answered the questions put to him under Section 38;

(b) all charges and penalties due in respect of that vessel or from the master thereof have been paid or the payment secured by such guarantee or deposit of such amount as the proper officer may direct;

(c) the master of the vessel has satisfied the proper officer that no penalty is leviable on him under Section 116 or the payment of any penalty that may be levied upon him under that Section has been secured by such guarantee or deposit of such amount as the proper officer may direct;

(d) the provisions of this Chapter and any rules and regulations relating to coastal goods and vessels carrying coastal goods have been complied with.

98. Application of certain provisions of this Act to coastal goods, etc.

(1) Sections 33, 34 and 36 shall, so far as may be, apply to coastal goods as they apply to imported goods or export goods.

(2) Sections 37 and 38 shall, so far as may be, apply to vessels carrying coastal goods as they apply to vessels carrying imported goods or export goods.

(3) The Central Government may, by notification in the Official Gazette, direct that all or any of the other provisions of Chapter VI and the provisions of Section 45 shall apply to coastal goods or vessels carrying coastal goods subject to such exceptions and modifications as may be specified in the notification.

98A. Power to relax. If the Central Government is satisfied that it is necessary in the public interest so to do it may, by notification in the Official Gazette, exempt generally, either absolutely or subject to such conditions as may be specified in the notification, coastal goods or vessels carrying coastal goods from all or any of the provisions of this Chapter.

99. Power to make rules in respect of coastal goods and coasting vessels. – The Central Government may make rules for -

(a) preventing the taking out of India of any coastal goods the export of which is dutiable or prohibited under this Act or any other law for the time being in force;

(b) preventing, in the case of a vessel carrying coastal goods as well as imported or export goods, the substitution of imported or export goods by coastal goods.

CHAPTER - XIII : SEARCHES, SEIZURE AND ARREST

100. Power to search suspected persons entering or leaving India, etc.

(1) If the proper officer has reason to believe that any person to whom this Section applies has secreted about his person, any goods liable to confiscation or any documents relating thereto, he may search that person.

(2) This Section applies to the following persons, namely : –

(a) any person who has landed from or is about to board, or is on board any vessel within the Indian customs waters;

(b) any person who has landed from or is about to board, or is on board a foreign-going aircraft;

(c) any person who has got out of, or is about to get into, or is in a vehicle, which has arrived from, or is to proceed to any place outside India;

(d) any person not included in clauses (a), (b) or (c) who has entered or is about to leave India;

(e) any person in a customs area.

101. Power to search suspected persons in certain other cases.

(1) Without prejudice to the provisions of Section 100, if an officer of customs empowered in this behalf by general or special order of the Commissioner of Customs, has reason to believe that any person has secreted about his person any goods of the description specified in sub-section (2) which are liable to confiscation, or documents relating thereto, he may search that person.

(2) The goods referred to in sub-section (1) are the following : –

(a) gold;

(b) diamonds;

(c) manufactures of gold or diamonds;

(d) watches;

(e) any other class of goods which the Central Government may, by notification in the Official Gazette, specify.

102. Persons to be searched may require to be taken before Gazetted Officer of customs or magistrate.

(1) When any officer of customs is about to search any person under the provisions of Section 100 or Section 101, the officer of customs shall, if such person so requires, take him without unnecessary delay to the nearest Gazetted Officer of customs or magistrate.

(2) If such requisition is made, the officer of customs may detain the person making it until he can bring him before the Gazetted Officer of customs or the magistrate.

(3) The Gazetted Officer of customs or the magistrate before whom any such person is brought shall, if he sees no reasonable ground for search, forthwith discharge the person but otherwise shall direct that search be made.

(4) Before making a search under the provisions of Section 100 or Section 101, the officer of customs shall call upon two or more persons to attend and witness the search and may issue an order in writing to them or any of them so to do; and the search shall be made in the presence of such persons and a list of all things seized in the course of such search shall be prepared by such officer or other person and signed by such witnesses.

(5) No female shall be searched by any one excepting a female.

103. Power to screen or X-ray bodies of suspected persons for detecting secreted goods.

(1) Where the proper officer has reason to believe that any person referred to in sub-section (2) of Section 100 has any goods liable to confiscation secreted inside his body, he may detain such person and produce him without unnecessary delay before the nearest magistrate.

(2) A magistrate before whom any person is brought under sub-section (1) shall, if he sees no reasonable ground for believing that such person has any such goods secreted inside his body, forthwith discharge such person.

(3) Where any such magistrate has reasonable ground for believing that such person has any such goods secreted inside his body and the magistrate is satisfied that for the purpose of discovering such goods it is necessary to have the body of such person screened or X-rayed, he may make an order to that effect.

(4) Where a magistrate has made any order under sub-section (3), in relation to any person, the proper officer shall, as soon as practicable, take such person before a radiologist possessing qualifications recognized by the Central Government for the purpose of this Section, and such person shall allow the radiologist to screen or X-ray his body.

(5) A radiologist before whom any person is brought under sub-section (4) shall, after screening or X-raying the body of such person, forward his report, together with any X-ray pictures taken by him, to the magistrate without unnecessary delay.

(6) Where on receipt of a report from a radiologist under sub-section (5) or otherwise, the magistrate is satisfied that any person has any goods liable to confiscation

secreted inside his body, he may direct that suitable action for bringing out such goods be taken on the advice and under the supervision of a registered medical practitioner and such person shall be bound to comply with such direction:

PROVIDED that in the case of a female no such action shall be taken except on the advice and under the supervision of a female registered medical practitioner.

(7) Where any person is brought before a magistrate under this Section, such magistrate may for the purpose of enforcing the provisions of this Section order such person to be kept in such custody and for such period as he may direct.

(8) Nothing in this Section shall apply to any person referred to in sub-section (1), who admits that goods liable to confiscation are secreted inside his body, and who voluntarily submits himself for suitable action being taken for bringing out such goods.

EXPLANATION: For the purposes of this Section, the expression "registered medical practitioner" means any person who holds a qualification granted by an authority specified in the Schedule to the Indian Medical Degrees Act, 1916 (7 of 1916), or notified under Section 3 of that Act, or by an authority specified in any of the Schedules to the Indian Medical Council Act, 1956 (102 of 1956).

104. Power to arrest.

(1) If an officer of customs empowered in this behalf by general or special order of the Commissioner of Customs has reason to believe that any person in India or within the Indian customs waters has committed an offence punishable under Section 132 or Section 133 or Section 135 or Section 135A or Section 136, he may arrest such person and shall, as soon as may be, inform him of the grounds for such arrest.

(2) Every person arrested under sub-section (1) shall, without unnecessary delay, be taken to a magistrate.

(3) Where an officer of customs has arrested any person under sub-section (1), he shall, for the purpose of releasing such person on bail or otherwise, have the same powers and be subject to the same provisions as the officer-in-charge of a police-station has and is subject to under the Code of Criminal Procedure, 1898 (5 of 1898).

(4) Notwithstanding anything contained in the Code of Criminal Procedure, 1898 (5 of 1898), an offence under this Act shall not be cognizable.

105. Power to search premises.

(1) If the Assistant Commissioner of Customs or Deputy Commissioner of Customs, or in any area adjoining the land frontier or the coast of India an officer of customs specially empowered by name in this behalf by the Board, has reason to believe that any goods liable to confiscation, or any documents or things which in his opinion will be useful for or relevant to any proceeding under this Act, are secreted in any place, he may authorise any officer of customs to search or may himself search for such goods, documents or things.

(2) The provisions of the Code of Criminal Procedure, 1898 (5 of 1898), relating to searches shall, so far as may be, apply to searches under this Section subject to the modification that sub-section (5) of Section 165 of the said Code shall have effect as if for the word "Magistrate", wherever it occurs, the words Commissioner of Customs were substituted.

106. Power to stop and search conveyances.

(1) Where the proper officer has reason to believe that any aircraft, vehicle or animal in India or any vessel in India or within the Indian customs waters has been, is being, or is about to be, used in the smuggling of any goods or in the carriage of any goods which have been smuggled, he may at any time stop any such vehicle, animal or vessel or, in the case of an aircraft, compel it to land, and –

(a) rummage and search any part of the aircraft, vehicle or vessel;

(b) examine and search any goods in the aircraft, vehicle or vessel or on the animal;

(c) break open the lock of any door or package for exercising the powers conferred by clauses (a) and (b), if the keys are withheld.

(2) Where for the purposes of sub-section (1) –

(a) it becomes necessary to stop any vessel or compel any aircraft to land, it shall be lawful for any vessel or aircraft in the service of the Government while flying her proper flag and any authority authorised in this behalf by the Central Government to summon such vessel to stop or the aircraft to land, by means of an international signal, code or other recognized means, and thereupon, such vessel shall forthwith stop or such aircraft shall forthwith land; and if it fails to do so, chase may be given thereto by any vessel or aircraft as aforesaid and if after a gun is fired as a signal the vessel fails to stop or the aircraft fails to land, it may be fired upon;

(b) it becomes necessary to stop any vehicle or animal, the proper officer may use all lawful means for stopping it, and where such means fail, the vehicle or animal may be fired upon.

106A. Power to inspect. Any proper officer authorised in this behalf by the Commissioner of Customs may, for the purpose of ascertaining whether or not the requirements of this Act have been complied with, at any reasonable time, enter any place intimated under Chapter IVA or Chapter IVB, as the case may be, and inspect the goods kept or stored therein and require any person found therein, who is for the time being in charge thereof, to produce to him for his inspection the accounts maintained under the said Chapter IVA or Chapter IVB, as the case may be, and to furnish to him such other information as he may reasonably require for the purpose of ascertaining whether or not such goods have been illegally imported, exported or are likely to be illegally exported.

107. Power to examine persons. Any officer of customs empowered in this behalf by general or special order of the Commissioner of Customs may, during the course of any enquiry in connection with the smuggling of any goods -

(a) require any person to produce or deliver any document or thing relevant to the enquiry;

(b) examine any person acquainted with the facts and circumstances of the case.

108. Power to summon persons to give evidence and produce documents.

(1) Any Gazetted Officer of customs shall have power to summon any person whose attendance he considers necessary either to give evidence or to produce a document or any other thing in any inquiry which such officer is making under this Act.

(2) A summons to produce documents or other things may be for the production of certain specified documents or things or for the production of all documents or things of a certain description in the possession or under the control of the person summoned.

(3) All persons so summoned shall be bound to attend either in person or by an authorised agent, as such officer may direct; and all persons so summoned shall be bound to state the truth upon any subject respecting which they are examined or make statements and produce such documents and other things as may be required :

PROVIDED *that the exemption under Section 132 of the Code of Civil Procedure, 1908 (5 of 1908), shall be applicable to any requisition for attendance under this Section.*

(4) Every such inquiry as aforesaid shall be deemed to be a judicial proceeding within the meaning of Section 193 and Section 228 of the Indian Penal Code, 1860 (45 of 1860).

109. Power to require production of order permitting clearance of goods imported by land. Any officer of customs appointed for any area adjoining the land frontier of India and empowered in this behalf by general or special order of the Board, may require any person in possession of any goods which such officer has reason to believe to have been imported into India by land, to produce the order made under Section 47 permitting clearance of the goods:

PROVIDED *that nothing in this Section shall apply to any imported goods passing from a land frontier to a land customs station by a route appointed under clause (c) of Section 7.*

110. Seizure of goods, documents and things.

(1) If the proper officer has reason to believe that any goods are liable to confiscation under this Act, he may seize such goods:

PROVIDED *that where it is not practicable to seize any such goods, the proper officer may serve on the owner of the goods an order that he shall not remove, part with, or otherwise deal with the goods except with the previous permission of such officer.*

(1A) The Central Government may, having regard to the perishable or hazardous nature of any goods, depreciation in the value of the goods with the passage of time, constraints of storage space for the goods or any other relevant considerations, by notification in the Official Gazette, specify the goods or class of goods which shall, as soon as may be after its seizure under sub-section (1), be disposed of by the proper officer in such manner as the Central Government may, from time to time, determine after following the procedure hereinafter specified.

(1B) Where any goods, being goods specified under sub-section (1A), have been seized by a proper officer under sub-section (1), he shall prepare an inventory of such goods containing such details relating to their description, quality, quantity, mark, numbers, country of origin and other particulars as the proper officer may consider relevant to the identity of the goods in any proceedings under this Act and shall make an application to a Magistrate for the purpose of –

(a) certifying the correctness of the inventory so prepared; or

(b) taking, in the presence of the Magistrate, photographs of such goods, and certifying such photographs as true; or

(c) allowing to draw representative samples of such goods, in the presence of the Magistrate, and certifying the correctness of any list of samples so drawn.

(1C) Where an application is made under sub-section (1B), the Magistrate shall, as soon as may be, allow the application.

(2) Where any goods are seized under sub-section (1) and no notice in respect thereof is given under clause (a) of Section 124 within six months of the seizure of the goods, the goods shall be returned to the person from whose possession they were seized :

PROVIDED that the aforesaid period of six months may, on sufficient cause being shown, be extended by the Commissioner of Customs for a period not exceeding six months.

(3) The proper officer may seize any documents or things which, in his opinion, will be useful for, or relevant to, any proceeding under this Act.

(4) The person from whose custody any documents are seized under sub-section (3) shall be entitled to make copies thereof or take extracts there from in the presence of an officer of customs.

110A. Provisional release of goods, documents and things seized pending adjudication. Any goods, documents or things seized under Section 110, may, pending the order of the adjudicating authority, be released to the owner on taking a bond from him in the proper form with such security and conditions as the adjudicating authority may require.

CHAPTER - XIV : CONFISCATION OF GOODS AND CONVEYANCES AND IMPOSITION OF PENALTIES

111. Confiscation of improperly imported goods, etc. The following goods brought from a place outside India shall be liable to confiscation: –

(a) any goods imported by sea or air which are unloaded or attempted to be unloaded at any place other than a customs port or customs airport appointed under clause (a) of Section 7 for the unloading of such goods;

(b) any goods imported by land or inland water through any route other than a route specified in a notification issued under clause (c) of Section 7 for the import of such goods;

(c) any dutiable or prohibited goods brought into any bay, gulf, creek or tidal river for the purpose of being landed at a place other than a customs port;

(d) any goods which are imported or attempted to be imported or are brought within the Indian customs waters for the purpose of being imported, contrary to any prohibition imposed by or under this Act or any other law for the time being in force;

(e) any dutiable or prohibited goods found concealed in any manner in any conveyance;

(f) any dutiable or prohibited goods required to be mentioned under the regulations in an import manifest or import report which are not so mentioned;

(g) any dutiable or prohibited goods which are unloaded from a conveyance in contravention of the provisions of Section 32, other than goods inadvertently unloaded but included in the record kept under sub-section (2) of Section 45;

(h) any dutiable or prohibited goods unloaded or attempted to be unloaded in contravention of the provisions of Section 33 or Section 34;

(i) any dutiable or prohibited goods found concealed in any manner in any package either before or after the unloading thereof;

(j) any dutiable or prohibited goods removed or attempted to be removed from a customs area or a warehouse without the permission of the proper officer or contrary to the terms of such permission;

(k) any dutiable or prohibited goods imported by land in respect of which the order permitting clearance of the goods required to be produced under Section 109 is not produced or which do not correspond in any material particular with the specification contained therein;

(l) any dutiable or prohibited goods which are not included or are in excess of those included in the entry made under this Act, or in the case of baggage in the declaration made under Section 77;

(m) any goods which do not correspond in respect of value or in any other particular with the entry made under this Act or in the case of baggage with the declaration made under Section 77 in respect thereof, or in the case of goods under transhipment, with the declaration for transhipment referred to in the proviso to sub-section (1) of Section 54;

(n) any dutiable or prohibited goods transited with or without transhipment or attempted to be so transited in contravention of the provisions of Chapter VIII;

(o) any goods exempted, subject to any condition, from duty or any prohibition in respect of the import thereof under this Act or any other law for the time being in force, in respect of which the condition is not observed unless the non-observance of the condition was sanctioned by the proper officer;

(p) any notified goods in relation to which any provisions of Chapter IVA or of any rule made under this Act for carrying out the purposes of that Chapter have been contravened.

112. Penalty for improper importation of goods, etc. Any person,—

(a) who, in relation to any goods, does or omits to do any act which act or omission would render such goods liable to confiscation under Section 111, or abets the doing or omission of such an act, or

(b) who acquires possession of or is in any way concerned in carrying, removing, depositing, harbouring, keeping, concealing, selling or purchasing, or in any other manner dealing with any goods which he knows or has reason to believe are liable to confiscation under Section 111, shall be liable, -

(i) in thc case of goods in respect of which any prohibition is in force under this Act or any other law for the time being in force, to a penalty not exceeding the value of the goods or five thousand rupees, whichever is the greater;

(ii) in the case of dutiable goods, other than prohibited goods, to a penalty not exceeding the duty sought to be evaded on such goods or five thousand rupees, whichever is the greater;

(iii) in the case of goods in respect of which the value stated in the entry made under this Act or in the case of baggage, in the declaration made under Section 77 (in either case hereafter in this Section referred to as the declared value) is higher than the value thereof, to a penalty not exceeding the difference between the declared value and the value thereof or five thousand rupees, whichever is the greater;

(iv) in the case of goods falling both under clauses (i) and (iii), to a penalty not exceeding the value of the goods or the difference between the declared value and the value thereof or five thousand rupees, whichever is the highest;

(v) in the case of goods falling both under clauses (ii) and (iii), to a penalty not exceeding the duty sought to be evaded on such goods or the difference between the declared value and the value thereof or five thousand rupees, whichever is the highest.

113. Confiscation of goods attempted to be improperly exported, etc. The following export goods shall be liable to confiscation:-

(a) any goods attempted to be exported by sea or air from any place other than a customs port or a customs airport appointed for the loading of such goods;

(b) any goods attempted to be exported by land or inland water through any route other than a route specified in a notification issued under clause (c) of Section 7 for the export of such goods;

(c) any goods brought near the land frontier or the coast of India or near any bay, gulf, creek or tidal river for the purpose of being exported from a place other than a land customs station or a customs port appointed for the loading of such goods;

(d) any goods attempted to be exported or brought within the limits of any customs area for the purpose of being exported, contrary to any prohibition imposed by or under this Act or any other law for the time being in force;

(e) any goods found concealed in a package which is brought within the limits of a customs area for the purpose of exportation;

(f) any goods which are loaded or attempted to be loaded in contravention of the provisions of Section 33 or Section 34;

(g) any goods loaded or attempted to be loaded on any conveyance, or water-borne, or attempted to be water-borne for being loaded on any vessel, the eventual destination of which is a place outside India, without the permission of the proper officer;

(h) any goods which are not included or are in excess of those included in the entry made under this Act, or in the case of baggage in the declaration made under Section 77;

(i) any goods entered for exportation which do not correspond in respect of value or in any material particular with the entry made under this Act or in the case of baggage with the declaration made under Section 77;

(ii) any goods entered for exportation under claim for drawback which do not correspond in any material particular with any information furnished by the exporter or manufacturer under this Act in relation to the fixation of rate of drawback under Section 75;

(j) any goods on which import duty has not been paid and which are entered for exportation under a claim for drawback under Section 74;

(k) any goods cleared for exportation which are not loaded for exportation on account of any wilful act, negligence or default of the exporter, his agent or employee, or which after having been loaded for exportation are unloaded without the permission of the proper officer;

(l) any specified goods in relation to which any provisions of Chapter IVB or of any rule made under this Act for carrying out the purposes of that Chapter have been contravened.

114. Penalty for attempt to export goods improperly, etc. Any person who, in relation to any goods, does or omits to do any act which act or omission would render such goods liable to confiscation under Section 113, or abets the doing or omission of such an act, shall be liable, -

(i) in the case of goods in respect of which any prohibition is in force under this Act or any other law for the time being in force, to a penalty not exceeding three times the value of the goods as declared by the exporter or the value as determined under this Act, whichever is the greater;

(ii) in the case of dutiable goods, other than prohibited goods, to a penalty not exceeding the duty sought to be evaded or five thousand rupees, whichever is the greater;

(iii) in the case of any other goods, to a penalty not exceeding the value of the goods, as declared by the exporter or the value as determined under this Act, whichever is the greater.

114A. Penalty for short-levy or non-levy of duty in certain cases. - Where the duty has not been levied or has been short-levied or the interest has not been charged or paid or has been part paid or the duty or interest has been erroneously refunded by reason of collusion or any wilful mis-statement or suppression of facts, the person who is liable to pay the duty or interest, as the case may be, as determined under sub-section (8) of Section 28 shall also be liable to pay a penalty equal to the duty or interest so determined:

PROVIDED that where such duty or interest, as the case may be, as determined under sub-section (8) of Section 28, and the interest payable thereon under Section 28AA, is paid within thirty days from the date of the communication of the order of the proper officer determining such duty, the amount of penalty liable to be paid by such person under this Section shall be twenty-five per cent of the duty or interest, as the case may be, so determined :

PROVIDED FURTHER that the benefit of reduced penalty under the first proviso shall be available subject to the condition that the amount of penalty so determined has also been paid within the period of thirty days referred to in that proviso :

PROVIDED ALSO that where the duty or interest determined to be payable is reduced or increased by the Commissioner (Appeals), the Appellate Tribunal or, as the case may be, the court, then, for the purposes of this Section, the duty or interest as reduced or increased, as the case may be, shall be taken into account :

PROVIDED ALSO that in case where the duty or interest determined to be payable is increased by the Commissioner (Appeals), the Appellate Tribunal or, as the case may be, the court, then, the benefit of reduced penalty under the first proviso shall be available if the amount of the duty or the interest so increased, along with the interest payable thereon under Section 28AA, and twenty-five percent of the consequential increase in penalty have also been paid within thirty days of the communication of the order by which such increase in the duty or interest takes effect :

PROVIDED ALSO that where any penalty has been levied under this Section, no penalty shall be levied under Section 112 or Section 114.

EXPLANATION: For the removal of doubts, it is hereby declared that –

(i) the provisions of this Section shall also apply to cases in which the order determining the duty or interest under sub-section (8) of Section 28 relates to notices issued prior to the date on which the Finance Act, 2000 receives the assent of the President;

(ii) any amount paid to the credit of the Central Government prior to the date of communication of the order referred to in the first proviso or the fourth proviso shall be adjusted against the total amount due from such person.

114AA. Penalty for use of false and incorrect material. If a person knowingly or intentionally makes, signs or uses, or causes to be made, signed or used, any declaration, statement or document which is false or incorrect in any material particular, in the transaction of any business for the purposes of this Act, shall be liable to a penalty not exceeding five times the value of goods.

115. Confiscation of conveyances.

(1) The following conveyances shall be liable to confiscation :-

(a) any vessel which is or has been within the Indian customs waters, any aircraft which is or has been in India, or any vehicle which is or has been in a customs area, while constructed, adapted, altered or fitted in any manner for the purpose of concealing goods;

(b) any conveyance from which the whole or any part of the goods is thrown overboard, staved or destroyed so as to prevent seizure by an officer of customs;

(c) any conveyance which having been required to stop or land under Section 106 fails to do so, except for good and sufficient cause;

(d) any conveyance from which any warehoused goods cleared for exportation, or any other goods cleared for exportation under a claim for drawback, are unloaded, without the permission of the proper officer;

(e) any conveyance carrying imported goods which has entered India and is afterwards found with the whole or substantial portion of such goods missing, unless the master of the vessel or aircraft is able to account for the loss of, or deficiency in, the goods.

(2) Any conveyance or animal used as a means of transport in the smuggling of any goods or in the carriage of any smuggled goods shall be liable to confiscation, unless the owner of the conveyance or animal proves that it was so used without the knowledge or connivance of the owner himself, his agent, if any, and the person in charge of the conveyance or animal:

PROVIDED that where any such conveyance is used for the carriage of goods or passengers for hire, the owner of any conveyance shall be given an option to pay in lieu of the confiscation of the conveyance a fine not exceeding the market price of the goods which are sought to be smuggled or the smuggled goods, as the case may be.

EXPLANATION: In this Section, "market price" means market price at the date when the goods are seized.

116. Penalty for not accounting for goods. If any goods loaded in a conveyance for importation into India, or any goods transhipped under the provisions of this Act or coastal goods carried in a conveyance, are not unloaded at their place of destination in India, or if the quantity unloaded is short of the quantity to be unloaded at that destination, and if the failure to unload or the deficiency is not accounted for to the satisfaction of the Assistant Commissioner of Customs or Deputy Commissioner of Customs, the person-in-charge of the conveyance shall be liable -

(a) in the case of goods loaded in a conveyance for importation into India or goods transhipped under the provisions of this Act, to a penalty not exceeding twice the amount of duty that would have been chargeable on the goods not unloaded or the deficient goods, as the case may be, had such goods been imported;

(b) in the case of coastal goods, to a penalty not exceeding twice the amount of export duty that would have been chargeable on the goods not unloaded or the deficient goods, as the case may be, had such goods been exported.

117. Penalties for contravention, etc., not expressly mentioned. Any person who contravenes any provision of this Act or abets any such contravention or who fails to comply with any provision of this Act with which it was his duty to comply, where no express penalty is elsewhere provided for such contravention or failure, shall be liable to a penalty not exceeding one lakh rupees.

118. Confiscation of packages and their contents.

(a) Where any goods imported in a package are liable to confiscation, the package and any other goods imported in that package shall also be liable to confiscation.

(b) Where any goods are brought in a package within the limits of a customs area for the purpose of exportation and are liable to confiscation, the package and any other goods contained therein shall also be liable to confiscation.

119. Confiscation of goods used for concealing smuggled goods. Any goods used for concealing smuggled goods shall also be liable to confiscation.

EXPLANATION: In this Section, "goods" does not include a conveyance used as a means of transport.

120. Confiscation of smuggled goods notwithstanding any change in form, etc.

(1) Smuggled goods may be confiscated notwithstanding any change in their form.

(2) Where smuggled goods are mixed with other goods in such manner that the smuggled goods cannot be separated from such other goods, the whole of the goods shall be liable to confiscation :

PROVIDED that where the owner of such goods proves that he had no knowledge or reason to believe that they included any smuggled goods, only such part of the goods the value of which is equal to the value of the smuggled goods shall be liable to confiscation.

121. Confiscation of sale-proceeds of smuggled goods. Where any smuggled goods are sold by a person having knowledge or reason to believe that the goods are smuggled goods, the sale-proceeds thereof shall be liable to confiscation.

122. Adjudication of confiscations and penalties. In every case under this Chapter in which anything is liable to confiscation or any person is liable to a penalty, such confiscation or penalty may be adjudged, -

(a) without limit, by a Commissioner of Customs or a Joint Commissioner of Customs;

(b) where the value of the goods liable to confiscation does not exceed two lakh rupees, by an Assistant Commissioner of Customs or Deputy Commissioner of Customs;

(c) where the value of the goods liable to confiscation does not exceed, ten thousand rupees, by a Gazetted Officer of Customs lower in rank than an Assistant Commissioner of Customs or Deputy Commissioner of Customs.

122A. Adjudication Procedure.

(1) The adjudicating authority shall, in any proceeding under this Chapter or any other provision of this Act, give an opportunity of being heard to a party in a proceeding, if the party so desires.

(2) The adjudicating authority may, if sufficient cause is shown at any stage of proceeding referred to in sub-section (1), grant time, from time to time, to the parties or any of them and adjourn the hearing for reasons to be recorded in writing:

PROVIDED that no such adjournment shall be granted more than three times to a party during the proceeding.

123. Burden of proof in certain cases.

(1) Where any goods to which this Section applies are seized under this Act in the reasonable belief that they are smuggled goods, the burden of proving that they are not smuggled goods shall be –

(a) in a case where such seizure is made from the possession of any person,-

(i) on the person from whose possession the goods were seized; and

(ii) if any person, other than the person from whose possession the goods were seized, claims to be the owner thereof, also on such other person;

(b) in any other case, on the person, if any, who claims to be the owner of the goods so seized.

(2) This Section shall apply to gold, and manufactures thereof, watches, and any other class of goods which the Central Government may by notification in the Official Gazette specify.

124. Issue of show-cause notice before confiscation of goods, etc. No order confiscating any goods or imposing any penalty on any person shall be made under this Chapter unless the owner of the goods or such person -

(a) is given a notice in writing with the prior approval of the officer of Customs not below the rank of an Assistant Commissioner of Customs, informing him of the grounds on which it is proposed to confiscate the goods or to impose a penalty;

(b) is given an opportunity of making a representation in writing within such reasonable time as may be specified in the notice against the grounds of confiscation or imposition of penalty mentioned therein; and

(c) is given a reasonable opportunity of being heard in the matter :

PROVIDED that the notice referred to in clause (a) and the representation referred to in clause (b) may, at the request of the person concerned be oral.

125. Option to pay fine in lieu of confiscation.

(1) Whenever confiscation of any goods is authorised by this Act, the officer adjudging it may, in the case of any goods, the importation or exportation whereof is prohibited under this Act or under any other law for the time being in force, and shall, in the case of any other goods, give to the owner of the

goods or, where such owner is not known, the person from whose possession or custody such goods have been seized, an option to pay in lieu of confiscation such fine as the said officer thinks fit :

PROVIDED that, without prejudice to the provisions of the proviso to sub-section (2) of Section 115, such fine shall not exceed the market price of the goods confiscated, less in the case of imported goods the duty chargeable thereon.

(2) Where any fine in lieu of confiscation of goods is imposed under sub-section (1), the owner of such goods or the person referred to in sub-section (1), shall, in addition, be liable to any duty and charges payable in respect of such goods.

126. On confiscation, property to vest in Central Government.

(1) When any goods are confiscated under this Act, such goods shall thereupon vest in the Central Government.

(2) The officer adjudging confiscation shall take and hold possession of the confiscated goods.

127. Award of confiscation or penalty by customs officers not to interfere with other punishments. The award of any confiscation or penalty under this Act by an officer of customs shall not prevent the infliction of any punishment to which the person affected thereby is liable under the provisions of Chapter XVI of this Act or under any other law.

CHAPTER XIV - A : SETTLEMENT OF CASES

127A. Definitions. In this Chapter, unless the context otherwise requires,

(a) "Bench" means a Bench of the Settlement Commission;

(b) "case" means any proceeding under this Act or any other Act for the levy, assessment and collection of customs duty, pending before an adjudicating authority on the date on which an application under sub-section (1) of Section 127B is made :

PROVIDED that when any proceeding is referred back in any appeal or revision, as the case may be, by any court, Appellate Tribunal or any other authority, to the adjudicating authority for a fresh adjudication or decision, as the case may be, then such proceeding shall not be deemed to be a proceeding pending within the meaning of this clause;

(c) "Chairman" means the Chairman of the Settlement Commission;

(d) "Commissioner (Investigation)" means an officer of the customs or a Central Excise Officer appointed as such Commissioner to conduct inquiry or investigation for the purposes of this Chapter;

(e) "Member" means a Member of the Settlement Commission and includes the Chairman and the Vice-Chairman;

(f) "Settlement Commission" means the Customs and Central Excise Settlement Commission constituted under Section 32 of the Central Excise Act, 1944 (1 of 1944); and

(g) "Vice-Chairman" means a Vice-Chairman of the Settlement Commission.

127B. Application for settlement of cases.

(1) Any importer, exporter or any other person (hereinafter referred to as the applicant in this Chapter) may, in respect of a case, relating to him make an application, before adjudication to the Settlement Commission to have the case settled, in such form and in such manner as may be specified by rules, and containing a full and true disclosure of his duty liability which has not been disclosed before the proper officer, the manner in which such liability has been incurred, the additional amount of customs duty accepted to be payable by him and such other particulars as may be specified by rules including the particulars of such dutiable goods in respect of which he admits short levy on account of misclassification, under-valuation or inapplicability of exemption notification or otherwise and such application shall be disposed of in the manner hereinafter provided :

PROVIDED that no such application shall be made unless, -

- *(a) the applicant has filed a bill of entry, or a shipping bill, in respect of import or export of such goods, as the case may be, and in relation to such bill of entry or shipping bill, a show cause notice has been issued to him by the proper officer;*
- *(b) the additional amount of duty accepted by the applicant in his application exceeds three lakh rupees; and*
- *(c) the applicant has paid the additional amount of customs duty accepted by him along with interest due under Section 28AB :*

PROVIDED FURTHER that no application shall be entertained by the Settlement Commission under this sub-section in cases which are pending in the Appellate Tribunal or any court:

PROVIDED ALSO that no application under this sub-section shall be made in relation to goods to which Section 123 applies or to goods in relation to which any offence under the Narcotic Drugs and Psychotropic Substances Act, 1985 (61 of 1985) has been committed:

PROVIDED ALSO that no application under this sub-section shall be made for the interpretation of the classification of the goods under the Customs Tariff Act, 1975 (51 of 1975).

(1A) Notwithstanding anything contained in sub-section (1), where an application was made under sub-section (1) before the 1st day of June, 2007 but an order under sub-section (1) of Section 127C has not been made before the said date, the applicant shall within a period of thirty days from the 1st day of June, 2007 pay the accepted duty liability failing which his application shall be liable to be rejected.

(2) Where any dutiable goods, books of account, other documents or any sale proceeds of the goods have been seized under Section 110, the applicant shall not be entitled to make an application under sub-section (1) before the expiry of one hundred and eighty days from the date of the seizure.

(3) Every application made under sub-section (1) shall be accompanied by such fees as may be specified by rules.

(4) An application made under sub-section (1) shall not be allowed to be withdrawn by the applicant.

127C. Procedure on receipt of an application under Section 127B.

(1) On receipt of an application under Section 127B, the Settlement Commission shall, within seven days from the date of receipt of the application, issue a notice to the applicant to explain in writing as to why the application made by him should be allowed to be proceeded with and after taking into consideration the explanation provided by the applicant, the Settlement Commission, shall, within a period of fourteen days from the date of the notice, by an order, allow the application to be proceeded with or reject the application, as the case may be, and the proceedings before the Settlement Commission shall abate on the date of rejection :

PROVIDED that where no notice has been issued or no order has been passed within the aforesaid period by the Settlement Commission, the application shall be deemed to have been allowed to be proceeded with.

(2) A copy of every order under sub-section (1) shall be sent to the applicant and to the Commissioner of Customs having jurisdiction.

(3) Where an application is allowed or deemed to have been allowed to be proceeded with under sub-section (1), the Settlement Commission shall, within seven days from the date of order under sub-section (1), call for a report along with the relevant records from the Commissioner of Customs having jurisdiction and the Commissioner shall furnish the report within a period of thirty days of the receipt of communication from the Settlement Commission :

PROVIDED that where the Commissioner does not furnish the report within the aforesaid period of thirty days, the Settlement Commission shall proceed further in the matter without the report of the Commissioner.

(4) Where a report of the Commissioner called for under sub-section (3) has been furnished within the period specified in that sub-section, the Settlement Commission may, after examination of such report, if it is of the opinion that any further enquiry or investigation in the matter is necessary, direct, for reasons to be recorded in writing, the Commissioner (Investigation) within fifteen days of the receipt of the report, to make or cause to be made such further enquiry or investigation and furnish a report within a period of ninety days of the receipt of the communication from the Settlement Commission, on the matters covered by the application and any other matter relating to the case :

PROVIDED that where the Commissioner (Investigation) does not furnish the report within the aforesaid period, the Settlement Commission shall proceed to pass an order under sub-section (5) without such report.

(5) After examination of the records and the report of the Commissioner of Customs received under sub-section (3), and the report, if any, of the Commissioner (Investigation) of the Settlement Commission under sub-section (4), and after giving an opportunity to the applicant and to the Commissioner of Customs

having jurisdiction to be heard, either in person or through a representative dulyauthorised in this behalf, and after examining such further evidence as may be placed before it or obtained by it, the Settlement Commission may, in accordance with the provisions of this Act, pass such order as it thinks fit on the matters covered by the application and any other matter relating to the case not covered by the application, but referred to in the report of the Commissioner of Customs and Commissioner (Investigation) under sub-section (3) or sub-section (4).

(6) An order under sub-section (5) shall not be passed in respect of an application filed on or before the 31st day of May, 2007, later than the 29th February, 2008 and in respect of an application made on or after the 1st day of June, 2007, after nine months from the last day of the month in which the application was made, failing which the settlement proceedings shall abate, and the adjudicating authority before whom the proceeding at the time of making the application was pending, shall dispose of the case in accordance with the provisions of this Act as if no application under Section 127B had been made.

PROVIDED that the period specified under this sub-section may, for reasons to be recorded in writing, be extended by the Settlement Commission for a further period not exceeding three months.

(7) Subject to the provisions of Section 32A of the Central Excise Act, 1944 (1 of 1944), the materials brought on record before the Settlement Commission shall be considered by the Members of the concerned Bench before passing any order under sub-section (5) and, in relation to the passing of such order, the provisions of Section 32D of the Central Excise Act, 1944 (1 of 1944) shall apply.

(8) The order passed under sub-section (5) shall provide for the terms of settlement including any demand by way of duty, penalty or interest, the manner in which any sums due under the settlement shall be paid and all other matters to make the settlement effective and in case of rejection contain the reasons therefore and it shall also provide that the settlement shall be void if it is subsequently found by the Settlement Commission that it has been obtained by fraud or misrepresentation of facts :

PROVIDED that the amount of settlement ordered by the Settlement Commission, shall not be less than the duty liability admitted by the applicant under Section 127B.

(9) Where any duty, interest, fine and penalty payable in pursuance of an order under sub-section (5) is not paid by the applicant within thirty days of receipt of a copy of the order by him, the amount which remains unpaid, shall be recovered along with interest due thereon, as the sums due to the Central Government by the proper officer having jurisdiction over the applicant in accordance with the provisions of Section 142.

(10) Where a settlement becomes void as provided under sub-section (8), the proceedings with respect to the matters covered by the settlement shall be

deemed to have been revived from the stage at which the application was allowed to be proceeded with by the Settlement Commission and the proper officer having jurisdiction may, notwithstanding anything contained in any other provision of this Act, complete such proceedings at any time before the expiry of two years from the date of the receipt of communication that the settlement became void.

127D. Power of Settlement Commission to order provisional attachment to protect revenue.

(1) Where, during the pendency of any proceeding before it, the Settlement Commission is of the opinion that for the purpose of protecting the interests of the revenue it is necessary so to do, it may, by order, attach provisionally any property belonging to the applicant in such manner as may be specified by rules.

(2) Every provisional attachment made by the Settlement Commission under sub-section (1) shall cease to have effect from the date the sums due to the Central Government for which such attachment is made are discharged by the applicant and evidence to that effect is submitted to the Settlement Commission.

127E.Power of Settlement Commission to reopen completed proceedings. If the Settlement Commission is of the opinion (the reasons for such opinion to be recorded by it in writing) that, for the proper disposal of the case pending before it, it is necessary or expedient to reopen any proceeding connected with the case but which has been completed under this Act before application for settlement under Section 127B was made, it may, with the concurrence of the applicant, reopen such proceeding and pass such order thereon as it thinks fit, as if the case in relation to which the application for settlement had been made by the applicant under that Section covered such proceeding also:

PROVIDED that no proceeding shall be reopened by the Settlement Commission under this Section after the expiry of five years from the date of application under sub-section (1) of Section 127B.

PROVIDED FURTHER that no proceeding shall be reopened by the Settlement Commission under this Section in a case where an application under Section 127B is made on or after the 1st day of June, 2007.

127F. Power and procedure of Settlement Commission.

(1) In addition to the powers conferred on the Settlement Commission under Chapter V of the Central Excise Act, 1944 (1 of 1944), it shall have all the powers which are vested in an officer of the customs under this Act or the rules made thereunder.

(2) Where an application made under Section 127B has been allowed to be proceeded with under Section 127C, the Settlement Commission shall, until an order is passed under sub-section (5) of Section 127C, have, subject to the provisions of sub-section [(4)] of that Section, exclusive jurisdiction to exercise the powers and perform the functions of any officer of customs or Central Excise Officer as the case may be, under this Act or in the Central Excise Act, 1944 (1 of 1944), as the case may be, in relation to the case.

(3) In the absence of any express direction by the Settlement Commission to the contrary, nothing in this Chapter shall affect the operation of the provisions of this Act in so far as they relate to any matter other than those before the Settlement Commission.

(4) The Settlement Commission shall, subject to the provisions of Chapter V of the Central Excise Act, 1944 (1 of 1944) and this Chapter, have power to regulate its own procedure and the procedure of Benches thereof in all matters arising out of the exercise of its powers, or of the discharge of its functions, including the places at which the Benches shall hold their sittings.

127G. Inspection, etc. of reports. No person shall be entitled to inspect, or obtain copies of, any report made by any officer of the Customs to the Settlement Commission; but the Settlement Commission may, in its discretion, furnish copies thereof to any such person on an application made to it in this behalf and on payment of such fee as may be specified by rules:

PROVIDED that, for the purpose of enabling any person whose case is under consideration to rebut any evidence brought on record against him in any such report, the Settlement Commission shall, on an application made in this behalf, and on payment by such person of such fee as may be specified by rules, furnish him with a certified copy of any such report or part thereof relevant for the purpose.

127H. Power of Settlement Commission to grant immunity from prosecution and penalty.

(1) The Settlement Commission may, if it is satisfied that any person who made the application for settlement under Section 127B has co-operated with the Settlement Commission in the proceedings before it and has made a full and true disclosure of his duty liability, grant to such person, subject to such conditions as it may think fit to impose, immunity from prosecution for any offence under this Act and also either wholly or in part from the imposition of any penalty and fine under this Act, with respect to the case covered by the settlement :

PROVIDED that no such immunity shall be granted by the Settlement Commission in cases where the proceedings for the prosecution for any such offence have been instituted before the date of receipt of the application under Section 127B.

EXPLANATION: For the removal of doubts, it is hereby declared that the application filed before the Settlement Commission on or before the 31st day of May, 2007 shall be disposed of as if the amendment in this Section had not come into force.

(2) An immunity granted to a person under sub-section (1) shall stand withdrawn if such person fails to pay any sum specified in the order of the settlement passed under "sub-section (5) of Section 127C within the time specified in such order or fails to comply with any other condition subject to which the immunity was granted and thereupon the provisions of this Act shall apply as if such immunity had not been granted.

(3) An immunity granted to a person under sub-section (1) may, at any time, be withdrawn by the Settlement Commission, if it is satisfied that such person had, in the course of the settlement proceedings, concealed any particulars, material to the settlement or had given false evidence, and thereupon such person may be tried for the offence with respect to which the immunity was granted or for any other offence of which he appears to have been guilty in connection with the settlement and shall also become liable to the imposition of any penalty under this Act to which such person would have been liable, had no such immunity been granted.

127-I. Power of Settlement Commission to send a case back to the proper officer.

(1) The Settlement Commission may, if it is of opinion that any person who made an application for settlement under Section 127B has not co-operated with the Settlement Commission in the proceedings before it, send the case back to the proper officer who shall thereupon dispose of the case in accordance with the provisions of this Act as if no application under Section 127B had been made.

(2) For the purpose of sub-section (1), the proper officer shall be entitled to use all the materials and other information produced by the assessee before the Settlement Commission or the results of the inquiry held or evidence recorded by the Settlement Commission in the course of the proceedings before it as if such materials, information, inquiry and evidence had been produced before such proper officer or held or recorded by him in the course of the proceedings before him.

(3) For the purposes of the time limit under Section 28 and for the purposes of interest under Section 28AA, in a case referred to in sub-section (1), the period commencing on and from the date of the application to the Settlement Commission under Section 127B and ending with the date of receipt by the officer of customs of the order of the Settlement Commission sending the case back to the officer of customs shall be excluded.

127J. Order of settlement to be conclusive. Every order of settlement passed under sub-section (5) of Section 127C shall be conclusive as to the matters stated therein and no matter covered by such order shall, save as otherwise provided in this Chapter, be reopened in any proceeding under this Act or under any other law for the time being in force.

127K. Recovery of sums due under order of settlement. Any sum specified in an order of settlement passed under sub-section (5) of Section 127C may, subject to such conditions, if any, as may be specified therein, be recovered, and any penalty for default in making payment of such sum may be imposed and recovered as sums due to the Central Government in accordance with the provisions of Section 142, by the proper officer having jurisdiction over the applicant.

127L. Bar on subsequent application for settlement in certain cases.

(1) where –

(i) an order of settlement passed under sub-section (7) of Section 127C as it stood immediately before the commencement of Section 102 of the Finance

Act, 2007(22 of 2007) or sub-section (5) of Section 127C provides for the imposition of a penalty on the applicant under Section 127B for settlement, on the ground of concealment of particulars of his duty liability; or

(ii) after the passing of an order of settlement under said sub-section (7) as it stood immediately before the commencement of Section 102 of the Finance Act, 2007 (22 of 2007) or sub-section (5) of Section 127C in relation to a case, such person is convicted of any offence under this Act in relation to that case; or

(iii) the case of such person is sent back to the proper officer by the Settlement Commission under Section 127-I, then such person shall not be entitled to apply for settlement under Section 127B in relation to any other matter.

(2) Where an applicant has made an application under sub-section (1) of Section 127B, on or after the 1st day of June, 2007 and if such application has been allowed to be proceeded with under sub-section (1) of Section 127C, such applicant shall not be entitled to apply for settlement under section 127B in relation to any other matter:

PROVIDED that such applicant shall not be prevented from filing an application for settlement if the issue in the subsequent application is, but for the period of dispute and amount, identical to the issue in respect of which the earlier application is pending before the Settlement Commission.".

127M. Proceedings before Settlement Commission to be judicial proceedings. Any proceedings under this Chapter before the Settlement Commission shall be deemed to be a judicial proceeding within the meaning of Sections 193 and 228, and for the purposes of Section 196, of the Indian Penal Code (45 of 1860).

127MA. omitted.

127N. Applications of certain provisions of Central Excise Act. The provisions of Chapter V of the Central Excise Act, 1944 (1 of 1944) insofar as it is not inconsistent with the provisions of this Chapter shall apply in relation to proceedings before the Settlement Commission under this Chapter.

CHAPTER - XV : APPEALS AND REVISION

128. Appeals to Commissioner (Appeals).

(1) Any person aggrieved by any decision or order passed under this Act by an officer of customs lower in rank than a Commissioner of Customs may appeal to the Commissioner (Appeals) within sixty days from the date of the communication to him of such decision or order:

PROVIDED that the Commissioner (Appeals) may, if he is satisfied that the appellant was prevented by sufficient cause from presenting the appeal within the aforesaid period of sixty days, allow it to be presented within a further period of thirty days.

(1A) The Commissioner (Appeals) may, if sufficient cause is shown at any stage of hearing of an appeal, grant time, from time to time, to the parties or any of them and adjourn the hearing of the appeal for reasons to be recorded in writing:

PROVIDED that no such adjournment shall be granted more than three times to a party during hearing of the appeal.

(2) Every appeal under this section, shall be in such form and shall be verified in such manner as may be specified by rules made in this behalf.

128A. Procedure in appeal.

(1) The Commissioner (Appeals) shall give an opportunity to the appellant to be heard if he so desires.

(2) The Commissioner (Appeals) may, at the hearing of an appeal, allow the appellant to go into any ground of appeal not specified in the grounds of appeal, if the Commissioner (Appeals) is satisfied that the omission of that ground from the grounds of appeal was not wilful or unreasonable.

(3) The Commissioner (Appeals) shall, after making such further inquiry as may be necessary, pass such order, as he thinks just and proper, confirming, modifying or annulling the decision or order appealed against:

PROVIDED that an order enhancing any penalty or fine in lieu of confiscation or confiscating goods of greater value or reducing the amount of refund shall not be passed unless the appellant has been given a reasonable opportunity of showing cause against the proposed order:

PROVIDED FURTHER that where the Commissioner (Appeals) is of opinion that any duty has not been levied or has been short-levied or erroneously refunded, no order requiring the appellant to pay any duty not levied, short-levied or erroneously refunded shall be passed unless the appellant is given notice within the time-limit specified in Section 28 to show cause against the proposed order.

(4) The order of the Commissioner (Appeals) disposing of the appeal shall be in writing and shall state the points for determination, the decision thereon and the reasons for the decision.

(4A) The Commissioner (Appeals) shall, where it is possible to do so, hear and decide every appeal within a period of six months from the date on which it is filed.

(5) On the disposal of the appeal, the Commissioner (Appeals) shall communicate the order passed by him to the appellant, the adjudicating authority, the Chief Commissioner of Customs and the Commissioner of Customs.

129. Appellate Tribunal.

(1) The Central Government shall constitute an Appellate Tribunal to be called the Customs, Excise and Service Tax Appellate Tribunal consisting of as many judicial and technical members as it thinks fit to exercise the powers and discharge the functions conferred on the Appellate Tribunal by this Act.

(2) A judicial member shall be a person who has for at least ten years held a judicial office in the territory of India or who has been a member of the Indian

Legal Service and has held a post in Grade I of that service or any equivalent or higher post for at least three years, or who has been an advocate for at least ten years.

EXPLANATION: For the purposes of this sub-section, -

(i) in computing the period during which a person has held judicial office in the territory of India, there shall be included any period, after he has held any judicial office, during which the person has been an advocate or has held the office of a member of a tribunal or any post, under the Union or a State, requiring special knowledge of law;

(ii) in computing the period during which a person has been an advocate, there shall be included any period during which the person has held a judicial office, or the office of a member of a tribunal or any post, under the Union or a State, requiring special knowledge of law after he became an advocate.

(2A) A technical member shall be a person who has been a member of the Indian Customs and Central Excise Service, Group A, and has held the post of Commissioner of Customs or Central Excise or any equivalent or higher post for at least three years.

(3) The Central Government shall appoint —

(a) a person who is or has been a Judge of a High Court; or

(b) one of the members of the Appellate Tribunal, to be the President thereof.

(4) The Central Government may appoint one or more members of the Appellate Tribunal to be the Vice-President, or, as the case may be, Vice-Presidents, thereof.

(4A) Omitted.

(5) A Vice-President shall exercise such of the powers and perform such of the functions of the President as may be delegated to him by the President by a general or special order in writing.

(6) On ceasing to hold office, the President, Vice-President or other Member shall not be entitled to appear, act or plead before the Appellate Tribunal.

129A. Appeals to the Appellate Tribunal.

(1) Any person aggrieved by any of the following orders may appeal to the Appellate Tribunal against such order -

(a) a decision or order passed by the Commissioner of Customs as an adjudicating authority

(b) an order passed by the Commissioner (Appeals) under Section 128A;

(c) an order passed by the Board or the Appellate Commissioner of Customs under Section 128, as it stood immediately before the appointed day;

(d) an order passed by the Board or the Commissioner of Customs, either before or after the appointed day, under Section 130, as it stood immediately before that day :

PROVIDED that no appeal shall lie to the Appellate Tribunal and the Appellate Tribunal shall not have jurisdiction to decide any appeal in respect of any order referred to in clause (b) if such order relates to, -

(a) any goods imported or exported as baggage;

(b) any goods loaded in a conveyance for importation into India, but which are not unloaded at their place of destination in India, or so much of the quantity of such goods as has not been unloaded at any such destination if goods unloaded at such destination are short of the quantity required to be unloaded at that destination;

(c) payment of drawback as provided in Chapter X, and the rules made thereunder :

PROVIDED FURTHER that the Appellate Tribunal may, in its discretion, refuse to admit an appeal in respect of an order referred to in clause (b) or clause (c) or clause (d) where –

(i) the value of the goods confiscated without option having been given to the owner of the goods to pay a fine in lieu of confiscation under Section 125; or

(ii) in any disputed case, other than a case where the determination of any question having a relation to the rate of duty of customs or to the value of goods for purposes of assessment is in issue or is one of the points in issue, the difference in duty involved or the duty involved; or

(iii) the amount of fine or penalty determined by such order, does not exceed fifty thousand rupees.

(1A) Every appeal against any order of the nature referred to in the first proviso to sub-section (1), which is pending immediately before the commencement of Section 40 of the Finance Act, 1984, before the Appellate Tribunal and any matter arising out of or connected with such appeal and which is so pending shall stand transferred on such commencement to the Central Government and the Central Government shall deal with such appeal or matter under Section 129DD as if such appeal or matter were an application or a matter arising out of an application made to itunder that Section.

(1B) (i) The Board may, by notification in the Official Gazette, constitute such Committees as may be necessary for the purposes of this Act.

(ii) Every Committee constituted under clause (i) shall consist of two Chief Commissioners of Customs or two Commissioners of Customs, as the case may be.

(2) The Committee of Commissioners of Customs may, if it is of opinion that an order passed by the Appellate Commissioner of Customs under Section 128, as it stood immediately before the appointed day, or by the Commissioner (Appeals) under Section 128A, is not legal or proper, direct the proper officer to appeal on its behalf to the Appellate Tribunal against such order.

PROVIDED that where the Committee of Commissioners of Customs differs in its opinion regarding the appeal against the order of the Commissioner (Appeals), it shall state the point or points on which it differs and make a reference to the jurisdictional Chief

Commissioner of Customs who shall, after considering the facts of the order, if is of the opinion that the order passed by the Commissioner (Appeals) is not legal or proper, direct the proper officer to appeal to the Appellate Tribunal against such order.

EXPLANATION: For the purposes of this sub-section, "jurisdictional Chief Commissioner" means the Chief Commissioner of Customs having jurisdiction over the adjudicating authority in the matter.

(3) Every appeal under this Section shall be filed within three months from the date on which the order sought to be appealed against is communicated to the Commissioner of Customs, or as the case may be, the other party preferring the appeal.

(4) On receipt of notice that an appeal has been preferred under this Section, the party against whom the appeal has been preferred may, notwithstanding that he may not have appealed against such order or any part thereof, file, within forty-five days of the receipt of the notice, a memorandum of cross-objections verified in such manner as may be specified by rules made in this behalf against any part of the order appealed against and such memorandum shall be disposed of by the Appellate Tribunal as if it were an appeal presented within the time specified in sub-section (3).

(5) The Appellate Tribunal may admit an appeal or permit the filing of a memorandum of cross-objections after the expiry of the relevant period referred to in sub-section (3) or sub-section (4), if it is satisfied that there was sufficient cause for not presenting it within that period.

(6) An appeal to the Appellate Tribunal shall be in such form and shall be verified in such manner as may be specified by rules made in this behalf and shall, irrespective of the date of demand of duty and interest or of levy of penalty in relation to which the appeal is made, be accompanied by a fee of, —

- (a) where the amount of duty and interest demanded and penalty levied by any officer of customs in the case to which the appeal relates is five lakh rupees or less, one thousand rupees;
- (b) where the amount of duty and interest demanded and penalty levied by any officer of customs in the case to which the appeal relates is more than five lakh rupees but not exceeding fifty lakh rupees, five thousand rupees;
- (c) where the amount of duty and interest demanded and penalty levied by any officer of customs in the case to which the appeal relates is more than fifty lakh rupees, ten thousand rupees :

  PROVIDED that no such fee shall be payable in the case of an appeal referred to in sub-section (2) or a memorandum of cross-objections referred to in sub-section (4).

(7) Every application made before the Appellate Tribunal, —

- (a) in an appeal for grant of stay or for rectification of mistake or for any other purpose; or

(b) for restoration of an appeal or an application, shall be accompanied by a fee of five hundred rupees :

PROVIDED that no such fee shall be payable in the case of an application filed by or on behalf of the Commissioner of Customs under this sub-section.

129B. Orders of Appellate Tribunal.

(1) The Appellate Tribunal may, after giving the parties to the appeal, an opportunity of being heard, pass such orders thereon as it thinks fit, confirming, modifying or annulling the decision or order appealed against or may refer the case back to the authority which passed such decision or order with such directions as the Appellate Tribunal may think fit, for a fresh adjudication or decision, as the case may be, after taking additional evidence, if necessary.

(1A) The Appellate Tribunal may, if sufficient cause is shown, at any stage of hearing of an appeal, grant time to the parties or any of them and adjourn the hearing of the appeal for reasons to be recorded in writing :

PROVIDED that no such adjournment shall be granted more than three times to a party during hearing of the appeal.

(2) The Appellate Tribunal may, at any time within six months from the date of the order, with a view to rectifying any mistake apparent from the record, amend any order passed by it under sub-section (1) and shall make such amendments if the mistake is brought to its notice by the Commissioner of Customs or the other party to the appeal :

PROVIDED that an amendment which has the effect of enhancing the assessment or reducing a refund or otherwise increasing the liability of the other party shall not be made under this sub-section, unless the Appellate Tribunal has given notice to him of its intention to do so and has allowed him a reasonable opportunity of being heard.

(2A) The Appellate Tribunal shall, where it is possible to do so, hear and decide every appeal within a period of three years from the date on which such appeal is filed :

PROVIDED that where an order of stay is made in any proceeding relating to an appeal filed under sub-section (1) of Section 129A, the Appellate Tribunal shall dispose of the appeal within a period of one hundred and eighty days from the date of such order:

PROVIDED FURTHER that if such appeal is not disposed of within the period specified in the first proviso, the stay order shall, on the expiry of that period, stand vacated.

(3) The Appellate Tribunal shall send a copy of every order passed under this Section to the Commissioner of Customs and the other party to the appeal.

(4) Save as otherwise provided in Section 130 or Section 130E, orders passed by the Appellate Tribunal on appeal shall be final.

129C. Procedure of Appellate Tribunal.

(1) The powers and functions of the Appellate Tribunal may be exercised and discharged by Benches constituted by the President from amongst the members thereof.

(2) Subject to the provisions contained in sub-section (4), a Bench shall consist of one judicial member and one technical member.

(3) Omitted

(4) The President or any other member of the Appellate Tribunal authorised in this behalf by the President may, sitting singly, dispose of any case which has been allotted to the Bench of which he is a member where -

  (a) the value of the goods confiscated without option having been given to the owner of the goods to pay a fine in lieu of confiscation under Section 125; or

  (b) in any disputed case, other than a case where the determination of any question having a relation to the rate of duty of customs or to the value of goods for purposes of assessment is in issue or is one of the points in issue, the difference in duty involved or the duty involved; or

  (c) the amount of fine or penalty involved, does not exceed ten lakhs rupees.

(5) If the members of a Bench differ in opinion on any point, the point shall be decided according to the opinion of the majority, if there is a majority; but if the members are equally divided, they shall state the point or points on which they differ and make a reference to the President who shall either hear the point or points himself or refer the case for hearing on such point or points by one or more of the other members of the Appellate Tribunal and such point or points shall be decided according to the opinion of the majority of these members of the Appellate Tribunal who have heard the case, including those who first heard it.

(6) Subject to the provisions of this Act, the Appellate Tribunal shall have power to regulate its own procedure and the procedure of the Benches thereof in all matters arising out of the exercise of its powers or of the discharge of its functions, including the places at which the Benches shall hold their sittings.

(7) The Appellate Tribunal shall, for the purposes of discharging its functions, have the same powers as are vested in a court under the Code of Civil Procedure, 1908 (5 of 1908), when trying a suit in respect of the following matters, namely:-

  (a) discovery and inspection;

  (b) enforcing the attendance of any person and examining him on oath;

  (c) compelling the production of books of account and other documents; and

  (d) issuing commissions.

(8) Any proceeding before the Appellate Tribunal shall be deemed to be a judicial proceedingwithin the meaning of Sections 193 and 228 and for the purpose of Section 196 of the Indian Penal Code (45 of 1860), and the Appellate Tribunal shall be deemed to be a Civil Court for all the purposes of Section 195 and Chapter XXVI of the Code of Criminal Procedure, 1973 (2 of 1974).

129D. Powers of Committee of Chief Commissioners of Customs or Commissioner of Customs to pass certain orders.

(1) The Committee of Chief Commissioners of Customs may, of its own motion, call for and examine the record of any proceeding in which a Commissioner of

Customs as an adjudicating authority has passed any decision or order under this Act for the purpose of satisfying itself as to the legality or propriety of any such decision or order and may, by order, direct such Commissioner or any other Commissioner to apply to the Appellate Tribunal for the determination of such points arising out of the decision or order as may be specified by the Committee of Chief Commissioners of Customs in its order.

PROVIDED that where the Committee of Chief Commissioners of Customs differs in its opinion as to the legality or propriety of the decision or order of the Commissioner of Customs, it shall state the point or points on which it differs and make a reference to the Board which, after considering the facts of the decision or order passed by the Commissioner of Customs, if is of the opinion that the decision or order passed by the Commissioner of Customs is not legal or proper, may, by order, direct such Commissioner or any other Commissioner to apply to the Appellate Tribunal for the determination of such points arising out of the decision or order, as may be specified in its order.

(2) The Commissioner of Customs may, of his own motion, call for and examine the record of any proceeding in which an adjudicating authority subordinate to him has passed any decision or order under this Act for the purpose of satisfying himself as to the legality or propriety of any such decision or order and may, by order, direct such authority or any officer of Customs subordinate to him to apply to the Commissioner (Appeals) for the determination of such points arising out of the decision or order as may be specified by the Commissioner of Customs in his order.

(3) Every order under sub-section (1) or sub-section (2), as the case may be, shall be made within a period of three months from the date of communication of the decision or order of the adjudicating authority.

(4) Where in pursuance of an order under sub-section (1) or sub-section (2), the adjudicating authority or any officer of customs authorised in this behalf by the Commissioner of Customs, makes an application to the Appellate Tribunal or the Commissioner (Appeals) within a period of one month from the date of communication of the order under sub-section (1) or sub-section (2) to the adjudicating authority, such application shall be heard by the Appellate Tribunal or the Commissioner (Appeals), as the case may be, as if such application were an appeal made against the decision or order of the adjudicating authority and the provisions of this Act regarding appeals, including the provisions of sub-section (4) of Section 129A shall, so far as may be, apply to such application.

(5) Omitted.

129DA. Omitted.

129DD. Revision by Central Government.

(1) The Central Government may, on the application of any person aggrieved by any order passed under Section 128A, where the order is of the nature referred to in the first proviso to sub-section (1) of Section 129A, annul or modify such order.

PROVIDED that the Central Government may in its discretion, refuse to admit an application in respect of an order where the amount of duty or fine or penalty, determined by such order does not exceed five thousand rupees.

EXPLANATION: For the purposes of this sub-section, "order passed under Section 128A" includes an order passed under that Section before the commencement of Section 40 of the Finance Act, 1984, against which an appeal has not been preferred before such commencement and could have been, if the said Section had not come into force, preferred after such commencement, to the Appellate Tribunal.

(1A) The Commissioner of Customs may, if he is of the opinion that an order passed by the Commissioner (Appeals) under Section 128A is not legal or proper, direct the proper officer to make an application on his behalf to the Central Government for revision of such order.

(2) An application under sub-section (1) shall be made within three months from the date of the communication to the applicant of the order against which the application is being made :

PROVIDED that the Central Government may, if it is satisfied that the applicant was prevented by sufficient cause from presenting the application within the aforesaid period of three months, allow it to be presented within a further period of three months.

(3) An application under sub-section (1) shall be in such form and shall be verified in such manner as may be specified by rules made in this behalf and shall be accompanied by a fee of, -

(a) two hundred rupees, where the amount of duty and interest demanded, fine or penalty levied by an officer of customs in the case to which the application relates is one lakh rupees or less;

(b) one thousand rupees, where the amount of duty and interest demanded, fine or penalty levied by an officer of customs in the case to which the application relates is more than one lakh rupees :

PROVIDED that no such fee shall be payable in the case of an application referred to in sub-section (1A).

(4) The Central Government may, of its own motion, annul or modify any order referred to in sub-section (1).

(5) No order enhancing any penalty or fine in lieu of confiscation or confiscating goods of greater value shall be passed under this Section, -

(a) in any case in which an order passed under Section 128A has enhanced any penalty or fine in lieu of confiscation or has confiscated goods of greater value, and

(b) in any other case, unless the person affected by the proposed order has been given notice to show cause against it within one year from the date of the order sought to be annulled or modified.

(6) Where the Central Government is of opinion that any duty of customs has not been levied or has been short-levied, no order levying or enhancing the duty

shall be made under this Section unless the person affected by the proposed order is given notice to show cause against it within the time limit specified in Section 28.

129E. Deposit, pending appeal, of duty and interest demanded or penalty levied. Where in any appeal under this Chapter, the decision or order appealed against relates to any duty and interest demanded in respect of goods which are not under the control of the customs authorities or any penalty levied under this Act, the person desirous of appealing against such decision or order shall, pending the appeal, deposit with the proper officer the duty and interest demanded or the penalty levied:

PROVIDED that where in any particular case, the Commissioner (Appeals) or the Appellate Tribunal is of opinion that the deposit of duty and interest demanded or penalty levied would cause undue hardship to such person, the Commissioner (Appeals) or, as the case may be, the Appellate Tribunal may dispense with such deposit subject to such conditions as he or it may deem fit to impose so as to safeguard the interests of revenue :

PROVIDED FURTHER that where an application is filed before the Commissioner (Appeals) for dispensing with the deposit of duty and interest demanded or penalty levied under the first proviso, the Commissioner (Appeals) shall, where it is possible to do so, decide such application within thirty days from the date of its filing.

129EE. Interest on delayed refund of amount deposited under the proviso to Section 129E. Where an amount deposited by the appellant in pursuance of an order passed by the Commissioner (Appeals) or the Appellate Tribunal (hereinafter referred to as appellate authority), under the first proviso to Section 129E, is required to be refunded consequent upon the order of the appellate authority and such amount is not refunded within three months from the date of communication of such order to the adjudicating authority, unless the operation of the order of the appellate authority is stayed by a superior court or tribunal, there shall be paid to the appellant interest at the rate specified in Section 27A after the expiry of three months from the date of communication of the order of the appellate authority, till the date of refund of such amount.

130. Appeal to High Court.

(1) An appeal shall lie to the High Court from every order passed in appeal by the Appellate Tribunal on or after the 1st day of July, 2003 (not being an order relating, among other things, to the determination of any question having a relation to the rate of duty of customs or to the value of goods for the purposes of assessment), if the High Court is satisfied that the case involves a substantial question of law.

(2) The Commissioner of Customs or the other party aggrieved by any order passed by the Appellate Tribunal may file an appeal to the High Court and such appeal under this sub-section shall be –

  (a) in any disputed case, other than filed within one hundred and eighty days from the date on which the order appealed against is received by the Commissioner of Customs or the other party;

(b) accompanied by a fee of two hundred rupees where such appeal is filed by the other party;

(c) in the form of a memorandum of appeal precisely stating therein the substantial question of law involved.

(2A) The High Court may admit an appeal after the expiry of the period of one hundred and eighty days referred to in clause (a) of sub-section (2), if it is satisfied that there was sufficient cause for not filing the same within that period.

(3) Where the High Court is satisfied that a substantial question of law is involved in any case, it shall formulate that question.

(4) The appeal shall be heard only on the question so formulated, and the respondents shall, at the hearing of the appeal, be allowed to argue that the case does not involve such question:

PROVIDED that nothing in this sub-section shall be deemed to take away or abridge the power of the Court to hear, for reasons to be recorded, the appeal on any other substantial question of law not formulated by it, if it is satisfied that the case involves such question.

(5) The High Court shall decide the question of law so formulated and deliver such judgment thereon containing the grounds on which such decision is founded and may award such cost as it deems fit.

(6) The High Court may determine any issue which –

(a) has not been determined by the Appellate Tribunal; or

(b) has been wrongly determined by the Appellate Tribunal, by reason of a decision on such question of law as is referred to in sub-section (1).

(7) When an appeal has been filed before the High Court, it shall be heard by a bench of not less than two Judges of the High Court, and shall be decided in accordance with the opinion of such Judges or of the majority, if any, of such Judges.

(8) Where there is no such majority, the Judges shall state the point of law upon which they differ and the case shall, then, be heard upon that point only by one or more of the other Judges of the High Court and such point shall be decided according to the opinion of the majority of the Judges who have heard the case including those who first heard it.

(9) Save as otherwise provided in this Act, the provisions of the Code of Civil Procedure, 1908 (5 of 1908) relating to appeals to the High Court shall, as far as may be, apply in the case of appeals under this Section.

130A. Application to High Court.

(1) The Commissioner of Customs or the other party may, within one hundred and eighty days of the date upon which he is served with notice of an order under Section 129B passed before the 1st day of July, 2003 (not being an order relating, among other things, to the determination of any question having a relation to the rate of duty of customs or to the value of goods for purposes of assessment),

by application in the prescribed form, accompanied, where the application is made by the other party, by a fee of two hundred rupees, apply to the High Court to direct the Appellate Tribunal to refer to the High Court any question of law arising from such order of the Tribunal.

(2) The Commissioner of Customs or the other party applying to the High Court under sub-section (1) shall clearly state the question of law which he seeks to be referred to the High Court and shall also specify the paragraph in the order of the Appellate Tribunal relevant to the question sought to be referred.

(3) On receipt of notice that an application has been made under sub-section (1), the person against whom such application has been made, may, notwithstanding that he may not have filed such application, file, within forty-five days of the receipt of the notice, a memorandum of cross-objections verified in the prescribed manner against any part of the order in relation to which an application for reference has been made and such memorandum shall be disposed of by the High Court as if it were an application presented within the time specified in sub-section (1).

(3A) The High Court may admit an application or permit the filing of a memorandum of cross-objections after the expiry of the relevant period referred to in sub-section (1) or sub-section (3), if it is satisfied that there was sufficient cause for not filing the same within that period.

(4) If, on an application made under sub-section (1), the High Court directs the Appellate Tribunal to refer the question of law raised in the application, the Appellate Tribunal shall, within one hundred and twenty days of the receipt of such direction, draw up a statement of the case and refer it to the High Court.

130B. Power of High Court or Supreme Court to require statement to be amended. If the High Court or the Supreme Court is not satisfied that the statements in a case referred to it are sufficient to enable it to determine the questions raised thereby, the Court may refer the case back to the Appellate Tribunal for the purpose of making such additions thereto or alterations therein as it may direct in that behalf.

130C. Case before High Court to be heard by not less than two judges.

(1) When any case has been referred to the High Court under Section 130 or Section 130A it shall be heard by a Bench of not less than two judges of the High Court and shall be decided in accordance with the opinion of such judges or of the majority, if any, of such judges.

(2) Where there is no such majority, the judges shall state the point of law upon which they differ and the case shall then be heard upon that point only by one or more of the other judges of the High Court, and such point shall be decided according to the opinion of the majority of the judges who have heard the case including those who first heard it.

130D. Decision of High Court or Supreme Court on the case stated.

(1) The High Court or the Supreme Court hearing any such case shall decide the questions of law raised therein, and shall deliver its judgment thereon containing

the grounds on which such decision is founded and a copy of the judgment shall be sent under the seal of the Court and the signature of the Registrar to the Appellate Tribunal which shall pass such orders as are necessary to dispose of the case in conformity with such judgment.

(1A) Where the High Court delivers a judgment in an appeal filed before it under Section 130, effect shall be given to the order passed on the appeal by the proper officer on the basis of a certified copy of the judgment.

(2) The costs of any reference to the High Court or an appeal to the High Court or the Supreme Court as the case may be which shall not include the fee for making the reference shall be in the discretion of the Court.

130E. Appeal to Supreme Court. An appeal shall lie to the Supreme Court from –

(a) any judgment of the High Court delivered –

(i) in an appeal made under Section 130; or

(ii) on a reference made under Section 130 by the Appellate Tribunal before the 1st day of July, 2003;

(iii) on a reference made under Section 130A,

in any case which, on its own motion or on an oral application made by or on behalf of the party aggrieved, immediately after passing of the judgment, the High Court certifies to be a fit one for appeal to the Supreme Court; or

(b) any order passed before the establishment of the National Tax Tribunal by the Appellate Tribunal relating, among other things, to the determination of any question having a relation to the rate of duty of customs or to the value of goods for purposes of assessment.

130F. Hearing before Supreme Court.

(1) The provisions of the Code of Civil Procedure, 1908 (5 of 1908), relating to appeals to the Supreme Court shall, so far as may be, apply in the case of appeals under Section 130E as they apply in the case of appeals from decrees of a High Court:

PROVIDED that nothing in this sub-section shall be deemed to affect the provisions of sub-section (1) of Section 130D or Section 131.

(2) The costs of the appeal shall be in the discretion of the Supreme Court.

(3) Where the judgment of the High Court is varied or reversed in the appeal, effect shall be given to the order of the Supreme Court in the manner provided in Section 130D in the case of a judgment of the High Court.

131. Sums due to be paid notwithstanding reference, etc. Notwithstanding that a reference has been made to the High Court or the Supreme Court or an appeal has been preferred to the Supreme Court, under this Act before the commencement of the National Tax Tribunal Act, 2005 sums due to the Government as a result of an order passed under sub-section (1) of Section 129B shall be payable in accordance with the order so passed.

131A. Exclusion of time taken for copy. In computing the period of limitation specified for an appeal or application under this Chapter, the day on which the order complained of was served, and if the party preferring the appeal or making the application was not furnished with a copy of the order when the notice of the order was served upon him, the time requisite for obtaining a copy of such order shall be excluded.

131B. Transfer of certain pending proceedings and transitional provisions.

(1) Every appeal which is pending immediately before the appointed day before the Board under Section 128, as it stood immediately before that day, and any matter arising out of or connected with such appeal and which is so pending shall stand transferred on that day to the Appellate Tribunal and the Appellate Tribunal may proceed with such appeal or matter from the stage at which it was on that day:

PROVIDED that the appellant may demand that before proceeding further with that appeal or matter, he may be re-heard.

(2) Every proceeding which is pending immediately before the appointed day before the Central Government under Section 131, as it stood immediately before that day, and any matter arising out of or connected with such proceeding and which is so pending shall stand transferred on that day to the Appellate Tribunal and the Appellate Tribunal may proceed with such proceeding or matter from the stage at which it was on that day as if such proceeding or matter were an appeal filed before it :

PROVIDED that if any such proceeding or matter relates to an order where

(a) the value of the goods confiscated without option having been given to the owner of the goods to pay a fine in lieu of confiscation under Section 125; or

(b) in any disputed case, other than a case where the determination of any question having a relation to the rate of duty of customs or to the value of goods for purposes of assessment is in issue or is one of the points in issue, the difference in duty involved or the duty involved; or

(c) the amount of fine or penalty determined by such order, does not exceed ten thousand rupees, such proceeding or matter shall continue to be dealt with by the Central Government as if the said Section 131 had not been substituted :

PROVIDED FURTHER that the applicant or the other party may make a demand to the Appellate Tribunal that before proceeding further with that proceeding or matter, he may be re-heard.

(3) Every proceeding which is pending immediately before the appointed day before the Board or the Commissioner of Customs under Section 130, as it stood immediately before that day, and any matter arising out of or connected with such proceeding and which is so pending shall continue to be dealt with by the Board or the Commissioner of Customs, as the case may be, as if the said Section had not been substituted.

(4) Any person who immediately before the appointed day was authorised to appear in any appeal or proceeding transferred under sub-section (1) or sub-section

(2) shall, notwithstanding anything contained in Section 146A, have the right to appear before the Appellate Tribunal in relation to such appeal or proceeding.

131BA. Appeal not to be filed in certain cases.

(1) The Board may, from time to time, issue orders or instructions or directions fixing such monetary limits, as it may deem fit, for the purposes of regulating the filing of appeal, application, revision or reference by the Commissioner of Customs under the provisions of this Chapter.

(2) Where, in pursuance of the orders or instructions or directions, issued under sub-section (1), the Commissioner of Customs has not filed an appeal, application, revision or reference against any decision or order passed under the provisions of this Act shall not preclude such Commissioner of Customs from filing any appeal, application, revision or reference in any other case involving the same or similar issues or questions of law.

(3) Notwithstanding the fact that no appeal, application, revision or reference has been filed by the Commissioner of Customs pursuant to the orders or instructions or directions issued under sub-section (1), no person, being a party in appeal, application, revision or reference shall contend that the Commissioner of Customs has acquiesced in the decision on the disputed issue by not filing appeal, application, revision or reference.

(4) The Appellate Tribunal or court hearing an appeal, application, revision or reference shall have regard to the circumstances under which the appeal, application, revision or reference was not filed by the Commissioner of Customs in pursuance of orders or instructions or directions issued under sub-section (1).

(5) Every order or instruction or direction issued by the Board on or after the 20th day of October, 2010, but before the date on which the Finance Bill, 2011 receives the assent of the President, fixing monetary limits for filing appeal, application, revision or reference shall be deemed to have been issued under sub-section (1), and the provisions of sub-sections (2), (3) and (4) shall apply 25 accordingly."

131C. Definitions. In this Chapter –

(a) "appointed day" means the date of coming into force of the amendments to this Act specified in Part I of the Fifth Schedule to the Finance (No. 2) Act, 1980 (44 of 1980) ;

(b) Omitted.

(c) "President" means the President of the Appellate Tribunal.

CHAPTER - XVI : OFFENCES AND PROSECUTIONS

132. False declaration, false documents, etc. Whoever makes, signs or uses, or causes to be made, signed or used, any declaration, statement or document in the transaction of any business relating to the customs, knowing or having reason to believe that such declaration, statement or document is false in any material particular, shall be punishable with imprisonment for a term which may extend to two years, or with fine, or with both.

133. Obstruction of officer of customs. If any person intentionally obstructs any officer of customs in the exercise of any powers conferred under this Act, such person shall be punishable with imprisonment for a term which may extend to two years, or with fine, or with both.

134. Refusal to be X-rayed. If any person –

(a) resists or refuses to allow a radiologist to screen or to take X-ray picture of his body in accordance with an order made by a Magistrate under Section 103, or

(b) resists or refuses to allow suitable action being taken on the advice and under the supervision of a registered medical practitioner for bringing out goods liable to confiscation secreted inside his body, as provided in Section 103, he shall be punishable with imprisonment for a term which may extend to six months, or with fine, or with both.

135. Evasion of duty or prohibitions. "(1) Without prejudice to any action that may be taken under this Act, if any person —

(a) is in relation to any goods in any way knowingly concerned in misdeclaration of value or in any fraudulent evasion or attempt at evasion of any duty chargeable thereon or of any prohibition for the time being imposed under this Act or any other law for the time being in force with respect to such goods; or

(b) acquires possession of or is in any way concerned in carrying, removing, depositing, harbouring, keeping, concealing, selling or purchasing or in any other manner dealing with any goods which he knows or has reason to believe are liable to confiscation under Section 111 or Section 113, as the case may be; or

(c) attempts to export any goods which he knows or has reason to believe are liable to confiscation under Section 113; or

(d) fraudulently avails of or attempts to avail of drawback or any exemption from duty provided under this Act in connection with export of goods, he shall be punishable, —

(i) in the case of an offence relating to, —

(A) any goods the market price of which exceeds one crore of rupees; or

(B) the evasion or attempted evasion of duty exceeding thirty lakh of rupees; or

(C) such categories of prohibited goods as the Central Government may, by notification in the Official Gazette, specify; or

(D) fraudulently availing of or attempting to avail of drawback or any exemption from duty referred to in clause (d), if the amount of drawback or exemption from duty exceeds thirty lakh of rupees, with imprisonment for a term which may extend to seven years and with fine:

PROVIDED that in the absence of special and adequate reasons to the contrary to be recorded in the judgment of the court, such imprisonment shall not be for less than one year;

(ii) in any other case, with imprisonment for a term which may extend to three years, or with fine, or with both.

(2) If any person convicted of an offence under this Section or under sub-section (1) of Section 136 is again convicted of an offence under this Section, then, he shall be punishable for the second and for every subsequent offence with imprisonment for a term which may extend to seven years and with fine:

PROVIDED that in the absence of special and adequate reasons to the contrary to be recorded in the judgment of the court such imprisonment shall not be for less than one year.

(3) For the purposes of sub-sections (1) and (2), the following shall not be considered as special and adequate reasons for awarding a sentence of imprisonment for a term of less than one year, namely :-

(i) the fact that the accused has been convicted for the first time for an offence under this Act;

(ii) the fact that in any proceeding under this Act, other than a prosecution, the accused has been ordered to pay a penalty or the goods which are the subject matter of such proceedings have been ordered to be confiscated or any other action has been taken against him for the same act which constitutes the offence;

(iii) the fact that the accused was not the principal offender and was acting merely as a carrier of goods or otherwise was a secondary party to the commission of the offence;

(iv) the age of the accused.

135A. Preparation. If a person makes preparation to export any goods in contravention of the provisions of this Act, and from the circumstances of the case it may be reasonably inferred that if not prevented by circumstances independent of his will, he is determined to carry out his intention to commit the offence, he shall be punishable with imprisonment for a term which may extend to three years, or with fine, or with both.

135B. Power of court to publish name, place of business, etc., of persons convicted under the Act.

(1) Where any person is convicted under this Act for contravention of any of the provisions thereof, it shall be competent for the court convicting the person to cause the name and place of business or residence of such person, nature of the contravention, the fact that the person has been so convicted and such other particulars as the court may consider to be appropriate in the circumstances of the case, to be published at the expense of such person in such newspapers or in such manner as the court may direct.

(2) No publication under sub-section (1) shall be made until the period for preferring an appeal against the orders of the court has expired without any appeal having been preferred, or such an appeal, having been preferred, has been disposed of.

(3) The expenses of any publication under sub-section (1) shall be recoverable from the convicted person as if it were a fine imposed by the court.

136. Offences by officers of customs.

(1) If any officer of customs enters into or acquiesces in any agreement to do, abstains from doing, permits, conceals or connive at any act or thing, whereby any fraudulent export is effected or any duty of customsleviable on any goods, or any prohibition for the time being in force under this Act or any other law for the time being in force with respect to any goods is or may be evaded, he shall be punishable with imprisonment for a term which may extend to three years, or with fine, or with both.

(2) If any officer of customs,-

(a) requires any person to be searched for goods liable to confiscation or any document relating thereto, without having reason to believe that he has such goods or document secreted about his person; or

(b) arrests any person without having reason to believe that he has been guilty of an offence punishable under Section 135; or

(c) searches or authorises any other officer of customs to search any place without having reason to believe that any goods, documents or things of the nature referred to in Section 105 are secreted in that place, he shall be punishable with imprisonment for a term which may extend to six months, or with fine which may extend to one thousand rupees, or with both.

(3) If any officer of customs, except in the discharge in good faith of his duty as such officer or in compliance with any requisition made under any law for the time being in force, discloses any particulars learnt by him in his official capacity in respect of any goods, he shall be punishable with imprisonment for a term which may extend to six months, or with fine which may extend to one thousand rupees, or with both.

137. Cognizance of offences.

(1) No court shall take cognizance of any offence under Section 132, Section 133, Section 134 or Section 135 or Section 135A, except with the previous sanction of the Commissioner of Customs.

(2) No court shall take cognizance of any offence under Section 136, -

(a) where the offence is alleged to have been committed by an officer of customs not lower in rank than Assistant Commissioner of Customs, except with the previous sanction of the Central Government;

(b) where the offence is alleged to have been committed by an officer of customs lower in rank than Assistant Commissioner of Customs except with the previous sanction of the Commissioner of Customs.

(3) Any offence under this Chapter may, either before or after the institution of prosecution, be compounded by the Chief Commissioner of Customs on payment,

by the person accused of the offence to the Central Government, of such compounding amount and in such manner of compounding as may be specified by rules.

PROVIDED that nothing contained in this sub-section shall apply to-

(a) a person who has been allowed to compound once in respect of any offence under Sections 135 and 135A;

(b) a person who has been accused of committing an offence under this Act which is also an offence under any of the following Acts, namely:—

(i) the Narcotic Drugs and Psychotropic Substances Act, 1985 (61 of 1985);

(ii) the Chemical Weapons Convention Act, 2000 (34 of 2000);

(iii) the Arms Act, 1959 (54 of 1959);

(iv) the Wild Life (Protection) Act, 1972 (53 of 1972);

(c) a person involved in smuggling of goods falling under any of the following, namely:—

(i) goods specified in the list of Special Chemicals, Organisms, Materials, Equipment and Technology in Appendix 3 to Schedule 2 (Export Policy) of ITC (HS) Classification of Export and Import Items of the Foreign Trade Policy, as amended from time to time, issued under Section 5 of the Foreign Trade (Development and Regulation) Act, 1992 (22 of 1992);

(ii) goods which are specified as prohibited items for import and export in the ITC (HS) Classification of Export and Import Items of the Foreign Trade Policy, as amended from time to time, issued under Section 5 of the Foreign Trade (Development and Regulation) Act, 1992 (22 of 1992);

(iii) any other goods or documents, which are likely to affect friendly relations with a foreign State or are derogatory to national honour;

(d) a person who has been allowed to compound once in respect of any offence under this Chapter for goods of value exceeding rupees one crore;

(e) a person who has been convicted under this Act on or after the 30th day of December, 2005.

138. Offences to be tried summarily. Notwithstanding anything contained in the Code of Criminal Procedure, 1898 (5 of 1898), an offence under this Chapter other than an offence punishable under clause (i) of sub-section (1) of Section 135 or under sub-section (2) of that Section may be tried summarily by a Magistrate.

138A. Presumption of culpable mental state.

(1) In any prosecution for an offence under this Act which requires a culpable mental state on the part of the accused, the court shall presume the existence of such mental state but it shall be a defence for the accused to prove the fact that he had no such mental state with respect to the act charged as an offence in that prosecution.

EXPLANATION: In this Section, "culpable mental state" includes intention, motive, knowledge of a fact and belief in, or reason to believe, a fact.

(2) For the purposes of this Section, a fact is said to be proved only when the court believes it to exist beyond reasonable doubt and not merely when its existence is established by a preponderance of probability.

138B. Relevancy of statements under certain circumstances.

(1) A statement made and signed by a person before any Gazetted Officer of customs during the course of any inquiry or proceeding under this Act shall be relevant, for the purpose of proving, in any prosecution for an offence under this Act, the truth of the facts which it contains, -

(a) when the person who made the statement is dead or cannot be found, or is incapable of giving evidence, or is kept out of the way by the adverse party, or whose presence cannot be obtained without an amount of delay or expense which, under the circumstances of the case, the court considers unreasonable; or

(b) when the person who made the statement is examined as a witness in the case before the court and the court is of opinion that, having regard to the circumstances of the case, the statement should be admitted in evidence in the interests of justice.

(2) The provisions of sub-section (1) shall, so far as may be, apply in relation to any proceeding under this Act, other than a proceeding before a court, as they apply in relation to a proceeding before a court.

138C. Admissibility of micro films, facsimile copies of documents and computer print outs as documents and as evidence.

(1) Notwithstanding anything contained in any other law for the time being in force, -

(a) a micro film of a document or the reproduction of the image or images embodied in such micro film (whether enlarged or not); or

(b) a facsimile copy of a document; or

(c) a statement contained in a document and included in a printed material produced by a computer (hereinafter referred to as a "computer printout"), if the conditions mentioned in sub-section (2) and the other provisions contained in this Section are satisfied in relation to the statement and the computer in question, shall be deemed to be also a document for the purposes of this Act and the rules made thereunder and shall be admissible in any proceedings thereunder, without further proof or production of the original, as evidence of any contents of the original or of any fact stated therein of which direct evidence would be admissible.

(2) The conditions referred to in sub-section (1) in respect of a computer printout shall be the following, namely :-

(a) the computer printout containing the statement was produced by the computer during the period over which the computer was used regularly to store or process information for the purposes of any activities regularly carried on over that period by the person having lawful control over the use of the computer;

(b) during the said period, there was regularly supplied to the computer in the ordinary course of the said activities, information of the kind contained in the statement or of the kind from which the information so contained is derived;

(c) throughout the material part of the said period, the computer was operating properly or, if not, then any respect in which it was not operating properly or was out of operation during that part of that period was not such as to affect the production of the document or the accuracy of the contents; and

(d) the information contained in the statement reproduces or is derived from information supplied to the computer in the ordinary course of the said activities.

(3) Where over any period, the function of storing or processing information for the purposes of any activities regularly carried on over that period as mentioned in clause (a) of sub-section (2) was regularly performed by computers, whether-

(a) by a combination of computers operating over that period; or

(b) by different computers operating in succession over that period; or

(c) by different combinations of computers operating in succession over that period; or

(d) in any other manner involving the successive operation over that period, in whatever order, of one or more computers and one or more combinations of computers, all the computers used for that purpose during that period shall be treated for the purposes of this Section as constituting a single computer; and references in this Section to a computer shall be construed accordingly.

(4) In any proceedings under this Act and the rules made thereunder where it is desired to give a statement in evidence by virtue of this Section, a certificate doing any of the following things, that is to say, -

(a) identifying the document containing the statement and describing the manner in which it was produced;

(b) giving such particulars of any device involved in the production of that document as may be appropriate for the purpose of showing that the document was produced by a computer;

(c) dealing with any of the matters to which the conditions mentioned in sub-section (2) relate, and purporting to be signed by a person occupying a responsible official position in relation to the operation of the relevant device or the management of the relevant activities (whichever is appropriate) shall be evidence of any matter stated in the certificate; and for the purposes of this sub-section it shall be sufficient for a matter to be stated to the best of the knowledge and belief of the person stating it.

(5) For the purposes of this Section, -

(a) information shall be taken to be supplied to a computer if it is supplied thereto in any appropriate form and whether it is so supplied directly or (with or without human intervention) by means of any appropriate equipment;

(b) whether in the course of activities carried on by any official, information is supplied with a view to its being stored or processed for the purposes of those activities by a computer operated otherwise than in the course of those activities, that information, if duly supplied to that computer, shall be taken to be supplied to it in the course of those activities;

(c) a document shall be taken to have been produced by a computer whether it was produced by it directly or (with or without human intervention) by means of any appropriate equipment.

EXPLANATION: For the purposes of this Section, -

(a) "computer" means any device that receives, stores and processes data, applying stipulated processes to the information and supplying results of these processes; and

(b) any reference to information being derived from other information shall be a reference to its being derived therefrom by calculation, comparison or any other process.

139. Presumption as to documents in certain cases. Where any document –

(i) is produced by any person or has been seized from the custody or control of any person, in either case, under this Act or under any other law, or

(ii) has been received from any place outside India in the course of investigation of any offence alleged to have been committed by any person under this Act, and such document is tendered by the prosecution in evidence against him or against him and any other person who is tried jointly with him, the court shall -

(a) presume, unless the contrary is proved, that the signature and every other part of such document which purports to be in the handwriting of any particular person or which the court may reasonably assume to have been signed by, or to be in the handwriting of, any particular person, is in that person's handwriting, and in the case of a document executed or attested, that it was executed or attested by the person by whom it purports to have been so executed or attested;

(b) admit the document in evidence, notwithstanding that it is not duly stamped, if such document is otherwise admissible in evidence;

(c) in a case falling under clause (i) also presume, unless the contrary is proved, the truth of the contents of such document.

EXPLANATION: For the purposes of this Section, "document" includes inventories, photographs and lists certified by a Magistrate under sub-section (1C) of Section 110.

140. Offences by companies.

(1) If the person committing an offence under this Chapter is a company, every person who, at the time the offence was committed was in charge of, and was responsible to, the company for the conduct of business of the company, as well as the company, shall be deemed to be guilty of the offence and shall be liable to be proceeded against and punished accordingly:

PROVIDED that nothing contained in this sub-section shall render any such person liable to such punishment provided in this Chapter if he proves that the offence was committed without his knowledge or that he exercised all due diligence to prevent the commission of such offence.

(2) Notwithstanding anything contained in sub-section (1), where an offence under this Chapter has been committed by a company and it is proved that the offence has been committed with the consent or connivance of, or is attributable to any negligence on the part of, any director, manager, secretary or other officer of the company, such director, manager, secretary or other officer shall also be deemed to be guilty of that offence and shall be liable to be proceeded against and punished accordingly.

EXPLANATION: For the purposes of this Section, -

(a) "company" means a body corporate and includes a firm or other association of individuals; and

(b) "director", in relation to a firm, means a partner in the firm.

140A. Application of Section 562 of the Code of Criminal Procedure, 1898, and of the Probation of Offenders Act, 1958.

(1) Nothing contained in Section 562 of the Code of Criminal Procedure, 1898 (5 of 1898), or in the Probation of Offenders Act, 1958 (20 of 1958), shall apply to a person convicted of an offence under this Act unless that person is under eighteen years of age.

(2) The provisions of sub-section (1) shall have effect notwithstanding anything contained in sub-section (3) of Section 135.

CHAPTER - XVII : MISCELLANEOUS

141. Conveyances and goods in a customs area subject to control of officers of customs.

(1) All conveyances and goods in a customs area shall, for the purpose of enforcing the provisions of this Act, be subject to the control of officers of customs.

(2) The imported or export goods may be received, stored, delivered, despatched or otherwise handled in a customs area in such manner as may be prescribed and the responsibilities of persons engaged in the aforesaid activities shall be such as may be prescribed.

142. Recovery of sums due to Government.

(1) Where any sum payable by any person under this Act including the amount required to be paid to the credit of the Central Government under Section 28B is not paid, -

(a) the proper officer may deduct or may require any other officer of customs to deduct the amount so payable from any money owing to such person which may be under the control of the proper officer or such other officer of customs; or

(b) the Assistant Commissioner of Customs or Deputy Commissioner of Customs may recover or may require any other officer of customs to recover the amount so payable by detaining and selling any goods belonging to such person which are under the control of the Assistant Commissioner of Customs or Deputy Commissioner of Customs or such other officer of customs; or

(c) if the amount cannot be recovered from such person in the manner provided in clause (a) or clause (b) -

   (i) the Assistant Commissioner of Customs or Deputy Commissioner of Customs may prepare a certificate signed by him specifying the amount due from such person and send it to the Collector of the district in which such person owns any property or resides or carries on his business and the said Collector on receipt of such certificate shall proceed to recover from such person the amount specified thereunder as if it were an arrear of land revenue; or

   (ii) the proper officer may, on an authorisation by Commissioner of Customs and in accordance with the rules made in this behalf, distrain any movable or immovable property belonging to or under the control of such person, and detain the same until the amount payable is paid; and in case, any part of the said amount payable or of the cost of the distress or keeping of the property, remains unpaid for a period of thirty days next after any such distress, may cause the said property to be sold and with the proceeds of such sale, may satisfy the amount payable and the costs including cost of sale remaining unpaid and shall render the surplus, if any, to such person.

   PROVIDED that where the person (hereinafter referred to as predecessor), by whom any sum payable under this Act including the amount required to be paid to the credit of the Central Government under Section 28B is not paid, transfers or otherwise disposes of his business or trade in whole or in part, or effects any change in the ownership thereof, in consequence of which he is succeeded in such business or trade by any other person, all goods, materials, preparations, plants, machineries, vessels, utensils, implements and articles in the custody or possession of the person so succeeding may also be attached and sold by the proper officer, after obtaining written approval from the Commissioner of Customs, for the purposes of recovering the amount so payable by such predecessor at the time of such transfer or otherwise disposal or change.

(2) Where the terms of any bond or other instrument executed under this Act or any rules or regulations made thereunder provide that any amount due under such instrument may be recovered in the manner laid down in sub-section (1), the amount may, without prejudice to any other mode of recovery, be recovered in accordance with the provisions of that sub-section.

142A. Liability under Act to be first charge. Notwithstanding anything to the contrary contained in any Central Act or State Act, any amount of duty, penalty, interest or any other sum payable by an assessee or any other person under this Act, shall, save as otherwise provided in Section 529A of the Companies Act, 1956, the Recovery of Debts Due to Banks and the Financial Institutions Act, 1993 and the Securitisation and Reconstruction of Financial Assets and the Enforcement of Security Interest Act, 2002, be the first charge on the property of the assessee or the person, as the case may be."

143. Power to allow import or export on execution of bonds in certain cases.

(1) Where this Act or any other law requires anything to be done before a person can import or export any goods or clear any goods from the control of officers of customs and the Assistant Commissioner of Customs or Deputy Commissioner of Customs is satisfied that having regard to the circumstances of the case, such thing cannot be done before such import, export or clearance without detriment to that person, the Assistant Commissioner of Customs or Deputy Commissioner of Customs may, notwithstanding anything contained in this Act or such other law, grant leave for such import, export or clearance on the person executing a bond in such amount, with such surety or security and subject to such conditions as the Assistant Commissioner of Customs or Deputy Commissioner of Customs approves, for the doing of that thing within such time after the import, export or clearance as may be specified in the bond.

(2) If the thing is done within the time specified in the bond, the Assistant Commissioner of Customs or Deputy Commissioner of Customs shall cancel the bond as discharged in full and shall, on demand, deliver it, so cancelled, to the person who has executed or who is entitled to receive it; and in such a case that person shall not be liable to any penalty provided in this Act or, as the case may be, in such other law for the contravention of the provisions thereof relating to the doing of that thing.

(3) If the thing is not done within the time specified in the bond, the Assistant Commissioner of Customs or Deputy Commissioner of Customs shall, without prejudice to any other action that may be taken under this Act or any other law for the time being in force, be entitled to proceed upon the bond in accordance with law.

143A. Duty deferment.

(1) When any material is imported under an import licence belonging to the category of Advance Licence granted under the Imports and Exports (Control) Act, 1947 (18 of 1947), subject to an obligation to export the goods as are specified in the said Licence within the period specified therein, the Assistant Commissioner of Customs or Deputy Commissioner of Customs may, notwithstanding anything

contained in this Act, permit clearance of such material without payment of duty leviable thereon.

(2) The permission for clearance without payment of duty under sub-section (1) shall be subject to the following conditions, that is to say -

(a) the duty payable on the material imported shall be adjusted against the drawback of duty payable under this Act or under any other law for the time being in force on the export of goods specified in the said Advance Licence; and

(b) where the duty is not so adjusted either for the reason that the goods are not exported within the period specified in the said Advance Licence, or within such extended period not exceeding six months as the Assistant Commissioner of Customs or Deputy Commissioner of Customs may, on sufficient cause being shown, allow, or for any other sufficient reason, the importer shall, notwithstanding anything contained in Section 28, be liable to pay the amount of duty not so adjusted together with simple interest thereon at the rate of twelve per cent per annum from the date the said permission for clearance is given to the date of payment.

(3) While permitting clearance under sub-section (1), the [Assistant Commissioner of Customs or Deputy Commissioner of Customs] may require the importer to execute a bond with such surety or security as he thinks fit for complying with the conditions specified in sub-section (2).

144. Power to take samples.

(1) The proper officer may, on the entry or clearance of any goods or at any time while such goods are being passed through the customs area, take samples of such goods in the presence of the owner thereof, for examination or testing, or for ascertaining the value thereof, or for any other purposes of this Act.

(2) After the purpose for which a sample was taken is carried out, such sample shall, if practicable, be restored to the owner, but if the owner fails to take delivery of the sample within three months of the date on which the sample was taken, it may be disposed of in such manner as the Commissioner of Customs may direct.

(3) No duty shall be chargeable on any sample of goods taken under this Section which is consumed or destroyed during the course of any test or examination thereof, if such duty amounts to five rupees or more.

145. Owner, etc., to perform operations incidental to compliance with customs law. All operations necessary for making any goods available for examination by the proper officer or for facilitating such examination shall be performed by, or at the expense of, the owner, importer or exporter of the goods, as the case may be.

146. Custom House agents to be licensed.

(1) No person shall carry on business as an agent relating to the entry or departure of a conveyance or the import or export of goods at any customs-station unless such person holds a licence granted in this behalf in accordance with the regulations.

(2) The Board may make regulations for the purpose of carrying out the provisions of this Section and, in particular, such regulations may provide for -

(a) the authority by which a licence may be granted under this Section and the period of validity of any such licence;

(b) the form of the licence and the fees payable therefor;

(c) the qualifications of persons who may apply for a licence and the qualifications of persons to be employed by a licensee to assist him in his work as an agent;

(d) the restrictions and conditions (including the furnishing of security by the licensee) subject to which a licence may be granted;

(e) the circumstances in which a licence may be suspended or revoked; and

(f) the appeals, if any, against an order of suspension or revocation of a licence, and the period within which such appeals shall be filed.

146A. Appearance by authorised representative.

(1) Any person who is entitled or required to appear before an officer of customs or the Appellate Tribunal in connection with any proceedings under this Act, otherwise than when required under Section 108 to attend personally for examination on oath or affirmation, may, subject to the other provisions of this Section, appear by an authorised representative.

(2) For the purposes of this Section, "authorised representative" means a person authorised by the person referred to in sub-section (1) to appear on his behalf, being -

(a) his relative or regular employee; or

(b) a custom house agent licensed under Section 146; or

(c) any legal practitioner who is entitled to practise in any civil court in India; or

(d) any person who has acquired such qualifications as the Central Government may specify by rules made in this behalf.

(3) Notwithstanding anything contained in this Section, no person who was a member of the Indian Customs and Central Excise Service -Group A and has retired or resigned from such Service after having served for not less than three years in any capacity in that Service shall be entitled to appear as an authorised representative in any proceedings before an officer of customs for a period of two years from the date of his retirement or resignation, as the case may be.

(4) No person -

(a) who has been dismissed or removed from Government service; or

(b) who is convicted of an offence connected with any proceeding under this Act, the Central Excise and Salt Act, 1944 (1 of 1944), or the Gold (Control) Act, 1968 (45 of 1968); or

(c) who has become an insolvent, shall be qualified to represent any person under sub-section (1), for all times in the case of a person referred to in clause (a), and for such time as the Commissioner of Customs or the competent authority under the Central Excises and Salt Act, 1944, or the Gold (Control) Act, 1968, as the case may be, may, by order, determine in the case of a person referred to in clause (b), and for the period during which the insolvency continues in the case of a person referred to in clause (c).

(5) If any person, -

(a) who is a legal practitioner, is found guilty of misconduct in his professional capacity by any authority entitled to institute proceedings against him, an order passed by that authority shall have effect in relation to his right to appear before an officer of customs or the Appellate Tribunal as it has in relation to his right to practice as a legal practitioner;

(b) who is not a legal practitioner, is found guilty of misconduct in connection with any proceedings under this Act by such authority as may be specified by rules made in this behalf, that authority may direct that he shall thenceforth be disqualified to represent any person under sub-section (1).

(6) Any order or direction under clause (b) of sub-section (4) or clause (b) of sub-section (5) shall be subject to the following conditions, namely :-

(a) no such order or direction shall be made in respect of any person unless he has been given a reasonable opportunity of being heard;

(b) any person against whom any such order or direction is made may, within one month of the making of the order or direction, appeal to the Board to have the order or direction cancelled; and

(c) no such order or direction shall take effect until the expiration of one month from the making thereof, or, where an appeal has been preferred, until the disposal of the appeal.

147. Liability of principal and agent.

(1) Where this Act requires anything to be done by the owner, importer or exporter of any goods, it may be done on his behalf by his agent.

(2) Any such thing done by an agent of the owner, importer or exporter of any goods shall, unless the contrary is proved, be deemed to have been done with the knowledge and consent of such owner, importer or exporter, so that in any proceedings under this Act, the owner, importer or exporter of the goods shall also be liable as if the thing had been done by himself.

(3) When any person is expressly or impliedly authorised by the owner, importer or exporter of any goods to be his agent in respect of such goods for all or any of the purposes of this Act, such person shall, without prejudice to the liability of the owner, importer or exporter, be deemed to be the owner, importer or exporter of such goods for such purposes :

PROVIDED that where any duty is not levied or is short-levied or erroneously refunded on account of any reason other than any willful act, negligence or default of the agent, such duty shall not be recovered from the agent unless in the opinion of Assistant Commissioner of Customs or Deputy Commissioner of Customs the same cannot be recovered from the owner, importer or exporter.

148. Liability of agent appointed by the person in charge of a conveyance.

(1) Where this Act requires anything to be done by the person in charge of a conveyance, it may be done on his behalf by his agent.

(2) An agent appointed by the person in charge of a conveyance and any person who represents himself to any officer of customs as an agent of any such person in charge, and is accepted as such by that officer, shall be liable for the fulfilment in respect of the matter in question of all obligations imposed on such person in charge by or under this Act or any law for the time being in force, and to penalties and confiscations which may be incurred in respect of that matter.

149. Amendment of documents. Save as otherwise provided in Sections 30 and 41, the proper officer may, in his discretion, authorise any document, after it has been presented in the custom house to be amended:

PROVIDED that no amendment of a bill of entry or a shipping bill or bill of export shall be so authorised to be amended after the imported goods have been cleared for home consumption or deposited in a warehouse, or the export goods have been exported, except on the basis of documentary evidence which was in existence at the time the goods were cleared, deposited or exported, as the case may be.

150. Procedure for sale of goods and application of sale proceeds.

(1) Where any goods not being confiscated goods are to be sold under any provisions of this Act, they shall, after notice to the owner thereof, be sold by public auction or by tender or with the consent of the owner in any other manner.

(2) The proceeds of any such sale shall be applied -

(a) firstly to the payment of the expenses of the sale,

(b) next to the payment of the freight and other charges, if any, payable in respect of the goods sold, to the carrier, if notice of such charges has been given to the person having custody of the goods,

(c) next to the payment of the duty, if any, on the goods sold,

(d) next to the payment of the charges in respect of the goods sold due to the person having the custody of the goods,

(e) next to the payment of any amount due from the owner of the goods to the Central Government under the provisions of this Act or any other law relating to customs, and the balance, if any, shall be paid to the owner of the goods.

PROVIDED that where it is not possible to pay the balance of sale proceeds, i any, to the owner of the goods within a period of six months from the date of sale of such goods or such further period as the Commissioner of Customs may allow, such balance of sale proceeds shall be paid to the Central Government.

151. Certain officers required to assist officers of customs. The following officers are hereby empowered and required to assist officers of customs in the execution of this Act, namely :-

(a) officers of the Central Excise Department;

(b) officers of the Navy;

(c) officers of Police;

(d) officers of the Central or State Governments employed at any port or airport;

(e) such other officers of the Central or State Governments or a local authority as are specified by the Central Government in this behalf by notification in the Official Gazette.

SECTION 151A. Instructions to officers of customs. The Board may, if it considers it necessary or expedient so to do for the purpose of uniformity in the classification of goods or with respect to the levy of duty thereon, or for the implementation of any other provisions of this Act or of any other law for the time being in force, insofar as they relate to any prohibition, restriction or procedure for import or export ofgoods issue such orders, instructions and directions to officers of customs as it may deem fit and such officers of customs and all other persons employed in the execution of this Act shall observe and follow such orders, instructions and directions of the Board:

Provided that no such orders, instructions or directions shall be issued -

(a) so as to require any such officer of customs to make a particular assessment or to dispose of a particular case in a particular manner; or

(b) so as to interfere with the discretion of the Commissioner of Customs (Appeals) in the exercise of his appellate functions.

152. Delegation of powers. The Central Government may, by notification in the Official Gazette, direct that subject to such conditions, if any, as may be specified in the notification-

(a) any power exercisable by the Board under this Act shall be exercisable also by a Chief Commissioner of Customs or a Commissioner of Customs empowered in this behalf by the Central Government;

(b) any power exercisable by a Commissioner of Customs under this Act may be exercisable also by a Joint Commissioner of Customs or an Assistant Commissioner of Customs or Deputy Commissioner of Customs empowered in this behalf by the Central Government;

(c) any power exercisable by a Joint Commissioner of Customs under this Act may be exercisable also by an Assistant Commissioner of Customs or Deputy Commissioner of Customs empowered in this behalf by the Central Government;

(d) any power exercisable by an Assistant Commissioner of Customs or Deputy Commissioner of Customs under this Act may be exercisable also by a Gazetted Officer of Customs empowered in this behalf by the Board.

153. Service of order, decision, etc. Any order or decision passed or any summons or notice issued under this Act, shall be served -

(a) by tendering the order, decision, summons or notice or sending it by registered post to the person for whom it is intended or to his agent; or

(b) if the order, decision, summons or notice cannot be served in the manner provided in clause (a), by affixing it on the notice board of the customs house.

154. Correction of clerical errors, etc. Clerical or arithmetical mistakes in any decision or order passed by the Central Government, the Board or any officer of customs under this Act, or errors arising therein from any accidental slip or omission may, at any time, be corrected by the Central Government, the Board or such officer of customs or the successor in office of such officer, as the case may be.

154A. Rounding off of duty, etc. The amount of duty, interest, penalty, fine or any other sum payable, and the amount of refund, drawback or any other sum due, under the provisions of this Act shall be rounded off to the nearest rupee and, for this purpose, where such amount contains a part of a rupee consisting of paise then, if such part is fifty paise or more, it shall be increased to one rupee and if such part is less than fifty paise it shall be ignored.

154B. Publication of information respecting persons in certain cases.

(1) If the Central Government is of opinion that it is necessary or expedient in the public interest to publish the names of any person and any other particulars relating to any proceedings or prosecutions under this Act in respect of such person, it may cause to be published such names and particulars in such manners as it thinks fit.

(2) No publication under this Section shall be made in relation to any penalty imposed under this Act until the time for presenting an appeal to the Commissioner (Appeals) under Section 128 or the Appellate Tribunal under Section 129A, as the case may be, has expired without an appeal having been presented or the appeal, if presented, has been disposal of.

EXPLANATION: In the case of a firm, company or other association of persons, the names of the partners of the firm, directors, managing agents, secretaries and treasures or managers of the company, or the members of the association, as the case may be, may also be published if, in the opinion of the Central Government, circumstances of the case justify it.

155. Protection of action taken under the Act.

(1) No suit, prosecution or other legal proceedings shall lie against the Central Government or any officer of the Government or a local authority for anything which is done, or intended to be done in good faith, in pursuance of this Act or the rules or regulations.

(2) No proceeding other than a suit shall be commenced against the Central Government or any officer of the Government or a local authority for anything purporting to be done in pursuance of this Act without giving the Central Government or such officer a month's previous notice in writing of the intended proceeding and of the cause thereof, or after the expiration of three months from the accrual of such cause.

156. General power to make rules.

(1) Without prejudice to any power to make rules contained elsewhere in this Act, the Central Government may make rules consistent with this Act generally to carry out the purposes of this Act.

(2) In particular and without prejudice to the generality of the foregoing power, such rules may provide for all or any of the following matters, namely:-

(a) the manner of determining the transaction value of the imported goods and export goods under sub-section (1) of Section 14;

(b) the conditions subject to which accessories of, and spare parts and maintenance and repairing implements for, any article shall be chargeable at the same rate of duty as that article;

(c) Omitted.

(d) the detention and confiscation of goods the importation of which is prohibited and the conditions, if any, to be fulfilled before such detention and confiscation and the information, notices and security to be given and the evidence requisite for the purposes of such detention or confiscation and the mode of verification of such evidence;

(e) the reimbursement by an informant to any public officer of all expenses and damages incurred in respect of any detention of any goods made on his information and of any proceedings consequent on such detention;

(f) the information required in respect of any goods mentioned in a shipping bill or bill of export which are not exported or which are exported and are afterwards re-landed;

(g) the publication, subject to such conditions as may be specified therein, of names and other particulars of persons who have been found guilty of contravention of any of the provisions of this Act or the rules.

(h) the amount to be paid for compounding and the manner of compounding under sub-section (3) of Section 137.

157. General power to make regulations.

(1) Without prejudice to any power to make regulations contained elsewhere in this Act, the Board may make regulations consistent with this Act and the rules, generally to carry out the purposes of this Act.

(2) In particular and without prejudice to the generality of the foregoing power, such regulations may provide for all or any of the following matters, namely :-

(a) the form of a bill of entry, shipping bill, bill of export, import manifest, import report, export manifest, export report, bill of transhipment, declaration for transhipment boat note and bill of coastal goods;

(ai) the manner of export of goods, relinquishment of title to the goods and abandoning them to customs and destruction or rendering of goods commercially valueless in the presence of the proper officer under clause (d) of sub-section (1) of Section 26A;

(aii) the form and manner of making application for refund of duty under sub-section (2) of Section 26A;

(aa) the form and manner in which an application for refund shall be made under Section 27;

(b) the conditions subject to which the transhipment of all or any goods under sub-section (3) of Section 54, the transportation of all or any goods under Section 56 and the removal of warehoused goods from one warehouse to another under Section 67, may be allowed without payment of duty;

(c) * * *

(d) the conditions subject to which any manufacturing process or other operations may be carried on in a warehouse under Section 65.

The manner of conducting audit of the assessment of duty of the imported or export goods at the office of the proper officer or the premises of the importer or exporter, as the case may be.

158. Provisions with respect to rules and regulations.

(1) All rules and regulations made under this Act shall be published in the Official Gazette.

(2) Any rule or regulation which the Central Government or the Board is empowered to make under this Act may provide -

(i) for the levy of fees in respect of applications, amendment of documents, furnishing of duplicates of documents, issue of certificates, and supply of statistics, and for rendering of any services by officers of customs under this Act;

(ii) that any person who contravenes any provision of a rule or regulation or abets such contravention or who fails to comply with any provision of a rule or regulation with which it was his duty to comply, shall be liable to a penalty which may extend to fifty thousand rupees.

159. Rules, certain notifications and orders to be laid before Parliament. Every rule or regulation made under this Act, every notification issued under Sections 11, 11B, 11H, 11-I, 11K, 11N, 14, 25, 28A, 43, 66, 69, 70, 74, 75, 76, 98, 98A, 101 and 123 and every order made under sub-section (2) of Section 25, other than an order relating to goods of strategic, secret, individual or personal nature, shall be laid, as soon as may be after it is made or issued, before each House of Parliament, while it is in session, for a total period of thirty days which may be comprised in one session, or in two or more successive sessions, and if, before the expiry of the session immediately following the session or the successive sessions aforesaid, both Houses agree in making any modification in the rule or regulation or notification or order, or both Houses agree that the rule or regulation should not be made or notification or order should not be issued or made, the rule or regulation or notification or order shall thereafter have effect only in such modified form or be of no effect, as the case may be; so, however, that any such modification or annulment shall be without prejudice to the validity of anything previously done under that rule or regulation or notification or order.

159A. Effect of amendments, etc., of rules, regulations, notifications or orders. Where any rule, regulation, notification or order made or issued under this Act or any notification or order issued under such rule or regulation, is amended, repealed, superseded or rescinded, then, unless a different intention appears, such amendment, repeal, supersession or rescinding shall not—

(a) revive anything not in force or existing at the time at which the amendment, repeal, supersession or rescinding takes effect; or

(b) affect the previous operation of any rule, regulation, notification or order so amended, repealed, superseded or rescinded or anything duly done or suffered thereunder; or

(c) affect any right, privilege, obligation or liability acquired, accrued or incurred under any rule, regulation, notification or order so amended, repealed, superseded or rescinded; or

(d) affect any penalty, forfeiture or punishment incurred in respect of any offence committed under or in violation of any rule, regulation, notification or order so amended, repealed, superseded or rescinded; or

(e) affect any investigation, legal proceeding or remedy in respect of any such right, privilege, obligation, liability, penalty, forfeiture or punishment as aforesaid, and any such investigation, legal proceeding or remedy may be instituted, continued or enforced and any such penalty, forfeiture or punishment may be imposed as if the rule, regulation, notification or order, as the case may be, had not been amended, repealed, superseded or rescinded.

160. Repeal and savings.

(1) The enactments specified in the Schedule are hereby repealed to the extent mentioned in the fourth column thereof.

(2) In the Indian Tariff Act, 1934 (32 of 1934) -

(a) for section 2, the following Section shall be substituted, namely :-

"2. **Duties specified in the Schedules to be levied.** – The rates at which duties of customs shall be levied under the Customs Act, 1962, are specified in the First and Second Schedules.

(b) sections 5 and 6 shall stand repealed.

(3) Notwithstanding the repeal of any enactment by this Section, -

(a) any notification, rule, regulation, order or notice issued or any appointment or declaration made or any licence, permission or exemption granted for any assessment made, confiscation adjudged or any duty levied or any penalty or fine imposed or any forfeiture, cancellation or discharge of any bond ordered or any other thing done or any other action taken under any repealed enactment shall, so far as it is not inconsistent with the provisions of this Act, be deemed to have been done or taken under the corresponding provision of this Act;

(b) any document referring to any enactment hereby repealed shall be construed as referring to this Act or to the corresponding provision of this Act.

(4) This Act shall apply to all goods which are subject to the control of customs at the commencement of this Act notwithstanding that the goods were imported before such commencement.

(5) Where the period prescribed for any application, appeal, revision or other proceeding under any repealed enactment had expired on or before the commencement of this Act, nothing in this Act shall be construed as enabling any such application, appeal or revision to be made or a proceeding to be instituted under this Act by reason only of the fact that a longer period therefore is prescribed or provision is made for extension of time in suitable cases by the appropriate authority.

(6) The provisions of Section 65 shall apply to goods warehoused before the commencement of this Act if the operations permissible under that Section were carried on after such commencement.

(7) Any duty or penalty payable under any repealed enactment may be recovered in a manner provided under this Act but without prejudice to any action already taken for the recovery of such duty or penalty under the repealed enactment.

(8) The mention of particular matters in sub-sections (4), (5), (6) and (7) shall not be held to prejudice or affect the general application of Section 6 of the General Clauses Act, 1897 (10 of 1897), with regard to the effect of repeals.

(9) Nothing in this Act shall affect any law for the time being in force relating to the constitution and powers of any Port authority in a major port as defined in the Indian Ports Act, 1908 (15 of 1908).

161. Removal of difficulties. If any difficulty arises in giving effect to the provisions of this Act, particularly in relation to the transition from the enactments repealed by this Act to the provisions of this Act, the Central Government may, by general or special order, do anything not inconsistent with such provisions which appears to be necessary or expedient for the purpose of removing the difficulty.

❑❑❑

4

Limited Liability Partnership Act, 2008 (6 OF 2009)

G.S.R. 229 (E). In exercise of the powers conferred by sub-sections (1) and (2) of Section 79 of the Limited Liability Partnership Act, 2008 (6 of 2009), the Central Government hereby makes the following rules, namely :-

CHAPTER -I : PRELIMINARY

1. Short title and commencement.

(1) These rules may be called the Limited Liability Partnership Rules, 2009.

(2) (a) Rules 1 to 31, rules 34 to 37 and rule 41 of these rules shall come into force on the 1st day of April, 2009;

(b) Rules 32 and 33, and rules 38 to 40 of these rules shall come into force on such date as the Central Government may, by notification in the Official Gazette, appoint.

2. Definitions.

(1) In these rules, unless the context otherwise requires,-

(i) "Act" means the Limited Liability Partnership Act, 2008 (6 of 2009);

(ii) "Annexure" means Annexure to these rules;

(iii) "Certifying Authority" means a person who has been granted a license to issue a Digital Signature Certificate under Section 24 of the Information Technology Act, 2000 (21 of 2000);

(iv) "Designated Partner Identification Number" (DPIN) means an identification number which the Central Government may allot to any individual or nominee of a body corporate, intending to be appointed as designated partner of a limited liability partnership (LLP), for the purpose of his identification as such;

(v) "digital signature" means authentication of any electronic record by a subscriber by means of an electronic method or procedure in accordance with the provisions of Section 3 of the Information Technology Act, 2000;

(vi) "Digital Signature Certificate" means a Digital Signature Certificate issued under sub-section (4) of Section 35 of the Information Technology Act, 2000;

(vii) "electronic record" means electronic record as defined under clause (t) of Section 2 of the Information Technology Act, 2000;

(viii) "electronic registry" means an electronic repository or storage system in which the information or documents are received, stored, protected and preserved in electronic form;

(ix) "Electronic mail (E-mail)" means message sent, received or forwarded in digital form via a computer-based communication mechanism;

(x) 'Officer' includes any partner, designated partner, employee of the LLP, any person in accordance with whose directions or instructions the partners of the LLP have been accustomed to act and any person authorized to accept any service on behalf of a foreign Limited Liability Partnership and partners of such foreign Limited Liability Partnership;

(xi) "Pre-fill" means the automated process of data input by the computer system from the database maintained in electronic registry;

(xii) "Provisional Designated Partner Identification Number" refers to the provisional identification number generated by the electronic system setup by the Ministry of Corporate Affairs;

(xiii) "Registrar" means a Registrar as defined under clause (s) of sub-section (1) of Section 2 of the Act;

(xiv) "Registrar's Front Office" means an office maintained by the Central Government or an agency authorized by it to facilitate e-filing of documents into the electronic registry and their inspection and viewing;

(xv) 'section' means Section of the Act;

(xvi) "website" means a location connected to the internet that maintains one or more web pages;

(2) Words and expressions used in these rules and not defined shall have the meaning respectively assigned to them in the Limited Liability Partnership Act, 2008 (6 of 2009) and the Information Technology Act, 2000 (21 of 2000).

3. Forms.

(1) Every LLP shall use the forms annexed to these rules for the purposes of the Act.

(2) Every LLP shall specify therein its limited liability partnership identification number (LLPIN).

4. Authentication of electronic forms. The electronic form shall be authenticated by authorized signatories using digital signatures, as defined under the Information Technology Act, 2000 (21 of 2000).

5. Fees.

(1) The fees payable in pursuance of the various provisions of the Act and these rules shall be as mentioned in Annexure 'A'.

(2) The fees payable in pursuance of the Act or any rule made or notification issued thereunder shall be paid into the Public Account of India:

PROVIDED that the fees payable to the Registrar may be paid also through postal orders (where the amount involved does not exceed fifty rupees) or through bank drafts payable at and/or drawn on post offices or banks, as the case may be, located at the same city or town where the office of the Registrar is situated:

PROVIDED FURTHER that, where a fee payable to the Registrar is paid through postal orders or bank drafts as aforesaid, it shall not be deemed to have been paid unless and until the relevant postal orders or drafts are cashed and the amount credited:

PROVIDED ALSO that, where application is filed through electronic media or through any other computer readable media, the user may choose any one of the following payment options namely, (i) Credit Card; or (ii) Internet Banking; or (iii) Remittance at the Bank Counter; or (iv) any other mode as approved by the Central Government.

6. The manner and conditions of filing, recording or registering of documents, forms, notices, statements, returns etc., shall be as laid down in Chapter XIII of these rules.

CHAPTER -II : NATURE OF LIMITED LIABILITY PARTNERSHIP

7. For the purposes of sub-section (3) of Section 7, an individual shall give his prior consent to act as a designated partner to the limited liability partnership in Form 9.

8. For the purposes of sub-section (4) of Section 7, the particulars of an individual who has given his consent to act as designated partner shall be filed in Form 4 along with fee as mentioned in Annexure 'A'.

9. (1) A person shall not be capable of being appointed as a designated partner of a limited liability partnership, if he -

(a) has at any time within the preceding five years been adjudged insolvent; or

(b) suspends, or has at any time within the preceding five years suspended payment to his creditors and has not at any time within the preceding five years made, a composition with them; or

(c) has been convicted by a Court for any offence involving moral turpitude and sentenced in respect thereof to imprisonment for not less than six months; or

(d) has been convicted by a Court for an offence involving Section 30 of the Act.

(2) The Central Government may, by notification in the Official Gazette, remove the disqualification incurred by any person by virtue of clauses (a) or (b) of sub-rule (1), either generally or in relation to any limited liability partnership or limited liability partnerships specified in the notification.

CHAPTER -III : DESIGNATED PARTNER'S IDENTIFICATION NUMBER

10. (1) Every individual or nominee of a body corporate, who is intending to be appointed as designated partner of a limited liability partnership shall make an application electronically in Form 7 to the Central Government for obtaining Designated Partner Identification Number (DPIN).

(2) The Central Government shall provide an electronic system to facilitate submission of application for the allotment of DPIN through a portal on the website of the Ministry of Corporate Affairs.

(3) The applicant shall access the Form 7 from the portal, fill-in the required particulars sought therein and use 'submit' function provided therein upon which the system will electronically generate and indicate in the space provided a Provisional DPIN.

(4) A provisional DPIN generated online under sub-rule (3) by the applicant will remain valid for a period of sixty days from the date on which it was generated.

(5) (i) The applicant shall, after the allotment of provisional DPIN, submit an application to the Central Government along with the fee as mentioned in Annexure 'A' for the allotment of regular DPIN within sixty days from the date on which provisional DPIN was generated on-line, failing which the provisional DPIN will lapse.

(ii) For making an application under sub-rule (i), the applicant shall take a print out of Form 7, affix his photograph in the space provided in that Form, enclose true copies of the proof of identity and proof of residence and physically sign the form at the place specified therein. The photograph and the proof of identity and residence shall be certified by any one of the following authorities:-

(a) Gazetted Officer of the Central or State Government,

(b) Notary Public,

(c) Chartered Accountant, Cost Accountant or Company Secretary holding a certificate of practice under the Chartered Accountants Act, 1949, the Cost and Works Accountants Act, 1959 and the Company Secretaries Act, 1980 respectively.

(6) The Central Government shall process the applications received for allotment of DPIN under sub-rule (5), decide on such application and communicate approval along with the DPIN allotted or rejection thereof to the applicant by way of a letter by post or electronically or in any other mode, within a period of one month from the receipt of such application.

(7) The DPIN so allotted is valid for the life time of such applicant and shall not be allotted to any other person in any case.

(8) Every designated partner shall intimate his consent to become a designated partner to the limited liability partnership and DPIN in Form 9 and the LLP shall intimate such DPIN to Registrar in Form 4.

(9) (a)(i) Every designated partner, who has been allotted a DPIN under these rules shall, in the event of any change in his particulars as stated in Form 7 under sub-rule (5), intimate such change(s) to the Central Government within a period of 30 days of such change(s) in Form 10.

(ii) The concerned designated partner shall also intimate such changes to the limited liability partnership or limited liability partnership(s) on which he is a designated partner within 30 days of such changes.

(b) The designated partners shall fill-in the relevant change(s) in prescribed Form 10, enclose a copy of the proof of the changed particulars duly certified in the manner specified in clause (ii) of sub-rule (5), affix signature at the place specified, and file the same to the Central Government. There shall be no fee for intimating the changes in particulars in Form 10.

(10) The Central Government, after being satisfied, through verification of such changed particulars from the enclosed copy of proof, shall incorporate the said change and inform the designated partner by way of a letter issued by post or electronically or in any other mode confirming the effect of such change in the electronic database maintained by the Ministry of Corporate Affairs.

CHAPTER -IV : INCORPORATION OF LIMITED LIABILITY PARTNERSHIP

11. For the purposes of Section 11, the incorporation document shall be filed in Form 2 with the Registrar having jurisdiction over the State in which the registered office of the limited liability partnership is to be situated alongwith the fee as provided in Annexure 'A'.

12. In case of foreign nationals residing outside India in countries signatory to the Hague Apostile Convention, 1961 and seeking to register a LLP in India, their signatures and address on the incorporation documents and proof of identity, where required, shall be notarized before the notary of the country of their origin and be duly apostillised in accordance with the said Hague Convention.

13. The statement to be filed along with the incorporation document under clause (c) of sub-section (1) of Section 11 shall be in the format provided in Part B of Form 2.

14.(1) In the office of Registrar there shall be maintained a Register of LLPs in which the names of LLPs shall be entered in the order in which they are registered.

(2) Every LLP so registered shall be assigned a LLP identification number (LLPIN) in one consecutive series.

15. (1) A document can be served on a limited liability partnership or a partner or designated partner thereof through the following other modes-

(i) electronic transmission;

(ii) courier.

(2) For the purposes of this rule,

(i) "electronic transmission" means a communication -

(a) delivered by -

(A) facsimile telecommunication or electronic mail when directed to the facsimile number of electronic mail address, respectively, which the partnership or the partner or the designated partner has provided from time to time for sending communications to the partnership or the partner or the designated partner respectively,

(B) posting on an electronic message board or network that the partnership or the partner or the designated partner has designated for those communications, and which transmission shall be validly delivered upon the posting, or

(C) other means of electronic communication as to which the LLP or the partner or the designated partner has placed in effect reasonable measures to verify that the sender is the person purporting to send the transmission, and

(b) that creates a record that is capable of retention, retrieval and review, and that may thereafter be rendered into clearly legible tangible form.

(ii) Courier means a document sent through a courier which provides the proof of delivery.

16. (1) A limited liability partnership shall give an address for service of documents within the jurisdiction of the Registrar where its registered office is situate. Such address shall include the postal code and e-mail address.

(2) The limited liability partnership, may, in addition to the registered office address, declare any other address as its address for service of documents, under sub-section (2) of Section 13, in the manner as laid down in the limited liability partnership agreement. Where the limited liability partnership agreement does not provide for such manner, consent of all partners shall be required for declaring any other address as the address for service of documents.

(3) The intimation of other address for service of documents to LLP shall be given to the Registrar in Form 12, within thirty days of complying with the requirements of sub-rule (2) above along with the fee as mentioned in Annexure 'A'.

(4) The effective date for the service of documents to LLP at the other address declared by the LLP cannot be prior to the date of filing of document under sub-rule (3).

17. (1) The limited liability partnership may change its registered office from one place to another by following the procedure as laid down in the limited liability partnership agreement. Where the limited liability partnership agreement does not provide for such procedure, consent of all partners shall be required for changing the place of registered office of limited liability partnership to another place:

PROVIDED that where the change in place of registered office is from one State to another State, the limited liability partnership having secured creditors shall also obtain consent of such secured creditors.

(2) For the purposes of sub-section (3) of Section 13, notice of change of place of registered office shall be given to Registrar in Form 15, within 30 days of complying with the requirements of sub-rule (1), in case of change of registered office within the same state, and within 30 days of complying with sub-rule (4) in case of change of registered office from one state to another state, along with fee mentioned in Annexure 'A'.

(3) Where there is any conviction, ruling, order or judgment of any Court, tribunal or other authority against the limited liability partnership, the particulars of such prosecutions initiated against or show-cause notices received by the limited liability partnership for the alleged offences under the LLP Act shall be stated in the notice of change of place of registered office to be filed with the Registrar.

(4) Where the change in place of registered office is from one state to another state, the limited liability partnership shall publish a general notice, not less than 21 days before filing any notice with Registrar, in a daily newspaper published in English and in the principal language of the district in which the registered office of the limited liability partnership is situated and circulating in that district giving notice of change of registered office.

(5) Where the change in place of registered office is from one place to another place within the state from the jurisdiction of one Registrar to the jurisdiction of another Registrar or from one state to another state, the limited liability partnership shall file the notice in Form 15 with the Registrar from where the limited liability partnership proposes to shift its registered office with a copy thereof for the information to the Registrar under whose jurisdiction the registered office is proposed to be shifted.

18. (1) The name of the limited liability partnership shall not be one prohibited under the Emblems and Names (Prevention of Improper Use) Act, 1950.

(2) A name shall not generally be reserved, if -

(i) it includes any word or words which are offensive to any Section of the people;

(ii) the proposed name is the exact Hindi or English translation of the name of an existing limited liability partnership in English or Hindi, as the case may be;

(iii) the proposed name has a close phonetic resemblance to the name of a LLP in existence, for example, J.K. LLP., Jay Kay LLP;

(iv) it includes the word Co-operative, Sahakari or the equivalent of word 'co-operative' in the regional languages of the country;

(v) it connotes the participation or patronage of the Central or State Government, unless circumstances justify to, e.g., a name may be deemed undesirable in certain context if it includes any of the words such as National, Union, Central, Federal, Republic, President, Rashtrapati, etc;

(vi) the proposed name contains the words 'British India';

(vii) the proposed name implies association or connection with any Embassy or Consulate or of a foreign government which suggests connection with local authorities such as Municipal, Panchayat, Zila Parishad or any other body connected with the Union or State Government;

(viii) the proposed name is vague like D.I.M.O. Limited liability partnership or I.V.N.R. Limited liability partnership or S.S.R.P Limited liability partnership;

(ix) it is different from the name or names of the existing limited liability partnership only to the extent of having the name of a place within brackets before the word 'limited liability partnership', for example, Indian Press (Delhi) LLP should not be allowed in view of the existence of the LLP named Indian Press LLP;

(x) it includes name of registered Trade mark, unless the consent of the owner of the trade mark has been produced;

(xi) the proposed name is identical with or too nearly resembles the name of a firm or LLP or company incorporated outside India and reserved by such firm, LLP or company with the registrar in accordance with these rules;

(xii) it is identical with or too nearly resembles the name of the limited liability partnership or a company in liquidation or it is identical with or too nearly resembles names of the LLP or a company which is struck off, up to the period of 5 years;

(xiii) it includes words like 'Bank', 'Insurance' and 'Banking', 'Venture capital' or 'mutual fund' or such similar names without the approval of the regulatory authority;

(xiv) it is intended or likely to produce a misleading impression regarding the scope or scale of its activities which would be beyond the resources at its disposal;

(xv) the proposed name includes words like French, British, German etc., unless the partners satisfy that there is some form of collaboration and connection with the foreigners of that particular country or place, the name of which is incorporated in the name;

(xvi) the proposed name of limited liability partnership includes the words company secretary, chartered accountant, advocates or such similar words as indicative of a profession, as part of the proposed name, the same shall be allowed only after obtaining approval from the Council governing such profession or such authority as may be nominated by the Central Government, in this behalf.

(3) A foreign LLP or a foreign company may on payment of fee as mentioned in Annexure 'A', apply in Form 25 to the Registrar for reserving its existing name by which it is registered in the country of its regulation or incorporation:

PROVIDED that such reservation shall be valid for three years but may be renewed on a fresh application along with payment of fee as provided in Annexure 'A'.

(4) An application for reservation of name with which the proposed limited liability partnership is to be registered or for change of name, as the case may be, shall be made to the Registrar having jurisdiction where the registered office of the limited liability partnership is to be situate.

(5) Every such application shall be in Form 1 and be accompanied by fee as mentioned in Annexure 'A' and the Registrar shall inform to the applicant for reservation or non reservation of the changed name or the name with which the proposed LLP is to be registered ordinarily within seven days of the receipt of application.

(6) Where the Registrar informs applicant about reservation of name with which the LLP is to be registered or changed name, as the case may be, such name shall be available for reservation for a period of three months from the date of intimation by the Registrar.

19. (1) A limited liability partnership or a body corporate or any other entity which already has a name which is similar to or which too nearly resembles the name of a limited liability partnership incorporated subsequently, may apply to the Registrar in Form 23 to give a direction to that limited liability partnership incorporated subsequently to change its name.

(2) The application under sub-rule (1) shall state -

(i) the LLPIN of limited liability partnership, or the CIN of the company or the registration number of the other entity as the case may be;

(ii) the name with which the limited liability partnership or the company or any other entity was incorporated or registered;

(iii) the grounds of objection to the name of the limited liability partnership incorporated subsequently.

(3) The application shall be verified by the person making it.

(4) The person making the application shall attach -

(a) the authority under which he is making such an application;

(b) a copy of the incorporation certificate of the limited liability partnership or the company or the registration certificate of the entity, as the case may be.

(5) The application shall be accompanied by a fee as mentioned in Annexure 'A'.

20. (1) The limited liability partnership may change its name by following the procedure as laid down in the limited liability partnership agreement. Where the limited liability partnership agreement does not provide such procedure, consent of all partners shall be required for changing the name of the limited liability partnership.

(2) Notice of change of name shall be given to the Registrar in Form 5, within 30 days of complying with requirement of sub-rule (1), along with a fee as mentioned in Annexure 'A'.

(3) The Registrar on being satisfied that the changed name is the one as reserved by him shall issue a fresh certificate of incorporation in the new name and the changed name shall be effective from the date of such certificate.

CHAPTER -V : PARTNERS AND THEIR RELATIONS

21. (1) For the purposes of sub-section (2) of Section 23, every limited liability partnership shall file information with regard to the limited liability partnership agreement in Form 3 with the Registrar within thirty days of the date of incorporation alongwith the fee as provided in Annexure 'A':

PROVIDED that any change made in the limited liability partnership agreement shall be filed in Form 3 within thirty days of such change alongwith the fee as provided in Annexure 'A'.

(2) For the purposes of sub-section (3) of Section 23, every limited liability partnership shall file information with regard to the limited liability partnership agreement referred to in such sub-section, in Form 3 with the Registrar within thirty days of the ratification by all the partners alongwith the fee as provided in Annexure 'A'.

22. (1) For the purposes of sub-section (1) of Section 25, every partner shall intimate change in his name or address to the limited liability partnership in Form 6.

(2) For the purposes of sub-section (2) of Section 25, where a person becomes or ceases to be a partner or where there is any change in the name or address of a partner, the limited liability partnership shall file with the Registrar, a notice in Form 4.

(3) For the purposes of sub-section (3) of Section 25, in respect of notice of a person becoming a partner, the Form 4 shall include a statement signed by the incoming partner that he consents to become a partner.

(4) The form shall be accompanied by a certificate from a Chartered Accountant in practice or Cost Accountant in practice or a Company Secretary in practice that he has verified the particulars from the books and records of the limited liability partnership and found them to be true and correct.

(5) The fees to be paid to the registrar in pursuance of sub-section (3) of Section 25 shall be as mentioned in Annexure 'A'.

CHAPTER -VI : FORM OF CONTRIBUTION

23. (1) The contribution of each partner shall be accounted for and disclosed in the Accounts of the LLP along with nature of contribution and amount.

(2) The contribution of a partner consisting of tangible, movable or immovable or intangible property or other benefits brought or contribution by way of an agreement or contract for services shall be valued by a practicing Chartered Accountant or by a practicing Cost Accountant or by approved valuer from the panel maintained by the Central Government.

CHAPTER -VII : FINANCIAL DISCLOSURES

24. (1) Every limited liability partnership shall keep books of accounts which are sufficient to show and explain the limited liability partnership's transactions and are such as to-

(a) disclose with reasonable accuracy, at any time, the financial position of the limited liability partnership at that time; and

(b) enable the designated partners to ensure that any Statement of Account and Solvency prepared under this rule complies with the requirements of the Act.

(2) The books of account shall contain-

(a) particulars of all sums of money received and expended by the limited liability partnership and the matters in respect of which the receipt and expenditure takes place;

(b) a record of the assets and liabilities of the limited liability partnership;

(c) statements of cost of goods purchased, inventories, work-in-progress, finished goods and cost of goods sold; and

(d) any other particulars which the partners may decide.

(3) The books of account which a limited liability partnership is required to keep shall be preserved for eight years from the date on which they are made.

(4) For the purposes of sub-section (3) of Section 34, every limited liability partnership shall file the Statement of Account and Solvency in Form 8 with the Registrar, within a period of thirty days from the end of six months of the financial year to which the Statement of Account and Solvency relates.

(5) The fees to be paid to the Registrar in pursuance of sub-section (3) of Section 34 for filing the Statement of Account and Solvency shall be as mentioned in Annexure 'A'.

(6) A limited liability partnership's Statement of Account and Solvency shall be signed on behalf of the limited liability partnership by its designated partners.

(7) The Statement of Account and Solvency of a limited liability partnership shall be signed by the designated partners of the LLP and each designated partner shall be taken to be a party to its approval unless he shows that he took all reasonable steps to prevent their being approved and signed.

(8) The accounts of every limited liability partnership shall be audited in accordance with these rules:

PROVIDED that a limited liability partnership whose turnover does not exceed, in any financial year, forty lakh rupees, or whose contribution does not exceed twenty-five lakh rupees shall not be required to get its accounts audited:

PROVIDED FURTHER that if partners of such limited liability partnership decide to get the accounts of such LLP audited, the accounts shall be audited in accordance with these rules:

PROVIDED ALSO that where the partners of such LLP do not decide for audit of the accounts of the LLP, such LLP shall include in the Statement of Account and Solvency a statement by the partners to the effect that the partners acknowledge their responsibilities for complying with the requirements of the Act and the Rules with respect to preparation of books of account and a certificate in the form specified in Form 8.

(9) A person shall not be qualified for appointment as an auditor of a limited liability partnership unless he is a Chartered Accountant in practice.

(10) An auditor or auditors of a limited liability partnership shall be appointed for each financial year of the LLP for auditing its accounts.

(11) The designated partners may appoint an auditor or auditors-

(a) at any time for the first financial year but before the end of the first financial year,

(b) at least 30 days prior to the end of the each financial year (other than the first financial year),

(c) to fill a casual vacancy in the office of auditor, including in the case when the turnover or contribution of a limited liability partnership exceeds the limits specified under sub-rule (8), or

(d) to fill up the vacancy caused by removal of an auditor.

(12) The partners may appoint an auditor or auditors where the designated partners have power to appoint under sub-rule (11) and have failed to appoint.

(13) An auditor or auditors of an LLP shall hold office in accordance with the terms of his or their appointment and shall continue to hold such office till the period-

(a) the new auditors are appointed, or

(b) they are re-appointed.

(14) Where no auditor has been appointed under sub-rule (11), any auditor in office shall be deemed to be re-appointed, unless -

(a) the limited liability partnership agreement requires actual re-appointment, or

(b) the majority of partners have determined that he should not be re-appointed and have given a notice to this effect to the LLP.

(15) Provisions of sub-rule (14) shall be applicable without prejudice to the provisions of the rules relating to removal and resignation of auditors under this chapter.

(16) A notice specified under clause (b) of sub-rule 14 -

(a) may be in hard copy or electronic form, and

(b) must be authenticated by the person or persons giving it.

(17) The remuneration of an auditor appointed by the limited liability partnership may be fixed by the designated partners or by following the procedure as laid down in the limited liability partnership agreement.

(18) (a) The partners of a limited liability partnership may remove an auditor from office at any time by following the procedure as laid down in the limited liability partnership agreement.

(b) Where the limited liability partnership agreement does not provide for removal of an auditor, consent of all the partners shall be required for removal of the auditor from his office.

(19) (a) An auditor of an LLP may resign his office by depositing a notice in writing to that effect at the LLP's registered office.

(b) Where an auditor is unwilling to be re-appointed, he shall give a notice in writing to that effect at the LLP's registered office, not less than 14 days before the end of the time allowed for appointing the new auditor.

(c) The notice under clause (a) or (b) is not effective unless it is accompanied by the statement of the circumstances connected with his ceasing to hold office.

(d) The auditor's term comes to an end as on the date on which the notice is deposited or on such later date as may be specified in the notice.

25. (1) For the purposes of sub-section (1) of Section 35, every limited liability partnership shall file an annual return with the Registrar in Form 11.

(2) The annual return of an LLP having turnover upto five crore rupees during the corresponding financial year or contribution upto fifty lakh rupees shall be accompanied with a certificate from a designated partner, other than the signatory to the annual return, to the effect that annual return contains true and correct information. In all other cases, the annual return shall be accompanied with a certificate from a Company Secretary in practice to the effect that he has verified the particulars from the books and records of the limited liability partnership and found them to be true and correct.

(3) The fees to be paid to the Registrar in pursuance of sub-section (1) of Section 35 for filing the annual return shall be as mentioned in Annexure 'A'.

26. The documents to be kept by the Registrar under Section 36 shall be available in the registry on payment of fee as mentioned in Annexure 'A' for inspection by any person and for obtaining any certified copy thereof.

CHAPTER -VIII : DESTRUCTION OF OLD RECORDS

27. (1) The Registrar shall preserve the documents permanently as specified in Annexure 'B' to these rules.

(2) Subject to previous order of the Registrar, the records in the office of Registrar may be destroyed after the expiry of the period of their preservation as specified below:-

(a) Records to be preserved for 21 years: All papers, registers, refund orders and correspondence relating to the limited liability partnership liquidation accounts.

(b) Records to be preserved for 5 years:

(i) copies of Government orders relating to limited liability partnership;

(ii) registered documents of limited liability partnership which have been fully wound up and finally dissolved together with correspondence relating to such limited liability partnership;

(iii) papers relating to legal proceedings from the date of disposal of the case and appeal, if any;

(iv) copies of statistical returns furnished to Government;

(v) all correspondences including correspondences relating to scrutiny of accounts, annual returns, prosecutions, reports to the Central Government and the Tribunal and the correspondences relating to complaints:

PROVIDED that in case of prosecution matter, the date is to be recorded from the date of disposal of the case and appeal, if any.

(c) Records to be preserved for three years-

(i) All books, records and papers, other than those specified in sub-rule (1), clauses (a) and (b) of sub-rule (2), sub-rule (3) and sub-rule (4).

(ii) Routine correspondence regarding payment of fees, additional filing fees and correspondence about the return of documents.

(3) The registered documents specified in Annexure 'C' to these rules relating to any limited liability partnership in operation shall be preserved for the period indicated against them in the said Annexure.

(4) Registered documents of foreign limited liability partnerships which cease to have any place of business in India shall be destroyed after expiry of three years from the date such limited liability partnerships cease to have any place of business in India.

(5) The Registrar shall maintain a Register of destroyed documents in two parts, in the form set out in the Annexure 'D' to these rules, wherein he shall enter brief particulars of the records destroyed and shall certify therein the date and mode of destruction.

(6) The provisions of these rules shall be in addition to and not in derogation of the rules for the destruction of office records connected with accounts (containing in Appendix 13 to the Compilation of the General Financial Rules) and the period prescribed under Record Retention Schedule for Records common to all departments and such other rules.

CHAPTER -IX : INVESTIGATIONS

28. For the purposes of clause (a) of sub-section (3) of Section 43, an application by the partners to investigate into the affairs of the limited liability partnership, shall be made, along with such security, for an amount calculated on the following scale but not exceeding twenty five lakh rupees, for payment of costs of the investigation:

Turnover (Rs.) [as stated in the Statement of Account of Solvency for the immediately preceding financial year]	**Amount of Security**
(i) Upto 1 Crore	2 Lakh
(ii) 1 Crore or more but less than 5 crore	5 Lakh
(iii) 5 Crore or more but less than 10 crore	10 Lakh
(iv) 10 Crore or more	25 Lakh

EXPLANATION. In the absence of Statement of Account and Solvency for the preceding financial year, such amount of security as may be fixed by the Central Government.

29. For the purposes of Section 44, an application by the partners under clause (a) of sub-section (1) of Section 43 to investigate the affairs of the limited liability partnership, shall be made alongwith the deposit of such security as calculated in the manner specified in rule 28.

30. The fee payable for furnishing a copy of the Inspector's report in pursuance of clause (b), sub-section (2), Section 49 shall be five rupees per page or fractional part thereof.

31. For the purposes of Section 54, a copy of the report of any inspector or inspectors, shall be authenticated either -

(a) by the common seal, if any, of the limited liability partnership whose affairs have been investigated into; or

(b) by a certificate of a public officer having the custody of the report, under and in accordance with the provisions of Section 76 of the Indian Evidence Act, 1872 (1 of 1872).

CHAPTER -X : CONVERSION TO LIMITED LIABILITY PARTNERSHIP

32. (1) The Registrar shall, on conversion of a firm, private company or an unlisted public company into limited liability partnership, issue a Certificate of Registration under his seal in Form 19.

(2) In the event, Registrar has refused the registration, the applicant firm or private company or unlisted public company, as the case may be, may apply to the Tribunal within sixty days from the date of receipt of such intimation of refusal.

33. For the purposes of the proviso to sub-section (1) of Section 58, where the firm, private company or unlisted public company has been converted into limited liability partnership, an intimation of such conversion to the concerned Registrar of firms or Registrar of Companies, as the case may be, shall be given in Form 14 within fifteen days of the date of registration of the LLP.

CHAPTER -XI : FOREIGN LIMITED LIABILITY PARTNERSHIP

34. (1) A foreign limited liability partnership shall, within thirty days of establishing a place of business in India, file with the Registrar in Form 27 -

(a) a copy of the certificate of incorporation or registration and other instrument(s) constituting or defining the constitution of the limited liability partnership;

(b) the full address of the registered or principal office of the limited liability partnership in the country of its incorporation;

(c) the full address of the office of the limited liability partnership in India which is to be deemed as its principal place of business in India; and

(d) list of partners and designated partners, if any, and the names and addresses of two or more persons resident in India, authorized to accept on behalf of the limited liability partnership, service of process and any notices or other documents required to be served on the limited liability partnership.

(2) (i) If the limited liability partnership is incorporated in any country which is a part of the Commonwealth, the copies of the documents referred to in sub-rule (1) shall be certified as true copies -

(a) by an official of the Government to whose custody the original is committed ;or

(b) by a Notary (Public) in that Part of the Commonwealth; or

(c) by an officer of the limited liability partnership, on oath before a person having authority to administer an oath in that part of the Commonwealth.

(ii) If the Limited Liability Partnership is incorporated in a country that falls outside the Commonwealth but is a party to the Hague Apostile Convention, 1961 -

(a) the copies of the documents referred to in sub-rule (1) shall be certified by an official of the Government to whose custody the original is committed and be duly apostillised in accordance with Hague Convention;

(b) a list of the partners and designated partners of the LLP, if any, the name and address of persons resident in India, authorized to accept notice on behalf of the Limited Liability Partnership shall be duly notarized and be apostillised in the country of their origin in accordance with Hague Convention.

(iii) If the limited liability partnership is incorporated in a country outside the Commonwealth and is not a party to the Hague Convention, the copy of the incorporation documents referred in sub-rule (1) shall be certified -

(a) by an official of the Government to whose custody the original is committed ; or

(b) a Notary (Public) of such country ; or

(c) by an officer of the limited liability partnership.

(iv) The signature or seal of the official referred to in sub-clause (a) of clause (iii) or the certificate of the Notary (Public) referred to in sub-clause (b) of that clause shall be authenticated by a Diplomatic or Consular Officer empowered in this behalf under Section 3 of the Diplomatic and Consular Officers (Oaths and Fees) Act, 1948 (XL of 1948), or where there is no such officer, by any of the officials mentioned in Section 6 of the Commissioners of Oaths Act, 1889 (52 and 53 Vic. C. 10), or in any Act amending the same.

(v) The certificate of the officer of the limited liability partnership referred to in sub-clause (c) of clause (iii) shall be signed before a person having authority to administer an oath as provided under Section 3 of the Diplomatic and Consular Officers (Oaths and Fees) Act, 1948 (XL of 1948), or as the case may be, by Section 3 of the Commissioners of Oaths Act, 1889 (52 and 53 Vic, C. 10) the status of the person administering the oath in the latter case being authenticated by any official specified in Section 6 of the Commissioners of Oaths Act, 1889 (52 and 53 Vic. C. 10) or in any Act amending the same.

(3) (i) If any alteration is made or occurs in-

(a) the instrument constituting or defining the constitution of a limited liability partnership incorporated or registered outside India;

(b) the registered or principal office of a limited liability partnership incorporated or registered outside India; or

(c) the partner or designated partner, if any, of a limited liability partnership incorporated or registered outside India, the foreign limited liability partnership shall file in Form 28 such alterations with the Registrar within sixty days of the close of the financial year.

(ii) If any alteration is made or occurs in-

(a) the certificate of incorporation or registration of limited liability partnership incorporated or registered outside India;

(b) the name or address of any of the persons authorized to accept service on behalf of a foreign limited liability partnership in India; or

(c) the principal place of business of foreign limited liability partnership in India, the foreign limited liability partnership shall file in Form 29 such alterations with the Registrar within thirty days from the date on which the alteration was made or occurred.

(4) Every foreign limited liability partnership shall file with the Registrar the Statement of Account and Solvency in Form 8 in accordance with provisions of Rule 24 duly signed by the authorized representatives within a period of 30 days from the end of six months of the financial year.

(5) (i) if any document as is mentioned in sub-rule (1) or (3) is not in the English language, there shall be annexed to it a certified translation thereof.

(ii) the translation of documents into English required to be filed with the Registrar in pursuance of sub-rule (1) or (3) shall be certified to be correct in the manner as provided in clause (iii) or clause (iv) of this sub-rule, as the case may be.

(iii) where any translation is made outside India, it shall be authenticated in the manner specified in sub-rule (2).

(iv) where such translation is made within India, it shall be authenticated-

(a) by an Advocate, Chartered Accountant, Company Secretary or Cost Accountant; or

(b) by an affidavit of a person who, in the opinion of the Registrar has adequate knowledge of the language of the original and of English.

(6) Every foreign limited liability partnership shall cause the name of the foreign limited liability partnership and of the country in which the limited liability partnership is incorporated, to be stated in legible English characters in all invoices, official correspondence and publications of the limited liability partnership.

(7) (a) where any such limited liability partnership makes default in delivering to the Registrar the names and addresses of persons resident in India who are authorized to accept on behalf of the limited liability partnership service of process, notices or other documents; or

(b) if at any time all the persons whose names and addresses have been so delivered are dead or have ceased so to reside, or refuse to accept service on behalf of the limited liability partnership or for any reason, cannot be served; a document may be served on the limited liability partnership by leaving it at, or sending it by post to, any place of business established by the limited liability partnership in India.

(8) If any foreign limited liability partnership ceases to have a place of business in India, it shall give notice to the Registrar in Form 29 within 30 days of its intention to close the place of business and as from the date on which notice is so given, the obligation of the limited liability partnership to file any document to the Registrar shall cease, provided it has no other place of business in India and it has filed all the documents due for filing as on the date of the notice.

(9) Every document which is required to be filed by any foreign limited liability partnership shall be filed in the electronic form to the Registrar having jurisdiction over New Delhi, through the portal maintained by the Ministry of Corporate Affairs on its website www.mca.gov.in.

(10) The Registrar shall, on registration of Form 27, issue a certificate for establishment of place of business in India by the foreign limited liability partnership in Form 30.

(11) There shall be paid to Registrar for filing or delivery or registering any form or document required by this Chapter the fee as mentioned in Annexure 'A'.

CHAPTER -XII : COMPROMISE, ARRANGEMENT OR RECONSTRUCTION OF LIMITED LIABILITY PARTNERSHIPS

35. (1) An application under sub-section (1) of Section 60 for an order convening a meeting of creditors or partners or creditors and partners shall be supported by an affidavit. A copy of the proposed compromise or arrangement shall be annexed to the affidavit as an exhibit thereto. The affidavit in support thereof shall be in Form 20.

(2) Where the limited liability partnership is not the applicant, a copy of the summons and of the affidavit shall be served on the limited liability partnership, or, where the limited liability partnership is being wound-up, on its liquidator, not less than 14 days before the date fixed for the hearing of the summons. The summons shall be in Form 21.

(3)(a) Upon the hearing of the summons or any adjourned hearing thereof, the Tribunal shall, by order, unless it thinks fit for any reason to dismiss the summons, give such directions as it may think necessary in respect of the following matters:

(i) determining the creditors and/or of partners whose meeting or meetings have to be held for considering the proposed compromise or arrangement;

(ii) fixing the time and place of such meeting or meetings;

(iii) appointing a Chairman for the meeting or chairmen for the meetings to be held;

(iv) fixing the quorum and the procedure to be followed at the meeting or meetings, including voting by proxy;

(v) determining the values of the creditors and/or the partners, as the case may be, whose meetings have to be held;

(vi) notice to be given of the meeting or meetings and the advertisement, if any, of such notice;

(vii) the time within which the chairman of the meeting is to report to the Tribunal the result of the meeting; and

(viii) such other matters as the Tribunal may deem necessary.

(b) The order made under clause (a) shall be in accordance with the rules as may be laid down in this behalf.

(4)(i) Voting by proxy shall be permitted, provided a proxy in Form 26 duly signed by the person entitled to attend and vote at the meeting is filed with the limited liability partnership at its registered office not later than 48 hours before the meeting.

(ii) Where a body corporate which is a partner or creditor of a limited liability partnership, authorizes any person to act as its representative at the meeting of the partners or creditors of the limited liability partnership, as the case may be, a copy of the authorization of such person to act as its representative at the meeting, and certified to be a true copy by a designated partner or other authorised officer of such body corporate, shall be lodged with the limited liability partnership at its registered office not later than 48 hours before the meeting.

(5) The notice of the meeting to be given to the creditors and/or partners, shall be in accordance with the rule laid down in this behalf, and shall be sent to them individually by the chairman appointed for the meeting, or, if the Tribunal so directs, by the limited liability partnership (or its Liquidator), or any other person as the Tribunal may direct, by post under certificate of posting to their last known address not less than 21 clear days before the date fixed for the meeting. It shall be accompanied by a copy of the proposed compromise or arrangement alongwith statement showing material interest of the designated partners, if any, and a form of proxy.

(6) The notice of the meeting shall be advertised, if so decided by the Tribunal, in such newspapers and in such manner as the Tribunal may direct.

(7) Every creditor or partner entitled to attend the meeting shall be furnished by the limited liability partnership, free of charge and within 48 hours of a requisition made for the same, with a copy of the proposed compromise or arrangement.

(8) The chairman appointed for the meeting or the limited liability partnership or other person directed to issue the advertisement and the notices of the meeting

shall file an affidavit not less than 7 days before the date fixed for the holding of the meeting or the holding of the first of the meetings, as the case may be, showing that the directions regarding the issue of notices and the advertisement have been duly complied with. In default thereof, the summons shall be posted before the Tribunal for such orders as it may think fit to make.

(9) The chairman of the meeting, or where there are separate meetings, the chairman of each meeting shall, within the time fixed by the Tribunal, or where no time has been fixed, within seven days after the conclusion of the meeting, report the result thereof to the Tribunal. The report shall state accurately the number of creditors or the partners, as the case may be, who were present and who voted at the meeting either in person or by proxy, their individual values and the way they voted.

(10)(i) Where the proposed compromise or arrangement is agreed to, with or without modification, as provided in sub-section (2) of Section 60, the limited liability partnership, or its Liquidator, as the case may be, shall, within seven days of the filing of the report by the chairman, present a petition to the Tribunal for confirmation of the compromise or arrangement:

PROVIDED that where a compromise or arrangement is proposed for the purposes of, or in connection with, a scheme for the reconstruction of any limited liability partnership or the amalgamation of any two or more limited liability partnerships, the petitioner shall pray for appropriate orders and directions under Section 62.

(ii) Where the limited liability partnership fails to present the petition under clause (i) for confirmation of the compromise or arrangement as aforesaid, it shall be open to any creditor or partner as the case may be, with the leave of the Tribunal, to present the petition for confirmation and the limited liability partnership shall be liable for the costs thereof.

(iii) Where no petition for confirmation of the compromise or arrangement is presented to, or where the compromise or arrangement has not been approved by the requisite majority under sub-section (2) of Section 60 and consequently no petition for confirmation could be presented, the report of the chairman as to the result of the meeting made under sub-rule (9) shall be placed for consideration before the Tribunal for such orders as may be necessary.

(11) An order made by the Tribunal as mentioned in sub-section (3) of Section 60 and sub-section (3) of Section 62 shall be filed with Registrar concerned in Form 22 along with fee as mentioned in Annexure 'A'.

EXPLANATION. In computing the period of 30 days from the date of order, the requisite time for obtaining a certified copy of order shall be excluded.

(12)(i) An arrangement for revival and rehabilitation of any LLP may be proposed -

(a) where on a demand by the creditors of the LLP representing fifty per cent or more of its outstanding amount of debt the LLP has failed to pay the debt, within thirty days of the service of the notice of demand or to secure or compound it to the reasonable satisfaction of the creditors; or

(b) where a petition for winding up of a LLP is pending before the Tribunal, in terms of the directions given by the Tribunal on the winding up petition; or

(c) where the liquidator has filed his report before the Tribunal, in terms of directions given by the Tribunal on the report of the Liquidator.

(ii) Without prejudice to clause (i), the LLP or any creditor or partner of the LLP, or in the case of a LLP which is being wound up, the Liquidator, may make an application for sanction of the arrangement for revival and rehabilitation before the Tribunal.

(13) (i) An application under sub-rule (12) shall be accompanied by-

(a) a statement of account and solvency of LLP for the immediately preceding financial year, in case the application under sub-rule (12) is made by the LLP;

(b) particulars and documents relevant to the scheme including commitments whether financial or otherwise expected from various parties or, proposed restructuring or rescheduling of the debts, or any undertaking or understanding, in case from bank or financial institution through a letter or in any other case through an affidavit of concerned party or parties, or in any other form as may be directed by the Tribunal; and

(c) proposed scheme of revival and rehabilitation of the LLP including proposal for appointment of an LLP Administrator.

(ii) An application under sub-rule (12) shall be made to the Tribunal within 90 days from the date of expiry of demand notice or from the date of the direction of the Tribunal referred to under clause (i) of sub-rule 12.

(14) (a) Within 60 days of receipt of an application under sub-rule (12), the Tribunal may hear all the parties concerned and admit or dismiss the application;

(b) where the Tribunal admits the application, it may make an order to that effect and make provisions in such order, for all or any of the following matters:-

(i) holding of meetings of the creditors for approval of scheme proposed for revival and rehabilitation of LLP;

(ii) procedure to be followed by the LLP Administrator proposed in the scheme in connection with holding of the meeting including the appointment of chairman for such meeting;

(iii) any other direction(s) or order(s) as may be considered necessary.

(c) The LLP Administrator proposed in the scheme shall submit his preliminary report including the decision of the meeting to the Tribunal within 60 days of order made under clause (b) of sub-rule 14.

(15) (i) On consideration of the report of the LLP Administrator under clause (c) of sub-rule (14), and other materials available, if the Tribunal is satisfied that the creditors representing three-fourths in value of the amount outstanding against that LLP have, with or without modification of the scheme, resolved

that it is not possible to revive and rehabilitate the LLP, the Tribunal may, within 60 days of the receipt of such report, order -

(a) that the proceedings for the winding up of the LLP be initiated; or

(b) the LLP be wound up, or the liquidator to continue; or

(c) sanction the arrangement for revival and rehabilitation of LLP as approved by such creditors with such modifications as may be considered necessary by the Tribunal, and make orders for continuation of the LLP Administrator or appointment of a new LLP Administrator:

PROVIDED that Tribunal may consider for its approval, the arrangement for revival and rehabilitation including the proposal for appointment of any other LLP Administrator moved by the LLP in the meeting of the creditors, in place of the arrangement proposed by the creditors or the Liquidator, provided the arrangement is approved by three-fourth majority, in value, of creditors.

PROVIDED FURTHER that where the arrangement of revival and rehabilitation relates to amalgamation of the LLP with any other LLP, no such scheme shall be sanctioned by the Tribunal unless the said scheme is approved with, or without modification by three-fourth majority of respective partners of transferor and transferee LLPs.

(ii) The order of sanction of the arrangement by the Tribunal under clause (i) may make provisions, for all or any of the following matters:-

(a) powers and functions of the LLP Administrator;

(b) the time period within which various actions proposed in the arrangement to be completed;

(c) any such direction to the LLP or its officers or to the creditors, or to the LLP Administrator or to any other person, as may be considered necessary, for the purpose of implementation of the arrangement of revival and rehabilitation; and

(d) any other order or orders as may be considered necessary.

(16) The LLP Administrator shall complete all the actions relating to implementation of the revival and rehabilitation arrangement and submit his final report before the Tribunal within such time directed by the Tribunal but not exceeding 180 days of the order under clause (i) of sub-rule (15);

(17)(i) The LLP administrator shall be appointed from a panel maintained by the Central Government for winding up and dissolution of LLPs.

(ii) The terms and conditions of the appointment including fee of LLP Administrator shall be such as may be ordered by the Tribunal.

(iii) The Tribunal may, on a reasonable cause being shown and for reasons to be recorded in writing, remove the LLP Administrator and may appoint another LLP Administrator.

(iv) In case of removal, death or incapacity of the LLP Administrator, the Tribunal may appoint another LLP Administrator.

(v) The LLP administrator shall, within 30 days of the making of order or orders under sub-rule (15) cause certified copy thereof to be filed with the Registrar concerned in Form 22 along with fee as mentioned in Annexure 'A'.

EXPLANATION. In computing the period of 30 days from the date of order, the requisite time for obtaining a certified copy of order shall be excluded.

CHAPTER -XIII : ELECTRONIC FILING OF DOCUMENTS

36. (1) (i) Every form or application or document or declaration required to be filed or delivered under the Act and rules made thereunder, shall be filed in computer readable electronic form, in portable document format (pdf) to the Registrar through the portal maintained by the Ministry of Corporate Affairs on its web-site www.mca.gov.in or through any other website approved by the Central Government and authenticated by a partner or designated partner of the limited liability partnership for such purpose by the use of a valid digital signature:

PROVIDED that where documents are required to be filed on Non-Judicial Stamp Paper, the LLP shall submit such documents in the physical form, in addition to their submission in electronic form, unless the Central Government, by an order, does not require submission in physical form.

(ii) Every designated partner, partner or person specified in the Act for authentication of e-form, documents or application etc., which are required to be filed or delivered under the Act or rules made thereunder, shall obtain a digital signature certificate from the Certifying Authority for the purpose of such authentication and such certificate shall not be valid unless it is of class II or Class III specification under the Information Technology Act, 2000.

(2) The Central Government shall set up and maintain -

(i) a website or portal to provide access to the electronic registry; and,

(ii) as many Registrar's Front Offices as may be necessary and at such places and for such time as Central Government may determine from time to time for filing of e-Forms, documents and applications, etc., viewing and inspection of documents in the electronic registry.

(3) (i) The Central Government shall set up and maintain a secure electronic registry in which all the documents filed electronically shall be stored. The electronic registry so set up shall enable public access and inspection of such documents as are required to be in the public domain under the Act on payment of the fees as mentioned in Annexure "A".

(ii) Every document or application or certificate or notice etc., required to be signed by the Registrar or an officer of the Central Government under the Act or rules made thereunder, shall be authenticated through a valid digital signature of such person or a system generated digital signature.

(iii) The Registrar or an officer of the Central Government, as the case may be, may send any communication either to the Limited Liability Partnership or its authorized representative, partners or both in the electronic manner for which the LLP shall create and maintain at all times a valid electronic address (e.g. E-mail, user Identification etc.) capable of receiving and acknowledging the receipt of such communication, automated or otherwise.

(4) The Registrar or an officer of the Central Government shall issue certificate, receipt, approval or communicate endorsement or acknowledgement in the electronic manner:

PROVIDED that where the Registrar or an officer of the Central Government, as the case may be, is not able to issue any certificate, receipt, endorsement, acknowledgement or approval in electronic manner for the reasons to be recorded in writing, he may issue such certificate, receipt, or communicate endorsement, acknowledgement or approval in the physical form under manual signature affixing seal of his office.

(5) The Registrar shall examine or cause to be examined every application or e-Form or document required or authorized to be filed by or delivered under the Act and rules made thereunder for approval, registration, taking on record or rectification by the Registrar as the case may be:

PROVIDED that the e-Forms or documents identified as informatory in nature and filed under Straight Through Process (STP) may be examined by the Registrar any time after its filing.

(6) Where the Registrar, on examining any application or e-Form or document referred to in sub-rule (5), finds it necessary to call further information or finds such application or e-Form or document to be defective or incomplete in any respect, he shall give intimation of such information called for or defects or incompleteness noticed electronically, by placing it on the website and also by e-mail on the last intimated e-mail address of the person or the limited liability partnership, which has filed such application or e-Form or document, directing him or it to furnish such information or to rectify such defects or incompleteness or to re-submit such application or e-Form or document within the period allowed under sub-rule (7):

PROVIDED that in case the e-mail address of the person or the Limited Liability Partnership in question is not available, such intimation shall be given by the Registrar by post at the last intimated address given in Form 12, or registered office address of the Limited Liability Partnership or the address of such person, as the case may be. The Registrar shall preserve the facts of such intimation in the electronic record.

(7) The Registrar shall allow such period or periods but not exceeding thirty days in aggregate to such person or LLP which has filed such application or e-Form or document under sub-rule (5) for furnishing further information or for rectification of the defects or incompleteness or for re-submission of such application or e-Form or document.

(8) In case where such further information called for has not been provided or has been furnished partially or has not been provided or defects or incompleteness has not been rectified or has been rectified partially or has not been rectified to the satisfaction of the Registrar within the period allowed under sub-rule (7),

the Registrar shall either reject or treat and label such application or e-Form or document as the case may be as "invalid" in the electronic record, and shall not take on record such invalid application or e-Form or document and shall inform such person or limited liability partnership as the case may be in the manner specified in sub-rule (6).

(9) Where any document has been recorded as invalid by the Registrar, such document may be rectified by the limited liability partnership only through fresh filing with payment of fee and additional fee as applicable, without prejudice to any other liability under the Act.

(10) Save as otherwise provided in the Act, the Registrar shall not keep any document pending for approval and registration or for taking on record or for rejection or otherwise for more than one hundred twenty days, from the date of its filing.

(11) The Registrar in case finds any e-Form or document filed under Straight Through Process (STP), referred to in proviso under sub-rule (5), as defective or incomplete in any respect, at any time, he shall treat and label such e-Form or document as "defective" in the electronic registry and shall also issue a notice pointing out such defects or incompleteness in such e-Form or document at the last intimated e-mail address (if available) of the person or the LLP which has filed the document and also in writing by post at the address of such person or address of such LLP or registered office address of LLP, calling upon such person or LLP to file such e-Form or document afresh with fee and additional fee as applicable, after rectifying such defects or incompleteness within a period of thirty days from the date of such notice.

CHAPTER -XIV : STRIKING OFF NAME OF DEFUNCT LLP

37. (1) Where a limited liability partnership is not carrying on any business or operation -

(a) for a period of two years or more and the Registrar has reasonable cause to believe the same, for the purpose of taking suo motu action for striking off the name of the LLP; or

(b) for a period of one year or more and has made an application in Form 24 to the Registrar, with the consent of all partners of the limited liability partnership for striking off its name from the register, the Registrar shall send a notice to the limited liability partnership and all its partners, of his intention to strike off the name of the limited liability partnership from the register and requesting them to send their representations along with copies of the relevant documents, if any, within a period of one month from the date of the notice:

PROVIDED that no such notice by Registrar shall be required under clause (b):

PROVIDED FURTHER that where the limited liability partnership is regulated under a special law, the application for removal of its name shall be accompanied by approval of the regulatory body constituted or established under that law.

(2) A notice issued under sub-rule (1) or contents of an application made by the LLP shall also be placed on the website of the Ministry of Corporate Affairs for the information of the general public for a period of one month.

(3) At the expiry of the time mentioned in the notice under sub-rule (1), or one month under sub-rule (2) above, the Registrar may, by an order, unless cause to the contrary is shown by the limited liability partnership, or the Registrar is satisfied that the name should not be struck off from the register, strike its name off the register, and shall publish notice thereof in the Official Gazette, and on the publication in the Official Gazette of this notice, the limited liability partnership shall stand dissolved.

(4) The Registrar, before passing an order under sub-rule (3), shall, where he has sufficient cause to believe that the limited liability partnership has any asset or liability, satisfy himself that sufficient provision has been made for the realization of all amount due to the limited liability partnership and for the payment or discharge of its liabilities and obligations by the limited liability partnership within a reasonable time and, if necessary, obtain necessary undertakings from the designated partner or partner or other persons in charge of the management of the limited liability partnership:

PROVIDED that notwithstanding the undertakings referred to in this sub-rule, the assets of the limited liability partnership shall be made available for the payment or discharge of all its liabilities and obligations even after the date of the order removing the name of the limited liability partnership from the register.

(5) The liability, if any, of every designated partner of the limited liability partnership dissolved under sub-rule (3), shall continue and may be enforced as if the limited liability partnership had not been dissolved.

(6) Nothing in this rule shall affect the power of the Tribunal to wind up a limited liability partnership the name of which has been struck off the register.

EXPLANATION. In computing the period of 30 days from the date of order, the requisite time for obtaining a certified copy of order shall be excluded.

CHAPTER -XV : CONVERSION FROM FIRM TO LIMITED LIABILITY PARTNERSHIP

38. (1) For the purposes of the Second Schedule, an application shall be made in the format provided in Part A of Form 17 together with the statement of partners in format provided in Part B of Form 17 alongwith the fee as mentioned in Annexure 'A'.

(2) The Registrar shall, on conversion of the firm into the limited liability partnership shall issue a certificate of registration under his seal in Form 19.

(3) For the purposes of para 5 of the Second Schedule, the limited liability partnership shall inform the concerned Registrar of firms about conversion of firm into limited liability partnership in Form 14.

CHAPTER -XVI : CONVERSION FROM PRIVATE COMPANY TO LIMITED LIABILITY PARTNERSHIP

39. (1) For the purposes of the Third Schedule, an application shall be made in the format provided in Part A of Form 18 together with the statement of shareholders in format provided in Part B of Form 18 alongwith the fee as mentioned in Annexure 'A'.

(2) The Registrar shall, on conversion of any private company into limited liability partnership shall issue a certificate of registration under his seal in Form 19.

(3) For the purposes of para 4 of the Third Schedule, the limited liability partnership shall inform the concerned Registrar of Companies about conversion of private company into limited liability partnership in Form 14.

CHAPTER -XVII : CONVERSION FROM UNLISTED PUBLIC COMPANY TO LIMITED LIABILITY PARTNERSHIP

40. (1) For the purposes of the Fourth Schedule, an application shall be made in the format provided in Part A of Form 18 together with the statement of shareholders in format provided in Part B of Form 18 alongwith the fee as mentioned in Annexure 'A'.

(2) The Registrar shall, on conversion of any unlisted public company into limited liability partnership shall issue a certificate of registration under his seal in Form 19.

(3) For the purposes of para 5 of the Fourth Schedule, the limited liability partnership shall inform the concerned Registrar of Companies about conversion of unlisted public company into limited liability partnership in Form 14.

CHAPTER -XVIII : COMPOUNDING OF OFFENCES

41. (1) Every application for the compounding of an offence shall be made in Form 31 to the Registrar who shall forward the same, together with his comments thereon, to the Central Government.

(2) Where any offence is compounded before the institution of any prosecution, no prosecution shall be instituted in relation to such offence, against the offender in relation to whom the offence is so compounded.

(3) Where the composition of any offence is made after the institution of any prosecution, such composition shall be brought by the Registrar in writing, to the notice of the Court in which the prosecution is pending.

(4) Where any offence is compounded under Section 39, whether before or after the institution of any prosecution, intimation thereof shall be given by the LLP to the Registrar in Form 22 within seven days from the date on which the offence is so compounded.

(5) The Central Government while dealing with an application for the compounding of the offence for a default in compliance with any provision of the Act which

requires a LLP or its partner or partners or designated partner or designated partners to file or register with, or send to, the Registrar any return, statement of account and solvency or other document, may, if it thinks fit to do so, direct, before allowing compounding under this rule, by order, any partner or designated partner of the LLP to file or register with, or on payment of the fee, and the additional fee, required to be paid under Section 69, such return, statement of account and solvency or other document within such time as may be specified in the order.

Form 1
[*See* rule 18(5)]
APPLICATION FOR RESERVATION OR CHANGE OF NAME

Note: All fields marked in *are to be mandatorily filled.

1. *Application for

Incorporating a new limited liability partnership (LLP) ______________ [ ]

Changing the name of an existing limited liability partnership. ______ [ ]

Part A: Reservation of name

2. Details of the applicant

(i) (a)* Whether applicant is an Individual as partner [ ] or nominee of a body corporate as a partner [ ]

(b) *Designated Partner Identification Number (DPIN) or Income-tax permanent account number (PAN) or passport number

(ii) (a) *Name

(b) *Occupation

(c) *Address

Line I

Line II

(d) *City

(e) *State

(f) *Pin code

(g) *ISO Country Code

(h) *Country

(i) *e-mail ID

(j) Phone

(k) Fax

3. Details of two proposed designated partners (one of them should be a resident in India)

(i) *Category (drop down) Individual, LLP, Company, LLP incorporated outside India (LIOI), Company incorporated outside India (CIOI).

(ii) *DPIN/Income-tax PAN/passport number; or LLPIN; or corporate identity number (CIN); or LIOI registration number; or CIOI registration number

(iii) *Name

(iv) *Name of nominee, in case of body corporate

(v) Details (number/date) of resolution authorizing nominee

(i) *Category (drop down) Individual, LLP, Company, LLP incorporated outside India (LIOI), Company incorporated outside India (CIOI).

(ii) *DPIN/Income-tax PAN/passport number; or LLPIN; or corporate identity number (CIN); or LIOI registration number; or CIOI registration number

(iii) *Name

(iv) *Name of nominee, in case of body corporate

(v) Details (number/date) of resolution authorizing nominee

4. *Name of the state in which the proposed LLP is to be registered

5. *Name of the office of Registrar in which the proposed LLP is to be situated

6. Whether the application is for conversion of firm or private company or unlisted public company into LLP

Yes [ ] No [ ]

If yes, enter the following details

____

(I) In case of conversion of firm:

(i) Name of the firm

(ii) Whether the firm is registered Yes [ ] No [ ]

If Yes, enter the following details:

____

(a) Name of the Statute/law under which firm is registered

(b) Name of the state in which firm is registered

(c) Date of registration DD/MM/YYYY

(d) Registration number

(II) In case of conversion of private company or unlisted public company

(a) CIN

(b) Name

7. *Proposed business of the Limited Liability Partnership (if the business includes banking and stock exchange, a copy of the in-principle approval of the appropriate authority should be attached)

8. * Proposed monetary value of contribution (in Rs) in figure ____________________ in words ______________________________________.

Part B: In case of change of name

9. *LLPIN of limited liability partnership______________________________

10.

(a) *Name of the limited liability partnership

(b) *Address of registered office of the limited liability partnership

*Line 1 ______________________________

*Line 2 ______________________________

*City ______________________ District ____________________

*State ______________________ *PIN Code ____________________

ISO Country Code ______________ *Country ____________________

*e-mail ID ______________________

Phone ______________________

Fax ______________________

11. *Reasons for change of name

____

____

12. * Existing monetary value of contribution (in Rs) in figure ______________ in words ______________________________.

Part C: Details regarding reservation of name or change of existing name of LLP

13. Proposed name of the LLP (please give six names in order of preference)

(a)* ______________________

(b) ______________________

(c) ______________________

(d) ______________________

(e) ______________________

(f) ______________________

14. State the significance of the key or coined word(s), if any; in the proposed name(s) (in brief)

(a) ______________________

(b) ______________________

(c) ______________________

(d) ______________________

(e) ______________________

(f) ______________________

(In case proposed name includes an activity, such activity should be reflective of the proposed business of the LLP)

15.(a) * Whether the proposed name(s) is/are based on a registered trade mark or is the subject matter of an application pending for registration under the Trade Marks Act.

(Please Tick) Yes [ ] No [ ]

(b) If yes, furnish particulars of trade mark or application

Attachments

1. In case of change of name of an existing limited liability partnership, a copy of the decision **Attach**

2. Copy of Trade Mark Registration/ acknowledgement of application for Trade Mark Registration/authorization to use Trade Mark **Attach**

3. If change is due to a direction received from the Central Government, then a copy of such direction **Attach**

4. Optional Attachment **Attach**

List of attachments

Remove attachment

VERIFICATION

To the best of my knowledge and belief, the information given in this Form and its attachments is correct and complete, and the proposed name is not undesirable, identical or too nearly resembles to that of any other partnership firm or limited liability partnership or body corporate or a registered trade mark or a trade mark which is subject of an application for registration of any other person under the Trade Marks Act, 1999.

I have gone through the provisions of the Limited Liability Partnership Act, 2008, and the rules framed thereunder and

I am authorised by the proposed partners to sign and submit this application.

OR

I have been authorized by ______________________ (firm/ private company/ unlisted public company) to sign and submit this application.

I have been authorised by the Limited Liability Partnership to sign and submit this application.

To be digitally signed by applicant.

Date:

Place:

Modify   Check form   Pre-scrutiny   Submit

For office use only

Digital signature of the authorizing officer ______________________

This e-form is hereby approved

This e-form is hereby rejected

Form 2
[*See* Rule 11]
INCORPORATION DOCUMENT AND STATEMENT

Note: All fields marked in *are to be mandatorily filled.

PART A : Incorporation Document

1.*Service Request Number (SRN) of Form 1

2.* Name of the limited liability partnership :

3.* State in which the registered office of the limited liability partnership is to be situated:

4.* Address of registered office of the limited liability partnership

*Line 1 ______________________________

*Line 2 ______________________________

*City ______________ District ______________

*State ______________ *PIN Code ______________

ISO Country Code ______________ *Country ______________

*e-mail ID ______________

Phone ______________

Fax ______________

5.*Business to be carried on by the limited liability partnership:

6. *Summary of Partners/designated partners

S. N.	Category	Number of Partners	Number of Designated partners	Number of designated partners resident in India
(i)	Individuals			
(ii)	LLPs			
(iii)	Companies			
(iv)	LLPs incorporated outside India			
(v)	Companies incorporated outside India			
	Total			

7. *Number of individual(s) as partner [ ] (Dynamic)

Note: In case individual(s) are more than five, attach details in respect of remaining partners in a separate sheet as an attachment.

Details in respect of individual(s). (First, enter details in respect of designated partners)

*Whether Designated partner Yes [ ] No [ ]

If yes, DPIN

*Whether resident in India Yes [ ] No [ ]

*Name :
*Father's / Husband's Name :
*Nationality :
*Date of birth :
*Occupation :
*Income-tax permanent account number (PAN):
Passport Number:
*Permanent residential address
*Address

*Line 1 ______________________________
*Line 2 ______________________________
*City ______________ *State ______________
*PIN Code ______________ *ISO Country Code* __________
*e-mail ID ______________
Phone ______________
Fax ______________

*Whether present residential address is same as the permanent residential address:
(Please Tick) Yes [ ] No [ ]
If no, present residential address
Address

*Line 1 ______________________________
*Line 2 ______________________________
*City ______________ *State ______________
*PIN Code ______________ *ISO Country Code* __________
*e-mail ID ______________
Phone ______________
Fax ______________

*Form of contribution

*Monetary value of contribution (in Rs.) (in figure) ______________ (in words) ______________________________.

If already a partner of limited liability partnership (LLP) or director of a company, specify the following. (In case partner or director in more than five LLP(s) and companies each, attach separate sheet as an attachment).

*No. of limited liability partnership(s) in which he is a partner
LLPIN ______________________________
Name ______________________________
No. of Company(s) in which he is a director ______________
CIN ______________________________
Name of the company ______________________________

8. Number of bodies corporate as partners [ ] (Dynamic)

Note: In case bodies corporate are more than five, attach details in respect of remaining bodies corporates in a separate sheet as an attachment.

*Details in respect of bodies corporate and their nominees. (First, enter details in respect of designated partners)

*Category (drop down) LLP, Company, LLP incorporated outside India (LIOI), Company incorporated outside India (CIOI)

*LLPIN or Corporate Identity Number (CIN), LIOI registration number or CIOI registration number

*Name of the body corporate ____________________

*Country where registered ____________________

*Full address of registered office ____________________

*Line 1 ____________________

*Line 2 ____________________

*City ____________ *State ____________

*PIN Code ____________ *ISO Country Code* ____________

*e-mail ID ____________

Phone ____________

Fax ____________

*Form of contribution

*Monetary value of contribution (in Rs.) (in figure) ____________ (in words) ____________.

*Name and particulars of the person signing on behalf of the body corporate as nominee

*Designation & authority

*Father's / Husband's Name

*Nationality :

*Date of birth :

*Occupation :

*Income-tax permanent account number (PAN)

Passport Number :

*Whether designated partner Yes [ ] No [ ]

If yes, DPIN

*Whether resident in India (Please Tick) Yes [ ] No [ ]

*Permanent residential address

*Address

*Line 1 ____________________

*Line 2 ____________________

*City ____________ *State ____________

*PIN Code ____________ *ISO Country Code* ____________

*e-mail ID ____________________

Phone ____________________

Fax ____________________

*Whether present residential address is same as the permanent residential address:

(Please Tick) Yes [ ] No [ ]

If no, present residential address

Address

*Line 1 ____________________

*Line 2 ____________________

*City ____________________ *State ____________________

*PIN Code ____________________ *ISO Country Code* ____________

*e-mail ID ____________________

Phone ____________________

Fax ____________________

9.*Total monetary value of contribution by partners in the LLP (in Rs.) ____________ (in figures) ____________________ (in words)

10.* We, the several partners whose names are subscribed below, are desirous of being formed into a limited liability partnership for carrying on a lawful business with a view to profit and have entered or agreed to enter into a limited liability partnership agreement in writing. We respectively agree to contribute money or other property or other benefit or to perform services for the limited liability partnership in accordance with the limited liability partnership agreement, the particulars of which are stated at serial number 7 or 8 against our respective names.

Name of each partner	Signature of Partner	Name, address and profession (alongwith professional membership number) of witness	Signature of witness
1	2	3	4

(Attach details in respect of names of partners/witnesses and their signatures in the above format as an attachment)

Attachments:.

1. Copy of authorization where the partner is a limited liability partnership, or company, or a limited liability partnership incorporated outside India or a company incorporated outside India.
2. Proof of address of registered office of limited liability partnership.
3. Details in respect of names of partners/witnesses and their signatures.
4. Attachments in respect of details of individuals/bodies corporate where the number exceeds five.
5. Optional attachment.

Part B : Statement

*Statement by a person who subscribed his name to the incorporation document :

I ________________ son/daughter/wife of ____________________________

do state as under:

(i) that I am a person named in the incorporation document as a designated partner/ partner of the limited liability partnership;

(ii) that the designated partners have given their prior consent to act as designated partners;

(iii) that all the requirements of the Limited Liability Partnership Act, 2008 and the rules made thereunder have been complied with, in respect of incorporation and matters precedent and incidental thereto;

(iv) that I make this statement conscientiously believing the same to be true.

To be digitally signed by
A designated partner
DPIN
Date: Place:

*Statement by an Advocate/Company Secretary/Chartered Accountant/Cost Accountant in practice:

I ________________ son/daughter/wife of ____________________________

do state as under:

(i) that I am

- an Advocate
- a Company Secretary
- a Chartered Accountant
- a Cost Accountant

engaged in the formation of the limited liability partnership and my membership number with ____________ (name of regulatory body) is ________________ (Membership Number);

(ii) that all the requirements of the Limited Liability Partnership Act, 2008 and the rules made thereunder have been complied with, in respect of incorporation and matters precedent and incidental thereto;

(iii) that I make this statement conscientiously believing the same to be true.

To be digitally signed by
Advocate / Company Secretary / Chartered Accountant / Cost Accountant in practice.
Date: Place:

Modify Check form Pre-scrutiny Submit

....

For office use only

This e-form is hereby registered

Digital signature of the authorizing officer ______________________________

Form 3

[*See* Rule 21]

INFORMATION WITH REGARD TO LIMITED LIABILITY PARTNERSHIP AGREEMENT AND CHANGES, IF ANY, MADE THEREIN

Note: All fields marked in *are to be mandatorily filled.

This Form is for : Filing information with regard to LLP Agreement For information with regard to changes in LLP Agreement

Part A -For filing information with regard to LLP Agreement

1.*LLPIN

2.*Name of Limited Liability Partnership

3.*Place at which the Limited Liability Partnership Agreement is made

4.(i) *Date of the Agreement

(ii) Date of ratification

5.*Address of Registered Office

*Line 1 ______________________________

*Line 2 ______________________________

*City ______________________ District ______________________

*State ______________________ *PIN Code ______________________

ISO Country Code ____________ *Country ______________________

*e-mail ID ______________________

6.*Business to be carried on by the Limited Liability Partnership

7. * Designated Partners

(i) Whether each of the partners from time to time is to be designated partner.

Yes [ ] No [ ]

(i) Names of persons who shall be designated partners on _______ incorporation.

Name DPIN

(ii) *Acts, matters or things required to be done by a designated partner in respect of the compliance of the provisions of the Act.

1.

2.

3.

(iii) *Powers in relation to acts, matters, or things which the designated partner can exercise only with the consent of all the partners/requisite number or percentage of partners.

1.

2.

3.

8. *Obligation to contribute

(i) Obligation of each partner to contribute money or property or other benefit or to perform services.

Sl. No.	Name of Partner	Nature and specification of obligation to contribute

(ii) Total Monetary value of contribution by partners in the LLP (in Rs.) ____________ (in figure) ______________________________ (in words)

9. *Partners' powers and duties

(i) Powers, duties and authority of each partner.

(a) Powers of the partners

(b) Duties of the partners

(c) Authority of the partners

(ii) Mutual rights and duties of partners

(iii) Mutual rights and duties of limited liability partnership and partners

10. *Restrictions, if any, on the partners' authority.

11. *Management and Administration of Limited Liability Partnership

(i) Acts, matters or things, if any, which can be done only with the consent of all the partners.

(ii) Acts, matters or things, if any, which can be done with the consent of majority of the partners.

(iii) Acts, matters or things, if any, which can be done only with the consent of requisite number or percentage of the partners.

(iv) Manner, if any, in which the consent of the partners is to be obtained.

(v) Procedure for calling, holding and conducting meetings, (where the decisions are to be made at meetings of partners)

12. *Whether the LLP has a common seal Yes [ ] No [ ]

If yes, authority to affix the seal

13. *Details of indemnity clause, if any -

14.*Clauses of the Agreement relating to -

(a) admission of a new partner

(b) retirement of a partner

(c) cessation of a partner

(d) expulsion of a partner

(e) resignation of a partner

15.*Details of obligations, rights, entitlements of a partner on admission, retirement, cessation, expulsion or resignation.

16.*Clauses relating to resolution of disputes

(a) Between the partners; or

(b) Between the partner and the LLP.

17.*Duration of Limited Liability Partnership, if any.

18.*Clauses, if any, relating to voluntary winding up

19. Information of clauses in the agreement:

(a) relating to rule 16 (2)

(b) relating to rule 17(1)

(c) relating to rule 20(1)

(d) relating to rule 24(18)(a)

20. Any other information or clause relating to the Limited Liability Partnership Agreement not covered above (optional).

B.For Filing information with regard to changes (addition, omission or alteration) in the Limited Liability Partnership Agreement

21.*LLPIN

22.*Name of the Limited Liability Partnership

23. *Address of the registered office of the Limited Liability Partnership

*Line 1 ______________________________

*Line 2 ______________________________

*City ______________ *State ______________

*PIN Code ______________ *ISO Country Code* ______________

*e-mail ID ______________

Phone ______________ Fax ______________

24. *Date of the modification of the agreement

25. *Please indicate the changes in the LLP agreement pertaining to any of the items 3 to 20 above:

26. Indicate any other change or changes in LLP agreement not covered under 25 above.

27.*Monetary value of contribution (in Rs) __________ (in figures) -

(i) Existing

(ii) Addition

(iii) Total

*Statement

I ______________________ (son/daughter/wife) of ________________ state as under :

(i) I am a person named in the Incorporation Document as a designated Partner/ I am a designated Partner of the limited liability partnership;

(ii) that the particulars given above are in accordance with the limited liability partnership agreement/ agreement relating to change in the limited liability partnership agreement;

(iii) the original Limited Liability Partnership Agreement will be produced whenever called for;

(iv) in case of change in contribution, the fees payable to Registrar has been/being paid;

(v) that I make this statement conscientiously believing the same to be true.

Attachment Optional.

To be digitally signed by designated partner

DPIN

Date: Place:

Certificate

It is hereby certified that I have verified the above particulars from the books and records of ______________________________ (name of the LLP) and found them to be true and correct.

Company Secretary in practice [ ]

Chartered Accountant in practice [ ]

Cost Accountant in practice [ ]

Whether associate or fellow: Associate [ ] Fellow [ ]

Membership Number or Certificate of Practice Number

To be digitally signed by

Company Secretary in practice/ Chartered Accountant in practice/ Cost Accountant in practice

Date: __/__/_____ (DDMMYYYY) Place:

Modify Check form Pre-scrutiny Submit

....

For office use only

This e-form is hereby registered

Digital signature of the authorizing officer

Form 4

[*See* Rule 8, 10(8), 22(2) and 22(3)]

NOTICE OF APPOINTMENT OF PARTNERS/ DESIGNATED PARTNER AND CHANGES AMONG THEM, INTIMATION OF DPIN BY THE LLP TO REGISTRAR AND CONSENT OF PARTNER TO BECOME A PARTNER /DESIGNATED PARTNER

Note: All fields marked in * are to be mandatorily filled.

PART A: Notice of appointment of partner/designated partner and changes among them and intimation of DPIN

1. * This form is for

New Limited Liability Partnership [ ]

Existing Limited Liability Partnership [ ]

2. * Service Request number (SRN) of Form 1 or LLPIN

3. * Name of the limited liability partnership

* Address of the registered office of the limited liability partnership

*Line 1 ______________________________

*Line 2 ______________________________

*City ________________ *State ________________

*PIN Code ________________ *ISO Country Code* ____________

*e-mail ID ________________

Phone ________________

Fax ________________

4.* Summary of partners and designated partners:

S. No.	Category	Number of Partners	Number of Designated partners	Number of designated partners resident in India
(i)	Individuals			
(ii)	LLPs			
(iii)	Companies			
(iv)	LLPs incorporated outside India			
(v)	Companies incorporated outside India			
	Total			

5. *Number of individual(s) as partner(s) [ ] (Dynamic)

Note: In case individual(s) are more than five, attach details in respect of remaining partners in a separate sheet as an attachment.

Details in respect of individual(s). (First, enter details in respect of designated partners)

*Whether designated partner Yes [ ] No [ ]

If yes, DPIN

*Whether resident in India Yes [ ] No [ ]

*Name

*Father's / Husband's Name

*Nationality

Appointment

Cessation [ ]

Change in name of partner [ ]

Change in name of designated partner [ ]

Change in designation [ ]

Change in address [ ]

Date of appointment

Date of Cessation

Changed name

Date of change in designation

New designation

(Please give address and other details of the partner in addendum to this Form)

6. * Number of bodies corporate as partners [ ] (Dynamic)

Note: In case bodies corporate are more than five, attach details in respect of remaining bodies corporates in a separate sheet as an attachment.

Details in respect of bodies corporate and their nominees. (First, enter details in respect of designated partners)

Category (drop down) LLP, Company, LLP incorporated outside India (LIOI), Company incorporated outside India (CIOI)

LLPIN or Corporate Identity Number (CIN), LIOI registration number or CIOI registration number

*Name

Country where registered

*Name and particulars of the person signing on behalf of the body corporate as nominee

*Designation

*Father's / Husband's Name :

*Nationality :

*Whether Designated partner Yes [ ] No [ ]

If yes, DPIN

*Whether resident in India Yes [ ] No [ ]

Appointment

Cessation [ ]

Change in name of partner [ ]

Change in name of designated partner [ ]

Change in designation [ ]

Change in address [ ]

Date of appointment

Date of Cessation

Changed name

Date of change in designation

New designation

(Please give address and other details of the partner and nominee in addendum to this Form)

Part B: Consent of partners/designated partners

Please attach the consent to become a partner/designated partner (separate consent for each partner/ designated partner) in the following format as an attachment:

"I, __________________ hereby give my consent to become a partner _____________ designated partner of the (name of the LLP) pursuant to Section 25(3)(c) / 7(4) of the Limited Liability Partnership Act, 2008.

I having consented to become a partner/designated partner of limited liability partnership also hereby undertake to contribute money or other property or other benefit or to perform services for limited liability partnership as per my obligations described in the limited liability partnership agreement."

Signed Designation

Attachment:

1. Consent to act as partner/designated partner
2. Evidence of cessation.
3. Affidavit or any other proof of change of name
4. Where the appointed partner is a body corporate, a copy of resolution of such body corporate and of the authority in favour of the nominee signing on behalf of body corporate.
5. Attachments in respect of details of individuals/bodies corporate where the number exceeds five.
6. Optional Attachment

Statement

To the best of my knowledge and belief, the information given in this form and its attachments is correct and complete.

I ______________________ a designated partner of the LLP, am authorized to sign and submit this form.

To be digitally signed by designated partner

DPIN

(The person signing the form should be different from the person in whose respect the form is being filed)

Date: Place:

Certificate

It is hereby certified that I have verified the above particulars from the books and records of _______________ (name of LLP) and found them to be true and correct.

Company Secretary in practice [ ]
Chartered Accountant in practice [ ]
Cost Accountant in practice [ ]

Whether associate or fellow Associate [ ] Fellow [ ]
Membership Number or Certificate of Practice Number

Date:

Place:

....

For office use only

This e-Form is hereby registered
Digital Signature of the authorizing officer
Submit to BO

Addendum to Form 4
Particulars of addresses and other details of partners/designated partners and changes therein

1. Number of individuals as partners

Note: In case individual(s) are more than five, attach details in respect of remaining partners in a separate sheet as an attachment.

Appointment

Cessation [ ]
Change in name of partner [ ]
Change in name of designated partner [ ]
Change in designation [ ]
Change in address [ ]

Details in respect of individual(s) (First, enter details in respect of designated partners)

(The details in this addendum should be in the order of names of partners given in Form 4)

*Whether Designated partner Yes [ ] No [ ]

If yes, DPIN

*Whether resident in India Yes [ ] No [ ]

*Name :

*Father's / Husband's Name :

*Nationality :

*Date of birth :

*Occupation :

*Income-tax permanent account number (PAN):

*Passport Number:

*Permanent residential address

Address

*Line 1 ______________________________

*Line 2 ______________________________

*City ______________ *State ______________

*PIN Code ______________ *ISO Country Code* __________

*e-mail ID ______________

Phone ______________

Fax ______________

*Whether present residential address is same as the permanent residential address:

(Please Tick) Yes [ ] No [ ]

If no, present residential address

Address

*Line 1 ______________________________

*Line 2 ______________________________

*City ______________ *State ______________

*PIN Code ______________ *ISO Country Code* __________

*e-mail ID ______________

Phone ______________

Fax ______________

2. Number of bodies corporate as partners

Note: In case bodies corporate are more than five, attach details in respect of remaining bodies corporate in a separate sheet as an attachment.

Appointment

Cessation [ ]

Change in name of partner [ ]

Change in name of designated partner [ ]

Change in designation [ ]
Change in address [ ]

Details in respect of bodies corporate and their nominees. (First, enter details in respect of designated partners)

(The details in this addendum should be in the order of names of partners given in Form 4)

Category (drop down) LLP, Company, LLP incorporated outside India (LIOI), Company incorporated outside India (CIOI).

LLPIN or Corporate Identity Number (CIN), LIOI registration number or CIOI registration number.

*Name of the body corporate

Country where registered

*Full address of registered office

*Line 1 ______________________

*Line 2 ______________________

*City ______________ *State ______________

*PIN Code ______________ *ISO Country Code* ______________

*e-mail ID ______________

Phone ______________

Fax ______________

*Name and particulars of the person signing on behalf of the body corporate as nominee

*Designation

*Father's/Husband's Name :

*Nationality :

*Date of birth :

*Occupation

*Income-tax permanent account number (PAN)

Passport Number

*Whether designated partner Yes [ ] No [ ]

If yes, DPIN

*Whether resident in India (Please Tick) Yes [ ] No [ ]

*Permanent residential address

Address

*Line 1 ______________________

*Line 2 ______________________

*City ______________ *State ______________

*PIN Code ______________ *ISO Country Code* ______________

*e-mail ID ______________

Phone ______________

Fax ______________

*Whether present residential address is same as the permanent residential address:
(Please Tick) Yes [ ] No [ ]

If no, present residential address

Address

*Line 1 ______________________________

*Line 2 ______________________________

*City ________________ *State ________________

*PIN Code ________________ *ISO Country Code* ____________

*e-mail ID ________________

Phone ________________

Fax ________________

Attachments:

1. Attachments in respect of details of addresses and other details of individuals/ bodies corporate where the number exceeds five.
2. Proof of address
3. Optional Attachment

Statement

To the best of my knowledge and belief, the information given in this form and its attachments is correct and complete.

I ________________ a designated partner of the ________________ (name of the LLP), am authorized to sign and submit this form.

To be digitally signed by designated partner

DPIN

(The person signing the form should be different from the person in whose respect the form is being filed)

Date:

Place:

Certificate

It is hereby certified that I have verified the above particulars from the books and records of ____________________ (name of the LLP) and found them to be true & correct.

Company Secretary in practice [ ]

Chartered Accountant in practice [ ]

Cost Accountant in practice [ ]

Whether associate or fellow Associate [ ] Fellow [ ]
Membership Number or Certificate of Practice Number

Date:

Place:

....

For office use only

This e-Form is hereby registered
Digital Signature of the authorizing officer
Submit to BO

Form 5
[*See* Rule 20(2)]
NOTICE OF CHANGE OF NAME

Note: All fields marked in * are to be mandatorily filled.

1. *LLPIN

2.

(a) *Name of the limited liability partnership

(b) Address of the registered office of the limited liability partnership

*Line 1 ____

*Line 2 ____

*City ____________________ *State ____________________

*PIN Code ________________ *ISO Country Code* __________

*e-mail ID ____________________

Phone ____________________

Fax ____________________

3. *Reasons/purpose for change of name

4. *Service Request Number (SRN) of Form 1

5. *Proposed name

6. *Date of compliance of sub-rule (1) of rule 20 (DD/MM/YYYY) __/__/____

Attachments

(i) Copy of the minutes of decision/resolution/consent of partners,

(ii) The extracts of the relevant provision of the Limited Liability Partnership Agreement, if any,

(iii) If change is due to a direction received from the Central Government/ Registrar, then a copy of such direction,

(iv) Optional attachment.

Statement

To the best of my knowledge and belief, the information given in this Form and its attachments is correct and complete.

I ____________________ a designated partner of the LLP, am authorized to sign and submit this form.

To be digitally signed by designated partner

DPIN

Date:

Place:

Certificate

It is hereby certified that I have verified the above particulars from the books and records of ______________________________ (name of the LLP) and found them to be true and correct.

Company Secretary in practice [ ]
Chartered Accountant in practice [ ]
Cost Accountant in practice [ ]

Digitally Signed

Certificate of Practice Number

Date:

Place:

Modify Check form Pre-scrutiny Submit

....

For office use only

This e-Form is hereby registered
Digital Signature of the authorizing officer
Submit to BO

Form 6

(*See* Rule 22(1)

INTIMATION OF PARTICULARS OF NAME OR ADDRESS OF A PARTNER/CHANGE IN SUCH PARTICULARS BY A PARTNER TO THE LIMITED LIABILITY PARTNERSHIP

Note: All fields marked in * are to be mandatorily filled.

1.*This form is for intimating to the Limited Liability Partnership

[ ] particulars

[ ] change in particulars by the partner.

Type of partner:

I. Individual

II. Limited liability partnership

III. Company

IV. Limited liability partnership incorporated outside India

V. Company incorporated outside India

Part A

I. Intimation of particulars -Individual

2. Name

(a) *First Name:

(b) *Last Name:

(c) *Middle Name:

(d) *Name as written:

3. *Father's Name/Husband's Name

4. *Whether citizen of India Yes [ ] No [ ]

5. *Nationality:

6. *Whether Resident in India: Yes [ ] No [ ]

7. *Date of Birth:

8. *Gender: M [ ] F [ ]

9. *Income-tax permanent account number

10. Voter's identity card

11. Passport number

12. Others (specify)

13. *Permanent Residential Address

*Line 1 ______________________________

*Line 2 ______________________________

*City ______________ District ______________

*State ______________ *PIN Code ______________

ISO Country Code __________ *Country ______________

*e-mail ID ______________

14. *Whether present residential address is the same as permanent residential address Yes [ ] No [ ]

15. Present residential address

*Line 1 ______________________________

*Line 2 ______________________________

*City ____________________ District ____________________

*State ____________________ *PIN Code ____________________

ISO Country Code ____________*Country ____________________

*e-mail ID ____________________

16.*Whether a partner of partnership firm or limited liability partnership or director of a company

Yes [ ] No [ ]

If Yes

(a) Names and addresses of the partnership firm(s)

Name Address of principal office

(b) LLPIN and name of the limited liability partnership(s)

LLPIN Name of limited liability partnership

(c) CIN and names of the companies in which he is a director

CIN DIN Name

II. Intimation of particulars -Limited liability partnership

LLPIN:

Name :

PAN number of the limited liability partnership

Full address of registered office

Name of the person who will be signing on behalf of the limited liability partnership

Designation and authority of the person signing on behalf of limited liability partnership

Please give particulars of the person authorized in the format as given in sub-part I of Part A from serial number 2 to 16.

III. Intimation of particulars -Company

CIN

Name

PAN number of the company

Full address of registered office

Name of the person who will be signing on behalf of the company

Designation and authority of the person signing on behalf of the company

Please give particulars of the person authorized in the format as given in sub-part I of Part A from serial number 2 to 16.

IV. Intimation of particulars -Limited liability partnership incorporated outside India

Name :

Country where the limited liability partnership is registered/incorporated

Registration/Incorporation Number

Full address of the registered office

The statute under which the limited liability partnership is registered

Name of the person who will be signing on behalf of the limited liability partnership incorporated outside India

Designation and authority of the person signing on behalf of limited liability partnership incorporated outside India

Please give particulars of the person authorized in the format as given in sub-part I of Part A from serial number 2 to 16.

V. Intimation of particulars -Company incorporated outside India

Name :

Country where the company is registered/incorporated

Registration/Incorporation Number

Full address of the registered office

The statute under which the company is registered

Name of the person who will be signing on behalf of the company incorporated outside India

Designation and authority of the person signing on behalf of company incorporated outside India

Please give particulars of the person authorized in the format as given in sub-part I of Part A from serial number 2 to 16.

PART B -Intimation of change in particulars relating to name or address of the partner

Please give below the particulars sought to be changed

____

____

The following documents in support of the above are attached

(a) ____________________

(b) ____________________

I ___________son/daughter of ______________________ declare and verify that the information given in the form and the documents enclosed is correct and complete.

Signature

Date

Place

Form 7

[*See* Rule 10)

APPLICATION FOR ALLOTMENT OF DESIGNATED PARTNER IDENTIFICATION NUMBER

Affix a latest passport size photograph and get it attested/ certified for submission of physical copy of the form with Central Government.

Note: All fields marked in * are to be mandatorily filled.

Provisional Designated Partner Identification Number (DPIN) (not to be filled by the applicant as it is generated by the system)

Applicant's name (enter full name and do not use abbreviations)

1. DIN (if allotted)

2. Name

(a) *First name :

(b) *Last name :

(c) *Middle name :

(d) *whether nominee of a body corporate Yes [ ] No [ ]

If Yes, the details of the body corporate:

Name of the body corporate

Registration Number

Address of the registered office of the body corporate

*Line 1 ______________________________

*Line 2 ______________________________

*City ______________ *State ______________

*PIN Code ______________ *ISO Country Code* ______________

*e-mail ID ______________

Phone ______________

Fax ______________

3. Father's /Husband's name

(a) *First name :

(b) *Last name :

(c) *Middle name :

4. *Whether a citizen of India : Yes [ ] No [ ]

5. *Nationality:

6.*Date of Birth (DD/MM/YYYY)

7. *Gender :

8. Place of birth

9. Income-tax permanent account number

10. Voter's identity card number :

11. Passport number :

12. Driving license number:

13. Other (please specify):

14. *Permanent Residential Address

*Line 1 ______________________________

*Line 2 ______________________________

*City ______________ *State ______________

*PIN Code ______________ *ISO Country Code* ______________

*e-mail ID ______________

Phone ______________

Fax ______________

15. *Whether present residential address is same as permanent residential address

Yes [ ] No [ ]

16. Present Residential Address

*Line 1 ______________________________

*Line 2 ______________________________

*City ______________ *State ______________

*PIN Code ______________ *ISO Country Code* ______________

*e-mail ID ______________

Phone ______________

Fax ______________

17. *Whether resident of India

Yes [ ] No [ ]

Specimen signature of the applicant
(within the box)

Instruction Kit Submit

Following documents are being enclosed :

Proof of Identity (Tick against the document being enclosed)

1. Passport [ ]
2. Election (voter identity) card [ ]
3. Driving license [ ]
4. Income-tax PAN card [ ]
5. Others-Please Specify [ ]

Proof of residence (Tick against the document being enclosed)

1. Passport [ ]
2. Election (voter identity) card [ ]
3. Ration card [ ]
4. Driving license [ ]

5. Electricity bill [ ]
6. Telephone bill [ ]
7. Bank account statement [ ]
8. Others-Please Specify [ ]

I ______________________ son/daughter of ______________________ resident of ______________________ hereby declare and verify that the information given in this application and the documents enclosed is correct and complete. I confirm that I do not possess and have not been allotted another Designated Partner Identification Number by the Central Government. I also confirm that no other application (including physical documents) submitted by me is pending for allotment of Designated Partner Identification Number.

Signature of the applicant
(to be signed for submission of physical copy of the form with Central Government)

Dated (DD/MM/YYYY) ____________

Place

General Guidelines for DPIN Application

1. Obtain Provisional DPIN -The applicant should first fill in the application on-line, generate a provisional DPIN and then take a print out for dispatch to the DPIN Processing Cell. All application without a provisional DPIN cannot be accepted for further process and would merit straight rejection.
2. Attestation/certification of photograph, proof identity and proof of residence - A Public Notary or a Gazetted Officer of a Government or a practising professional (Chartered Accountant/ Company Secretary/Cost Accountant) or a Company Secretary in full time employment of the company.
3. Particulars of the attesting/certifying authority -The attesting authority must indicate the following while attesting the documents : (i) Signatures; (ii) Name in full in Capitals; (iii) Registration No; and (iv) Seal/ Stamp.
4. Language of proofs for identity and residence -In case the proof of identity and proof of residence is in a language other than Hindi or English, a certified copy of translation of the same in Hindi or English should be enclosed and the translation be also certified by the professional who has otherwise certified the said proofs.
5. Date of Birth -The proof of identify enclosed with DPIN Form should also contain the Date of Birth of the applicant and the same should match the Date of Birth filled in the application form. In case the proof of identify does not indicate the

Date of Birth then additional proof of Date of Birth, duly certified/attested, should be attached.

6. **Father's Name** - The proof of identify enclosed with DPIN Form should also contain the Father's Name of the applicant and the same should match the Father's Name filled in the application form. In case the proof of identify does not indicate the Father's Name then additional proof of Father's Name, duly certified /attested, should be attached.
7. Process for applications who are (i) Indian citizens residing abroad; (ii) foreign nationals residing in India; and (iii) foreign nationals residing outside India - While general conditions as mentioned at Sr.No.1,3,4 and 5 would be applicable in these categories also, the certification of attached documents and the photograph may be done by a notary in the home country of the applicant or the designated partner of the LLP. Further, in the case of a Foreign National, certified copy of the valid passport should be enclosed.

....

For office use only

Signature of the Authorizing Officer

Dated

Place

Form 8
[*See* Rule 24]
STATEMENT OF ACCOUNT & SOLVENCY

Note: All fields marked in *are to be mandatorily filled.

Annual or interim

If Annual -Statement of Account and Solvency as at

LLPIN/FLLPIN

Name of the Limited Liability Partnership/ Foreign Limited Liability Partnership

Part A: Statement of Solvency

We ____________________ being the designated partners or authorized representatives of ____________________ (name of the LLP/FLLP) do solemnly affirm and sincerely declare that we have made a full inquiry into the affairs of this Limited Liability Partnership/ Foreign Limited Liability Partnership, and that, having done so, have formed the opinion that the Limited Liability Partnership/Foreign Limited Liability Partnership is/is not able to pay its debts in full as they become due in the normal course of business.

We append a Statement of the Assets and Liabilities as at ____________________ and Income and Expenditure for the period ended on ____________________ being the latest practicable date before the making of this declaration.

We append a Statement indicating creation of charges or modification or satisfaction thereof during the financial year.

We declare that the turnover does not exceed/exceeds 40 lakh or the contribution does not exceed/exceeds 25 lakh rupees. The partners/authorized representatives have taken proper care and responsibility for maintenance of adequate accounting records and preparation of accounts in accordance with the provisions of the LLP Act and the Rules made thereunder.

We ____________________ being the authorized representatives of ________________ (name of the foreign LLP) do solemnly affirm and sincerely declare that we have made a full enquiry into the affairs of the limited liability partnership incorporated outside India, and that, having done so, have formed the opinion that such foreign limited liability partnership incorporated outside India is/is not able to pay its debts in full as they become due in the normal course of business.

We make this statement conscientiously believing it to be true, and by virtue of the provisions of the Limited Liability Partnership Act, 2008, the rules made thereunder.

Made on this _______________ day of _____________.

Place:

Signature of Designated Partners of LLP or authorized representatives (AR) of a Foreign LLP

DPINs

Part B: Statement of Account

Statement of Assets and Liabilities

Of ______________ as at ______________ (period)

(In Rupees ____)

	Particulars	Figures as at the end of the current reporting period	Figures as at the end of the previous reporting period
	1	2	3
I.	**CONTRIBUTION AND LIABILITIES**		
(1)	**Partners' funds**		
	(a) Contribution		
	(b) Reserves and surplus (Surplus being the profit/loss made during the year)		
(2)	**Liabilities**		
	(a) Secured loans		
	(b) Unsecured loans		
	(c) Short term borrowings		
	(d) Creditors/trade payables		
	- Advance from customers		
	(e) other liabilities (to specify)		
	(f) Provisions		
	(i) for taxation		
	(ii) for contingencies		
	(iii) for insurance		
	(iv) other provisions (if any)		
	TOTAL		
II.	**ASSETS**		
	(a) Fixed assets		
	(b) Investments		
	(c) Loans and advances		
	(d) Inventories		
	(e) Debtors/trade receivables		
	(f) Cash and cash equivalents		
	(g) other assets (to specify)		
	TOTAL		

Notes:

(a) Contingent liabilities not provided for.

(b) The disclosures under provisions of Section 22 of the Micro, Small and Medium Enterprises Development Act, 2006 may be added as attachment to this Form.

(c) Any other disclosures the LLP thinks proper to disclose.

Signature of Designated Partners of LLP or authorized representatives (AR) of a Foreign LLP

DPINs

Statement of Income and Expenditure

Of ____________ for the period from ____________ to ______________.

Income	Current year	Previous year
Turnover		
Other income (to specify)		
Increase/(decrease) in stocks [including for raw materials, work in progress and finished goods]		
TOTAL INCOME		
Expenses		
Purchases		
Personnel expenses		
Administrative expenses		
Selling expenses		
Depreciation		
Interest		
Other expenses (to specify)		
Profit before taxes		
Provision for Tax		
Profit after Tax		
Profit transferred to Partners'account		
Profit transferred to Reserves and surplus		

Note:

(a) Turnover means the aggregate of the gross value of the realization made from the sales, supply or distribution of the goods or on account of services rendered or both during the financial year. The amount of total excise duty/service tax deducted from turnover shall be disclosed separately.

(b) Any other disclosures the LLP thinks proper to disclose.

Signature of Designated Partners of LLP or authorized representatives (AR) of a Foreign LLP

DPINs

Certificate by the Designated partner or the auditor

It is hereby certified that I have verified the particulars contained in the Statement of Account and Solvency including the Statements of assets and liabilities as at __________ and the income and expenditure for the period ending __________ from the accounting records and other books and papers of _____________ (name of the LLP) and found them to be true and fair.

Name of the auditor/designated partner

*Line 1 ____

*Line 2 ____

*City _______________________*State _______________________

*PIN Code ___________________*ISO Country Code* ____________

*e-mail ID ________________________

Phone _________________________

Fax _________________________

Membership number/DPIN

Place:

Date:

Modify Check form Pre-scrutiny Submit

....

For office use only

This e-form is hereby registered

Digital signature of the authorizing officer

Appendix to Statement of Account and Solvency

PARTICULARS FOR CREATION OR MODIFICATION OR SATISFACTION OF CHARGES BY AN LLP

1.*LLPIN

2.(a) This form is for

creation of charge [ ]

modification of charge [ ]

satisfaction of charge [ ]

*(b) charge identification ID number of the charge to be modified or satisfied

3. *Type of charge

Immoveable property	Ship
Any interest in immoveable property	Goodwill
Book debts	Patent, licence under a patent
Moveable property (not being pledge)	Trade marks
Floating charge	Copyright or licence under copy right
If others, specify	

4. *Whether joint charge is involved Yes [ ] No [ ]

5. *Number of charge holders

6. Particulars of the charge holders

CIN/LLPIN ____________________

*Name

*Address

*Line 1 ____

*Line 2 ____

*City ____________________ *State ____________________

*PIN Code ____________________ *ISO Country Code* ____________

*e-mail ID ____________________

Phone ____________________

Fax ____________________

7.*Nature or description of instrument(s) creating or modifying the charge.

8.*Date of the instrument creating or modifying the charge (DD/MM/YYYY)

9. (a) *whether charge created or modified outside India

Yes [ ] No [ ]

(b) In case charge created or modified outside India on the property situated outside India, the date of receipt of the documents in India (DD/MM/YYYY)

10.*Amount secured by charge in Rs.

11. Brief particulars of the principal terms and conditions and extent and operation of the charge

(a) *Rate of interest

(b) *terms of repayment

(c) *margin

(d) *extent and operation of the charge

(e) others

12. In case of acquisition of property, subject to charge, furnish the following details relating to existing charge on the property so acquired:

(a) date of instrument creating or evidencing the charge,

(b) description of the instrument creating or evidencing the charge,

(c) date of acquisition of the property,

(d) amount of the charge in rupees,

(e) particulars of the property charged.

13.*Short particulars of the property charged (including location of the property)

14.(a)*whether any of the property or interest therein under reference is not registered in the name of the company.

Yes [ ] No [ ]

(b) If yes, in whose name it is registered

Note: If more than one charge holder involved, details of extent of charge, particulars of property charged, amount secured to be provided in attachment.

15. Date of latest modification prior to present modification DD/MM/YYYY

16. Particulars of present modification

17. Date of satisfaction in full (DD/MM/YYYY)

Attachments:

(i) instrument of creation or modification

(ii) instrument evidencing creation or modification of charge in case of acquisition of property which is already subject to charge

(iii) particulars of all joint charge holders

(iv) letter of charge holder stating that the amount has been satisfied

(v) optional attachment.

Signature of Designated Partner

DPIN

Form 9

[*See* Rule 7 and 10(8)]

CONSENT TO ACT AS DESIGNATED PARTNER

Note: All fields marked in *are to be mandatorily filled.

To

Limited Liability Partnership

(Name and address of the limited liability partnership)

Date: DD/MM/YYYY

Subject :Consent to act as Designated Partner

I, ___________________ hereby give my consent to act as designated partner of the (name of the LLP) pursuant to Section 7(3) of the Act.

Particulars

1. *Designated Partner Identification Number (DPIN)

2. *Name

3. *Father's /Husband's Name

4. *Present residential address

5.*e-mail ID

6. Name of the Partnership Firm

Or

LLPIN & Name of Limited Liability Partnership

Or

CIN & Name of the Company

Or

Name of any other body corporate whose nominee the designated partner is.

I hereby state that I satisfy the conditions and requirements for being eligible to be a designated partner and I have not been disqualified to act as a designated partner.

To be signed by the designated partner:

DPIN

Date:

Place:

Form 10

[*See* Rule 10(9)]

INTIMATION OF CHANGES IN PARTICULARS BY DESIGNATED PARTNERS

Note: All fields marked in *are to be mandatorily filled.

Affix a latest passport size photograph and get it attested/ certified for submission of the form with MCA

1. *Designated Partner Identification Number (DPIN)

2. Please identify (tick) and fill-in particulars sought to be changed:

Applicant name
Nationality
Date of birth
Income-tax permanent account number:
Voter's identity card number :
Passport number :
Driving licence number:
Permanent residential address:
Present residential address:
Other (please specify):

3. Applicant's name (enter full name and do not use abbreviations)

First name :
Last name :
Middle name :

4. Whether a resident of India Yes [ ] No [ ]

5. Nationality:

6. Date of birth (DD/MM/YYYY)

7. Income-tax permanent account number

8. Voter's identity card number :

9. Passport number :

10. Driving licence number:

11. Permanent residential address

Line I
Line II

(a) City :
(b) State :
(c) Country :
(d) Pin code :
(e) Phone :
(f) Fax :

12. Present residential address

Line I

Line II

(a) City :

(b) State :

(c) Country :

(d) Pin code :

(e) Phone :

(f) Fax :

NOTE I: Enclose necessary documents attested by a Notary or gazetted officer or a Company Secretary, a Chartered Accountant, a Cost Accountant holding a certificate of practice under the Company Secretaries Act, 1980, Chartered Accountants Act, 1949, and the Cost and Works Accountants Act, 1959 respectively.

NOTE II: In case any proof enclosed is in language other than Hindi or English then the translated copy of the same in English or Hindi shall be required to be enclosed. It should be certified by the same professional who has certified other proof.

NOTE III: In case the designated partner submitting change in particulars is not residing in India, the certification of attached documents and the photograph may be done by a notary in the home country of the applicant. Further, in the case of a foreign national, certified copy of the valid passport should be enclosed.

NOTE IV: The photograph of the applicant being affixed on the form should also be attested.

IF ANY OF THE REQUIREMENTS ARE NOT MET, CHANGES WILL NOT BE CONSIDERED.

I ____________________ son/daughter of ____________________ resident of ____________________ hereby declare and verify that the information given in this Form and the documents enclosed is correct and complete.

Signature of the applicant

Date Place

....

For office use only

Signature of the Authorizing Officer

Date Place

Form 11
[*See* Rule 25(1)]
ANNUAL RETURN OF LIMITED LIABILITY PARTNERSHIP

Note: All fields marked in *are to be mandatorily filled.

*Annual Return made upto 31st day of March of ______________ (Year).

1.*LLPIN

2.*Name of limited liability partnership

3.*Address of registered office

*Line 1 ____

*Line 2 ____

*City ______________________ *State ______________________

*PIN Code ____________________ *ISO Country Code* ____________

*e-mail ID ________________________

Phone ________________________

Fax ________________________

4. Other address if declared under Section 13(2) for service of documents

*Line 1 ____

*Line 2 ____

*City ______________________ *State ______________________

*PIN Code ____________________ *ISO Country Code* ____________

*e-mail ID ________________________

Phone ________________________

Fax ________________________

5. Date of closure of Financial Year to which the Annual Return relates

(DD/MM/YYYY)

6. Business classification

(with reference to one or more categories prescribed for business, trade, profession, service or occupation classification)

7. Principal business activities of the Limited Liability Partnership

8.*Summary of partners and designated partners for whom this Form is filed.

SN	Category	Number of Partners	Number of Designated partners	Number of designated partners resident in India
(i)	Individuals			
(ii)	LLPs			
(iii)	Companies			
(iv)	LLPs incorporated outside India			
(v)	Companies incorporated outside India			
	Total			

9. Number of individual(s) as partner for [ ] (Dynamic)

Note: (In case individual(s) are more than ten, attach details in respect of remaining individual partners in a separate sheet as an attachment.

Details in respect of individual(s). (First, enter details in respect of designated partners)

*Whether Designated partner Yes [ ] No [ ]

If yes, DPIN

*Whether resident in India Yes [ ] No [ ]

*Name :

*Father's / Husband's Name :

*Nationality :

Date of appointment

Date of Cessation

Changed name

Date of change in designation

New designation

(Please give address and other details of the partner in Addendum to this Form)

Whether a partner of partnership firm or limited liability partnership or director of a company

Yes [ ] No [ ]

Names and addresses of the partnership firm(s)

Name ________________ Address of principal office ________________

LLPIN and name of the limited liability partnership(s)

LLPIN ________________

Name of limited liability partnership ______________

CIN and names of the companies in which he is a director

CIN ___________ DIN ______________ Name______________

Whether nominee of a body corporate

Yes [ ] No [ ]

10. *Number of bodies corporate as partners [ ] (Dynamic)

Note: In case bodies corporate are more than five, attach details in respect of remaining bodies corporate in a separate sheet as an attachment.

Details in respect of bodies corporate and their nominees (First, enter details in respect of designated partners)

Category (drop down) LLP, Company, LLP incorporated outside India (LIOI), Company incorporated outside India (CIOI).

LLPIN or Corporate Identity Number (CIN) or LIOI registration number or CIOI registration number

*Name

*Country where registered

*Name and particulars of the person signing on behalf of the body corporate as nominee

*Designation

*Father's / Husband's Name

*Nationality

*Whether Designated partner Yes [ ] No [ ]

If yes, DPIN

*Whether resident in India Yes [ ] No [ ]

Date of appointment

Date of Cessation

Changed name, if any

Date of change in designation

New designation

(Please give address and other details of the partner and nominee in Addendum to this Form)

Whether a partner of partnership firm or limited liability partnership or director of a company

Yes [ ] No [ ]

Names and addresses of the partnership firm(s)

Name ____________ Address of principal office ______________

LLPIN and name of the limited liability partnership(s)

LLPIN ___________

Name of limited liability partnership

CIN and names of the companies in which he is a director

CIN ___________ DIN ____________ Name ____________

11. *Obligations of the partners to contribute

Sr. No.	Name of Partner	Obligation and form of contribution	Contributions received and accounted for (in Rs.)

12. *Particulars of penalties imposed on the :

(i) Limited liability partnership

Section No.	offence	Penalty imposed

(ii) Partners/ Designated partners

Name of the Partner/ Designated Partner	Section No.	offence	Penalty imposed

13. *Particulars of compounding of offences

Section No.	Offence	Date of Compounding of offence

Attachments:

Optional Attachment.

Verification

To the best of my knowledge and belief, the information given in this Form and its attachments is correct and complete.

To be digitally signed by

Designated Partner ____________________

DPIN

Date:

Place:

Certificate

I certify that Annual Return contains true and correct information.

To be signed by a Designated partner

DPIN

or

I certify that all the particulars mentioned above are true as per the books and records of ________________________ (name of the LLP) and found them to be true and correct.

Company Secretary in practice

Certificate of Practice Number

Date: Place: ______________

Modify Check form Pre-scrutiny Submit

....

For office use only

This e-form is hereby registered

Digital signature of the authorizing officer

Addendum to Form 11

Particulars of addresses and other details of partners/designated partners

1. Number of individuals as partners

(In case individual(s) are more than ten, attach details in respect of remaining individual partners in a separate sheet as an attachment.

Details in respect of individual(s) (First, enter details in respect of designated partners)

(The details in this Addendum should be in the order of names of partners given in Form 11)

*Whether Designated partner Yes [ ] No [ ]

If yes, DPIN

*Whether resident in India Yes [ ] No [ ]

*Name :

*Father's / Husband's Name :

*Nationality

*Date of birth

*Occupation

*Income-tax permanent account number (PAN)

Passport Number

*Permanent residential address

Address

*Line 1 ______________________________

*Line 2 ______________________________

*City ________________ *State ________________

*PIN Code ________________ *ISO Country Code* __________

*e-mail ID ________________

Phone ________________

Fax ________________

*Whether present residential address is same as the permanent residential address:

(Please Tick) Yes [ ] No [ ]

If no, present residential address

Address

*Line 1 ______________________________

*Line 2 ______________________________

*City ________________ *State ________________

*PIN Code ________________ *ISO Country Code* __________

*e-mail ID ________________

Phone ________________

Fax ________________

2. Number of bodies corporate as partner

(In case bodies corporate are more than five, attach details in respect of remaining bodies corporate in a separate sheet as an attachment. First, enter details in respect of designated partners)

Details in respect of Bodies Corporate and their nominees.

(The details in this Addendum should be in the order of names of partners given in Form 11).

Category (drop down) LLP, Company, LLP incorporated outside India (LIOI), Company incorporated outside India (CIOI).

LLPIN or Corporate Identity Number (CIN) or LIOI registration number or CIOI registration number

*Name of the body corporate

*Country where registered

*Full address of registered office

*Line 1 ______________________________

*Line 2 ______________________________

*City ______________ *State ______________

*PIN Code ______________ *ISO Country Code* __________

*e-mail ID ______________

Phone ______________ Fax ______________

*Name and particulars of the person signing on behalf of the body corporate as nominee

*Designation

*Father's / Husband's Name

*Nationality

*Date of birth

*Occupation

*Income-tax permanent account number (PAN)

Passport Number

*Whether designated partner: Yes [ ] No [ ]

If yes, DPIN

*Whether resident in India (Please Tick) Yes [ ] No [ ]

*Permanent residential address

Address

*Line 1 ______________________________

*Line 2 ______________________________

*City ______________ *State ______________

*PIN Code ______________ *ISO Country Code* __________

*e-mail ID ______________

Phone ______________ Fax ______________

*Whether present residential address is same as the permanent residential address:
(Please Tick) Yes [ ] No [ ]

If no, present residential address

Address

*Line 1 ____________________

*Line 2 ____________________

*City ____________________ *State ____________________

*PIN Code ____________________ *ISO Country Code* ____________

*e-mail ID ____________________

Phone ____________________ Fax ____________________

Attachments

Optional Attachment.

Verification

To the best of my knowledge and belief, the information given in this form and its attachments is correct and complete.

To be digitally signed by

Designated Partner

DPIN

Certificate

I certify that annual return contains true and correct information.

To be signed by a designated partner

DPIN

Or

I certify that all the particulars mentioned above are true as per the books and records of ____________________ (name of the LLP) and found them to be true and correct.

Company Secretary in practice

Certificate of Practice Number

Modify Check form Pre-scrutiny Submit

....

For office use only

This e-form is hereby registered

Digital signature of the authorizing officer

Form 12

[*See* Rule 16(3)]

FORM FOR INTIMATING OTHER ADDRESS FOR SERVICE OF DOCUMENTS

Note: All fields marked in *are to be mandatorily filled.

1. *LLPIN

2. *Name of the Limited Liability Partnership

3.*Address of Registered Office

*Line 1 ____________________

*Line 2 ____________________

*City ____________ *State ____________

*PIN Code ____________ *ISO Country Code* ____________

*e-mail ID ____________

Phone ____________ Fax ____________

4. Pursuant to Section 13(2) of the Limited Liability Partnership Act, 2008, the above named Limited Liability Partnership declares the following address, other than the address of its Registered Office, for serving a document on it or its partner or designated partner:

Other address:

*Line 1 ____________________

*Line 2 ____________________

*City ____________ *State ____________

*PIN Code ____________ *ISO Country Code* ____________

*e-mail ID ____________

Phone ____________ Fax ____________

Date of complying with sub-rule(2) of Rule 16 :

Attachments.

(i) Copy of the minutes of decision/resolution/consent of partners,

(ii) The extracts of the relevant provision of the Limited Liability Partnership Agreement, if any,

(iii) Proof of address,

(iv) Optional Attachment.

Verification

To the best of my knowledge and belief, the information given in this Form and its attachments is correct and complete.

I ____________ a designated partner of ____________________ (name of the LLP) am authorized to sign and submit this form.

To be digitally signed by designated partner

DPIN

Date:

Place:

Modify Check form Pre-scrutiny Submit

For office use only

This e-form is hereby registered
Digital signature of the authorizing officer

Form 13

[Refer Section 24(1) of the Act]

SPECIMEN OF NOTICE OF CESSATION BY A CEASING PARTNER TO OTHER PARTNERS

Note: All fields marked in *are to be mandatorily filled.

To

All Partners
.... Limited Liability Partnership
(Registered Address)

All Partners
.... Limited Liability Partnership
(Other address declared by the Limited Liability Partnership for service of documents)

Date: (DDMMYYYY) _______________
[Date should be at least 30 days before the date partner intends to resign]

In accordance with the provisions of Section 24(1) of the Limited Liability Partnership Act, 2008, I _________________________ (Name of Partner) do hereby give notice of my intention to resign as a partner of the (name of the LLP) with effect from (DDMMYYY).

Name of the partner

Address

Name of the Authorised Signatory

Signatures

#Applicable where the partner is a body corporate. Copy of authorization to be attached.

Date:

Place:

Form 14

[*See* Rule 33]

FORM FOR INTIMATING THE REGISTRAR OF FIRMS/REGISTRAR OF COMPANIES OF CONVERSION OF FIRM/COMPANY INTO LIMITED LIABILITY PARTNERSHIP

Note: All fields marked in *are to be mandatorily filled.

This form is for intimating

- ❒ Conversion of firm into limited liability partnership.
- ❒ Conversion of private company into limited liability partnership
- ❒ Conversion of unlisted public company into limited liability partnership

Part A : Conversion of firm into limited liability partnership

1. *Name of the firm

2. *Principal address of the firm

3. *Whether the firm is registered under the Partnership Act, 1932

Yes [ ] No [ ]

If yes, date of registration

Registration No.

If no, whether the firm is registered under any other law

Yes [ ] No [ ]

If yes, the name of the Statute

Date of registration

Registration No.

Part B : Conversion of private company/ unlisted public company into limited liability partnership

1. *Name of the company

2. *CIN

3. Address of registered office of the company

*Line 1 ____________________

*Line 2 ____________________

*City ____________ *State ____________

*PIN Code ____________ *

Part C : Particulars of the Limited liability partnership into which the aforesaid firm/company has been converted.

1. *LLPIN

2. *Name of the limited liability partnership

3. *Date of incorporation ___/___/______ (DDMMYYYY)

4. Address of registered office

*Line 1 ____

*Line 2 ____

*City ______________________*State ____________________

*PIN Code ________________*ISO Country Code* ____________

*e-mail ID ____________________

Phone ______________________ Fax ____________________

Attachments:

(1) Copy of the certificate of incorporation of Limited Liability Partnership.

(2) Optional Attachment.

Certificate

I,____________________ partner of the (name of the LLP) hereby give notice of conversion of the ____________________ (name of converted firm or company) into the said limited liability partnership on __________ day of ____________________.

To be digitally signed by a partner of the LLP who, in case of conversion of firm, was one of the partners, or who, in case of conversion of a private or unlisted public company, was one of the directors in the company.

DIN/DPIN

Date:

Place:

Modify Check form Pre-scrutiny Submit

....

For office use only

This e-form is hereby registered

Digital signature of the authorizing officer

FORM 15

[*See* Rule 17]

NOTICE OF CHANGE OF PLACE OF REGISTERED OFFICE

Note: All fields marked in *are to be mandatorily filled.

1.*LLPIN

2.*Name of the Limited Liability Partnership

3.*Present address of the registered office of the limited liability partnership

*Line 1 ____________________

*Line 2 ____________________

*City ____________ *State ____________

*PIN Code ____________ *ISO Country Code* ____________

*e-mail ID ____________

Phone ____________ Fax ____________

4.*New address of the registered office of the limited liability partnership

*Line 1 ____________________

*Line 2 ____________________

*City ____________ *State ____________

*PIN Code ____________ *ISO Country Code* ____________

*e-mail ID ____________

Phone ____________ Fax ____________

5.*The full address of the police station under whose jurisdiction the new registered office address of the limited liability partnership is situated

*Name

*Address

*Line I

*Line II

*City/Town/village:

*Tehsil:

*District:

*State:

*Pin code:

6. Particulars of prosecutions initiated against or show cause notices received by the LLP for alleged offences under the Act.

7. *Change of place of registered office is -

(   ) Within the same city/town/village.

(   ) From one place to another place within the same State.

(   ) Within the State from the jurisdiction of one Registrar to the jurisdiction of another Registrar.

(   ) Change of place of the registered office from one State to another State.

8. Dates of publication of public notice in the newspapers

(Applicable where change of place of the registered office is from one State to another).

9. *Date of complying with sub-rule (1) or sub-rule (4) of Rule 17.

Attachments.

(i) Proof of changed address of registered office.

(ii) Copy of the minutes of decision/resolution/consent of partners

(iii) The extracts of the relevant provision of the Limited Liability Partnership Agreement, if any.

(iv) Copies of public notice, if applicable.

(v) Consent of secured creditors, if applicable.

(vi) Optional attachment.

Verification

To the best of my knowledge and belief, the information given in this Form and its attachments is correct and complete.

I ______________ a designated partner of ____________________ (name of the LLP), am authorized to sign and submit this form.

To be digitally signed by designated partner

DPIN

Date: Place: __________

Certificate

It is hereby certified that I have verified the above particulars from the books and records of __________________ (name of the LLP) and found them to be true and correct.

Company Secretary in practice [ ]

Chartered Accountant in practice [ ]

Cost Accountant in practice [ ]

To be digitally signed by

Certificate of Practice Number

Date: Place: ___________

....

For office use only

This e-form is hereby registered

Digital signature of the authorizing officer

Submit to BO

Form 16
[Refer Section 12(1)(b) of the Act]
CERTIFICATE OF INCORPORATION

LLPIN ________ of 20____

I hereby certify that ____________________________ Limited Liability Partnership is incorporated pursuant to Section 12(1) of the Limited Liability Partnership Act, 2008.

Given under my hand at __________ this _________ day of ____________, Two thousand _____________.

Registrar
(Seal)

Form 17
[*See* paragraphs 2, 3, 4 and 16 of the Second Schedule of the Act and Rule 38(1)]
APPLICATION AND STATEMENT FOR THE CONVERSION OF A FIRM INTO LIMITED LIABILITY PARTNERSHIP

Note: All fields marked in *are to be mandatorily filled.

Part A : Application

1. *Name of the firm

2. *Principal address of the firm

*Line 1 ____

*Line 2 ____

*City ____________________________ *State ______________________

*PIN Code ___________________ *ISO Country Code* ____________

*e-mail ID _________________________

Phone ________________________ Fax ________________________

3. (a) *Whether the firm is registered under the Partnership Act, 1932.

Yes [ ] No [ ]

If yes, date of registration

Registration No.

If no, whether the firm is registered under any other law

Yes [ ] No [ ]

If yes, the name of the Statute under which registered

Date of registration

Registration No.

(b) *Date of agreement by which firm was formed DD/MM/YYYY

4. *Total number of partners in the firm

5. *Names and addresses of the partners (Dynamic).

Name	Address (House Number, city/town/village, District, State, Pin code.)	Amount of capital held in the firm

6. *Service Request Number (SRN) of Form 1

7. *Name of the proposed limited liability partnership

8. *Address of registered office of the proposed limited liability partnership

*Line 1 ______________________________

*Line 2 ______________________________

*City ______________ *State ______________

*PIN Code ______________ *ISO Country Code* ______________

*e-mail ID ______________

Phone ______________ Fax ______________

9. *Total number of partners in the LLP

10. *Whether all the partners of firm have given their consent for conversion of the firm into the limited liability partnership.

Yes [ ] No [ ]

If yes, attach the copy of the consent.

11. *Whether all the partners of the limited liability partnership comprise all the partners of the Firm and no one else.

Yes [ ] No [ ]

12. *Whether up to date Income-tax return is filed under the Income-tax Act, 1961.

Yes [ ] No [ ]

If Yes, indicate the period upto which such return is filed

DD/MM/YYYY

13. *Whether any proceedings by or against the firm are pending in any Court or Tribunal or any other Authority.

Yes [ ] No [ ]

If yes, particulars of such proceedings in the following manner :-

Name of Court/ Tribunal/ Authority	Particulars

(In case the number of proceedings is more than five, separate sheet(s) in the above manner may be attached as an attachment)

14. Whether any earlier application for conversion of the said firm into limited liability partnership was refused by the Registrar. Yes [ ] No [ ]

If yes, give SRN of earlier Form 17 and the reasons for refusal:-

(i) SRN

(ii) Reasons

15. *Whether any conviction, ruling, order, judgment of any Court, Tribunal or other authority in favour of or against the firm are subsisting.

Yes [ ] No [ ]

If Yes, details thereof in following manner:-

Section and the title of relevant Act	Particulars	Name of Court/ Tribunal/ Authority

(In case the number of proceedings is more than five, separate sheet(s) in the above manner may be attached as an attachment)

16. *Whether consent of all the creditors for conversion of the firm into limited liability partnership has been obtained.

Yes [ ] No [ ]

If Yes, attach the list and consent of such creditors.

17. *Whether any clearance, approval or permission for conversion of the firm into limited liability partnership is required from any other body/authority.

Yes [ ] No [ ]

If Yes, whether the applicable approvals from the concerned body/authority or authorities have been obtained.

Yes [ ] No [ ]

18. *Whether the Statement of assets and liabilities of the firm duly certified as true and correct by a Chartered Accountant in practice and made upto a date not preceding 30 days of the date of filing the application for conversion attached.

To be digitally signed by designated partner

DPIN

Date

Place ______________

Part B : Statement

I ____________ partner of M/s __________________ (name of the firm) registered under the Indian Partnership Act, 1932 or under ____________________________ (name of the law) at ____________ (name of the place) in the State /UT of ____________ (name of the State or Union Territory) on _________ (date); registration number __________ and also named in the incorporation document of __________________ (name of the LLP) as a partner or designated partner give my consent for the conversion of the said firm M/s (name of the firm) into the limited liability partnership.

2.I state that I shall be personally liable (jointly and severally with the limited liability partnership) for the liabilities and obligations of the firm which were incurred prior to the conversion or which arose from any contract entered into prior to the conversion.

I further state as under:

(i) that all the requirements of the Limited Liability Partnership Act, 2008 and the Rules made thereunder have been complied with, in respect of conversion of firm into limited liability partnership and matters precedent and incidental thereto;

(ii) that all the partners of the limited liability partnership comprise all the partners of the firm and no one else;

(iii) that the applicable clearances, approvals or permissions for conversion of the firm into a limited liability partnership from any body/authority have been obtained;

(iv) that the consent of all the creditors for conversion of the firm into limited liability partnership has been obtained;

(v) that to the best of my knowledge and belief, the information given in this form and its attachments is correct and complete.

Attachments

1. Statement of partners of the firm (may be attached in a tabular form)
2. Incorporation Document & Statement in Form 2 filed electronically.
3. Statement of Assets and Liabilities of the firm duly certified as true and correct by the Chartered Accountant in practice.
4. List of all the creditors along with their consent to the conversion (may be given in the form of a tabular statement).
5. Approval from any body/authority.
6. Optional attachment.

To be digitally signed by a partner or designated partner

Date:

Place:

(The statement(s) of remaining partner(s) shall be given in the above format as a tabular statement as an attachment)

Certificate

It is hereby certified that I have verified the above particulars from the books and records of M/s __________________ Name of the firm) and found them to be true and correct.

Company Secretary in practice [ ]
Chartered Accountant in practice [ ]
Cost Accountant in practice [ ]

To be digitally signed by

Certificate of Practice Number

Date:

Place:

....

For office use only

Digital signature of the authorizing officer
This e-form is hereby approved
This e-form is hereby rejected

Form 18

[*See* paragraphs 2 and 3 of Third Schedule, paragraphs 2, 3 and 4 of Fourth Schedule of the Act and Rule 39(1) and 40(1)]

APPLICATION AND STATEMENT FOR CONVERSION OF A PRIVATE COMPANY/UNLISTED PUBLIC COMPANY INTO LIMITED LIABILITY PARTNERSHIP

Note: All fields marked in *are to be mandatorily filled.

Part A: Application

1. *CIN

2. *Name of the Company

3. *Date of incorporation

4. *Name of office of Registrar of Companies

5. *Address of registered office of the company

*Line 1 ________________________________

*Line 2 ________________________________

*City ______________ *State ______________

*PIN Code ______________ *ISO Country Code* __________

*e-mail ID ______________

Phone ______________ Fax ______________

6. *Total number of shareholders in the company

7. *Names and addresses of the shareholders

Name	Address (House Number, city/town/village, District, State, Pin code.)	Number of shares held in the company.

(In case number of shareholders is more than ten, separate sheet(s) in the above manner may be attached as an attachment)

8. *Service Request Number (SRN) of Form 1

9. *Name of the proposed limited liability partnership

10. *Address of registered office of the proposed limited liability partnership

*Line 1 ________________________________

*Line 2 ________________________________

*City ______________ *State ______________

*PIN Code ______________ *ISO Country Code* __________

*e-mail ID ______________

Phone ______________ Fax ______________

11. *Total number of partners in the LLP

12. *Whether all the shareholders of the company have given their consent for conversion of the company into the limited liability partnership.

Yes [ ] No [ ]

13. *Whether all the partners of the limited liability partnership comprise all the shareholders of the company and no one else.

Yes [ ] No [ ]

14. *Whether any security interest in the assets of the company is subsisting or in force.

Yes [ ] No [ ]

If yes, give details

____

____

15. *Whether up to date Income-tax return is filed under the Income-tax Act, 1961.

Yes [ ] No [ ]

If Yes, indicate the period upto which such return is filed

DD/MM/YYYY ______________

16. *Whether any prosecution initiated against or show cause notice received by the company for alleged offences under the Companies Act, 1956.

Yes [ ] No [ ]

If Yes, give details in the following manner:-

S. No.	Section of the Companies Act under which action being initiated	Date of issue of show cause notice	Status (reply sent/ under examination by concerned authority)

(In case number of prosecution initiated/ show cause notice received is more than five, separate sheet(s) in the above manner may be attached as an attachment)

17. *Whether any proceeding by or against the company is pending in any Court or Tribunal or any other Authority.

Yes [ ] No [ ]

If Yes, details thereof in following manner:-

Name of Court/ Tribunal/ Authority	Particulars

(In case number of proceedings is more than five, separate sheet(s) in the above manner may be attached as an attachment)

18. *Whether any earlier application for conversion of the said company into limited liability partnership was refused by the Registrar.

Yes [ ] No [ ]

If yes, give SRN of earlier Form 18 and the reasons for refusal:

(i) SRN

(ii) Reasons

19. *Whether any conviction, ruling, order, judgment of any Court, Tribunal or other authority in favour of or against the company is subsisting.

Yes [ ] No [ ]

If Yes, details thereof in following manner:-

Section and the title of relevant Act	Particulars	Name of Court/ Tribunal/ Authority

(In case number of proceedings is more than five, separate sheet(s) in the above manner may be attached as an attachment)

20. *Whether consent of all the unsecured creditors for conversion of the company into limited liability partnership has been obtained.

Yes [ ] No [ ]

If yes, a copy thereof.

21. *Whether any clearance, approval or permission for conversion of the company into limited liability partnership is required from any body/ authority.

Yes [ ] No [ ]

If Yes, whether the applicable approvals from the concerned body/authority or authorities have been obtained.

Yes [ ] No [ ]

22. *Whether upto date documents including immediately preceding balance sheet and annual returns under the Companies Act, 1956 have been filed.

Yes [ ]

23. *Whether the statement of assets and liabilities of the company duly certified as true and correct by the auditor made up to a date not preceding 30 days of the date of filing the application attached.

Yes [ ]

To be digitally signed by designated partner

DPIN

Date

Place

Part B: Statement

I ________________ shareholder of ______________ and also (name of the company) and also named in the incorporation document of ________________________ (name of the LLP) as a partner or designated partner give my consent for the conversion of the said company ____________________________________ (name of the company) into the limited liability partnership.

I state as under:

(i) that all the requirements of the Limited Liability Partnership Act, 2008 and the rules made thereunder have been complied with, in respect of conversion of private company/ unlisted public company into limited liability partnership and matters precedent and incidental thereto;

(ii) that all the partners of the limited liability partnership comprise all the shareholders of the company and no one else;

(iii) that the applicable clearances, approvals or permissions for conversion of the company into a limited liability partnership from any authority/authorities have been obtained;

(iv) that the consent of all the unsecured creditors for conversion of the company into limited liability partnership has been obtained;

(v) that all the documents due for filing including balance sheet and annual return for the immediately preceding financial year have been filed under the provision of the Companies Act, 1956;

(vi) that to the best of my knowledge and belief, the information given in this form and its attachments is correct and complete.

Attachments

1. Statement of shareholders (may be given in a tabular form)
2. Incorporation Document & Statement in Form 2 filed electronically.
3. Statement of Assets and Liabilities of the company duly certified as true and correct by the auditor.
4. List of all the unsecured creditors along with their consent. (may be attached in a tabular form)
5. Approval from any other body/authority.
6. Optional attachment.

To be digitally signed by a partner or designated partner

Date:

Place:

(The statement(s) of remaining shareholder (s) shall be given in the above format as a tabular statement as an attachment)

Certificate

It is hereby certified that I have verified the above particulars from the books and records of ______________________________ (name of the company) and found them to be true and correct.

Company secretary in practice [ ]
Chartered Accountant in practice [ ]
Cost Accountant in practice [ ]

Digitally Signed

Certificate of Practice Number

Date:

Place:

....

For office use only

Digital signature of the authorizing officer
This e-form is hereby approved
This e-form is hereby rejected

Form 19
[*See* Rule 32(1)]

Certificate of Registration on Conversion of .... [Firm/ company] to .... [Insert name of limited liability partnership] LLPIN ________ of 20__-__

I hereby certify that ______________________Limited Liability Partnership is this day registered pursuant to Section 58(1) of the Limited Liability Partnership Act, 2008.

Given under my hand at __________ this _________ day of ___________, Two thousand _____________.

Registrar

Form 20
[*See* Rule 35(1)]

Limited liability partnership application No..... of 20......... Applicants

Affidavit in support of Summons

I,.......... of .... solemnly affirm and state as follows:

1. I am the designated partner/ partner of the said limited liability partnership, or the liquidator of the said limited liability partnership in liquidation.

(Where the application is not by the limited liability partnership or its liquidator, but by a partner or creditor, the above paragraph should be suitably altered).

2. The limited liability partnership was incorporated on....20___. The document now produced and shown to me is a copy of the incorporation document of the said limited liability partnership.

3. The registered office of the limited liability partnership is situated at......

4. The limited liability partnership commenced the business of......(e.g..., manufacture of auto parts etc) and has been carrying on the same, since.....

5. (Here set out in separate paragraphs the circumstances that have necessitated the proposed compromise or arrangement, the objects sought to be achieved by it, and the terms of the compromise or arrangement. A copy of the proposed compromise or arrangement should be marked as an exhibit and annexed to the affidavit).

6. (Here set out the class of creditors or partners with whom the compromise or arrangement is to be made; where the arrangement is between the limited liability partnership and its partners, it should be stated whether any creditors or class of creditors are likely to be affected by it)

7. It may be necessary that a meeting (or meetings) of the creditors or partners (if the meeting is only to be of a class of creditors, it should be so stated), should be called to consider and approve the proposed compromise or arrangement.

8. It is suggested that the meeting (or meetings) may be held at the premises of the registered office of the limited liability partnership or at such other place as may be determined by the Tribunal, and on such date(s) and at such time(s) as this Tribunal may direct; and that a chairman may be appointed for the meeting (or for each of the meetings) to be held.

9. It is suggested that notice of the proposed compromise or arrangement and of the meeting may be published once in (here set out the newspapers) and in such other manner as the Tribunal may direct.

10. It is prayed that necessary directions may be given as to the issue and publication of notices and the convening, holding and conducting of the meeting(s) proposed above.

Solemnly affirmed.

Sd/-A.B.
Before me

Before me
Sd/-Commissioner for Oaths

Date:

Place:

Form 21

[*See* Rule 35(2)]

Limited liability partnership application No..... of 20......... Applicants

Summons for directions to convene a meeting under Section 60(1)

Let all parties concerned attend the Member of the Tribunal in Chamber on............... day, the .... Day of 20..., at .....o' clock in the ..... noon on the hearing of the applicant of the above named limited liability partnership [or of the applicant(s) above named] for an order that a meeting (or separate meetings) be held at .... of [Here enter the class or classes of creditors or the partners of which the meetings have to be held] of the above limited liability partnership, for the purpose of considering, and if thought fit, approving, with or without modification, a scheme of compromise or arrangement proposed to be made between the limited liability partnership and the said (here mention the class or classes of creditors or partners) of the said limited liability partnership;

And that directions may be given as to the method of convening, holding and conducting the said meeting(s) and as to the notices and advertisements to be issued.

And that a chairman (or chairmen) may be appointed of the said meeting(s), who shall report the result thereof to the Tribunal.

Authorized representative for the applicant(s)

Officer of the Tribunal.

The affidavit of......will be used in support of the summons.

Note: Where the limited liability partnership is not the applicant, the summons should be served on the limited liability partnership, or, where it is being wound up, on its liquidator.

Date:

Place:

FORM 22

[*See* Rule 35(11) and (17) and 41(4)]

NOTICE OF INTIMATION OF ORDER OF COURT/ TRIBUNAL/CLB/CENTRAL GOVERNMENT TO THE REGISTRAR

Note: All fields marked in *are to be mandatorily filled.

1. *LLPIN

2. *Name of the limited liability partnership

3. Address of registered office

*Line 1 ____________________

*Line 2 ____________________

*City ____________ *State ____________

*PIN Code ____________ *ISO Country Code* ____________

*e-mail ID ____________

Phone ____________ Fax ____________

4. *Order of Court/ Tribunal/CLB/Central Government

5. *Date of order

6. *Date of receipt of certified copy

7. *Section or rule reference

8. *Description of order

9. *Submitted by or on behalf of ;-

Name

Address

*Line 1 ____________________

*Line 2 ____________________

*City ____________ *State ____________

*PIN Code ____________ *ISO Country Code* ____________

*e-mail ID ____________

Phone ____________ Fax ____________

Attachment

(i) *Certified copy of the order.

(ii) Optional attachment.

VERIFICATION

To the best of my knowledge and belief, the information given in this Form and its attachments is correct and complete.

I have gone through the provisions of the Limited Liability Partnership Act, 2008 and the rules framed thereunder.

I have been authorised to sign and submit this form.

To be digitally signed by
(Designated partner in case of LLP or by authorized representative in other cases)
DPIN, if applicable

Dated:

Place:

....

For office use only

This e-form is hereby registered
Digital signature of the authorizing officer __________submit to BO______

FORM 23

[*See* Rule 19(1)]

APPLICATION FOR DIRECTION TO LLP TO CHANGE ITS NAME

1. *Name of the applicant

2. *Address of the applicant

*Line 1 ______________________________

*Line 2 ______________________________

*City ______________ *State ______________

*PIN Code ______________ *ISO Country Code* ______________

*e-mail ID ______________

Phone ______________ Fax ______________

3. *LLPIN of limited liability partnership or the CIN of the company or Registration No. of other entity, if any

4. (a) *The name with which the limited liability partnership or the company or any other entity was incorporated or registered

(b) *Address

*Line 1 ______________________________

*Line 2 ______________________________

*City ______________ *State ______________

*PIN Code ______________ *ISO Country Code* ______________

*e-mail ID ______________

Phone ______________ Fax ______________

5. Grounds of objection

Attachments.

1. Copy of the authority to make application.
2. Copy of incorporation/registration certificate of limited liability partnership or the company or registration certificate of other entity, if any.
3. Optional attachment.

VERIFICATION

To the best of my knowledge and belief, the information given in this Form and its attachments is correct and complete.

I have gone through the provisions of the Limited Liability Partnership Act, 2008, the rules framed there under.

I have been authorized to sign and submit this application.

To be digitally signed by the applicant

Date

Place

For office use only

This e-Form is hereby approved
This e-Form is hereby rejected

Digital Signature of the authorizing officer
Submit to BO

FORM 24

[*See* Rule 37(1)(b)]

APPLICATION TO THE REGISTRAR FOR STRIKING OFF NAME

Note: All fields marked in *are to be mandatorily filled.

1.*LLPIN

2.*Name of the limited liability partnership

3. *Registered office address

*Line 1 ____________________

*Line 2 ____________________

*City ____________________ *State ____________________

*PIN Code ____________________ *ISO Country Code* ____________________

*e-mail ID ____________________

Phone ____________________ Fax ____________________

4. *Name and address of the designated partners (In case of more than 5 designated partners, attach details of such designated partners in a separate sheet as an attachment)

*Name

*Address

*Line 1 ____________________

*Line 2 ____________________

*City ____________________ *State ____________________

*PIN Code ____________________ *ISO Country Code* ____________________

*e-mail ID ____________________

Phone ____________________ Fax ____________________

5. *Name and address of other partners (In case of more than 5 partners, attach details of remaining partners in a separate sheet as an attachment)

*Name

Address

*Line 1 ____________________

*Line 2 ____________________

*City ____________________ *State ____________________

*PIN Code ____________________ *ISO Country Code* ____________________

*e-mail ID ____________________

Phone ____________________ Fax ____________________

6. *Whether up to date Income-tax returns filed.

Yes [ ] No [ ]

7. *Whether consent of all the partners obtained.

Yes [ ] No [ ]

8. *Copy of the latest statement of assets and liabilities not preceding 30 days of the date of filing application attached.

Yes [ ]

Attachments

1. *Copy of detailed application
2. Copy of authority to make the application
3. Copy of consent of all partners or creditors.
4. Copy of the undertaking in case of striking off name.
5. Optional attachment.

VERIFICATION

To the best of my knowledge and belief, the information given in this Form and its attachments is correct and complete.

I have gone through the provisions of the Limited Liability Partnership Act, 2008 and the rules framed thereunder.

I have been authorized to sign and submit this application.

To be digitally signed by the designated partner

DPIN

Date

Place

Modify Check form Pre-scrutiny Submit

....

For office use only

Digital signature of the authorizing officer

This e-form is hereby approved

This e-form is hereby rejected

FORM 25
[*See* Rule 18(3)]
APPLICATION FOR RESERVATION/RENEWAL OF NAME BY A FOREIGN LLP/FOREIGN COMPANY

Note: All fields marked in *are to be mandatorily filled.

Reservation [ ]

Renewal of Reservation [ ]

SRN of reservation ______________

1. *Name of the applicant

Address of the applicant

*Line 1 ______________

*Line 2 ______________

*City ______________ *State ______________

*PIN Code ______________ *ISO Country Code* ______________

*e-mail ID ______________

Phone ______________ Fax ______________

2. Name of the foreign limited liability partnership or foreign company.

3. Registered office address or principal place of business address of foreign limited liability partnership or foreign company

*Line 1 ______________

*Line 2 ______________

*City ______________ *State ______________

*PIN Code ______________ *ISO Country Code* ______________

*e-mail ID ______________

Phone ______________ Fax ______________

4. *Date of incorporation/ registration (DD/MM/YYYY)

5. *Incorporation or registration number

6. *Country of incorporation or registration

Attachments

1. Certified copy of the incorporation or registration certificate.
2. Certified copy of the authority to submit the application
3. Optional attachment.

VERIFICATION

To the best of my knowledge and belief, the information given in this Form and its attachments is correct and complete.

I have gone through the provisions of the Limited Liability Partnership Act, 2008, the rules framed thereunder.

I have been authorized to sign and submit this application.

To be digitally signed by applicant

Date:

Place:

Modify   Check form   Pre-scrutiny   Submit

....

For office use only

Digital signature of the authorizing officer
This e-form is hereby approved
This e-form is hereby rejected

Form 26
[*See* Rule 35(4)]
FORM OF PROXY

(Name of limited liability partnership)

I .... being a partner of the above named limited liability partnership hereby appoint .... or failing him, ... as my proxy to vote for me on my behalf at the meeting of the partners of the limited liability partnership to be held on the .... day of .... 20......

Signed this .... day of ...... 20....   Signature of Partner

Place: ____________

FORM 27
[*See* Rule 34(1)]
FORM FOR REGISTRATION OF PARTICULARS BY FOREIGN LIMITED LIABILITY PARTNERSHIP

Note: All fields marked in *are to be mandatorily filled.

1.*Name of the limited liability partnership incorporated or registered outside India :

2. (i) *Country where the limited liability partnership is incorporated

(ii) *Details of relevant Statute under which the limited liability partnership has been incorporated

(iii) *Details of the authority under which limited liability partnership is establishing a place of business in India

3. *State of principal place of business in India

4. (i) *Date of establishment of principal place of business in India

(ii) *Date on which approval of Reserve Bank of India obtained

5. Full address of the registered or principal office of the limited liability partnership incorporated or registered outside India:

*Line 1 ____________________________

*Line 2 ____________________________

*City ____________________ *State ____________________

*PIN Code ____________________ *ISO Country Code* ____________

*e-mail ID ____________________

Phone ____________________ Fax ____________________

6. *Full address of the office of the limited liability partnership in India which is deemed as its principal place of business in India

*Line 1 ____________________

*Line 2 ____________________

*City ____________________ *State ____________________

*PIN Code ____________________ *ISO Country Code* ____________

*e-mail ID ____________________

Phone ____________________ Fax ____________________

7. *List of persons resident in India and authorised to accept on behalf of the limited liability partnership service of process and any notices or other documents required to be served on the limited liability partnership;

*Number of persons authorized [ ] [drop down]

Particulars of person authorized

1. Income-tax permanent account number(PAN)

Name of person resident in India authorized to accept on behalf of the foreign limited liability partnership

*First Name

*Surname

*Father's / Husband's Name:

*Designation:

*Nationality:

*Where the Nationality of origin is different from the above mentioned nationality,

*Nationality of origin:

*Date of birth :

Others (please specify)

If already a partner of partnership firm or limited liability partnership or director of a company, specify the following:

No. of partnership firms in which he is a partner [ ] Drop down

Names & addresses of the partnership firm(s)

Name:

Address of principal office:

No. of limited liability partnership(s) in which he is a partner [ ] Drop down

LLPIN and name of the limited liability partnership(s)

LLPIN____________ Name of limited liability partnership

No. of Company (ies) in which he is a director [ ] Drop down

DIN

Name and CIN of the Company(ies)

CIN ______________ Name of Company

Permanent residential address

Address

*Line 1 ______________________________

*Line 2 ______________________________

*City ________________ *State ________________

*PIN Code ________________ *ISO Country Code* ____________

*e-mail ID ________________

Phone ________________ Fax ________________

*Whether present residential address is same as the permanent address

Yes [ ] No [ ]

Present residential address

*Line 1 ______________________________

*Line 2 ______________________________

*City ________________ *State ________________

*PIN Code ________________ *ISO Country Code* ____________

*e-mail ID ________________

Phone ________________ Fax ________________

Note: In case the authorized representatives are more than five, attach details in respect of remaining representatives in separate sheet as attachment.

8. List of partners & designated partners, if any,-

*Number of partners

*Number of designated partners, if any

*Particulars of partners;-

Present Name

*First name :

*Last name :

*Middle name :

Former Name(if any)

*First name :

*Last name :

*Middle name :

*Father's / Husband's Name :

*Nationality :

*Where the Nationality of origin is different from the above mentioned nationality,

*Nationality of origin:

*Date of birth :

*Business/occupation :

Others (please specify)
*Whether designated partner Yes [ ] No [ ]
Usual residential address
Address
*Line 1 ______________________________
*Line 2 ______________________________
*City ______________ *State ______________
*PIN Code ______________ *ISO Country Code* ____________
*e-mail ID ______________
Phone ______________ Fax ______________
*Whether nominee of a body corporate Yes [ ] No [ ]
If Yes,
(i) Name of the body corporate
(ii) Address of registered or principal office of the body corporate
*Line 1 ______________________________
*Line 2 ______________________________
*City ______________ *State ______________
*PIN Code ______________ *ISO Country Code* ____________
*e-mail ID ______________
Phone ______________ Fax ______________

Note: In case the partners/ designated partners are more than five, attach details in respect of remaining partners/ designated partners in separate sheet as attachment.

Attachments

1. Copy of the incorporation document or other instrument constituting or defining the constitution of the limited liability partnership certified in the manner specified in the sub-rule (2) of Rule 34.
2. Extracts of the Statute under which the foreign limited liability partnership has been set up.
3. Copy of authority under which the foreign limited liability partnership is establishing the place of business in India.
4. Copy of approval of Reserve Bank of India for allowing the foreign limited partnership to establish place of business in India.
5. If the above instrument is not in English then the translated version of the documents, certified in the manner specified in the sub-rule (5) of Rule 34.
6. Power of attorney in favour of authorized representative.
7. Optional attachment.

VERIFICATION

To the best of my knowledge and belief, the information given in this Form and its attachments is correct and complete.

I have gone through the provisions of the Limited Liability Partnership Act, 2008 and the rules framed thereunder in respect of establishment of place of business by a foreign limited liability partnership.

I am authorised to sign and submit this form.

To be digitally signed by:

Authorized representative of foreign limited liability partnership

Date:

Place:

Modify Check form Pre-scrutiny Submit

For office use only

Digital signature of the authorizing officer

This e-form is hereby registered

Form 28
[*See* Rule 34(3)]

Alteration in the -

(A) the incorporation document, or other instrument constituting or defining the constitution of a limited liability partnership incorporated or registered outside India; or

(B) the registered or principal office of a limited liability partnership incorporated or registered outside India; or

(C) the partner or designated partner if any of a limited liability partnership incorporated or registered outside India.

Note: All fields marked in *are to be mandatorily filled.

*Name of the LLP incorporated or registered outside India:

*Country where the LLP is incorporated

*Financial year ended on

(name of the foreign LLP) having established a place of business in India at hereby gives you notice of the alteration in -

- ❐ the incorporation document, or other instrument constituting or defining the constitution of a limited liability partnership incorporated or registered outside India; or
- ❐ the registered or principal office of a limited liability partnership incorporated or registered outside India; or
- ❐ the partner or designated partner if any of a limited liability partnership incorporated or registered outside India.

(A) the incorporation document, or other instrument constituting or defining the constitution of a limited liability partnership incorporated or registered outside India

A brief description of the alteration is given hereunder:

As per decision taken by LLP on ______________________ Shri ______________________ was authorised to file this alteration with the Registrar.

[Certified copy of the decision and/or the copy of the amended document should be enclosed. If the decision is not in English, a certified translation thereof must be enclosed.]

(B) the registered or principal office of a limited liability partnership incorporated or registered outside India

(i) The registered/principal office of the LLP in the country of incorporation has been shifted with effect from

(ii) The new address is as under:-

*Line 1 ____

*Line 2 ____

*City ___________________________ *State ___________________________

*PIN Code _______________________ *ISO Country Code* _______________

*e-mail ID __________________________

Phone ___________________________ Fax ___________________________

(C) the partner or designated partner of a limited liability partnership incorporated or registered outside India

(i) partner/designated partner of the LLP (if individual)

Name and surname in full	Usual residential address, email ID	Nationality	Business/ occupation or if there is no business/ occupation, particulars of other partnership/ directorships held, if any	Remarks as to alteration

(ii) partner/designated partner of the LLP (if bodies corporate)

Corporate Name	Registered office or principal office of body corporate	Names of directors/partners of body corporate		Remarks as to alteration
		Full name and address of each director or partner	Nationality of each director or partner and nationality of origin if different from present nationality	

Attachments:

1. Copy of the decision or other document through which alteration has been made
2. If the above instrument is not in English then the translated version of the documents, certified in the manner specified in the sub-rule (5) of Rule 34.
3. Power of attorney in favour of authorized representative
4. Optional Attachment.

VERIFICATION

To the best of my knowledge and belief, the information given in this Form and its attachments is correct and complete.

I have gone through the provisions of the Limited Liability Partnership Act, 2008 and the rules framed thereunder in respect of establishment of place of business by a foreign Limited Liability Partnership.

I am authorised to sign and submit this form.

To be digitally signed by:

Authorized representative of foreign limited liability partnership

Date: Place:

Modify Check form Pre-scrutiny Submit

....

For office use only

This e-form is hereby registered

Digital signature of the authorizing officer

Form 29
[*See* Rule 34(3) and (8)]

(A) Alteration in the certificate of incorporation or registration of limited liability partnership incorporated or registered outside India;

(B) Alteration in the name or address of any of the persons authorized to accept service on behalf of a foreign limited liability partnership in India;

(C) Alteration in the principal place of business of foreign limited liability partnership in India;

(D) Cessation to have place of business in India

Note: All fields marked in *are to be mandatorily filled.

*Name of the foreign LLP:

* FLLPIN

*Country where the foreign LLP is incorporated

The above mentioned foreign LLP having established a place of business in India at hereby gives notice for -

- ❐ alteration in the certificate of incorporation or registration of limited liability partnership incorporated or registered outside India
- ❐ alteration in the name or address of any of the persons authorized to accept service on behalf of a foreign limited liability partnership in India;
- ❐ alteration in the principal place of business of foreign limited liability partnership inIndia;

Cessation to have place of business in India

(A) alteration in the certificate of incorporation or registration of limited liability partnership incorporated or registered outside India

*A brief description of the alteration is given hereunder:

Date of Alteration

(B) alteration in the name or address of any of the persons authorized to accept service on behalf of a foreign limited liability partnership in India;

(1)

Present name and surname in full	Usual residential address	Remarks as to alteration (give date)

(2) Date of alteration

(C) alteration in the address of principal place of business of the foreign limited liability partnership in India.

(1) The principal place of business in India was shifted ____________________ with effect from

(2) Date of alteration

(3) The changed address is as under:-

*Line 1 ____________________

*Line 2 ____________________

*City ______________ *State ______________

*PIN Code ______________ *ISO Country Code* __________

*e-mail ID ______________

Phone ______________ Fax ______________

(D) (1) that it intends to close its place of business in India at the following places—

*Line 1 ____________________

*Line 2 ____________________

*City ______________ *State ______________

*PIN Code ______________ *ISO Country Code* __________

*e-mail ID ______________

Phone ______________ Fax ______________

(2) Date of intention to close

(3) That the LLP is not maintaining the place of business at any other place in India.

(4) That the LLP has filed with the Registrar all documents due for filing.

Attachments

(i) Copy of the decision or other document through which alteration has been made

(ii) Copy of approval of Reserve Bank of India for cessation of place of establishment of office in India of the foreign limited liability partnership

(iii) Power of attorney in favour of authorized representative

(iv) Optional Attachment.

VERIFICATION

To the best of my knowledge and belief, the information given in this Form and its attachments is correct and complete.

I have gone through the provisions of the Limited Liability Partnership Act, 2008 and the rules framed there under in respect of establishment of place of business by a foreign Limited Liability Partnership.

I am authorised to sign and submit this form.

To be digitally signed by:

Authorized representative of foreign limited liability partnership

Date: Place:

Modify Check form Pre-scrutiny Submit

....

For office use only

This e-form is hereby registered

Digital signature of the authorizing officer

Form 30

[*See* Rule 34(10)]

CERTIFICATE FOR ESTABLISHMENT OF PLACE OF BUSINESS IN INDIA

Foreign Limited Liability Partnership Registration Number: __________

Year __________

I hereby certify that Form No 27 dated ________ filed pursuant to Rule 34 of the Limited Liability Partnership Rules, 2009 informing establishment of place of business in India at __________________ with effect from ________ by __________, a Limited Liability Partnership originally incorporated in _______ has been registered.

Given under my hand at _______ this ______ day of _____ Two Thousand _____.

Registrar

(Seal)

Form 31
[*See* Rule 41(1)]
APPLICATION FOR COMPOUNDING OF AN OFFENCE UNDER THE ACT

Note: All fields marked in *are to be mandatorily filled.

1. *LLPIN

2. *Name of the limited liability partnership

3. Registered Office Address

*Line 1 ______________________________

*Line 2 ______________________________

*City ______________ *State ______________

*PIN Code ______________ *ISO Country Code* ______________

*e-mail ID ______________

Phone ______________ Fax ______________

4. *Name and address of the persons seeking compounding of the offence

(In case of more than 5 persons, attach details of such persons in a separate sheet as an attachment)

*Name

*Address

*Line 1 ______________________________

*Line 2 ______________________________

*City ______________ *State ______________

*PIN Code ______________ *ISO Country Code* ______________

*e-mail ID ______________

Phone ______________ Fax ______________

5. Name and address of the persons who have received the show cause notice, if any.

(In case of more than five persons, attach details of remaining persons in a separate sheet as an attachment)

Name

Address

*Line 1 ______________________________

*Line 2 ______________________________

*City ______________ *State ______________

*PIN Code ______________ *ISO Country Code* ______________

*e-mail ID ______________

Phone ______________ Fax ______________

6. *(i) Please indicate the Section of the Act under which offence has been committed:

*(ii) indicate the relevant penalty provisions of the Act

7. Whether the offence has been made good as on date of application, if applicable.

Yes [ ] No [ ]

If yes, the date of making the default good.

8. Copy of the latest statement of assets and liabilities attached.

Yes [ ]

Attachments

1. *Copy of detailed application
2. Copy of authority to make the application on behalf of the LLP
3. Copy of authority to make the application on behalf of other persons
4. Optional attachment.

VERIFICATION

To the best of my knowledge and belief, the information given in this Form and its attachments is correct and complete.

I have gone through the provisions of the Limited Liability Partnership Act, 2008 and the rules framed there under.

I have been authorized to sign and submit this application on behalf of the

(name of persons on whose behalf application is made)

To be digitally signed by the designated partner or

Authorized representative

DPIN

Date Place

Modify Check form Pre-scrutiny Submit

....

For office use only

Digital signature of the authorizing officer

This e-form is hereby approved

This e-form is hereby rejected

ANNEXURE 'A'

1. For registration of Limited Liability Partnership including conversion of a firm or a private company or an unlisted public company into Limited Liability Partnership:

(a)	Limited Liability Partnership whose contribution does not exceed Rs. 1 lakh	Rs. 500/-
(b)	Limited Liability Partnership whose contribution exceeds Rs. 1 lakh but does not exceed Rs. 5 lakhs	Rs. 2000/-
(c)	Limited Liability Partnership whose contribution exceeds Rs. 5 lakhs but does not exceed Rs. 10 lakhs	Rs. 4000/-
(d)	Limited Liability Partnership whose contribution exceeds Rs. 10 lakh	Rs. 5000/-

2. The difference between the fees payable on the increased slab of contribution and the fees paid on the preceding slab of contribution shall be paid through Form 3.

3.For filing, registering or recording any document, form, statement, notice, Statement of Accounts and Solvency, annual return and an application alongwith the Statement for conversion of a firm or a private company or an unlisted public company into LLP by this Act or by these rules required or authorized to be filed, registered or recorded:

(a)	Limited Liability Partnership whose contribution does not exceed Rs. 1 lakh	Rs. 50/-
(b)	Limited Liability Partnership whose contribution exceeds Rs. 1 lakh but does not exceed Rs. 5 lakhs	Rs. 100/-
(c)	Limited Liability Partnership whose contribution exceeds Rs. 5 lakhs but does not exceed Rs. 10 lakhs	Rs. 150/-
(d)	Limited Liability Partnership whose contribution exceeds Rs. 10 lakh	Rs. 200/-

4. Fee for any application other than application for conversion of a firm or a private company or an unlisted public company into LLP shall be as under:-

(a)	An application for reservation of name u/s 16	Rs. 200/-
(b)	An application for direction to change the name	Rs. 10000/-
(c)	Application for reservation of name under Rule 18(3)	Rs. 10,000/-
(d)	Application for renewal of name under rule 18(3)	Rs. 5000/-
(e)	Application for obtaining DPIN under rule 10(5)	Rs.100/-

5. Fee for inspection of documents or for obtaining certified copy thereof shall be as under:-

(a)	For inspection of documents of an LLP under section 36	Rs. 50/-
(b)	For Copy or extract of any document under section 36 to be certified by Registrar	Rs. 5/- per page or fractional part thereof

6. Fee for filing any form or a Statement of Account and Solvency or a notice or a document by foreign limited liability partnership

(a)	For filing a document under rule 34(1)	Rs. 5000/-
(b)	Any other form or Statement of Account and Solvency or notice or document	Rs. 1000/-

ANNEXURE 'B'
No.

No. (1)	NAME OF DOCUMENT (2)	PERIOD OF PRESERVATION (3)
1.	Incorporation document [Section 11(1)(b)]	Permanent
2.	Notice of situation of registered office [Section 13]	Permanent
3.	Information with regard to Limited Liability Partnership Agreement or any changes made therein [Section 23(2)]	Permanent
4.	Notice of other address of any limited liability partnership at which documents to be served [Section 13(2)]	Permanent

ANNEXURE 'C'

No. (1)	NAME OF DOCUMENT (2)	PERIOD OF PRESERVATION (3)
1.	Statement of compliance with requirements of the Act by an Advocate or Company Secretary or Chartered Accountant or Cost Accountant in whole-time practice and by any person who subscribed his name to the incorporation document [Section 11(1)(c)]	5 years
2.	Notice of a person ceasing to be a partner and any change in the name or address of a partner	5 years
3.	Registered documents relating to LLP struck off under Section 75 together with correspondence or copy of the order of restoration of the LLP into the register	5 years
4.	Annual return of a limited liability partnership	5 years
5.	Consent of candidates to act as designated partner to be filed with the Registrar [section 7(4)]	5 years
6.	Consent to act as a partner	5 years
7.	Statement by all the partners of firm containing particulars of firm along with application for its conversion into limited liability partnership	5 years
8.	Statement by all the shareholders containing particulars of private company/unlisted public company along with application for its conversion into limited liability partnership	5 years
9.	Certified copy of the order(s) of the Tribunal under section 60/61/62.	5 years
10.	Copy of the order of dissolution of a LLP by Tribunal [Section 63]	5 years
11.	Statement of Account and Solvency	8 years

ANNEXURE 'D'

PARTICULARS OF DOCUMENTS RELATING TO LIMITED LIABILITY PARTNERSHIP

PART I

Name Of Limited Liability Partnership	Act Under Which Registered	Date On Which Finally Dissolved Or Wound Up Or Struck Off	Description Of Documents Destroyed	Date And Mode Of Destruction With Remarks
(1)	(2)	(3)	(4)	(5)

Particulars of documents other than those specified in Part I

PART II

No. Of The File Of Documents Destroyed	Subject To Which The Document Refers	Description Of Documents Destroyed	Date And Mode Of Destruction With Remarks
(1)	(2)	(3)	(4)

❑❑❑

5

Sugar Special Excise Duty Act, 1959

AN ACT to provide for the imposition of a special duty of excise on certain sugar.

Be it enacted by Parliament in the Tenth Year of the Republic of India as follows: -

1. Short title and commencement.

(1) This Act may be called the Sugar (Special Excise Duty) Act, 1959.

(2) It shall be deemed to have come into force on the 25th day of October, 1959.

2. Definitions. In this Act, unless the context otherwise requires, -

(a) "Central Excises Act" means the Central Excise Act, 1944;

(b) "factory" means any premises, including the precincts thereof, wherein or in any part of which sugar, is being manufactured, or wherein or in any part of which, any manufacturing process connected with the production of sugar is being carried on or is ordinarily carried on, and includes any premises wherein sugar in respect of which the duty of excise payable under the Central Excises Act or the Additional Duties of Excise (Goods of Special Importance) Act, 1957 has not been paid, is stored;

(c) "sugar" means any form of sugar, whether wholly or partially manufactured, but does not include -

(i) khandsari sugar, that is to say, sugar in the manufacture of which neither a vacuum pan nor a vacuum evaporator is employed; or

(ii) palmyra sugar, that is to say sugar, manufactured from jaggery obtained by boiling the juice of the palmyra palm.

3. Imposition of special additional duty on certain sugar.

(1) There shall be levied and collected in respect of that quantity of sugar removed from any factory on or after the commencement of this Act as is

equivalent to the quantity of sugar lying in stock on such commencement within the precincts of the factory, a special duty of excise at the rate of rupees two and fifty-two naye paise per cwt.

(2) The duty of excise referred to in sub-section (1) shall be in addition to the duties of excise chargeable on sugar under the Central Excises Act or any other law for the time being in force.

(3) The provisions of the Central Excises Act and the rules thereunder, including those relating to refunds and exemptions from duty shall, so far as may be, apply in relation to the levy and collection of the special duty of excise referred to in sub-section (1) as they apply in relation to the levy and collection of the duties of excise on sugar under the Central Excises Act.

4. Effect of levy of duty on certain transactions. Where, in compliance with an order made with reference to clause (f) of sub-section (2) of Section 3 of the Essential Commodities Act, 1955 (10 of 1955), a person is required to sell any sugar, the price of the sugar so required to be sold shall, if he has paid the special duty of excise leviable under section 3 on such sugar, include an amount equivalent to the duty so paid, and he shall be entitled to be paid such amount by the buyer.

5. Repeal. The Sugar (Special Excise Duty) Ordinance, 1959 is repealed.

❑❑❑

6

Taxation on Income (Investigation Commission) Act, 1947

ACT NO. XXX OF 1947 [18TH APRIL, 1947]

AN ACT to provide for an investigation into matters relating to taxation on income.

WHEREAS it is expedient, for the purpose of ascertaining whether the actual incidence of taxation on income is and has been in recent years in accordance with the provisions of law, and the extent to which the existing law and procedure for the assessment and recovery of such taxation is adequate to prevent the evasion thereof, to make provision for an investigation to be made into such matters;

It is hereby enacted as follows:-

1. Short title, extent and commencement.

(1) This Act may be called the Taxation on Income (Investigation Commission) Act, 1947.

(2) It extends to the whole of British India.

(3) It shall come into force on such date as the Central Government may, by notification in the Official Gazette, appoint.

2. Interpretation. In this Act, "taxation on income" means any tax chargeable under the Indian Income-tax Act, 1922 (XI of 1922) or the Excess Profits Tax Act, 1940 (XV of 1940).

3. Constitution and functions of commission. The Central Government may constitute a Commission to be called the Income-tax Investigation Commission (hereinafter referred to as the Commission) whose duties it shall be -

(a) to investigate and report to the Central Government on all matters relating to taxation on income, with particular reference to the extent to which the existing law relating to, and procedure for, the assessment and collection of such taxation is adequate to prevent the evasion thereof;

(b) to investigate in accordance with the provisions of this Act any case referred to it under Section 5 and report thereon to the Central Government.

4. Composition of Commission.

(1) The Commission shall consist of a Chairman (being a person who is or has been a Judge of a High Court) and two other Commissioners, appointed by the Central Government.

(2) On the occurrence from any cause of a vacancy among the Commissioners, the Central Government may, if it thinks fit, appoint a person to fill the vacancy.

5. Power of Central Government to refer cases for investigation.

(1) The Central Government may, at any time before the 31st day of December, 1947, refer to the Commission for investigation and report any case in which the Central Government has *prima facie* reasons for believing that a person has to a substantial extent evaded payment of taxation on income, together with such material as may be available in support of such belief.

(2) If in the course of investigation into a case referred to it under sub-section (1), the Commission has reason to believe that some person other than the person whose case is being investigated has himself evaded payment of taxation on income, it may make a report to the Central Government stating its reasons for such belief, and on receipt of such report the Central Government may at any time refer the case of such other person to the Commission for investigation and report.

6. Powers of Commission.

(1) The Commission shall have power to administer oaths, and shall have all the powers of a Civil Court under the Code of Civil Procedure, 1908 (V of 1908), for the purposes of taking evidence on oath, enforcing the attendance of witnesses and of persons whose cases are being investigated, compelling the production of documents and issuing commissions for the examination of witnesses, and shall be deemed to be a Civil Court for all the purposes of Section 195 and Chapter XXXV of the Code of Criminal Procedure, 1898 (V of 1898); and any reference in the said Chapter to the presiding officer of a Court shall be deemed to include a reference to the Chairman of the Commission.

(2) If in the course of any investigation under this Act it appears to the Commission to be necessary to examine any accounts or documents which it cannot itself conveniently examine, the Commission may authorise any person qualified in its opinion to make such examination to examine the accounts or documents and interrogate for that purpose any person having charge or custody thereof and make a report thereon to the Commission; and any person having charge or custody of such accounts or documents shall be bound to produce them to

the person so authorised and to give to such person any information in respect thereof which the person so authorised may require.

(3) The Commissioners and all persons authorised by the commission under this Section shall be deemed to be public servants within the meaning of Section 21 of the Indian Penal Code (XLV of 1860).

7. Procedure of Commission.

(1) The Commission shall, subject to the provisions of this Act, have power to regulate its own procedure (including the fixing of places and times of its sittings and deciding whether to sit in public or in private) and may act notwithstanding a vacancy in the number of the Commissioners.

(2) In making an investigation under clause (b) of Section 3, the Commission shall act in accordance with the principles of natural justice, shall follow as far as practicable the principles of the Indian Evidence Act, 1872 (1 of 1872), and shall give the person whose case is being investigated a reasonable opportunity of rebutting any evidence adduced against him.

(3) Any person whose case is being investigated the Commission may be represented by a pleader duly authorised to act on his behalf.

(4) Except with the previous sanction of the Central Government,-

(a) no suit, prosecution or other legal proceeding shall be instituted against any person in any civil or criminal court for any evidence given by him in any proceedings before the Commission, and

(b) no evidence so given shall be admissible in evidence against such person in any suit, prosecution or other proceeding before such Court.

(5) No document shall be inadmissible in evidence in any proceedings before the Commission on the ground that it is not duly stamped or registered.

(6) Nothing in Section 54 of the Indian Income-tax Act, 1922 (XI of 1922) or in that Section as applied to excess profits tax by Section 21 of the Excess Profits Tax Act, 1940 (XV of 1940) shall apply to the disclosure of any of the particulars referred to therein in any proceeding before the Commission or in any report made by the Commission to the Central Government or in any report made to the Commission by a person authorised under sub-section (2) of Section 6.

8. Power to direct reopening of assessment proceedings.

(1) After considering any report made to it under clause (b) of Section 3, the Central Government may, by order in writing, direct that proceedings to assess in respect of the income of any period commencing after the 31st day of December, 1938 the person to whose case the report relates to income-tax, super-tax or excess profits tax shall be taken or reopened; and upon such a direction being made, such assessment proceedings may be taken and completed under the appropriate law, notwithstanding anything contained in Section 34 of the Indian Income-tax Act, 1922 (XI of 1922), or Section 15 of the Excess Profits Tax Act, 1940 (XV of 1940), or any other law, and notwithstanding any lapse of time.

(2) On a direction being made under sub-section (1), a copy of the report of the Commission so far as it relates to the case of the person concerned, shall be furnished to him.

(3) Notwithstanding anything to the contrary contained in any other law, in any proceedings directed to be taken under sub-section (1), any evidence in the case adduced before the Commission or a person authorised by it under sub-section (2) of Section 6 shall be admissible in evidence.

9. Bar of jurisdiction. No act or proceeding of the Commission or any person authoriced by it under sub-section (2) of Section 6 shall be called in question in any manner by any Court, and no suit, prosecution or other legal proceeding shall lie against the Crown or any Commissioner or any other person for anything in good faith done or intended to be done under this Act.

10. Power to make rules. The Central Government may, by notification in the Official Gazette, make rules for carrying out the purposes of this Act.

❑❑❑

7

The Agricultural Produce Cess Act, 1940

ACT NO. 27 OF 1940 [15TH APRIL, 1940]

AN ACT to make better financial provision for the Indian Council of Agricultural Research.

WHEREAS it is expedient to make better financial provision for the carrying out by the Indian Council of Agricultural Research of the objects for which it is established as set forth in the memorandum of Association of that body, and for this purpose to impose on certain articles a cess by way of customs duty on export, the proceeds of which shall be paid to the Council.

It is hereby enacted as follows —

1. Short title and commencement.

2. Definitions. In this Act, unless there is anything repugnant in the subject or context,— (8 of 1878) (19 of 1924)

(a) "Collector" means a customs-collector as defined in clause (c) of Section 3 of Sea customs Act, 1878, or a Collector of Land Customs as defined in clause (c) of Section 2 of the Land Customs Act, 1924, as the case may be, and

(b) "Council" means the Indian Council of Agricultural Research.

3. Imposition of cess.

(1) A customs duty at the rate of one-half of one per cent.ad valorem shall be levied on all article included in the Schedule which are exported from the territories to which this act extends;

PROVIDED that the said duty shall not be levied on articles proved to the satisfaction of the Collector not to have been produced in India.

(2) The Central Government may, by by notification in the Official Gazette, fix for the purposes of levying the said duty tariff values of any articles included in the Schedule, and may alter any tariff values for the time being in force.

4. Power to exclude articles from Schedule. The Central Government may after previous consultation with the council, by [1]notification in the Official Gazette, direct that any article specified in the Schedule shall cease to the subject to the duty imposed by Section 3, and thereupon, so long as the notification remains in force, that article shall deemed not to be included in the schedule.

5. Refund of, and exemption from cess. The Central Board of Revenue may make[1] rules providing, on such conditions as may be specified, in the rules, for —

(a) The refund of duty levied where articles are exported by land and subsequently imported into India, and

(b) The export by land, without payment of the duty of the articles, which are subsequently be imported into India.

6. Payment of Cess to Council and expenditure of Cess by Council.

(1) The proceeds of the levied under this Act reduced by the cost of collection as determined by the Central Government shall be paid to the council.

(2) The amount so due shall be paid by the Central Government to the Council at the intervals of not more than six months.

(3) The expenditure of the money so paid to the council shall be subject to such limitation as may be imposed by rules made in this behalf by the Central Government.

7. Standing Finance Committee.

(1) The Council shall constitute a Standing Finance Committee, of which one member shall be chosen among the representatives of the Central Legislature on the governing body of the council, and one member shall be an officer appointed by the Central Government.

(2) Subject to the provisions of the sub-section (1) the constitution, functions and procedure of the Standing Finance Committee shall be regulated in such manner as the Council may with the previous approval of the Central Government determine.

8. Reserve fund. The Council shall in accordance with the rules made in this behalf by the Central Government create and maintain a reserve fund.

9. Power of Central Government to make rules.

(1) Central Government may, after consultation with the council, by notification in the Official Gazette, make rules to carry out the purposes of the Act.

(2) In particular and without prejudice to the generality of the foregoing power, the Central Government may make rules regulating the expenditure of money paid to the council under Section 6 and providing for the creation, maintenance and management of the reserve fund referred to in Section 8.

(3) All rules made under this act shall be laid before Parliament as soon as may be after they are made.

THE SCHEDULE

[*See* Section 3]

1. BONES
2. BRISTLES
3. BUTTER
4. CEREALS, other than Rice and Wheat.
5. DRUGS
6. FIBRE for brushes.
7. FISH
8. FRUITS
9. GHEE
10. HIDES, raw.
11. MANURES
12. OILCAKES
13. PULSES
14. SEEDS
15. SKINS, raw.
16. SPICES
17. TOBACCO, unmanufactured
18. VEGETABLES
19. WHEAT
20. WHEAT FLOUR
21. WOOL, raw.

□□□

8

The Central Board of Direct Taxes (Validation of Proceedings) Act, 1971

ACT NO. 37 OF 1971 [14TH AUGUST 1971]

AN ACT to provide for validation of certain proceedings in relation to direct taxes and for matters connected therewith.

The objective of the Act is *to provide for validation of certain proceedings in relation to direct taxes.*

Be it enacted by Parliament in the twenty-second year of the Republic of India as follows:-

1. Short title. This Act may be called the Central Board of Direct Taxes (Validation of Proceedings) Act, 1971.

2. Validation of certain proceedings. Notwithstanding any judgement decree or order of any court, tribunal or any other authority no approval, declaration, determination, recognition, direction, instruction, notification, order or rule, or other thing or acting given, made, granted issued, done or taken or purporting to have been given, made granted, issued, done or taken by the Central Board of Direct Taxes, constituted under the Central Boards of Revenue Act, 1963 (54 of 1963) in the exercise of the powers or the performance of the duties entrusted to it by the Central Government or by or under nay law (not being the Estate Duty Act, 1953 (34 of 1953)) shall be deemed to be invalid or ever to have been invalid by reason only of the fact that such approval, declaration, determination, recognition, direction, instruction, notification, order rule, thing or action was given, made granted, issued, done or taken by the Chairman and other members of the said Board, either singly or jointly, without having been validly entrusted with the powers or duties in that behalf in accordance with the provisions of the aforesaid 1963- Act or the rules made thereunder and accordingly-

(a) all acts, proceedings or things done or taken in pursuance of such approval, declaration, determination, recognition, direction, instruction, notification, order rule, thing or action shall, for all purposes, be deemed to be, and to have always been, done or taken in accordance with law; and

(b) no suit or other proceeding shall be instituted or continued against the government or any person or authority whatsoever on the ground that any such act, proceeding or thing was not done or taken in accordance with law.

❑❑❑

9

The Central Boards of Revenue Act, 1963

Act No. 54 of 1963 [30th December, 1963]

AN ACT to provided to provide for the constitution of separate Boards of Revenue for Direct Taxes and for Excise and Customs and to amend certain enactments for the purpose of conferring powers and imposing duties on the said Boards.

Be it enacted by Parliament in the Fourteenth Year of the Republic of India as follows:-

1. Short title and commencement.

(1) This Act may be called the Central Boards of Revenue Act, 1963.

(2) It shall come into force on such date [1-1-1964; *vide* Notification No. S.O. 3606, dated 30-12-1964, Gazette of India, Extraordinary Pt. II, Sec. 3 (ii), p.897.] as the Central Government may, by notification in the Official Gazette, appoint.

2. Definitions. In this Act, unless the context otherwise requires,-

(a) "Board" means the Central Board of Direct Taxes or the Central Board of Excise and Customs constituted under Section 3;

(b) "Central Board of Revenue" means the Central Board of Revenue constituted under the Central Board of Revenue Act, 1924 (4 of 1924.);

(c) "direct tax" means-

(1) any duty leviable or tax chargeable under-

(i) the Estate Duty Act, 1953 (34 of 1953.);

(ii) the Wealth-tax Act, 1957 (27 of 1957.);

(iii) the Expenditure-tax Act, 1957 (29 of 1957.);

(iv) the Gift-tax Act, 1958 (18 of 1958.);

(v) the Income-tax Act, 1961 (43 of 1961);

(vi) the Super Profits Tax Act, 1963 (14 of 1963); and

(2) any other duty or tax which, having regard to its nature or incidence, may be declared by the Central Government, by notification in the Official Gazette, to be a direct tax.

3. Constitution of separate Central Boards for Direct Taxes and for Excise and Customs.

(1) The Central Government shall, in place of the Central Board of Revenue, constitute two separate Board of Revenue to be called the Central Board of direct Taxes and the Central Board of Excise and Customs, and each such Board shall, subject to the control of the Central Government, exercise such powers and perform such duties, as may be entrusted to that Board by the Central Government or by or under any law.

(2) Each Board shall consist of such number of persons not exceeding five as the Central Government may think fit to appoint.

4. Procedure of the Board.

(1) The Central Government may make rules for the purpose of regulating the transaction of business by each Board and every order made or act done in accordance with such rules shall be deemed to be the order or act, as the case may be, of the Board.

(2) Every rule made under this Section shall be laid as soon as may be after it is made before each House of Parliament while it is in session for a total period of thirty days which may be comprised in one session or in two successive sessions, and if, before the expiry of the session in which it is so laid or the session immediately following, both Houses agree in making any modification in the rule or both Houses agree that the rule should not be made, the rule shall thereafter have effect only in such modified form or be of no effect, as the case may be, so however, that any modification or annulment shall be without prejudice to the validity of anything previously done under that rule.

5. Amendment of certain enactments.

(1) In the Estate Duty Act, 1953, (34 of 1953), the Wealth-tax Act, 1957, (27 of 1957), the Expenditure-tax Act, 1957 (29 of 1957), the Gift-tax Act, 1958 (18 of 1958), the Income-tax Act 1961 (43 of 1961) and the Super Profits Tax Act, 1963 (14 of 1963) for the words and figures 'Central Board of Revenue constituted under the Central Board of Revenue Act 1924' (4 of 1924) or 'Central Board of Revenue', wherever they occur, the words and figures 'Central Board of Direct Taxes constituted under the Central Boards of Revenue Act, 1963' shall be substituted.

(2) In the Central Excises and Salt Act, 1944, (1 of 1944) and the Customs Act, 1962, (52 of 1962) for the words and figures "Central Board of Revenue constituted under the Central Board of Revenue Act, 1924", (4 of 1924) or "Central Board of Revenue" wherever they occur, the words and figures "Central

Board of Excise and Customs constituted under the Central Boards of Revenue Act, 1963" shall be substituted.

(3) The functions entrusted to the Central Board of Revenue by or under any other enactment shall,-

(a) if such functions relate to matters connected with direct taxes, be discharged by the Central Board of Direct Taxes; and

(b) if such functions relate to any other matter, unless they are entrusted by the Central Government to the Central Board of Direct Taxes, be discharged by the Central Board of Excise and Customs.

6. Transfer of certain proceedings.

(1) Every proceeding pending at the commencement of this Act, before the Central Board of Revenue shall-

(a) if it is a proceeding relating to direct taxes, stand transferred to the Central Board of Direct Taxes; and

(b) in any other case, stand transferred to the Central Board of Excise and Customs.

(2) If any question arises as to whether any proceeding stands transferred to the Central Board of Direct Taxes or to the Central Board of Excise and Customs, it shall be referred to the Central Government whose decision thereon shall be final.

(3) In any legal proceeding pending at the commencement of this Act to which the Central Board of Revenue is a party,-

(a) if it is a proceeding relating to direct taxes, the Central Board of Direct Taxes shall be deemed to be substituted for the Central Board of Revenue in such proceeding; and

(b) if it is a proceeding relating to any other matter, the Central Board of Excise and Customs shall be deemed to be substituted for the Central Board of Revenue in such proceeding.

7. Power to remove difficulties.

(1) If any difficulty arises in giving effect to the provisions of this Act, the Central Government may, by order published in the Official Gazette, make such provisions not inconsistent with the purposes of this Act, as appear to it to be necessary or expedient for removing the difficulty.

(2) An order under sub-section (1) may be made so as to have retrospective effect from a date not earlier than the date of the commencement of this Act.

8. Repeal and saving.

(1) The Central Board of Revenue Act, 1924, is hereby repealed (4 of 1924)

(2) Nothing contained in sub-section (1) shall affect any appointment, assessment, order (Including quasi-judicial order) or rule made, or exemption, approval or recognition granted, or any notice, notification, direction or instruction issued, or any duty levied, or penalty or fine imposed, or confiscation adjudged, or any

form prescribed, or any other thing done or action taken by the Central Board, of Revenue under any law and any such appointment, assessment, order, rule, exemption, approval, recognition, notice, notification, direction, instruction, duty, penalty fine, confiscation, form, thing or action shall be deemed to have been made, granted, issued, levied, imposed, adjudged, prescribed, done or taken by the Central Board of Direct Taxes, or as the case may be, by the Central Board of Excise and Customs and shall continue to be in force unless and until it is revised, withdrawn or superseded by the concerned Board.

□□□

10

The Central Excises and Salt Act, 1944

ACT NO. 1 OF 1944 [24TH FEBRUARY, 1944]

AN ACT to consolidate and amend the law relating to Central duties of excise and to salt.

WHEREAS it is expedient to consolidate and amend the law relating to Central duties of excise on goods manufactured or produced in certain parts of India and to salt.

It is hereby enacted as follows:-

CHAPTER - I

1. Short title extent and commencement.

(1) This Act may be called the Central Excises and Salt Act, 1944;

(2) It extends to the whole of India;

(3) It shall come into force on such date [1] as the Central Government may, by notification in the Official Gazette, appoint in this behalf.

2. Definitions. In this Act, unless there is anything repugnant in the subject or context,-

(a) [2]["adjudicating authority" means any authority competent to pass any order or decision under this Act, but does not include the Central Board of Excise and Customs constituted under the Central Boards of Revenue Act, 1963, (54 of 1963) Collector of Central Excise (Appeals) or Appellate Tribunal;

(aa) "Appellate Tribunal" means the Customs, Excise and Gold (Control) Appellate Tribunal constituted under Section 129 of the Customs Act, 1962] (52 of 1962);

(aaa) "broker" or" commission agent" means a person who in the ordinary course of business makes contracts for the sale or purchase of excisable goods for others;

(b) "Central Excise Officer" means any officer of the Central Excise Department, or any person (including an officer of the State Government) invested by the Central Board of Excise and Customs constituted under the Central Boards of Revenue Act, 1963 (54 of 1963) with any of the powers of a Central Excise Officer under this Act;

(c) "curing" includes wilting, drying, fermenting and any process for rendering an unmanufactured product fit for marketing or manufacture;

(d) "excisable goods" means goods specified in the Schedule to the Central Excise Tariff Act, 1985] as being subject to a duty of excise and includes salt (5 of 1986);

(e) " factory" means any premises, including the precincts thereof, wherein or in any part of which excisable goods other than salt are manufactured, or wherein or in any part of which any manufacturing process connected with the production of these goods is being carried on or is ordinarily carried on;

(ee) "Fund" means the Consumer Welfare Fund established under Section 12C;

(f) "manufacture" includes any process,-

(i) incidental or ancillary to the completion of a manufactured product;

(ii) which is specified in relation to any goods in the Section or Chapter notes of the Schedule to the Central Excise Tariff Act, 1985 as amounting to manufacture, (5 of 1986) and the word" manufacturer" shall be construed accordingly and shall include not only a person who employs hired labour in the production or manufacture of excisable, goods, but also any person who engages in their production or manufacture on his own account;

(g) "Prescribed" means prescribed by rules made under this Act;

(h) "sale" and "purchase", with their grammatical variations and cognate expressions, mean any transfer of the possession of goods by one person to another in the ordinary course of trade or business for cash or deferred payment or other valuable consideration;

(i) "saltpeter" includes rasi, sajji, and all other substances manufactured from saline earth, and kharinun and every form of sulphate or carbonate of soda;

(j) "salt factory" includes-

(i) a place used or intended to be used in the manufacture of salt and all embankments, reservoirs, condensing and evaporating pans, buildings and waste places situated within the limits of such place as defined from time to time by the Collector of Central Excise;

(ii) all drying grounds and storage platforms and storehouses appertaining to any such place;

(iii) land on which salt is spontaneously produced; and a "private salt factory" is one not solely owned or not solely worked by the Central Government;

(k) ' wholesale dealer" means a person who buys or sells excisable goods wholesale for the purpose of trade or manufacture, and includes a broker or commission agent who, in addition to making contracts for the sale or purchase of excisable goods for others, stocks such goods belonging to others as an agent for the purpose of sale.

CHAPTER - II : LEVY AND COLLECTION OF DUTY

3. Duties specified in the Schedule to the Central Excise Tariff Act, 1985 to be levied.

(1) There shall be levied and collected in such manner as may be prescribed duties of excise on all excisable goods other than salt which are produced or manufactured in [3][India] and a duty on salt manufactured in, or imported by land into, any part of India as, and at the rates, set forth in the Schedule to the Central Excise Tariff Act, 1985 (5 of 1986);

PROVIDED that the duties of excise which shall be levied and collected on any [4][excisable goods] which are produced or manufactured -

(i) in a free trade zone and brought to any other place in India; or

(ii) by a hundred per cent., export-oriented undertaking and allowed to be sold in India, shall be an amount equal to the aggregate of the duties of customs which would be leviable under Section 12 of the Customs Act, 1962 (52 of 1962) on like goods produced or manufactured outside India if imported into India, and where the said duties of customs are chargeable by reference to their value, the value of such excisable goods shall, notwithstanding anything contained in any other provision of this Act, be determined in accordance with the provisions of the Customs Act, 1962 and the Customs Tariff Act, 1975 (51 of 1975).

EXPLANATION 1. Where in respect of any such like goods, any duty of customs leviable under the said Section 12 is leviable at different rates, then, such duty shall, for the purposes of this proviso, be deemed to be leviable under the said Section 12 at the highest of those rates.

[5]*[EXPLANATION 2.* In this proviso,-

(i) " free trade zone" means the Kandla Free Trade Zone and the Santa Cruz Electronics Export Processing Zone and includes any other free trade zone which the Central Government may, by notification in the Official Gazette, specify in this behalf;

(ii) "hundred per cent. export-oriented undertaking" means an undertaking which has been approved as a hundred per cent. export-oriented undertaking by the Board appointed in this behalf by the Central Government in exercise of the powers conferred by Section 14 of the Industries (Development and Regulation) Act, 1951, (65 of 1951) and the rules made under that Act.

(1A) The provisions of sub-section (1) shall apply in respect of all excisable goods other than salt which are produced or manufactured in India by, or on behalf of, Government, as they apply in respect of goods which are not produced or manufactured by Government.

(2) The Central Government may, by notification in the Official Gazette, fix, for the purpose of levying the said duties, tariff values of any articles enumerated, either specifically or under general headings, in the Schedule to the Central Excise Tariff Act, 1985 (5 of 1986) as chargeable with duty *ad valorem* and may alter any tariff values for the time being in force.

(3) Different tariff values may be fixed-

(a) for different classes or descriptions of the same excisable goods; or

(b) for excisable goods of the same class or description-

(i) produced or manufactured by different classes of producers or manufacturers; or

(ii) sold to different classes of buyers: Provided that in fixing different tariff values in respect of excisable goods falling under sub-clause (i) or sub-clause (ii), regard shall be had to the sale prices charged by the different classes of producers or manufacturers or, as the case may be, the normal practice of the wholesale trade in such goods.

Emergency. power of Central Government to increase duties of excise. *Rep. by the Repealing and Amending Act, 1960 (58 of 1960), s. 2 and Sch. I.*

4. Valuation of excisable goods for purposes of charging of duty of excise.

(1) Where under this Act, the duty of excise is chargeable on any excisable goods with reference to value, such value shall, subject to the other provisions of this Section, be deemed to be-

(a) the normal price thereof, that is to say, the price at which such goods are ordinarily sold by the assessee to a buyer in the course of wholesale trade for delivery at the time and place of removal, where the buyer is not a related person and the price is the sole consideration for the sale:

Provided that -

(i) where, in accordance with the normal practice of the wholesale trade in such goods, such goods are sold by the assessee at different prices to different classes of buyers (not being related persons) each such price shall; subject to the existence of the other circumstances specified in clause (a), be deemed to be the normal price of such goods in relation to each such class of buyers;

(ii) where such goods are sold by the assessee in the course of wholesale trade for delivery at the time and place of removal at a price fixed under any law for the time being in force or at a price, being the maximum, fixed under any such law, then, notwithstanding anything contained in clause (iii) of this proviso, the price or the maximum price, as the case may be, so fixed, shall, in relation to the goods so sold, be deemed to be the normal price thereof;

(iii) where the assessee so arranges that the goods are generally not sold by him in the course of wholesale trade except to or through a related person, the normal price of the goods sold by the assessee to or through such related person shall be deemed to be

the price at which they are ordinarily sold by the related person in the course of wholesale trade at the time of removal, to dealers (not being related persons) or where such goods are not sold to such dealers, to dealers (being related persons) who sell such goods in retail;

(b) where the normal price of such goods is not ascertainable for the reason that such goods are not sold or for any other reason, the nearest ascertainable equivalent thereof determined in such manner as may be prescribed.

(2) Where, in relation to any excisable goods the price thereof for delivery at the Place of removal is not known and the value thereof is determined with reference to the price for delivery at a place other than the place of removal, the cost of transportation from the place of removal to the place of delivery shall be excluded from such price.

(3) The provisions of this Section shall not apply in respect of any excisable goods for which a tariff value has been fixed under sub-section (2) of Section 3.

(4) For the purposes of this Section,-

(a) "assessee" means the person who is liable to pay the duty of excise under this Act and includes his agent;

(b) "place of removal" means-

(i) a factory or any other place or premises of production or manufacture of the excisable goods; or

(ii) a warehouse or any other place or premises wherein the excisable goods have been permitted to be deposited without payment of duty, from where such goods are removed;

(c) " related person" means a person who is so associated with the assessee that they have interest, directly or indirectly, in the business of each other and includes a holding company, a subsidiary company, a relative and a distributor of the assessee, and any sub-distributor of such distributor.

EXPLANATION: In this clause "holding company", "subsidiary company" and "relative" have the same meanings as in the Companies Act, 1956 (1 of 1956);

(d) "value", in relation to any excisable goods,-

(i) where the goods are delivered at the time of removal in a packed condition, includes the cost of such packing except the cost of the packing which is of a durable nature and is returnable by the buyer to the assessee.

EXPLANATION: In this sub-clause, "packing" means the wrapper, container, bobbin, pirn, spool, reel or warp beam or any other thing in which or on which the excisable goods are wrapped, contained or wound;

(ii) does not include the amount of the duty of excise, sales tax and other taxes, if any, payable on such goods and, subject to such rules as may be made, the trade discount (such discount not being refundable on any account whatsoever) allowed in accordance with the normal practice of the wholesale trade at the time of removal in respect of such goods sold or contracted for sale.

[6][*EXPLANATION:* For the purposes of this sub-clause, the amount of the duty of excise payable on any excisable goods shall be the sum total of-

(a) the effective duty of excise payable on such goods under this Act; and

(b) the aggregate of the effective duties of excise payable under other Central Acts, if any, providing for the levy of duties of excise on such goods, and the effective duty of excise on such goods under each Act referred to in clause (a) or clause (b) shall be -

(i) in a case where a notification or order providing for any exemption (not being an exemption for giving credit with respect to, [7][or reduction of duty of excise under such Act on such goods equal to, any duty of excise under such Act, or the additional duty under Section 3 of the Customs Tariff Act, 1975, (51 of 1975) already paid] on the raw material or component parts used in the production or manufacture of such goods) from the duty of excise under such Act is for the time being in force, the duty of excise computed with reference to the rate specified in such Act in respect of such goods as reduced so as to give full and complete effect to such exemption; and

(ii) in any other case, the duty of excise computed with reference to the rate specified in such Act in respect of such goods;

(e) "wholesale trade" means sales to dealers, industrial consumers Government, local authorities and other buyers, who or which purchase their requirements otherwise than in retail.]

5. [8][Remission of duty on goods found deficient in quantity.

(1) The Central Government may, by rules made under this Section, provide for remission of duty of excise leviable on any excisable goods which due to any natural cause are found to be deficient in quantity.

(2) Any rules made under sub-section (1) may, having regard to the nature of the excisable goods or of processing or of curing thereof, the period of their storage or transit and other relevant considerations, fix the limit or limits of percentage beyond which no such remission shall be allowed:

PROVIDED that different limit or limits of percentage may be fixed for different varieties of the same excisable goods or for different areas or for different seasons.]

5A. Power to grant exemption from duty of excise.

(1) If the Central Government is satisfied that it is necessary in the public interest so to do, it may, by notification in the Official Gazette, exempt generally either absolutely or subject to such conditions (to be fulfilled before or after removal) as may be specified in the notification, excisable goods of any specified description from the whole or any part of the duty of excise leviable thereon:

PROVIDED that, unless specifically provided in such notification, no exemption. therein shall apply to excisable goods which are produced or manufactured -

(i) in a free trade zone and brought to any other place in India; or

(ii) by a hundred per cent. export-oriented undertaking and allowed to be sold in India.

EXPLANATION. In this proviso, "free trade zone" and "hundred per cent export-oriented undertaking" shall have the same meanings as in Explanation 2 to sub-section (1) of Section 3.

(2) If the Central Government is satisfied that it is necessary in the public interest so to do, it may, by special order in each case, exempt from the payment of duty of' excise, under circumstances of an exceptional nature to be stated in such order, any excisable goods on which duty of excise is leviable.

(3) An exemption under sub-section (1) or sub-section (2) in respect of any excisable goods from any part of the duty of excise leviable thereon (the duty of excise leviable thereon being hereinafter referred to as the statutory duty) may be granted by providing for the levy of a duty on such goods at a rate expressed in a form or method' different from the form or method in which the statutory duty is leviable and any exemption granted in relation to any excisable goods in th manner provided in this sub-section shall have effect subject to the condition that the duty of excise chargeable on such goods shall in no case exceed the statutory duty.

EXPLANATION: "Form or method", in relation to a rate of duty of excise means. the basis, namely, valuation, weight, number, length, area, volume or other measure with reference to which the duty is leviable.

(4) Every notification issued under sub-rule (1), and every order made under sub-rule (2), of Rule 8 of the Central Excise Rules, 1944, and in force immediately before the commencement of the Customs and Central Excises Laws (Amendment) Act, 1987 shall be deemed to have been issued or made under the provisions of this Section and shall continue to have the same force and effect after such commencement until it is amended, varied rescinded or superseded under the provisions of this Section.

6. Registration of certain persons. Any prescribed person who is engaged in -

(a) the production or manufacture or any process of production or manufacture of any specified goods included in the Schedule to the Central Excise Tariff Act, 1985, or

(b) the wholesale purchase or sale (whether on his own account or as a broker or commission agent) or the storage of any specified goods included in the Schedule to the Central Excise Tariff Act, 1985, shall get himself registered with the proper officer in such manner as may be prescribed.

7. * * * *

8. Restriction on possession of goods specified in the Second Schedule. From such date as may be specified in this behalf by the Central Government by notification in the Official Gazette, no person shall, except as provided by rules made under this Act, have in his possession [9][any goods specified in the Second Schedule in excess of such quantity as may be prescribed for the purposes of this Section as the maximum amount of such goods or of any variety of such goods which may be possessed at any one time by such a person.

9. Offences and penalties.

(1) Whoever commits any of the following offences, namely.-

(a) contravenes any of the provisions of Section 8 or of a rule made under clause (iii) or clause (xxvii) of sub-section (2) of Section 37;

(b) evades the payment of any duty payable under this Act;

(bb) removes any excisable goods in contravention of any of the provisions of this Act or any rule made thereunder or in any way concerns himself with such removal;

(bbb) acquires possession of, or in any way concerns himself in transporting, depositing, keeping, concealing, selling or purchasing, or in any other manner deals with, any excisable goods which he knows or has reason to believe are liable to confiscation under this Act or any rule made thereunder,

(c) fails to supply any information which he is required by rules made under this Act to supply, or (unless with a reasonable belief, the burden of proving which shall be upon him, that the information supplied by him is true) supplies false information;

(d) attempts to commit, or abets the commission of, any of the offences mentioned in clauses (a) and (b) of this Section; shall be punishable,-

(i) in the case of an offence relating to any excisable goods, the duty leviable thereon under this Act exceeds one lakh of rupees, with imprisonment for a term which may extend to seven years and with fine:

PROVIDED that in the absence of special and adequate reasons to the contrary to be recorded in the judgment of the Court such imprisonment shall not be for a term of less than six months;

(ii) in any other case, with imprisonment for a term which may extend to three years or with fine or with both.

(2) If any person convicted of an offence under this Section is again convicted of an offence under this Section, then, he shall be punishable for the second and for every subsequent offence with imprisonment for a term which may extend to seven years and with fine:

PROVIDED that in the absence of special and adequate reasons to the contrary to be recorded in the judgment of the Court such imprisonment shall not be for a term of less than six months.

(3) For the purposes of sub-sections (1) and (2), the following shall not be considered as special and adequate reasons for awarding a sentence of imprisonment for a term of less than six months, namely:-

(i) the fact that the accused has been convicted for the first time for an offence under this Act;

(ii) the fact that in any proceeding under this Act, other than a prosecution, the accused has been ordered to pay a penalty or the goods in relation to such proceedings have been ordered to be confiscated or any other action has been taken against him for the same act which constitutes the offence;

(iii) the fact that the accused was not the principal offender and was acting merely as a carrier of goods or otherwise was a secondary party in the commission of the offence;

(iv) the age of the accused.

9A. Certain offences to be non-cognisable. Notwithstanding anything contained in the Code of Criminal Procedure, 1898 (5 of 1898) offences under Section 9 shall be deemed to be non-cognisable within the meaning of that Code.

9AA. Offences by companies.

(1) Where an offence under this Act has been committed by a company, every person who at the time the offence was committed was in charge of, and was responsible to, the company for the conduct of the business of the company, as well as the company, shall be deemed to be guilty of the offence and shall be liable to be proceeded against and punished accordingly:

PROVIDED that nothing contained in this sub-section shall render any such person liable to any punishment provided in this Act, if be proves that the offence was committed without his knowledge or that he had exercised all due diligence to prevent the commission of such offence.

(2) Notwithstanding anything contained in sub-section (1), where an offence under this Act has been committed by a company and it is proved that the offence has been committed with the consent or connivance of, or is attributable to any neglect on the part of, any director, manager, secretary or other officer of the company, such director, manager, secretary or other officer shall also be deemed to be guilty of that offence and shall be liable to be proceeded against and punished accordingly.

EXPLANATION: For the purposes of this Section -

(a) "company" means any body corporate and' includes a firm or other association of individuals; and

(b) "director" in relation to a firm means a partner in the firm.]

9B. Power of Court to publish name, place of business etc., of persons convicted under the Act.

(1) Where any person is convicted under this Act for contravention of any of the provisions thereof, it shall be competent for the Court convicting the person to cause the name and place of business or residence of such person, nature of the contravention, the fact that the person has been so convicted and such other particulars as the Court may consider to be appropriate in the circumstances of the case, to be published at the expense of such person, in such newspapers or in such manner as the Court may direct.

(2) No publication under sub-section (1) shall be made until the period for preferring an appeal against the orders of the Court has expired without any appeal having been preferred, or such an appeal, having been preferred, has been disposed of.

(3) The expenses of any publication under sub-section (1) shall be recoverable from the convicted person as if it were a fine imposed by the Court.

9C. Presumption of culpable mental state.

(1) In any prosecution for an offence under this Act which requires a culpable mental state on the part of the accused, the Court shall presume the existence of such mental state but it shall be a defence for the accused to prove the fact that he had no such mental state with respect to the act charged as an offence in that prosecution.

EXPLANATION: In this Section, "culpable mental state" includes intention motive, knowledge of a fact, and belief in, or reason to believe, a fact.

(2) For the purposes of this Section, a fact is said to be proved only when the Court believes it to exist beyond reasonable doubt and not merely when its existence is established by a preponderance of probability.

9D. Relevancy of statements under certain circumstances.

(1) A statement made arid signed by a person before any Central Excise Officer of a gazetted rank during the course of any inquiry or proceeding under this Act shall be relevant, for the purpose of proving, in any prosecution for an offence under this Act, the truth of the facts which it contains,-

(a) when the person who made the statement is dead or cannot be found, or is incapable of giving evidence, or is kept out of the way by the adverse party, or whose presence cannot be obtained without an amount of delay or expense which, under the circumstances of the case, the Court considers unreasonable; or

(b) when the person who made the statement is examined as a witness in the case before the Court and the Court is of opinion that, having regard to the circumstances of the case, the statement should be admitted in evidence in the interests of justice.

(2) The provisions of sub-section (1) shall, so far as may be, apply in relation to any proceedings under this Act, other than a proceeding before a Court, as they apply in relation to a proceeding before a Court.

9E. Application of Section 562 of the Code of Criminal Procedure, 1898, and of the Probation of offenders Act, 1958.

(1) Nothing contained in Section 562 of the Code of Criminal Procedure 1898 (5 of 1898) or in the Probation of Offenders Act, 1958 (20 of 1958) shall apply to a person convicted of an offence under this Act unless that person is under eighteen years of age.

(2) The provisions of sub-section (1) shall have effect notwithstanding anything contained in sub-section (3) of Section 9.

10. Power of Courts to order forfeiture. Any Court trying an offence under this Chapter may order the forfeiture to Government of any goods in respect of which the Court is satisfied that an offence under this Chapter has been committed, and may also order the forfeiture of any receptacles, packages or coverings in which such goods are contained and the animals, vehicles, vessels or other conveyances, used in carrying the goods and any implements or machinery used in the manufacture of the goods.

11. Recovery of sums due to Government. In respect of duty and any other sums of any kind payable to the Central Government under any of the provisions of this Act or of the rules made thereunder, the officer empowered by the Central Board of Excise and Customs constituted under the Central Boards of Revenue Act, 1963 (54 of 1963) to levy such duty or require the payment of such sums may deduct the amount so payable from any money owing to the person from whom such sums may be recoverable or due which may be in his hands or under his disposal or control, or may recover the amount by attachment and sale of excisable goods belonging to such person; and if the amount payable is not so recovered he may prepare a certificate signed by him specifying the amount due from the person liable to pay the same and send it to the Collector of the district in which such person resides or conducts his business and the said Collector, on receipt of such certificate, shall proceed to recover from the said person the amount specified therein as if it were an arrear of land revenue.

11A. Recovery of duties not levied or not paid or short levied or short paid or erroneously refunded.

(1) When any duty of excise has not been levied or paid or has been short-levied or short-paid or erroneously refunded, a Central Excise Officer may, within six months from the relevant date, serve notice on the person chargeable with the duty which has not been levied or paid or which has been short-levied or short-paid or to whom the refund has erroneously been made, requiring him to show cause why he should not pay the amount specified in the notice (54 of 1963):

PROVIDED that where any duty of excise has not been levied or paid or has been short-levied or short-paid or erroneously refunded by reason of fraud, collusion or any wilful misstatement or suppression of facts, or contravention of any of the provisions of this Act or of the rules made thereunder with intent to evade payment of duty, by such person or his agent, the provisions of this sub-section shall have effect, as if (5 xxx), for the words "six months", the words "five years" were substituted.

EXPLANATION. Where the service of the notice is stayed by an order of a Court, the period of such stay shall be excluded in computing the aforesaid period of six months or five years, as the case may be.

(2) The Central Excise Officer shall, after considering the representation, if any, made by the person on whom notice is served under sub-section (1), determine the amount of duty of excise due from such person (not being in excess of the amount specified in the notice) and thereupon such person shall pay the amount so determined.

(3) For the purposes of this Section-

(i) " refund" includes rebate of duty of excise on excisable goods exported out of India or on excisable materials used in the manufacture of goods which are exported out of India;

(ii) " relevant date" means,.-

(a) in the case of excisable goods on which duty of excise has not been levied or paid or has been short-levied or short-paid-

(A) where under the rules made under this Act a monthly return, showing particulars of the duty paid on the excisable goods removed during the month to which the said return relates, is to be filed by a manufacturer or producer or a licensee of a warehouse, as the case may be, the date on which such return is so filed;

(B) where no monthly return as aforesaid is filed, the last date on which such return is to be filed under the said rules;

(C) in any other case, the date on which the duty is to be paid under this Act or the rules made thereunder;

(b) in a case where duty of excise is provisionally assessed under this Act or the rules made thereunder, the date of adjustment of duty after the final assessment thereof;

(c) in the case of excisable goods on which duty of excise has been erroneously refunded, the date of such refund.

11B. Claim for refund of duty.

(1) Any person claiming refund of any duty of excise may make an application for refund of such duty to the Assistant Collector of Central Excise before the expiry of six months from the relevant date in such form as may be prescribed and the application shall be accompanied by such documentary or other evidence (including the documents referred to in Section 12A) as the applicant may furnish to establish that the amount of duty of excise in relation to which such refund is claimed was collected from, or paid by, him and the incidence of such duty had not been passed on by him to any other person:

PROVIDED that where an application for refund has been made before the commencement of the Central Excises and Customs Laws (Amendment) Act, 1991, such application shall be deemed to have been made under this sub-section as amended by the said Act and the same shall be dealt with in accordance with the provisions of sub-section (2) as substituted by that Act:

PROVIDED FURTHER that the limitation of six months shall not apply where any duty has been paid under protest.

(2) if, on receipt of any such application, the Assistant Collector of Central Excise is satisfied that the whole or any part of the duty of excise paid by the applicant is refundable, he may make an order accordingly and the amount so determined shall be credited to the Fund:

PROVIDED that the amount of duty of excise as determined by the Assistant Collector of Central Excise under the foregoing provisions of this sub-section shall, instead of being credited to the Fund, be paid to the applicant, if such amount is, relatable to—

(a) rebate of duty of excise on excisable goods exported out of India or, on excisable materials used in the manufacture of goods which are exported out of India;

(b) unspent advance deposits lying in balance in the applicant's account current maintained with the Collector of Central Excise;

(c) refund of credit of duty paid on excisable goods used as inputs in accordance with the rules made, or any notifica-tion issued, under this Act;

(d) the duty of excise paid by the manufacturer, if he had not passed on the incidence of such duty to any other person;

(e) the duty of excise borne by the buyer, if he had not passed on the incidence of such duty to any other person;

(f) the duty of excise borne by any other such class of applicants as the Central Government may, by notification in the Official Gazette, specify:

PROVIDED FURTHER that no notification under clause (f) of the first proviso shall be issued unless in the opinion of the Central Government the incidence of duty has not been passed on by the persons concerned to any other person.

(3) Notwithstanding anything to the contrary contained in any judgment, decree, order or direction of the Appellate Tribunal or any Court or in any other provision of this Act or the rules made thereunder or any other law for the time being in force, no refund shall be made except as provided in sub-section (2).

(4) Every notification under clause (f) of the first proviso to sub-section (2) shall be laid before each House of Parliament, if it is sitting, as soon as may be after the issue of the notification, and, if it is not sitting, within seven days of its reassembly, and the Central Government shall seek the approval of Parliament to the notification by a resolution moved within a period of fifteen days beginning with the day on which the notification is so laid before the House of the People and if Parliament makes any modification in the notification or directs that

the notification should cease to have effect, the notification shall thereafter have effect only in such modified form or be of no effect, as the case may be, but without prejudice to the validity of anything previously done thereunder.

(5) For the removal of doubts, it is hereby declared that any notification issued under clause (f) of the first proviso to sub-section (2), including any such notification approved or modified under sub-section (4), may be rescinded by the Central Government at any time by notification in the Official Gazette."

EXPLANATION: For the purposes of this Section,-

(A) "refund" includes rebate of duty of excise on excisable goods exported out of India or on excisable materials used in the manufacture of goods which are exported out of India;

(B) "relevant date" means,-

(a) in the case of goods exported out of India where a refund of excise duty paid is available in respect of the goods themselves or, as the case may be, the excisable materials used in the manufacture of such goods -

(i) if the goods are exported by sea or air, the date on which the ship or the aircraft in which such goods are loaded, leaves India, or

(ii) if the goods are exported by land, the date on which such goods pass the frontier, or

(iii) if the goals arc exported by post, the date of despatch of goods by the Post Office concerned to a place outside India;

(b) in the case of goods returned for being remade, refined, reconditioned, or subjected to any other similar process, in any factory, the date of entry into the factory for the purposes aforesaid;

(c) in the case of goods to which banderols are required to be affixed if removed for home consumption but not so required when exported outside India, if returned to a factory after having been removed from such factory for export out of India, the date of entry into the factory;

(d) in a, case where a manufacturer is required to pay a sum, for a certain period, on the basis of the rate fixed by the Central Government by notification in the Official Gazette in full discharge of his liability for the duty leviable on his production of certain goods, if after the manufacturer has made the payment on the basis of such rate for any period but before the expiry of that period such rate is reduced, the date of such reduction;

(e) in the case of a person, other than the manufacturer, the date of purchase of the goods by such person;"

(f) in any other case, the date of payment of duty.

11C. Power not to recover duty of excise not levied or short-levied as a result of general practice.

(1) Notwithstanding anything contained in this Act, if the Central Government is satisfied-

(a) that a practice was, or is, generally prevalent regarding levy of duty of excise (including non-levy thereof)on any excisable goods; and

(b) that such goods were, or are, liable-

(i) to duty of excise, in cases where according to the said practice the duty was not, or is not being, levied, or

(ii) to a higher amount of duty of excise than what was, or is being, levied, according to the said practice, then, the Central Government may, by notification in the Official Gazette, direct that the whole of the duty of excise payable on such goods, or, as the case may be, the duty of excise in excess of that payable on such goods, but for the said practice, shall not be required to be paid in respect of the goods on which the duty of excise was not, or is not being, levied, or was, or is being, short-levied, in accordance with the said practice.

(2) Where any notification under sub-section (1) in respect of any goods has been issued, the whole of the duty of excise paid on such goods or, as the case may be, the duty of excise paid in excess of that payable on such goods, which would not have been paid if the said notification had been in force, shall be dealt with in accordance in force, shall be dealt with in accordance with the provisions of sub-section (2) of Section 11B:

Provided that the person claiming the refund of such duty or, as the case may be, excess duty, makes an application in this behalf to the Assistant Collector of Central Excise, in expiry of six months in sub-section (1) of Section 11B, before the expiry of six months from the date of issue of the said notification."

11D. Duties of excise collected from the buyer to be deposited with the Central Government.

(1) Notwithstanding anything to the contrary contained in any order or direction of the Appellate Tribunal or any Court or in any other provision of this Act or the rules made thereunder, every person who has collected any amount from the buyer of any goods in any manner as representing duty of excise, shall forthwith pay the amount so collected to the credit of the Central Government.

(2) The amount paid to the credit of the Central Government under sub-section (1) shall be adjusted against the duty of excise payable by the person on finalisation of assessment and where any surplus is left after such adjustment, the amount of such surplus shall either be credited to the Fund or, as the case may be, refunded to the person who has borne the incidence of such amount, in accordance with the provisions of Section 11B and the relevant date for making an application under that Section in such cases shall be the date of the public notice to be issued by the Assistant Collector of Central Excise.

12. Application of the provisions of Act 8 of 1878 to Central excise duties. The Central Government may, by notification in the Official Gazette, declare that any of the provisions of the Sea Customs Act, 1878, relating to the levy of and exemption from customs duties, drawback of duty, warehousing, offences and penalties, confiscation, and procedure relating to offences and appeals shall, with such modifications and alterations as it may consider necessary or desirable to adapt them to the circumstances, be applicable in regard to like matters in respect of the duties imposed by Section 3.

CHAPTER -IIA : INDICATING AMOUNT OF DUTY IN THE PRICE OF GOODS, ETC., FOR PURPOSE OF REFUND AND CREDITING CERTAIN AMOUNTS TO THE FUND

12A. Price of goods to indicate the amount of duty paid thereon. Notwithstanding anything contained in this Act or any other law for the time being in force, every person who is liable to pay duty of excise on any goods shall, at the time of clearance of the goods, prominently indicate in all the documents relating to assessment, sales invoice, and other like documents, the amount of such duty which will form part of the price at which such goods are to be sold.

12B. Presumption that incidence of duty has been passed on to the buyer. Ever person who has paid the duty of excise on any goods under this Act shall, unless the, contrary is proved by him, be deemed to have passed on the full incidence of such duty to the buyer of such goods.

12C. Consumer Welfare Fund.

(1) There shall be established by the Central Government a fund, to be called the Consumer Welfare Fund.

(2) There shall be credited to the Fund, in such manner as may be prescribed,—

(a) the amount of duty of excise referred to in sub-section (2) of Section 11B or sub-section (2) of Section 11C or sub-section (2) of Section 11D;

(b) the amount of duty of customs referred to in sub-section (2) of Section 27 or sub-section (2) of Section 28A, or sub-section (2) of Section 28B of the Customs Act, 1962 ;

(c) any income from investment of the amount credited to the Fund and any other monies received by the Central Government for the purposes of this Fund.

12D. Utilisation of the Fund.

(1) Any money credited to the Fund shall be utilised by the Central Government for the welfare of the consumers in accordance with such rules as that Government may make in this behalf.

(2) The Central Government shall maintain or, if it thinks fit, specify the authority which shall maintain, proper and separate ac-count and other relevant records in relation to the Fund in such form as may be prescribed in consultation with the Comptroller and Auditor-General of India."

CHAPTER -III : POWERS AND DUTIES OF OFFICERS AND LANDHOLDERS

12E. Powers of Central Excise Officers.

(1) A Central Excise Officer may exercise the powers and discharge the duties conferred or imposed under this Act on any other Central Excise Officer who is subordinate to him.

(2) Notwithstanding anything contained in sub-section (1), the Collector of Central Excise (Appeals) shall not exercise the powers and discharge the duties conferred or imposed on a Central Excise Officer other than those specified in Section 14 or Chapter VIA.

13. Power to arrest.

(1) Any Central Excise Officer duly empowered by the Central Government in this behalf may arrest any person whom he has reason to believe to be liable to punishment under this Act.

(2) Any person accused or reasonably suspected' of committing an offence under this Act or any rules made thereunder, who on demand of any officer duly empowered by the, Central Government in this behalf refuses to give his name and residence, or who gives a name or residence which such officer has reason to believe to be false, may be arrested by such officer in order that his name and residence may be ascertained.

14. Power to summon persons to give evidence and produce documents in inquiries under this Act.

(1) Any Central Excise Officer duly empowered by the Central Government in this behalf shall have power to summon any person whose attendance he considers necessary either to give evidence or to produce a document or any other thing in any inquiry which such officer is making for any of the purposes of this Act. A summons to produce documents or other things may be for the production of certain specified documents or things or for the production of all documents or things of a certain description in the possession or under the control of the person summoned.

(2) All persons so summoned shall be bound to attend, either in person or by an authorised agent, as such officer may, direct; and all persons so summoned shall be bound to state the truth upon any subject respecting which they are examined or make statements and to produce such documents and other things as may be required:

PROVIDED that the exemptions under Sections 132 and 133 of the Code of Civil Procedure shall be applicable to requisitions for attendance under this Section (5 of 1980).

(3) Every such inquiry as aforesaid shall be deemed to be a "judicial proceeding" within the meaning of Section 193 and Section 228 of the Indian Penal Code (45 of 1860).

15. Officers required to assist Central Excise Officers. All officers of Police and Customs and all officers of Government engaged in the collection of land revenue, and all village officers are hereby empowered and required to assist the Central Excise Officers in the execution of this Act.

16. Owners or occupiers of land to report manufacture of contraband excisable goods. Every owner or occupier of land, and the agent of any such owner or occupier, in charge of the management of that land, if contraband excisable goods are manufactured thereon, shall in the absence of reasonable excuse be bound to give notice of such manufacture to a Magistrate, or to an officer of the Central Excise, Customs, Police, or Land Revenue Department, immediately the fact comes to his knowledge.

17. Punishment or connivance at offences. Any owner or occupier of land, or any agent of such owner or occupier in charge of the management of that land, who wilfully connives at any offence against the provisions of this Act or of any rules made thereunder shall for every such offence be punishable with imprisonment for a term which may extend to six months, or with fine which may extend to five hundred rupees, or with both.

18. Searches and arrests how to be made. All searches made under this Act or any rules' made thereunder and all arrests made under this Act shall be carried out in accordance with the provisions of the Code of Criminal Procedure, 1898, relating respectively to' searches and arrests made under that Code (5 of 1898).

19. Disposal of persons arrested. Every person arrested under this Act shall be forwarded without delay to the nearest Central Excise Officer empowered to send persons so arrested to a Magistrate, or, if there is no such Central Excise Officer within a reasonable distance,-to the officer-in-charge of the nearest police-station.

20. Procedure to be followed by officer-in-charge of police station. The officer-in-charge of a police-station to whom any person is forwarded under Section 19 shall either admit him to bail to appear before the Magistrate having jurisdiction, or in default of bail forward him in custody to such Magistrate.

21. Inquiry how to be made by Central Excise Officers against arrested persons forwarded to them under Section 19.

(1) When any person is forwarded under Section 19 to a Central Excise Officer empowered to send persons so arrested to a Magistrate, the Central Excise Officer shall proceed to inquire into the charge against him.

(2) For this purpose the Central Excise Officer may exercise the same powers and shall be subject to the same provisions as the officer-in-charge of a police-station may exercise and is subject to under the Code of Criminal Procedure, 1898, when investigating a cognizable case (5 of 1898) :

Provided that-

(a) if the Central Excise Officer is of opinion that there is sufficient evidence or reasonable ground of suspicion against the accused person, he shall either admit him to bail to appear before a Magistrate having jurisdiction in the case, or forward him in custody to such Magistrate;

(b) if it appears to the Central Excise Officer that there is not sufficient evidence or reasonable ground of suspicion against the accused person, he shall release the accused person on his executing a bond, with or without sureties as the Central Excise Officer may

direct, to appear, if and when so required before the Magistrate having jurisdiction, and shall make a full report of all the particulars of the case to his official superior.

22. Vexatious search, seizure, etc., by Central Excise Officer. Any Central Excise or other officer exercising powers under this Act or under the rules made thereunder who-

(a) without reasonable ground of suspicion searches or causes to be searched any house, boat or place;

(b) vexatiously and unnecessarily detains, searches or arrests any person;

(c) vexatiously and unnecessarily seizes the movable property of any person, on pretence of seizing or searching for any article liable to confiscation under this Act;

(d) commits, as such officer, any other act to the injury of any person, without having reason to believe that such act is required for the execution of his duty; shall, for every such offence, be punishable with fine which may extend to two thousand rupees. Any person wilfully and maliciously giving false information and so causing an arrest or a search to be made under this Act shall be punishable with fine which may extend to two thousand rupees or with imprisonment for a term which may extend to two years or with both.

23. Failure of Central Excise Officer in duty. Any Central Excise Officer who ceases or refuses to perform or withdraws himself from the duties of his office, unless he has obtained the express written permission of the Collector of Central Excise, or has given to his superior officer two months' notice in writing of his intention or has other lawful excuse, shall on conviction before a Magistrate be punishable with imprisonment for a term which may extend to three months or with fine which may extend to three months' pay, or with both.

CHAPTER -IV : TRANSPORT BY SEA

24. Penalties for carrying excisable goods in certain vessels. When any excisable goods are carried by sea in any vessel other than a vessel of the burden of three hundred tons and upwards, the owner and master of such vessel shall each be punishable with imprisonment for a term which may extend to six months, or with fine which may extend to one thousand rupees, or with both.

25. Exceptions. Nothing in Section 24 applies to -

(a) any excisable goods covered bv a permit granted under rules made under this Act;

(b) any excisable goods covered by a pass granted by any officer whom the Central Board of Excise and Customs constituted under the Central Boards of Revenue Act, 1963 may appoint in this behalf; (54 of 1963)

(c) such amount of excisable goods carried on board any vessel for consumption by her crew or by the passengers or animals (if any) on board as the Central Board of Excise and Customs constituted under the Central Boards of Revenue Act, 1963 may from time to time exempt from the operation of Section 24 (54 of 1963).

26. Power of stoppage, search and arrest. When any officer-empowered by the Central Board of Excise and Customs constituted under the Central Boards of Revenue Act, 1963, (54 of 1963) to act Under this Section has reason to believe, from personal knowledge or from information taken down in writing, that any excisable goods are being carried, or have within the previous twenty-four hours been carried, in any vessel so as to render the owner or master of such vessel liable to the penalties imposed by Section 24, he may require such vessel to be brought-to and thereupon may-

(a) enter and search the vessel;

(b) require the master of the vessel to produce any documents in his possession relating to the vessel or the cargo thereof;

(c) seize the vessel if the officer has reason to believe it liable to confiscation under this Act, and cause it to be brought with its crew and cargo into any port in India; and

(d) where any excisable goods are found on board the vessel, search and arrest without a warrant any person on board the vessel whom he has reason to believe to be punishable under Section 24.

27. Penalties for resisting officer. Any master of a vessel refusing or neglecting to bring-to the vessel or to produce his papers when required to do so by an officer acting under Section 26, and any person obstructing any such officer in the performance of his duty, may be arrested by such officer without a warrant, and shall be punishable with imprisonment for a term which may extend to six months or with fine which may extend to one thousand rupees, or with both.

28. Confiscation of vessel and cargo.

(1) Every vessel (including all appurtenances) in which any excisable goods are carried so as to render the owner or master of such vessel liable to penalties imposed by Section 24, the cargo on board such vessel and the excisable goods in respect of which an offence under this Act has been committed shall be liable to confiscation on the orders of the officer empowered in this behalf by the Central Government.

(2) Whenever any Customs Officer is satisfied that any article is liable to confiscation under this Section he may seize such article, and shall at once report the seizure to his superior officer for the information of the officer empowered to order confiscation under sub-section (1) and such officer may, if satisfied on such report or after making such inquiry as he thinks fit, that the article so seized is liable, to confiscation, either declare it to be confiscated, or impose a fine in lieu thereof not exceeding the value of the article.

29. Jurisdiction. Any offence punishable under Section 24 or Section 27 may be deemed to have been committed within the limits of the jurisdiction of the Magistrate of any place where the offender is found, or to which, if arrested under Section 26 or Section 27, he may be brought.

30. Power to exempt from operation of his Chapter. The Central Government may, by notification in the Official Gazette, exempt the carriage of excisable goods within any local limits or in any class of vessels from the operation of this Chapter, and, by like notification, again subject such carriage to the operation of this Chapter.

CHAPTER -V : SPECIAL PROVISIONS RELATING TO SALT

31. Special and permanent rights of manufacturing salt to be recognised. The proprietor of a private salt factory who has by virtue of a sanad granted by the Government or any former Government, a special and permanent right to manufacture salt, or to excavate or collect natural salt, shall on application made in accordance with the rules made under this Act be entitled to a licence for such purpose and to the annual renewal thereof, unless on a breach of the provisions of this Act, his licence has been cancelled by an officer duly empowered by the Central Government in this behalf.

32. Rights of ordinary proprietors of existing salt-works. Every proprietor of a private salt-work, other than a private salt factory, to which Section 31 applies, of which, under the provisions of Section 17 of the Bombay Salt Act, 1890, (Bom. Act 11 of 1890) the proprietor was entitled on application to a licence to manufacture or to excavate or collect natural salt at such factory, shall continue to be entitled, on, application made in accordance with the rules made under this Act, to a licence for such purpose and to the annual renewal thereof, unless on a breach of the provisions of this Act his licence has been cancelled by an officer duly empowered by the Central Government in this behalf:

PROVIDED that the Collector of Central Excise may at any time withdraw or withhold a licence from the proprietor of any such salt factory, if no salt has been manufactured, excavated or collected in such salt factory for the three years ending on the thirtieth day of June last preceding the date of his order, or, with the previous sanction of the Central Board of Excise and Customs constituted under the Central Boards of Revenue Act, 1963, (54 of 1963) if such salt factory has not produced, on an average, during the said three years, at least five thousand maunds. of salt per annum.

CHAPTER -VI : ADJUDICATION OF CONFISCATIONS AND PENALTIES

33. Power of adjudication. Where by the rules made under this Act anything is liable to confiscation or any person is liable to a penalty, such confiscation or penalty may be adjudged-

(a) without limit, by a Collector of Central Excise;

(b) up to confiscation of goods not exceeding five hundred rupees in value and imposition of penalty not exceeding two hundred and fifty rupees, by an Assistant Collector of Central Excise:

PROVIDED that the Central Board of Excise and Customs constituted under the Central Boards of Revenue Act, 1963 (54 of 1963) may, in the case of any officer performing the duties of an Assistant Collector of Central Excise, reduce the limits indicated in clause (b) of this Section and may confer on any officer the powers indicated in clause (a) or (b) of this Section.

34. Option to pay fine in lieu of confiscation. Wherever confiscation is adjudged under this Act or the rules made thereunder, the officer adjudging it shall give the owner of the goods an option to pay in lieu of confiscation such fine as the officer thinks fit.

34A. Confiscation or penalty not to interfere with other punishments. No confiscation made or penalty imposed under the provisions, of this Act or of any rule made thereunder shall prevent the infliction of any other punishment to which the person affected thereby is liable under the provisions of this Act or under any other law.

CHAPTER -VIA : APPEALS

35. Appeals to Collector (Appeals).

(1) Any person aggrieved by any decision or order passed under this Act by a Central Excise Officer lower in rank than a Collector, of Central Excise may appeal to the Collector of Central, Excise (Appeals)[hereafter in this Chapter referred to as the Collector (Appeals)] within three months from the date of the communication to him of such decision or order:

PROVIDED that the Collector (Appeals) may, if he is satisfied that the appellant was prevented by sufficient cause from presenting the appeal within the aforesaid period of three months, allow it to be presented within a further period of three months.

(2) Every appeal under this Section shall be in the prescribed form and shall be verified in the prescribed manner.

35A. Procedure in appeal.

(1) The Collector (Appeals) shall give an opportunity to the appellant to be heard, if he so desires.

(2) The Collector (Appeals) may, at the hearing of an appeal, allow an appellant to go into any ground of appeal not specified in the grounds of appeal, if the Collector (Appeals) is satisfied that the omission of that ground from the grounds of appeal was not wilful or unreasonable.

(3) The Collector (Appeals), may, after making such further inquiry as may be necessary, pass such order as he thinks fit confirming, modifying or annulling the decision or order appealed against, or may refer the case back to the adjudicating authority with such directions as he may think fit for a fresh adjudication or decision, as the case may be, after taking additional evidence, if necessary:

PROVIDED that an order enhancing any penalty or fine in lieu of confiscation or confiscating goods of greater value or reducing the amount of refund shall not be passed unless the appellant has been given a reasonable opportunity of showing cause against the proposed order:

PROVIDED FURTHER that where the Collector (Appeals) is of opinion that any duty of excise has not been levied or paid or has been short-levied or short-paid or erroneously refunded, no order requiring the appellant to pay any duty not levied or paid, short-levied or short-paid or erroneously refunded shall be passed unless the appellant is given notice within the time limit specified in Section 11 A to show cause against the proposed order.

(4) The order of the Collector (Appeals) disposing of the appeal shall be in writing and shall state the points for determination the decision thereon and the reasons for the decision.

(5) On the disposal of the appeal, the Collector (Appeals) shall communicate the order passed by him to the appellant, the adjudicating authority and the Collector of Central Excise.

35B. Appeals to the Appellate Tribunal.

(1) Any person aggrieved by any of the following orders may appeal to the Appellate Tribunal against such order-

(a) a decision or order passed by the Collector of Central Excise as an adjudicating authority;

(b) an order passed by the Collector (Appeals) under Section 35A;

(c) an order passed by the Central Board of Excise and Customs constituted under the Central Boards of Revenue Act, 1963 (54 of 1963) (hereafter in this Chapter referred to as the Board) or the Appellate Collector of Central Excise under Section 35, as it stood immediately before the appointed day;

(d) an order passed by the Board or the Collector of Central Excise, either before or after the appointed day, under Section 35A, as it stood immediately before that day:

PROVIDED that no appeal shall lie to the Appellate Tribunal and the Appellate Tribunal shall not have jurisdiction to decide any appeal in respect' of any order referred to in clause (b) if such order relates to -

(a) a case of loss of goods, where the loss occurs in transit from a factory to a warehouse or to another factory, or from one warehouse to another, or during the course of processing of the goods in a warehouse or in storage, whether in a factory or in a warehouse;

(b) a rebate of duty of excise on goods exported to any country or territory outside India or on excisable materials used in the manufacture of goods which are exported to any country or territory outside India;

(c) goods exported outside India (except to Nepal or Bhutan) without payment of duty.

PROVIDED FURTHER that the Appellate Tribunal may, in its discretion, refuse, to admit an appeal in respect of an order referred to in clause (b) or clause (c) or clause (d) where-

(i) in any disputed case, other than a case where the determination of any question having a relation to the rate of duty of excise or to the value, of goods for purposes of assessment is in issue or is one of the points in issue, the difference in duty involved or the duty involved; or

(ii) the amount of fine or penalty determined by such order, does not exceed fifty thousand rupees.

(1A) Every appeal against any order of the nature referred to in the first proviso to sub-section (1), which is pending immediately before the commencement of Section 47 of the Finance Act, 1984 (21 of 1984), before the Appellate Tribunal and any matter arising out of, or connected with, such appeal and which is so pending shall stand transferred on such commencement to the Central Government, and the Central Government shall deal with such appeal or matter under Section 35EE as if such appeal or matter were an application or a matter arising out of' an application made to it under that Section.

(2) The Collector of Central Excise may, if he is of opinion that an order passed by the Appellate Collector of Central Excise tinder Section 35, as it stood immediately before the appointed day, or the Collector (Appeals) under Section 35A, is not legal or proper, direct any Central Excise Officer authorised by him in this behalf (hereafter in this Chapter referred to as the authorised officer) to appeal on his behalf to the Appellate Tribunal against such order.

(3) Every appeal under this Section shall be filed within three months from the date on which the order sought to be appealed against is communicate to the Collector of Central Excise, or, as the case may be, the other party preferring the appeal.

(4) On receipt of notice that an appeal has been preferred under this Section, the party against whom the appeal has been preferred may, notwithstanding that. he may not have appealed against such order or any part thereof, file, within forty-five days of the receipt of the notice, a memorandum of cross objections verified in the prescribed manner against any part of the order appealed against and such memorandum shall be disposed of by the Appellate Tribunal as if it were an appeal, presented within the time specified in sub-section (3).

(5) The Appellate Tribunal may admit an appeal or permit the filing of a memorandum of cross-objections after the expiry of the relevant period referred to in sub-section (3) or sub-section (4), if it is satisfied that there was sufficient cause for not presenting it within that period.

(6) An appeal to the Appellate Tribunal shall be in the prescribed form and shall be verified in the prescribed manner and shall, in the case of an appeal made on or after the 1st day of June, 1993, irrespective of the date of demand of duty or of levy of penalty in relation to which the appeal is made, be accompanied by a fee of,-

   (a) where the amount of duty demanded and penalty levied by any Central Excise Officer in the case to which the appeal relates is one lakh rupees or less, two hundred rupees:

   (b) where the amount of duty demanded and penalty levied by any Central Excise Officer in the case to which the appeal relates is more than one lakh rupees, one thousand rupees:

   PROVIDED that no such fee shall be payable in the case of an appeal referred to in sub-section (2) or a memorandum of cross-objections referred to in sub-section (4)."

35C. Orders of Appellate Tribunal.

(1) The Appellate Tribunal may, after giving the parties to the appeal an opportunity of being, heard, pass such orders thereon as it thinks fit, confirming, modifying

or annulling the decision or order appealed against or may refer the case back to the authority which passed such decision or order with such directions as the Appellate Tribunal may think fit, for a fresh adjudication or decision, as the case may be, after taking additional evidence, if necessary.

(2) The Appellate Tribunal may, At any time within four years from the date of the order, with a view to rectifying any mistake apparent from the record, amend any order passed by it under sub-section (1) and shall make such amendments if the mistake is brought to its notice by the Collector of Central Excise or thc other party to the appeal:

PROVIDED that an amendment which has the effect of enhancing an assessment or reducing a refund or otherwise increasing the liability of the other party, shall not be made under this sub-section, unless the Appellate Tribunal has given notice to him of its intention to do so and has allowed him a reasonable opportunity of being heard.

(3) The Appellate Tribunal shall send a copy of every order passed under this Section to the Collector of Central Excise and the other party to the appeal.

(4) Save as provided in Section 35G or Section 35L, orders passed by the Appellate Tribunal on appeal shall be final.

35D. Procedure of Appellate Tribunal.

(1) The provisions of sub-sections (1), (2), (5) and (6) of Section 129C of the Customs Act, 1962, shall apply to the Appellate Tribunal in the discharge of its functions under this Act as they apply to it in the discharge of its functions under the Customs Act, 1962 (52 of 1962).

(2) Every appeal against a decision or order relating, among other things, to the determination of any question having a relation to the rate of duty of excise or to the value of goods for purposes of assessment, shall be heard by a Special Bench constituted by the President for hearings such appeals and such Bench shall consist of not less than [two members] and shall include at least one judicial member and one technical member.

(3) The President or any other member of the Appellate Tribunal authorised in this behalf by the President may, sitting singly, dispose of any case which has been allotted to the Bench of which he is a member where-

   (a) in any disputed case, other than a case where the determination of any question having a relation to the rate of duty of excise or to the value of goods for purposes of assessment is in issue or is one of the points in issue, the difference in duty involved or the duty involved; or

   (b) the amount of fine or penalty involved, does not exceed one lakh rupees

35E. Powers of Board or Collector of Central Excise to pass certain orders.

(1) The Board may, of its own motion, call for and examine the record of any proceeding in which a Collector of Central Excise as an adjudicating authority has passed any decision or order under this Act for the purpose of satisfying itself as to the legality or propriety of any such decision or order and may, by order, direct such Collector to' apply to the, Appellate Tribunal or, as the case

may be, the Customs and Excise Revenues Appellate Tribunal established under Section 3 of the Customs and Excise Revenues Appellate Tribunal Act, 1986 (62 of 1986) for the determination of such points arising out of the decision or order as may be specified by the Board in its order.

(2) The Collector of Central Excise may, of his own motion, call for and examine the record of any proceeding in which an adjudicating authority subordinate to him has passed any decision or order under this Act for the purpose of satisfying himself as to the legality or propriety of any such decision or order and may, by order, direct such authority to apply to the Collector (Appeals) for the determination of such points arising' out of the decision or order as may be specified by the Collector of Central Excise in his order.

(3) No order shall be made under sub-section (1) or sub-section (2) after the expiry of one year from the date of the decision or order of the adjudicating authority.

(4) Where in pursuance of an order under sub-section (1) or sub-section the adjudicating authority or the authorised officer makes an application to the Appellate Tribunal or, as the case may be, the Customs and Excise Revenues Appellate Tribunal established under Section 3 of the Customs and Excise Revenues Appellate Tribunal Act, 1986] (62 of 1986) or the Collector (Appeals) within a period of three months from the date of communication of the order under sub-section (1) or sub-section (2) to the adjudicating authority, such application shall be heard by the Appellate Tribunal or, as the case may be, the Customs and Excise Revenues Appellate Tribunal established under Section 3 of the Customs and Excise Revenues Appellate Tribunal Act, 1986 or the Collector (Appeals), as the case may be, as if such application were an appeal made against the decision or order of the adjudicating authority and the provisions of this Act regarding appeals, including the provisions of sub-section (4) of Section 35B or, as the case may be the provisions of the Customs and Excise Revenues Appellate Tribunal Act, 1986 shall, so far as may be, apply to such application.

(5) The provisions of this Section shall not apply to any decision or order in which the determination of any question having a relation to the rate of duty of excise or to the value of goods for the purposes of assessment of any duty is in issue or is one of the points in issue.

EXPLANATION. For the purposes of this sub-section, the determi-nation of a rate of duty in relation to any goods or valuation of any goods for the purposes of assessment of duty includes the determination of a question-

(a) relating to the rate of duty of excise for the time being in force, whether under the Central Excise Tariff Act, 1985 or under any other Central Act providing for the levy and collection of any duty of excise, in relation to any goods on or after the 28th day of February, 1986 ; or

(b) relating to the value of goods for the purposes of assessment of any duty of excise in cases where the assessment is made on or after the 28th day of February, 1986 ; or

(c) whether any goods are excisable goods or whether the rate of duty of excise on any goods is nil; or

(d) whether any goods fall under a particular heading or sub-heading of the Schedule to the Central Excise Tariff Act, 1985 (5 of 1986), or the Additional Duties of Excise (Goods of Special Importance) Act, 1957 (58 of 1957) or the Additional Duties of Excise (Textiles and Textile Articles) Act, 1978 (40 of 1978), or that any goods are or not covered by a particular notification or order issued by the Central Government or the Board, as the case may be, granting total or partial exemption from duty; or

(e) whether the value of any goods for the purposes of assessment of duty of excise shall be enhanced or reduced by the addition or reduction of the amounts in respect of such matters as are specifically provided in this Act.]

35EA. Powers of revision of Board or Collector of Central Excise in certain cases.

(1) The Board may, of its own motion or on the application of any aggrieved person or otherwise, call for and examine the record of any proceeding in which a Collector of Central Excise has passed any decision or order not being a decision or order passed under sub-section (2) of this Section of the nature referred to in sub-section (5) of Section 35E for the purpose of satisfying itself as to correctness, legality or propriety of such decision or order and may pass such order thereon as it thinks fit.

(2) The Collector of Central Excise may, of his own motion or on the application of any aggrieved person or otherwise, call for and examine the record of any proceeding in which an adjudicating authority subordinate to him has passed any decision or order of the nature referred to in sub-section (5) of Section 35E for the purpose of satisfying himself as to the correctness, legality or propriety of such decision or order and may pass such order thereon as he thinks fit.

(3) (a) No decision or order under this Section shall be made so as to prejudicially affect any person unless such person is given a reasonable opportunity of making representation and if, he so desires, of being heard in his defence.

(b) Where the Board or, as the case may be, the Collector of Central Excise is of the opinion that any duty of excise has not been levied or has been short-levied or short-paid or erroneously refunded, no order requiring the affected person to pay any duty not levied or paid, short-levied or short-paid or erroneously refunded shall be passed under this Section unless such person is given notice within the time limit specified in Section 11A to show cause against the proposed order.

(4) No proceedings shall be initiated under sub-section (1) or sub-section (2) in respect of any decision or order after the expiry of a period of six months from the date of communication of such decision or order:

PROVIDED that in respect of any decision or order passed before the commencement of the Customs and Central Excises Laws (Amendment) Act, 1987, the provisions of this sub-

section shall have effect as if for the words "six months", the words "one year" were substituted.

(5) Any person aggrieved by any decision or order passed under sub-section (1) or sub-section (2) may appeal to the Customs and Excise Revenues Appellate Tribunal established under Section 3 the Customs and Excise Revenues Appellate Tribunal Act, 1986, against such decision or order."

35EE. Revision by Central Government.

(1) The Central Government may, on the application of any person aggrieved by any order passed under Section 35A, where the order is of the nature referred to in the first proviso to, sub-section (1) of Section 35B, annul or modify such order.

EXPLANATION. For the purposes of this sub-section, "order passed under Section 35A" includes an order passed under that Section before the commencement of Section 47 of the Finance Act, 1984 (21 of 1984) against which an appeal has not been preferred before such commencement and could have been if the said Section had not come into force, preferred after such commencement, to the Appellate Tribunal.

(2) An application under sub-section (1) shall be made within three months from the date of the communication to the applicant of the order against which the application is being made:

PROVIDED that the Central Government may, if it is satisfied that the applicant was prevented by sufficient cause from presenting the application within the. aforesaid period of three months, allow it to be presented within a further period of three months.

(3) An application under sub-section (1) shall be in such form and shall be verified in such manner as may be specified by rules made in this behalf and shall be accompanied by a fee of two hundred rupees.

(4) The Central Government may, of its own motion, annul or modify any order referred to in sub-section (1).

(5) No order enhancing any penalty or fine in lieu of confiscation or confiscating goods of greater value shall be passed under this Section,-

(a) in any case, in which an order passed under Section 35A has enhanced any penalty or fine in lieu of confiscation or has confiscated goods of greater value, and

(b) in any other case, unless the person affected by the proposed order has been given notice to show cause against it within one year from the date of the order sought to be annulled or modified.

(6) Where the Central Government is of opinion that any duty of excise has not been levied or has been short-levied, no order levying or enhancing the duty shall be made under this Section unless the person affected by the proposed order is given notice to show cause against it within the time limit specified in Section 11A.

35F. Deposit, pending appeal of duty demanded or penalty levied. Where in any appeal under this Chapter, the decision or order appealed against relates to any duty demanded in respect of goods which are not under the control of central excise authorities or any penalty levied under this Act, the person desirous of appealing against such decision or order shall, pending the appeal, deposit with the adjudicating authority the duty demanded or the penalty levied:

PROVIDED that where in any particular case, the Collector (Appeals) or the Appellate Tribunal is of opinion that the deposit of duty demanded or penalty levied would cause undue hardship to such person, the Collector (Appeals) or, as the case may be, the Appellate Tribunal, may dispense with such deposit subject to such conditions as he or it may deem fit to impose so as to safeguard the interests of revenue.

35G. Statement of case to High Court.

(1) The Collector of Central Excise or the other party may, within sixty days of the date upon which he is served with notice of an order under Section 35C (not being an order relating, among other things, to the determination of any question having a relation to the rate of duty of excise or to the value of goods for purposes of assessment), by application in the prescribed form, accompanied, where the application is made by the other party, by a fee of two hundred rupees, require the Appellate Tribunal to refer to the High Court any question of law arising out of such order and, subject to the other provisions contained in this Section, the Appellate Tribunal shall, within one hundred and twenty days of the receipt of such application, draw up a statement of the case and refer it to the High Court:

PROVIDED that the Appellate Tribunal may, if it is satisfied that the applicant was prevented by sufficient cause from presenting the application within the period hereinbefore specified, allow it to be presented within a further period not exceeding thirty days.

(2) On receipt of notice that an application has been made under sub-section (1), the person against whom such application has been made, may, notwithstanding that he may not have filed such an application, file, within forty-five days of the receipt of the notice, a memorandum of cross-objections verified in the prescribed manner against any part of the order in relation to which an application for reference has been made and such memorandum shall be disposed of by the Appellate Tribunal as if it were an application presented within the time specified in sub-section (1).

(3) If, on an application made under sub-section (1), the Appellate Tribunal refuses to state the case on the ground that no question of law arises, the Collector of Central Excise, or, as the case may be, the other party may, within six months from the date on which he is served with notice of such refusal, apply to the High Court and the High Court may, if it is not satisfied with the correctness of the decision of the Appellate Tribunal, require the Appellate Tribunal to state the case and to refer it, and on receipt of any such requisition, the Appellate Tribunal shall state the case and refer it accordingly.

(4) Where in the exercise of its powers under sub-section (3), the Appellate Tribunal refuses to state a case which it has been required by an applicant to state, the applicant may, within thirty days from the date on which he receives notice of

such refusal, withdraw his application and, if he does so, the fee, if any, paid by him shall be refunded.

35H. Statement of case to Supreme court in certain cases. If, on an application made under Section 35G, the Appellate Tribunal is of opinion that, on account of conflict in the decisions of High Courts in respect of any particular question of law, it is expedient that a reference should be made direct to the Supreme Court, the Appellate Tribunal may draw up a statement of the case and refer it through the President direct to the Supreme Court.

35I. Power of High Court or Supreme Court to require statement to be amended. If the High Court or the Supreme Court is not satisfied that the statements in a case referred to it are sufficient to enable it to determine the questions raised thereby, the Court may refer the case back to the Appellate Tribunal, for the purpose of making such additions thereto or alterations therein as it may direct in that behalf.

35J. Case before High Court to be heard by not less than two Judges.

(1) When any case has been referred to the High Court under Section 35G, it shall be heard by a Bench of not less than two Judges of the High Court and shall be decided in accordance with the opinion of such Judges or of the majority, if any, of such Judges.

(2) Where there is no such majority, the Judges shall state the point of law upon which they differ and the case shall then be heard upon that point only by one or more of the other Judges of the High Court, and such point shall be decided according to the opinion of the majority of the Judges who have heard the case including those who first heard it.

35K. Decision of High Court or Supreme Court on the case stated.

(1) The High Court or the Supreme Court hearing any such case shall decide the questions of law raised therein and shall deliver its judgment thereon containing the grounds on which such decision is founded and a copy of the judgment shall be sent under the seal of the Court and the signature of the Registrar to the Appellate Tribunal which shall pass such orders as are necessary to dispose of the case in conformity with such judgment.

(2) The costs of any reference to the High Court or the Supreme Court which shall not include the fee for making the reference shall be in the discretion of the Court.

35L. Appeal to Supreme Court. An appeal shall lie to the Supreme Court from-

(a) any judgment of the High Court delivered on a reference made under Section 35G in any case which, on its own motion or on an oral application made by or on behalf of the party aggrieved, immediately after the passing of the judgment, the High Court certifies to be a fit one for appeal to the Supreme Court; or

(b) any order passed by the Appellate Tribunal relating, among other things, to the determination of any question having a relation to the rate of duty of excise or to the value of goods for purposes of assessment.

35M. Hearing before Supreme Court.

(1) The provisions of the Code of Civil Procedure, 1908 1, (5 of 1908) relating to appeals to the Supreme Court shall, so far as may be, apply in the case of appeals under Section 35L a, they apply in the case of appeals from decrees of a High Court:

PROVIDED that nothing in this sub-section shall be deemed to affect the provisions of sub-section (1) of Section 35K or Section 35N.

(2) The costs of the appeal shall be in the discretion of the Supreme Court.

(3) Where the judgment of the High Court is varied or reversed in the appeal, effect shall be given to the order of the Supreme Court in the manner provided in Section 35K in the case of a judgment of the High Court.

35N. Sums due to be paid notwithstanding reference, etc. Notwithstanding that a reference has been made to the High Court or the Supreme Court or an appeal has been preferred to the Supreme Court, sums due to the Government as a result of ail order passed under sub-section (1) of Section 35C shall be payable in accordance with the order so passed.

35O. Exclusion of time taken for copy. In computing the period of limitation prescribed for an appeal or application under this Chapter, the day on which the order complained of was served, and if the party preferring the appeal or making the application was not furnished with a copy of the order when the notice of the order was served upon him, the time requisite for obtaining a copy of such order shall be excluded.

35P. Transfer of certain pending proceedings and transitional provisions.

(1) Every appeal which is pending immediately before the appointed day before the Board under Section 35, as it stood immediately before that day, and any matter arising out of or connected with such appeal and which is so pending shall stand transferred on that day to the Appellate Tribunal and the Appellate Tribunal may proceed with such appeal or matter from the stage at which it was on that day:

PROVIDED that the appellant may demand that before proceeding further with that appeal or matter, he may be reheard.

(2) Every proceeding which is pending immediately before the appointed day before the Central Government under Section 36, as it stood immediately before that day, and any matter arising out of or connected with such proceeding and which is so pending shall stand transferred on that day to the Appellate Tribunal and the Appellate Tribunal may proceed with such proceeding or matter from the stage at which it was on that day as if such proceeding or matter were an appeal filed before it:

Provided that if any such proceeding or matter relates to an order where-

(a) in any disputed case, other than a case where the determination of any question having a relation to the rate of duty of excise or to the value of goods for purposes of assessment is in issue or is one of the points in issue, the difference in duty involved or the duty involved; or

(b) the amount of fine or penalty determined by such order, does not exceed ten thousand rupees, such proceeding or matter shall continue to be dealt with by the Central Government as if the said Section 36 had not been substituted:

Provided further that the applicant or the other party may make a demand to the Appellate Tribunal that before proceeding further with that proceeding or matter, he may be reheard.

(3) Every proceeding which is pending immediately before the appointed day before the Board or the Collector of Central Excise under Section 35A, as it stood immediately before that day, and any matter arising out of or connected with such proceeding and which is so pending shall continue to be dealt with by the Board or the Collector of Central Excise, as the case may be, as if the said Section had not been substituted.

(4) Any person who immediately before the appointed day was authorised to appear in any appeal or proceeding transferred under sub-section (1) or sub-section (2) shall, notwithstanding anything contained in Section 35Q, have the right to appear before the Appellate Tribunal in relation to such appeal or proceeding.

35Q. Appearance by authorised representative.

(1) Any person who is entitled or required to appear before a Central Excise Officer or the Appellate Tribunal in connection with any proceedings under this Act, otherwise than when required under this Act to appear personally for examination on oath or affirmation, may, subject to the other provisions of this Section, appear by an authorised representative.

(2) For the purposes of this Section, "authorised representative" means a person authorised by the person referred to in sub-section (1) to appear on his behalf, being -

(a) his relative or regular employee; or

(b) any legal practitioner who is entitled to practise in any civil court in India; or

(c) any person who has acquired such qualifications as the Central Government may prescribe for this purpose.

(3) Notwithstanding anything contained in this Section, no person who was a member of the Indian Customs and Central Excise Service-Group A and has retired or resigned from such Service after having served for not less than three years in any capacity in that Service, shall be entitled to appear as an authorised representative in any proceedings before a Central Excise Officer for a period of two years from the date of his retirement or resignation, as the case may be.

(4) No person,-

(a) who has been dismissed or removed from Government service; or

(b) who is convicted of an offence connected with any proceeding under this Act, the Customs Act, 1962 (52 of 1962) or the Gold (Control) Act, 1968 ; or (45 of 1968).

(c) who has become an insolvent, shall be qualified to represent any person under sub-section (1), for all times in the case of a person referred to in clause (a), and for such time as the Collector of Central Excise or the competent authority under the Customs Act, 1962 (52 of 1962) or the Gold (Control) Act, 1968 (45 of 1968), as the case may be, may, by order, determine in the case of a person referred to in clause (b), and for the period during which the insolvency continues in the case of a person referred to in clause (c).

(5) If any person,-

(a) who is a legal practitioner, is found guilty of misconduct in his professional capacity by any authority entitled to institute proceedings against him, an order passed by that authority shall have effect in relation to his right to appear before a Central Excise Officer or the Appellate Tribunal as it has in relation to his right to, practise as a legal practitioner;

(b) who is not a legal practitioner, is found guilty of misconduct in connection with any proceedings under this Act by the prescribed authority, the prescribed authority may direct that he shall thenceforth be disqualified to represent any person under sub-section (1).

(6) Any order or direction under clause (b) of sub-section (4) or clause (b) of sub-section (5) shall be subject to the following conditions, namely:-

(a) no such order or direction shall be made in respect of any person unless he has been given a reasonable opportunity of being heard;

(b) any person against whom any such order or direction is made may, within one month of the making of the order or direction, appeal to the Board to have the order or direction cancelled; and

(c) no such order or direction shall take effect until the expiration of one month from the making thereof, or, where an appeal has been preferred, until the disposal of the appeal.

36. Definitions. In this Chapter-

(a) "appointed day" means the date of coming into force of the amendments to this Act specified in Part II of the Fifth Schedule to the Finance (No. 2) Act, 1980 (44 of 1980);

(b) "High Court" means,—

(i) in relation to any State, the High Court for that State;

(ii) in relation to a Union territory to which the jurisdiction of the High Court of a State has been extended by law, that High Court;

(iii) in relation to the Union territories of Dadra and Nagar Haveli and Goa, Daman and Diu, the High Court at Bombay;

(iv) in relation to another Union territory, the highest court of civil appeal for that territory other than the Supreme Court of India;

(c) "President" means the President of the Appellate Tribunal.

CHAPTER -VIB : PRESUMPTION AS TO DOCUMENTS

36A. Presumption as to documents in certain cases. Where any document is produced by any person or has been seized from the custody or control of any person, in either case, under this Act or under any other law and such document is tendered by the prosecution in evidence against him or against him and any other person who is tried jointly with him, the Court shall -

(a) unless the contrary is proved by such person, presume—

(i) the truth of the contents of such document;

(ii) that the signature and every other part of such document which purports to be in the handwriting of any particular person or which the Court may reasonably assume to have been signed by, or to be in the handwriting of, any particular person, is in that person' s handwriting, and in the case of a document executed or attested, that it was executed or attested by the person by whom it purports to have been so executed or attested;

(b) admit, the document in evidence, notwithstanding that it is not duly stamped, if such document is otherwise admissible in evidence.

36B. Admissibility of micro films, facsimile copies of documents and computer print outs as documents and as evidence.

(1) Notwithstanding anything contained in any other law for the time being in force -

(a) a micro film of a document or the reproduction of the image or images embodied in such micro film (whether enlarged or not); or

(b) a facsimile copy of a document; or

(c) a statement contained in a document and included in a printed material produced by a computer (hereinafter referred to as a "computer print out"), if the conditions mentioned in sub-section (2) and the other provisions contained in this Section are satisfied in relation to the statement and the computer in question, shall be deemed to be also a document for the purposes of this Act and the rules made thereunder and shall be admissible in any proceedings thereunder, without further proof or production of the original, as evidence of any contents of the original or of any fact stated therein of which direct evidence would be admissible.

(2) The conditions referred to in sub-section (1) in respect of a computer print out shall be the following, namely:-

(a) the computer print out containing the statement was produced by the computer during the period over which the computer was used regularly to store or process information for the purposes of any activities regularly carried on over that period by the person having lawful control over the use of the computer;

(b) during the said period, there was regularly supplied to the computer in the ordinary course of the said activities, information of the kind contained In the statement or of the kind from which the information so contained is derived;

(c) throughout the material part of the said period, the computer was operating properly or, if not, then any respect in which it was not operating properly or was out of operation during that part of that period was not such as to affect the production of the document or the accuracy of the contents; and

(d) the information contained in the statement reproduces or is derived from information supplied to the computer in the ordinary course of the said activities.

(3) Where over any period, the function of storing or processing information for the purposes of any activities regularly carried on over that period as mentioned in clause (a) of sub-section (2) was regularly performed by computers, whether-

(a) by a combination of computers operating over that period; or

(b) by different computers operating in succession over that period; or

(c) by different combinations of computers operating in succession over that period; or

(d) in any other manner involving the successive operation over that period, in whatever order, of one or more computers and one or more combinations of computers, all the computers used for that purpose during that period shall be treated for the purposes of this Section as constituting a single computer; and references in this Section to a computer shall be construed accordingly.

(4) In any proceedings under this: Act and the rules made thereunder where it is desired to give a statement in evidence, by virtue of this Section, a certificate doing any of the following things, that is to say —

(a) identifying the document containing the statement and describing the manner in which It was produced;

(b) giving such particulars of any device involved in the production of that document as may be appropriate for the purpose of showing that the document was produced by a computer;

(c) dealing with any of the matters to which the conditions mentioned in sub-section (2) relate, and purporting to be signed by a person occupying a responsible official position in relation to the operation of the relevant device or the management of the relevant activities (whichever is appropriate) shall be evidence of any matter stated in the certificate; and for the purposes of this sub-section it shall be sufficient for a matter to; be stated to the best of the knowledge and belief of the person stating it.

(5) For the purposes of this Section —

(a) information shall be taken to be supplied, to a computer if it is supplied thereto in any appropriate form and whether it is so supplied directly or (with or without human intervention) by means of any appropriate equipment;

(b) whether in the course of activities carried on by any official, information is supplied with a view to its, being stored or processed for the purposes of those activities by a computer operated otherwise than in the course of those activities, that information, if duly supplied to that computer, shall be taken to be supplied to it in the course of those activities;

(c) a document shall be taken to have been produced by a computer whether it was produced by it directly or (with or without human intervention) by means of any appropriate equipment.

EXPLANATION. For the purposes of this Section,-

(a) "computer" means any device that receives, stores and processes data, applying stipulated processes to the information and supplying results of these processes; and

(b) any reference to information being derived from other information shall be a reference to its being derived therefrom by calculation comparison or an other process.

CHAPTER -VII : SUPPLEMENTAL PROVISIONS

37. Power of Central Government to make rules.

(1) The Central Government may make rules to carry into effect the purposes of this Act.

(2) In particular, and without prejudice to the generality of the foregoing power, such rules may—

(i) provide for determining under Section 4 the nearest ascertainable equivalent of the normal price;

(ia) having regard to the normal practice of the wholesale trade, define or specify the kinds of trade discount to be excluded from the value under Section 4 including the circumstances in which and the conditions subject to which such discount is to be so excluded;

(ib) provide for the assessment and collection of duties of excise, the authorities by whom functions under this Act are to be discharged, the issue of notices requiring payment, the manner in which the duties shall be payable, and the recovery of duty not paid;

(ic) provide for the remission of duty of excise leviable on any excisable goods, which due to any natural cause are found to be deficient in quantity, the limit or limits of percentage beyond which no such remission shall be allowed and the different limit or limits of percentage for different varieties of the same excisable goods or for different areas or for different seasons;

(ii) prohibit absolutely, or with such exceptions, or subject to such conditions as the Central Government thinks fit, the production or manufacture, or any process of the production or manufacture, of excisable goods, or of any component parts or ingredients or containers thereof, except on land or premises approved for the purpose;

(iii) prohibit absolutely, or with such exceptions, or subject to such conditions as the Central Government thinks fit, the transit of excisable goods from any part of a India to any other part thereof;

(iv) regulate the removal of excisable goods from the place where produced, stored or manufactured or subjected to any process of production or manufacture and their transport to or from the premises of a registered or a bonded warehouse, or to a market;

(v) regulate the production or manufacture, or any process of the production or manufacture, the possession, storage and sale of salt, and so far as such regulation is essential for the proper levy and collection of the duties imposed by this Act, of any other excisable goods, or of any component parts or ingredients or containers thereof;

(vi) provide for the employment of officers of the Government to supervise the carrying out of any rules made under this Act;

(vii) require a manufacturer or the licensee of a warehouse to provide accommodation within the precincts of his factory or warehouse for officers employed to supervise the carrying out of regulations made under this Act and prescribe the scale of such accommodation;

(viii) provide for the appointment, licensing, management, and supervision of bonded warehouses and the procedure to be followed in entering goods into and clearing goods from such warehouses;

(ix) provide for the distinguishing of goods which have been manufactured after registration of materials which have been imported under licence, and of goods on which duty has been paid, or which are exempt from duty under this Act;

(x) impose on persons engaged in the production or manufacture, storage or sale (whether on their own account or as brokers or commission agents) of salt, and, so far as such imposition is essential for the proper levy and collection of the duties imposed by this Act, of any other excisable goods, the duty of furnishing information, keeping records and making returns, and prescribe the nature of such information and the form of such records and returns, the particulars to be contained therein, and the manner in which they shall be verified;

(xi) require that excisable goods shall not be sold or, offered or kept for sale in India except in prescribed containers, bearing a banderol, stamp or label of such nature and affixed in such manner as may be prescribed;

(xii) provide for the issue of registration certificates and transport permits and the fees, if any, to be charged therefor:

PROVIDED that the fees for the licensing of the manufacture and refining of salt and saltpetre shall not exceed. in the case of each such licence, the following amounts, namely:-RS. Licence to manufacture and refine saltpetre and to separate and purify salt in the process of such manufacture and refining 50 Licence to manufacture salt petre. Licence to manufacture sulphate of soda (kharinun) by solar heat in evaporating pans 10 Licence to manufacture sulphate of soda (knarinun) by artificial heat 2 Licence to manufacture other saline substances 2;

(xiii) provide for the detention of goods, plant, machinery or material, for the purpose of exacting the duty, the procedure in connection with the confiscation, otherwise than under Section 10 or Section 28, of goods in respect of which breaches of the Act or rules have been committed, and the disposal of goods so detained or confiscated;

(xiv) authorise and regulate the inspection of factories and provide for the taking of samples, and for the making of tests, of any substance produced therein, and for the inspection or search of any place or conveyance used for the production, storage, sale or transport of salt, and so far as such inspection or search is essential for the proper levy and collection of the duties imposed by this Act, of any other excisable goods;

(xv) authorise and regulate the composition of offences against, or liabilities incurred under, this Act or the rules made thereunder;

(xvi) provide for the grant of a rebate of the duty paid on goods which are exported out of India or shipped for consumption on a voyage to any port outside India;

(xvia) provide for the credit of duty paid or deemed to have been paid on the goods used in, or in relation to, the manufacture of excisable goods;

(xvib) provide for the giving of credit of sums of money with respect to raw materials used in the manufacture of excisable goods;

(xvii) exempt any goods from the whole or any part of the duty imposed by this Act;

(xviia) provide incentives for increased production or manufacture of any goods by way of remission of, or any concession with respect to, duty payable under this Act;

(xviii) define an area no point in which shall be more than one hundred yards from the nearest point of any place in which salt is stored or sold by or on behalf of the Central Government, or of any factory in which saltpetre is manufactured or refined, and regulate the possession, storage and sale of salt within such area;

(xix) define an area round any other place in which salt is manufactured, and regulate the possession, storage and sale of salt within such area;

(xx) authorise the 5[Central Board of Excise and Customs constituted under the Central Boards of Revenue Act, 1963] (54 of 1963) or Collectors of Central Excise appointed for the purposes of this Act to provide, by written instructions, for supplemental matters arising out of any rule made by the Central Government under this Section;

(xxi) provide for the publication, subject to such conditions as may be specified therein, of names and other particulars of persons who have been found guilty of contravention of any of the provisions of this Act or of any rule made thereunder;

(xxii) provide for the charging of fees for the examination of excisable goods intended for export out of India and for rendering any other service by a Central Excise Officer under this Act or the rules made thereunder.

(xxiii) specify the form in which application for refund shall be made under Section 11B;

(xxiv) provide for the manner in which money is to be credited to the Fund;

(xxv) provide for the manner in which the Fund shall be utilised for the welfare of the consumers;

(xxvi) specify the form in which the account and records relating to the Fund shall be maintained.

(xxvii) specify the persons who shall get themselves registered under Section 6 and the manner of their registration.]

(3) In making rules under this Section, the Central Government may provide that any person committing a breach of any rule shall, where no other penalty is provided by this Act, be liable to a penalty not exceeding two thousand rupees and that any article in respect of which any such breach is committed shall be confiscated.

(4) Notwithstanding anything contained in sub-section (3), and without, prejudice to the provisions of Section 9, in making rules under this Section, the Central Government may provide that if any manufacturer, producer or licensee of a warehouse —

(a) removes any excisable goods in contravention of the provisions of any such rule; or

(b) does not account for all such goods manufactured, produced or stored by him; or

(c) engages in the manufacture, production or storage of such goods without having applied for the registration as required Section 6; or

(d) contravenes the provisions of any such rule with intent to evade payment of duty, then-

(i) any land, building, plant, machinery, materials, conveyance, animal or any other thing used in connection with the manufacture, production, storage, removal or disposal of such goods, and

(ii) all excisable goods on such land or in such building or produced or manufactured with such plant, machinery, materials or thing, belonging to such manufacturer, producer or licensee shall be liable to confiscation and the manufacturer, producer or licensee shall be liable to a penalty not exceeding three times the value of the excisable goods in respect of which any contravention of the nature referred to in clause (a), (b), (c) or (d) has been committed, or five' thousand rupees, whichever is greater.]

(5) Notwithstanding anything contained in sub-section (3), the Central Government any make rules to provide for the imposition upon any person-

who acquires possession of, or is in any way concerned in transporting, removing, depositing, keeping, concealing, selling or purchasing, or in any other manner deals with, any excisable goods which he knows or has reason to believe are liable to confiscation under this Act or the rules made thereunder, a penalty not exceeding three times the value of such goods or five thousand rupees, whichever is greater.

37A. Delegation of powers. The Central Government may, by notification in the Official Gazette, direct that subject to such conditions, if any, as may be specified in the notification —

(a) any power exercisable by the Board under this Act may be exercisable also by a Principal Collector of Central Excise or a Collector of Central Excise] empowered in this behalf by the Central Government;

(b) any power exercisable by a Collector of Central Excise under this Act may be exercisable also by a Deputy Collector of Central Excise or an Assistant Collector of Central Excise empowered in this behalf by the Central Government;

(c) any power exercisable by a Deputy Collector of Central Excise under this Act may be exercisable also by an Assistant Collector of Central Excise empowered in this behalf by the Central Government; and

(d) any power exercisable by an Assistant Collector of Central Excise under this Act may be exercisable also by a Gazetted Officer of Central Excise empowered in this behalf by the Board.

37B. Instructions to Central Excise Officers. The Central Board of Excise and Customs constituted under the Central Boards of Revenue Act, 1963 (54 of 1963) may, if it considers it necessary or expedient so to do for the purpose of uniformity in the classification of excisable goods or with respect to levy of duties of excise on such goods, issue such orders, instructions and directions to the Central Excise Officers as it may deem fit, and such officers and all other persons employed in the execution of this Act shall observe and follow such orders, instructions and directions of the said Board:

PROVIDED that no such orders, instructions or directions shall be issued-

(a) so as to require any Central Excise Officer to make a particular assessment or to dispose of a particular case in a particular manner; or

(b) so as to interfere with the discretion of the Collector of Central Excise (Appeals) in the exercise of his appellate functions.

37C. Service of decisions, orders, summons, etc.

(1) Any decision or order passed or any summons or notice issued under this Act or the rules made thereunder, shall be served,-

(a) by tendering the decision, order, summons or notice, or sending it by registered post with acknowledgement due, to the person for whom it is intended or his authorised agent, if any;

(b) if the decision, order, summons or notice cannot be served in the manner provided in clause (a), by affixing a copy thereof to some conspicuous part of the factory or warehouse or other place of business or usual place of residence of the person for whom such decision, order, summons or notice, as the case may be, is intended;

(c) if the decision, order, summons or notice cannot be served in the manner provided in clauses (a) and (b), by affixing a copy thereof on the notice board of the officer or authority who or which passed such decision or order or issued such summons or notice.

(2) Every decision or order passed or any summons or notice issued under this Act or the rules made thereunder, shall be deemed to have been served on the date on which the decision, order, summons or notice is tendered or, delivered by post or a copy thereof is affixed in the manner provided in sub-section (1),

37D. Rounding off of duty, etc. The amount of duty, interest, penalty, fine or any other sum payable, and the amount of refund or any other sum due, tinder the provisions of this Act shall be rounded off to the nearest rupee and, for this purpose, where such amount contains a part of a rupee consisting of paise then, if such part is fifty paise or more, it shall be increased to one rupee and if such part is less than fifty paise it shall be ignored.

38. Publication of rules and notifications and laying of rules before Parliament.

(1) All rules made and notifications issued under this Act shall be published in the Official Gazette.

(2) Every rule made under this Act and every notification issued under sub-section (1) of Section 5A and Section 11C shall be laid, as soon as may be after it is made or issued, before each House of Parliament, while it is in session, for a total period of thirty days which may be comprised in one session or in two or more successive sessions, and if, before the expiry of the session immediately following the session or the successive sessions aforesaid, both Houses agree in making any modification in the rule or notification or both Houses agree that the rule should not be made or the notification should not be issued, the rule or notification shall thereafter have effect only in such modified form or be of no effect, as the case may be; so, however, that any such modification or annulment shall be without prejudice to the validity of anything previously done under that rule or notification."

39. Repeal of enactments. *Rep. by the Repealing and Amending Act, 1947 (2 of 1948), s. 2 and Sch.*

40. Protection of action taken under the Act.

(1) No suit, prosecution or other legal proceeding shall lie against the Central Government or any officer of the Central Government or a State Government for anything which is done, or intended to be done, in good faith, in pursuance of this Act or any rule made thereunder.

(2) No proceeding, other than a suit, shall be commenced against the Central Government or any officer of the Central Government or a State Government

for anything done or purported to have been done in pursuance of this Act or any rule made thereunder, without giving the Central Government or such officer a month' s previous notice in writing of the intended proceeding and of the cause thereof or after the expiration of three months from the accrual of such cause.

The First Schedule. *Rep. by the Central Excise Tariff Act, 1985 (5 of 1986), s. 4 (w. e. f 28-2-1986).*

THE SECOND SCHEDULE
[*See* Sections 6 and 8]

PART A

Excisable goods specified for the purposes of Section 6 –

1. Tobacco
2. Betel-nuts when supplied by a curor to a wholesale dealer,
3. Coffee whether directly or through a broker or commission agent.

PART B

Excisable goods specified for the purposes of Section 8 –

1. Tobacco.

[The Third Schedule.] *Rep. by the Repealing and Amending Act, 1947 (2 of 1948), s. 2 and Sch.*

❑❑❑

11

The Central Sales Tax (Amendment) Act, 2001

ACT NO. 41 OF 2001 [11TH SEPTEMBER, 2001]

AN ACT further to amend the Central Sales Tax Act, 1956.

Be it enacted by Parliament in the Fifty-second Year of the Republic of India as follows:-

1. Short title and commencement.

(1) This Act may be called the Central Sales Tax (Amendment) Act, 2001.

(2) It shall come into force on such date as the Central Government may, by notification in the Official Gazette, appoint.

2. Amendment of Section 13. In the Central Sales Tax Act, 1956 (74 of 1956) (hereinafter referred to as the principal Act), in Section 13, in sub-section 1, after clause (g), the following clauses shall be inserted, namely:-

"(h) the proper functioning of the Authority constituted under Section 19;

(i) the salaries and allowances payable to, and the terms and conditions of service of the Chairman and Members under sub-section (3) of Section 19;

(j) any other matter as may be prescribed."

3. Insertion of new Chapter after Chapter V. After Chapter V of the principal Act, the following Chapter shall be inserted, namely:- "CHAPTER VI AUTHORITY TO SETTLE DISPUTES IN COURSE OF INTER-STATE TRADE OR COMMERCE".

19. Central Sales Tax Appellate Authority.

(1) The Central Government shall constitute, by notification in the Official Gazette, an Authority to settle inter-state disputes falling under Section 6A or Section

9 of this Act, to be known as "the Central Sales Tax Appellate Authority (hereinafter referred to as the Authority)".

(2) The Authority shall consist of the following Members appointed by the Central Government, namely:-

   (a) a Chairman, who is a retired Judge of the Supreme Court, or a retired Chief Justice of a High Court;

   (b) an officer of the Indian Legal Service who is, or is qualified to be, an Additional Secretary to the Government of India; and

   (c) an officer of a State Government not below the rank of Secretary or an officer of the Central Government not below the rank of Additional Secretary, who is an expert in sales tax matters.

(3) The salaries and allowances payable to, and the terms and conditions of service of, the Chairman and Members shall be such as may be prescribed.

(4) The Central Government shall provide the Authority with such officers and staff as may be necessary for the efficient exercise of the powers of the Authority under this Act.

20. Appeals.

(1) The provisions of this Chapter shall apply to appeals filed by the aggrieved dealer against any order of the assessing authority made under Section 6A or Section 9 of this Act.

(2) Notwithstanding anything contained in the general sales tax laws, the Authority shall adjudicate an appeal filed by a dealer aggrieved against any order of the assessing authority rejecting his claim under Section 6A or Section 9 of this Act.

(3) An appeal against the order of the assessing authority rejecting the claim of the dealer under Section 6A or Section 9 of this Act may be filed by the aggrieved dealer within forty-five days from the date on which the order is served on him:

PROVIDED that the Authority may entertain any appeal after the expiry of the said period of forty-five days, but not later than sixty days, from the date aforesaid if it is satisfied that the appellant was prevented by sufficient cause from filing the ap eal in time.

(4) The application shall be made in quadruplicate and be accompanied by a fee of five thousand rupees.

21. Procedure on receipt of application.

(1) On receipt of an appeal, the Authority shall cause a copy thereof to be forwarded to the assessing authority concerned and to call upon it to furnish the relevant records:

PROVIDED that such records shall, as soon as possible, be returned to the assessing authority.

(2) The Authority shall adjudicate and decide upon the appeal filed against an order of the assessing authority.

(3) The Authority, after examining the appeal and the records called for, by order, either allow or reject the appeal:

PROVIDED that no appeal shall be rejected unless an opportunity has been given to the appellant of being heard in person or through a duly authorised representative: Provided further that whether an appeal is rejected or accepted, reasons for such rejection or acceptance shall be given in the order.

(4) The Authority shall make an endeavour to pronounce its order in writing within six months of the receipt of the appeal.

(5) A copy of every order made under sub-section (3) shall be sent to the appellant and to the assessing authority.

22. Powers of the Authority.

(1) The Authority shall have the same powers as are vested in a court under the Code of Civil Procedure, 1908 (5 of 1908), while trying a suit in respect of the following matters, namely:-

(a) enforcing the attendance of any person, examining him on oath or affirmation;

(b) compelling the production of accounts and documents;

(c) issuing commission for the examination of witnesses;

(d) the reception of evidence on affidavits;

(e) any other matter which may be prescribed.

(2) Every proceeding before the Authority shall be deemed to be a judicial proceeding within the meaning of Sections 193 and 228 of the Indian Penal Code (45 of 1860) and the Authority shall be deemed to be Code of Criminal Procedure, 1973 (2 of 1974), a civil court for the purposes of Section 195.

23. Procedure of Authority. The Authority shall, subject to the provisions of this Chapter, have power to regulate its own procedure in all matters arising out of the exercise of powers under this Act.

24. Authority for Advance Rulings to function as Authority under this Act.

(1) Notwithstanding anything contained in any other law for the time being in force and in Section 19 of this Act, the Authority for Advance Rulings constituted under Section 245 of the Income-tax Act, 1961 (43 of 1961) shall be notified by the Central Government in the Official Gazette, with such modifications as may be necessary, to make its composition in conformity with Section 19 of this Act, as the Authority under this Act till such time an Authority is constituted under that Section.

(2) On and from the date of the constitution of the Authority in accordance with the provisions of Section 19 of this Act, the proceedings pending with the Authority for Advance Rulings shall stand transferred to the Authority constituted under that section from the stage at which such proceedings stood before the date of constitution of the said Authority.

25. Transfer of pending proceedings. On and from the date when the Authority is constituted under Section 19, every appeal arising out of the provisions contained in this Chapter -

(i) which is pending immediately before the constitution of such Authority before the appellate authority constituted under the general sales tax law of a State or of the Union territory, as the case may be; or

(ii) which would have been required to be taken before such appellate Authority, shall stand transferred to such Authority on the date on which it is established.

26. Applicability of order passed. An order passed by the Authority under this Chapter shall be binding on the assessing authorities and other authorities created by or under any law relating to general sales tax, in force for the time being in any State or Union territory.

❑❑❑

12

The Central Sales Tax (Amendment) Act, 2005

Act No. 3 of 2006 [16th January, 2006]

AN ACT further to amend the Central Sales Tax Act, 1956.

BE it enacted by Parliament in the Fifty-sixth Year of the Republic of India as follows:-

1. Short title and commencement.

(1) This Act may be called the Central Sales Tax (Amendment) Act, 2005.

(2) It shall come into force on such date as the Central Government may, by notification in the Official Gazette, appoint.

2. Amendment of Section 19. In the Central Sales Tax Act, 1956 (74 of 1956) (hereinafter referred to as the principal Act), in Section 19, after sub-section (2), the following sub-section shall be inserted, namely:-

"(2A) Notwithstanding anything contained in sub-section (2), the Chairman or a Member holding a post as such in the Authority for Advance Rulings appointed under clause (a) or clause (c), as the case may be, of sub-section (2) of Section 245-O of the Income-tax Act, 1961 (43 of 1961) may, in addition to his being the Chairman or a Member of that Authority, be appointed as the Chairman or a Member, as the case may be, of the Authority under this Act."

3. Insertion of new Section 19A. After Section 19 of the principal Act, the following Section shall be inserted, namely:-

"**19A. Vacancies, etc., not to invalidate proceedings.** No proceeding before the Authority shall be questioned or shall be invalid on the ground merely of the existence of any vacancy or defect in the constitution of the Authority."

4. Substitution of new Section for Section 20. For Section 20 of the principal Act, the following Section shall be substituted, namely:-

"20. Appeals.

(1) The provisions of this Chapter shall apply to appeals filed by any aggrieved person against any order of the highest appellate authority of a State, made under Section 6A read with Section 9.

EXPLANATION: For the purposes of this Section and Sections 21, 22 and 25 "highest appellate authority of a State" means any authority or tribunal or court (except the High Court) established or constituted under the general sales tax law of a State, by whatever name called.

(2) Notwithstanding anything contained in the general sales tax law of a State, the Authority shall adjudicate an appeal filed under sub-section (1).

(3) An appeal under sub-section (1) may be filed within ninety days from the date on which the order referred to in that sub-section is served on any aggrieved person:

PROVIDED that the Authority may entertain any appeal after the expiry of the said period of ninety days, but not later than one hundred and fifty days from the date of such service, if it is satisfied that the appellant was prevented by sufficient cause from filing the appeal in time:

PROVIDED FURTHER that the Authority may entertain any appeal from an aggrieved person within sixty days from the commencement of the Central Sales Tax (Amendment) Act, 2005, where such aggrieved person had the right to file an appeal against the order of the highest appellate authority of the State under sub-section (1) as it stood immediately before the commencement of the said Act, but has not availed of the right to file the appeal during the period commencing on and from the 3rd day of December, 2001 and ending with the 16th day of March, 2005.

(4) The application shall be made in quadruplicate and be accompanied by a fee of five thousand rupees.'.

5. Amendment of Section 21. In Section 21 of the principal Act,-

(i) in sub-section (2), for the words "assessing authority", the words "highest appellate authority" shall be substituted;

(ii) in sub-section (5), for the words "appellant and to the assessing authority", the words "appellant, assessing authority, respondent and highest appellate authority of the State Government concerned" shall be substituted.

6. Amendment of Section 22. In Section 22 of the principal Act, for sub-section (1A), the following sub-section shall be substituted, namely:-"(1A) The Authority may grant stay of the operation of the order of the highest appellate authority against which the appeal is filed before it or order the pre-deposit of the tax before entertaining the appeal and while granting such stay or making such order for the pre-deposit of the tax, the Authority shall have regard, if the assessee has made pre-deposit of the tax under the general sales tax law of the State concerned, to such pre-deposit or pass such appropriate order as it may deem fit.".

7. Substitution of new Section for Section 25. For Section 25 of the principal Act, the following Section shall be substituted, namely:-

"25. Transfer of pending proceedings.

(1) On and from the commencement of the Central Sales Tax (Amendment) Act, 2005, all appeals (except appeals against orders of the highest appellate authority of the State) pending before the Authority notified under sub-section (1) of Section 24 shall stand transferred together with the records thereof to the highest appellate authority of the concerned State.

(2) Such highest appellate authority of the State to which such appeal has been transferred under sub-section (1) on receipt of such records shall proceed to deal with such appeal so far as may be in the same manner as in the case of an appeal filed before such highest appellate authority of the State according to the general sales tax law of the appropriate State, from the stage which was reached before such transfer or from any earlier stage or de novo as such highest appellate authority of the State may deem fit:

PROVIDED that where the highest appellate authority finds that the appellant has not availed of the opportunity of filing first appeal before the appellate authority, such case shall be forwarded to such authority.".

8. Amendment of Section 26. In Section 26 of the principal Act, the words" or Union territory" shall be omitted.

❏❏❏

13

The Central Sales Tax Act, 1956

(74 OF 1956) (21ST DECEMBER, 1956)

AN ACT to formulate principals for determining when a sale or purchase of goods takes place in the course of inter-State trade or commerce or outside a State or in the course of import into or export from India, to provide for the levy, collection and distributions of taxes on sales of goods in the course of inter-State trade or commerce and to declared certain goods to be of special importance in inter-State trade or commerce and specify the restrictions and conditions to which laws imposing taxes on the sale or purchase of such goods of special importance shall be subject.

Be it enacted by Parliament in the Seventh Year of the Republic of India as follows:-

CHAPTER - I : PRELIMINARY

1. Short tile, extent and commencement.

(1) This Act may be called The Central Sales Tax Act, 1956.

(2) It extends to the whole of India.

(3) It shall come into force on such date as the Central Government may, by notification if the Official Gazette, appoint, and different dates may be appointed for different provisions of this Act.

2. Definitions. In this Act, unless the context otherwise requires,-

(a) "appropriate State" means -

(i) In relation to a dealer who has one or more places of business situated in the same State, that State;

(ii) In relation to a dealer who has places of business situate in different States, every such State with respect to the place or places of business situate within its territory;

(aa) "business" includes-

(i) any trade, commerce or manufacture, or any adventure or concern in the nature of trade, commerce or manufacture, whether or not such trade, commerce, manufacture, adventure or concern is carried on with a motive to make gain or profit and whether or not any gain or profit accrues from such trade, commerce, manufacture, adventure or concern; and

(ii) any transaction in connection with, or incidental or ancillary to, such trade, commerce, manufacture, adventure or concern;

(ab) "crossing the customs frontiers of India" means crossing the limits of the area of a customs station in which imported goods or export goods are ordinarily kept before clearance by customs authorities.

EXPLANATION: For the purposes of this clause, "custom station" and "customs authorities" shall have the same meanings as in the Customs Act, 1962 (52 of 1962);

(b) "dealer" means any person who carries on (whether regularly or otherwise) the business of buying, selling, supplying or distributing goods, directly or indirectly, for cash, or for deferred payment, or for commission, remuneration or other valuable consideration, and includes-

(i) a local authority, a body corporate, a company, any co-operative society or other society, club, firm, Hindu undivided family or other association of persons which carries on such business;

(ii) a factor, broker, commission agent, del credere agent, or any other mercantile agent, by whatever name called, and whether of the same description as herein before mentioned or not, who carries on the business of buying, selling, supplying or distributing goods belonging to any principal whether disclosed or not; and

(iii) an auctioneer who carries on the business of selling or auctioning goods belonging to any principal, whether disclosed or not and whether the offer of the intending purchaser is accepted by him or by the principal or a nominee of the principal.

EXPLANATION 1: Every person who acts as an agent, in any State, of a dealer residing outside that State and buys, sells, supplies or distributes, goods in the State or acts on behalf of such dealer as -

(i) a mercantile agent as defined in the Sale of Goods Act, 1930, (3 of 1930); or

(ii) an agent for handling of goods or documents of title relating to goods; or

(iii) an agent for the collection or the payment of the sale price of goods or as a guarantor for such a collection or payment, and every local branch or office in a State of a firm registered outside that State or a company or other body corporate, the principal office or headquarters whereof is outside that State, shall be deemed to be a dealer for the purposes of this Act.

EXPLANATION 2: A Government which, whether or not in the course of business, buys, sells, supplies or distributes goods, directly or otherwise for cash or for deferred payment or for commission, remuneration or other valuable consideration, shall except in relation to any sale, supply or distribution of surplus, unserviceable or old stores or materials or waste products or obsolete or discarded machinery or parts or accessories thereof, be deemed to be a dealer for the purposes of this Act;

(c) "declared goods" means goods declared under Section 14 to be of special importance in inter-State trade or commerce;

(d) "goods" includes all materials, articles, commodities and all other kinds of movable property, but does not include newspapers, actionable claims, stocks, shares and securities;

(dd) "place of business" includes-

(i) in any case where a dealer carries on business through an agent (by whatever name called), the place of business of such agent;

(ii) a warehouse, godown, or other place where a dealer stores his goods; and

(iii) a place where a dealer keeps his books of account;]

(e) "prescribed" means prescribed by rules made under this Act;

(f) "registered dealer" means a dealer who is registered under sec.7;

(g) "sale" with its grammatical variations and cognate expressions, means any transfer of property in goods by one person to another for cash or for deferred payment or for any other valuable consideration, and includes,-

(i) a transfer, otherwise than in pursuance of a contract, of property in any goods for cash, deferred payment or other valuable consideration;

(ii) a transfer of property in goods (whether as goods or in some other form) involved in the execution of a works contract;

(iii) a delivery of goods on hire-purchase or any system of payment by instalments;

(iv) a transfer of the right to use any goods for any purpose (whether or not for a specified period) for cash, deferred payment or other valuable consideration;

(v) the supply of goods by any unincorporated association or body of persons to a member thereof for cash, deferred payment or other valuable consideration;

(vi) a supply, by way of or as a part of any service or in any other manner whatsoever, of goods, being food or any other article for human consumption or any drink (whether or not intoxicating), where such supply or service, is for cash, deferred payment or other valuable consideration, [but does not include a mortgage or hypothecation of or a charge or pledge on goods].

(h) "sale price" means the amount payable to a dealer as consideration for the sale of any goods, less any sum allowed as cash discount according to the practice normally prevailing in the trade, but inclusive of any sum charged for anything done by the dealer in respect of the goods at the time of or before the delivery thereof other than the cost of freight or delivery or the cost of installation in cases where such cost is separately charged;

"PROVIDED that in the case of a transfer of property in goods (whether as goods or in some other form) involved in the execution of a works contract, the sale price of such goods shall be determined in the prescribed manner by making such deduction from the total consideration for the works contract as may be prescribed and such price shall be deemed to be the sale price for the purposes of this clause.

(i) "sales tax law" means any law for the time being in force in any State or part thereof which provides for the levy of taxes on the sale or purchase of goods generally or on any specified goods expressly mentioned in that behalf and includes value added tax law, and 'general sales tax law' means any law for the time being in force in any State or part thereof which provides for the levy of tax on the sale or purchase of goods generally and includes value added tax law;

(j) "turnover" used in relation to any dealer liable to tax under this Act means the aggregate of the sale prices received and receivable by him in respect of sales of any goods in the course of inter-State trade or commerce made during any prescribed period and determined in accordance with the provisions of this Act and the rules made there under;

(ja) 'works contract' means a contract for carrying out any work which includes assembling, construction, building, altering, manufacturing, processing, fabricating, erection, installation, fitting out, improvement, repair or commissioning of any movable or immovable property;

(k) "Year", in relation to a dealer, means the year applicable in relation to him under the general sales tax law of the appropriate State, and where there is no such year applicable, the financial year.

CHAPTER - II : FORMULATION OF PRINCIPLES FOR DETERMINING WHEN A SALE OR PURCHASE OF GOODS TAKES PLACE IN THE COURSE OF INTER-STATE TRADE OR COMMERCE OR OUTSIDE A STATE OR IN THE COURSE OF IMPORT OR EXPORT

3. When is a sale or purchase of goods said to take place in the course of inter-State trade or commerce. A sale or purchase of goods shall be deemed to take place in the course of inter-State trade or commerce if the sale or purchase-

(a) occasions the movement of goods from one State to another; or

(b) is effected by a transfer of documents of title to the goods during their movement from one State to another.

EXPLANATION 1: Where goods are delivered to a carrier or other bailee for transmission, the movement of the goods shall, for the purposes of clause (b), be deemed to commence at the time of such delivery and terminate at the time when delivery is taken from such carrier or bailee.

EXPLANATION 2. Where the movement of goods commences and terminates in the same State it shall not be deemed to be a movement of the goods from one State to another by reason merely of the fact that in the course of such movement the goods pass through the territory of any other State.

4. When is a sale or purchase of goods said to take place outside a State.

(1) Subject to the provisions contained in Section 3, when a sale or purchase of goods is determined in accordance with sub-section (2) to take place inside a State, such sale or purchase shall be deemed to have taken place outside all other States.

(2) A sale or purchase of goods shall be deemed to take place inside a State, if the goods are within the State-

(a) in the case of specific or ascertained goods, at the time of the contract of sale is made; and

(b) in the case of unascertained or future goods, at the time of their appropriation to the contract of sale by the seller or by the buyer, whether assent of the other party is prior or subsequent to such appropriation.

EXPLANATION: Where there is a single contract of sale or purchase of goods situated at more places than one, the provisions of this sub-section shall apply as if there were separate contracts in respect of the goods at each of such places.

5. When is a sale or purchase of goods said to take place in the course of import or export.

(1) A sale or purchase of goods shall be deemed to take place in the course of the export of the goods out of the territory of India only if the sale or purchase either occasions such export or is affected by a transfer of documents of title to the goods after the goods have crossed the customs frontiers of India.

(2) A sale or purchase of goods shall be deemed to take place in the course of the import of the goods into the territory of India only if the sale or purchase either occasions such import or is effected by a transfer of documents of title to the goods before the goods have crossed the customs frontiers of India.

(3) Notwithstanding anything contained in sub-section (1), the last sale or purchase of any goods preceding the sale or purchase occasioning the export of those goods out of the territory of India shall also be deemed to be in the course of such export, if such last sale or purchase took place after, and was for the purpose of complying with, the agreement or order for or in relation to such export.

(4) The provisions of sub-section (3) shall not apply to any sale or purchase of goods unless the dealer selling the goods furnishes to the prescribed authority in the prescribed manner a declaration duly filled and signed by the exporter

to whom the goods are sold in a prescribed form obtained from the prescribed authority.

(5) Notwithstanding anything contained in sub-section (1), if any designated Indian carrier purchases Aviation Turbine Fuel for the purposes of its international flight, such purchase shall be deemed to take place in the course of the export of goods out of the territory of India.

EXPLANATION: For the purposes of this sub-section, 'designated Indian carrier' means any carrier which the Central Government may, by notification in the Official Gazette, specify in this behalf.

CHAPTER - III : INTER-STATE SALES TAX

6. Liability to tax on inter-state sales.

(1) Subject to the other provisions contained in this Act, every dealer shall, with effect from such date as the Central Government may, by notification in the Official Gazette, appoint, not being earlier than thirty days from the date of such notification, be liable to pay tax under this Act on all sales of goods other than electrical energy effected by him in the course of inter-State trade or commerce during any year on and from the date so notified:

PROVIDED that a dealer shall not be liable to pay tax under this Act on any sale of goods which, in accordance with the provisions of sub-section (3) of Section 5 is a sale in the course of export of those goods out of the territory of India.

(1A) A dealer shall be liable to pay tax under this Act on a sale of any goods effected by him, in the course of inter-State trade or commerce notwithstanding that no tax would have been leviable (whether on the seller or the purchaser) under the sales tax law of the appropriate State if that sale had taken place inside that State.

(2) Notwithstanding anything contained in sub-section (1) or sub-section (1A), where a sale of any goods in the course of inter-State trade or commerce has either occasioned the movement of such goods from one State to another or has been effected by a transfer of documents of title to such goods during their movement from one State to another, any subsequent sale during such movement effected by a transfer of documents of title to such goods,-

(a) to the Government, or

(b) to a registered dealer other than the Government, if the goods are of the description referred to in sub-section (3) of Section 8 shall be exempt from tax under this Act:

PROVIDED that no such subsequent sale shall be exempt from tax under this sub-section unless the dealer effecting the sale furnishes to the prescribed authority in the prescribed manner and within the prescribed time or within such further time as that authority may, for sufficient cause, permit,-

(a) a certificate dully filled and signed by the registered dealer from whom the goods

were purchased containing the prescribed particulars in a prescribed form obtained from the prescribed authority; and

(b) If the subsequent sale is made- (i) to a registered dealer, a declaration referred to in clause (a) of sub-section (4) of Section 8, or (ii) to the Government, not being a registered dealer, a certificate referred to in clause (b) of sub-section (4) of Section 8:

PROVIDED FURTHER that it shall not be necessary to furnish the declaration or the certificate referred to in clause (b) of the preceding proviso in respect of a subsequent sale of goods if :-

(a) the sale or purchase of such goods is, under the sales tax law of the appropriate State, exempt from tax generally or is subject to tax generally at a rate which is lower than four per cent (whether called a tax or fee or by any other name); and

(b) the dealer effecting such subsequent sale proves to the satisfaction of the authority referred to in the preceding proviso that such sale is of the nature referred to in clause (a) or clause (b) of this sub-section.

(3) Notwithstanding anything contained in this Act, no tax under this Act shall be payable by any dealer in respect of sale of any goods made by such dealer, in the course of inter-state trade or commerce, to any official, personnel, consular or diplomatic agent of-

(i) any foreign diplomatic mission or consulate in India; or

(ii) the United Nations or any other similar international body, entitled to privileges under any convention or agreement to which India is a party or under any law for the time being in force, if such official, personnel, consular or diplomatic agent, as the case may be, has purchased such goods for himself or for the purposes of such mission, consulate, United Nations or other body.

(4) The provisions of sub-section (3) shall not apply to the sale of goods made in the course of inter-State trade or commerce unless the dealer selling such goods furnishes to the prescribed authority a certificate in the prescribed manner on the prescribed form duly filled and signed by the official, personnel, consular or diplomatic agent, as the case may be.

6A. Burden of proof, etc., In case of transfer of goods claimed otherwise than by way of sale.

(1) Where any dealer claims that he is not liable to pay tax under this Act, in respect of any goods, on the ground that the movement of such goods from one State to another was occasioned by reason of transfer of such goods by him to any other place of his business or to his agent or principal, as the case may be and not by reason of sale, the burden of proving that the movement of those goods was so occasioned shall be on that dealer and for this purpose he may furnish to the assessing authority, within the prescribed time or within such further time as that authority may, for sufficient cause, permit, a declaration, duly filled and signed by the principal officer of the other place of business, or

his agent or principal, as the case may be, containing the prescribed particulars in the prescribed form obtained from the prescribed authority, along with the evidence of dispatch of such goods and if the dealer fails to furnish such declaration, then, the movement of such goods shall be deemed for all purposes of this Act to have been occasioned as a result of sale.

(2) If the assessing authority is satisfied after making such inquiry as he may deem necessary that the particulars contained in the declaration furnished by a dealer under sub-section (1) are true, he may, at the time of, or at any time before, the assessment of the tax payable by the dealer under this Act, make an order to that effect and thereupon the movement of goods to which the declaration relates shall be deemed for the purposes of this Act to have been occasioned otherwise than as a result of sale.

EXPLANATION: In this Section, "assessing authority", in relation to a dealer, means the authority for the time being competent to assess the tax payable by the dealer under this Act.

7. Registration of dealers

(1) Every dealer liable to pay tax under this Act, shall within such time as may be prescribed for the purpose, make an application for registration under this Act to such authority in the appropriate State as the Central Government may, by general or special order, specify, and every such application shall contain such particulars as may be prescribed.

(2) Any dealer liable to pay tax under the sales tax law of the appropriate State, or where there is no such law in force in the appropriate State or any part thereof, any dealer having a place of business in that State or part, as the case may be, may, notwithstanding that he is not liable to pay tax under this Act, apply for registration under this Act to the authority referred to in sub-section (1), and every such application shall contain such particulars as may be prescribed.

EXPLANATION: For the purpose of this sub-section, a dealer shall be deemed to be liable to pay tax under the sales tax law of the appropriate State notwithstanding that under such law a sale or purchase made by him is exempt from tax or a refund or rebate of tax is admissible in respect thereof.

(2A) Where it appears necessary to the authority to whom an application is made under sub-section (1) or sub-section (2) so to do for the proper realisation of the tax payable under this Act or for the proper custody and use of the forms referred to in clause (a) of the first proviso to sub-section (2) of Section 6 or sub-section (1) of Section 6A or clause (a) of the sub-section (4) of Section 8, he may, by an order in writing and for reasons to be recorded therein, impose as a condition for the issue of a certificate of registration a requirement that the dealer shall furnish in the prescribed manner and within such time as may be specified in the order such security as may be so specified, for all or any of the aforesaid purposes.

(3) If the authority to whom an application under sub-section (1) or sub-section (2) is made is satisfied that the application is in conformity with the provisions of this Act and the rules made thereunder and the condition, if any, imposed under sub-section (2A), has been complied with, he shall register the applicant and grant to him a certificate of registration in the prescribed form which shall specify the class or classes of goods for the purposes of sub-section (1) of Section 8.

(3A) Where it appears necessary to the authority granting a certificate of registration under this Section so to do for the proper realisation of tax payable under this Act or for the proper custody and use of the forms referred to in sub-section (2A), he may, at any time while such certificate is in force, by an order in writing and for reasons to be recorded therein, require the dealer, to whom the certificate has been granted, to furnish within such time as may be specified in the order and in the prescribed manner such security, or, if the dealer has already furnished any security in pursuance of an order under this sub-section or sub-section (2A), such additional security, as may be specified in the order, for all or any of the aforesaid purposes.

(3B) No dealer shall be required to furnish any security under sub-section (2A) or any security or additional security under sub-section (3A) unless he has been given an opportunity of being heard.

(3BB) The amount of security which a dealer may be required to furnish under sub-section (2A) or sub-section (3A) or the aggregate of the amount of such a security and the amount of additional security which he may be required to furnish under sub-section (3A), by the authority referred to therein shall not exceed-

(a) in the case of a dealer other than a dealer who has made an application, or who has been registered in pursuance of an application, under sub-section (2), a sum equal to the tax payable under this Act, in accordance with the estimate of such authority, on the turnover of such dealer for the year in which such security or, as the case may be, additional security is required to be furnished, and

(b) in the case of a dealer who has made an application, or who has been registered in pursuance of an application, under sub-section (2), a sum equal to the tax leviable under this Act, in accordance with the estimate of such authority on the sales to such dealer in the course of inter-State trade or commerce in the year in which such security or, as the case may be, additional security is required to be furnished, had such dealer been not registered under this Act.

(3C) Where the security furnished by the dealer under sub-section (2A) or sub-section (3A) is in the form of a surety bond and the surety becomes insolvent or dies, the dealer shall, within thirty days of the occurrence of any of the aforesaid events, inform the authority granting the certificate of registration and shall within ninety days of such occurrence furnish a fresh surety bond or furnish in the prescribed manner other security for the amount of the bond.

(3D) The authority granting the certificate of registration may by order and for good and sufficient cause forfeit the whole or any part of the security furnished by a dealer-

(a) for realizing any amount of tax or penalty payable by the dealer,

(b) if the dealer is found to have misused any of the forms referred to in sub-section (2A) or to have failed to keep them in proper custody:

PROVIDED that no order shall be passed under this sub-section without giving the dealer an opportunity of being heard.

(3E) Where by reason of an order under sub-section (3D), the security furnished by any dealer is rendered insufficient, he shall make up the deficiency in such manner and within such time as may be prescribed.

(3F) The authority issuing the forms referred to in sub-section (2A) may refuse to issue such a forms to a dealer who has failed to comply with an order under that sub-section or sub-section (3A), or with the provisions of sub-section (3C) or sub-section (3E), until the dealer has complied with such order or such provisions as the case may be.

(3G) The authority granting a certificate of registration may, on application by the dealer to whom it has been granted, order the refund of any amount or part thereof deposited by the dealer by way of security under this Section, if it is not required for the purposes of this Act.

(3H) Any person aggrieved by an order passed under sub-section (2A), sub-section (3A), sub-section (3D) or sub-section (3G) may, within thirty days of the service of the order on him, but after furnishing the security, prefer, in such form and manner as may be prescribed, an appeal against such order to such authority (hereinafter in this Section referred to as the "appellate authority") as may be prescribed:

PROVIDED that the appellate authority may, for sufficient cause, permit such person to present the appeal -

(a) after the expiry of the said period of thiry days; or

(b) without furnishing the whole or any part of such security.

(3I) The procedure to be followed in hearing any appeal under sub-section (3H), and the fees payable in respect of such appeals shall be such as may be prescribed.

(3J) The order passed by the appellate authority in any appeal under sub-section (3H) shall be final.]

[30A. Sub-sections 3(C) to 3(J) were inserted by Act 61 of 1979 (w.e.f.1.4.1973).

(4) A certificate of registration granted under this Section may-

(a) either on the application of the dealer to whom it has been granted or, where no such application has been made, after due notice to the dealer, be amended by the authority granting it if he satisfied that by reason of the registered dealer having changed the name, place or nature of his business or the class or classes of goods in which he carries on business or for any other reason the certificate or registration granted to him requires to be amended; or

(b) be cancelled by the authority granting it where he is satisfied, after due notice to the dealer to whom it has been granted, that he has ceased to carry on business or has ceased to exist or has failed without sufficient cause to comply with an order under sub-section (3A) or with the provisions of sub-section (3C) or sub-section (3E) or has failed to pay any tax or penalty payable under this Act, or in the case of a dealer registered under sub-section (2) has ceased to be liable to pay tax under the sales tax law of the appropriate State or for any other sufficient reason.

(5) A registered dealer may apply in the prescribed manner not latter than six months before the end of a year to the authority which granted his certificate of registration for the cancellation of such registration, and the authority shall, unless the dealer is liable to pay tax under this Act, cancel the registration accordingly, and where he does so, the cancellation shall take effect from the end of the year.

8. Rates of tax on sales in the course of inter-State trade or commerce.

(1) Every dealer, who in the course of inter-State trade or commerce

(a) sells to the Government any goods; or

(b) sells to a registered dealer other than the Government, goods of the description referred to in sub-section (3) shall be liable to pay tax under this Act, which shall be four per cent of his turnover or at the rate applicable to the sale or purchase of such goods inside the appropriate State under the sales tax law of that State, whichever is lower :

PROVIDED that the rate of tax payable under this sub-section by a dealer shall continue to be four percent, of his turnover, until the rate of two percent takes effect under this sub-section.

(2) The tax payable by any dealer on his turnover in so far as the turnover or any part thereof relates to the sale of goods in the course of inter-State trade or commerce not falling within sub-section (1) -

(a) in the case of declared goods, shall be calculated (at twice the rate) applicable to the sale or purchase of such goods inside the appropriate State;

(b) in the case of goods other than declared goods, shall be calculated at the rate of ten per cent or at the rate applicable to the sale or purchase of such goods inside the appropriate State, whichever is higher; and

(c) in the case of goods, the sale or, as the case may be, the purchase of which is, under the sales tax law of the appropriate State, exempt from tax generally shall be *nil,* and for the purpose of making any such calculation under clause(a) or clause (b), any such dealer shall be deemed to be a dealer liable to pay tax under the sales tax law of the appropriate State, notwithstanding that he, if in fact, may not be so liable under that law.

EXPLANATION: For the purposes of this sub-section, a sale or purchase of any goods shall not be deemed to be exempt from tax generally under the sales tax law of the appropriate State if under that law the sale or purchase of such goods is exempt only in specified circumstances or under specified conditions or tax is levied on the sale or purchase of such goods at specified stages or otherwise than with reference to the turnover of the goods.

(2A) Omitted.

(3) The goods referred to in clause (b) of sub-section (1)-

are goods of the class or classes specified in the certificate of registration of the registered dealer purchasing the goods as being intended for re-sale by him or subject to any rules made by the [Central Government in this behalf, for use by him in the manufacture or processing of goods for sale or in the telecommunications network or] in mining or in generation or distribution of electricity or any other form of power;

are containers or other materials specified in the certificate of registration of the registered dealer purchasing the goods, being containers or materials intended for being used for the packing of goods for sale;

are containers or other materials used for the packing of any goods or classes of goods specified in the certificate of registration referred to in clause (b) or for the packing of any containers or other materials specified in the certificate of registration referred to in clause (c).

(4) The provisions of sub-section (1) shall not apply to any sale in the course of inter-State trade or commerce unless the dealer selling the goods furnishes to the prescribed authority in the prescribed manner -

(a) a declaration duly filled and signed by the registered dealer to whom the goods are sold containing the prescribed particulars in the prescribed form obtained from the prescribed authority; or

(b) if the goods are sold to the Government, not being a registered dealer, a certificate in the prescribed form duly filled and signed by a duly authorised officer of the Government.

PROVIDED that the declaration referred to in clause (a) is furnished within the prescribed time or within such further time as that authority may, for sufficient cause, permit.

(5) Notwithstanding anything contained in this Section, the State Government may, on the fulfilment of the requirements laid down in sub-section (4) by the dealer if it is satisfied that it is necessary so to do in the public interest, by notification in the Official Gazette, and subject to such conditions as may be specified therein direct-

(a) that no tax under this Act shall be payable by any dealer having his place of business in the State in respect of the sales by him, in the course of inter-State trade or commerce, to a registered dealer or the Government from any such place of business of any such goods or classes of goods as may be specified in the notification, or that the tax on such sales shall be calculated at such lower rates than those specified in sub-section (1) or sub-section (2) as may be mentioned in the notification;

(b) that in respect of all sales of goods or sales of such classes of goods as may be specified in the notification, which are made, in the course of inter-State trade or commerce, to a registered dealer or [the Government] by any dealer having his place of business in the State or by any class of such dealers as may be specified in the notification to any person or to such class of persons as may be specified in the notification, no tax under this Act shall be payable or the tax on such sales shall be calculated at such lower rates than those specified in sub-section (1) or sub-section (2) as may be mentioned in the notification.

(6) Notwithstanding anything contained in this Section, no tax under this Act shall be payable by any dealer in respect of sale of any goods made by such dealer, in the course of inter-State trade or commerce to a registered dealer for the purpose of setting up operation, maintenance, manufacture, trading, production, processing, assembling, repairing, reconditioning, re-engineering, packaging or for use as packing material or packing accessories in an unit located in any special economic zone or for development, operation and maintenance of Special Economic zone by the developer of the Special Economic zone, if such registered dealer has been authorised to establish such unit or to develop, operate and maintain such Special Economic Zone by the authority specified by the Central Government in this behalf.

(7) The goods referred to in sub-section (6) shall be the goods of such class or classes of goods as specified in the certificate of registration of the registered dealer referred to in that sub-section.

(8) The provisions of sub-sections (6) and (7) shall not apply to any sale of goods made in the course of inter-State trade or commerce unless the dealer selling such goods furnishes to the prescribed authority referred to in sub-section (4), a declaration in the prescribed manner on the prescribed form obtained from the authority specified by Central Government under sub-section (6), duly filled in and signed by the registered dealer to whom such goods are sold.

EXPLANATION: For the purpose of sub-section (6), the expression "special economic zone" has the meaning assigned to it in clause (iii) to Explanation 2 to the proviso to Section 3 of the Central Excise Act, 1944.

8A. Determination of turnover.

(1) In determining the turnover of a dealer for the purpose of this Act, the following deductions shall be made from the aggregate of the sale prices, namely:-

(a) the amount arrived at by applying the following formula -

$$\frac{\text{rate of tax} \times \text{aggregate of sale prices}}{100 + \text{rate of tax}}$$

PROVIDED that no deduction on the basis of the above formula shall be made if the amount by way of tax collected by a registered dealer, in accordance with the provisions of this Act, has been otherwise deducted from the aggregate of sale prices.

EXPLANATION: Where the turnover of a dealer is taxable at different rates, the aforesaid formula shall be applied separately in respect of each part of the turnover liable to a different rate of tax;

(b) the sale price of all goods returned to the dealer by the purchasers of such goods -

(i) within a period of three months from the date of delivery of the goods, in the case of goods returned before the 14th day of May, 1966;

(ii) within a period of six months from the date of delivery of the goods, in the case of goods returned on or after the 14th day of May, 1966:

PROVIDED that satisfactory evidence of such return of goods and of refund or adjustment in accounts of the sale price thereof is produced before the authority competent to assess or, as the case may be, re-assess the tax payable by the dealer under this Act; and

(c) such other deductions as the Central Government may, having regard to the prevalent market conditions, facility of trade and interests of consumers, prescribe.

(2) Save as otherwise provided in sub-section (1), in determining the turnover of a dealer for the purposes of this Act, no deduction shall be made from the aggregate of the sale prices.

9. Levy and collection of tax and penalties.

(1) The tax payable by any dealer under this Act on sales of goods effected by him in the course of inter-State trade or commerce, whether such sales fall within clause (a) or clause (b) of Section 3, shall be levied by the Government of India and the tax so levied shall be collected by the Government in accordance with the provisions of sub-section (2), in the State from which the movement of the goods commenced.

PROVIDED that, in the case of a sale of goods during their movement from one State to another, being a sale subsequent to the first sale in respect of the same goods and being also a sale which does not fall within sub-section (2) of Section 6, the tax shall be levied and collected.

(a) where such subsequent sale has been effected by a registered dealer, in the State from which the registered dealer obtained or, as the case may be, could have obtained, the form prescribed for the purposes of clause (a) of sub-section (4) of Section 8 in connection with the purchase of such goods, and,

(b) where such subsequent sale has been effected by an unregistered dealer in the State from which such subsequent sale has been effected.

(2) Subject to the other provisions of this Act and the rules made thereunder, the authorities for the time being empowered to assess, re-assess, collect and enforce payment of any tax under general sales tax law of the appropriate State shall, on behalf of the Government of India, assess, re-assess, collect and enforce payment of tax, including any interest or penalty], payable by a dealer under this Act as if the tax or interest or penalty] payable by such a dealer under this Act is a tax or interest or penalty payable under general sales tax law of the State; and for this purpose they may exercise all or any of the powers they have under the general sales tax law of the State; and the provisions of such law, including provisions relating to returns, provisional assessment, advance payment of tax registration of the transferee of any business, imposition of the tax liability of a person carrying on business on the transferee of, or successor to, such business, transfer of liability of any firm or Hindu undivided family to pay tax in the event of the dissolution of such firm or partition of such family, recovery of tax from third parties, appeals, reviews, revisions, references, refunds, rebates, penalties, charging or payment of interest, compounding of offences and treatment of documents furnished by a dealer as confidential, shall apply accordingly:

PROVIDED that if in any State or part thereof there is no general sales tax law in force, the Central Government may, by rules made in this behalf make necessary provisions for all or any of the matters specified in this sub-section.

(2A) All the provisions relating to offences, interest and penalties (including provisions relating to penalties in lieu of prosecution for an offence or in addition to the penalties or punishments for an offence but excluding the provisions relating to matters provided for in Section 10 and 10A) of the general sales tax law of each State shall, with necessary modifications, apply in relation to the assessment, re-assessment, collection and the enforcement of payment of any tax required to be collected under this Act in such State or in relation to any processes connected with such assessment, re-assessment, collection or enforcement of payment as if the tax under this Act were a tax under such sales tax law.

(2B) If the tax payable by any dealer under this Act is not paid in time, the dealer shall be liable to pay interest for delayed payment of such tax and all the provisions for delayed payment of such tax and all the provisions relating to due date for payment of tax, rate of interest for delayed payment of tax, of the general sales tax law of each state, shall apply in relation to due date for payment of tax, rate of interest for delayed payment of tax, and assessment and collection of interest for delayed payment of tax under this Act in such states as if the tax and the interest payable under this Act were a tax and an interest under such sales tax law.

(3) The proceeds in any financial year of any tax, including any interest or penalty including any penalty, levied and collected under this Act in any State (other than a Union Territory on behalf of the Government of India shall be assigned to that State and shall be retained by it; and the proceeds attributes to Union Territories shall form part of the Consolidated Funds of India.

Validation of Section 9

(1) The provisions of Section 9 of the Central Sales Tax' 1956 (hereafter in this Section referred to as the Central Sales Tax Act) shall have effect, and shall be deemed always to have had effect, as if that Section also provided –

(a) That all the provisions relating to interest of the general sales tax law of each state shall, with necessary modifications, apply in relation to –

(i) the assessment, re-assessment, collection and enforcement of payment of any tax required to be collected under the Central Sales Tax Act, in such State; and

(ii) any process connected with such assessment, re-assessment, collection or enforcement of payment; and

(b) that for the purpose of the application of the provisions of such law, the tax under the Central Sales Tax Act shall be deemed to be tax under such law.

(2) Notwithstanding anything contained in any judgment, decree or order of any court, tribunal or other authority, general sales tax law of any State imposed or purporting to have been imposed in pursuance of the provisions of Section 9 of the Central Sales Tax Act, and all proceedings, acts or things taken or done for the purposes of, or in relation to the imposition or collection of such interest, before the commencement of this Section, shall for all purposes, be deemed to be and to have always been imposed, taken or done as validly and effectively as if the provisions of sub-section (1) had been in force when such interest was imposed or proceedings or acts or things were taken or done and, accordingly;

(a) no suit or other proceedings shall be maintained or continued in, or before, any court, tribunal or other authority for the refund of any amount received or realized by way of such interest;

(b) no court, tribunal or other authority shall enforce any decree or order directing the refund of any amount received or realized by way of such interest;

(c) where any amount which had been received or realized by way of such interest is refunded before the date on which the Finance Act, 2000 receives the assent of the President and such refund would not have been allowed if the provisions of sub-section (1) had been in force on the date on which the order for such refund was passed, the amount so refunded may be recovered as an arrear of tax under the Central Sales Tax Act;

(d) any proceeding, act or thing which could have been validly taken, continued or done for the imposition of collection of such interest at any time before the commencement of this Section if the provisions of sub-section (1) had then been in force but which had not been taken, continued or done, may after such commencement, be taken, continued or done.

(3) Nothing in sub-section (2) shall be construed as preventing any person

(a) from questioning the imposition or collection of any interest or any proceedings, act or thing in connection therewith; or

(b) from claiming any refund, in accordance with the provisions of the Central Sales Tax Act, read with sub-section (1).

EXPLANATION: For this purposes of this Section, "general sales tax law" shall have the same meaning assigned to it in the Central Sales Tax Act.

9A. Collection of tax to be only by registered dealers. No person who is not a registered dealer shall collect in respect of any sale by him of goods in the course of inter-State trade or commerce any amount by way of tax under this Act, and no registered dealer shall make any such collection except in accordance with this Act and the rules made there under.

9B. Rounding off of tax, etc. The amount of tax, interest, penalty, fine or any other sum payable, and the amount of refund due, under the provisions of this Act shall be rounded off to the nearest rupee and, for this purpose, where such amount contains a part of a rupee consisting of paise, then, if such part is fifty paise or more, it shall be increased to one rupee and if such part is less than fifty paise it shall be ignored.

PROVIDED that nothing in this Section shall apply for the purpose of collection by a dealer of any amount by way of tax under this Act in respect of any sale by him of goods in the course of inter-State trade or commerce.

10. Penalties. If any person-

(a) furnishes a certificate or declaration under sub-section (2) of Section 6 or sub-section (1) of Section 6A or sub-section (4) or sub-section (8) of Section 8, which he knows, or has reason to believe, to be false; or

(aa) fails to get himself registered as required by Section 7 or fails to comply with an order under sub-section (3A) or with the requirements of sub-section (3C) or sub-section (3E), of that Section,

(b) being a registered dealer, falsely represents when purchasing any class of goods that goods of such a class are covered by his certificate of registration, or

(c) not being a registered dealer, falsely represents when purchasing goods in the course of inter-State trade or commerce that he is a registered dealer; or

(d) after purchasing any goods for any of the purposes specified in clause (b) or clause(c) or clause (d) of sub-section (3) or sub-section (6)] of Section 8 fails, without reasonable excuse to make use of the goods for any such purpose,

(e) has in his possession any form prescribed for the purpose of sub-section (4) or sub-section (8) of Section 8 which has not been obtained by him or by his principal or by his agent in accordance with the provisions of this Act or any rules made thereunder;

(f) collects any amount by way of tax in contravention of the provisions contained in Section 9A, he shall be punishable with simple imprisonment which may extend to six months or with fine or with both, and when the offence is a continuing offence, with a daily fine which may extend to fifty rupees for every day during which the offence continues.

10A. Imposition of penalty in lieu of prosecution.

(1) If any person purchasing goods is guilty of an offence under clause (b) or clause (c) or clause (d) of Section 10, the authority who granted to him or, as the case may be, is competent to grant to him a certificate of registration under this Act may, after giving him a reasonable opportunity of being heard, by order in writing, impose upon him by way of penalty a sum not exceeding one and a half times the tax which would have been levied under sub-section (2) of Section 8 in respect of the sale to him of the goods, if the sale had been a sale falling within that sub-section.

PROVIDED that no prosecution for an offence under Section 10 shall be instituted in respect of the same facts on which a penalty has been imposed under this Section.

(2) The penalty imposed upon any dealer under sub-section (1) shall be collected by the Government of India in the manner provided in sub-section (2) of Section 9 -

(a) in the case of an offence falling under clause (b) or clause (d) of Section 10, in the State in which the person purchasing the goods obtained the form prescribed for the purposes of clause (a) of sub-section (4) of Section 8 in connection with the purchase of such goods;

(b) in the case of an offence falling under clause (c) of Section 10, in the State in which the person purchasing the goods should have registered himself if the offence had not been committed.

11. Cognizance of offences.

(1) No court shall take cognizance of any offence punishable under the Act or the rules made thereunder except with the previous sanction of the Government within the local limits of whose jurisdiction the offence has been committed or such officer of that Government as it may, by general or special order, specify in this behalf; and no court inferior to that of a presidency magistrate or a magistrate of the first class shall try any such offence.

(2) All offences punishable under this Act shall be cognizable and bailable.

12. Indemnity. No suit, prosecution or other legal proceeding shall lie against any officer of Government for anything which is in good faith done or intended to be done under this Act or the rules made thereunder.

13. Power to make rules.

(1) The Central Government may, by notification in the Official Gazette, make rules providing for-

(a) the manner in which applications for registration may be made under this Act, the particulars to be contained therein, the procedure for the grant of such registration, the circumstances in which registration may be refused and the form in which the certificate of registration may be given;

(aa) The manner of determination of the sale price and the deductions from the total consideration for a works contract under the proviso to clause (h) of Section 2;

(ab) the form and the manner for furnishing declaration under sub-section (8) of Section 8;

(b) the period of turnover, the manner in which the turnover in relation to the sale of any goods under this Act shall be determined, and the deductions which may be made under clause (c) of sub-section (1) of Section 8A in the process of such determination;

(c) the cases and circumstances in which, and the conditions subject to which, any registration granted under this Act may be cancelled;

(d) the form in which and the particulars to be contained in any declaration or certificate to be given under this Act, the State of origin of such form or certificate and the time within which any such certificate or declaration shall be produced or furnished

(e) the enumeration of goods or class of goods used in the manufacture or processing of goods for sale or in mining or in the generation or distribution of electricity or any other form of power;

(f) the matters in respect of which provisions may be made under the proviso to sub-section (2) of Section 9;

(g) the fees payable in respect of applications under this Act.

(h) the proper functioning of the authority constituted under Section 19.

(i) the salaries and allowances payable to, and the terms and conditions of service of, the Chairman and Members under sub-section (3) of Section 19.

(j) any other matter as may be prescribed.

(2) Every rule made by the Central Government under sub-section (1) shall be laid as soon as may be after it is made, before each House of Parliament, while it is in session, for a total period of thirty days which may be comprised in one session or in two or more successive sessions, and if, before the expiry of the session immediately following the sessions or the successive sessions aforesaid, both Houses agree in making any modification in the rule or both Houses agree that the rule should not be made, the rule shall thereafter have effect only in such modified form or be of no effect, as the case may be; so

however, that any such modification or annulment shall be without prejudice to the validity of anything previously done under that rule.

(3) The State Government may make rules, not inconsistent with the provisions of this Act and the rules made under sub-section (1), to carry out the purposes of this Act.

(4) In particular and without prejudice to the powers conferred by sub-section (3), the State Government may make rules for all or any of the following purposes namely:-

(a) the publication of lists of registered dealers, of the amendments made in such lists from time to time, and the particulars to be contained in such lists;

(aa) the manner of determination of the sale price and the deductions from the total consideration for a works contract under the proviso to clause (h) of Section 2;"

(ab) the manner in which security may be furnished under sub-section (2A) or sub-section (3A) or sub-section (3C) of Section 7 and the manner in which and the time within which any deficiency may be made up under sub-section (3E) of that Section;

(b) the form and manner in which accounts relating to sales in the course of inter-State trade or commerce shall be kept by registered dealers;

(c) the furnishing of any information relating to the stocks of goods of, purchase, sales and deliveries of books by any dealer or any other information relating to his business as may be necessary for the purposes of this Act;

(d) the inspection of any books, accounts or documents required to be kept under this Act, the entry into any premises at all reasonable time for the purposes of searching for any such books, accounts or documents kept or suspected to be kept in such premises and the seizure of such books, accounts or documents;

(e) the authority from whom, the conditions subject to which and the fees subject to payment of which any form of certificate prescribed under clause (a) of the first proviso to sub-section (2) of Section 6 or of declaration prescribed under sub-section (1) of Section 6A or sub-section (4) of Section 8 may be obtained, the manner in which such forms shall be kept in custody and records relating thereto maintained and the manner in which any such form may be used and any such certificate or declaration may be furnished;

(ee) the form and manner in which, and the authority to whom, an appeal may be preferred under sub-section (3H) of Section 7, the procedure to be followed in hearing such appeals and the fees payable in respect of such appeals;

(f) in the case of an undivided Hindu family, association, club, society, firm or company or in the case of a person who carries on business as guardian or trustee or otherwise on behalf of another person, the furnishing of a declaration stating the name of the person who shall be deemed to be the manager in relation to the business of the dealer in the State and the form in which such declaration may be given,

(g) the time within which, the manner in which and the authorities to whom any change in the ownership of any business or in the name, place, or nature of any business carried on by any dealer shall be furnished.

(5) In making any rule under this Section the Central Government, or, as the case may be, the State Government may direct that a breach thereof shall be punishable with fine which may extend to five hundred rupees and when the offence is a continuing offence, with a daily fine which may extend to fifty rupees for every day during which the offence continues.

CHAPTER - IV : GOODS OF SPECIAL IMPORTANCE IN INTER-STATE TRADE OR COMMERCE

14. Certain goods to be of special importance in Inter-State trade or commerce. It is hereby declared that the following goods are of special importance in inter-State trade or commerce :-

(a) cereals, that is to say.-

(i) paddy (Oryza sativa L);

(ii) rice (Oryza sativa L);

(iii) wheat (Triticum vulgare, T.compactum, T.sphaerococcum, T. durum, T. aestivum L.T. discoccum);

(iv) jowar or milo (Sorghum vulgare pers);

(v) bajara (Pennisetum typhoideum L);

(vi) maize (Zea malys D);

(vii) ragi (Eleusine coracana Gaertn);

(viii) kodon (Paspalum scrobiculatum L);

(ix) kutki (Panicum miliare L);

(x) barely (Hordeum vulgare L);]

(aa)] coal, including coak in all its forms, but excluding char-coal:

PROVIDED that during the period commencing on the 23rd day of February, 1967 and ending with the date of commencement of Section 11 of the Central Sales Tax (Amendment) Act, 1972, this clause shall have effect subject to the modification that the words "but excluding charcoal" shall be omitted;

(b) cotton, that is to say, all kinds of cotton (indigenous or imported in its unmanufactured state, whether ginned or unginned baled pressed or otherwise, but not including cotton waste;

(i) cotton fabrics covered under heading Nos. 52.05, 52.06, 52.07, 52.08,

52.09, 52.10, 52.11, 52.12, 58.01, 58.02, 58.03, 58.04, 58.05, 58.06, 59.01, 59.03, 59.05, 59.06 and 60.01 of the Schedule to the Central Excise Tariff Act, 1985;

(ii) cotton yarn but not including cotton yarn waste;

(iii) crude oil, that is to say, crude petroleum oils and crude oils obtained from bituminous minerals such as shale, calcareous rock, sand), whatever their composition, whether obtained from normal or condensation oil-deposits or by the destructive distillation of bituminous minerals and whether or not subject to all or any of the following processes:-

(1) decentration;

(2) de-salting;

(3) dehydration;

(4) stabilisation in order to normalise the vapour pressure,

(5) elimination of very light fractions with a view to returning them to the oil-deposits in order to improve the drainage and maintain the pressure;

(6) the addition of only those hydrocarbons previously recovered by physical methods during the course of above-mentioned processes;

(7) any other minor process (including addition of pour point depressants or flow improves) which does not change the essential character of the substance;

(iv) Aviation Turbine fuel sold to a Turbo-Prop Aircraft.

EXPLANATION: For the purposes of this clause, "Turbo-Prop Aircraft" means an aircraft deriving thrust, mainly from propeller, which may be driven by either turbine engine or piston engine.

(c) hides and skins, whether in a raw or dressed state;

(d) Iron and steel i.e. to say:-

(i) pig iron sponge iron and cast iron including ingot moulds, bottom plates, iron scrap, cast iron scrap, runner scrap and iron skull scrap;

(ii) steel semis (ingots, slabs, blooms and billets of all qualities, shapes and sizes);

(iii) skelp bars, tin bars, sheet bars, hoe-bars and sleeper bars;

(iv) steel bars (rounds, rods, squares, flats, octagons and hexagons, plain and ribbed or twisted, in coil form as well as straight lengths);

(v) steel structural (angles, joists, channels, tees, sheet, pilling Section, Z Sections or any other rolled Sections);

(vi) sheets, hoops, strips and skelp, both black and galvanised, hot and cold rolled, plain and corrugated in all qualities, in straight lengths and in coil form, as rolled and in rivetted condition;

(vii) plates both plain and chequered in all qualities;

(viii) discs, rings, forgings and steel castings;

(ix) tool, alloy and special steels of any of the above categories;

(x) steel melting scrap in all forms including steel skull, turnings and borings;

(xi) steel tubes both welded and seamless, of all diameters and lengths including tube fittings;

(xii) tin-plates, both hot dipped and electrolytic and tin-free plates;

(xiii) fish plates bars, bearing plates bars, crossing sleeper bars, fish plates, bearing plates, crossing sleepers and pressed steel sleepers, rails-heavy and light crane rails;

(xiv) wheels, tyres, axels and wheels sets;

(xv) wire rods and wire-rolled, drawn, galvanised, aluminised, tinned or coated such as by copper;

(xvi) defectives, rejects, cuttings or end pieces of any of the above categories;

(e) jute, that is to say, the fibre extracted from plants belonging to the species corchorus capsularies, and Corchorus olitorius and the fibre known as mesta or bimli extracted from plants of the species Hibiscus cannabinus and Hibiscus sabdariffa- Varaltissima and the fibre known as Summ or Sunn-hemp extracted from plants of the species Crotalaria Juncea whether baled or otherwise;

(va) Liquified Patroleum Gas for domestic use

(f) Oilseeds, that is to say:-

(i) Groundnut or peanut (Arachis hypogaea);

(ii) Sesamum or Til (Sesamum orientale);

(iii) Cotton seed (Gossypium Spp);

(iv) Soyabean (Glycine seja);

(v) Rapseed and Mustared

1. Torta (Brassica campestris var toria);
2. Rai (Brassica juncea);
3. Jamba-Taramira(Eruca Saatiya);
4. Sarson, yellow and brown (Brassica campestris var sarson);
5. Banarsi Rai or True Mustured (Brassica nigra);

(vi) Linseed (Linum usitatissimum);

(vii) Castor (Ricinus communis);

(viii) Coconut (i.e. Copra excluding tender coconuts) (Cocosnucifers);

(ix) Sunflower (Helianthus annus);

(x) Nigar seed (Guizotia abyssinica);

(xi) Neem, vepa (Azadirachta indica);

(xii) Mahua, illupai, Ippe (Medhuca indica M. Latifolia, Bassia, Latifolia and Madhuca longifolia syn. M. Longifolia);

(xiii) Karanja; Pongam, Honga (Pongamia pinnata syn.P. Glabra);

(xiv) Kusum (Schleichera oleosa, syn S. Trijuga);

(xv) Punna, Undi (Calophyllum inophyllum);

(xvi) Kokum (Carcinia indica);

(xvii) Sal (Shorea robusta);

(xviii) Tung (Aleurites fordii and A.montanna)

(xix) Red palm (Elaeis guinensis);

(xx) Safflower (Carthanus tincotorius);

(fa) pulses, that is to say:-

(i) gram or gulab (Cicerarietinum L);

(ii) tur or arhar (Cajanus cajan);

(iii) moong or green gram (Phaseolus aureus);

(iv) masuri or lentil (Lens esculenta Moench, Lens culinaris Mdeic);

(v) urad or black gram (Phaseolus mungo);

(vi) moth (Phaseolus aconitifolius Jacq);

(vii) lakh or khesari (Lathyrus sativus L);

(g) man-made fabrics covered under heading Nos. 54.08, 54.09, 54.10, 54.11, 54.12, 55.07, 55.08, 55.09, 55.10, 55.11, 55.12, 58.01, 58.02, 58.03, 58.04, 58.05, 58.06, 59.01, 59.02, 59.03, 59.05, 59.06 and 60.01 of the Schedule to the Central Excise Tariff Act, 1985 (5 of 1986);

(h) sugar covered under sub-heading Nos. 1701.20, 1701.31, 1701.39 and 1702.11 of the Schedule to the Central Excise Tariff Act, 1985 (5 of 1986);

(i) unmanufactured tobacco and tobacco refuse covered under sub-heading No. 2401.00, cigars and cheroots of tobacco covered under heading No.24.02, cigarette and cigarillos of tobacco covered under sub-heading Nos. 2403.11 and 2403.21 and other manufactured tobacco covered under sub-heading Nos. 2404.11, 2404.12, 2404.13, 2404.19, 2404.21, 2404.29, 2404.31, 2404.39, 2404.41, 2404.50 and 2404.60, of the Schedule to the Central Excise Tariff Act, 1985 (5 of 1986);

(j) woven fabrics of wool covered under heading Nos. 51.06, 51.07, 58.01, 58.02, 58.03 and 58.05 of the Schedule to the Central Excise Tariff Act, 1985.

[****]

15. Restrictions and conditions in regard to tax on sale or purchase of declared goods within a State. Every sales tax law of a State shall, insofar as it imposes or authorises the imposition of a tax on the sale or purchase of declared goods, be subject to the following restrictions and conditions, namely:-

(a) the tax payable under that law in respect of any sale or purchase of such goods inside the State shall not exceed four percent of the sale or purchase price thereof [****]

(b) where a tax has been levied under that law in respect of the sale or purchase inside the State of any declared goods and such goods are sold in the course of inter-State trade or commerce, and tax has been paid under this Act in respect of the sale of such goods in the course of inter-State trade or commerce, the tax levied under such law shall be reimbursed to the person making such sale in the course of inter-State trade or commerce in such manner and subject to such conditions as may be provided in any law in force in that State;

(c) where a tax has been levied under that law in respect of the sale or purchase inside the State of any paddy referred to in sub-clause (i) of clause (i) of Section 14, the tax leviable on rice procured out of such paddy shall be reduced by the amount of tax levied on such paddy;

(ca) Where a tax on sale or purchase of paddy referred to in sub-clause(i) or clause (a) of Section 14 is leviable under that law and the rice procured out of such paddy is exported out of India, then for the purposes of sub-section (3) of Section 5, the paddy and rice shall be treated as a single commodity.

(d) each of the pulses referred to in clause (fa) of Section 14, whether whole or separated, and whether with or without husk, shall be treated as a single commodity for the purposes of levy of tax under this law.

CHAPTER - V : LIABILITY IN SPECIAL CASES

16. Definitions. In this Chapter,-

(a) "appropriate authority", in relation to a company means the authority competent to assess tax on the company;

(b) "company" and "private company" have the meanings respectively assigned to them by clauses (i) and (iii) of sub-section (1) of Section 3 of the Companies Act, 1956.

17. Company in liquidation.

(1) Every person (a) who is the liquidator of any company which is being wound up, whether under the orders of a court or otherwise; or (b) who has been appointed the receiver of any assets of a company, (hereinafter referred to as the liquidator) shall, within thirty days after he has become such liquidator, give notice of his appointment as such to the appropriate authority.

(2) The appropriate authority shall, after making such inquiry or calling for such information as it may deem fit, notify to the liquidator within three months from the date on which he receives notice of the appointment of the liquidator the amount which, in the opinion of the appropriate authority would be sufficient to provide for any tax which is then, or is likely thereafter to become, payable by the company.

(3) The liquidator shall not part with any of the assets of the company or the properties in his hands until he has been notified by the appropriate authority under sub-section (2) and on being so notified, shall set aside an amount equal to the amount notified and, until he so set aside such amount, shall not part with any of the assets of the company or properties in his hands:

PROVIDED that nothing contained in this sub-section shall debar the liquidator from parting with such assets or properties in compliance with any order of a court or for the purpose of the payment of the tax payable by the company under this Act or for making any payment to secured creditors whose debts are entitled under law to priority of payment over debts due to Government on the date of liquidation or for meeting such costs and expenses of the winding up of the company as are in the opinion of the appropriate authority reasonable.

(4) If the liquidator fails to give the notice in accordance with sub-section (1) or fails to set aside the amount as required by, or parts with any of the assets of the company or the properties in his hands in contravention of the provisions of sub-section (3), he shall be personally liable for the payment of the tax which the company would be liable to pay:

PROVIDED that if the amount of any tax payable by the company is notified under sub-section (2), the personal liability of the liquidator under this sub-section shall be to the extent of such amount.

(5) Where there are more liquidators than one, the obligations and liabilities attached to the liquidator under this Section shall attach to all the liquidators jointly and severally.

(6) The provisions of this Section shall have effect notwithstanding anything to the contrary contained in any other law for the time being in force.

18. Liability of directors of private company in liquidation. Notwithstanding anything contained in the Companies Act, 1956 when any private company is wound up after the commencement of this Act, and any tax assessed on the company under this Act for any period, whether before or in the course of or after its liquidation, cannot be recovered, then, every person who was a director of the private company at any time during the period for which the tax is due shall be jointly and severally liable for the payment of such tax unless he proves that the non-recovery cannot be attributed to any gross neglect, misfeasance or breach of duty on his part in relation to the affairs of the company.

CHAPTER - VI : AUTHORITY TO SETTLE DISPUTES IN COURSE OF INTER-STATE TRADE OR COMMERCE

19. Central Sales Tax Appellate Authority.

(1) The Central Government shall constitute, by notification in the Official Gazette, an Authority to settle inter-State disputes falling under Section 6A read with Section 9 of this Act, to be known as "the Central Sales Tax Appellate Authority (hereinafter referred to as the Authority)".

(2) The Authority shall consist of the following Members appointed by the Central Government, namely:-

(a) a Chairman, who is a retired Judge of the Supreme Court, or a retired Chief Justice of a High Court;

(b) an officer of the Indian Legal Service, who is, or is qualified to be, an Additional Secretary to the Government of India; and

(c) an officer of a State Government not below the rank of Secretary or an officer of the Central Government not below the rank of Additional Secretary, who is an expert in sales tax matters.

(2A) Notwithstanding anything contained in sub-section (2), the Chairman or a member holding a post as such in the Authority for Advance Rulings appointed under clause (a) or clause (c), as the case may be, of sub-section (2) of Section 245-O of the Income-Tax Act, 1961 may, in addition to his being the Chairman or a Member of that Authority, be appointed as the Chairman or a Member, as the case may be, of the Authority under this Act.

(3) The salaries and allowances payable to, and the terms and conditions or service of the Chairman and Members shall be such as may be prescribed.

(4) The Central Government shall provide the Authority with such officers and staff as may be necessary for the efficient exercise of the powers of the Authority under this Act.

19A. Vacancies etc., not to invalidate proceedings. "No proceeding before the Authority shall be questioned or shall be invalid on the ground merely of the existence of any vacancy or defect in the constitution of the Authority".

20. Appeals.

(1) The provisions of this Chapter shall apply to appeals filed by any aggrieved person against any order of the highest appellate authority of a state, made under Section 6A read with Section 9.

EXPLANATION: For the purpose of this Section and Sections 21, 22 and 25 "highest appellate authority of a state" means any authority or tribunal or court (except the High Court) established or constituted under the general sales tax law of a State, by whatever name called.

(2) Notwithstanding anything contained in the general sales tax law of a state, the Authority shall adjudicate an appeal filed under sub Section (1).

(3) An appeal under sub-section (1) may be filed within ninety days from the date on which the order referred to in that sub-section is served on any aggrieved person :

PROVIDED that the Authority may entertain any appeal after the expiry of the said period of ninety days, but not later than one hundred and fifty days from the date of such service, if it is satisfied that the appellant was prevented by sufficient cause from filing the appeal in time.

PROVIDED FURTHER that the authority may entertain any appeal from an aggrieved person within sixty days from the commencement of the Central Sales Tax Act (Amendment) Act, 2005, where such aggrieved person had the right to file an appeal against the order of the highest appellate authority of the state under sub-section (1) as it stood immediately before the commencement of the said act, but has not availed of the right to file the appeal during the period commencing on and from the 3rd day of December, 2001 and ending with the 16th day of March, 2005.

(4) The application shall be made in quadruplicate and be accompanied by a fee of five thousand rupees.

21. Procedure on receipt of application.

(1) On receipt of an appeal, the Authority shall cause a copy thereof to be forwarded to the assessing authority concerned and to call upon it to furnish the relevant records:

PROVIDED that such records shall, as soon as possible, be returned to the assessing authority.

(2) The Authority shall adjudicate and decide upon the appeal filed against an order of the highest appellate authority.

(3) The Authority, after examining the appeal and the records called for, by order, either allow or reject the appeal:

PROVIDED that no appeal shall be rejected unless an opportunity has been given to the appellant of being heard in person or through a duly authorised representative.

PROVIDED FURTHER that whether an appeal is rejected or accepted, reasons for such rejection or acceptance shall be given in the order.

(4) The Authority shall make an endeavour to pronounce its order in writing within six months of the receipt of the appeal.

(5) A copy of every order made under sub-section (3) shall be sent to the appellant, assessing authority, respondent and highest appellate authority of the State Government concerned.

22. Powers of the Authority.

(1) The Authority shall have the same powers as are vested in a court under the Code of Civil Procedure, 1908, while trying a suit in respect of the following matters, namely:-

(a) enforcing the attendance of any person, examining him on oath or affirmation;

(b) compelling the production of accounts and documents;

(c) Issuing the commission for the examination of witnesses;

(d) the reception of evidence on affidavits;

(e) any other matter which may be prescribed.

(1A) the Authority may grant stay of the operation of the order of the highest appellate authority against which the appeal is filed before it or order the pre-deposit of the tax before entertaining the appeal and while granting such stay or making such order for the pre-deposit of the tax, the Authority shall have regard, if the assessee has made pre-deposit of the tax under the general sales tax law of the state concerned, to such pre-deposit or pass such appropriate order as it may deem fit.

(2) Every proceeding before the Authority shall be deemed to be a judicial proceeding within the meaning of Section 193 and 228 of the Indian Penal Code and the Authority shall be deemed to be a civil court for the purpose of Section 195 and Chapter XXVI of the Code of Criminal Procedure, 1973.

23. Procedure of authority. The Authority shall, subject to the provisions of this Chapter, have power to regulate its own procedure in all matters arising out of the exercise of powers under this Act.

24. The Authority for Advance Rulings to function as authority under this Act.

(1) Notwithstanding anything contained in any other law for the time being in force and in Section 19 of this Act, the Authority for Advance Rulings constituted under Section 245-O of the Income Tax Act, 1961 shall be notified by the Central Government in the Official Gazette, with such modifications as may be necessary, to make its composition in conformity with Section 19 of this Act, as the Authority under this Act till such time an Authority is constituted under that Section.

(2) On and from the date of the constitution of the Authority in accordance with the provisions of Section 19 of this Act, the proceedings pending with the Authority for Advance Rulings shall stand transferred to the Authority constituted under that Section from the stage at which such proceedings stood before the date of constitution of the said Authority.

25. Transfer of pending proceedings.

[(1) on and from the commencement of the Central Sales Tax (Amendment)Act'2005, all appeals (except appeals against orders of the highest appellate authority of the state) pending before the Authority notified under sub-section (1) of Section 24 shall stand transferred together with the records thereof to the highest appellate authority of the concerned state.

(2) such highest appellate authority of the state to which such appeal has been transferred under sub-section (1) on receipt of such records shall proceed to deal with such appeal so far as may be in the same manner as in the case of an appeal filed before such highest appellate authority of the state according to the general sales tax law of the appropriate state, from the stage which was reached before such transfer or from any earlier stage or de novo as such highest appellate authority of the state may deem fit:

PROVIDED that where the highest appellate authority finds that the appellant has not availed of the opportunity of filing first appeal before the appellate authority, such case shall be forwarded to such authority.

26. Applicability of Orders passed. An order passed by the Authority under this Chapter shall be binding on each State Government concerned, the assessing authorities and other authorities created by or under any law relating to general sales tax, in force for the time being in any State (***).

□□□

14

The Cess and Other Taxes on Minerals (Validation) Act, 1992

ACT NO. 16 OF 1992 [4TH APRIL, 1992]

AN ACT to validate the imposition and collection of cesses and certain other taxes on minerals under certain State laws.

Be it enacted by Parliament in the Forty- third Year of the Republic of India as follows:—

1. Short title, extent and commencement.

(1) This Act may be called the Cess and Other Taxes on Minerals (Validation) Act, 1992 .

(2) It extends to the whole of India.

(3) It shall be deemed to have come into force on the 15th day of February, 1992 .

2. Validation of certain State laws and actions taken and things done thereunder.

(1) The laws specified in the Schedule to this Act shall be, and shall be deemed always to have been, as valid as if the provisions contained therein relating to cesses or other taxes on minerals had been enacted by Parliament and such provisions shall be deemed to have remained in force up to the 4th day of April, 1991.

(2) Notwithstanding any judgment, decree or order of any court, all actions taken, things done, rules made, notifications issued or purported to have been taken, done, made or issued and cesses or other taxes on minerals realised under any such laws shall be deemed to have been validly taken, done, made, issued or realised, as the case may be, as if this section had been in force at all material times when such actions were taken, things were done, rules were made,

notifications were issued, or cesses or other taxes were realised, and no suit or other proceeding shall be maintained or continued in any court for the refund of the cesses or other taxes realised under any such laws.

(3) For the removal of doubts, it is hereby declared that nothing in sub-section (2) shall be construed as preventing any person from claiming refund of any cess or tax paid by him in excess of the amount due from him under any such laws.

3. Repeal and savings.

(1) The Cess and Other Taxes on Minerals (Validation) Ordinance, 1992 (Ord. 7 of 1992) is hereby repealed.

(2) Notwithstanding such repeal, anything done or any action taken under the said Ordinance shall be deemed to have been done or taken under the corresponding provisions of this Act.

❏❏❏

15

The Cess Laws (Repealing and Amending) Act, 2006

ACT NO. 24 OF 2006 [1ST JUNE, 2006]

AN ACT to repeal certain enactments and to amend certain other enactments relating to levy of cess on certain items.

Be it enacted by Parliament in the Fifty-seventh Year of the Republic of India as follows:-

1. Short title. This Act may be called the Cess Laws (Repealing and Amending) Act, 2006.

2. Repeal of certain enactment. The enactments specified in the First Schedule are hereby repealed to the extent mentioned in the fourth column thereof.

3. Amendment of Act 26 of 1975. The enactment specified in the Second Schedule is hereby amended to the extent and in the manner mentioned in the fourth column thereof.

4. Savings.

(1) The repeal or amendment by this Act of any enactment shall not-

(a) affect any other enactment in which the repealed enactment has been applied, incorporated or referred to;

(b) affect the validity, invalidity, effect or consequences of anything already done or suffered, or any right, title, obligation or liability already acquired, accrued or incurred or any remedy or proceeding in respect thereof, or any release or discharge of or from any debt, penalty, obligation, liability, claim or demand, or any indemnity already granted, or the proof of any past act or thing;

(c) affect any principle or rule of law, or established jurisdiction, form or course of pleading, practice or procedure, or existing usage, custom, privilege, restriction, exemption, office or appointment, notwithstanding that the same respectively may have been in any manner affirmed or recognised or derived by, in or from any enactment hereby repealed;

(d) revive or restore any jurisdiction, office, custom, liability, right, title, privilege, restriction, exemption, usage, practice, procedure or other matter or thing not now existing or in force.

(2) The mention of particular matters in sub-section (1) shall not be held to prejudice or affect the general application of Section 6 of the General Clauses Act, 1897, with regard to the effect of repeals.

5. Collection and payment of arrears of duties. Notwithstanding the repeal of the enactments specified in the First Schedule or the amendments in the enactment as specified in the Second Schedule, the proceeds of duties levied under the said enactments immediately preceding the date on which the Cess Laws (Repealing and Amending) Bill, 2006 receives the assent of the President -

(i) if collected by the collecting agencies but not paid into the Reserve Bank of India; and

(ii) if not collected by the collecting agencies, shall be paid or as the case may be, collected and paid into the Reserve Bank of India for being credited to the Consolidated Fund of India.

FIRST SCHEDULE

[*See* Section 2]

Repeals Year No. Short title Extent of repeal 1, 2, 3, 4, 1942 7 The Coffee Act, 1942 Sections 11 and 13. 1972 13 The Marine Products Export Development Authority Act, 1972 Sections 14 and 15. 1986 3 The Agricultural and Processed Food Products Export Cess Act, 1985 The whole. 1986 11 The Spices Cess Act, 1986 The whole.

SECOND SCHEDULE

[*See* Section 3]

Amendments Year No. Short title Amendments 1 2 3 4 1975 26 The Tobacco Cess Act, 1975.

(i) Section 4 shall be omitted.

(ii) In Section 5, for the words and figures "duties of excise and customs levied under sections 3 and 4 respectively", the words and figure "duty of excise levied under section 3" shall be substituted.

❑❑❑

16

The Compulsory Deposit Scheme (Income-Tax Payers) Act, 1974

AN ACT to provide, in the interest of national economic development, for compulsory deposit by certain classes of income-tax payers and for the framing of a scheme in relation thereto, and for matters connected therewith of incidental thereto.

Be it enacted by Parliament in the Twenty-fifth Year of the Republic of India as follows:

1. Short title, extent and commencement.

(1) This Act may be called the Compulsory Deposit Scheme (Income-tax Payers) Act, 1974.

(2) It extends to the whole of India.

(3) It shall be deemed to have come into force on the 17th day of July, 1974.

2. Definitions. In this Act, unless the context otherwise requires -

(a) "compulsory deposit" means compulsory deposit under this Act;

(b) "deposit" means a deposit of money;

(c) "depositor" means a person who is liable to, make a compulsory deposit;

(d) "Income-tax Act" means the Income-tax Act, 1961; (43 of 1961)

(dd) "Income-tax Officer" has the same meaning as in clause (25) of Section 2 of the Income-tax Act, and includes an Inspecting Assistant Commissioner who exercises or performs the powers or functions conferred on, or assigned to, him under Section 125 or Section 125A of the said Act;]

(e) all other words and expression herein but not defined and defined in the Income-tax Act shall have the meanings, respectively, assigned to them in that Act.

3. Tax authorities.

(1) The income-tax authorities specified in Section 116 of the come-tax Act shall be the authorities for the purpose of this the Act and every such authority shall exercise the power and perform the functions of a tax authority under this Act in respect of any company, and for this purpose his jurisdiction under this Act shall be the same as he has under the Income-Tax Act by virtue of orders or directions issued under Section 120 of that Act (Including orders or directions assigning concurrent jurisdiction) or under any other provision of that Act.

(2) The Board may, from time to time, issue such orders,instructions and directions to other tax authorities as it may deem fit for the proper administration of this Act, and such authorities and all other persons employed in the execution of this Act shall observe and follow such orders, instructions and directions of the Board:

PROVIDED that no such orders, instructions or directions shall be issued-

(a) so as to require any tax authority to make a particular assessment or to dispose of a particular case in a particular manner; or

(b) so as to interfere with the discretion of the Commissioner (Appeals) in the exercise of his appellate functions."

3. Persons liable to make compulsory deposits.

(1) Subject to the provisions of this Act, the persons specified in sub-section (2) shall be liable to make compulsory deposits "for the assessment year commencing on the 1st day of April, 1975 and every subsequent assessment year (not being an assessment year commencing on or after the 1st day of April, 1986.

(2) The persons referred to in sub-section (1) are the following namely: -

(a) every person, being-

(i) an individual, who is a citizen of India;

(ii) a Hindu undivided family;

(iii) a trustee appointed under a trust declared by a duly executed instrument in writing, whether testamentary or otherwise (including any Wakf deed which is valid under the Mussalman Wakf Validating Act, 1913), (6 of 1913) if the income in respect of which the trustee is liable to income-tax as a representative assessee or any part thereof is not specifically receivable on behalf or for the benefit of any one person or where the individual shares of the persons on whose behalf or for whose benefit such income or such part thereof is receivable are indeterminate or unknown; and

(b) every person who is assessable under the Income-tax Act in respect of the total income of an individual, or a Hindu undivided family or a trustee specified in clause (a).

(3) Notwithstanding anything contained in sub-section (1),-

(a) an individual specified in sub-clause (i) of clause (a) of sub-section (2), or

(b) any person specified in clause (b) of sub-section (2) who is assessable under the Income-tax Act in respect of the total income of the individual aforesaid, shall not be liable to make any compulsory deposit for any assessment year where, in either case, such individual is more than [sixty-five years of age on the first day of the financial year immediately preceding that assessment year".

4. Requirement as to compulsory deposit.

(1) Where, in relation to an assessment year referred to in sub-section (1) of Section 3, the current income of any person, being an individual or a Hindu undivided family or a trustee specified in clause (a) of sub-section (2) of that Section, exceeds fifteen thousand rupees, such person, or if any other person is assessable under the Income-tax Act in respect of the total income of such person, the person so assessable, shall make, in accordance with and subject to the provisions of this Act and any scheme framed thereunder, [1][a compulsory deposit -

(i) for the assessment year commencing on the 1st day of April 1975 and the assessment year commencing on the 1st day of April, 1976, at the rates specified in Paragraph A of the Schedule (4 ***);

(ii) for the assessment year commencing on the 1st day of April, 1977 and the assessment year commencing on the 1st day of April 1978, at the rates specified in Paragraph B of the Schedule (7 ***);

"(iii) for the assessment year commencing on the 1st day of April, 1979, the assessment year commencing on the 1st day of April, 1980, and the assessment year commencing on the 1st day of April, 1981, at the rates specified in Paragraph C of the Schedule; and

(iv) for the assessment year commencing on the 1st day of April, 1982, at the rates specified in Paragraph D of the Schedule."

(2) Where, in the case of any person specified in sub-section (2) of Section 3, a deduction is required to be made under the Additional Emoluments (Compulsory Deposit) Ordinance, 1974, (8 of 1974) the amount of the compulsory deposit which such person is liable to make under this Act for any assessment year shall be reduced by the amount deducted under that Ordinance during the financial year immediately preceding that assessment year; and where such deduction is equal to or exceeds the amount of such compulsory deposit, it shall not be necessary for such person to make a compulsory deposit for that assessment year.

EXPLANATION. When any Central Act repeals and replaces (with or without any modification) the Additional Emoluments (Compulsory Deposit) Ordinance, 1974, (8 of 1974) the references to the said Ordinance in this sub-section shall be construed as references to such Central Act.

(3) For the purposes of this Section, "current income", in relation to an assessment year, means,-

[1][in a case where a statement is sent by the person to clause (a) of sub-section (1) of Section 209A of the Income-tax Act in the financial year immediately preceding that assessment year or where the Income-tax Officer has made an order under sub-section (1) or sub-section (3) of Section 210 of that Act requiring the person to pay advance tax during the financial year immediately preceding that assessment year and the person has not sent an estimate under Section 209A or, as the case may be, Section 212 of that Act]

(i) if the total income of the latest previous year in respect of which the person has been assessed by way of regular assessment forms the basis of computation of advance tax payable by him. such total income [exclusive of capital gains and income referred to in sub-clause (ix) of clause (24) of Section 2 [2][and in clause (c) of Section 115C] of the Income-tax Act] as increased by the net agricultural income if any, which has been taken into account for the purposes of charging income-tax for the assessment year relevant to that previous year; or

(ii) if the total income of the previous year on the basis of which income-tax has been paid by the person under Section 140A of the Income-tax Act forms the basis of computation of advance tax, such total income [exclusive of capital gains and income referred to in sub-clause (ix) of clause (24) of Section 2 and in clause (c) of Section 115C of the Income-tax Act as increased by the net agricultural income, if any, returned by the person in the return of income for the assessment year relevant to that previous year;

(b) in a case where an estimate is sent by the person under [1][section 209A or Section 212 of the Income-tax Act the total income [exclusive of capital gains and income referred to in sub-clause (ix) of clause (24) of Section 2 [2][and in clause (c) of Section 115C] of the Income-tax Act] as estimated by him of the period which would be the previous year for that assessment creased by the net agricultural income, if any, of that estimated by him;

(c) in any other case, if the total income of the person, as estimated by him, of the period which would be the previous year for that assessment year exceeds the maximum amount rot chargeable to income-tax in his case, such total income [exclusive of capital gains and income referred to in sub-clause (ix) of clause (24) of Section 2 [2][and in clause (c) of Section 115C] of the Income-tax Act] as increased by the net agricultural income, if any, of that period, as estimated by him.

EXPLANATION: In this sub-section, "net agricultural income" means the net agricultural income as defined in the- Finance Act of the relevant year.

5. Time for making compulsory deposit. A depositor shall make the compulsory deposit for an assessment year referred to in sub-section (1) of Section 3,-

(a) in a case where such depositor is required to pay advance tax under the Income-tax Act in the financial year immediately preceding that assessment year, at any time (in one sum or in instalments of his choice) before the expiry of the date on which the last instalment of advance tax is payable by him in accordance with the provisions of [1][section 211 or sub-section (4) of Section 209A] or, as the case may be, sub-section (3A) of Section 212 of that Act;

(b) in any other case, at any time (in one sum or in instalments of his choice) before the end of the financial year immediately preceding that assessment year.

6. Order by Income-tax Officer for compulsory deposit in certain cases.

(1) If, in relation to an assessment year referred to in sub-section (1) of Section 3, the correct income of a person falling under clause (c) of sub-section (3) of Section 4 exceeds fifteen thousand rupees and such person has failed to make the compulsory deposit for that assessment year, the Income-tax Officer shall, by order in writing, direct that such person shall make the compulsory deposit with reference to his correct income.

(2) For the purposes of this Section, "correct income" of a person, in relation to an assessment year, means-

(i) in a case where the person has furnished the return of income under Section 139 of the Income-tax Act, the total income [exclusive of capital gains and income referred to in sub-clause fix) of clause (24) of Section 2 [2][and in clause (c) of Section 115C] of the Income-tax Act] returned by him, as increased by the net agricultural income, if any, returned by him;

(ii) in a case where the person has failed to furnish the return of income under Section 139 of the Income-tax Act and assessment is made under Section 144 of that Act, the total income [exclusive of capital gains and income referred to in sub-clause (ix) of clause (24) of Section 2 [2][and in clause (c) of Section 115C] of the Income-tax Act] determined on assessment, as increased by the net agricultural income, if any, determined on assessment.

EXPLANATION. In this sub-section, "net agricultural income" has the meaning assigned to it in the Explanation to sub-section (3) of Section 4.

7. Compulsory deposit to carry simple interest.

(1) Every compulsory deposit made by or recovered from a depositor shall carry simple interest at a rate equal to the bank deposit rate.

EXPLANATION: In this sub-section, "bank deposit rate" means the highest of the maximum rates at which interest may be paid on different classes of deposits (other than those maintained in savings account or those maintained by charitable or religious institutions) by different classes of scheduled banks in accordance with the directions given or issued to banking companies generally by the Reserve Bank of India under the Banking Regulation Act, 1949 (10 of 1949).

(2) The interest shall be calculated in such manner as may be specified in the scheme framed under Section 19.

(3) For the purposes of the deduction under Section 80L of the Income-tax Act, interest received on a compulsory deposit shall be deemed to be interest received on a deposit with a banking company to which the Banking Regulation Act, 1949, applies.

"7A. For the purposes of exemption under Section 5 of the Wealth-tax Act, 1957, the amount of compulsory deposit shall be deemed to be a deposit with a banking company to which the Banking Regulation Act, 1949 (10 of 1949) applies."]

8. Repayment compulsory deposit.

[2][(1)] The amount of compulsory deposit made by or recovered from a depositor in any financial year shall be repayable in five equal annual instalments commencing from the expiry of two years from the end of that financial year, together with the interest due on the whole or, as the case may be, part of the amount of the compulsory deposit which has remained unpaid:

"PROVIDED that no depositor shall be entitled to withdraw before the expiry of the financial year 1985-86 any amount which, in accordance with the foregoing provisions of this sub-section, is repayable or payable during that financial year and the provisions of sub-section (2) shall apply in relation to such amount as they apply in relation to any amount referred to in that sub-section:"

PROVIDED FURTHER that nothing in this Section shall prevent earlier repayment of the deposit or any instalment thereof together with the interest due in any case in which the Income-tax Officer is satisfied that extreme hardship will be caused unless such repayment is made.

"(1A) Notwithstanding anything contained in sub-section (1) -

(a) the amount of compulsory deposit made by or recovered from an individual; or

(b) the amount of compulsory deposit made by or recovered from any person who is assessable under the Income-tax Act in respect of the total income of an individual on behalf of such individual, shall, to the extent it has remained unpaid, be repayable, together with interest thereon -

"(i) Where such individual has attained the age of sixty-five years before the 1st day of April, 1983, on the 1st day of June, 1983; and

(ii) in any other case, on the first day of the financial year immediately succeeding the financial year in which such individual attained sixty-five years of age".

"(2) Where any amount has become repayable or payable under sub-section (1), "or sub-section (1A)," the depositor may, at his option, not withdraw such amount after it has become so repayable or payable, and if he does so, such amount shall carry interest for the period it is not withdrawn as if it were a compulsory deposit, and the provisions of this Act shall, so far as may be, apply in relation to such amount or interest thereon as they apply in relation to a compulsory deposit or as the case may be, interest on such deposit."

9. Intimation regarding compulsory deposit. Every depositor shall send to the Income-tax Officer, along with the return of income for the assessment year for which he is liable to make a compulsory deposit, proof of the fact of such deposit having been made.

10. Penalty for failure to make compulsory deposit.

(1) If, in relation to an assessment year referred to in sub-section (1) of Section 3, any person who is liable to make a compulsory deposit [being a person falling under clause (a) or clause (b) of sub-section (3) of Section 4]-

(a) has without reasonable cause failed to make the compulsory deposit within the time allowed under Section 5, or

(b) has made the compulsory deposit within such time but the deposit so made falls short of [1][“the requisite amount and there is no reasonable cause for making such short payment” the Income-tax Officer may, by order in writing, direct that such person shall pay, by way of penalty, a sum -

(i) which, in the case referred to in clause (a), shall be equal to twenty-five per cent. of the compulsory deposit which he is liable to make; and

(ii) which, in the case referred to in clause (b), shall be equal to twenty-five per cent of the amount by which the compulsory deposit made by him falls short of the requisite amount.

(2) If, in relation to an assessment year referred to in sub-section (1) of Section 3, the correct income of a person falling under clause (c) of sub-section (3) of Section 4, exceeds fifteen thousand rupees and such person-

(a) [1][“has, without reasonable cause, failed to make”] the compulsory deposit within the time allowed under Section 5, or

(b) has made the compulsory deposit within such time on the basis of his own estimate but the deposit so made falls short of seventy-five per cent. of the compulsory deposit which he would have been liable to make on the basis of [1][“his correct income and there is no reasonable cause for making such short payment”;

“the Income-tax Officer may” by order in writing, direct that such person shall pay by way of penalty a sum-

(i) which, in the case referred to in clause (a), shall be equal to twenty-five per cent of the compulsory deposit calculated with reference to his correct income; and

(ii) which, in the case referred to in clause (b), shall be equal to twenty-five per cent. of the amount by which the compulsory deposit made by him falls short of the compulsory deposit calculated with reference to his correct income.

EXPLANATION: In this sub-section, “correct income” has the meaning assigned to it in sub-section (2) of Section 6.

(3) No order imposing a penalty under this Section shall be made against any person

unless such person has been heard or has been given a reasonable opportunity of being heard.

11. Authorities.

(1) Every Director of Inspection, Commissioner of Income-tax [2][Commissioner of income-tax (Appeal)], Appellate Assistant Commissioner of Income-tax, Inspecting Assistant Commissioner of Income-tax, Income-tax Officer and Inspector of Income-tax, shall have the like powers and perform the like functions under this Act as he has and performs under the Income-tax Act, and for the exercise of his powers and the performance of his functions, his jurisdiction under this Act shall be the same as he has under the Income-tax Act and for this purpose compulsory deposit under this Act shall be deemed to be tax chargeable under that Act.

(2) All officers and persons employed in the execution of this Act shall observe and follow the orders, instructions and directions of the Board:

Provided that no such orders, instructions or directions shall be issued-

(a) so as to require any authority referred to in sub-section (1) to dispose of a particular case in a particular manner; or

(b) so as to interfere with the discretion of the [2]["Commissioner (Appeals) or the Appellate Assistant Commissioner"] in the exercise of his appellate functions.

(3) Every Income-tax Officer employed in the execution of this Act shall observe and follow the orders, instructions and directions, issued guidance by the Director of Inspection or by the Commissioner or by the Inspecting Assistant Commissioner within whose jurisdiction he performs his functions.

12. Appeals and revision.

(1) "Subject to the provisions of sub-section (2), any depositor" aggrieved by any order of the Income-tax Officer under Section 10, may Appeal to the Appellate Assistant Commissioner and the provisions of the Income-tax Act relating to appeals, reference and revision shall, so far as may be, Apply in relation as they apply in relation to an order of the Income-tax sing a penalty under Section 221 of that Act.

(2) Where an order referred to in sub-section (1) is made by an Inspecting Assistant Commissioner in exercise of the powers or functions conferred on or assigned to him under Section 125 or Section 125A of the Income-tax Act, the provisions of that sub-section shall have effect as if for the words "Appellate Assistant Commissioner", the words and brackets "Commissioner (Appeals)" were substituted."

12(1) Where any order imposing a penalty under Section 10 made by the Income-tax Officer before the date on which the Finance (No. 2) Act, 1980 received the assent of the President (such order being hereafter in this Section referred to as pre-amendment penalty order) has not been made the subject matter any subsequent proceeding by way of appeal or revision under this Act, then, the depositor aggrieved by such order may, if the considers that no such penalty would have been levied if the amendments made to Section 10 by the Finance (No. 2) Act, 1980 had been in force on the date of passing of such order, make an application to the Income-tax Officer for a special review.

(2) Where a pre-amendment penalty order has been made the subject matter of any subsequent proceeding by way of an appeal or revision under this Act, the depositor aggrieved by the order passed in any such proceeding or as the case may beg the last of such proceedings may, if he considers that no such penalty would have been levied if the amendments made to Section 10 by the Finance (No. 2) Act, 1980 had been in force on the date of passing of the pre-amendment penalty order, make an application to the authority which passed the order in such proceeding or, as the case may be, the last of such proceedings for a special review.

(3) The application referred to in sub-section (1) or sub-section (2) shall be presented before the 1st day of January, 1981:

PROVIDED that the Income-tax Officer or the other authority to whom an application for special review is made may admit such application after the said date if he or it is satisfied that the depositor had sufficient cause for not presenting it before the said date.

(4) The income-tax Officer or other authority to whom the application for special review is made under sub-section (1) or sub-section (2), may make such enquiry or cause such enquiry to be made and, subject to the provisions of this Act, may pass such order as he or it thinks fit.

(5) The provisions of Section 12 shall, so far as may be, apply in relation to an order passed under sub-section (4) as they apply in relation to a pre-amendment penalty order or, as the case may be, an order passed by any other authority under that Section.

(6) The special review under this Section shall be in addition to and not in derogation of any other remedy which an aggrieved depositor may have under this Act.

EXPLANATION: For the purposes of this Section, "authority" includes the Appellate Tribunal.

10. Opportunity of being heard. No order imposing a penalty under Section 9 [2][or Section 9A] shall be made unless the assessee has been given a reasonable opportunity of being heard.

11. Appeals to the Appellate Assistant Commissioner.

(1) Any person objecting to the amount of surtax for which he is liable as assessed by the Income-tax Officer or denying his liability to be assessed under this Act, or objecting to any penalty or fine imposed by the Income-Tax Officer, [3]["or objecting to the interest levied by the Income-Tax Officer under Section 7D"], or to the amount allowed by the Income-tax Officer by way of any relief under any provisions of this Act, or to any refusal by the Income-tax Officer to grant relief or to an order of rectification or amendment having the effect of enhancing the assessment or reducing the refund, or to an order refusing to allow the claim

made by the assessee for a rectification under Section 13 or amendment under Section 14 may appeal to the Commissioners Appeals

(2) Every appeal shall be in the prescribed form and shall be verified in the prescribed manner.

(3) An appeal shall be presented within thirty days of the following date, that is to say-

(a) where the appeal relates to assessment or penalty or fine, the date of service of the notice of demand relating to the assessment or penalty or fine, or

(b) in any other case, the date on which the intimation of the order sought to be appealed against is served:

PROVIDED that the [1][Commissioners Appeals] may admit an appeal after the expiration of the said period if he is satisfied that the appellant had sufficient cause for not presenting it within that period.

(4) The Commissioner (Appeals) shall hear and determine the appeal and, subject to the provisions of this Act, pass such orders as he thinks fit and such orders may include an order enhancing the assessment or penalty:

PROVIDED that an order enhancing the assessment or penalty shall not be made unless the person affected thereby has been given a reasonable opportunity of showing cause against such enhancement.

(5) The procedure to be adopted in the hearing and determination of the appeals shall, with any necessary modification, be in accordance with the procedure applicable in relation to income-tax.

13. Rectification of mistakes.

(1) With a view to rectifying any mistake apparent from the record, the Income-tax Officer, the Appellate Assistant Commissioner, the Commissioner (Appeals) the Commissioner and the appellate Tribunal may, of his, or its, own motion or on an application by the depositor in this behalf, amend any order passed by him or it in any proceeding under this Act, [2][“within four years from the end of the financial year in which such order was passed”.

(2) An amendment which has the effect of enhancing the compulsory deposit or any penalty imposed under this Act shall not be made under this Section unless the authority concerned has given notice to the depositor of its intention so to do and has allowed the depositor a reason able opportunity of being heard.

(3) Where an amendment is made-under this Section, the order shall be passed in writing by the authority concerned.

(4) Where any such amendment has the effect of enhancing the compulsory deposit or the penalty imposed under this Act, the Income-tax Officer shall serve on the depositor a notice specifying the sum which has to be deposited or paid.

14. Collection and recovery of compulsory deposit and penalty.

(1) When, in consequence of any order passed under this Act, any compulsory deposit or penalty has to be made or paid, the income-tax Officer shall serve upon the depositor a notice specifying the sum which has to be deposited or paid.

(2) The sum specified in a notice under sub-section (1) shall be deposited or, as the case may be, paid within thirty-five days of the service of the notice at the place and with or to the person mentioned in the notice:

PROVIDED that on an application made by the depositor before the expiry of the said period of thirty-five days, the Income-tax Officer may extend the time for making the deposit or payment or allow tile deposit or payment to be made by instalments subject to such conditions as he may think fit to impose in the circumstances of the case.

(3) If a depositor fails to make the compulsory deposit within the time allowed under Section 5, or if he fails to deposit or, as the case may be, pay the amount which he is required to deposit or pay by notice under sub-section (1) within the time allowed under sub-section (2) (whether fixed originally or on extension), at the place and with or to the person mentioned in the said notice, the depositor shall be deemed to be in default.

(4) Any arrear of compulsory deposit and any penalty imposed under this Act shall be recoverable in the manner provided in Chapter XVII-D of the Income-tax Act for recovery of arrears of tax and for this purpose the provisions of that Chapter shall apply as if references to the assessee therein were references to the depositor.

15. Rounding off.

(1) The amount of the current income, correct income and compulsory deposit shall be rounded off to the nearest multiple of ten rupees and, for this purpose, any part of a rupee consisting of paise shall be ignored and thereafter if such amount is not a multiple of ten, then, if the last figure in that amount is five or more, the amount shall be increased to the next higher amount which is a multiple of ten and if the last figure is less than five. The amount shall be reduced to the next lower amount which is a multiple of ten.

EXPLANATION. In this sub-section, "current income" and "correct income" have the meanings respectively assigned to them in sub-section (3) of Section 4 and sub-section (2) of Section 6.

(2) The amount of penalty payable under the provisions of this Act shall be rounded off to the nearest rupee and, for this purpose, where such amount contains a part of a rupee consisting of paise, then, if such part is fifty paise or more, it shall be increased to one rupee and if such part is less than fifty paise, it shall be ignored.

16. Applicability of Chapter XV of Income-tax Act. The provisions of Chapter XV of the Income-tax Act relating to liability in special cases shall, so far as may be, apply in relation to compulsory deposits and penalties impassable under this Act as they apply in relation to income-tax payable and penalties impassable under that Act.

17. Protection against attachment.

(1) The amount of compulsory deposit and interest thereon standing to the credit of any depositor shall not be liable to attachment under a decree or order of any court in respect of any debt or liability incurred by the depositor.

(2) The amount of compulsory deposit and interest thereon standing to the credit of a depositor at the time of his death and payable to his nominee shall vest in the nominee and shall be free from debt or other liability incurred by the deceased or incurred by the nominee before the death of the depositor.

18. Protection of action taken in good faith. No suit, prosecution or other legal proceeding shall lie against the Government or against any officer of the Government for anything which is in good faith done or intended to be done under this Act or any scheme framed thereunder.

19. Compulsory Deposit Scheme.

(1) The Central Government shall, by notification in the Official Gazette, frame a scheme or schemes, to. be called Compulsory Deposit (Income-tax Payers) Scheme or Schemes, in relation to compulsory deposits.

(2) A scheme framed under sub-section (1) may provide for-

(a) the manner in which compulsory deposits shall be made;

(b) the documents to be issued to persons by whom deposits have been made as evidence of such deposits;

(c) the authority or authorities by or through whom the deposits may be collected;

(d) the nomination of any person to receive the amount standing to the credit of a depositor in the event of his death or in cancellation or change of such nomination;

(e) the issue of duplicate of any document issued as evidence of any deposit in the event of loss or destruction of the original and the fee (not exceeding two rupees) on the payment of which such duplicate may be issued;

(f) any other matter which may be necessary or Proper for the effective implementation of the scheme.

(3) The Central Government may, by notification in the Official Gazette, add to, amend or vary any scheme framed under sub-section (1).

(4) A scheme framed under sub-section (1) or a notification issued under sub-section (3) may provide that all or any of its provisions shall take effect either prospectively or retrospectively on such date as may be specified in this behalf in the scheme or notification.

(5) Any scheme framed under sub-section (1) or any notification issued under sub-section (3) shall have effect notwithstanding anything contained in any law for the time being in force (other than this Act) or any instrument having effect by virtue of any law other than this Act.

(6) Every scheme framed under sub-section (1) and every notification issued under sub-section (3) shall be laid, as soon as may be, after it is framed or issued before each House of Parliament while it is in session for a total period of thirty days which may be comprised in one session or in two or more successive sessions, and if, before the expiry of the session immediately following the session or the successive sessions aforesaid, both Houses agree in making any

modification in the scheme or notification or both Houses agree that the scheme or notification should not be framed or issued, the scheme or notification shall thereafter have effect only in such modified form or be of no effect, as the case may be; so, however, that any such modification or annulment shall be without prejudice to the validity of anything previously done under that scheme or notification.

20. Power to remove difficulties. If any difficulty arises in giving effect to the provisions of this Act, the Central Government may, by order, not inconsistent With the provisions of this Act, remove the difficulty:

PROVIDED that no such order shall be made after the expiry of a period of two years from the commencement of this Act.

21. Repeal and saving.

(1) The Compulsory Deposit Scheme (Income-tax Payers) Ordinance, 1974, (10 of 1974) is hereby repealed.

(2) Notwithstanding such repeal, anything done or any action taken under the Ordinance so repealed shall be deemed to have been done or taken under the corresponding provisions of this Act.

THE SCHEDULE

[*See* Section 4(1)]

RATES OF COMPULSORY DEPOSIT

Paragraph A

(1) Where the current income 4 per cent. of the current exceeds Rs. 15,000 but income does not exceed Rs. 25, 000.

(2) Where the current income Rs. 1,000 plus 6 per cent of exceeds Rs. 25,000 but the amount by which the does not exceed Rs. 70,000 current income exceeds Rs. 25,000;

(3) Where the current income Rs.3,700 plus 8 per cent. of exceeds Rs. 70,000 the amount by which the current income exceeds Rs. 70,000:

[1][**Paragraph B**

(1) Where the current income exceeds 4 percent. of the current Rs. 15,000 but does not exceed income Rs. 25,000.

(2) Where the current income exceeds Rs. 1,000 plus 10 per cent. Rs. 25,000 but does not exceed of the amount by which the Rs. 70,000 current income exceeds Rs. 25,000.

(3) Where the current income exceeds Rs. 5,500 plus 12 per cent. of Rs. 70,000 the amount by which the current income exceeds Rs. 70,000.

[2] [**Paragraph C**

(i) Where the current income exceeds 4.5 per cent. of the current Rs. 15,000 but does not exceed income Rs. 25,000.

(ii) Where the current income exceeds Rs. 1,125 plus 11 per cent. of Rs. 25,000 but does not exceed the amount by which the Rs. 35,000 current income exceeds Rs. 25,000.

(iii) Where the current income Rs.2,225 plus 12.5 per cent. exceeds Rs. 35,000 but does of the amount by which the not exceed Rs. 70,000 current income exceeds Rs. 35,000.

(iv) Where the current income Rs. 6,600 plus 12.5 per cent. exceeds Rs. 70,000 of the amount by which the current income exceeds Rs. 70,000.

"Paragraph D

(i) Where the current income 4.5 per cent. of the current exceeds Rs. 15,000 but income does not exceed Rs. 25,000.

(ii) Where the current income Rs. 1,125 plus 11 per cent. exceeds Rs. 25,000 but of the amount by which the does not exceed Rs. 35,000 current income exceeds Rs. 25, 000.

(iii) Where the current income Rs. 2,225 plus 12.5 per cent. exceeds Rs. 35,000 but of the amount by which the does not exceed Rs. 50,000 current income exceeds Rs. 35,000.

(iv) Where the current income Rs. 4,100 plus 15 per cent. of exceeds Rs. 50,000 but the amount by which the does not exceed Rs. 70,000 current income exceeds Rs. 50,000.

(v) Where the current income Rs. 7,100 plus 18 per cent. exceeds Rs. 70,000 of the amount by which the current income exceeds Rs. 70,000."]

PROVIDED that—

(a) in a case falling under Paragraph A or Paragraph B, where the current income exceeds Rs. 15,000 but does not exceed Rs. 15,620, the compulsory deposit shall in no case exceed the amount by which the current income exceeds Rs. 15,000;

(b) in a case falling under Paragraph C, [or Paragraph D][3], where the current income exceeds Rs. 15,000 but does not exceed Rs. 15,710, the compulsory deposit shall in no case exceed the amount by which the current income exceeds Rs. 15,000;

(c) where the amount of compulsory deposit calculated in accordance with the foregoing provisions is less than Rs.100, it shall not be necessary for the taxpayer concerned to make such deposit."]

EXPLANATION: In this Schedule, "current income" has the meaning assigned to it in sub-section (3) of Section 4.

1 Ins. by Act 66 of 1976, S.43 (w.e.f. 1-4-1976).

❑❑❑

17

The Compulsory Deposit Scheme Act, 1963

ACT NO.21 OF 1963 [22ND MAY, 1963]

AN ACT to provide in the interest of national economic development for compulsory deposit and for the framing of a scheme in relation thereto.

Be it enacted by Parliament in the Fourteenth Year of the Republic of India as follows:—

1. Short title, extent and commencement.

(1) This Act may be called the Compulsory Deposit Scheme Act, 1963.

(2) It extends to the whole of India.

(3) It shall come into force on such date {*11-6-1963; vide Notification No. G.S.R. 887, dated 25-5-1963, Gazette of India Extraordinary, Pt. II, Sec.3(i), p.439.*} as the Central Government may, by notification in the Official Gazette, appoint.

2. Persons to whom Act applies. This Act shall apply to the following categories of persons, namely:

(a) persons liable to payment of land-revenue (whether known as land-revenue, rent, tax or by any other name) under any law with respect to land-revenue whether or not such persons are liable to pay tax under the Income-tax Act;

(b) persons liable to payment of tax under the Income-tax Act;

(c) holders of immovable properties situated in urban areas assessed to tax (whether known as property tax, house tax or by any other name) who are not liable to payment of tax under the Income-tax Act;

(d) employees of—

(i) the Central and State Governments,

(ii) local authorities,

(iii) companies as defined in Section 3 of the Companies Act, 1956, including foreign companies within the meaning of Section 591 and Government companies as defined in Section 617 of that Act,

(iv) any other corporation (including a co-operative society) established by or under a Central, Provincial or State Act,

(v) individuals or associations of persons or bodies of individuals liable to payment of tax under the Income-tax Act, and entitled to deduct the salary paid to their employees for the purpose of computing their income under that Act, whose annual income from salary is one thousand five hundred rupees or more and who are not liable to payment of tax under the Income-tax Act;

(e) dealers whose annual turnover, determined in accordance with the provisions of any State Act with respect to tax on the sale of goods, is fifteen thousand rupees or more and who are not liable to payment of tax under the Income-tax Act:

PROVIDED that where by or under any such State Act any amount higher than fifteen thousand rupees has been fixed as the minimum annual turnover for the purpose of registration under that Act the reference to fifteen thousand rupees in this clause shall be construed as a reference to that amount.

EXPLANATION: In this clause, -

(a) "dealer" has the same meaning as in the respective State Acts with respect to tax on the sale of goods;

(b) "State Act" includes a Provincial Act;

(f) such other categories of persons [than those referred to in clauses (a) to (e)] whose annual income is one thousand five hundred rupees or more and who are not liable to payment of tax under the Income-tax Act, as may be specified by the Central Government by notification in the Official Gazette.

3. Definitions. In this Act, unless the context otherwise requires, -

(a) "additional surcharge" means additional surcharge for the purposes of the Union referred to in the annual Finance Act;

(b) "deposit" means a deposit of money;

(c) "Income-tax Act" means the Income-tax Act, 1961 (43 of 1961);

(d) "Person" shall have the same meaning as in clause (31) of Section 2 of the Income-tax Act;

(e) "salary" has the same meaning as in Section 17 of the Income-tax act, but in relation to a person falling under clause (d) of Section 2 does not include any gratuity or annuity or pension;

(f) "urban area" means any area within the local limits of a municipality (by whatever name called), a notified area committee, a town area committee, a city and town committee, a small town committee, a Cantonment Board or a Panchayat constituted by reorganisation of any of the aforesaid local authorities and having a population of ten thousand or more;

(g) "year" means the financial year.

4. Requirement as to compulsory deposit.

(1) As from such date as the Central Government may, by notification in the Official Gazette, appoint in this behalf, every person to whom this Act applies, other than a person falling under clause (b) of Section 2, shall make a compulsory deposit at such rate as may be provided for in a scheme framed under this Act:

PROVIDED that different notifications may be issued under this sub-section on different dates in relation to different categories of persons:

PROVIDED FURTHER that the rate of compulsory deposit shall not exceed the maximum rate specified in sub-section (2).

(2) The maximum rate of deposit shall be—

(a) in the case of a person falling under clause (a) of Section 2, fifty per cent of the land-revenue (including surcharge thereon, if any), payable in respect of the land or lands held by him in the year for which deposit is required to be made.

EXPLANATION: In this clause "year" means the year with reference to which land-revenue is payable under any law with respect to land-revenue;

(b) in the case of a person falling under clause (c) of that section, three per cent of the annual rental value of the property with reference to which the property is assessed to the tax referred to in that clause in the year in which the deposit is required to be made:

PROVIDED that where the property is assessed to such tax not with reference to its annual rental value, the maximum rate of deposit under this clause shall be twelve and a half per cent of such tax;

(c) in the case of a person falling under clause (d) of that section, three per cent of his annual income from salary;

(d) in the case of a person falling under clause (e) of that section, one-third of one percent of his turnover during the year immediately preceding the year in which the deposit is required to be made;

(e) in the case of a person falling under clause (f) of that section, a sum of sixty rupees per annum.

(3) A person falling under clause (b) of Section 2 by whom any additional surcharge is payable in respect of any assessment year may make a deposit under this Act in respect of that year and if he does so, then, he shall, on production of proof before the income-tax officer concerned of the fact of such deposit having been made, be entitled to deduction from the additional surcharge of a sum which shall be equal to -

(a) the sum so deposited, or

(b) (i) where his residual income is six thousand rupees or less, three per cent of such residual income, or

(ii) where his residual income exceeds six thousand rupees, three per cent of the first six thousand rupees of such residual income and two per cent of the balance thereof, whichever is less.

EXPLANATION: In this sub-section "residual income" has the same meaning as in Section 2 of the Finance Act, 1963 (13 of 1963).

(4) Any person falling under clause (b) of Section 2 who is in receipt of any income under the head "salaries" during any financial year may make a deposit under this Act in that year and if he does so, then, notwithstanding anything in the Income-tax Act, the person responsible for paying that income shall, on production of proof of the fact of such deposit having been made, reduce the amount of additional surcharge included in the tax to be deducted in accordance with the provisions of Section 192 of that Act by a sum which shall be equal to -

(a) the sum so deposited, or

(b) the sum calculated in accordance with clause(b) of sub-section (3), whichever is less.

(5) Any person falling under clause(b) of Section 2 who is liable to pay advance tax under the Income-tax Act in any financial year may make a deposit under this Act in that year and if he does so, then, notwithstanding anything contained in the Income-tax Act, he shall, on production of proof before the income-tax officer concerned of the fact of such deposit having been made, be entitled to deduction from the additional surcharge included in the advance tax, of a sum which shall be equal to -

(a) the sum so deposited, or

(b) the sum calculated in accordance with clause (b) of sub-section (3), whichever is less.

EXPLANATION: In this sub-section, "advance tax" shall have the same meaning as in Section 207 of the Income-tax Act.

(6) Where a person falling under clause (d) of Section 2 pays in any year any sum -

(i) to effect or to keep in force any insurance on the life of such person or on the life of the wifc or husband of such person; or

(ii) as a contribution to any provident fund to which the Provident Funds Act, 1925, (19 of 1925) applies or to any "recognised provident fund" as defined in clause (38) of Section 2 of the Income tax Act; or

(iii) in a ten-year account or a fifteen-year account under the Post Office Savings Bank (Cumulative Time Deposit) Rules, 1959, as amended from time to time, he shall not be liable to make any compulsory deposit under this section for that year if such sum is not less than eleven per cent.of his annual income from salary.

(7) Where any person falls under any two or more categories referred to in Section 2 other than the category referred to in clause (b) of that section, then, he shall make a compulsory deposit at the rate applicable to each of those categories.

(8) Any deposit made under this section shall bear simple interest at the rate of four per cent.per annum to be calculated from the first day of the month immediately following the month in which the deposit is made to the last day of the month immediately preceding the month in which it is repaid (both days inclusive) and notwithstanding anything in the Income-tax Act, the amount of such interest shall be free of any tax under that Act.

(9) Any deposit made under this section during any year shall be repayable with interest thereon at any time after the expiry of five years from the end of the year in which the deposit has been made:

PROVIDED that nothing in this sub-section shall prevent earlier repayment of any deposit with interest thereon in any case in which the authority empowered to make such repayment is satisfied that genuine hardship will be caused unless such repayment is made.

(10) If any doubt or dispute arises as to the amount to be deposited by any person under this Act or as to the date on which such amount is to be deposited or as to any other matter in relation to any deposit to be made under this Act, the decision thereon of the Government or any authority empowered by the Government in this behalf shall be final.

5. Compulsory Deposit Scheme.

(1) The Central Government shall, by notification in the Official Gazette, frame one or more scheme or schemes to be called Compulsory Deposit Schemer or Scheme in relation to deposits under this Act.

(2) A scheme framed under sub-section (1) may provide for, -

(a) the rates at which and the period for which compulsory deposits shall be made by the several categories of persons to whom this Act applies and the extension of such period;

(b) the manner (including the deduction of deposit at source) in which and the intervals at which such deposits shall be made;

(c) the documents to be issued to persons by whom deposits have been made as evidence of such deposits;

(d) the authority or authorities by or through whom deposits may be collected or by whom penalties for failure to make deposits may be levied;

(e) the accounts to be maintained with respect to such deposits and the officers by whom such accounts shall be maintained;

(f) the nomination of any person to receive the amount standing to the credit of a depositor in the event of his death and the cancellation or change of such nomination;

(g) the issue of duplicate of any document issued as evidence of any deposit in the event of loss or destruction of the original the fee on the payment of which such duplicate may be

(h) the exemptions, if any, to be granted in exercise of the powers under Section 9;

(i) the delegation of powers in pursuance of Section 10;

(j) the repayment and withdrawal of deposits with interest thereon and the conditions, if any, under which such repayment or withdrawal may be made;

(k) any other matter which may be necessary or proper for the effective implementation of the Scheme.

(3) A scheme framed under this section may provide that all or any of its provisions shall take effect either prospectively or retrospectively on such date as may be specified in this behalf in the Scheme.

(4) Any scheme framed under this section shall have effect notwithstanding anything contained in any law for the time being in force, other than this Act, or in any instrument having effect by virtue of any law other than this Act.

6. Modification of Scheme. The Central Government may, by notification in the Official Gazette, add to amend or vary any scheme framed under this Act.

7. Rounding off. Where the amount of any deposit to be made under this Act contains a part of a rupee, then, if such part is *fifty naye paise* or more, it shall be increased to one complete rupee and if such part is less than *fifty naye paise*, it shall be ignored.

8. Power to suspend, reduce or remit the amount of compulsory deposit. Where the State Government has suspended payment of land-revenue, or reduced or remitted the amount of land-revenue, payable in any year in respect of any land, then, the Central Government may, by order, suspend payment of the compulsory deposit, or reduce or remit the amount of such deposit payable in that year under Section 4 by a person falling under clause (a) of Section 2.

9. Power to exempt. Where the Central Government is of the opinion that it is necessary or expedient so to do, either in the public interest or having regard to the peculiar circumstances of any case, it may, by notification in the Official Gazette and subject to such conditions, if any, as it may specify in the notification —

(a) exempt any person or class of persons from the operation of all or any of the provisions of this Act; and

(b) cancel any such notification and again subject, by a like notification, the person or class of persons to the operation of such provisions.

10. Power to delegate. The Central Government may, by notification in the Official Gazette, direct that any power which may be exercised by it under attainder this Act, other than the power under Section 5 or the power under this section, shall, subject to such restrictions and conditions, if any as it may specify in the notification, be exercised also by -

(a) such officer or authority subordinate to the Central Government, or

(b) such State Government or such officer or authority subordinate to a State Government, or

(c) such other officer or authority, as may be specified in the notification.

11. Protection against attachment.

(1) The amount standing to the credit of any depositor shall not be liable to attachment under any decree or order of any court in respect of any debt or liability incurred by the depositor.

(2) Any amount standing to the credit of a depositor at the time of his death and payable to his nominee under a scheme shall vest in the nominee and shall be free from any debt or other liability incurred by the deceased or incurred by the nominee before the death of the depositor.

12. Penality for failure to make deposit.

(1) If any person who is liable to make a deposit under this Act fails to make the same within the time specified therefor, he shall be liable to pay by way of penalty an amount not exceeding half the amount of deposit which he is liable to make:

PROVIDED that before levying any such penalty such person shall be given a reasonable opportunity of being heard in respect of the same.

(2) Where any person is responsible for paying any income falling under the head "Salaries" as mentioned in the Income-tax Act, then, notwithstanding anything on that Act, in computing the total income of that person under that Act for any assessment year commencing on or after the 1st day of April, 1964, no deduction shall be allowed in respect of payment of any income under that head which in the case of any employee exceeds one thousand five hundred rupees but from which no tax is deductible under the heading "B-Deduction at source" in Chapter XVII of that Act unless a sum equal to the amount which such employee is required to deposit under this Act is deducted from such income at source and is deposited in accordance with the provisions of this Act and the Scheme framed thereunder.

13. Recovery of arrears of deposit and penalty. Any arrear of deposit and any penalty for failure to make such deposit under this Act shall be recoverable in the same manner as an arrear of land-revenue.

14. Protection of action taken in good faith. No suit, prosecution or other legal proceedings shall lie against any person for anything which is in good faith done or intended to be done under this Act or any scheme framed thereunder.

15. Power to remove difficulties. If any difficulty arises in giving effect to the provisions of this Act or of any scheme framed thereunder, the Central Government may, by order, as occasion requires, do anything (not inconsistent with this Act) which appears to it to be necessary for removing the difficulty.

16. Scheme to be laid before the House of Parliament. Any scheme framed under this Act shall be laid, as soon as may be, after it is framed before each House of Parliament while it is in session for a total period of thirty days which may be comprised in one session or in two or more successive sessions, and if before the expiry of that session in which it is so laid or the session or sessions immediately following both Houses agree in asking any modification in any provision of the scheme or both Houses agree that any provision in the scheme should not be made, the provision of the scheme shall thereafter have effect only in such modified form or be of no effect, as the case may be, so, however that any such modification or annulment shall be without prejudice to the validity of anything previously done under that provision.

❑❑❑

18

The Customs and Central Excise Laws (Repeal) Act, 2004

ACT NO. 25 OF 2004 [21ST DECEMBER, 2004]

AN ACT to repeal certain Customs and Central Excise enactments.

Be it enacted by Parliament in the Fifty-fifth Year of the Republic of India as follows:-

1. Short title. This Act may be called the Customs and Central Excise Laws (Repeal) Act, 2004.

2. Repeal of certain enactments. The enactments specified in the Schedule are hereby repealed.

3. Savings.

(1) The repeal by this Act of any enactment shall not affect any other enactment in which the repealed enactment has been applied, incorporated or referred to; and this Act shall not effect the validity, invalidity, effect or consequences of anything already done or suffered, or any right, title, obligation or liability already acquired, accrued or incurred, or any remedy or proceedings in respect thereof, or any release or discharge of or from any debt, penalty, obligation, liability, claim or demand, or any indemnity already granted, or the proof of any past act or thing; nor shall this Act affect any principle or rule of law, or established jurisdiction, form or course of pleading, practice or procedure, or existing usage, custom, privilege, restriction, exemption, office or appointment, notwithstanding that the same respectively may have been in any manner affirmed or recognised or derived by, in or from any enactment hereby repealed; nor shall the repeal by this Act of any enactment revive or restore any jurisdiction, office, custom, liability, right, title, privilege, restriction,

exemption, usage, practice, procedure or other matter or thing not now existing or in force.

(2) Sub-section (1) shall not be held to prejudice or affect the general application of section 6 of the General Clauses Act, 1897 (10 of 1897) with regard to the effect of repeal of the Acts specified in the Schedule.

THE SCHEDULE

[*See* Section 2]

Year	**Number**	**Short title**
(1)	(2)	(3)
1958	27	The Mineral Oils (Additional Duties of Excise and Customs) Act, 1958.
1959	58	The Sugar (Special Excise Duty) Act, 1959.
1986	45	The Central Duties of Excise (Retrospective Exemption) Act, 1986.
1986	62	The Customs and Excise Revenues Appellate Tribunal Act, 1986.
1988	29	The Customs and Central Excise Laws (Amendment) Act, 1988.

❑❑❑

19

The Customs Duties and Cesses (Conversion to Metric Units) Act, 1960

ACT NO. 40 OF 1960 [21ST SEPTEMBER, 1960)

AN ACT further to amend certain laws relating to customs duties and cesses for the purpose of adopting metric units in those laws.

Be it enacted by Parliament in the Eleventh Year of the Republic of India as follows:-

1. Short title and Commencement.

(1) This Act may be called the Customs Duties and Cesses (Conversion to Metric Units) Act, 1960.

(2) It shall come into force on such date as the Central Government may, by notification in the Official Gazette, appoint.

2. Amendment of Act 14 of 1923. In the Indian Cotton Cess Act, 1923 (14 of 1923) in sub-section (1) of section 3, for the words "at the rate of four annas per standard bale of four hundred pounds avoirdupois, or in the case of unbaled cotton, of one anna per hundred pounds avoirdupois", the following words and figures shall be substituted, namely -

"at the rate of twenty-five naye paise per bale of 181.4 kilograms or, in the case of unbaled cotton, of seven naye paise per fifty kilograms".

3. Amendment of Act 24 of 1930. In the Indian Lac Cess Act, 1930 (14 of 1930) in section 3, for the words "a cess at the rate of fourteen annas per maund in the case of lac, and ten annas per maund in the case of refuse lac", the following words shall be substituted, namely -

"a cess at the rate of two rupees and thirty naye paise per quintal in the case of lac, nd one rupee and seventy naye paise per quintal in the case of refuse lac".

4. Amendment of Act 32 of 1934. The Indian Tariff Act, 1934 (32 of 1934) shall be amended in the manner specified in the Schedule.

5. Amendment of Act 7 of 1942. In the Coffee Act, 1942, (7 of 1942)-

(i) in section 11, for the words "at such rate not exceeding six rupees per hundred weight", the words "at such rate not exceeding eleven rupees and eighty naye paise per quintal" shall be substituted;

(ii) in section 12, for the words "at such rate not exceeding six rupees per hundred weight", the words "at such rate not exceeding eleven rupees and eighty naye paise per quintal" shall be substituted;

(iii) in section 13, in sub-section (5), for the word "hundredweight", the word "quintals" shall be substituted;

(iv) in the proviso to section 20,-

(a) in clause (ii), for the words "two pounds avoirdupois", the words "one kilogram" shall be substituted;

(b) in clause (iii), for the words "ten pounds avoirdupois", the words "five kilograms" shall be substituted;

(c) in clause (iv), for the words "one pound avoirdupois", the words "five hundred grams" shall be substituted.

6. Amendment of Act 10 of 1944. In the Indian Coconut Committee Act, 1944 (10 of 1944) in sub-section (1) of section 3, for the words and letters "not exceeding four annas per cwt.", the words "not exceeding forty-nine naye paise per quintal", shall be substituted.

7. Amendment of Act 9 of 1946. In the Indian Oilseeds Committee Act, 1946 (9of 1946) in sub-section (1) of section 3,-

(i) in clause (a), for the words "at the rate of one anna per maund", the words "at the rate of seventeen naye paise per quintal" shall be substituted; and

(ii) in clause (b), for the words "at the rate of two annas per maund", the words "at the rate of thirty-three naye paise per quintal" shall be substituted.

8. Amendment of Act 29 of 1953. In the Tea Act, 1953 (29 of 1953) -

(i) in section 24, in clause (c), for the words "not exceeding ten pounds avoirdupois", the words "not exceeding five kilograms" shall be substituted, and

(ii) in section 25, in sub-section (1), for the words "at the rate of four rupees per one hundred pounds", the words "at the rate of eight rupees and eighty naye paise per quintal" shall be substituted.

9. Amendment of Act 45 of 1953. In the Coir Industry Act, 1953 (45 of 1953) in sub-section (1) of section 13, for the words "at such rate not exceeding one rupee per hundred weight", the words "at such rate not exceeding two rupees per quintal" shall be substituted.

10. Savings. Nothing contained in this Act shall be deemed to affect the validity of any notification, rule or order issued under any of the enactments amended thereby and in force immediately before the commencement of this Act merely by reason of the fact that the rate of any customs duty or cess specified therein has been expressed in terms of annas, pice or pies or with reference to any weight or measure other than a standard mass or measure under the Standards of Weights and Measures Act, 1956 (89 of 1956) and every such notification, rule or order shall, until altered, repealed or amended by the Central Government or other competent authority, continue to have effect as if this Act had not been passed.

THE SCHEDULE
[*See* Section 4]

Item	Name of article	Nature of duty	Standard rate of duty	Preferential rate of duty if the article is the produce or manufacture of		Duration on of protective rates of duty
				The United Kingdom	A British colony	
			For the existing entries, substitute			
3(1)	-	-	Rs. 2.70 per quintal plus 10 per cent. ad valorem	-	-	-
8(1) 9	-	-	Rs. 1.97 per quintal 40 per cent. *ad valorem* plus 13 naye paise per kilogram.	-	-	-
9(2)	-	-	Rs. 1.32 per kilogram 06 per kilogram	-	Rs. 1	-
9(5)	-	-	Rs. 2.27 per kilogram	-	Rs 2.20 per kilogram	-
13(6)	-	-	Rs. 42.90 per kilogram or 25 per cent. *Ad valorem,* whichever is higher.	-	-	-
15(5)	-	-	Rs. 19.68 per quintal	-	-	-
17	-	-	The rate at which excise duty is for the time being leviable on sugar, other than *Khandsari* or *palmyra* sugar, produced in India *plus* Rs. 19.70 per quintal.			
17(3)	-	-	The rate at which excise duty is for the time being leviable on sugar, other than *Khansari* or *palmyra* sugar, produced in India *plus* Rs. 19.70 per quintal	-	-	-
18(b)	-	-	50 per cent. *ad valorem* or Rs. 2.20 per kilogram, whichever is higher.	-	-	-

22(1) (a)	for27 0z.", substitute "767 millilitres".	-	Rs. 1.30 per litre	-	-	-
22(1) (b)	for *"27 oz."* and "20 oz.", substitute "767 millilitres" and "568 milliltres" respectively.	-	-	-	-	-
22(1) (c)	for "13-1/2 oz." and "10 oz."substitute "384 millilitres" and 284 millilitres" respectively.	-	-	-	-	-
22(1) (d)	for "6-3/4 oz." and "5 oz.", substitute "192 millilitres" and "142 millilitres" respectively.	-	-	-	-	-
22(1) (e)	-	-	Rs. 1.60 per litre	-	-	-
22(2) (a)	for *"27 oz."*, substitute "767 millilitres".	-	Rs. 2.60 per litre	-	-	
22(2) (b)	for "27 oz," and "20 oz." substitute "767 millilitres" and "568 milliliters" respectively	-	-	-	-	-
22(2) (c)	for "13 1/2 oz," and "10 oz." substitute "384 millilitres" and "284 millilitres" respectively	-	-	-	-	-
22(2) (d)	for "6 3/4 oz." and "5 oz," substitute 192 millilitres" and "142 millilitres respectively.	-	-	-	-	-
22(2) (e)	-	-	Rs. 3.30 per litre	-	-	-
22(3) (a)	-	-	Rs. 17.00 per litre	-	-	-
22(3) (b)	-	-	Rs. 11.00 per litre	-	-	-
22(4) (a)	-	-	Rs. 33.00 per litre of the strength of London proof or 125 per cent. *ad valorem,* whichever is higher.	-	-	-
22(4) (b) (i)	-	-	Rs. 44.00 per litre or 125 per cent *ad valorem,* whichever is higher.	-	-	-
22(4) (b) (ii)	-	-	Rs. 33.00 per litre of the strength of London proof or 125 per cent *ad valorem,* whichever is higher.	-	-	-

22 (5) (a) (I)	-	-	Rs. 16.06 per litre of 45 per cent. *ad valorem*, whichever is higher.	-	Rs. 14.96 Per litre or 35 per cent. *Ad valorem*, whichever is higher	-
22 (5) (b) (ii)	-	-	Rs. 12.15 per litre of the strength of London proof or 45 per cent. *ad valorem*, whichever is higher.	-	Rs. 11.33 per litre of the strength of London proof or 35 per cent. *Ad valorem*, whichever is higher.	-
24	-	-	Rs. 37.50 per kilogram	-	-	-
24 (1)	-	-	40 per cent *ad valorem*, plus Rs. 36.40 per kilogram.	-	-	-
24 (2)	-	-	40 per cent *ad valorem*, plus Rs.41 per thousand or Rs.36.40 per kilogram, whichever is higher.	-	-	-
24 (3)	-	-	Rs. 22.05 per kilogram,		Rs. 22.05 per kilogram.	
25 (5)	-	-	Rs. 29.50 per tonne	-	-	-
27	-	-	80 naye paise per tonne	-	-	-
27 (4) (b)	-	-	Rs. 45 per kilolitre at 15 degrees of centigrade thermometer.	-	-	-
27 (7) (*a*)	-	-	Rs. 19.70 per tonne or 16 per cent. *ad valorem*, whichever is higher.	-	-	-
27 (8)	-	-	Rs. 44.50 per kilolitre at 15 degrees of centigrade thermometer, or 16 per cent. *ad valorem*, whichever is higher.	-	-	-
28 (4) (a)	-	-	Rs. 8.37 per quintal	-	-	-
28 (4) (*b*)	-	-	Rs. 11.32 per quintal	-	-	-
28 (9)	-	-	Rs. 17.60 per kilogram	-	-	-
28 (10	-	-	25 per cent. *ad valorem*, or Rs. 17.60 per kilogram of saccharine content, whichever is higher.	-	-	-

29 (15) (a)	-	-	Rs. 6.89 per quintal	-	-	-
28 (15) (b)	-	-	Rs. 9.84 per quintal	-	-	-
28 (20) (a)	-	-	35 per cent *ad valorem,* or Rs. 1.10 per kilogram, whichever is higher.	-	-	-
28 (20 (b)	-	-	35 per cent *ad valorem,* or Rs. 1.10 per kilogram, whichever is higher.	-	-	-
28 (20) (c)	-	-	35 per cent *ad valorem,* or Rs. 1.10 per kilogram, whichever is higher.	-	-	-
28 (20) (d)	-	-	35 per cent *ad valorem,* or whichever is higher.	-	-	-
28 (20) (e)	-	-	35 per cent *ad valorem,* or whichever is higher.	-	-	-
28 (22)	for "14" substitute "6.36 kilograms".	-		-	-	-
29	-	-	Rs. 6.60 per 100 linear metres	-	-	-
29 (1)	-	-	Rs. 1.60 per linear metre *plus* the excise duty for the time being leviable on like articles if produced or manufactured in India and where such duty is leviable at different rates, the highest duty.	-	-	-
30 (2) (cc)(1)	for "1 lb.", substitute "453 grams"	-	30 per cent *ad valorem,* or Rs. 16.70 per quintal, whichever is higher, *plus,* the excise duty for the time being leviable on like articles if produced or manufactured in India and where such duty is leviable at different rates, the highest duty.	-	-	-

30 (2) (cc)(ii)	for "1/2 lb". and "1 lb.," substitute "226 grams" and "453 grams" respedtively.	-	30 per cent *ad valorem,* or Rs. 22.10 per quintal, whichever is higher, *plus* the excise duty for the time being leviable on like articles if produced or manufactured in India and where such duty is leviable at different rates, the highest duty.	-	-	-
30 (2) (cc)(iii)	for "1/4 lb,"and "1/2 lb," substitute "113 grams" and "226 grams" respectively.	-	30 per cent *ad valorem,* or Rs. 33.46 per quintal, whichever is higher, *plus* the excise duty for the time being leviable on like articles if produced or manufactured in India, and where such duty is leviable at different rates, the highest duty.	-	-	-
30 (2) (cc) (iv)	for "1/4 lb.", substitute "113 grams".	-	30 per cent. *ad valorem,* or Rs. 47.20 per quintal, whichever is higer, *plus* the excise duty for the time being leviable on like articles if produced or manufactured in India, and where such duty is leviable at different rates, the highest duty.	-	-	-
30 (7)	-	-	15 naye paise for every length or 190.5 millimetres or part thereof, or 75 per cent. *ad valorem,* whichever is higher.	-	-	-
34 (4 (b)	-	-	Rs. 1.10 per kilogram	-	-	-
34 (4) (c)	-	-	Rs. 1.33 per kilogram	-	-	-

44 (7)	-	-	75 per cent. *ad valorem,* or Rs. 31.50 per quintal, whichever is higher.	-	-	-
45 (4)	-	-	15 naye paise for every length of 190.5 mm or part thereof, or 75 per cent. *ad valorem,* whichever is higher.	-	-	-
46	-	-	35 per cent *ad valorem,* plus Rs. 8.80 per kilogram.	-	-	-
46 (3)	-	-	26 naye paise per kg	-	-	-
47 (a)	-	-	35 per cent. *ad valorem,* plus Rs. 8.80 per kilogram.	-	-	-
47 (b)	-	-	35 per cent *ad valorem* plus Rs. 11.60 per kg	-	-	-
47 (2)	-	-	Rs. 6.60 per kilogram or 50 per cent. *ad valorem,* whichever is higher, *plus* the excise duty for the time being leviable on like articles if produced or manufactured in India, and where such duty is leviable at different rates, the highest duty.	-	-	-
47 (6) (b) (I)	-	-	6 1/4 per cent, *ad valorem,* or 22 naye paise per kilogram, whichever is higher.	-	-	-
47 (6)	-	-	7 1/2 per cent *ad valorem,* plus Rs 18.70 per kilogram whichever is higher.	-	-	-
48 (a)	-	-	120 per cent. *ad vlaorem* plus Rs.18.70 per cent kilogram *plus* the excise duty for the time being leviable on like articles if produced or manufactured in India, and where such duty is leviable at different rates, the highest duty.	-	-	-

48 (b)	-	-	120 per cent *ad valorem,* plus Rs. 18.70 per kilogram *plus* the excise duty for the time being leviable on like articles if produced or manufactured in India, and where such duty is leviable at different rates, the highest duty.	-	-	-
48 (c)	-	-	120 per cent. *ad valorem,* plus Rs. 13.80 per Kilogram *plus* the excise duty for the time being leviable on like articles if produced or manufactured in India, and where such duty is leviable at different rates, the highest duty.	-	-	-
48 (1) (a)	-	-	80 per cent. *ad valorem,* or 54 naye paise per square metre, whichever is higher.	-	-	-
48 (1) (b)	-	-	100 per cent *ad vlaorem,*or Rs. 1.08 per suarc metre, whichever is higher.	-	-	-
48 (4) (a)	-	-	100 per cent *ad valorem,* plus Rs. 6.60 per kilogram *plus* the excise duty for the time being leviable on like articles if prouced or manufactured in India, and where such duty is leviable at different rates, the highest duty.	-	-	-
48 (4) (b) (I)	-	-	100 per cent. *ad valorem,* or Rs. 6.60 per kilogram, whichever is higher, *plus* the excise duty			

			for the time being leviable on like articles if produced or manufactured in India, and where such duty is leviable at different rates, the highest duty.			
48 (5) (a) (I)	-	-	80 per cent. *ad vlaorem,*or 42 naye paise per square metre, whichever is higher, *plus* the excise duty for the time being leviable on like articles if produced or manufactured in India, and where such duty is leviable at different rates, the highest duty.	-	-	-
48 (5) (*a*) (*ii*)	-	-	100 per cent. *ad vlaorem,* or 84 naye paise per square metre whichever is higher, *plus* the excise duty for the time being leviable on like articles if produced or manufactured in India, and where such duty is leviable at different rates, the highest duty.	-	-	-
48(5) (b)(i)	-	-	80 percent ad valorem or 54 naye paise per square metre, whichever is higher, *plus*)the excise duty for the time being leviable on like articles if produced or manufactured in India, and where such duty is leviable at different rates, the highest duty.	-	-	-

48(5) (b)(ii)	-	-	100 percent. advalorem or Rs.1.08 per square metre, whichever is highers, *plus* the excise duty for the time being leviable on like articles if produced or manufactured in India, and where such duty is leviable at different rates, the highest duty.	-	-	-
49 (1) (a)	for "4 yards",substitute "3.66 metres".	-	-	-	-	-
49 (1) (b)	for ":2 1/2 yards", substitute"2,29 metres"	-	-	-	-	-
49 (1) (c)	for "4 yards", substitute"3.66 metres"	-	-	-	-	-
49 (5)	-	-	Rs.1.10 per kilograms	-	-	-
51 (1)	-	-	100 percent *ad valorem* or Rs11.00 per kilogram, whichever is higher.	-	-	-
51 (2) (a)	for "4Ibs"., substitute "1.815 kilograms".		100 percent.*ad valorem or Rs.*11.00 per kilogram, whichever is higher.	-	-	-
51 (2) (b)	for "4Ibs". substitute "1.815 kilograms".		100 percent *ad valorem* or Rs. 8.80 per kilogram, whichever is higher.	-	-	-
51 (3)	-	-	100 percent. *ad valorem* o Rs. 11.00 per kilogram, whichever is higher.	-	-	-
59(4)	-	-	75 per cent *ad valorem,* or Rs. 8.60 per square metre, whichever is higher.	-	-	-
60 (1) (b)	for "one inch", substitute "25.4millimetres".	-	-	-	-	-
61 (2)	-	-	Rs. 1.80 per 100 grams	-	-	-
61 (3)	-	-	Rs. 25.70 per 10 grams	-	-	-
62 (1)	-	-	Rs. 1.80 per 100 grams	-	-	-

62 (2)	-	-	Rs. 25.70 per 10 grams	-	-	-
63 (2) (*a*) (*I*)	-	-	Rs. 21.65 per tonne or 10 per cent. *ad valorem,* whichever is higher.	-	-	-
63 (2) (*a*) (*ii*)	-	-	Rs. 63.97 per tonne	-	-	-
63 (2) (b)	-	-	Rs. 59.10 per tonne.	-	-	-
63 (3) (i)	-	-	Rs. 30.51 per tonne or 10 per cent *ad valorem,* whichever is higher.	-	-	-
63 (3) (ii)	-	-	Rs. 59.05 per tonne or 21 per cent. *ad valorem,* whichever is higher.	-	-	-
63 (6) (ii)	-	-	Rs. 73.80 per tonne.	-	-	-
63 (8)	for "1 1/2 inches", substitute "38.1 millimetres"		Rs. 4.90 per tonne or 20 per cent *ad valorem,* whichever is higher.	-	-	-
63 (9)	-	-	Rs. 59.10 per tonne	-	-	-
63 (10) (i)	-	-	Rs. 59.10 per tonne *plus* the excise duty for the time being leviable on like articles if produced or manufactured in India, and where such duty is leviable at different rates, the highest duty.	-	-	-
63 (10) (ii)	-	-	Rs. 79.70 per tonne *plus* the excise duty for the time being leviable on like articles if produced or manufactured in India, and where such duty is leviable at different rates, the highest duty.	-	-	-
63 (17) (i)	-	-	Rs. 31.50 per tonne or 10 per cent *ad valorem,* whichever is higher.	-	-	-

63 (17) (ii)	-	-	Rs. 54.10 per tonne	-	-	-
63 (19 (a) (i)	-	-	Rs. 14.80 per tonne or to per cent. *ad valorem,* whichever is higher.	-	-	-
63 (19) (a) (ii)	-	-	39.40 per tonne	-	-	-
63 (19) (b)	-	-	Rs. 59.10 Per tonne	-	-	-
63 (20) (a) (I) (i)	-	-	Rs. 28.54 per tonne or 10 per cent. *ad valorem,* whichever is higher.	-	-	-
63 (20) (a) (I) (ii)	-	-	Rs. 49.21 per tonne	-	-	-
63 (20) (a) (2) (i)	-	-	Rs. 29.53 per tonne or 10 per cent. *ad valorem,* whichever is higher.	-	-	-
63 (20) (a) (2) (ii)	-	-	Rs. 59.05 per tonne	-	-	-
63 (20) (b) (1) (i)	-	-	Rs. 31.50 per tonne or 10 per cent. *ad valorem,* whichever is higher.	-	-	-
63 (20) (b (1) (ii)	-	-	Rs. 54.10 per tonne	-	-	-
63 (20) (b) (2) (i)	-	-	Rs. 31.49 per tonne or 10 per cent *ad valorem,* whichever is higer	-	-	-
63 (20) (b) (2) (ii)	-	-	Rs. 63.97 per tonne	-	-	-
63 (21) C (i)	-	-	Rs. 9.80 per tonne or 10	-	-	-
63 (21) C (ii)	-	-	Rs. 9.80 per tonne or 20 per cent. *ad valorem,* whichever is higher.	-	-	-
63 (21) D (i)	-	-	Rs. 30.51 per tonne or 10 per cent. *ad valorem,* whichever is higher.	-	-	-
63 (21 D (ii)	-	-	Rs. 59.05 per tonne	-	-	-

63 (21) E (i)	-	-	Rs. 29.50 per tonne or 10 per cent. *ad valorem,* whichever is higher.	-	-	-
63 (21 E (ii)	-	-	Rs. 78.70 per tonne	-	-	-
63 (21) F (i)	-	-	Rs. 29.50 per tonne or 10 per cent. *ad valorem,* whichever is higher.	-	-	-
63 (21) F (ii)	-	-	Rs. 78.70 per tonne.	-	-	-
63 (25) (ii)	-	-	25 per cent. *ad valorem,* plus Rs.34.45 per tonne.	-	-	-
63 (27) (i)	-	-	Rs. 14.80 per tonne or 15 per cent. *ad valorem,* whichever is higher.	-	-	-
63 (27) (ii)	-	-	Rs. 41.80 per tonne or 25 per cent. *ad valoram,* whichever is higher.	-	-	-
63 (31) (a)	-	-	Rs. 28.54 per tonne or 10 per cent. *ad valorem,* whichever is higher	-	-	-
63 (31) (b)	-	-	Rs. 49.21 per tonne	-	-	-
63 (32) (a)	-	-	Rs 49.21 per tonne	-	-	-
63 (32) (b)	-	-	Rs. 83.66 per tonne	-	-	-
70 (3)	-	-	45 per cent. *ad valorem,* or Rs. 88.60 per quintal, whichever is higher.	-	-	-
71 (4)	-	-	22 naye paise per kilogram	-	-	-
71 (8)	For "24 inches", "9 inches and 1/32 inch", substitute "610 millimetres" "228.6 millimetre" respectively.	-		-	-	-

71 (13) (1) (a)	-	-	100 per cent. *ad valorem,* or Rs. 3.30 per metre, whichever is higher.	-	-	-
71 (13) (1)(b)	*for* "inch, *substitute* "25.4 millimeters"	-	100 per cent *ad valorem,* or Rs 3.30 per metre, whichever is higher.	-	-	-
71 (13) (1)(c)			100 per cent *ad valorem,* or Rs. 3.30 per metre, whichever is higher.	-	-	-
71 (14)	for"3 7/8 inches", substitute "98 millimetres"; for 5 1/2 inches", wherever they occur, substitute "140 millimeters"; for "7 inches"; wherever they occur, substitute "178 millimetres"; for "8 inches", wherever they ocur, substitute "204 millimeters"; for "10 inches wherever they occur, substitute "254 millimeters";for "12 inches", wherever they occur, substitute "305 millimaters"; for "14 inches", wherever they occur, substitute "356 millimetres"; and for "18 inches", substitute "458 millmetres".	-	-	-	-	-
72 (35)	for "2", substitute "51 millimeters".	-	-	-	-	-
72 (36)	for "2" substitute "51 millimetres".	-	-	-	-	-
72 (37)	for "2", substitute "51 millimetres".	-	-	-	-	-
72 (38)	for "2" substitute "51 millimetres".	-	-	-	-	-
73 (1)	for "one-eightieth part of a square inch", substitute "8.0645 square millimetres".	-	-	-	-	-
73 (6)	for "one-eightieth Part of a square inch", substitute "8.0645 square millimetres".	-	-	-	-	-

73 (18)	for "24", substitute "61 centimetres".	-	-	-	-	-
74 (a)	-	-	Rs 19.68 per tonne or 15 per cent. *ad valorem*, whichever is higher.	-	-	-
74 (b)	-	-	Rs . 59.05 per tonne or 25 cent. *ad valorem*, whichever is higher.	-	-	-
75 (7A)	for "1/2'*1/8 " and "1/2 3/16", substitute "12.7 mm 3.175 mm". and "12.7 mm 4.7625 mm." respectively	-	-	-	-	-
75 (12) (b)	for "6 inches", wherever they occur, substitute "153 millimeters".	-	-	-	-	-
75 (18) (b)	for "one inch", substitute "25.4 millmetres".	-	-	-	-	-

(i) In the First Schedule to the Indian Tariff Act, 1934, in the second column, in clause (b) of the proviso to each of the Items Nos. 22(4) and 22(5), for the words "Imperial gallon", the word "litre" 4 shall be substituted.

(ii) In the First Schedule to the Indian Tariff Act, 1934, for Item No.27(5), the following Item shall be substituted, namely;-

Item	**Name of article**	**Nature of duty**	**Standard rate of duty**	**Preferential rate of duty if the article is the produce or manufacture of**		**Duration on of protective rates of duty**
				The United Kingdom	**A British colony**	
27 (5)	High Speed Diesel Oil and vaporizing Oil, that is to say, mineral oil (excluding mineral colza oil and turpentine substitute) which has its flashing point at or above seventy-six degrees of Fahrenheit's thermometer, and satisfies either of the following requirements, namely;- (i) the oil has a flame height of ten millimetres or more but less than eighteen millimeters, or.					

	(ii) the oil has a flame height of less than ten millimeters, but has a viscosity of less than fifty seconds by Redwood I Viscometer at one hundred degrees of fahrenheit's thermometer, and contains less than one quarter of one per cent by weight of any bituminous substance					
	(a) High Speed Diesel Oil thermometer or 16 per cent *ad valorem*, whichever is higher, plus the excise duty for the time being leviable on like articles if produced or manufactured in India	Revenue	Rs. 44.60 per kilolitre at 15 degrees of centigrade			
	(b) Vaporizing Oil	Revenue	Rs. 44.70 per kilolitre at 15 degrees of centigrade thermometer or 16 per cent *ad valorem*, whichever is higher, plus the excise duty for the time being leviable on like articles if produced or manufacture in India			

EXPLANATION. The expressions "mineral oil", "flame height" and "flashing point" have the meanings respectively assigned to them in Explanation I, II, and III to Item No. 27(4).

(iii) In the First Schedule to the Indian Tariff Act, 1934, in Item No.63(21)A,-

(a) in the second column, for the figures, letters and words "30 lbs.per yard", wherever they occur, the figures and words "14.881 kilograms per metre" shall be substituted; and

(b) in the fourth column, for the letters, figures and words "Rs. 10 per ton", "Rs. 31 per ton" and "Rs. 60 per ton", wherever they occur, the letters, figures and words "Rs. 9.80 per tonne", "Rs. 30.51 per tonne" and "Rs. 59.05 per tonne" shall respectively be substituted.

(iv) in the First schedule to the Indian Tariff Act, 1934, in Item No.63(21)B,-

(a) in the second column, for the figures, letters and words "30 lbs.per yard", wherever they occur, the figures and words "14.881 kilograms per metre" shall be substituted; and

(b) in the fourth column, for the letters, figures and words "Rs. 10 per ton", "Rs. 33 per ton", and "Rs. 65 per ton", wherever they occur, the letters, figures and words "Rs. 9.80 per tonne", "Rs. 32.48 per tonne" and "Rs. 63. 97 per tonne" shall respectively be substituted.

PART II

The Second schedule to the Indian Tarrif Act, 1934, shall be amended in the manner and to the extent specified in the Table below, and the existing entries in any column thereof which have not been so amended shall continue unaltered.

TABLE

Item No.	**Name of article**	**Rate of duty**
	For the existing entries, substitute-	
1(1)	—	Rs. 4.50 per bale of 181.43696 kilograms.
1(2)	—	Rs. 15 per bale of 181.43696 kilograms.
2(I)	—	Rs. 344.50 per tonne.
2 (ii)	—	Rs. 1476.30 per tonne.
2(iii)	—	Rs. 78.70 per tonne.
3	—	Rs. 400 per bale of 181.43696 kilograms.
5	—	Not exceeding 66 naye paise per kilogram as the Central Government may, by notification in the Official Gazette, fix.
6	*for* "inch", wherever it occurs, *substitute* "25.4 millimetres".	
9	—	Rs. 1.10 per kilogram.
9 (1)	—	Rs. 344.50 per tonne.
13	—	Rs. 295.30 per tonne.
14	—	Rs. 147.60 per tonne.
15	—	Rs. 295.30 per tonne.
16	—	Rs. 300 per flask of 34.01943 kilograms.
17	—	Rs. 123.00 per quintal.
18	—	Rs. 226.40 per tonne.
19	—	Rs. 172.20 per tonne.
20	—	Rs. 98.40 per tonne.
21	—	Rs. 49.20 per tonne.

❑❑❑

20

The Customs Tariff Act, 1975

Act No. 51 of 1975 [18th August, 1975]

AN ACT to consolidate and amend the law relating to customs duties.

Be, it enacted by Parliament in the Twenty-sixth Year of the Republic of India as follows:-

1. Short title, extent and commencement.

(1) This Act may be called the Customs Tariff Act, 1975.

(2) It extends to the whole of India.

(3) It shall come into force on such date' as the Central Government may, by notification in the Official Gazette, appoint.

2. Duties specified in the Schedule to be levied. The rates at which duties of customs shall be levied under the Customs Act, 1962, (52 of 1962) are specified in the First and Second Schedules.

3. Levy of additional duty equal to excise duty.

(1) Any article which is imported into India shall, in addition, be liable to a duty (hereafter in this section referred to as the additional duty) equal to the excise duty for the time being leviable on a like article if produced or manufactured in India and if such excise duty on a like article is leviable at any percentage of its value, the additional duty to which the imported article shall be so liable shall be calculated at that percentage, of the value of the imported article.

EXPLANATION: In this section, the expression "the excise duty for the time being leviable on a like article if produced or manufactured in India" means the excise duty for the time being in force which would be leviable on a like article if produced or manufactured in India or, if a like article is not so produced or manufactured, which would be leviable on the class or description of articles to which the imported article belongs, and where such duty is leviable at different rates, the highest duty.

(2) For the purpose of calculating - under this section the additional duty on any imported article, where such duty is leviable at any percentage of its value, the value of the imported article shall, notwithstanding anything contained in Section 14 of the Customs Act, 1962, (52 of 1962) be the aggregate of-

(i) the value of the imported article determined under sub-section (1) of the said Section 14 or the tariff value of such article fixed under sub-section (2) of that section, as the case may be; and

(ii) any duty of customs chargeable on that article under Section 12 of the Customs Act, 1962 (52 of 1962) and any sum chargeable on that article under any law for the time being in force as an addition to, and in the same manner as, a duty of customs, but not including the duty referred to in sub-section (1).

(3) If the Central Government is satisfied that it is necessary in the public interest to levy on any imported article [whether on such article duty is leviable under sub-section (1) or not] such additional duty as would counter-balance the excise duty leviable on any raw materials, components and ingredients of the same nature as, or similar to those, used in the production or manufacture of such article, it may, by notification in the Official Gazette, direct that such imported article shall, in addition, be liable to an additional duty representing such portion of the excise duty leviable on such raw materials, components and ingredients as, in either case, may be determined by rules made by the Central Government in this behalf.

(4) In making any rules for the purposes of sub-section (3), the Central Government shall have regard to the average quantum of the excise duty payable on the raw materials, components or ingredients used in the production or manufacture of such like article.

(5) The duty chargeable under this section shall be in addition to any other duty imposed under this Act or under any other law for the time being in force.

(6) The provisions of the Customs Act, 1962, (52 of 1962) and the rules and regulations thereunder, including those relating to drawbacks, refunds and exemption duties, shall, so far as may be, apply to the duty chargeable under this section as they apply in relation to the duties leviable under that Act.

4. Levy of duty where standard rate and preferential rate are specified.

(1) Where in respect of any Article a preferential rate of revenue' duty is specified in the First Schedule, or is admissible by virtue of a notification under Section 25 of the Customs Act, 1962 (52 of 1962) the duty to be levied and collected shall be at the standard rate, unless the owner of the article claims at the time of importation that it is chargeable with a preferential rate of duty, being [1][the produce or manufacture of such preferential area] as is notified under subsection'

(3) and the article is determined, in accordance with the rules made under sub-section (2), to be such produce or manufacture.

(2) The Central Government may, by notification in the Official Gazette, make rules for determining if any article is 1[the produce or manufacture of any preferential area].

(3) For the purposes of this Section and the First Schedule, [1][preferential area'] means any country or territory which the Central Government may, by Notification from in the Official Gazette, declare to be such area.

(4) Notwithstanding anything contained ins sub-section (1), where the Central Government is satisfied that, that in the interests of trade including promotion of exports, it is necessary to take immediate action for discontinuing the preferential rate, or increasing the preferential rate to a rate not exceeding the standard rate, or decreasing the preferential rate, in respect of an article specified in the First Schedule, the Central Government may, by notification in the Official Gazette, direct an amendment of the said Schedule to be made so as to provide for, such discontinuance of, or increase or decrease, as the case may be, in, the preferential rate.

(5) Every notification issued under sub-section (3) or sub-section (4) shall, 'as soon as may be after it is issued, be' laid before each House of Parliament.

5. Levy of a lower rate of duty under a trade agreement.

(1) Where under a trade agreement between the Government of India and the Government of a foreign country or territory, duty at a rate lower than that specified in the First Schedule is to be charged on articles which are the produce or manufacture of such foreign country or territory, the Central Government may, by notification in the Official Gazette, make rules for determining if any article is the produce or manufacture of such foreign country or territory and for requiring the owner to make a claim at the time of importation, supported by such evidence as may be prescribed in the said rules, for assessment at the appropriate lower rate under such Agreement.

(2) If any question arises whether any trade agreement applies to any country or territory, or whether it has ceased to apply to India or any foreign country or territory, it shall be referred to the Central Government for decision and the decision of the Central Government shall be final and shall not be liable to be questioned in any court of law.

6. Power of Central Government to levy protective duties in certain cases.

(1) Where the Central Government, upon a recommendation made to it in this behalf by the Tariff Commission established under the Tariff Commission Act, 1951 (50 of 1951) is satisfied that circumstances exist which render it necessary to take immediate action to provide for the protection of the interests of any industry established in India, the Central Government may, by notification in the Official Gazette, impose on any goods imported into India in respect of which the said recommendation is made, a duty of customs of such

amount, not exceeding the amount proposed in the said recommendation, as it thinks fit.

(2) Every duty imposed on any goods under sub-section (1) shall, for the purposes of this Act, be deemed to have been specified in the First Schedule as the duty leviable in respect of such goods.

(3) Where a notification has been issued under sub-section (1), the Central Government shall, unless the notification is in the meantime rescinded, have a Bill introduced in Parliament, as soon as may be, but in any case during the next session of Parliament following the date of the issue of the notification to give effect to the proposals in regard to the continuance of a protective duty of customs on the goods to which the notification relates, and the notification shall cease to have effect when such Bill becomes law, whether with or without modifications, but without prejudice to the validity of anything previously done thereunder:

PROVIDED that if the notification under sub-section (1) is issued when Parliament is in session, such a Bill shall be introduced in Parliament during that session:

PROVIDED FURTHER that where for any reason a Bill as aforesaid does not become law within six months from the date of its introduction in Parliament, the notification shall cease to have effect on the expiration of the said period of six months, but without prejudice to the validity of anything previously done thereunder.

7. Duration of protective duties and power of Central Government to alter them.

(1) When the duty specified in respect of any article in the First Schedule is characterised as protective in [1][column (5)] of that Schedule, that duty shall have effect only up to and inclusive of the date, if any, specified in that Schedule.

(2) Where in respect of any such article the Central Government is satisfied after such inquiry as it thinks necessary that such duty has become ineffective or excessive for the purpose of securing the protection intended to be afforded by it' to be a similar article manufactured in India and that circumstances exist which render it necessary to take immediate action, it may, by notification in the Official Gazette, increase of reduce such duty to such extent as it thinks necessary.

(3) Every notification under sub-section (2), in so far as it relates to increase of such duty, shall be laid before each House of Parliament if it is sitting as soon as may be after the issue of the notification, and if it is not sitting within seven days of its re-assembly, and the Central Government shall seek the approval of Parliament to the notification by a resolution moved within a period of fifteen days beginning with the day on which the notification is so laid before the House of the People and if Parliament make' s any modification in the notification or directs that the notification should cease to have effect, the notification shall thereafter have effect only in such modified form or be of no effect, as the case may be, but without prejudice to the validity of anything previously done thereunder.

(4) For the removal of doubts, it is hereby declared that any notification issued under sub-section (2), including any such notification approved or modified under sub-section (3), may be rescinded by the Central Government at any time by notification in the Official Gazette.

8. Emergency power of Central Government to increase or levy export duties.

(1) Where, in respect of any article, whether included in the Second Schedule or not, the Central Government is satisfied that the export duty leviable thereon should be increased or that an export duty should be levied, and that circumstances exist which render it necessary to take immediate action, the Central Government may, by notification in the Official Gazette, direct and amendment of the Second Schedule to be made so as to provide for an increase the export duty leviable or, as the case may be, for the levy of an export duty, on that article.

(2) The provisions of sub-section (3) and (4) of Section 7 shall apply to any notification issued under sub-section (1) as they apply in relation to any notification increasing duty issued under sub-section (2) of Section 7.

8A. 3[Emergency power of Central Government to increase import duties.

(1) Where in respect of any article included in the First Schedule, the Central Government is satisfied that the import duty leviable thereon under Section 12 of the Customs Act, 1962 should be increased and that circumstances exist which render it necessary to take immediate action, it may, by notification in the Official Gazette direct an amendment of that Schedule to be made so as to provide for an increase in the import duty leviable on such article to such extent as it thinks necessary:

PROVIDED that the Central Government shall not issue any notification under this sub soction for substituting the rate of, import duty in respect of any article as specified by an earlier notification issued under this sub-section be that Government before such earlier notification has been approved with or without modifications under sub-section (2).

(2) The provisions of sub-sections (3) and (4) of Section 7 shall apply to any notification issued under sub-section (1) as they apply in relation to any notification increasing duty issued under sub-section (2) of Section 7."]

9. Additional import duty on bountyfed articles.

(1) Where any country or territory pays, or bestows, directly or indirectly, any bounty or Subsidy upon the manufacture or production therein or the exportation therefrom of any article, then, upon the importation of any such article into India, whether the same is imported directly from the country of manufacture, production or otherwise, and whether it is imported in the same condition as when exported from the country of manufacture or production or has been changed in condition by manufacture, production or otherwise, the Central Government may, by notification in the Official Gazette, impose,-

(i) if the article is not otherwise chargeable with duty under the provisions of this Act, a duty or

(ii) if the article is otherwise so chargeable, an additional duty, not exceeding the amount of such bounty or subsidy:

PROVIDED that the Central Government may, pending the determination in accordance with the provisions of this section and the rules made thereunder of the amount of such bounty or grant, impose a duty or additional duty under this sub-section not exceeding the amount of such bounty or subsidy as provisionally estimated by it and if such duty or additional duty exceeds such bounty or subsidy as so determined -

(a) the Central Government shall, having regard to such determination and as soon as may be after such determination, reduce such duty or additional duty; and

(b) refund shall be made of so much of such duty or additional duty which has been collected as is in excess of the duty or additional duty as so reduced;

(2) The amount of any such bounty or subsidy as aforesaid shall, from time to time, be ascertained, determined, and declared by the Central Government, after such inquiry as it may consider necessary and the Central Government may, by notification in the Official Gazette, make rules for the identification of such articles and for the assessment and collection of any [1][duty or additional duty, as the case may be, imposed upon the importation thereof under sub-section (1).

(3) Every notification issued under sub-section (1) shall, as soon as may be after it is issued, be laid before each House of Parliament.

9A. Antidumping duty.

(1) Where any article is exported from any country or territory (hereafter in this section referred to as the exporting country or territory) to India at less than its normal value, then, upon the importation of such article into India, the Central Government may, by notification in the Official Gazette, impose,—

(a) if the article is not otherwise chargeable with duty under the provisions of this Act, a duty; or

(b) if the article is otherwise so chargeable, an additional duty, not exceeding the margin of dumping in relation to such article not exceeding the margin of dumping in relation to such article:

(1) **Sub-section (1) and (2) of Section 9 shall stand amended as follows when Section 2 of Act No. 52 of 1982 comes into force:** "(1) Where any country or territory pays, or bestows, directly or indirectly, any bounty or subsidy upon the manufacture or production therein or the exportation therefrom of any article, then, upon the importation of any such article into India, whether the same is imported directly from the country of manufacture, production or otherwise, and whether it is imported in the same condition as when exported from the country of manufacture, production or has been changed in condition by manufacture, production or otherwise, the Central

Government may, by notification in the Official Gazette, impose —

(i) if the article is not otherwise chargeable with duty under the provisions of this Act, a duty; or

(ii) if the article is otherwise so chargeable, an additional duty, not exceeding the amount of such bounty or subsidy:

Provided that the Central Government may, pending the determination in accordance with the provisions of this section and the rules made thereunder of the amount of such bounty or grant, impose a duty or additional duty under this sub-section not exceeding the amount of such bounty or subsidy as provisionally estimated by it and if such duty or additional duty exceeds such bounty or subsidy as so determined —

(a) the Central Government shall, having regard to such determination and as soon as may be after such determination, reduce such duty or additional duty; and

(b) refund shall be made of so much of such duty or additional duty which has been collected as is in excess of the duty of the duty or additional duty as so reduced."

(c) in sub-section (2),—

(i) for the words "not amount of any such bounty or grant", the words "amount of any such bounty or subsidy" shall be substituted;

(ii) for the words "additional duty", the words "duty or additional duty, as the case may be," shall be substituted. Provided that the, Central Government may, pending the determination in accordance with the provisions of this section and the rules made thereunder of the normal value and the margin of dumping in relation to any article, impose on the importation of such article into India a duty or additional duty under this sub-section on the basis of a provisional estimate of such value and margin and if such duty or additional duty exceeds the margin as so determined -

(a) the Central Government shall, having regard to such determination and as soon as may be after such determination, reduce such duty or additional duty; and

(b) refund shall be made of so much of such duty or additional duty which has been collected as is in excess of such duty or additional duty as so reduced.

EXPLANATION. For the purposes of this section,-

(a) "margin of dumping", in relation to an article, means the difference between the price at which such article is exported and its normal value;

(b) "normal value", in relation to an article, means-

(i) the comparable price in the ordinary course of trade for the said article or like article when meant for consumption in the exporting country or territory-as determined under sub-section (2); or

(ii) where such comparable price cannot be ascertained because of the particular market situation or for any other reason, such value shall be either-

(A) the highest comparable price for the said article or like article from the exporting country or territory to any third country in the ordinary course of trade as determined under sub-section (2); or

(B) the cost of production of the said article or like article in the country of origin along with reasonable addition for selling and any other cost, and for profits, as determined under sub-section (2).

(2) Subject to any rules made under sub-section (3), the Central Government shall, after making due allowance in each case for differences in conditions and terms of sale, for differences in taxation and for other differences affecting price comparability, and, after such inquiry as it may consider necessary, determine, for the purposes of sub-section (1), the export price and the normal value of, and the margin of dumping in relation to, any article.

(3) The Central Government may, by notification in the Official Gazette, make rules for the purposes of this section, and without prejudice to the generality of the foregoing, such rules may provide for the manner in which articles liable for any duty or additional duty under sub-section (1) may be identified, and for the manner in which the export price and the normal value of, and the margin of dumping in relation to, such articles may be determined and for the assessment and collection of such duty or additional duty.

(4) Every notification issued under sub-section (1) shall, as soon as may be after it is issued, be laid before each House of Parliament.

9B. No levy under Section 9 or Section 9A in certain cases in the absence of injury to industry in India.

(1) Notwithstanding anything contained in Section 9 or Section 9A, the Central Government shall not levy any duty or additional duty under either of those sections on the import into India of any article from any country or territory to which this section applies unless that Government, after making investigation in accordance with the rules made under sub-section (3), declares, by notification in the Official Gazette, that the import of such article into India causes or threatens material injury to any industry established in India or materially retards the establishment of any industry in India.

(2) This section applies to every country or territory which is specified by the Central Government by notification in the Official Gazette to be a country, or territory

which, by reason of its being a party to the General Agreement on Tariff and Trade or by reason of any agreement between it and India for giving the most-favoured nation treatment or for any other reason, levies duty or additional duty of the nature referred to in Section 9 or Section 9A on articles imported from India only when such import causes or threatens any material injury to any industry established in such country or territory or material retards the establishment of such industry in such country or territory.

(3) The Central Government may, by notification in the Official Gazette, make rules for the purposes of this Section, and without Prejudice, to the generality of the foregoing, such rules may provide for the manner in which any investigation may be made for the purposes of sub-section(1), the factors to which regard shall be had in any such investigation and for all matters connected with such investigation.

(4) Every notification issued under, sub-Section, (1) or sub-section(2) shall, as soon as may be after it is issued, be laid before each House of Parliament.

EXPLANATION: For the purposes of this Section, "industry", in relation to any article, includes the manufacture or production of like articles, any activity connected therewith find the persons engaged in such production, manufacture or activity.

10. Rules to be laid before Parliament. Every rule made under this Act shall be laid, as soon as may be after it is made, before each House of Parliament, while it is in session for a total period of thirty days which may be comprised in one session or in two or more successive sessions, and if before the expiry of the session immediately following the session or the successive sessions aforesaid, both Houses agree in making any modification in the rule, or both House agree that the rule should not be made, the rule shall, thereafter, have effect only in such modified form or be of no effect, as the case may be; so, however, that any such modification or annulment shall be without prejudice to the validity of anything previously done under that rule.

11. Power of Central Government to alter duties under certain circumstances.

(1) Where the Central Government is satisfied that it is necessary so to do for the purpose of giving effect to any agreement entered into before the commencement of this Act with a foreign Government, it may, by notification in the Official Gazette, increase or reduce the duties referred to in Section 2 to such extent as each case may require:

PROVIDED that not notification under this sub-sectionincreasing or reducing the duties as aforesaid shall be issued by the Central Government after the expiration of a period of one year from the commencement of this Act.

(2) Every notification issued under sub-section(1) shall, as soon as may be after it is issued, be laid before each House of Parliament.

12. Repeal and saving.

(1) The Indian Tariff Act, 1934 (32 of 1934) and the Indian Tariff (Amendment) Act, 1949 (1 of 1949) are hereby repealed.

(2) Notwithstanding the repeal of any of the Acts mentioned in sub-section(1), anything done or any action taken (including any notification published and any rules and orders made or deemed to have been made under the provisions of those Acts and in force immediately before the commencement of this Act) shall, insofar as such thing or action is not inconsistent with the provisions of this Act, be deemed to have been done or taken under the provisions of this Act and shall continue in force accordingly until superseded by anything done or any action taken under this Act.

13. Consequential amendment of Act 52 of 1962. In the Customs Act, 1962, in sub-section (1) of Section 12 and in sub-section(1) of Section 14, for the words and figures "Indian Tariff Act, 1934", (32 of 1934) the words and figures "Customs Tariff Act, 1975" shall be substituted.

❑❑❑

21

The Export (Quality Control And Inspection) Act, 1963

Act No. 22 of 1963 [24th August, 1963]

AN ACT to provide for the sound development of the export trade of India through quality control and inspection and for matters connected therewith.

Be it enacted by Parliament in the Fourteenth Year of the Republic of India as follows:—

1. Short title, extent and commencement.

(1) This Act may be called the Export (Quality Control and Inspection) Act, 1963.

(2) It extends to the whole of India.

(3) It shall come into force on such date as the Central Government may, by notification in the Official Gazette, appoint.

2. Definitions. In this Act, unless the context otherwise requires,—

(a) "adjudicating authority"means the authority specified in, or under, Section 10K;

(ab) "Appellate authority"means the Appellate authority referred to in Section 10M;

(ac) "Council" means the Export Inspection Council established under Section 3;

(b) "export", with its grammatical variations and cognate expressions, means taking out of India to a place outside India;

(c) "inspection", in relation to a commodity, means the process of determining whether a batch of goods in that commodity complies with the standard specifications applicable to it or any other specifications stipulated in the export contract generally by inspecting either the whole batch or a selected sample or samples which purport to represent the whole batch;

(d) "notified commodity"means any commodity notified under clause (a) of Section 6;

(e) "prescribed" means prescribed by rules made under this Act;

(f) "quality control" means any activity having for its object the determination of the quality of a commodity (whether during the process of manufacture or production or subsequently) in order to ascertain whether it satisfies the standard specifications applicable to it or any other specifications stipulated in the export contract and whether it may be accepted for purposes of export.

3. Establishment of Export Inspection Council.

(1) The Central Government may, by notification in the Official Gazette, establish, with effect from such date as may be specified in the notification, a Council to be known as the Export Inspection Council, which shall consist of—

(a) a Chairman to be appointed by the Central Government;

(b) the Director of Inspection and Quality Control, *ex officio*, who shall be the Secretary;

(c) the Honorary Adviser on Standardization to the Government of India and Director of Indian Standards Institution, ex officio;

(d) the Agricultural Marketing Adviser to the Government of India, *ex officio*;

(e) the Director-General of Commercial Intelligence and Statistics, *ex officio*;

(f) fifteen other members nominated by the Central Government three of whom shall be persons representing the agencies referred to in Section 7.

(2) The Council shall be a body corporate by the name aforesaid, having perpetual succession and a common seal, with power to acquire, hold and dispose of property and to contract, and shall by the said name sue and be sued.

(3) The term of office of, and the manner of filling casual vacancies among, the members of the Council referred to in clauses (a) and (f) of sub-section (1) and the travelling and daily allowances payable to the members of the Council and the procedure to be followed in the discharge of its functions by the Council shall be such as may be prescribed.

(4) No act or proceeding of the Council shall be invalidated merely by reason of any vacancy in, or any defect in the constitution of, the Council.

(5) Subject to such rules as may be made by the Central Government in this behalf, the Council may appoint such officers and other employees as it considers necessary for the purpose of discharging its functions under this Act.

4. Director of Inspection and Quality Control. The Central Government shall appoint a Director of Inspection and Quality Control to exercise such powers and perform such duties under this Act as may be prescribed.

5. Functions of the Council.

(1) The functions of the Council shall generally be to advise the Central Government regarding measures for the enforcement of quality control and

inspection in relation to commodities intended for export and to draw up programmes therefor, to make, with the concurrence of the Central Government, grants-in-aid to the agencies established or recognised under Section 7 and to perform such other functions as may be assigned to it by or under this Act.

(2) For the purpose of performing its functions, the Council may co-opt as members such number of persons as it thinks fit who have special knowledge and practical experience in matters relating to any commodity or trade therein and any such person shall have the right to take part in the discussions of the Council but shall not have the right to vote and shall not be a member for any other purpose.

(3) The Council may also constitute specialist committees for conducting investigations on special problems connected with its functions.

(4) In the performance of its functions under this Act, the Council shall be bound by such directions as the Central Government may give to it in writing from time to time.

6. Powers of the Central Government in regard to quality control and inspection. If the Central Government, after consulting the Council, is of opinion that it is necessary or expedient so to do for the development of the export trade of India, it may, by order published in the Official Gazette,—

(a) notify commodities which shall be subject to quality control or inspection or both prior to export;

(b) specify the type of quality control or inspection which will be applied to a notified commodity;

(c) establish, adopt or recognise one or more standard specifications for a notified commodity;

(d) prohibit the export in the course of international trade of a notified commodity unless it is accompanied by a certificate issued under Section 7 that the commodity satisfies the conditions relating to quality control or inspection, or it has affixed or applied to it a mark or seal recognised by the Central Government as indicating that it conforms to the standard specifications applicable to it under clause (c).

7. Machinery for quality control and inspections.

(1) The Central Government may, by notification in the Official Gazette, establish, or recognise subject to such conditions as it may deem fit, agencies for quality control or inspection or both:

Provided that if the Central Government is of opinion that any recognition granted to any agency under this sub-section should, in the public interest, be withdrawn, the Central Government may, after giving a reasonable opportunity to that agency to make representations in the matter, withdraw, by like notification, the recognition granted to it.

(2) Any agency referred to in sub-section (1) may, on application made to it or otherwise, hold or cause to be held such examination as it thinks fit relating to quality control or inspection of notified commodities, either at the time of export or earlier, in such testing houses or by such surveyors or samplers as are

approved by the Central Government in this behalf and may charge such fees as may be prescribed for the purpose of such examination.

(3) If, after the examination, the agency is of opinion that the commodity satisfies the standard specifications laid down in respect of it under Section 6 or, as the case may be, any other specifications stipulated in the export contract, it may issue a certificate that the commodity satisfies the conditions relating to quality control and inspection.

(3A) Where the agency has reason to believe that a certificate issued under sub-section (3) has been obtained fraudulently or by misrepresentation, or the commodity in relation to which the certificate is issued has been changed or has deteriorated in quality, the agency may, by order amend, suspend or cancel the certificate in such manner and subject to such procedure as may be prescribed:

PROVIDED that before amending, suspending or cancelling any such certificate the holder thereof shall be given a reasonable opportunity of being heard;

(4) Any person aggrieved by the refusal of any agency referred to in sub-section (1) to issue a certificate, or by the amendment, suspension or cancellation of a certificate under sub-section (3A), may prefer an appeal within such time as may be prescribed to such authority as the Central Government may, by notification in the Official Gazette, constitute for the purpose of hearing appeals.

(5) Subject to the provisions of sub-section (6), the decision of the agency where no appeal is filed, and the decision of the appellate authority where an appeal is filed, shall be final and shall not be questioned in any court of law.

(6) The Central Government may, at any time, call for and examine the record of any proceeding relating to any decision of an agency or appellate authority under this Section for the purpose of satisfying itself as to the legality or propriety of such decision and may pass such order thereon as it thinks fit.

8. Power to recognise or establish marks to denote conformity with standard specifications.

(1) The Central Government may, by notification in the Official Gazette, recognise or establish any mark or seal in relation to a notified commodity for the purpose of denoting that such commodity conforms to a standard specification applicable to it.

(2) Any such mark or seal affixed or applied to a notified commodity or to any covering containing, or label attached to, such commodity shall be deemed to be evidence of the commodity being in conformity with the standard specifications applicable to it under this Act:

PROVIDED that nothing in this sub-section shall prevent any officer of customs from examining any consignment of a notified commodity intended for export if he has reason to believe that the seal or mark is not genuine or has been affixed or applied fraudulently or if such an examination is necessary for the purpose of any other law for the time being in force.

9. Power to obtain information from exporters, etc. The Central Government or any officer or authority authorised by it in this behalf may, by notice published in the Official Gazette, require—

(i) persons manufacturing, dealing in or exporting notified commodities; and

(ii) such other persons as may be prescribed, to furnish any information, return or report which the Central Government or such officer or authority may consider necessary for carrying out the purposes of this Act.

10. Finance, accounts and audit.

(1) For the purpose of enabling the Council to discharge its functions under this Act, the Central Government may, after due appropriation made by Parliament by law in this behalf, pay to the Council such sums of money as that Government considers necessary by way of grants, loans or otherwise.

(2) For the purpose of discharging its functions under this Act, the Council may receive grants or donations from bodies and institutions approved by the Central Government in this behalf.

(3) The Council shall have its own fund to which shall be credited the sums of money referred to in sub-sections (1) and (2) and the moneys in the fund shall be applied for —

  (a) meeting the pay and allowances of the officers and other employees of the Council and other administrative expenses of the Council;

  (b) carrying out the functions of the Council under this Act.

(4) The Council shall prepare, before the commencement of each financial year, a statement of programme of its activities during that year as well as a financial estimate in respect thereof.

(5) A statement prepared under sub-section (4) shall, not later than three months before the commencement of each financial year, be submitted for approval to the Central Government.

(6) The Council shall maintain such accounts and prepare the balance-sheet in such form as may, in consultation with the Comptroller and Auditor-General of India, be prescribed.

(7) The accounts of the Council shall be audited in such manner and at such times as may, in consultation with the Comptroller and Auditor-General of India, be prescribed.

10A. Power to enter and inspect. The Director of Inspection and Quality Control or any officer of the Central Government authorised by him in writing in this behalf (hereinafter referred to as the"authorised officer") may enter at any reasonable time, any premises in which —

(a) any commodity which has been changed after inspection by any agency, referred to in sub-section (1) of Section 7; or

(b) any books of account or other documents or things which, in his opinion, will be useful for, or relevant to, any proceeding under this Act, are suspected to have been kept or concealed, and inspect such commodity, books of account, other documents or things and may take such notes or extracts from such books of account or other documents as he may think fit.

10B. Power to search. If the authorised officer has any reason to believe that—

(a) any commodity which has been changed after inspection by any agency referred to in sub-section (1), of Section 7; or

(b) any books of account or other documents or things which, in his opinion, will be useful for, or relevant to, any proceeding under this Act, are secreted in any place, he may enter into and search such place or premises for such commodity, books of account, other documents or fsthings.

10C. Power to seize commodities, etc.

(1) If the authorised officer has any reason to believe that any commodity is liable to confiscation under this Act, he may seize such commodity together with the package, covering or receptacle, if any, in which such commodity is found and where such commodity is found to have been mixed with any other goods or materials, he may seize such commodity together with the goods or materials with which it is so mixed:

PROVIDED that where it is not practicable to seize any such commodity, the authorised officer may serve on the owner of the commodity an order that he shall not remove, part with, or otherwise deal with, the commodity except with the previous permission of such authorised officer.

(2) Where any commodity is seized under sub-section (1) and no notice in respect thereof is given under Section 10L within six months of the seizure of such commodity, it shall be returned to the person from whose possession it was seized:

PROVIDED that the aforesaid period of six months may, on sufficient cause being shown, be extended by the Director of Inspection and Quality Control by a further period not exceeding six months.

(3) The authorised officer may seize any documents or things which, in his opinion, will be useful for, or relevant to, any proceeding under this Act.

(4) The person from whose custody any documents are seized under sub-section (3) shall be entitled to make copies thereof or take extracts therefrom in the presence of the authorised officer.

(5) If any person legally entitled to the documents or things seized under sub-section (3) objects, for any reason, to the retention by the authorised officer of the documents or things, he may make an application to the Central Government stating therein the reasons for such objection and requesting for the return of the documents or things.

(6) On receipt of an application under sub-section (5), the Central Government may, after giving the applicant an opportunity of being heard, pass such order as it may think fit.

(7) Where any document—

(a) is produced or furnished by any person or has been seized from the custody or control of any person under this Act or any other law for the time being in force; or

(b) has been received from any place outside India (duly authenticated by such authority or person and in such manner as may be prescribed) in the course of the investigation of any offence alleged to have been committed by any person against this Act, and such document is tendered in evidence against the person by whom it is produced or from whom it was seized or against such person and any other person who is jointly tried, or proceeded against, with him, the court, or, as the case may be, the adjudicating authority shall, notwithstanding anything to the contrary contained in any other law for the time being in force,—

(i) presume, unless the contrary is proved, that the signature and every other part of such document which purports to be in the handwriting of any particular person or which the court or the adjudicating authority may reasonably assume to have been signed by, or to be in the handwriting of, any particular person, is under that person' s handwriting, and, in the case of a document executed or attested, it was executed or attested by the person by whom it purports to have been so executed or attested;

(ii) admit the document in evidence notwithstanding that it is not duly stamped, if such document is otherwise admissible in evidence.

10D. Power to stop and seize conveyances. Any authorise officer may, if he has any reason to suspect that any conveyance or animal is being, or is about to be, used for the transportation of any commodity which is liable to confiscation under this Act and that by such transportation any provision of this Act has been, is being, or is about to be, contravened, at any time, stop such conveyance or animal or, in the case of an aircraft, compel it to land, and

(a) rummage and search the conveyance or any part thereof,

(b) examine and search any goods or materials in the conveyance or on the animal,

(c) if it becomes necessary to stop any conveyance or animal, he may use all lawful means for stopping it and where such means fail, the conveyance or animal may be fired upon, and where he is satisfied that it is necessary so to do to prevent the contravention of any provision of this Act, he may seize such conveyance or animal.

EXPLANATION: Any reference in this Section to a conveyance shall, unless the context otherwise requires, be construed as including a reference to an aircraft, vehicle or vessel.

10E. Search and seizure to be made in accordance with the Code of Criminal Procedure 1973. The provisions of the Code of Criminal Procedure, 1973, relating to searches and seizures shall, so far as may be, apply to every search or seizure made under this Act.

10F. Confiscation. Any commodity in respect of which—

(a) a certificate has been obtained from an agency referred to in sub-section (1) of Section 7 fraudulently or by misrepresentation, or

(b) any provision of this Act has been, is being, or is attempted to be, contravened, shall, together with any package, covering or receptacle in which such commodity is found, be liable to confiscation and, where such commodity is so mixed with any other goods or materials that it cannot be readily separated, such other goods or materials shall also be liable to confiscation:

PROVIDED that where it is established to the satisfaction of the adjudicating authority that any commodity, which is liable to confiscation under this Act, belongs to a person other than the person who has, by any act or omission, rendered it liable to confiscation, and such act or omission was without the knowledge or connivance of the person to whom it belongs, such commodity shall not be ordered to be confiscated; but such other action as is authorised by this Act may be taken against the person who has, by such act or omission, rendered such commodity liable to confiscation.

10G. Confiscation of conveyance. Any conveyance or animal which has been, is being, or is attempted to be, used for the transport of any commodity which is liable to confiscation under this Act, shall be liable to confiscation unless the owner of the conveyance or animal proves that it was, is being, or is about to be, so used without the knowledge or connivance of the owner himself, his agent, if any, and the person in charge of the conveyance or animal and that each of them had taken all reasonable precautions against such use:

PROVIDED that in the case of a conveyance or animal used for the transport of goods or passengers for hire, the owner of the conveyance or animal shall be given an option to pay, in lieu of confiscation of the conveyance of animal, a fine not exceeding the value of the commodity which has been, is being, or is attempted to be, transported by such conveyance or animal.

10H. Option to pay fine in lieu of confiscation. Whenever confiscation of any commodity is authorised by this Act, the officer adjudging it shall, without prejudice to the provisions of the proviso to Section 10G, give to the owner of the commodity an option to pay in lieu of confiscation such fine not exceeding the value of the commodity.

10I. Liability to penalty. Any person,—

(a) who, in relation to any commodity, does or omits to do any act which act or omission would render such commodity liable to confiscation under this Act, or abets the doing or omission of such an act; or

(b) who acquires possession of or is in any way concerned in carrying, removing, depositing, keeping, concealing, selling or purchasing, or in any manner dealing with, any commodity which he knows or has reason to believe is liable to confiscation under this Act, shall be liable to a penalty not exceeding five times the value of the commodity or five thousand rupees, whichever is more, whether or not such commodity has been confiscated or is available for confiscation.

10J. Confiscation or penalty not to interfere with other punishments. No confiscation made or penalty imposed under the foregoing provisions of this Act shall prevent the infliction of any other punishment to which the person affected thereby is liable under the provisions of this Act or under any other law for the time being in force.

10K. Adjudication. Any confiscation may be adjudged or penalty, may be imposed under this Act by the Director of Inspection and Quality Control, or, where he so directs, by a general or special order, by any officer subordinate to him.

10L. Giving of opportunity to the owner of goods, etc. No order of adjudication of confiscation or imposing a penalty shall be made unless the owner of the commodity, conveyance or animal or other person concerned, is given a notice in writing—

(a) informing him of the grounds on which it is proposed to confiscate such commodity, conveyance or animal or to impose a penalty;

(b) giving him a reasonable opportunity of making a representation in writing within such reasonable time as may be specified in the notice against the confiscation or imposition of penalty mentioned therein, and, if he so desires, of being heard in the matter.

10M. Appeal.

(1) Any person aggrieved by any decision or order made under this Act may prefer an appeal,—

(a) Where the decision or order has been made by the Director of Inspection and Quality Control, to the Central Government;

(b) where the decision or order has been made by any officer subordinate to the Director of Inspection and Quality Control, to the Director of Inspection and Quality Control, within a period of forty-five days from the date on which the decision or order is served on such person:

PROVIDED that the Appellate authority may, if it is satisfied that the appellant was prevented by sufficient cause from preferring the appeal within the aforesaid period of forty-five days, allow such appeal to be preferred within a further period of forty-five days:

PROVIDED FURTHER that in the case of an appeal against an order imposing a penalty, no such appeal shall be entertained unless the amount of the penalty has been deposited by the appellant: Provided also that where the Appellate authority is of the opinion that the deposit to be made will cause undue hardship to the appellant, it may, at its discretion, dispense with such deposit either unconditionally or subject to such conditions as it may impose.

(2) The Appellate authority may, after giving to the appellant a reasonable opportunity of being heard, if he so desires, and after making such further inquiries, if any, as it may consider necessary, pass such orders as it thinks fit, confirming, modifying or reversing the decision or order appealed against, or may send back the case, with such directions as it may think fit, for a fresh adjudication or decision, as the case may be, after taking additional evidence, if necessary:

PROVIDED that an order enhancing or imposing a penalty or confiscating commodity of a greater value shall not be made under this Section unless the appellant has had an opportunity of making a representation and, if he so desires, of being heard, in his defence.

10N. Powers of revision. The Central Government may, on its own motion or otherwise, call for and examine the records of any proceeding in which an order of adjudication of confiscation or imposing any penalty has been made by any officer under this Act and against which no appeal has been preferred, for the purpose of satisfying itself as to the correctness, legality or propriety of such order or decision and pass such orders thereon as it may think fit:

PROVIDED that no decision or order shall be varied under this Section so as to prejudicially affect any person unless such person—

(a) has, within a period of two years from the date of such decision or order, received a notice to show cause why such decision or order shall not be varied, and

(b) has been given a reasonable opportunity of making a representation and, if he so desires, of being heard in his defence.

10O. Powers of adjudicating and other authorities.

(1) Every authority making any adjudication or hearing any appeal or exercising any powers of revision under this Act shall have all the powers of a civil court under the Code of Civil Procedure, 1908, while trying a suit, in respect of the following matters, namely:—

(a) summoning and enforcing the attendance of witnesses;

(b) requiring the discovery and production of any document;

(c) requisitioning any public record or copy thereof from any court or office;

(d) receiving evidence on affidavits; and

(e) issuing commissions for the examination of witnesses or documents.

(2) Every authority making any adjudication or hearing any appeal or exercising any powers of revision under this Act shall be deemed to be a Civil Court for the purposes of Sections 345 and 346 of the Code of Criminal Procedure, 1973.

(3) Every authority making any adjudication or hearing any appeal or exercising any powers of revision under this Act shall have the power to make such orders of an interim nature as it may think fit and may also, for sufficient cause, order the stay of operation of any decision or order.

10P. Continuance of proceedings in the event of death or insolvency.

(1) Where a penalty has been imposed by the adjudicating authority and—

(a) no appeal against the order imposing such penalty has been preferred to the Appellate authority and the person entitled to file such appeal dies or is adjudicated an insolvent before the expiry of the period within which the appeal can be preferred; or

(b) an appeal has been preferred to the Appellate authority against the order imposing such penalty but the appellant dies or is adjudicated an insolvent during the pendency of the appeal, then, it shall be lawful for the legal representatives of such person or the Official Assignee or the Official Receiver as the case may be, to prefer an appeal to the Appellate authority or as the case may be to continue the appeal before the Appellate authority in place of such person and the provisions of Section 10M shall so far as may be, apply or continue to apply to such appeal.

(2) The powers of the Official Assignee or the Official Receiver under sub-section (1) shall be exercised by him subject to the provisions of the Presidency-towns Insolvency Act, 1909, or the Provincial Insolvency Act, 1909, or the Provincial Insolvency Act, 1920, as the case may be.]

11. Penalty.

(1) If any person contravenes any order under clause (d) of Section 6, or fraudulently obtains a certificate under Section 7, or fraudulently affixes or applies any such mark or seal as is referred to in sub-section (1) of Section 8, he shall, on conviction, be punishable—

(i) for the first offence, with imprisonment for a term which may extend to two years, or with fine which may extend to five thousand rupees, or with both;

(ii) for the second or subsequent offence, with imprisonment for a term which may extend to [2][three years] and also with fine which may extend to five thousand rupees and in the absence of special and adequate reasons to be mentioned in the judgment of the court, such imprisonment shall not be less than three months.

(2) Any person who attempts to commit or abets the commission of an offence punishable under sub-section (1) shall be deemed to have committed such offence.

(3) If any person contravenes or attempts to contravene or abets the contravention of any other provision of this Act or any rules or orders made thereunder, he shall be punishable with fine which may extend to one thousand rupees.

11A. Penalty for contravention of order made by adjudicating authority or Appeallate authority. If any person fails to pay the penalty imposed by the adjudicating or the Appellate authority or fails to comply with any direction or order made, or deemed to have been made, under this Act, he shall, on conviction, be punishable with imprisonment for a term which may extend to two years, or with fine, or with both.

11B. Offences by officers and employees of agency, etc.

(1) If any officer or employee of the Council or of any agency referred to in sub-section (1) of Section 7, or any surveyor, sampler or employee of any testing house, referred to in sub-section (2) of that Section enters into, or acquiesces in, any agreement to do, abstains from doing, permits, conceals or connives at, any act or thing whereby any provision of this Act is or may be contravened, he shall, on conviction, be punishable with imprisonment for a term which may extend to two years, or with fine which may extend to five thousand rupees, or with both.

(2) If any officer searches or authorises any other officer of the Central Government to search any place without having reason to believe that any commodity, books of account or documents or things of the nature referred to in Section 10B are secreted in that place, he shall, on conviction, be punishable with imprisonment for a term which may extend to six months, or with fine which may extend to one thousand rupees, or with both.

(3) If any officer or employee of the Council or of any agency referred to in sub-section (1) of Section 7, or any surveyor, sampler or employee of any testing house, referred to in sub-section (2) of that Section, except in the discharge in good faith of his duty as such officer or employee or in compliance with any

requisition made under any law for the time being in force discloses any particulars learnt by him in his official capacity in respect of any commodity, he shall on conviction be punishable with imprisonment for a term which may extend to six months or with fine which may extend to one thousand rupees or with both.

11C. Correction of clerical or arithmetical mistakes. Clerical or arithmetical mistakes in any decision or order, or errors arising therein from any accidental slip or omission may, at any time, be corrected by the authority by which the decision or order was made either on its own motion or on the application of the aggrieved person:

PROVIDED that where any correction proposed to be made under this Section will have the effect of prejudicially affecting any person, no such correction shall be made except after giving to that person a reasonable opportunity of making a representation in the matter and no such correction shall be made after the expiry of a period of two years from the date on which such decision or order was made.

12. Offences by companies.

(1) Where an offence under this Act has been committed by a company, every person who, at the time the offence was committed, was in charge of, and was responsible to, the company for the conduct of the business of the company, as well as the company, shall be deemed to be guilty of the offence and shall be liable to be proceeded against and punished accordingly:

PROVIDED that nothing contained in this sub-section shall render any such person liable to any punishment, if he proves that the offence was committed without his knowledge or that he exercised all due diligence to prevent the commission of such offence.

(2) Notwithstanding anything contained in sub-section (1), where an offence under this Act has been committed by a company and it is proved that the offence has been committed with the consent or connivance of, or is attributable to any negligence on the part of, any director, manager, secretary or other officer of the company, such director, manager, secretary or other officer shall also be deemed to be guilty of that offence and shall be liable to be proceeded against and punished accordingly.

EXPLANATION: For the purposes of this Section—

(a) "company"means a body corporate and includes a firm or other association of individuals; and

(b) "director", in relation to a firm, means a partner in the firm.

13. Delegation of powers. The Central Government may, by notification in the Official Gazette, direct that any power exercisable by it under this Act shall, in relation to such matters and subject to such conditions, if any, as may be specified in the direction, be exercisable also by—

(a) the Council;

(b) such officer or authority subordinate to the Central Government, or such State Government or such officer or authority subordinate to a State Government as may be specified in the direction.

14. Procedure for prosecution. No prosecution for an offence punishable under this Act shall be instituted except by or with the consent of an officer authorised by the Central Government by general or special order in this behalf.

15. Officers and employees of agency to be public servants. All officers and employees of the Council or of any agency established or recognised under sub-section

(1) of Section 7 and all surveyors, samplers and employees of testing houses, referred to in sub-section (2) of that Section shall, while acting or purporting to act in pursuance of the provisions of this Act or any rule or order made thereunder, be deemed to be public servants within the meaning of Section 21 of the Indian Penal Code (45 of 1860).

16. Protection of action taken in good faith.

(1) No suit, prosecution or other legal proceeding shall lie against the Council or any officer or employee of the Government or the Council or any agency referred to in sub-section (1) of Section 7 for anything which is in good faith done or intended to be done in pursuance of this Act or any rule or order made thereunder.

(2) No suit or other legal proceeding shall lie against the Government for any damage caused or likely to be caused by anything which is in good faith done or intended to be done in pursuance of this Act or any rule or order made thereunder.

16A. Suspension, etc., of operation of the provisions of the Act.

(1) If the Central Government is satisfied that circumstances exist which render it necessary or expedient so to do in the public interest, it may, by notification in the Official Gazette, suspend or relax to a specified extent the operation of all or any of the provisions of this Act in respect of such notified commodity or commodities generally or in respect of any area and for such period as may be specified in the notification.

(2) Where the operation of any provision of this Act has, under sub-section (1), been suspended or relaxed, such suspension or relaxation may, at any time be removed by the Central Government by a like notification.

(3) Every notification issued under this section shall be laid, as soon as may be after it is issued before each House of Parliament, while it is in session, for a total period of thirty days which may be comprised in one session or in two or more successive sessions, and if, before the expiry of the session immediately following the session or the successive sessions aforesaid, both Houses agree in making any modification in the notification or both Houses agree that the notification should not be issued, the notification shall thereafter have effect only in such modified form or be of no effect, as the case may be; so, however, that any such modification or annulment shall be without prejudice to the validity of anything previously done under that notification.

17. Power to make rules.

(1) The Central Government may, by notification in the Official Gazette, make rules to carry out the purposes of this Act.

(2) In particular and without prejudice to the generality of the foregoing power,

such rules may provide for—

(a) the travelling and daily allowances payable to members of the Council, persons co-opted under sub-section (2) of Section 5, and members of specialist committees referred to in sub-section (3) of that section;

(b) the functions of the Council and the procedure to be followed by it;

(c) the appointment of officers and other employees of the Council;

(d) the procedure to be followed for various types of quality control and inspection;

(e) the conditions which a testing house, surveyor or sampler should satisfy for purposes of approval by the Central Government;

(f) the fees chargeable for purposes of examination and issue of certificates under Section 7;

(ff) the manner in which, and the procedure subject to which, any certificate issued under sub-section (3) of Section 7 shall be amended, suspended or cancelled;];

(g) the filing of appeals under Section 7 and the fees payable therefor;

(gg) the authority or person by which or by whom, and the manner in which, any document received from a place outside India shall be authenticated;

(h) the manner in which the accounts of the Council shall be maintained and audited;

(i) any other matter which is required to be, or may be, prescribed.

(3) Every rule made by the Central Government under this section shall be laid as soon as may be after it is made before each House of Parliament while it is in session for a total period of thirty days which may be comprised in one session or in two or more successive sessions, and if, before the expiry of the session [1][immediately following the session] or the successive sessions aforesaid, both Houses agree in making any modification in the rule or both Houses agree that the rule should not be made, the rule shall thereafter have effect only in such modified form or be of no effect, as the case may be; so, however, that any such modification or annulment shall be without prejudice to the validity of anything previously done under that rule.

18. Act to override other enactments. As from the date on which a commodity is notified under clause (a) of Section 6, the provisions of this Act or anything done or any action taken thereunder shall have effect in relation to that commodity notwithstanding any provisions (relating to quality control and inspection prior to the export of such commodity) contained in any enactment other than this Act or in any instrument having effect by virtue of any enactment other than this Act.

❑❑❑

22

The Finance (No. 2) Bill, 1996

ACT NO. 33 OF 1996 [28TH SEPTEMBER 1996]

AN ACT to give effect to the financial proposals of the Central Government for the financial year 1996-97.

Be it enacted by Parliament in the Forty-seventh Year of the Republic of India as follows:

CHAPTER - I : PRELIMINARY

1. Short title and commencement.

(1) This Act may be called the Finance (No. 2) Act, 1996.

(2) Save as otherwise provided in this Act, Sections 2 to 58 and Section 88 shall be deemed to have come into force on the 1st day of April, 1996.

CHAPTER - II : RATES OF INCOME-TAX

2. Tax

(1) Subject to the provisions of sub-sections (2) and (3), for the assessment year commencing on the 1st day of April, 1996, (tax) income-tax shall be charged at the rates specified in Part I of the First Schedule and such tax shall be increased, in the cases to which Paragraph E, of that Part applies by a surcharge calculated in the manner provided therein.

(2) In the cases to which Sub-Paragraph I or Sub-Paragraph 11 of Paragraph A of Part I of the First Schedule applies, where the assessee has, in the previous year, any net agricultural income exceeding six hundred rupees, in addition to total income, and the total income exceeds -

(i) in a case to which the said Sub-Paragraph I applies, forty thousand rupees, and

(ii) in a case to which the said Sub-Paragraph II applies, eighteen thousand rupees, then,-

(a) the net agricultural income shall be taken into account, in the manner provided in clause (b)[that is to say, as if the net agricultural income were comprised in the total income after,-

(i) in a case to which the said Sub-Paragraph I applies, the first forty thousand rupees, and

(ii) in a case to which the said Sub-Paragraph II applies, the first eighteen thousand rupees, of the total income but without being liable to tax, only for the purpose of charging income-tax in respect of the total income; and

(b) the income-tax chargeable shall be calculated as follows:-

(i) the total income and the net agricultural income shall be aggregated and the amount of income-tax shall be determined in respect of the aggregate income at the rates specified in Sub-Paragraph I or, as the case may be, Sub-Paragraph II of the said Paragraph A, as if such aggregate income were the total income;

(ii) the net agricultural income shall be increased,-

(A) in a case to which the said Sub-Paragraph I applies, by a sum of forty thousand rupees; and

(B) in a case to which the said Sub-Paragraph II applies, by a sum of eighteen thousand rupees, and the amount of income-tax shall be determined in respect of the net agricultural income as so increased at the rates specified in Sub-Paragraph I or, as the case may be, Sub-Paragraph 11 of the said Paragraph A, as if the net agricultural income as so increased were the total income;

(iii) the amount of income-tax determined in accordance with sub-clause (i) shall be reduced by the amount of income-tax determined in accordance with sub-clause (ii) and the sum so arrived at shall be the income-tax in respect of the total income.

(3) In cases to which the provisions of Chapter XII or Chapter XII-A or sub-section (1A) of Section 161 or Section 164 or Section 164A or Section 167B of the Income-tax Act, 1961 (hereinafter referred to as the Income-tax Act) (43 of 1961). apply, the tax chargeable shall be determined as provided in that Chapter or that Section, and with reference to the rates imposed by sub-section (1) or the rates as specified in that Chapter or Section, as the case may be:

PROVIDED that the amount of income-tax computed in accordance with the provisions of Sections 112 and 113 of the Income-tax Act shall be increased in the case of a domestic company by a surcharge as provided in Paragraph E of Part I of the First Schedule:

PROVIDED FURTHER that in respect of any income chargeable to tax under Section 115B, or in the case of a domestic company having a total income exceeding seventy-five thousand rupees under Section 115BB, of the Income-tax Act, the income-tax computed shall be increased by a surcharge calculated at the rate of fifteen per cent. of such income-tax.

(4) In cases in which tax has to be deducted under Sections 193, 194, 194A, 194B, 194BB, 194D and 195 of the Income-tax Act at the rates in force, the deduction shall be made at the rates specified in Part II of the First Schedule and shall be increased, in the cases to which the provisions of sub-item (a) of item 2 of that Part apply, by a surcharge calculated in the manner provided therein.

(5) In cases in which tax has to be deducted under Sections 194C, 194G, 194-I, 194J and 194K of the Income-tax Act, the deduction shall be made at the rates specified in those Sections and shall be increased in the case of an assessee, being a domestic company, by a surcharge calculated at the rate of seven-and-a-half per cent. of such deduction.

(6) In cases in which tax has to be collected under Section 206C of the Income-tax Act, the collection shall be made at the rates specified in that Section and shall be increased in the case of a buyer, being a domestic company, by a surcharge calculated at the rate of seven-and-a-half per cent. of such collection.

(7) Subject to the provisions of sub-section (8), in cases in which income-tax has to be calculated under the first proviso to sub-section (5) of Section 132 of the Income-tax Act or charged under sub-section (4) of Section 172 or sub-section (2) of Section 174 or Section 175 or Sub-section (2) of Section 176 of the said Act or deducted under Section 192 of the said Act from income chargeable under the bead "Salaries"or in which the "advance tax" payable under Chapter XVII-C of the said Act has to be computed, at the rate or rates in force, such income-tax or, as the case may be, "advance tax"shall be so calculated, charged, deducted or computed at the rate or rates specified in Part III of the First Schedule and such tax shall be increased, in the cases to which Paragraph E of that Part applies, by a surcharge calculated in the manner provided therein:

PROVIDED that in the cases to which the provisions of Chapter XII or Chapter XII-A or sub-section (1A) of Section 161 or Section 164 or Section 164A or Section 167B of the Income-tax Act apply, "advance tax" shall be computed with reference to the rates imposed by this sub-section or the rates as specified in that Chapter or Section, as the case may be:

PROVIDED FURTHER that the amount of income-tax computed in accordance with the provisions of Sections 112 and 113 of the Income-tax Act shall be increased in the case of a domestic company by a surcharge as provided in Paragraph E of Part III of the First Schedule:

PROVIDED ALSO that in respect of any income chargeable to tax under Section 115B, or in the case of a domestic company, under Section 115BB of the Income-tax Act, having a total income exceeding seventy-five thousand rupees, the "advance tax"computed under the first proviso shall be increased by a surcharge calculated at the rate of seven-and-a-half per cent of such "advance tax".

(8) In the cases to which Paragraph A of Part III of the First Schedule applies, where the assessee has, in the previous year or, if by virtue of any provision of the Income-tax Act, income-tax is to be charged in respect of the income of a period other than the previous year, in such other period, any net agricultural income exceeding six hundred rupees, in addition to total income and the total income exceeds forty thousand rupees, then, in calculating income-tax under the first proviso to sub-section (5) of Section 132 of the Income-tax Act or in charging income-tax under sub-section (2) of Section 174 or Section 175 or sub-section (2) of Section 176 of the said Act or in computing the "advance tax"payable under Chapter XVII-C of the said Act, at the rate or rates in force,-

(a) the net agricultural income shall be taken into account, in the manner provided in clause (b) [that is to say, as if the net agricultural income were comprised in the total income after the first forty thousand rupees of the total income but without being liable to tax], only for the purpose of calculating, charging or computing such income-tax or, as the case may be, "advance tax"in respect of the total income; and

(b) such income-tax or, as the case may be, "advance tax"shall be so calculated, charged or computed as follows:-

(i) the total income and the net agricultural income shall be aggregated and the amount of income-tax or "advance tax"shall be determined in respect of the aggregate income at the rates specified in the said Paragraph A as if such aggregate income were the total income;

(ii) the net agricultural income shall be increased by a sum of forty thousand rupees, and the amount of income-tax or "advance tax"shall be determined in respect of the net agricultural income as so increased at the rates specified in the said Paragraph A as if the net agricultural income as so increased were the total income;

(iii) the amount of income-tax or "advance tax"determined in accordance with sub-clause (i) shall be reduced by the amount of income-tax or, as the case may be, "advance tax"determined in accordance with sub-clause (ii) and the sum so arrived at shall be the income-tax or, as the case may be, "advance tax"in respect of the total income.

(9) For the purposes of this Section and the First Schedule,-

(a) "domestic company"means an Indian company, or any other company which, in respect of its income liable to income-tax under the Income-tax Act for the assessment year commencing on the 1st day of April, 1996, has made the prescribed arrangements for the declaration and payment within India of the dividends (including dividends on preference shares) payable out of such income in accordance with the provisions of Section 194 of the Act;

(b) "insurance commission" means any remuneration or reward, whether by way of commission or otherwise, for soliciting or procuring insurance business (including business relating to the continuance, renewal or revival of policies of insurance);

(c) "net agricultural income", in relation to a person, means the total amount of agricultural income, from whatever source derived, of that person computed in accordance with the rules contained in Part IV of the First Schedule;

(d) all other words and expressions used in this Section or in the First Schedule but not defined in this sub-section and defined in the Income-tax Act shall have the meanings respectively assigned to them in that Act.

CHAPTER - III : DIRECT TAXES INCOME-TAX

3. Amendment of Section 2. In Section 2 of the Income-tax Act, with effect from the 1st day of October, 1996,-

(a) in clause (7A), for the words "Assistant Commissioner" and "Deputy Commissioner", the words "Assistant Commissioner" or "Assistant Director" and "Deputy Commissioner" or "Deputy Director" shall respectively be substituted;

(b) in clause (24), after sub-clause (x), the following sub-clause shall be inserted, namely: '(xi) any sum received under a Keyman insurance policy including the sum allocated by way of bonus on such policy.

EXPLANATION. For the purposes of this clause, the expression "Keyman insurance policy" shall have the meaning assigned to it in the Explanation to clause (10D) of Section 10'.

4. Amendment of Section 10. In Section 10 of the Income-tax Act,-

(a) in clause (10A), after sub-clause (ii), the following sub-clause shall be inserted with effect from the 1st day of April, 1997, namely:- "(iii) any payment in commutation of pension received from a fund under clause (23AAB);"

(b) in clause (10D), after the words, brackets, figures and letters "other than any sum received under sub-section (3) of Section 80DDA", the following shall be inserted with effect from the 1st day of October, 1996, namely or under a Keyman insurance policy.

EXPLANATION.-For the purposes of this clause, "Keyman insurance policy" means a life insurance policy taken by a person on the life of another person who is or was the employee of the first mentioned person or is or was connected in any manner whatsoever with the business of the first mentioned person;';

(c) in clause (15), in sub-clause (iv), after item (i), in the Explanation, for clause (e), the following clause shall be substituted with effect from the 1st day of April, 1997, namely:- "(e) the operation of ships or aircrafts or construction or operation of rail systems;"

(d) after clause (23AAA), the following clause shall be inserted with effect from the 1st day of April, 1997, namely: (23AAB) any income of a fund, by whatever name called, set up by the Life Insurance Corporation of India on or after the 1st day of August, 1996 under a pension scheme,-

(i) to which contribution is made by any person for the purpose of receiving pension from such fund;

(ii) which is approved by the Controller of Insurance.

EXPLANATION. For the-purposes of this clause, the expression "Controller of Insurance" shall have the meaning assigned to it in clause (5B) of Section 2 of the Insurance Act, 1938 (4 of 1938);

(e) after clause (23BBB), the following clause shall be inserted and shall be deemed to have been inserted with effect from the 1st day of April, 1992, namely:-

"(23BBC) any income of the SAARC Fund for Regional Project set up by Colombo Declaration issued on the 21st day of December, 1991 by the Heads of State or Government of the Member Countries of South Asian Association for Regional Cooperation established on the 8th day of December, 1985 by the Charter of the South Asian Association for Regional Cooperation;";

(f) after clause (23F), the following clause shall be inserted with effect from the 1st day of April, 1997, namely:-

(G) any income by way of dividends, interest or long-term capital gains of an infrastructure capital fund or an infrastructure capital company from investments made by way of shares or long-term finance in any enterprise carrying on the business of developing, maintaining and operating any infrastructure facility, which fulfils the conditions specified in sub-section (4A) of Section 80-IA.

EXPLANATION: For the purposes of this clause,-(a) "infrastructure capital company" means such company as has made investments by way of acquiring shares or providing long-term finance to an enterprise carrying on the business of developing, maintaining and operating infrastructure facility; (b) "infrastructure capital fund" means such fund operating under a trust deed, registered under the provisions of the Registration Act, 1908 (16 of 1908), established to raise monies by the trustees for investment by way of acquiring shares or providing long-term finance to an enterprise carrying on the business of developing, maintaining and operating infrastructure facility; (c) "infrastructure facility" shall have the meaning assigned to it in clause (ca) of sub-section (12) of Section 80-IA; (d)"long-term finance" shall have the meaning assigned to it in clause (viii) of sub-section (1) of Section 36;'

(g) for clause (24), the following clause shall be substituted with effect from the 1st day of April, 1997, namely: '(24) any income chargeable under the heads "income from house property" and "Income from other sources" of-

(a) a registered union within the meaning of the Trade Unions Act, 1926 (16 of 1926) formed primarily for the purpose of regulating the relations between workmen and employers or between workmen and workmen;

(b) an association of registered unions referred to in subclause (a);'.

5. Amendment of Section 12A. In Section 12A of the Income-tax Act, in clause (a), for the words "whichever is later", the words, figures and letters"whichever is later and such trust or institution is registered under Section 12AA"shall be substituted with effect from the 1st day of April, 1997.

6. Insertion of new Section 12AA. After Section 12A of the Income-tax Act, the following Section shall be inserted with effect from the 1st day of April, 1997, namely:-

"12AA. Procedure for registration.

(1) The Chief Commissioner or Commissioner, on receipt of an application for registration of a trust or institution made under clause (a) of Section 12A, shall-

(a) call for such documents or information from the trust or institution as he thinks necessary in order to satisfy himself about the genuineness of activities of the trust or institution and may also make such inquiries as he may deem necessary in this behalf, and

(b) after satisfying himself about the objects of the trust or institution and the genuineness of its activities, be-

(i) shall pass an order in writing registering the trust or institution;

(ii) shall, if he is not so satisfied, pass an order in writing refusing to register the trust or institution, and a copy of such order shall be sent to the applicant:

PROVIDED that no order under sub-clause (ii) shall be passed unless the applicant has been given a reasonable opportunity of being heard.

(2) Every order granting or refusing registration under clause (b) of sub-section (1) shall be passed before the expiry of six months from the end of the month in which the application was received under clause (a) of Section 12A.".

7. Amendment of Section 16. In Section 16 of the Income-tax Act, for clause (i), the following clauses shall be substituted with effect from the 1st day of April, 1997, namely:-' (i) in the case of an assessee whose income from salary, before allowing a deduction under this clause, does not exceed sixty thousand rupees, a deduction of a sum equal to thirty-three and one-third per cent. of the salary or eighteen thousand rupees, whichever is less;

(ia) in any other case, a deduction of a sum equal to thirty-three and one-third per cent of the salary or fifteen thousand rupees, whichever is less:

PROVIDED that in the. case of an assessee, being a woman, whose total income before making any deduction under this clause, does not exceed seventy-five thousand rupees, the provisions of this clause shall have effect as if for the words "fifteen thousand rupees", the words "eighteen thousand rupees" had been substituted.

EXPLANATION. For the removal of doubts, it is hereby declared that where, in the case of an assessee, salary is due from, or paid or allowed by, more than one employer, the deduction under this clause shall be computed with reference to the aggregate salary due, paid or allowed to the assessee and shall in no case exceed the amount specified under clause (i) or clause (ia), as the case may be.'

8. Amendment of Section 17. In Section 17 of the Income-tax Act, in clause (3), in sub-clause (ii), for the words "interest on such contributions", the following shall be substituted with effect from the 1st day of October, 1996, namely: 'interest on such contributions or any sum received under a Keyman insurance policy including the sum allocated by way of bonus on such policy.

EXPLANATION. For the purposes of this sub-clause, the expression "Keyman insurance policy" shall have the meaning assigned to it in clause (10D) of Section 10.'

9. Amendment of Section 24. In Section 24 of the Income-tax Act, in sub-section (2), in the proviso,-

(a) for the words "ten thousand rupees", the words "fifteen thousand rupees" shall be substituted with effect from the 1st day of April, 1997 ;

(b) after the words, brackets, figures and letters "sub-clause (i) of clause (a) of sub-section (2) of Section 23", the words, brackets and figures "or sub-section (3) of Section 23" shall be inserted and shall be deemed to have been inserted with effect from the 1st day of April, 1995.

10. Amendment of Section 28. In Section 28 of the Income-tax Act, after clause (v), the following clause shall be inserted with effect from the 1st day of October, 1996, namely:- '(vi) any sum, received under a Keyman insurance policy including the sum allocated by way of bonus on such policy.

EXPLANATION: For the purposes of this clause, the expression "Keyman insurance policy" shall have the meaning assigned to it in clause (10D) of Section 10'.

11. Amendment of Section 32. In Section 32 of the Income-tax Act, with effect from the 1st day of April, 1997 -

(a) in sub-section (1), after the words "plant or furniture owned", the words "wholly or partly", shall be inserted;

(b) in sub-section (1), after the third proviso, the following proviso shall be inserted, namely:-

"PROVIDED ALSO that the aggregate deduction, in respect of depreciation of buildings, machinery, plant or furniture allowable to the predecessor and the successor in the case of succession, referred to in Section 170 or the amalgamating company and the amalgamated company in the case of amalgamation, as the case may be, shall not exceed in any previous year the deduction calculated at the prescribed rates as if the succession or the amalgamation had not taken place, and such deduction shall be apportioned between the predecessor and the successor, or the amalgamating company and the amalgamated company, as the case may be, in the ratio of the number of days for which the assets were used by them."

(c) for sub-section (2), the following sub-section shall be substituted, namely:- "(2) Where in the assessment of the assessee full effect cannot be given to any allowance under clause (ii) of sub-section (1) in any previous year owing to there being no profits or gains chargeable for that previous year or owing to the profits or gains being less than the allowance, then, the allowance or the part of allowance to which effect has not been given (hereinafter referred to as unabsorbed depreciation allowance), as the case may be,-

(i) shall be set off against the profits and gains, if any, of any business or profession carried on by him and assessable for that assessment year;

(ii) if the unabsorbed depreciation allowance cannot be wholly set off, under clause (i), the amount not so set off shall be set off from the income under any other bead, if any, assessable for that assessment year;

(iii) if the unabsorbed depreciation allowance cannot be wholly set off under clause (i) and clause (ii), the amount of allowance not so set off shall be carried forward to the following assessment year and-(a) it shall be set off against the profits and gains, if any, of any business or profession carried on by him and assessable for that assessment year;

(b) if the unabsorbed depreciation allowance cannot be wholly so set off, the amount of unabsorbed depreciation allowance not so set off shall be carried forward to the following assessment year not being more than eight assessment years immediately succeeding the assessment year for which the aforesaid allowance was first computed:

PROVIDED that the business or profession for which the allowance was originally computed continued to be carried on by him in the previous year relevant for that assessment year:

PROVIDED FURTHER that the time limit of eight assessment years specified in sub-clause (b) shall not apply in the case of a company for the assessment year beginning with the assessment year relevant to the previous year in which the said company has become a sick industrial company under sub-section (1) of Section 17 of the Sick Industrial Company (Special Provisions) Act, 1985 (1 of 1986). and ending with the assessment year relevant to the previous year in which the entire networth of such company becomes equal to or exceeds the accumulated losses.

EXPLANATION. For the purposes of this clause, "networth" shall have the meaning assigned to it in clause (ga) of subsection (1) of Section 3 of the Sick Industrial Companies (Special Provisions) Act, 1985 (1 of 1986),.

12. Amendment of Section 35. In Section 35 of the Income-tax Act, in subsection (2AA), for the provisos, the following proviso shall be substituted with effect from the 1st day of October, 1996, namely:-

PROVIDED that the prescribed authority shall, before granting approval, satisfy itself about the, feasibility or carrying out the scientific research and shall submit its report to the Director General in Such form as may be prescribed."

13. Amendment of Section 35AC. In Section 35AC of the Income-tax Act, after sub-section (3) and before the Explanation, the following sub-sections shall be inserted with effect from the 1st day of October, 1996, namely:-

"(4) Where an association or institution is approved by the National Committee under sub-section (1), and subsequently that Committee is satisfied that the project or the scheme is not being carried on in accordance with all or any of the conditions subject to which approval was granted, it may, at any time, after giving a reasonable opportunity of showing cause against the proposed withdrawal to the concerned association or institution, withdraw the approval.

(5) Where any project or scheme has been notified as an eligible project or scheme under clause (b) of the Explanation and subsequently the National Committee is satisfied that the project or the scheme is not being carried out in accordance with all or any of the

conditions subject to which such project or scheme was notified, such notification may be withdrawn in the same manner in which it was issued:

> *PROVIDED that a reasonable opportunity of showing cause against the proposed withdrawal shall be given by the National Committee to the concerned association, institution, public sector company or the local authority, as the case may be."*

14. Amendment of Section 36. In Section 36 of the Income-tax Act, in sub-section 1, in clause (viii),-

- (a) for the words"before making any deduction under this Section", the words"before making any deduction under this clause"shall be substituted and shall be deemed to have been substituted;
- (b) in the second proviso, for the brackets and words"(excluding the amounts capitalised from reserves)", the words"and of the general reserves"shall be substituted with effect from the 1st day of April, 1997 ;
- (c) in the Explanation, after clause (d), the following clause shall be inserted and shall be deemed to have been inserted, namely:-' (e)"long-term finance"means any loan or advance where the terms under which moneys are loaned or advanced provide for repayment along with interest thereof during a period of not less than seven years.'

15. Amendment of Section 40A. In Section 40A of the Income-tax Act, in sub-section (3), for the words "ten thousand" wherever they occur, the words "twenty thousand" shall be substituted with effect from the 1st day of April, 1997.

16. Amendment of Section 41. In Section 41 of the Income-tax Act, Explanation occurring below sub-section (1) shall be renumbered as Explanation 2, and before Explanation 2 as so renumbered, the following Explanation shall be inserted with effect from the 1st day of April, 1997, namely:-

'*EXPLANATION 1:* For the purposes of this sub-section, the expression "loss or expenditure or some benefit in respect of any such trading liability by way of remission or cessation thereof" shall include the remission or cessation of any liability by a unilateral act by the first mentioned person under clause (a) or the successor in business under clause (b) of that sub-section by way of writing off such liability in his accounts.'

17. Amendment of Section 43. In Section 43 of the Income-tax Act, in clause 1, after Explanation 4, the following Explanation shall be inserted with effect from the 1st day of October, 1996, namely:

"*EXPLANATION 4A:* Where before the date of acquisition by the assessee (hereinafter referred to as the first mentioned person), the assets were at any time used by any other person (hereinafter referred to as the second mentioned person) for the purposes of his business or profession and depreciation allowance has been claimed in respect of such assets in the case of the second mentioned person and such person acquires on lease, hire or otherwise assets from the first mentioned person, then, notwithstanding anything contained in Explanation 3, the actual cost of the transferred assets, in the case of first mentioned person, shall be the same as the written down value of the said assets at the time of thereof by the second mentioned person."

18. Amendment of Section 43B. In Section 43B of the Income-tax Act, with effect from the 1st day of April, 1997 -

(a) in clause (d), after the words "governing such loan or borrowing" the words "governing such loan or borrowing" or shall be substituted;

(b) after clause (d), the following clause shall be inserted, namely:-"(e) any sum payable by the assessee as interest on any term loan from a scheduled bank in accordance with the terms and conditions of the agreement governing such loan";

(c) after Explanation 3, the following Explanation shall be inserted, namely:-

EXPLANATION 3A: For the removal of doubts, it is hereby declared that where a deduction in respect of any sum referred to in clause (e) of this Section is allowed in computing the income referred to in Section 28 of the previous year (being a previous year relevant to the assessment year commencing on the 1st day of April, 1996, or any earlier assessment year) in which the liability to pay such sum was incurred by the assessee, the assessee shall not be entitled to any deduction under this Section in respect of such sum in computing the income of the previous year in which the sum is actually paid by him";

(d) in Explanation 4, after clause (a), the following clause shall be inserted, namely:-

(aa) "scheduled bank" shall have the meaning assigned to it in clause (ii) of the Explanation to clause (viia) of sub-section (1) of the Section 36'.

19. Amendment of Section 45: In Section 45 of the Income-tax Act, in sub-section 1, after the figures and letter "54E", the figures and letters "54EA, 54EB", shall be inserted with effect from the 1st day of October, 1996.

20. Insertion of new Sections 54 EA and 54 EB. After Section 54E of the Income-tax Act, the following Sections shall be inserted with effect from the 1st day of October, 1996, namely:-

54EA. Capital gain on transfer of long-term capital assets not to be charged in the case of investment in specified bonds or debentures.

(1) Where the capital gain arises from the transfer of a long-term capital asset (the capital asset so transferred being hereafter in this Section referred to as the original asset) and the assessee has, at any time within a period of six months after the date of such transfer, invested the whole or any part of the net consideration in any of the bonds, debentures or units of any mutual fund referred to in clause (23D) of Section 10 specified by the Board in this behalf by notification in the Official Gazette (such assets hereafter in this Section referred to as the specified bonds or debentures), the capital gain shall be dealt with in accordance with the following provisions of this Section, that is to say -

(a) if the cost of the specified bonds or debentures is not less than the net consideration in respect of the original asset, the whole of such capital gain shall not be charged under Section 45;

(b) if the cost of the specified bonds or debentures is less than the net consideration in respect of the original asset, so much of the capital gain as bears to the whole of the capital gain the same proportion as the cost of acquisition of the specified bonds or debentures bears to the net consideration shall not be charged under Section 45.

(2) Where the specified bonds or debentures are transferred or converted (otherwise than by transfer) into money at any time within a period of three years from the date of their acquisition, the amount of capital gain arising from the transfer of the original asset not charged under Section 45 on the basis of the cost of such specified bonds or debentures as provided in clause (a) or clause (b) of sub-section (1) shall be deemed to be the income chargeable under the head "capital gains" relating to long-term capital assets of the previous year in which the specified bonds or debentures are transferred or converted (otherwise than by transfer) into money.

EXPLANATION: In a case where the original asset is transferred and the assessee invests the whole or any part of the net consideration in respect of the original asset in any specified bonds or debentures and such assessee takes any loan or advance on the security of such specified bonds or debentures, he shall be deemed to have converted (otherwise than by transfer) such specified bonds or debentures into money on the date on which such loan or advance is taken:

(3) Where the cost of the specified bonds or debentures has been taken into account for the purposes of clause (a) or clause (b) of sub-section (1), a rebate with reference to such cost shall not be allowed under Section 88.

EXPLANATION. For the purposes of this Section -

(a) "cost", in relation to any specified bonds or debentures, means the amount invested in such specified bonds or debentures out of the net consideration received or accruing as a result of the transfer of the original asset;

(b) "net consideration", in relation to the transfer of a capital asset, means the full value of the consideration received or accruing as a result of the transfer of the capital asset as reduced by the expenditure incurred wholly and exclusively in connection with such transfer.

54EB. Capital gain on transfer of long-term capital assets not to be charged certain cases.

(1) Where the capital gain arises from the transfer of a long-term capital asset (the capital asset so transferred being hereafter in this Section referred to as the original asset), and the assessee has, at any time within a period of six months after the date of such transfer invested the whole or any part of capital gains, in any of the assets specified by the Board in this behalf by notification in the Official Gazette (such assets hereafter in this Section referred to as the long-term specified assets), the capital gain shall be dealt with in accordance with the following provisions of this Section, that is to say,-

(a) if the cost of the long-term specified asset is not less than the capital gain arising from the transfer of the original asset, the whole of such capital gain shall not be charged under Section 45;

(b) if the cost of the long-term specified asset is less than the capital gain arising from the transfer of the original asset, so much of the capital gain as bears to the whole of the capital gain the same proportion as the cost of acquisition of the long-term specified asset bears to the whole of the capital gain, shall not be charged under Section 45.

EXPLANATION: "Cost", in relation to any long-term specified asset, means the amount invested in such spęcified asset out of capital gains received or accruing as a result of the transfer of the original asset.

(2) Where the long-term specified asset is transferred or converted (otherwise than by transfer) into money at any time within a period of seven years from the date of its acquisition, the amount of capital gains arising from the transfer of the original asset not charged under Section 45 on the basis of the cost of such long-term specified asset as provided in clause (a), or as the case may be, clause (b) of sub-section (1) shall be deemed to be the income chargeable under the bead"Capital gains"relating to long-term capital assets of the previous year in which the long-term specified asset is transferred or converted (otherwise than by transfer) into money. Explanation.-In a case where the original asset is transferred and the assessee invests the whole or any part of the capital gain received or accrued as a result of transfer of the original asset in any long-term specified asset and such assessee takes any loan or advance on the security of such specified asset, he shall be deemed to have converted (otherwise than by transfer) such specified asset into money oh the date on which such loan or advance is taken.

(3) Where the cost of the long-term specified asset has been taken into account for the purposes of clause (a) or clause (b) of sub-section (1), a deduction from the amount of income-tax with reference to such cost shall not be allowed under Section 88.'.

21. Amendment of Section 56. In Section 56, in sub-section (2), after clause (iii), the following clause shall be inserted with effect from the 1st day of October, 1996, namely:-(iv) income referred to in sub-clause (xi) of clause (24) of Section 2, if such income is not chargeable to income-tax under the head "Profits and gains of business or profession" or under the head "Salaries".'.

22. Omission of Section 80CC. Section 80CC of the Income-tax Act shall be omitted and shall be deemed to have been omitted with effect from the 1st day of April, 1993.

23. Insertion of new Section 80CCC. After Section 80CCB of the income-tax Act, the following Section shall be insert with effect from the 1st day of April, 1997, namely:-

80CCC. Deduction respect of contribution to certain pension funds.

(1) Where an assessee being an individual has in the previous year paid or deposited any amount out of his income chargeable to tax to effect or keep in force a contract for any annuity plan of Life Insurance Corporation of India for receiving pension from the fund referred to in clause (23AAB) of Section 10, he shall, in accordance with, and subject to the provisions of this Section be allowed a deduction in the computation of his total income of the whole of the amount paid or deposited (excluding interest or bonus accrued or credited to the

assessee's account if any) as does not exceed the amount of ten thousand rupees in the previous year.

(2) Where any amount standing to the credit of the assessee in a fund, referred to in sub-section (1) in respect of which a deduction has been allowed under sub-section (1), together with the interest or bonus accrued or credited to the assessee' s account, if any, is received by the assessee or his nominee-

(a) on account of the surrender of the annuity plan whether in whole or in part, in any previous year, or

(b) as pension received from the annuity plan, an amount equal to the whole of the amount referred to in clause (a) or clause (b) shall be deemed to be the income of the assessee or his nominee, as the case may be, in that previous year in which such withdrawal is made or, as the case may be, pension is received, and shall accordingly be chargeable to tax as the case may be, pension is received, and shall accordingly be chargeable to tax as income of that previous year.

(3) Where any amount paid or deposited by the assessee has been taken into account for the purposes of this Section, a rebate with reference to such amount shall not be allowed under Section 88."

24. Amendment of Section 80D. In Section 80D of the Income-tax Act, in sub-section (1), for the words "six thousand rupees", wherever they occur, the words "ten thousand rupees" shall be substituted with effect from the 1st day of April, 1997, namely:-

25. Insertion of new Section 80 DDB. After Section 80DDA of the Income-tax Act, the following Section shall be inserted with from the 1st day of April, 1997, namely:-

80DDB. Deduction in respect of medical treatment, etc. Where an assessee who is resident in India has, during the previous year, incurred any expenditure for the medical treatment of such disease or ailment as may be specified in the rules made in this behalf by the Board-

(a) for himself or a dependent relative, in case the assessee is an individual; or

(b) for any member of a Hindu undivided family, in case the assessee is Hindu Undivided family. the assessee shall be allowed a deduction of a sum of fifteen thousand rupees in respect of that previous year in which such expenditure was incurred:

PROVIDED that no such deduction shall be allowed unless the assessee furnishes a certificate in such from and from such authority as may be prescribed.

EXPLANATION. For the purposes of this Section, "dependant" means a person who is not dependant for his support or maintenance on any person other than the assessee.'

26. Amendment of Section 80G. In Section 80G of the Income-tax Act with, effect from the 1st day of April, 1997,-

(a) in sub-section (1) in clause (i), after the words brackets figures and letter sub-clause (iiih) or, the words, brackets, figures and letters sub-clause (iiiha) or sub-clause (iiihb) or sub-clause (iiihc) or shall be inserted;

(b) in sub-section (2), in clause (a), after sub-clause (iiih), the following subclauses shall be inserted, namely:-

'(iiiha) the National Blood Transfusion Council or to any State Blood Transfusion Council which has its sole object the control, supervision, regulation or encouragement in India of the services related to operation and requirements of blood banks.

EXPLANATION: For the purposes of this sub-clause,-

(a) "National Blood Transfusion Council" means a society registered under the Societies Registration Act, 1860 (21 of 1860). and has an officer not below the rank of an Additional Secretary to the Government of India dealing with the AIDS Control Project as its Chairman, by whatever name called;

(b) "State Blood Transfusion Council" means a society registered, in consultation with the National Blood Transfusion Council, under the Societies Registration Act, 1860 (21 of 1860) or under any law corresponding to that Act in force in any part of India and has Secretary to the Government of that State dealing with the Department of Health, as its Chairman, by whatever name called; or

(iiihb) any fund set up by a State Government to provide medical relief to the poor; or

(iiihc) the Army Central Welfare Fund or the Indian Naval Benevolent Fund or the Air Force Central Welfare Fund established by the armed forces of the Union for the welfare of the past and present members of such forces or their dependents; or'.

27. Amendment of Section 80GG. In Section 80GG of the Income-tax Act, for the words "one thousand rupees", the words "two thousand rupees" shall be substituted with effect from the 1st day of April, 1997.

28. Amendment of Section 80-IA. In Section 80-IA of the Income-tax Act, with effect from the 1st day of April, 1997,-

(a) in subsection (1), after the words "infrastructure facility", the words "or scientific and industrial research and development" shall be inserted;

(b) after sub-section (4A), the following sub-section shall be inserted, namely:- "(4B) This Section applies to any company registered in India carrying on scientific and industrial research and development which fulfils all the following conditions, namely:-

(i) the company has the main object of scientific and industrial research and development;

(ii) the company is for the time being approved by the prescribed authority at any time before the 1st day of April, 1998.";

(c) in sub-section (5), after clause (ia), the following clause shall be inserted, namely:- "(ib) in the case of a company referred to in sub-section (4B), hundred percent of the profits and gains derived from such business";

(d) in sub-section (6), after clause (iv), the following clause shall be inserted, namely: "(v) five in the case of an assessee, being a company referred to in sub-section (4B), deriving profits and gains from scientific and industrial research and development";

(e) in sub-section (12),-

 (i) in clause (c), after sub-clause (2), the following sub-clause, shall be inserted, namely: "(3) in the case of a company carrying on scientific and industrial research and development, means the assessment year relevant to the previous year in which the company is approved by the prescribed authority for the purposes of sub-section (4B)";

 (ii) for clause (ca), the following clause shall be substituted, namely- '(ca) "infrastructure facility"means-

  (i) a road, highway, bridge, airport, port, rail system or any other public facility of a similar nature as may be notified by the Board in this behalf in the Official Gazette;

  (ii) a water supply project, irrigation project, sanitation and sewerage system'.

29. Omission of Section 80J. Section 80J of the Income-tax shall be omitted and shall be deemed to have been omitted with effect from the 1st day of April, 1989.

30. Amendment of Section 80L. In Section 80L of the Income-tax Act, in sub-section

(1) with effect from the 1st day of April, 1997.-

 (a) in caluse (1) and (2), for the words "thirteen thousand", the words "twelve thousand" shall be substituted;

 (b) after caluse (2), the following, proviso shall be inserted, namely:-

"PROVIDED that where any income referred in clause (iv), clause (v) or clause (va) remains unallowed after the deduction under the foregoing provision of this Section, there shall be allowed in computing the total income of the assessee, an additional deduction of an amount equal to so much of such income as has remained unallowed so, however, that the amount of such additional deduction shall not exceed three thousand rupees."

31. Amendment of Section 80R. In Section 80R of the Income-tax Act, for the portion beginning with the words "equal. to" and ending with the words "whichever is higher", the following shall be substituted with effect from the 1st day of April, 1997, namely:- "equal to seventy-five per cent of such remuneration, as is brought into India by, or on behalf of, the assessee in convertible foreign exchange within a period of six months from the end of the previous year or where the Chief Commissioner or Commissioner is satisfied (for reasons to be recorded in writing) that the assessee is, for reasons beyond his control unable to do so within the said period of six months, within such further period as the Chief Commissioner or Commissioner may allow in this behalf:

PROVIDED that no deduction under this Section shall be allowed unless the assessee furnishes a certificate, in the prescribed form, along with the return of income, certifying that the deduction has been correctly claimed in accordance with the provisions of this Section".

32. Amendment of Section 80RR. In Section 80RR of the Income-tax Act, for the portion beginning with the words "equal to" and ending with the words "whichever is higher", the following shall be substituted with effect from the 1st day of April, 1997, namely;-"equal to seventy-five per cent of such income, as is brought into India by, or on behalf of, the assessee in convertible foreign exchange within a period of six months from the end of the previous year or where the Chief Commisioner or Commissioner is satisfied (for reasons to be recorded in writing) that the assessee is, for reasons beyond his control unable to do so within the said period of six months, within such further period as the Chief Commissioner or Commissioner may allow in this behalf:

> *PROVIDED that no deduction under this Section shall be allowed unless the assessee furnishes a certificate, in the prescribed form along with the return of income certifying that the education has been correctly claimed in accordance with the provisions of this Section."*

33. Amendment of Section 80RRA. In Section 80RRA of the Income-tax Act, in sub-section 1, for the portion beginning with the words "equal to" and ending with the words "whichever is higher", the following shall be substituted with effect from the 1st day of April 1997, namely - "equal to seventy-five per cent of such remuneration, as is brought into India by, or on behalf of, the assessee in convertible foreign exchange within a period of six months from the end of the previous year or where the Chief Commissioner or Commissioner is satisfied (for reasons to be recorded in writing) that the assessee is, for reasons beyond his control unable to do so within the said period of six months within such further period as the Chief Commissioner or Commissioner may allow in this behalf:

> *PROVIDED that no deduction under this sub-section shall be allowed unless the assessee furnishes a certificate in the prescribed form along with the return of income, certifying that the deduction has been correctly claimed in accordance with the provisions of this Section."*

34. Amendment of Section 88. In Section 88 of the Income-tax Act, with effect from the 1st day of April, 1997,-

(a) in sub-section (2) after clause (xv), the following clause shall be inserted namely:-

(xvi) as subscription to equity shares or debentures forming part of any eligible issue of capital approved by the Board on an application made by a public company in the prescribed form:

PROVIDED that where a deduction is claimed and allowed under this clause with reference to the cost of any equity shares or debentures, the cost of such shares of debentures shall not be taken into account for the purposes of Sections 54EA and 54EB.

EXPLANATION. For the purposes of this clause,-

(i) "eligible issue of capital" means an issue made by a public company formed and registered in India and the issue is wholly and exclusively for the purposes of developing, maintaining and operating an infrastructure facility or for generating, or for generating and distributing, power;

(ii) "infrastructure facility" shall have the meaning assigned to it in clause (ca) of sub-section (12) of Section 80-IA;

(iii) "public company" shall have the meaning assigned to it in Section 3 of the Companies Act, 1956 (1 of 1956);.

(xvii) as subscription to any units of any mutual fund referred to in clause (23D) of Section 10 and approved by the Board on an application made by such mutual fund in the prescribed form:

PROVIDED that where a deduction is claimed and allowed under this clause with reference to, the cost of units, the cost of such units shall not be taken into account for the purposes of Section 54EA and 54EB:

PROVIDED FURTHER that this clause shall apply if the amount of subscription to such units is subscribed only in the eligible issue of capital of any company.

EXPLANATION. For the purposes of this clause, "eligible issue of capital" means an issue referred to in clause (i) of Explanation to clause (xvi) of sub-section (2) of Section 88.';

(b) after sub-section (5), the following sub-section shall be inserted, namely:- "(5A) Where the aggregate of any sums specified in clause (i) to clause (xv) of sub-section (2) exceeds an amount of sixty thousand rupees, a deduction under sub-section (1) shall be allowed with reference to so much of the aggregate as does not exceed an amount of sixty thousand rupees:

PROVIDED that, in the case of an individual referred to in the proviso to sub-section (1) the provisions of this sub-section shall have effect as if for the words "sixty thousand rupees", the words "seventy thousand rupees" had been substituted".

(c) in sub-section (6), in clause (ii), for the words "twelve thousand rupees", the words "fourteen thousand rupees" shall be substituted;

(d) after sub-section (7), the following sub-section shall be inserted, namely:- "(7A) If any equity shares or debentures, with reference to the cost of which a deduction is allowed under sub-section (1), are sold or otherwise transferred by the assessee to any person at any time within a period of three years from the date of their acquisition, the aggregate amount of the deductions of income-tax so allowed in respect of such equity shares or debentures in the previous year or years preceding the previous year in which such sale or transfer has taken place shall be deemed to be tax payable by the assessee for the assessment year relevant to such previous year and shall be added to the amount of income-tax on the total income of the assessee with which he is chargeable for such assessment year.

EXPLANATION. A person shall be treated as having acquired any shares or debentures on the date on which his name is entered in relation to those shares or debentures in the register of members or of debenture-holders, as the case may be, of the public company."

35. Omission of Section 88A. Section 88A of the Income-tax Act shall be omitted and shall be deemed to have been omitted with effect from the 1st day of April, 1994.

36. Amendment of Section 88B. In Section 88B of the Income-tax Act, for the words "one hundred thousand rupees", the words, "one hundred and twenty thousand rupees" shall be substituted with effect from the 1st day of April, 1997.

37. Amendment of Section 112. In Section 112 of the Income-tax Act, in sub-section (1) with effect from the 1st day of April, 1997,-

(a) in clause (b), in sub clause (ii), for the words "thirty per cent", the words "twenty per cent" shall be substituted;

(b) in clause (d), in sub-clause (ii), for the words "thirty per cent", the words "twenty per cent" shall be substituted.

38. Amendment of Section 115AC. In Section 115AC of the Income-tax Act, in sub-section 1, in clause (a), after the words "specify in this behalf", the words "or on bonds or shares of a public sector company, sold by the Government" shall be inserted with effect from the 1st day of October, 1996.

39. Insertion of new Section 115JA. After Section 115J of the Income-tax Act, the following Section shall be inserted with effect from the 1st day of April, 1997, namely:-

115JA. Deemed income relating to certain companies.

(1) Notwithstanding anything contained in any other provisions of this Act, where in the case of an assessee, being a company, the total income, as computed under this Act in respect of any previous year relevant to the assessment year commencing on or after the 1st day April, 1997 (hereafter in this Section referred to as the relevant previous year) is less than thirty per cent. of its book profit the total income of such assessee chargeable to tax for the relevant previous year shall be deemed to be an amount equal to thirty per cent. of such book profit.

(2) Every assessee, being a company, shall, for the purposes of this Section prepare its profit and loss account for the relevant previous year in accordance with the provisions of Parts II and III of Schedule VI to the Companies Act, 1956 (1 of 1956):

PROVIDED that while preparing profit and loss account, the depreciation shall be calculated on the same method and rates which have been adopted for calculating the depreciation for the purpose of preparing the profit and loss account laid before the company at its annual general meeting in accordance with the provisions of Section 210 of the Companies Act, 1956 (1 of 1956):

PROVIDED FURTHER that where a company has adopted or adopts the financial year under the Companies Act, 1956 (1 of 1956) which is different from the previous year under the Act, the method and rates for calculation of depreciation shall correspond to the method and rates which have been adopted for calculating the depreciation for such financial year or part of such financial year falling within the relevant previous year.

EXPLANATION. For the purposes of this Section, "book profit" means the net profit as shown in the profit and loss account for the relevant previous year prepared under sub-section (2), as increased by -

(a) the amount of income-tax paid or payable, and the provision therefor; or

(b) the amounts carried to any reserves by whatever name called; or

(c) the amount or amounts set aside to provisions made for meeting liabilities, other than ascertained liabilities; or

(d) the amount by way of provision for losses of subsidiary companies; or

(e) the amount or amounts of dividends paid or proposed; or

(f) the amount or amounts of expenditure relatable to any income to which any of the provisions of Chapter III applies;

if any amount referred to in clauses (a) to (f) is debited to the profit and loss account, and as reduced by -

(i) the amount withdrawn from any reserves or provisions if any such amount is credited to the profit and loss account:

PROVIDED that, where this Section is applicable to an assessee in any previous year (including the relevant previous year), the amount withdrawn from reserves created or provisions made in a previous year relevant to the assessment year commencing on or after the 1st day of April, 1997 shall not be reduced from the book-profit unless the book profit of such year has been increased by those reserves or provisions (out of which the said amount was withdrawn) under this Explanation; or

(ii) the amount of income to which any of the provisions of Chapter III applies, if any such amount is credited to the profit and loss account; or

(iii) the amount of loss brought forward or unabsorbed depreciation, whichever is less as per books of account.

EXPLANATION. For the purposes of this clause, the loss shall not include depreciation; or

(iv) the amount of profits derived by an industrial undertaking from the business of, generation or generation and distribution of power; or

(v) the amount of profits derived by an industrial undertaking located in an industrially backward State or district as referred to in sub-clause (b) or subclause (c) of clause (iv) of sub-section (2) of Section 80-IA, for the assessment years such industrial undertaking is eligible to claim a deduction of hundred per cent. of the profits and gains under sub-section (5) of Section 80-IA; or

(vi) the amount of profits derived by an industrial undertaking from the business of developing, maintaining and operating any infrastructure facility as defined under sub-section (12) of Section 80-1A, and subject to fulfilling the conditions laid down in sub-section (4A) of Section 80-IA; or

(vii) the amount of-profits of a sick industrial company for the assessment year commencing from the assessment year relevant to the previous. year in which the said company has become a sick industrial company under sub-section (1) of Section 17 of the Sick Industrial Companies (Special Provisions) Act, 1985 (1 of 1986) and ending with the assessment year during which the entire net worth of such company becomes equal to or exceeds the accumulated losses.

EXPLANATION. For the purposes of this clause, "net worth" shall have the meaning assigned to it in clause (ga) of sub-section (1) of Section 3 of the Sick Industrial Companies (Special Provisions) Act, 1985 (1 of 1986).

(3) Nothing contained in subsection (1) shall affect the determination of the amounts in relation to the relevant previous year to be carried forward to the subsequent year or years under the provisions of sub-section (2) of Section 32 or sub-section (3) of Section 32A or clause (ii) of sub-section (1) of Section 72 or Section 73 or Section 74 or sub-section (3) of Section 74A.

(4) Save as otherwise provided in this Section, all other provisions of this Act shall apply to every assesses, being a company, mentioned in this Section'.

40. Amendment of Section 115K. In Section 115K of the Income-tax Act, with effect from the 1st day of April, 1997,-

(a) for the words "forty-seven thousand rupees", wherever they occur, the words "forty-nine thousand three hundred and thirty rupees" shall be substituted;

(b) for the words "six lakh rupees", at both the places where they occur, the words "seven lakh rupees" shall be substituted.

41. Amendment of Section 120. In Section 120 of the Income-tax Act, in sub-section (4), in clause (b), for the words "a Deputy Commissioner" and "such Deputy Commissioner", the words "a Deputy Commissioner or a Deputy Director" and "such Deputy Commissioner or Deputy Director" shall respectively be substituted with effect from the 1st day of October, 1996.

42. Amendment of Section 139. In Section 139 of the Income-tax Act, in sub-section 1, with effect from the 1st day of April, 1997,-

(a) the Explanation shall be renumbered as Explanation 1 and in the Explanation 1 as so renumbered, in clause (b), for sub-clause (i), the following sub-clause shall be substituted, namely:- "(i) in a case where the accounts of the assessee are required under this Act or any other law to be audited or where the report of an accountant is required to be furnished under Section 80HHC or Section 80HHD or where the prescribed certificate is required to be furnished under Section 80R or Section 80RR or sub-section (1) of Section 80RRA, or in the case of a co-operative society or in the case of a working partner of a firm whose accounts are required under this Act or any other law to be audited, the 31st day of October of the assessment year";

(b) after Explanation 1 as so renumbered, the following Explanation shall be inserted, namely:-

EXPLANATION 2. For the purposes of sub-clause (i) of clause (b) of Explanation 1, the expression "working partner" shall have the meaning assigned to it in Explanation 4 of clause (b) of Section 40.'.

43. Amendment of Section 148. In Section 148 of the Income-tax Act, in sub-section 1, the words"not being less than thirty days,"shall be omitted and shall be deemed to have been omitted with effect from the 1st day of April, 1989.

44. Amendment of Section 153. In Section 153 of the Income-tax Act, in Explanation 1, in clause (iii), for the words "the date on which the assessee furnishes", the words "the last date on which the assessee is required to furnish" shall be substituted with effect from the 1st day of April, 1997.

45. Amendment of Section 158B. In Section 158B of the Income-tax Act, in clause (a), for the words "period of ten previous years", the words "previous years relevant to ten assessment years" shall be substituted and shall be deemed to have been substituted with effect from the 1st day of July, 1995.

46. Amendment of Section 158BB. In Section of the Income-tax Act, in sub-section (1), in the Explanation, for clause (b), the following clause shall be substituted and shall be deemed to have been substituted with effect from the 1st day of July, 1995, namely:- "(b) of a firm, returned income and total income assessed for each of the previous years falling within the block period shall be the income determined before allowing deduction of salary, interest, commission, bonus or remuneration by whatever name called:

PROVIDED that undisclosed income of the firm so determined shall not be chargeable to tax in the hands of the partners, whether on allocation or on account of enhancement".

47. Amendment of Section 158BE. In Section 158BE of the Income-tax Act, after sub-section (2), the following Explanation shall be inserted and shall be deemed to have been inserted with effect from the 1st day of July, 1995, namely:-

"*EXPLANATION.* In computing the period of limitation for the purposes of this Section, the period-

(i) during which the assessment proceeding is stayed by an order or injunction of any court, or

(ii) commencing from the day on which the Assessing Officer directs the assessee to get his accounts audited under sub-section (2A) of Section 142 and ending on the day on which the assessee is required to furnish a report of such audit under that sub-section, shall be excluded".

48. Amendment of Section 158G. In Section 158BG of the Income-tax Act, for the proviso, the following proviso shall be substituted with effect from the 1st day of October, 1996, namely:-

"PROVIDED that no such order shall be passed without the previous approval of the Commissioner or Director, as the case may be".

49. Amendment of Section 194A. In Section 194A of the Income-tax Act, in sub-section (3), in clause (i), for the proviso, the following proviso shall be substituted with effect from the 1st day of October, 1996, namely:-

"PROVIDED that in respect of the income credited or paid in respect of-

(a) time deposits with a banking company to which the Banking Regulation Act, 1949 (10 of 1949) applies (including any bank or banking institution referred to in Section 51 of that Act); or

(b) time deposits with a co-operative society engaged in carrying on the business of banking;

(c) deposits with a public company which is formed and registered in India with the main object of carrying on the business of providing long-term finance for construction or purchase of houses in India for residential purposes and which is for the time being approved by the Central Government for the purpose of clause (viii) of sub-section (1) of Section 36, the provisions of this clause shall have effect as if for the words "two thousand five hundred rupees", the words "ten thousand rupees" had been substituted and the aforesaid amount

shall be computed with reference to the income credited or paid by a branch of the banking company or the co-operative society or the public company, as the case may be".

50. Amendment of Section 199. In Section 199 of the Income-tax Act, with effect from the 1st day of April, 1997 -

(i) for the words "owner of the security", the words "owner of the security, or depositor or owner of property or of unit-holder" shall be substituted;

(ii) in the first proviso, for the word "owner", the words "owner or depositor or unit-holder" shall be substituted;

(iii) for the second proviso, the following proviso shall be substituted, namely:-

PROVIDED FURTHER that where any property, deposit, security, unit or share is owned jointly by two or more persons not constituting a partnership, the payment shall be deemed to have been made on behalf of, and credit shall be given to, each such person in the same proportion in which rent, interest on deposit or on security or income in respect of unit or dividend on share is assessable as his income".

51. Omission of Section 206A and 206B. Sections 206A and 206B of the Income-tax Act shall be omitted with effect from the 1st day of October, 1996.

52. Amendment of Section 206C. In Section 206C of the Income-tax Act, in sub-section 1, for the Table, the following Table shall be substituted with effect from the 1st day of October, 1996, namely:-"

S. No.	Nature of Goods	Percentage
(1)	**(2)**	**(3)**
(i)	Alcoholic liquor for human consumption (other than Indian-made foreign liquor) and tendu leaves Ten per cent.	
(ii)	Timber obtained under a forest lease Fifteen per cent.	
(iii)	Timber obtained by any mode other than under a forest lease Five per cent.	
(iv)	Any other forest produce not being timber or tendu leaves Fifteen per cent."	

53. Amendment of Section 208. In Section 208 of the Income-tax Act, for the words "one thousand five hundred rupees", the words "five thousand rupees" shall be substituted with effect from the 1st day of October, 1996.

54. Amendment of Section 234C. In Section 234C of the Income-tax Act, in sub-section 1, with effect from the 1st day of April, 1997,-

(a) in the first proviso, for the words "instalment of advance tax which is immediately due or where no such instalment is so due", the words "remaining instalments of advance tax which are due or where no such instalments are due" shall be substituted;

(b) the second proviso shall be omitted.

55. Amendment of Section 272A. In Section 272A of the Income-tax Act, in sub-section (2), in clause (c), the words, figures and letters "or Section 206A or Section 206B" shall be omitted with effect from the 1st day of October, 1996 Wealth-tax.

56. Amendment of Section 2. In Section 2 of the Wealth-tax Act, 1957 (27 of 1957) (hereinafter referred to as the Wealth-tax Act), in clause (ea), for sub-clause (i), the following sub-clause shall be substituted with effect from the 1st day of April, 1997, narnely:-

(i) any building or land appurtenant thereto (hereinafter referred to as "house"), whether used for residential or commercial purposes or for the purpose of maintaining a guest-house or otherwise including a farmhouse situated within twenty-five kilometers from local limits of any municipality (whether known as municipality, municipal corporation or by any other name) or a cantonment board, but does not include-

(1) a house meant exclusively for residential purposes and which is allotted by a company to an employee or an officer or director who is in whole-time employment, having a gross annual salary of less than two lakh rupees;

(2) any house for residential or commercial purposes which forms part of stock-in-trade;

(3) any house which the assessee may occupy for the purposes of any business or profession carried on by him;'.

57. Amendment of Section 4. In Section 4 of the Wealth-tax Act, with effect from the 1st day of April, 1997, for subsection (7), the following sub-sections shall be substituted, namely:-

"(7) Where the assessee is a member of a co-operative society, company or other association of persons and a building or part thereof is allotted or leased to him under a house building scheme of the society, company or association, as the case may be, the assessee shall, notwithstanding anything contained in this Act or any other law for the time being in force, be deemded to be the owner of such building or part and the value of such building or part shall be included in computing the net wealth of the assessee; and, in determining the value of such building or part, the value of any outstanding instalments of the amount payable under such scheme by the assessee to the society, company or association towards the cost of such building or part and the land appurtenant thereto shall, whether the amount so payable is described as such or in any other manner in such scheme, be deducted as a debt owed by him in relation to such building or part.

(8) A person-

(a) who is allowed to take or retain possession of any building or part thereof in part performance of a contract of the nature referred to in Section 53A of the Transfer of Property Act, 1882 (43 of 1882);

(b) who acquires any rights (excluding any rights by way of a lease from month to month or for a period not exceeding one year) in or with respect to any building or part thereof by virtue of any such transaction as is referred to in clause (f) of Section 269UA of the Income-tax Act, shall be deemed to be the owner of that building or part thereof and the value of such building or part shall be included in computing the net wealth of such person."

58. Amendment of 21A. In Section 21A of the Wealth-tax Act, for the words "Where any property is held", the words, brackets and figures "Notwithstanding anything contained in clause (i) of Section 5, where any property is held" shall be substituted and shall be deemed to have been substituted with effect from the 1st day of April, 1993.

CHAPTER -IV : INDIRECT TAXES CUSTOMS

59. Amendment of Section 15. In the Customs Act, 1962 (52 of 1962) (hereinafter referred to as the Customs Act), in Section 15, in sub-section 1, for the proviso, the following proviso shall be substituted, namely:-

> *"PROVIDED that if a bill of entry has been presented before the date of entry inwards of the vessel or the arrival of the aircraft by which the goods are imported, the, bill of entry shall be deemed to have been presented on the date of such entry inwards or the arrival, as the case may be".*

60. Amendment of Section 27. In Section 27 of the Customs Act, in sub-section 1, after the second proviso, the following proviso shall be inserted, namely:-

> *"PROVIDED ALSO that in the case of goods which are exempt from payment of duty by a special order issued under sub-section (2) of Section 25, the limitation of one year or six months, as the case may be, shall be computed from the date of issue of such order".*

61. Amendment of Section 28AA. In Section 28AA of the Customs Act, in the opening paragraph, for the words "Where a person", the words, figures and letters "Subject to the provisions contained in Section 28AB, where a person" shall-be substituted.

62. Insertion of new Section 28AB. After Section 28AA of the Customs Act, the following Section shall be inserted, namely:-

28AB. Interest on delayed payment of duty in special cases.

(1) Where any duty has not been levied or has been short levied or erroneously refunded by reason of collusion or any wilful mis-statement or suppression of facts, the person who is liable to pay the duty as determined under sub-section (2) of Section 28, shall, in addition to the duty, be liable to pay interest at such rate not below ten per cent. and not exceeding thirty per cent. per annum, as is for the time being fixed by the Board, from the first day of the month succeeding the month in which the duty ought to have been paid under this Act, or from the date of such erroneous refund, as the case may be, but for the provisions contained in sub-section (2) of Section 28, till the date of payment of such duty.

(2) For the removal of doubts, it is hereby declared that the provisions of sub-section (1) shall not apply to cases where the duty became payable before the date on which the Finance (No. 2) Bill, 1996 receives the assent of the President.

EXPLANATION 1: Where the duty determined to be payable is reduced by the Commissioner (Appeals), the Appellate Tribunal or, as the case may be, the court, the interest shall be payable on such reduced amount of duty.

EXPLANATION 2: Where the duty determined to be payable is increased or further increased by the Commissioner (Appeals), the Appellate Tribunal or, as the case may be, the court, the interest shall be payable on such increased or further increased amount of duty.".

63. Amendment of Section 46. In Section 46 of the Customs Act, in sub-section (3), for the second proviso, the following proviso shall be substituted, namely:-

"PROVIDED FURTHER that a bill of entry may be presented even before the delivery of such manifest if the vessel or the aircraft by which the goods have been shipped for importation into India is expected to arrive within thirty days from the date of such presentation."

64. Insertion of new Section 114A. After Section 114 of the Customs Act, the following Section shall be inserted, namely:-

"114A. Penalty for short-levy or non-levy of duty in certain cases. Where the duty has not been levied or has been short-levied or the interest has not been charged or paid or has not been part paid or the duty or interest has been erroneously refunded by reason of collusion or any wilful misstatement or suppression of facts, the person who is liable to pay the duty or interest, as the case may be, as determined under sub-section (2) of Section 28 shall also be liable to pay a penalty equal to the duty or interest so determined;

PROVIDED that where the duty or interest determined to be payable is reduced or increased by the Commissioner (Appeals), the Appellate Tribunal or, as the case may be, the court, then, for the purposes of this Section, the duty or interest as reduced or increased, as the case may be, shall be taken into account:

PROVIDED FURTHER that where any penalty has been levied under this Section, no penalty shall be levied under Section 112 or Section 114."

65. Amendment of Section 129. In Section 129 of the Customs Act, for sub-section (3), the following sub-section shall be substituted, namely:-

"(3) The Central Government shall appoint-

(a) a person who is or has been a Judge of a High Court; or

(b) one of the members of the Appellate Tribunal, to be the President thereof."

66. Amendment of Section 129C. In Section 129C of the Customs Act, in sub-section (4), for the words"one lakh rupees", the words"ten lakh rupees"shall be substituted.

67. Amendment of Act 51 of 1975. The Customs Tariff Act, 1975 (hereinafter referred to as the Customs Tariff Act) shall be amended in the manner specified in the Second Schedule.

68. Special duties of customs.

(1) In the case of goods mentioned in the First Schedule to the Customs Tariff Act, or in that Schedule, as amended from time to time, there shall be levied and collected as a special duty of customs, an amount equal to two per cent. of the value of the goods as determined in accordance with the provisions of Section 14 of the Customs Act.

(2) Sub-section (1) shall cease to have effect after the 31st day of March, 1999, and upon such cesser, Section 6 of the General Clauses Act, 1897 (10 of 1897) shall apply as if the said subsection had been repealed by Central Act.

(3) The special duties of customs referred to in sub-section (1) shall be in addition to any duties of customs chargeable on such goods under the Customs Act or any other law for the time being in force.

(4) The provisions of the Customs Act and the rules and regulations made thereunder including those relating to refunds and exemptions from duties shall, as far as may be, apply in relation to the levy and collection of the special duties of customs leviable under this Section in respect of any goods as they apply in relation to the levy and collection of-the duties of customs on such goods under that Act or those rules and regulations, as the case may be.

69. Amendment of long title. In the Central Excises and Salt Act, 1944 (1 of 1944). (hereinafter referred to as the Central Excises Act), in the long tide, the words "and to salt" shall be omitted.

70. Amendment of preamble. In the preamble to the Central Excises Act, the words "and to salt" shall be omitted.

71. Amendment of Section 1. In Section 1 of the Central Excises Act, for sub-section 1, the following subsection shall be substituted, namely:- "(1) This Act may be called the Central Excise Act, 1944."

72. Amendment of Section 2. In Section 2 of the Central Excises Act, clauses (i) and (j) shall be omitted.

73. Amendment of Section 3. In Section 3 of the Central Excises Act, in sub-section 1, for the words "other than salt which are produced or manufactured in India and a duty on salt manufactured in, or imported by land into, any part of India", the words "which are produced or manufactured in India" shall be substituted.

74. Amendment of Section 4. In Section 4 of the Central Excises Act -

(a) in sub-section (1), in clause (a), in the proviso, after clause (i), the following clause shall be inserted, namely:- "(ia) where the price at which such goods are ordinarily sold by the assessee is different for different places of removal, each such price shall, subject to the existence of other circumstances specified in clause (a), be deemed to be the normal price of such goods in relation to each such place of removal";

(b) in sub-section (4),-

(i) in clause (b),-

(A) in sub-clause (i), the word"or"occurring at the end shall be omitted;

(B) after sub-clause (ii), the following sub-clause shall be inserted, namely:-

(ii) a depot, premises of a consignment agent or any other place or premises from where the excisable goods are to be sold after their clearance from the factory and";

(iii) after clause (b), the following clause shall be inserted, namely:-

(ba) "time of removal", in respect of goods removed from the place of removal referred to in sub-clause (iii) of clause (b), shall be deemed to be the time at which such goods are cleared from the factory'.

75. Amendment of Section 11AA. In Section 11AA of the Central Excises Act, in the opening paragraph, for the words "Where a person", the words figures and letters "Subject to the provisions contained in Section 11AB, where a person" shall be substituted.

76. Insertion of new Sections 11AB and 11AA. After Section 11AA of the Central Excises Act, the following Sections shall be inserted, namely:-

"11AB. Interest on delayed payment of duty.

(1) Where any duty of excise has not been levied or paid or has been short-levied or short-paid or erroneously refunded by reason of fraud, collusion or any wilful misstatement or suppression of facts, or contravention of any of the provisions of this Act or the rules made thereunder with intent to evade payment of duty, the person liable to pay duty as determined under sub-section (2) of Section 11A shall, in addition to the duty, be liable to pay interest at such rate not below ten per cent and not exceeding thirty per cent. per annum, as is for the time being fixed by the Board, from the first day of the month succeeding the month in which the duty ought to have been paid under this Act or the rules made thereunder or from the date of such erroneous refund, as the case may be, but for the provisions contained in sub-section (2) of Section 11A, till the date of payment of such duty.

(2) For the removal of doubts, it is hereby declared that the provisions of subsection (1) shall not apply to cases where the duty became payable before the date on which the Finance (No. 2) Bill, 1996 receives the assent of the President.

EXPLANATION 1.- Where the duty determined to be payable is reduced by the Commissioner (Appeals), the Appellate Tribunal or, as the case may be, the court, the interest shall be payable on such reduced amount of duty.

EXPLANATION 2.- Where the duty determined to be payable is increased or further increased by the Commissioner (Appeals), the Appellate Tribunal or, as the case may be, the court, the interest shall be payable on such increased or further increased amount of duty.

11AC. Penality for short-levy or non-levy, of duty in certain cases. Where any duty of excise has not been levied or paid or has been shortlevied or short-paid or erroneously refunded by reasons of fraud, collusion or any wilful mis-statement or suppression of facts, or contravention of any of the provisions of this Act or of the rules made thereunder with intent to evade payment of duty, the person who is liable to pay duty as determined under sub-section (2) of Section 11A, shall also be liable to pay a penalty equal to the duty so determined:

> *PROVIDED that where the duty determined to be payable is reduced or increased by the Commissioner (Appeals), the Appellate Tribunal or, as the case may be, the court, then, for the purposes of this Section, the duty as reduced or increased. as the case may be, shall be taken into account".*

77. Amendment of Section 11B. In Section 11B of the Central Excises Act, in the Explanation, in clause (B), after sub-clause (e), the following sub-clause shall be inserted, namely:- "(e) in the case of goods which are exempt from payment of duty by a special order issued under sub-section (2) of Section 5A, the date of issue of such order".

78. Amendment of Section 12. In Section 12 of the Central Excises Act, for the words and figures "Sea Customs Act, 1878 (8 of 1878)", the words and figures "Customs Act, 1962 (52 of 1962)" shall be substituted.

79. Omission of Chapter V. Chapter V of the Central Excises Act shall be omitted.

80. Amendment of Section 35D. In Section 35D of the Central Excises Act, in sub-section (3), for the words "one lakh rupees", the words "ten lakh rupees" shall be substituted.

81. Amendment of Act 32 of 1985. In the Finance Act, 1985,-

(a) sections 44 and 49 shall be omitted;

(b) Fifth Schedule shall be omitted.

82. Amendment of Act 5 of 1986. The Central Excise Tariff Act, 1985 (hereinafter referred to as the Central Excise Tariff Act) shall be amended in the manner specified in the Third Schedule.

83. Amendment of Act 58 of 1986. The Additional Duties of Excise (Goods of Special Importance) Act, 1957 (hereinafter referred to as the Additional Duties of Excise Act) shall be amended in the manner specified in the Fourth Schedule.

84. Amendment of Act 40 of 1978. In the Additional Duties of Excise (Textiles and Textile Articles) Act, 1978 -

(a) in Section 3, in sub-section (1), for the words "twenty per cent", the words "fifteen per cent" shall be substituted;

(b) the Schedule shall be amended in the manner specified in the Fifth Schedule.

CHAPTER -V : SERVICE TAX

85. Amendment of Act 32 of 1994. In the Finance Act, 1994, with effect from such date as the Central Government may, by notification in the Official Gazette, appoint,-

(1) in Section 65,-

(a) clause (1) shall be renumbered as clause (1B) and before the clause as so renumbered, the following clauses shall be inserted, namely:-

(1) 'advertisement"includes any notice, circular, label, wrapper, document, boarding or any other audio or visual representation made by means of light, sound, smoke or gas;

(1A) "advertising agency"means any commercial concern engaged in providing any service connected with the making, preparation, display or exhibition of advertisement and includes an advertising consultant';

(b) after clause (4), the following clause shall be inserted, namely:-

(4A) "courier agency"means a commercial concern engaged in the door-to-door transportation of time-sensitive documents, goods or articles utilising the services of a person, either directly or indirectly, to carry or accompany such documents, goods or articles';

(c) after clause (6), the following clause shall be inserted, namely:-

(6A) "pager" means an instrument, apparatus or appliance which is a non-speech, one way personal calling system with alert and has the capability of receiving, storing and displaying numeric or alpha-numeric messages.';

(d) in clause (15), for the words "telephone connection", the words "telephone connection or pager" shall be substituted;

(e) in clause (16),-

(i) after sub-clause (b), the following sub-clause shall be inserted, namely:- "(ba) to a subscriber, by the telegraph authority, in relation to a pager;";

(ii) after sub-clause (c), the following sub-clauses shall be inserted, namely:-"(d) to a client, by an advertising agency, in relation to advertisements in any manner;

(f) to a customer, by a courier agency, in relation to door-to-door transportation of time-sensitive documents, goods or articles";

(2) for Section 66, the following Section shall be substituted, namely:-

66. Charge of service tax.

(1) On and from the commencement of this Chapter, there shall be charged a tax (hereinafter referred to as the service tax), at the rate of five per cent of the value of the taxable services referred to in sub-clauses (a), (b) and (c) of clause (16) of Section 65 which are provided to any person by the person responsible for collecting the service tax.

(2) With effect from the date notified under Section 85 of the Finance (No. 2) Act, 1996, there shall be charged a service tax at the rate of five per cent of the value of the taxable services referred to in sub-clauses (ba), (d) and (e) of clause (16) of Section 65 which are provided to any person by the person responsible for collecting the service tax";

(3) in Section 67,-

(i) in clause (b), for the words "telephone connections", at both the places where they occur, the words "telephone connections or pagers" shall be substituted;

(ii) after clause (c) the following clauses shall be inserted, namely:-"(d) in relation to service provided by an advertising agency to a client shall be the gross amount charged by such agency from the client for services in relation to advertisements; (e) in relation to service provided by a courier agency to a customer shall be the gross amount charged by such agency from the customer for services in relation to door-to-door transportation of time sensitive documents, goods and articles";

(4) in Section 68, in sub-section (1), for the words "or the insurer", the words, "the insurer, the advertising agency or the courier agency" shall be substituted.

86. Validation: Notwithstanding anything contained in Section 93 of the Finance

Act, 1994 (32 of 1994), the notification of the Government of India in the Ministry of Finance, Department of Revenue No. G. S. R. 174 (E), dated the 3rd April, 1996, shall have and shall be deemed always to have had, effect on and from the 1st day of July, 1994.

CHAPTER - VI : MISCELLANEOUS

87. Amendment of Act 74 of 1956. In Section 15 of the Central Sales Tax Act, 1956, after clause (c), the following clause shall be inserted, namely:-"(ca) where a tax on sale or purchase of paddy referred to in sub-clause (i) of clause (1) of Section 14 is leviable under that law and the rice procured out of such paddy is exported out of India, then, for the purposes of sub-section (3) of Section 5, the paddy and rice shall be treated as a single commodity.".

88. North-Eastern Development Finance Corporation Limited to be exempt for a certain period from liability to pay income-tax. Notwithstanding anything contained in the Income-tax Act, the North-Eastern Development Finance Corporation Limited (a company formed and registered under the Companies Act, 1956) (1 of 1956) shall not be liable to pay tax on its income for the previous year relevant to the assessment year commencing on the 1st day of April, 1996 and for the nine previous years next following that previous year.

❑❑❑

23

The Finance Act, 1996

ACT No. 5 OF 1996 [27TH MARCH, 1996]

AN ACT to continue the existing rates of income-tax for the financial year 1996-97.

Be it enacted by Parliament in the Forty-seventh Year of the Republic of India as follows:-

1. Short title and commencement.

(1) This Act may be called the Finance Act, 1996.

(2) It shall come into force on the 1st day of April, 1996.

2. Income-tax. The provisions of Section 2 of, and the First Schedule to the Finance Act, 1995 (22 of 1995) shall apply in relation to income-tax for the assessment year or, as the case may be, the financial year commencing on the 1st day of April, 1996, as they apply in relation to income tax for the assessment year or, as the case may be, the financial year commencing on the 1st day of April, 1995, with the following modifications, namely :

(a) in Section 2 -

(i) for the figures "1995", wherever they occur, the figures "1996" shall be substituted;

(ii) in sub-section (2), for the words "thirty-five thousand rupees", wherever they occur, the words "forty thousand rupees" shall be substituted;

(iii) in the first proviso to sub-section (3), for the word and figures "section 112", the words and figures "sections 112 and 113 of the Income-tax Act" shall be substituted;

(b) in the First Schedule -

(i) for Part I, the following Part shall be substituted, namely:-

PART - I : INCOME-TAX

Paragraph A - Sub-Paragraph I. In the case of every individual or Hindu undivided family or association of persons or body of individuals, whether incorporated or not, or every artificial juridical person referred to in sub-clause (vii) of clause (31) of Section 2 of the Income-tax Act, not being a case to which Sub-Paragraph II of this Paragraph or any other Paragraph of this Part applies, Rates of income-tax

(1) where the total income does not Nil; exceed Rs. 40,000;

(2) where the total income exceeds 20 per cent of the amount by Rs. 40,000 but does not exceed which the total income exceeds Rs. 60,000 Rs. 40,000;

(3) where the total income exceeds Rs. 4,000 plus 30 per cent. of Rs. 60,000 but does not exceed the a mount by which the total Rs. 1,20,000 income exceeds Rs. 60,000;

(4) where the total income exceeds Rs. 22, 000 plus 40 per cent. Rs. 1,20,000 of the amount by which the total income exceeds Rs. 1,20,000.

Sub-Paragraph II. In the case of every Hindu undivided family which at any time during the previous year has at least one member whose total income of the previous year relevant to the assessment year commencing on the 1st day of April, 1996 exceeds Rs. 40,000, Rates of income-tax

(1) where the total income does not Nil; exceed Rs. 18,000;

(2) where the total income exceeds 30 per cent of the total income-Rs. 18,000 but does not exceed me exceeds Rs. 18,000; Rs. 1,00,000;

(3) where the total income exceeds Rs. 24,600 plus 40 per cent. of Rs. 1,00,000 the amount by which the total income exceeds Rs. 1,00,000. Paragraph B In the case of every co-operative society, Rates of income-tax

(1) where the total income does not 10 per cent of the total exceed Rs. 10,000 income;

(2) where the total income exceeds Rs. 1,000 plus 20 per cent of Rs. 10,000 but does not exceed the amount by which the total Rs. 20,000 income exceeds Rs. 10,000;

(3) where the total income exceeds Rs. 3, 000 plus 35 per cent. of Rs. 1, 00, 000 the amount by which the total income exceeds Rs. 20,000.

Paragraph C. In the case of every firm, Rate of Income tax On the whole of the total income 40 per cent. **Paragraph D.** In the case of every local authority,- Rate of income-tax On the whole of the total income 30 per cent. **Paragraph E.** In the case of a company,-Rates of income-tax I. In the case of a domestic company 40 per cent. of the total income; II. In the case of a company other than a domestic company,-

(i) on so much of the total income as consists of -

(a) royalties received from Government or an Indian concern in pursuance of an agreement made by it with the Government or the Indian concern after the 31st day of March, 1961 but before the 1st day of April, 1976, or

(b) fees for rendering technical services received from Government or an Indian concern in pursuance of an agreement made by it with the Government or the Indian concern after the 29th day of February, 1964 but before the 1st day of April, 1976, and where such agreement has, in either 50 per cent has been approved by the Central Government.

(ii) on the balance, if any, of the 55 per cent. total income Surcharge on income-tax The amount of income-tax computed in accordance with the provisions of this Paragraph or Sections 112 and 113 of the Income-tax Act shall, in the case of every domestic company having a total income exceeding seventy-five thousand rupees, be increased by a surcharge calculated at the rate of fifteen per cent of such income-tax.";

(ii) in Part III, Sub-Paragraph II of Paragraph A, for the figures "1996", the figures "1997" shall be substituted;

(iii) in Part IV, in Rule 8,-

(A) for sub-rules (1) and (2), the following sub-rules shall be substituted, namely:-" (1) Where the assessee has, in the previous year relevant to the assessment year commencing on the 1st day of April, 1996, any agricultural income and the net result of the computation of the agricultural income of the assessee for any one or more of the previous years relevant to the assessment years commencing on the 1st day of April, 1988 or the 1st day of April, 1989 or the 1st day of April, 1990 or the 1st day of April, 1991 or the 1st day of April, 1992 or the 1st day of April, 1993 or the 1st day of April, 1994 or the 1st day of April, 1995, is a loss, then, for the purposes of sub-section (2) of Section 2 of this Act,-

(i) the loss so computed for the previous year relevant to the assessment year commencing on the 1st day of April, 1988, to the extent, if any, such loss has not been set off, against the agricultural income for the previous year relevant to the assessment year commencing on the 1st day of April. 1989 or the 1st day of April, 1990 or the 1st day of April, 1991. or the 1st day of April, 1992 or the 1st day of April, 1993 or the 1st day of April, 1994 or the 1st day of April, 1995;

(ii) the loss so computed for the previous year relevant to the assessment year commencing on the 1st day of April, 1989 to the extent, if any, such loss has not been set off against the agricultural income for the previous year relevant to the assessment year commencing on the 1st day of April, 1990 or the 1st day of April, 1991 or the 1st day of April, 1992 or the 1st day of April, 1993 or the 1st day of April, 1994 or the 1st day of April, 1995;

(iii) die loss so computed for the previous year relevant to the assessment year commencing on the 1st day of April, 1990, to the extent, if any, such loss has not been set off against the agricultural income for the previous year relevant to the assessment year commencing on the 1st day of April, 1991 or the 1st day of April, 1992 or the 1st day of April, 1993 or the 1st day of April, 1994 or the 1st day of April, 1995;

(iv) the loss so computed for the previous year relevant to the assessment year commencing on the 1st day of April, 1991 to the extent, if any, such loss has not been set off against the agricultural income for the previous year relevant to the assessment year commencing on the 1st day of April, 1992 or the 1st day of April, 1993 or the 1st day of April, 1994 or the 1st day of April, 1995;

(v) the loss so computed for the previous year relevant to the assessment year commencing oil the 1st clay of April, 1992 to the extent, in any, such loss has not been set off against the agricultural income for the previous year relevant to the assessment year commencing on the 1st day of April, 1993 or the 1st day of April, 1994 or the 1st day of April, 1995;

(vi) the loss so computed for the previous year relevant to the assessment year commencing on the 1st day of April, 1993, to the extent, if any, such loss has not been set off against the agricultural income for the previous year relevant to the assessment year commencing on the 1st day of April, 1994 or the 1st day of April, 1995;

(vii) the loss so computed for the previous year relevant to the assessment year commencing on the 1st day of April, 1994, to the extent, if any, such loss has not been set off against the agricultural income for the previous year relevant to the assessment year commencing on the 1st day of April, 1995;

(viii) the loss so computed for the previous year relevant to the assessment year commencing on the 1st day of April, 1995, shall be set off against the agricultural income of the assessee for the previous year relevant to the assessment year commencing on the 1st day of April, 1996.

(2) Where the assessee has, in the previous year relevant to the assessment year commencing on the 1st day of April, 1997 or, if by virtue of any provision of the Income-tax Act, income-tax is to be charged in respect of the income of a period other than that previous year. In such other period, any agricultural income and the net result of the computation of the agricultural income of the assessee for any one or more of the previous year relevant to the assessment years commencing on the 1st day of April, 1989 or the 1st day of April, 1990 or the 1st day of April, 1991 or the 1st day of April, 1992 or the 1st day of April, 1993 or the 1st day of April, 1994 or the 1st day of April, 1995 or the 1st day of April, 1996, is a loss, then, for the purposes of sub-section (8) of Section 2 of this Act -

(i) the loss so computed for the previous year relevant to the assessment year commencing on the 1st day of April, 1989, to the extent, if any, such loss has not been set off against the agricultural income for the previous year relevant to the assessment year commencing on the 1st day of April, 1990 or the 1st day of April, 1991 or the 1st day of April, 1992 or the 1st day of April, 1993 or the 1st day of April, 1994 or the 1st day of April, 1995 or the 1st day of April, 1996;

(ii) the loss so computed for the previous year relevant to the assessment year commencing on the 1st day of April, 1990, to the extent, if any, such loss has not been set off against the agricultural income for the previous year relevant to the assessment year commencing on the 1st day of April, 1991 or the 1st day of April, 1992 or the 1st day of April, 1993 or the 1st day of April, 1994 or the 1st day of April, 1995 or the 1st day of April, 1996;

(iii) the loss so computed for the previous year relevant to the assessment year commencing on the 1st day of April, 1991, to the extent, if any, such loss has not been set off against the agricultural income for the previous year relevant to the assessment year commencing on the 1st day of April, 1992 or the 1st day of April, 1993 or the 1st day of April, 1994 or the 1st day of April, 1995 or the 1st day of April, 1996;

(iv) the loss so computed for the previous year relevant to the assessment year commencing on the 1st day of April, 1992, to the extent, if any, such loss has not been set off against the agricultural income for the previous year relevant to the assessment year commencing on the 1st day of April, 1993 or the 1st day of April, 1994 or the 1st day of April, 1995 or the 1st day of April, 1996;

(v) the loss so computed for the previous year relevant to the assessment year commencing on the 1st day of April, 1993, to the extent, if any, such loss has not been set off against the agricultural income for the previous year relevant to the assessment year commencing on the 1st day of April, 1994 or the 1st day of April, 1995 or the 1st day of April, 1996;

(vi) the loss so computed for the previous year relevant to the assessment year commencing on the 1st day of April, 1994, to the extent, if any, such loss has not been set off against the agricultural income for the previous year relevant to the assessment year commencing on the 1st day of April, 1995 or the 1st day of April, 1996;

(vii) the loss so computed for the previous year relevant to the assessment year commencing on the 1st day of April, 1995, to the extent if any such loss has not been set off against the agricultural income for the previous year relevant to the assessment year commencing on the 1st day of April, 1996;

(viii) the loss so computed for the previous year relevant to the assessment year commencing on the 1st day of April, 1996, shall be set off against the agricultural income of the assessee for the previous year relevant to the assessment year commencing on the 1st day of April, 1997".

(B) for sub-rule (4), the following sub-rule shall be substituted, namely:- "(4) Notwithstanding anything contained in this rule, no loss which has not been determined by the Assessing Officer under the provisions of these rules or the rules contained in Part IV of the First Schedule to the Finance Act, 1988 (26 WA 988), or of the First Schedule to the Finance Act, 1989 (13 of 1989), or of the First Schedule to the Finance Act, 1990 (12 of 1990), or of the First Schedule to the Finance (No. 2) Act, 1991 (49 of 1991), or of the First Schedule to the Finance Act, 1992 (18 of 1992), or of the First Schedule to the Finance Act, 1993 (38 of 1993), or of the First Schedule to the Finance Act, 1994 (32 of 1994), or of the First Schedule to the Finance Act, 1995 (22 of 1995) shall be set off under sub-rule (1) or, as the case may be, sub-rule (2)."

❑❑❑

24

The Finance Commission (Miscellaneous Provisions) Act, 1951

Act No. 33 of 1951 [16th May, 1951]

AN ACT to determine the qualifications requisite for appointment as members of the Finance Commission and the manner in which they shall be selected, and to prescribe their powers.

Be it enacted by Parliament as follows:—

1. Short title. This Act may be called the Finance Commission (Miscellaneous Provisions) Act, 1951.

2. Definition. In this Act, "the Commission" means the Finance Commission constituted by the President pursuant to clause (1) of article 280 of the Constitution.

3. Qualifications for appointment as, and the manner of selection of, members of the commission. The Chairman of the Commission shall be selected from among persons who have had experience in public affairs, and the four other members shall be selected from among persons who—

(a) are, or have been, or are qualified to be appointed as Judges of a High Court; or

(b) have special knowledge of the finances and accounts of Government; or

(c) have had wide experience in financial matters and in administration; or

(d) have special knowledge of economics.

4. Personal interest to disqualify members. Before appointing a person to be a member of the Commission, the President shall satisfy himself that that person will have no such financial or other interest as is likely to affect prejudicially his functions as a member of the commission; and the President shall also satisfy himself from time to time with respect to every member of the Commission that he has no such interest and any person who is, or whom the President proposes to appoint to be, a member of the Commission shall, whenever required by the President so to do, furnish to him such information as the President considers necessary for the performance by him of his duties under this section.

5. Disqualifications for being a member of the Commission. A person shall be disqualified for being appointed as, or for being, a member of the Commission —

(a) if he is of unsound mind;

(b) if he is an undischarged insolvent;

(c) if he has been convicted of an offence involving moral turpitude;

(d) if he has such financial or other interest as is likely to affect prejudicially his functions as a member of the Commission.

6. Term of office of members and eligibility for reappointment. Every member of the Commission shall hold office for such period as may be specified in the order of the President appointing him, but shall be eligible for reappointment:

PROVIDED that he may, by letter addressed to the President, resign his office.

7. Conditions of service and salaries and allowances of members.

(1) The members of the Commission shall render whole-time or part-time service to the Commission as the President may in each case specify, and there shall be paid to the members of the Commission such fees or salaries and such allowances as the Central Government may, by rules made [2][by notification in the Official Gazette], in this behalf determine.

(2) Every rule made under this section shall be laid, as soon as may be after it is made, before each House of Parliament, while it is in session, for a total period of thirty days which may be comprised in one session or in two or more successive sessions, and if, before the expiry of the session immediately following the session or the successive sessions aforesaid, both Houses agree in making any modification in the rule or both Houses agree that the rule should not be made, the rule shall thereafter have effect only in such modified form or be of no effect, as the case may be; so, however, that any such modification or annulment shall be without prejudice to the validity of anything previously done under that rule.

8. Procedure and powers of the Commission.

(1) The Commission shall determine their procedure and in the performance of their functions shall have all the powers of a civil court under the Code of Civil Procedure, 1908 (5 of 1908), while trying a suit in respect of the following matters, namely:—

(a) summoning and enforcing the attendance of witnesses;

(b) requiring the production of any document;

(c) requisitioning any public record from any court or office.

(2) The Commission shall have power to require any person to furnish information on such points or matters as in the opinion of the Commission may be useful

for, or relevant to, any matter under the consideration of the Commission and any person so required shall, notwithstanding anything contained in sub-section (2) of Section 54 of the Indian Income-tax Act, 1922 (11 of 1922), or in any other law for the time being in force, be deemed to be legally bound to furnish such information within the meaning of Section 176 of the Indian Penal Code (45 of 1860).

(3) The Commission shall be deemed to be a civil court for the purposes of sections 480 and 482 of the Code of Criminal Procedure, 1898 (5 of 1898).

EXPLANATION: For the purposes of enforcing the attendance of witnesses, the local limits of the Commission' s jurisdiction shall be the limits of the territory of India.

❑❑❑

25

The Foreign Aircraft (Exemption from Taxes and Duties on Fuel and Lubricants) Act, 2002

ACT NO. 36 OF 2002 [11TH JUNE, 2002]

AN ACT to implement Agreements entered into by India with other countries in pursuance of the Convention on International Civil Aviation opened for signatures at Chicago on the 7th December, 1944.

WHEREAS a Convention on International Civil Aviation was signed by India on the 7th December, 1944;

AND WHEREAS India, having signed the said Convention, entered into Agreements with the parties to the said Convention to exempt the taxes and duties on fuel and lubricants supplied in India to the aircraft of the contracting parties.

Be it enacted by Parliament in the Fifty-third Year of the Republic of India as follows :-

1. Short title and extent.

(1) This Act may be called the Foreign Aircraft (Exemption from Taxes and Duties on Fuel and Lubricants) Act, 2002.

(2) It extends to the whole of India.

2. Definitions. In this Act, unless the context otherwise requires,-

(a) "Agreements" means the Air Services Agreements or Air Transport Agreements entered into by India with parties to the Convention;

(b) "Convention" means the Convention on International Civil Aviation opened for signatures at Chicago on the 7th December, 1944.

3. Exemption from levy of taxes and duties on fuel and lubricants supplied to aircraft of other countries. Where, in pursuance of the Convention or Agreement with any other country or countries, it is necessary to grant exemption from levy of taxes and duties on fuel and lubricants filied into receptacles forming part of any aircraft of any other country or countries under any law of a State or Union territory in India, the Central Government may, by notification in the Official Gazette, make such provi ions as may be necessary for giving effect to the said Convention or Agreement and thereupon the said provision shall apply accordingly and, notwithstanding anything contrary contained in any other law, shall in such application have the force of law in India.

❑❑❑

26

The Government Trading Taxation Act, 1926

ACT NO. 3 OF 1926 [24TH FEBRUARY, 1926]

AN ACT to determine the liability of certain Governments to taxation 2 in respect of trading operations.

WHEREAS it is expedient to determine the liability to taxation for the time being in forces 2 of the Government of any part of His Majesty's Dominions, 3 4 in respect of any trade or business carried on by or on behalf of such Government;

It is hereby enacted as follows:-

1. Short title and commencement.

(1) This Act may be called the Government Trading Taxation Act, 1926.

(2) It shall come into force on such date [5][as the Central Government may, by notification in the Official Gazette, appoint.

2. Liability of certain Governments to taxation in respect of trading operations.

(1) Where a trade or business of any kind is carried on by or on behalf of the Government of any part of His Majesty' s Dominions, [3][that Government shall, in respect of the trade or business and of all operations connected therewith, all property occupied in [6][India] and all goods owned in [6][India] for the purposes thereof, and all income arising in connection therewith, be liable-

(a) to taxation under the Indian Income-tax Act, 1922, (11 of 1922) in the same manner and to the same extent as in the like case a company would be liable;

(b) to all other taxation for the time being in force in [6][India] in the same manner as in the like case any other person would be liable.

(2) For the purposes of the levy and collection of income-tax under the Indian Income-tax Act, 1922 (11 of 1922), in accordance with the provisions of sub-section (1), any Government to which that sub-section applies shall be deemed to be a company within the meaning of that Act, and the provisions of that Act shall apply accordingly.

(3) In this section the expression "His Majesty' s Dominions" includes any territory which is under His Majesty' s protection or in respect of which a mandate is being exercised by the Government of any part of His Majesty's Dominions.

3. Application of the Act to existing liability of Acceding or other Indian States. Where any Acceding State or other Indian State was liable for any tax under this Act in respect of any period before the 26th day of January, 1950 , and such liability has, after that date, devolved upon a Part B State, the provisions of Section 2 shall apply in relation to that Part B State as they applied in relation to the corresponding Acceding State or other Indian State.

❑❑❑

27

The Indian Lac Cess Act, 1930

ACT NO. 24 OF 1930

On the dissolution of the Committee constitued under this Act w.e.f. Ist April, 1966, by Notification No. S.O. 881, dated the 18th March, 1966, Gazette of India, Part II, Section 3(ii), p. 815, the Act is deemed to have been repealed.

□□□

28

The Indian Tolls Act, 1888

ACT NO. 8 OF 1888 [5TH SEPTEMBER, 1888]

AN ACT to remove doubts as to the legality of the levy of certain Tolls.

WHEREAS doubts have been raised as to the operation of the Acts of the Governor General in Council, No. VIII of 1851 (an Act for enabling Government to levy Tolls on Public Roads and Bridges) and No. XV of 1864 (an Act to amend Act VIII of 1851);

It is hereby enacted as follows:—

1. Enforcement of Acts VIII of 1851 and XV of 1864 in the Punjab. Act VIII of 1851 and XV of 1864 shall be deemed to be in force throughout the territories now administered by the Lieutenant-Governor of the Punjab, and from the twenty-first day of August, 1857, , and the twenty-fourth day of March, 1864, respectively, to have been in force in the territories for the time being administered as part of the Punjab as it existed immediately before the 1st November, 1956.

2. Operation of the Act in the Punjab and certain other parts of the States. (1) In any part of India beyond the limits of the territories administered by the Governor of Fort St. George in Council, and the Lieutenant-Governors of Bengal and the North-Western Provinces, to or in which Acts VIII of 1851 and XV of 1864 may be or have been extended, or may be or have been declared to be in force, under the latter of those Acts or by this Act or by or under any other enactment, the State Government shall be deemed to have and, where the Acts have been in force the passing of this Act, to have had the same authority as if it had been included among the State Governments specified in Section 2 of Act VIII of 1851.

3. Validation of past levy of tolls. All tolls levied, or purporting to have been levied, under Acts VIII of 1851 and XV of 1864 , or either of those Acts, before the passing of this

Act, shall be deemed to have been lawfully levied.

4. Saving. Nothing in the foregoing sections shall affect any proceedings commenced in any Civil Court before the first day of July, 1888.

5. Amendment of Section 2, Act VIII, 1851. *Rep. by the A. O. 1937.*

❑❑❑

29

The Interest Tax Act, 1974

(Act No. 45 of 1974)

PREAMBLE

AN ACT to impose a special tax on interest in certain cases.

Be it enacted by Parliament in the Twenty-fifth Year of the Republic of India as follows:

1. Short title and Extent.

(1) This Act may be called the Interest-tax Act, 1974.

(2) It extends to the whole of India.

2. Definitions. In this Act, unless the context otherwise requires, -

(1) "**assessee**" means a person by whom interest-tax, or any other sum of money, is payable under this Act and includes -

(a) every person in respect of whom any proceeding under this Act has been taken for the assessment of his chargeable interest or of the amount of refund due to him or of the chargeable interest of any other person in respect of which he is assessable or of the amount of refund due to such other person;

(b) every person who is deemed to be an assessee in default under any provision of this Act;

(2) "**assessment**" includes reassessment;

(3) "**assessment year**" means the period of twelve months commencing on the 1st day of April every year;

(4) "**Board**" means the Central Board of Direct Taxes constituted under the Central Boards of Revenue Act, 1963 (54 of 1963);

(5) **"chargeable interest"** means the total amount of interest referred to in Section 5, computed in the manner laid down in Section 6;

(5A) **"credit institution"** means, -

(i) a banking company to which the Banking Regulation Act, 1949 (10 of 1949) applies (including any bank or banking institution referred to in Section 51 of that Act);

(ii) a public financial institution as defined in Section 4A of the Companies Act, 1956 (1 of 1956);

(iii) a State financial corporation established under Section 3 or Section 3A or an institution notified under Section 46 of the State Financial Corporations Act, 1951 (63 of 1951); and

(iv) any other financial company;

(5B) **"financial company"** means a company, other than a company referred to in sub-clause (i), (ii) or (iii) of clause (5A), being -

(i) a hire-purchase finance company, that is to say, a company which carries on, as its principal business, hire-purchase transactions or the financing of such transactions;

(ii) an investment company, that is to say, a company which carries on, as its principal business, the acquisition of shares, stock, bonds, debentures, debenture stock, or securities issued by the Government or a local authority, or other marketable securities of a like nature;

(iii) a housing finance company, that is to say, a company which carries on, as its principal business, the business of financing of acquisition or construction of houses, including acquisition or development of land in connection therewith;

(iv) a loan company, that is to say, a company [not being a company referred to in sub-clauses (i) to (iii)] which carries on, as its principal business, the business of providing finance, whether by making loans or advances or otherwise;

(v) a mutual benefit finance company, that is to say, a company which carries on, as its principal business, the business of acceptance of deposits from its members and which is declared by the Central Government under Section 620A of the Companies Act, 1956 (1 of 1956), to be a Nidhi or Mutual Benefit Society;

(va) a residuary non-banking company [other than a financial company referred to in subclause (i), (ii), (iii), (iv) or (v)], that is to say, a company which receives any deposit under any scheme or arrangement, by whatever name called, in one lump sum or in instalments by way of contributions or subscriptions or by sale of units or certificates or other instruments or in any other manner;

(vi) a miscellaneous finance company, that is to say, a company which carries on exclusively, or almost exclusively, two or more classes of business referred to in the preceding sub-clauses;

(6) **"Income-tax Act"** means the Income-tax Act, 1961 (43 of 1961);

(7) **"interest"** means interest on loans and advances made in India and includes -

(a) commitment charges on unutilised portion of any credit sanctioned for being availed of in India; and

(b) discount on promissory notes and bills of exchange drawn or made in India, but does not include -

(i) interest referred to in sub-section (1B) of Section 42 of the Reserve Bank of India Act, 1934 (2 of 1934);

(ii) discount on treasury bills;

(8) **"prescribed"** means prescribed by rules made under this Act;

(9) all other words and expressions used herein but not defined and defined in the Income-tax Act shall have the meanings respectively assigned to them in that Act.

3. Tax authorities.

(1) The income-tax authorities specified in Section 116 of the Income-tax Act shall be the interest-tax authorities for the purposes of this Act.

(1A) Every such authority shall exercise the powers and perform the functions of an interest-tax authority under this Act in respect of any person within his jurisdiction.

(1B) The jurisdiction of an interest-tax authority under this Act shall be the same as he has under the Income-tax Act by virtue of orders or directions issued under Section 120 of that Act (including orders or directions assigning the concurrent jurisdiction) or under any other provision of that Act.

(1C) The interest-tax authority having jurisdiction in relation to a credit institution which has no income assessable to income-tax under the Income-tax Act shall be the interest-tax authority having jurisdiction in respect of the area in which that institution carries on its business or has its principal place of business.

(1D) Section 118 of the Income-tax Act and any notification issued thereunder shall apply in relation to the control of interest-tax authorities as they apply in relation to the control of the corresponding income-tax authorities, except to the extent to which the Board may, by notification in the Official Gazette, otherwise direct in respect of any interest-tax authority.

(2) All officers and persons employed in the execution of this Act shall observe and follow the orders, instructions and directions of the Board:

PROVIDED that no such orders, instructions or directions shall be issued -

(a) so as to require any tax authority to make a particular assessment or to dispose of a particular case in a particular manner; or

(b) so as to interfere with the discretion of the Commissioner (Appeals) in the exercise of his appellate functions.

(3) Every Income-tax Officer or Assistant Commissioner employed in the execution of this Act shall observe and follow the orders, instructions and directions issued for his guidance by the Director or by the Commissioner or by the Additional Commissioner of Income-tax or the Deputy Commissioner within whose jurisdiction he performs his functions.

4. Charge of tax.

(1) Subject to the provisions of this Act, there shall be charged on every scheduled bank for every assessment year commencing on or after the 1st day of April, 1975, a tax in this Act referred to as interest-tax in respect of its chargeable interest of the previous year at the rate of seven per cent of such chargeable interest:

PROVIDED that the rate at which interest-tax shall be charged in respect of any chargeable interest accruing or arising after the 31st day of March, 1983 shall be three and a half per cent of such chargeable interest.

(2) Notwithstanding anything contained sub-section (1) but subject to the other provisions of this Act, there shall be charged on every credit institution for every assessment year commencing on and from the 1st day of April, 1992, interest-tax in respect of its chargeable interest of the previous year at the rate of three per cent of such chargeable interest.

PROVIDED that the rate at which interest-tax shall be charged in respect of any chargeable interest accruing or arising after the 31st day of March, 1997, shall be two per cent. of such chargeable interest.

5. Scope of chargeable interest. Subject to the provisions of this Act, the chargeable interest of any previous year of a credit institution shall be the total amount of interest (other than interest on loans and advances made to other credit institutions or to any co-operative society engaged in carrying on the business of banking) accruing or arising to the credit institution in that previous year:

PROVIDED that any interest in relation to categories of bad or doubtful debts referred to in Section 43D of the Income-tax Act shall be deemed to accrue or arise to the credit institution in the previous year in which it is credited by the credit institution to its profit and loss account for that year or, as the case may be, in which it is actually received by the credit institution, whichever is earlier.

6. Computation of chargeable interest.

(1) Subject to the provisions of sub-section (2), in computing the chargeable interest of a previous year, there shall be allowed from the total amount of interest (other than interest on loans and advances made to credit institutions) accruing or arising to the assessee in the previous year, a deduction in respect of the amount of interest which is established to have become a bad debt during the previous year:

PROVIDED that such interest has been taken into account in computing the chargeable interest of the assessee of an earlier previous year and the amount has been written off as irrecoverable in the accounts of the assessee for the previous year during which it is established to have become a bad debt.

EXPLANATION: For the removal of doubts, it is hereby declared that in computing the chargeable interest of a previous year, no deduction, other than the deduction specified in this sub-section, shall be allowed from the total amount of interest accruing or arising to the assessee.

(2) In computing the chargeable interest of a previous year, the amount of interest which accrues or arises to the assessee before the 1st day of August, 1974, or after the 28th day of February, 1978 during the period commencing on the 1st day of March, 1978, and ending with the 30th day of June, 1980 during the period commencing on the 1st day of April, 1985 and ending with the 30th day of September, 1991, shall not be taken into account.

7. Return of chargeable interest.

(1) In the case of every credit institution, its principal officer, or where in the case of a non-resident credit institution any person has been treated at its agent under Section 163 of the Income-tax Act, such person, shall furnish a return of the chargeable interest of the credit institution of the previous year in the prescribed form 17 and verified in the prescribed manner and setting forth such other particulars as may be prescribed, before the 31st day of December of the assessment year.

(2) Without prejudice to the provisions of sub-section (1), the Assessing Officer may, before the end of the relevant assessment year, serve a notice upon the principal officer of any credit institution, or where in the case of a non-resident credit institution any person has been treated as its agent under Section 163 of the Income-tax Act, upon such person, requiring him to furnish within thirty days from the date of service of the notice a return of the chargeable interest of the credit institution of the previous year in the prescribed form and verified in the prescribed manner and setting forth such other particulars as may be prescribed.

(3) Any assessee who has not furnished a return within the time allowed under sub-section (1) or sub-section (2), or having furnished a return under sub-section (1) or sub-section (2), discovers any omission or wrong statement therein, may furnish a return or a revised return, as the case may be, at any time before the expiry of one year from the end of the relevant assessment year or before the completion of the assessment, whichever is earlier.

8. Assessment.

(1) For the purposes of making an assessment under this Act, the Assessing Officer may serve on any person who has furnished a return under Section 7 or upon whom a notice has been served under sub-section (2) of Section 7 (whether a return has been furnished or not) a notice requiring him on a date therein to

be specified to produce or cause to be produced such accounts or documents or evidence as the Assessing Officer may require for the purposes of this Act and may, from time to time, serve further notices requiring the production of such further accounts or documents or other evidence as he may require.

(2) The Assessing Officer, after considering such accounts, documents or evidence, if any, as he has obtained under sub-section (1) and after taking into account any relevant material which he has gathered, shall, by an order in writing, assess the chargeable interest and the amount of the interest-tax payable on the basis of such assessment.

(3) If any person -

(a) fails to make a return as required under sub-section (1) of Section 7 and has not made a return or a revised return under sub-section (3) of that Section, or

(b) fails to comply with all the terms of notice under sub-section (2) of that Section, the Assessing Officer shall, after taking into account all the relevant material which he has gathered and after giving the assessee an opportunity of being heard, make the assessment of the total chargeable interest to the best of his judgment and determine the sum payable by the assessee on the basis of such assessment :

PROVIDED that such opportunity shall be given by the Assessing Officer by serving a notice calling upon the assessee to show cause, on a date and time to be specified in the notice, why the assessment should not be completed to the best of his judgment:

PROVIDED FURTHER that it shall not be necessary to give such opportunity in a case where a notice under sub-section (1) has been issued prior to the making of an assessment under this Section.

9. Self-assessment.

(1) Where interest-tax is payable on the basis of any return required to be furnished under Section 7 or Section 10, after taking into account the amount of interest-tax, if any, already paid under any provision of this Act, the assessee shall be liable to pay such interest-tax, together with interest payable under any provision of this Act for any delay in furnishing the return or any default or delay in payment of advance interest-tax, before furnishing the return and the return shall be accompanied by proof of payment of such interest-tax and interest.

EXPLANATION: Where the amount paid by the assessee under this sub-section falls short of the aggregate of the interest-tax and interest as aforesaid, the amount so paid shall first be adjusted towards the interest payable as aforesaid and the balance, if any, shall be adjusted towards the interest-tax payable.

(2) After the assessment under Section 8 has been made, any amount paid under sub-section (1) shall be deemed to have been paid towards such assessment.

(3) If any assessee fails to pay the whole or any part of interest-tax or interest or both in accordance with the provisions of sub-section (1), he shall, without

prejudice to any other consequences which he may incur, be deemed to be an assessee in default in respect of the interest-tax or interest or both remaining unpaid, and all the provisions of this Act shall apply accordingly.

10. Interest escaping assessemnt. If -

(a) the Assessing Officer has reason to believe that by reason of the omission or failure on the part of the assessee to make a return under Section 7 for any assessment year or to disclose fully and truly all material facts necessary for his assessment for any assessment year, chargeable interest for that year has escaped assessment or has been under-assessed or has been made the subject of excessive relief under this Act, or

(b) notwithstanding that there has been no omission or failure as mentioned in clause (a) on the part of the assessee, the Assessing Officer has, in consequence of information in his possession, reason to believe that chargeable interest assessable for any assessment year has escaped assessment or has been under-assessed or has been the subject of excessive relief under this Act, he may, in cases falling under clause (a), at any time, and in cases falling under clause (b), at any time within four years of the end of that assessment year, serve on the assessee a notice containing all or any of the requirements which may be included in a notice under Section 7, and may proceed to assess or reassess the amount chargeable to interest-tax and the provisions of this Act shall, so far as may be, apply, as if the notice were a notice issued under that Section.

10A. Time limit for completion of assessments and reassessments.

(1) No order of assessment shall be made under Section 8 at any time after the expiry of two years from the end of the assessment year in which the interest was first assessable.

(2) No order of assessment or reassessment shall be made under Section 10 after the expiry of two years from the end of the financial year in which the notice under that Section was served.

(3) Notwithstanding anything contained in sub-sections (1) and (2), an order of fresh assessment in pursuance of an order passed under Section 15, Section 16, Section 19 or Section 20, setting aside or cancelling an assessment, may be made at any time before the expiry of two years from the end of the financial year in which the order under Section 15 or Section 16 is received by the Commissioner or, as the case may be, the order under Section 19 or Section 20 is passed by the Commissioner.

(4) The provisions of sub-sections (1) and (2) shall not apply to the assessment or reassessment made in consequence of, or to give effect to, any finding or direction contained in an order under Section 15 or Section 16 or Section 19 or Section 20 of this Act or Section 256 or Section 260 of the Income-tax Act as applicable to this Act by virtue of Section 21 of this Act or in an order of any Court in a proceeding otherwise than by way of appeal or reference under this Act and such assessment or reassessment may, subject to the provisions of sub-section (3), be completed at any time.

EXPLANATION 1: In computing the period of limitation for the purposes of this Section -

(i) the time taken in reopening the whole or any part of the proceeding; or

(ii) the period during which the assessment proceeding is stayed by an order or injunction of any court, shall be excluded.

EXPLANATION 2: Where, by an order referred to in sub-section (4), any interest is excluded from the chargeable interest for an assessment year in respect of an assessee, then, an assessment of such interest for another assessment year shall, for the purposes of Section 10 and this Section, be deemed to be one made in consequence of, or to give effect to, any finding or direction contained in the said order.

11. Advance payment of interest-tax.

(1) Interest-tax shall be payable in advance during the financial year in respect of the chargeable interest for the assessment year immediately following that financial year in accordance with the provisions of this Section.

(2) Interest-tax shall be payable in advance in three instalments during each financial year, the due date of, and the amount payable in, each such instalment being as specified in the following Table :

TABLE

Due date of instalment Amount payable

On or before the 15th Not less than twenty per cent of September such interest-tax payable in advance.

On or before the 15th Not less than fifty per cent of such December interest-tax payable in advance, as reduced by the amount, if any, paid in the earlier instalment.

On or before the 15th The whole amount of such interest-tax March payable in advance as reduced by the amount or amounts, if any, paid in the earlier instalment or instalments:

PROVIDED that any amount paid by way of interest-tax payable in advance on or before the 31st day of March shall also be treated as interest-tax paid in advance during the financial year ending on that day for all the purposes of this Act.

12. Interest for default in furnishing return of chargeable interests.

(1) Where the return of chargeable interest for any assessment year under sub-section (1) of Section 7, or in response to a notice under sub-section (2) of that Section is furnished after the due date, or is not furnished, the assessee shall be liable to pay simple interest at the rate of two per cent for every month or part of a month comprised in the period commencing on the date immediately following the due date, and, -

(a) where the return is furnished after the due date, ending on the date of the furnishing of the return; or

(b) where no return has been furnished, ending on the date of completion of assessment under sub-section (3) of Section 8, on the amount of the interest-tax on the chargeable interest as determined under sub-section (2) or sub-section (3) of Section 8 as reduced by the interest-tax paid in advance.

EXPLANATION 1: In this Section, "**due date**" means the 31st day of December of the relevant assessment year or, as the case may be, the date on which return in response to a notice under sub-section (2) of Section 7 is due to be filed.

EXPLANATION 2: Where in relation to an assessment year, an assessment is made for the first time under Section 10, the assessment so made shall be regarded as assessment made under sub-section (2), or, as the case may be, sub-section (3) of Section 8.

EXPLANATION 3: For the purposes of computing the interest payable under Section 9, interest-tax on the chargeable interest declared in the return shall be deemed to be the interest-tax on total chargeable interest determined under sub-section (2) or sub-section (3) of Section 8.

(2) The interest payable under sub-section (1) shall be reduced by the interest, if any, paid under Section 9 towards the interest chargeable under this Section.

(3) Where the return of chargeable interest for any assessment year, required by a notice under Section 10 issued after the completion of assessment under sub-section (2) or sub-section (3) of Section 8 or Section 10 is furnished after the expiry of the time allowed under such notice or is not furnished, the assessee shall be liable to pay simple interest at the rate of two per cent for every month or part of a month comprised in the period commencing on the date immediately following the expiry of time allowed as aforesaid, and, -

(a) where the return is furnished after the expiry of the time aforesaid, ending on the date of furnishing the return; or

(b) where no return has been furnished, ending on the day of completion of the reassessment under Section 10, on the amount by which the interest-tax on the chargeable interest as determined on the basis of such reassessment exceeds the interest-tax on chargeable interest on the basis of earlier assessment aforesaid.

(4) Where, as a result of an order under Section 15 or Section 17 of this Act or Section 254 or Section 260 or Section 262 of the Income-tax Act, as applicable to this Act by virtue of Section 21 of this Act, the amount on which interest was payable under sub-section (1) or sub-section (3) has been increased or reduced, as the case may be, the interest shall be increased or reduced accordingly, and-

(i) in a case where the interest is increased, the Assessing Officer shall serve on the assessee a notice of demand in the prescribed form specifying the sum payable and such notice of demand shall be deemed to be a notice under Section 156 of the Income-tax Act as applicable to this Act by virtue of Section 21, and the provisions of this Act shall apply accordingly;

(ii) in a case where the interest is reduced, the excess interest paid, if any, shall be refunded.

(5) The provisions of this Section shall apply in respect of assessments for the assessment year commencing on the 1st day of April, 1992 and subsequent years.

12A. Interest for default in payment of interest-tax in advance.

(1) Subject to the other provisions of this Section, where in any financial year, an assessee, who is liable to pay interest-tax in advance under Section 11 has failed to pay such tax, or where the interest-tax paid in advance by such assessee is less than ninety per cent of the assessed interest-tax, the assessee shall be liable to pay simple interest at the rate of two per cent for every month or part of a month comprised in the period from the 1st day of April next following such financial year to the date of determination of chargeable interest under sub-section (2) or, as the case may be, sub-section (3) of Section 8 on an amount equal to the assessed interest-tax or, as the case may be, on the amount by which the interest-tax payable in advance falls short of the assessed interest-tax.

EXPLANATION 1: In this Section, "assessed interest-tax" means -

(a) for the purpose of computing the interest payable under Section 9, the interest-tax on the chargeable interest as declared in the return referred to in that Section;

(b) in any other case, interest-tax on chargeable interest as determined under sub-section (2) or, as the case may be, sub-section (3) of Section 8.

EXPLANATION 2: Where, in relation to an assessment year, an assessment is made for the first time under Section 10, the assessment so made shall be regarded as assessment made under sub-section (2) or, as the case may be, sub-section (3) of Section 8.

(2) Where, before the date of completion of assessment under sub-section (2) or sub-section (3) of Section 8, interest-tax is paid by the assessee under Section 9 or otherwise, -

(i) interest shall be calculated in accordance with the foregoing provisions of this Section up to the date on which the tax is so paid, and reduced by the interest, if any, paid under Section 9 towards the interest chargeable under this Section;

(ii) thereafter, interest shall be calculated at the rate aforesaid on the amount by which the tax so paid together with interest-tax paid in advance falls short of the assessed interest-tax.

(3) Where, as a result of an order of reassessment under Section 10, the amount on which the interest was payable under sub-section (1) is increased, the assessee shall be liable to pay simple interest at the rate of two per cent for

every month or part of a month comprised in the period commencing on the day following the completion of the assessment under sub-section (2) or, as the case may be, sub-section (3) of Section 8 referred to in sub-section (1) and ending on the date of reassessment under Section 10, on the amount by which the interest-tax on the basis of the reassessment exceeds the interest-tax on the chargeable interest determined on the basis of assessment under sub-section (2) or, as the case may be, sub-section (3) of Section 8.

(4) Where, as a result of an order under Section 15 or Section 17 of this Act or Section 254 or Section 260 or Section 262 of the Income-tax Act as applicable to this Act by virtue of Section 21 of this Act, the amount on which interest was payable under sub-section (1) or sub-section (3) has been increased or reduced, as the case may be, the interest shall be increased or reduced accordingly, and-

  (i) in a case where the interest is increased, the Assessing Officer shall serve on the assessee a notice of demand in the prescribed form specifying the sum payable and such notice of demand shall be deemed to be a notice under Section 156 of the Income-tax Act as applicable to this Act by virtue of Section 21 of this Act, and provisions of this Act shall apply accordingly;

  (ii) in a case where the interest is reduced, the excess interest paid, if any, shall be refunded.

(5) The provisions of this Section shall apply in respect of assessments for the assessment year commencing on the 1st day of April, 1992 and subsequent assessment years.

12B. Interest for department of interest-tax payable in advance.

(1) Where in any financial year, the assessee who is liable to pay interest-tax in advance under Section 11 has failed to pay the interest-tax and where such tax paid by the assessee on his chargeable interest on or before the 15th day of September is less than twenty per cent of the interest-tax due on the returned chargeable interest or the amount of such interest-tax paid on or before the 15th day of December is less than fifty per cent of the tax due on the returned chargeable interest, then, the assessee shall be liable to pay simple interest at the rate of one and one-half per cent per month of the shortfall for a period of three months on the amount of shortfall from twenty per cent or, as the case may be, fifty per cent of the interest-tax due on the returned chargeable interest.

(2) The provisions of this Section shall apply in respect of assessments for the assessment year commencing on the 1st day of April, 1992 and subsequent assessment years.

13. Penalty for concealment of chargeable interest. If the Assessing Officer or the Commissioner (Appeals) in the course of any proceeding under this Act, is satisfied that any person has concealed the particulars of chargeable interest or has furnished inaccurate particulars of such interest, he may direct that such person shall pay by way of penalty, in addition to any interest-tax payable by him, a sum which shall not be less than, but shall not exceed three times, the amount of interest-tax sought to be evaded by reason of the concealment of particulars of his chargeable interest or the furnishing of inaccurate particulars of such chargeable interest.

14. Opportunity of being head. No order imposing a penalty under Section 12 or Section 13 shall be made unless the assessee has been heard, or has been given a reasonable opportunity of being heard.

15. Appeals to the commissioner (Appeals).

(1) Any person objecting to the amount of interest-tax for which he is assessed by the Assessing Officer or denying his liability to be assessed under this Act, or objecting to any penalty or fine imposed by the Assessing Officer, or to the amount allowed by the Assessing Officer by way of any relief under any provision of this Act, or to any refusal by the Assessing Officer to grant relief or to an order of rectification having the effect of enhancing the assessment or reducing the refund, or to an order refusing to allow the claim made by the assessee for a rectification under Section 17, may appeal to the Commissioner (Appeals).

(2) Every appeal shall be in the prescribed Form 27 and shall be verified in the prescribed manner.

(3) An appeal shall be presented within thirty days of the following date, that is to say,-

(a) where the appeal relates to assessment or penalty or fine, the date of service of the notice of demand relating to the assessment or penalty or fine, or

(b) in any other case, the date on which the intimation of the order sought to be appealed against is served :

PROVIDED that the Commissioner (Appeals) may admit an appeal after the expiration of the said period if he is satisfied that the appellant had sufficient cause for not presenting it within that period.

(4) The Commissioner (Appeals) shall hear and determine the appeal and, subject to the provisions of this Act, pass such orders as he thinks fit and such orders may include an order enhancing the assessment or penalty:

PROVIDED that an order enhancing the assessment or penalty shall not be made unless the person affected thereby has been given a reasonable opportunity of showing cause against such enhancement.

(5) The procedure to be adopted in the hearing and determination of the appeals shall, with any necessary modification, be in accordance with the procedure applicable in relation to income-tax.

15A. [Omitted by the finance (No. 2) act, 1991, w.e.f. 1-10-1991.

16. Appeals to appellate tribunal.

(1) Any assessee aggrieved by an order passed by a Commissioner under Section 19, or an order passed by a Commissioner (Appeals) under any provision of this Act, may appeal to the Appellate Tribunal against such order.

(2) The Commissioner may, if he objects to any order passed by the Commissioner (Appeals) under any provision of this Act, direct the Assessing Officer to appeal to the Appellate Tribunal against the order.

(3) Every appeal under sub-section (1) or sub-section (2) shall be filled within sixty days of the date on which the order sought to be appealed against is communicated to the assessee or to the Commissioner, as the case may be.

(4) The Assessing Officer or the assessee, as the case may be, on receipt of notice that an appeal against the order of the Commissioner (Appeals) has been preferred under sub-section (1) or sub-section (2) by the other party may, notwithstanding that he may not have appealed against such order or any part thereof, within thirty days of the receipt of the notice, file a memorandum of cross-objections 32, verified in the prescribed manner, against any part of the order of the Commissioner (Appeals), and such memorandum shall be disposed of by the Appellate Tribunal as if it were an appeal presented within the time specified in sub-section (3).

(5) The Appellate Tribunal may admit an appeal or permit the filing of a memorandum of cross-objections after the expiry of the relevant period referred to in sub-section (3) or sub-section (4), if it is satisfied that there was sufficient cause for not presenting it within that period.

(6) An appeal to the Appellate Tribunal shall be in the prescribed Form 33, and shall be verified in the prescribed manner and, shall, except in the case of an appeal referred to in sub-section (2) or a memorandum of cross-objections referred to in sub-section (4), be accompanied by a fee of two hundred rupees.

(7) Subject to the provisions of this Act, in hearing and making an order on any appeal under this Section, the Appellate Tribunal shall exercise the same powers and follow the same procedure as it exercises and follows in hearing and making an order on any appeal under the Income-tax Act.

17. Rectification of mistakes.

(1) With a view to rectifying any mistake apparent from the record, the Commissioner, the Assessing Officer, the Commissioner (Appeals) and the Appellate Tribunal may, of his, or its, own motion or on an application by the assessee in this behalf, amend any order passed by him or it in any proceeding under this Act within four years from the end of the financial year in which such order was passed.

(2) An amendment which has the effect of enhancing the assessment or reducing a refund or otherwise increasing the liability of the assessee shall not be made under this Section unless the authority concerned has given notice to the assessee of its intention so to do and has allowed the assessee a reasonable opportunity of being heard.

(3) Where an amendment is made under this Section, the order shall be passed in writing by the authority concerned.

(4) Subject to the other provisions of this Act, where any such amendment has the effect of reducing the assessment, the Assessing Officer shall make any refund, which may be due to such assessee 38.

(5) Where any such amendment has the effect of enhancing the assessment or reducing the refund already made, the Assessing Officer shall serve on the assessee a notice of demand 39, in the prescribed form specifying the sum payable.

18. Interest-tax deductible in computing total income under the income-tax act. Notwithstanding anything contained in the Income-tax Act, in computing the income of a credit institution chargeable to income-tax under the head "**Profits and gains of business or profession**" or under the head "**Income from other sources**", the interest-tax payable by the credit institution for any assessment year shall be deductible from the income, under the respective heads, of the credit institution assessable for that assessment year.

19. Revision of order prejudicial to revenue.

(1) The Commissioner may call for and examine the record of any proceeding under this Act, and if he considers that any order passed therein by the Assessing Officer is erroneous in so far as it is prejudicial to the interests of the Revenue, he may, after giving the assessee an opportunity of being heard and after making or causing to be made such enquiry as he deems necessary, pass such order thereon as the circumstances of the case justify, including an order enhancing or modifying the assessment, or cancelling the assessment and directing a fresh assessment.

EXPLANATION: For the removal of doubts, it is hereby declared that, for the purposes of this sub-section, -

(a) "**record**" shall include and shall be deemed always to have included all records relating to any proceeding under this Act available at the time of examination by the Commissioner;

(b) where any order referred to in this sub-section is the subject-matter of any appeal, the power of the Commissioner under this sub-section shall extend to all such matters as had not been considered and decided in such appeal.

(2) No order shall be made under sub-section (1) after the expiry of two years from the end of the financial year in which the order sought to be revised was passed.

(3) Notwithstanding anything contained in sub-section (2), an order in revision under this Section may be passed at any time in the case of an order which has been passed in consequence of, or to give effect to, any finding or direction contained in an order of the Appellate Tribunal, the High Court or the Supreme Court.

EXPLANATION: In computing the period of limitation for the purposes of sub-section (2), the time taken in giving an opportunity to the assessee to be reheard under the proviso to Section 129 of the Income-tax Act, as applicable to this Act by virtue of Section 21 of this Act, any period during which any proceeding under this Section is stayed by an order or injunction of any court shall be excluded.

20. Revision of orders by commissioner.

(1) The Commissioner may, either of his own motion or on an application by the assessee for revision, call for the record of any proceeding under this Act which has been taken by an Assessing Officer subordinate to him and may make such enquiry or cause such enquiry to be made and, subject to the provisions of this Act, may pass such order thereon, not being an order prejudicial to the assessee, as he thinks fit.

(2) The Commissioner shall not of his own motion revise any order under this Section if the order has been made more than one year previously.

(3) In the case of an application for revision under this Section by the assessee, the application shall be made within one year from the date on which the order in question was communicated to him or the date on which he otherwise came to know of it, whichever is earlier:

PROVIDED that the Commissioner may, if he is satisfied that the assessee was prevented by sufficient cause from making the application within that period, admit an application made after the expiry of that period.

(4) The Commissioner shall not revise any order under this Section in the following cases -

(a) where an appeal against the order lies to the Commissioner (Appeals) or to the Appellate Tribunal but has not been made and the time within which such appeal may be made has not expired, or the assessee has not waived his right of appeal; or

(b) where the order has been made the subject of an appeal to the Commissioner (Appeals) or to the Appellate Tribunal.

(5) Every application by an assessee for revision under this Section shall be accompanied by a fee of twenty-five rupees.

EXPLANATION 1: An order by the Commissioner declining to interfere shall, for the purposes of this Section, be deemed not to be an order prejudicial to the assessee.

21. Application of provisions of income-tax act. The provisions of the following Sections and Schedules of the Income-tax Act and the Income-tax (Certificate Proceedings) Rules, 1962, as in force from time to time, shall apply with necessary modifications as if the said provisions and the rules referred to interest-tax instead of to income-tax: -

2(44) [50a, 119 50a], 129, 131, 132, 132A, 132B, 133 to 136 (both inclusive), 138, 140 145, 156, 160, 161, 162, 163, 166, 167, 170, 173, 175, 176, 178, 179, 220 to 227 (both inclusive), 228A, 229, 232, 237 to 245 (both inclusive), 254 to 262 (both inclusive), 265, 266, 268, 269, 281, 281B, 282, 284, 287, 288, 288A, 288B, 289 to 293 (both inclusive), the Second Schedule and the Third Schedule :

PROVIDED that references in the said provisions and the rules to the "assessee" shall be construed as references to an assessee as defined in this Act.

22. Income-tax papers to be available for the purposes of this act.

(1) Notwithstanding anything contained in the Income-tax Act, all information contained in any statement or return made or furnished under the provisions of that Act or obtained or collected for the purposes of that Act may be used for the purposes of this Act.

(2) All information contained in any statement or return made or furnished under the provisions of this Act or obtained or collected for the purposes of this Act may be used for the purposes of the Income-tax Act.

23. Failure to comply with notices. If any person fails, without reasonable cause, to produce or cause to be produced, any accounts or documents required to be produced under Section 8, he shall pay by way of penalty, a sum which shall not be less than one thousand rupees, but which may extend to twenty-five thousand rupees for each such failure.

24. False statements. If a person makes a statement in any verification under this Act or any rule made thereunder, or delivers an account or statement which is false, and which he either knows or believes to be false or does not believe to be true, he shall be punishable with rigorous imprisonment for a term which shall not be less than three months but which may extend to seven years and with fine.

25. Wilful attempt to evade tax, etc. If a person wilfully attempts in any manner whatsoever to evade any interest-tax, penalty or interest chargeable or imposable under this Act, he shall, without prejudice to any penalty that may be imposable on him under any other provision of this Act, be punishable with rigorous imprisonment for a term which shall not be less than three months but which may extend to seven years and with fine.

EXPLANATION: For the purposes of this Section, a wilful attempt to evade any interest-tax, penalty or interest chargeable or imposable under this Act or the payment thereof shall include a case where any person -

(i) has in his possession or control any books of account or other documents (being books of account or other documents relevant to any proceeding under this Act) containing a false entry or statement; or

(ii) makes or causes to be made any false entry or statement in such books of account or other documents; or

(iii) wilfully omits or causes to be omitted any relevant entry or statement in such books of account or other documents; or

(iv) causes any other circumstances to exist which will have the effect of enabling such person to evade any interest-tax, penalty or interest chargeable or imposable under this Act or the payment thereof.

26. Abetment of false returns, etc. If a person abets or induces in any manner another person to make and deliver any account or a statement or declaration relating to any chargeable interest which is false and which he either knows or believes to be false or does not believe to be true or to commit an offence under Section 25, he shall be punishable with rigorous imprisonment for a term which shall not be less than three months but which may extend to seven years and with fine.

26A. Offences by credit intitutions.

(1) Where an offence under this Act has been committed by a credit institution, every person who, at the time the offence was committed, was in charge of, and was responsible to, the credit institution for the conduct of the business of the credit institution as well as the credit institution shall be deemed to be guilty of the offence and shall be liable to be proceeded against and punished accordingly:

PROVIDED that nothing contained in this sub-section shall render any such person liable to any punishment if he proves that the offence was committed without his knowledge or that he had exercised all due diligence to prevent the commission of such offence.

(2) Notwithstanding anything contained in sub-section (1), where an offence under this Act has been committed by a credit institution and it is proved that the offence has been committed with the consent or connivance of, or is attributable to any neglect on the part of, any director, manager, secretary or other officer of the credit institution, such director, manager, secretary or other officer shall also be deemed to be guilty of that offence and shall be liable to be proceeded against and punished accordingly.

EXPLANATION: For the purposes of this Section, "**director**", in relation to a co-operative society, means any member controlling the affairs thereof.

26B. Institutions of proceedings and composition of offfences.

(1) A person shall not be proceeded against for any offence under Section 24 or Section 25 or Section 26 or for any offence under the Indian Penal Code, except with the previous sanction of the Commissioner or Commissioner (Appeals) :

PROVIDED that the Chief Commissioner or, as the case may be, Director General may issue such instructions or directions to the aforesaid interest-tax authorities as he may deem fit for institution of proceedings under this sub-section.

(2) Any offence under the Sections referred to in sub-section (1) may, either before or after the institution of proceedings, be compounded by the Chief Commissioner or Director General.

EXPLANATION: For the removal of doubts, it is hereby declared that the power of the Board to issue orders, instructions or directions under this Act shall include the power to issue instructions or directions (including instructions or dircctions to obtain the previous approval of the Board) to other interest-tax authorities for the proper composition of offences under this Section.

26C. Power of credit institutions to vary certain agreements. Notwithstanding anything contained in any agreement under which any term loan has been sanctioned by the credit institution before the 1st day of October, 1991, it shall be lawful for the credit institution to vary the agreement so as to increase the rate of interest stipulated therein to the extent to which such institution is liable to pay the interest-tax under this Act in relation to the amount of interest on the term loan which is due to the credit institution.

EXPLANATION: For the purposes of this Section, **"term loan"** means a loan which is not repayable on demand.

27. Power to make rules.

(1) The Board may, subject to the control of the Central Government, by notification in the Official Gazette, make rules for carrying out the purposes of this Act.

(2) In particular, and without prejudice to the generality of the foregoing power, such rules may provide for all or any of the following matters, namely: -

(a) the form in which returns under Section 7 may be furnished and the manner in which they may be verified;

(b) the form in which appeals under Section 15 or Section 16 may be filed and the manner in which they may be verified;

(c) the procedure to be followed on applications for rectification of mistakes and applications for refunds;

(d) any other matter which by this Act is to be, or may be, prescribed.

(3) The power to make rules conferred by this Section shall on the first occasion of the exercise thereof include the power to give retrospective effect to the rules or any of them from a date not earlier than the date of commencement of this Act.

(4) The Central Government shall cause every rule made under this Section to be laid, as soon as may be, after it is made before each House of Parliament while it is in session for a total period of thirty days which may be comprised in one session or in two or more successive sessions, and if, before the expiry of the session immediately following the session or the successive sessions aforesaid, both Houses agree in making any modification in the rule or both Houses agree that the rule should not be made, the rule shall thereafter have effect only in such modified form or be of no effect, as the case may be; so, however, that any such modification or annulment shall be without prejudice to the validity of anything previously done under that rule.

28. Power to exempt. Where the Central Government is of the opinion that it is necessary or expedient so to do either in the public interest or having regard to the peculiar circumstances of the case, it may, by notification, and subject to conditions, if any, as may be specified in the notification, exempt any credit institution or any class of credit institutions or any interest on any category of loans or advances from the levy of interest-tax :

PROVIDED that no such exemption shall be made except on the recommendation of the Reserve Bank of India.

29. Power to remove difficulty.

(1) If any difficulty arises in giving effect to the provisions of this Act, the Central Government may, by order, not inconsistent with the provisions of this Act, remove the difficulty:

PROVIDED that no such order shall be made after the expiry of a period of two years from the commencement of this Act.

(2) If any difficulty arises in giving effect to the provisions of this Act, as amended by the Finance (No. 2) Act, 1991, the Central Government may, by order, do anything not inconsistent with such provisions for the purpose of removing the difficulty:

PROVIDED that no such order shall be made after the expiry of two years from the 1st day of October, 1991.

(3) Every order made under sub-section (2) shall be laid before each House of Parliament.

30. Consequential amendments.

(1) In Section 2 of the Central Boards of Revenue Act, 1963 (54 of 1963), in sub-clause (1) of clause (c), -

(a) in item (vi), the word "and" occurring at the end shall be omitted; and

(b) after item (vi) as so amended, the following item shall be inserted, namely:

"(vii) the Interest-tax Act, 1974; and"

(2) In the Economic Offences (Inapplicability of Limitation) Act, 1974 (12 of 1974), in the Schedule, after entry 2 relating to the Income-tax Act, 1961 (43 of 1961), the following entry shall be inserted, namely:

"2A. THE INTEREST-TAX ACT, 1974".

❐❐❐

30

The Jute Manufactures Cess (Amendment) Act, 2002

ACT NO. 13 OF 2002 [27TH MARCH, 2002]

AN ACT to amend the Jute Manufactures Cess Act, 1983.

Be it enacted by Parliament in the Fifty- third Year of the Republic of India as follows:-

1. Short title and commencement.

(1) This Act may be called the Jute Manufactures Cess (Amendment) Act, 2002.

(2) It shall come into force on such date as the Central Government may, by notification in the Official Gazette, specify.

2. Substitution of a new Schedule for Schedule to Act 28 of 1983. For the Schedule to the Jute Manufactures Cess Act, 1983, the following Schedule shall be substituted, namely :

THE SCHEDULE

[*See* Sections 2 (a) and 3.1]

Sl. No.	Articles of jute	The maximum rate at Actual rate at which No. manufacture which duty of excise duty of excise is to may be collected be collected until a different rate is specified by the Central Government
1.	Carpet Backing	Two per cent ad One per cent ad valorem Valorem
2.	Hessian	Two per cent ad One per cent ad valorem Valorem
3.	Sacking	Two per cent ad One per cent ad valorem Valorem
4.	Yarn and Twine	Two per cent ad One per cent ad valorem Valorem
5.	D. W. Tarpaulin	Two per cent ad One per cent ad valorem Valorem
6.	Decorative	Two per cent ad One per cent ad Fabrics valorem Valoremd valorem
7.	Cotton Bagging	Two per cent ad One per cent adorem valorem Valorem
8.	Soil saver	Two per cent ad One per cent ad valorem Valorem ad valorem
9.	Japanese Rice	Two per cent ad One per cent ad Bags valorem Valorem ad valorem
10.	Any other article	Two per cent ad One per cent ad of Jute valorem Valorem ad valorem Manufacture.

❑❑❑

31

The Jute Manufactures Development Council Act, 1983

ACT NO. 27 OF 1983 [7TH SEPTEMBER, 1983]

AN ACT to provide for the establishment of a Council for the development of production of jute manufactures by increasing the efficiency and productivity in the jute industry, the financing of activities for such development and for matters connected therewith.

Be it enacted by Parliament in the Thirty-fourth Year of the Republic of India as follows:—

CHAPTER - I : PRELIMINARY

1. Short title, extent and commencement.

(1) This Act may be called the Jute Manufactures Development Council Act, 1983.

(2) It extends to the whole of India.

(3) It shall come into force on such date as the Central Government may, by notification in the Official Gazette, appoint.

2. Definitions. In this Act, unless the context otherwise requires,—

(a) "Chairman" means the Chairman of the Council;

(b) "Council" means the Jute Manufactures Development Council established under Section 3;

(c) "jute manufacture" shall have the same meaning as assigned to it in the Jute Manufactures Cess Act, 1983 ;

(d) "member" means a member of the Council and includes the Chairman;

(e) "prescribed" means prescribed by rules made under this Act;

(f) "year" means the year commencing on the 1st day of July and ending on the 30th day of June next following.

CHAPTER - II : THE JUTE MANUFACTURES DEVELOPMENT COUNCIL

3. Establishment and constitution of the Council.

(1) With effect from such date as the Central Government may, by notification in the Official Gazette, appoint in this behalf, there shall be established for the purposes of this Act, a Council to be called the Jute Manufactures Development Council.

(2) The Council shall be a body corporate by the name aforesaid, having perpetual succession and a common seal, with power to acquire, hold and dispose of property, both movable and immovable, and to contract, and shall by the said name sue and be sued.

(3) The head office of the Council shall be at Calcutta in the State of West Bengal, and the Council may, with the previous approval of the Central Government, establish offices or agencies at other places in or outside India.

(4) The Council shall consist of the following members, namely:—

(a) a Chairman to be appointed by the Central Government;

(b) such number of members not exceeding eight as the Central Government may think fit to be appointed by it from among the Ministries of the Central Government dealing with—

(i) agriculture;

(ii) commerce (textiles);

(iii) finance;

(iv) industry;

(v) civil supplies;

(vi) co-operation;

(c) six members to be appointed by the Central Government by rotation in the alphabetical order to represent respectively the Governments of the States of Andhra Pradesh, Assam, Bihar, Meghalaya, Orissa, Tripura and West Bengal in which jute is cultivated on a large scale:

PROVIDED that such appointment shall be made on the recommendation of the Government of the State concerned;

(d) four members to be appointed by the Central Government to represent the producers of jute manufactures;

(e) two members to be appointed by the Central Government to represent the exporters of jute manufactures;

(f) three members to be appointed by the Central Government to represent the growers of jute;

(g) three members to be appointed by the Central Government to represent the interests of workmen employed in factories producing jute manufactures;

(h) five members to be appointed by the Central Government from amongst persons who, in the opinion of the Central Government, are experts in jute technological research, jute marketing or agricultural economics.

(5) The Council shall elect, from amongst its members, a Vice-Chairman who shall exercise such of the powers and perform such of the functions of the Chairman as may be prescribed or as may be delegated to him by the Chairman.

(6) The term of office and other conditions of service of the members and the manner of filling vacancies among, and the procedure to be followed in the discharge of their functions by the members shall be such as may be prescribed.

(7) Any officer of the Central Government, not being a member of the Council, when deputed by that Government in this behalf, shall have the right to attend the meetings of the Council and take part in the proceedings thereof, but shall not have the right to vote.

(8) The Council may associate with itself, in such manner, subject to such conditions and for such purposes as may be prescribed, any person whose assistance or advice it may desire in complying with any of the provisions of this Act and a person so associated shall be entitled to receive such allowances or fees as may be fixed by the Central Government and shall have the right to take part in the proceedings of the Council relevant to the purpose for which he has been associated, but shall not have the right to vote.

(9) No act or proceeding of the Council or any committee appointed by it under Section 5 shall be invalidated merely by reason of—

(a) any vacancy in, or any defect in the constitution of, the Council or such committee; or

(b) any defect in the appointment of a person acting as a member of the Council or such committee; or

(c) any irregularity in the procedure of the Council or such committee not affecting the merits of the case.

(10) The Council shall meet at such times and places and shall observe such rules of procedure in regard to the transaction of business at its meetings (including the quorum at meetings) as may be prescribed.

4. Salary and allowances and other conditions of service of Chairman and other members.

(1) The Chairman shall be entitled to such salary and allowances and shall be subject to such conditions of service in respect of leave, pension, provident fund and other matters as may from time to time be fixed by the Central Government.

(2) The other members of the Council shall receive such allowances as may be fixed by the Central Government.

5. Committees of the Council.

(1) The Council may appoint such committees as may be necessary for the efficient discharge of its duties and performance of its functions under this Act.

(2) The Council shall have the power to co-opt as members of any committee appointed under sub-section (1) such number of persons who are not members of the Council as it may think fit and the persons so co-opted shall have the right to attend meetings of the committee and take part in its proceedings but shall not have the right to vote.

(3) The persons co-opted as members of a committee under sub-section (2) shall be entitled to receive such allowances or fees for attending the meetings of the committee as may be fixed by the Central Government.

6. Officers of the Council and other staff.

(1) Subject to the provisions of this Act, every person employed by the Jute Manufactures Development Council established under sub-section (1) of Section 6 of the Industries (Development and Regulation) Act, 1951, (65 of 1951) immediately before the date of establishment of the Council under Section 3 of this Act, shall, on and from such date, become an employee of the Council with such designation as the Council may determine and shall hold his office or service therein by the same tenure, at the same remuneration and upon the same terms and conditions as he would have held on such date if the Council had not been established and shall continue to do so unless and until his employment in the Council is terminated or until such tenure, remuneration and terms and conditions are duly altered by the Council:

PROVIDED that the tenure, remuneration and terms and conditions of service of any such person shall not be altered to his disadvantage without the previous approval of the Central Government.

(2) Every employee holding any office under the Central Government immediately before the date of establishment of the Council solely or mainly for or in connection with such matters as are relevant to the functions of the Council under this Act, shall, on and from such date, be treated as on deputation with the Council but shall hold his office in the Council by the same tenure and upon the same terms and conditions of service as respects remuneration, leave, provident fund, retirement or other terminal benefits as he would have held such office, if the Council had not been established and shall continue to do so until the Central Government, either on its own motion or at the request of the Council, recalls such employee to its service or until the Council, with the concurrence of the Central Government, duly absorbs such employee in its regular service, whichever is earlier:

PROVIDED that during the period of deputation of any such employee with the Council, the Council shall pay to the Central Government, in respect of every such employee, such contribution towards his leave salary, pension and gratuity as the Central Government may, by order, determine:

PROVIDED FURTHER that any such employee, who has, in respect of the proposal of the Council to absorb him in its regular service, intimated within such time as may be specified in this behalf by the Council his intention of not becoming a regular employee of the Council, shall not be absorbed by the Council in its regular service.

(3) If any dispute or doubt arises as to which of the employees serving under the Central Government are to be treated as on deputation with the Council under this Section, such dispute or doubt shall be decided by the Central Government in consultation with the Council and the decision of the Central Government thereon shall be final.

(4) For the purposes of enabling it efficiently to discharge its functions under this Act, the Council shall, subject to the other provisions of this Section and to such rules as may be made in this behalf by the Central Government, appoint (whether on deputation or otherwise) such number of officers and other employees as it may consider necessary:

PROVIDED that the appointment of such category of officers as may be specified in such rules, shall be subject to the approval of the Central Government.

(5) Subject to the other provisions of this Section, every officer or other employee appointed by the Council shall be subject to such conditions of service and shall be entitled to such remuneration as may be prescribed.

7. Functions of the Council.

(1) It shall be the duty of the Council to promote, by such measures as it thinks fit, the development of production of jute manufactures by increasing the efficiency and productivity in the jute industry.

(2) Without prejudice to the generality of the provisions of sub-section (1), the measures referred to therein may provide for—

(a) evolving an integrated approach to jute cultivation in the matter of formulation of schemes, extension work, implementation and evaluation of schemes aimed at increasing the yield of jute and improving the quality thereof;

(b) promoting arrangements for better marketing and sale of jute;

(c) recommending targets for production for jute industry, co-ordinating production programmes and reviewing progress from time to time;

(d) suggesting norms of efficiency for jute industry with a view to eliminating waste, obtaining optimum production, improving quality and reducing costs;

(e) promoting standardisation of jute manufactures;

(f) maintenance and improvement of existing markets and development of new markets outside India for jute manufactures and devising marketing strategy in consonance with the demand for such manufactures outside India;

(g) sponsoring, assisting, co-ordinating or encouraging scientific, technological and economic research into the matters relating to materials, equipment, methods of production, product development, including discovery and development of new materials, equipment and methods and of improvements in those already in use in the jute industry;

(h) ensuring stabilisation of prices of jute manufactures in and outside India;

(i) promoting or undertaking the collection and formulation of statistics regarding jute industry;

(j) propagating information useful to the growers, dealers and exporters of jute and producers or manufacturers of jute goods;

(k) such other matters as may be prescribed.

(3) The Council shall perform its functions under this Section in accordance with and subject to such rules as may be made by the Central Government and such rules may be in particular make provisions for ensuring that the Council functions in close liaison with Union agencies, institutions and authorities concerned with the jute manufactures (including cultivation of jute) and avoids duplication of effort.

8. Dissolution of the Council.

(1) The Central Government may, by notification in the Official Gazette and for reasons to be specified therein, direct that the Council shall be dissolved from such date and for such period as may be specified in the notification:

PROVIDED that before issuing any such notification, the Central Government shall give a reasonable opportunity to the Council to make representations against the proposed dissolution and shall consider the representations, if any, of the Council.

(2) When the Council is dissolved under the provisions of sub-section (1),—

(a) all the members, notwithstanding that their term of office has not expired, shall, from the date of dissolution, vacate their offices as such members;

(b) all the powers and duties of the Council shall, during the period of dissolution, be exercised and performed by such person or persons as the Central Government may appoint in this behalf and their remuneration shall be such as may be prescribed;

(c) all funds and other properties vested in the Council shall, during the period of dissolution, vest in the Central Government; and

(d) as soon as the period of dissolution expires, the Council shall be reconstituted in accordance with the provisions of this Act.

CHAPTER - III : FINANCE, ACCOUNTS AND AUDIT

9. Grants and loans by the Central Government Jute Fund. The Central Government may, after due appropriation made by Parliament by law in this behalf, pay to the Council by way of grants or loans such sums of money as the Central Government may think fit for being utilised for the purposes of this Act.

10.

(1) There shall be formed a Fund to be called the Jute Fund and there shall be credited thereto—

(a) any fees that may be levied and collected under this Act or the rules made thereunder;

(b) any sums of money paid or any grants or loans granted by the Central Government for the purposes of this Act;

(c) any grants or loans that may be made by any person for the purposes of this Act.

(2) The Fund shall be applied—

(a) for meeting the cost of the measures referred to in Section 7;

(b) for meeting the salaries, allowances and other remuneration of the officers and other employees of the Council;

(c) for meeting the other administrative expenses of the Council;

(d) for repayment of any loans.

11. Borrowing powers of the Council. Subject to such rules as may be made in this behalf by the Central Government, the Council shall have the power to borrow on the security of the Jute Fund or any other asset for carrying out the purposes of this Act.

12. Accounts and audit.

(1) The Council shall maintain proper accounts and other relevant records and prepare an annual statement of accounts, including the profit and loss account, and the balance sheet, in such form and in such manner as may be prescribed by the Central Government in consultation with the Comptroller and Auditor-General of India.

(2) The accounts of the Council shall be audited by the Comptroller and Auditor-General of India at such intervals as may be specified by him and any expenditure incurred in connection with such audit shall be payable by the Council to the Comptroller and Auditor-General.

(3) The Comptroller and Auditor-General of India and any other person appointed by him in connection with the audit of the accounts of the Council shall have the same rights and privileges and authority in connection with such audit as the Comptroller and Auditor-General has in connection with the audit of the Government accounts and, in particular, shall have the right to demand the production of books, accounts, connected vouchers and other documents and papers and to inspect any of the offices of the Council.

(4) The accounts of the Council as certified by the Comptroller and Auditor-General of India or any other person appointed by him in this behalf together with the audit report thereon shall be forwarded annually to the Central Government and that Government shall cause the same to be laid before each House of Parliament.

CHAPTER - IV : CONTROL BY CENTRAL GOVERNMENT

13. Directions by Central Government. The Council shall carry out such directions as may be issued to it from time to time by the Central Government for the efficient administration of this Act.

14. Returns and reports of activities of the Council.

(1) The Council shall furnish to the Central Government at such time and in such form and manner as may be prescribed, such returns and statements and such particulars in regard to any proposed or existing programme for the development of jute manufactures, as the Central Government may, from time to time, require.

(2) The Council shall furnish a programme of its activities for each year to the Central Government for its information and directions, if any.

(3) Without prejudice to the provisions of sub-section (1), the Council shall, as soon as possible, after the end of each year, submit to the Central Government a report in such form, and before such date, as may be prescribed, giving a true and full account of its activities, policy and programmes during the previous year.

(4) A copy of the report received under sub-section (3) shall be laid, as soon as may be, after it is received, before each House of Parliament.

CHAPTER - V : MISCELLANEOUS

15. Power to call for reports and returns. The Council may require a producer of a jute manufacture to furnish, for the purposes of this Act, such statistical or other information in such form and within such period as may be specified by the Council.

16. Power of inspection. Any person authorised in this behalf by the Central Government or by the Council or any officer of the Council authorised by the Chairman in writing, may enter, at all reasonable times, any place or premises where jute manufactures are stored, kept or exposed for sale and may require the production for inspection of any book, register, record or other paper kept therein and ask for any information relating to the production, storage or keeping for sale of jute manufactures.

17. Penalties. Whoever fails to comply with any order or direction given under this Act, within such time as may be specified in the said order or direction, or contravene or attempts to contravene or abets the contravention of any of the provisions of this Act or any rules made thereunder, shall be punishable with imprisonment for a term which may extend to one year or with fine which may extend to one thousand rupees, or with both.

18. Offences by companies.

(1) Where an offence under this Act has been committed by a company, every person who at the time the offence was committed was in charge of, and was responsible to, the company for the conduct of the business of the company, as well as the company, shall be deemed to be guilty of the offence and shall be liable to be proceeded against and punished accordingly:

PROVIDED that nothing contained in this sub-section shall render any such person liable to any punishment provided in this Act, if he proves that the offence was committed without his knowledge or that he had exercised all due diligence to prevent the commission of such offence.

(2) Notwithstanding anything contained in sub-section (1), where an offence under this Act has been committed by a company and it is proved that the offence

has been committed with the consent or connivance of, or is attributable to any neglect on the part of, any director, manager, secretary or other officer shall also be deemed to be guilty of that offence and shall be liable to be proceeded against and punished accordingly.

EXPLANATION: For the purposes of this Section,—

(a) "company" means any body corporate and includes a firm or other association of individuals; and

(b) "director", in relation to a firm, means a partner in the firm.

19. Cognizance of offences. No court inferior to that of a Metropolitan Magistrate or a Judicial Magistrate of the first class shall try any offence punishable under this Act.

20. Sanction for prosecutions. Notwithstanding anything contained in the Code of Criminal Procedure, 1973 (2 of 1974), no court shall take cognizance of any offence punishable under this Act except with the previous sanction of the Central Government.

21. Protection of action taken in good faith. No suit, prosecution or other legal proceeding shall lie against the Central Government, or the Council or any committee appointed by it, or any member of the Council or such committee, or any officer or other employee of the Central Government or the Council or any other person authorised by the Central Government or the council or the Chairman for anything which is in good faith done or intended to be done under this Act or the rules made thereunder.

22. Members, officers and employees of the Council to be public servants. All the members and all officers and other employees of the Council when acting or purporting to act in pursuance of the provisions of this Act or the rules made thereunder shall be deemed to be public servants within the meaning of Section 21 of the Indian Penal Code (45 of 1860).

23. Suspension of operation of Act.

(1) If the Central Government is satisfied that circumstances have arisen rendering it necessary that certain of the restrictions imposed by this Act should cease to be imposed and if it considers it necessary or expedient so to do in the public interest, the Central Government may, by notification in the Official Gazette, suspend or relax to a specified extent and for such period as may be specified in the notification, the operation of all or any of the provisions of this Act, in all or any of the territories to which this Act extends.

(2) Where the operation of any provision of this Act has, under sub-section (1), been suspended or relaxed, such suspension or relaxation may, at any time while this Act remains in force, be removed by the Central Government by notification in the Official Gazette.

(3) Every notification issued under this Section shall be laid, as soon as may be after it is issued, before each House of Parliament, while it is in session, for a total period of thirty days which may be comprised in one session or in two or more successive sessions, and if, before the expiry of the session immediately following the session or the successive sessions aforesaid, both Houses agree in making any modification in the notification or both Houses agree that the

notification should not be issued, the notification shall thereafter have effect only in such modified form or be of no effect, as the case may be; so, however, that any such modification or annulment shall be without prejudice to the validity of anything previously done under that notification.

24. Application of other laws not barred. The provisions of this Act shall be in addition to, and not in derogation of, the provisions of any other law for the time being in force.

25. Power to make rules.

(1) The Central Government may, by notification in the Official Gazette, make rules for carrying out the purposes of this Act.

(2) In particular and without prejudice to the generality of the foregoing power, such rules may provide for all or any of the following matters, namely:—

(a) the powers and functions of the Vice-Chairman of the Council under sub-section (5) of Section 3;

(b) the term of office and other conditions of service of members, the manner of filling vacancies among, and the procedure to be followed in the discharge of their functions by, members, under sub-section (6) of Section 3;

(c) the manner in which, the conditions subject to which and the purposes for which persons may be associated by the Council under sub-section (8) of Section 3;

(d) the times and places at which the Council shall meet, the rules of procedure to be observed in regard to the transaction of business at its meetings and the number of members which shall form a quorum at a meeting under sub-section (10) of Section 3;

(e) the conditions and limitations subject to which the Council may appoint officers and other employees under sub-section (4) of Section 6;

(f) the conditions of service and the remuneration of officers and other employees appointed by the Council under sub-section (5) of Section 6;

(g) the matters in respect of which the Council may undertake measures in the discharge of its functions under clause (k) of sub-section (2) of Section 7;

(h) the remuneration payable to the person or persons referred to in clause (b) of sub-section (2) of Section 8;

(i) the conditions subject to which the Council shall borrow on the security of the Jute Fund or any other asset under Section 11;

(j) the form and manner in which the accounts of the Council shall be maintained under sub-section (1) of Section 12;

(k) the time at which and the form and manner in which the Council shall furnish returns, statements and other particulars under sub-section (1) of Section 14;

(l) the form in which and the date before which the Council shall furnish to the Central Government the report of its activities, policy and programmes under sub-section (3) of Section 14;

(m) any other matter which is to be or may be prescribed or provided for by rules under this Act.

(3) Every rule made under this Act shall be laid, as soon as may be after it is made, before each House of Parliament, while it is in session, for a total period of thirty days which may be comprised in one session or in two or more successive sessions, and if, before the expiry of the session immediately following the session or the successive sessions aforesaid, both Houses agree in making any modification in the rule or both Houses agree that the rule should not be made, the rule shall thereafter have effect only in such modified form or be of no effect, as the case may be; so, however, that any such modification or annulment shall be without prejudice to the validity of anything previously done under that rule.

❑❑❑

32

The Land Customs Act, 1924

ACT NO. 19 OF 1924

This Act has been repealed by the Customs Act, 1962 (52 of 1962), s.160 and the Sch. (w.e.f. Ist February, 1963).

33

The Mineral Products (Additional Duties of Excise and Customs) Act, 1958

ACT NO. 27 OF 1958 [4TH SEPTEMBER, 1958]

AN ACT to provide for the levy and collection of additional duties of excise and customs on certain mineral products.

Be it enacted by Parliament in the Ninth Year of the Republic of India as follows:-

1. Short title and commencement.

(1) This Act may be called the Mineral Products (Additional Duties of Excise and Customs) Act, 1958.

(2) It shall be deemed to have come into force on the twentieth day of May, 1958.

2. Definitions. In this Act, "motor spirit", "kerosene", "refined diesel oils and vaporizing oil", "diesel oil, not otherwise specified" and "furnace oil" shall have the meanings respectively assigned to them in items Nos. 6, 7, 8, 9 and 10 of the First Schedule to the Central Excises and Salt Act, 1944 (1 of 1944)

3. Levy and collection of additional duties of excise on certain mineral oils.

(1) There shall be levied and collected in respect of the goods mentioned in column 1 of the Table hereunder duties of excise at such rates not exceeding those specified in relation thereto in column 2 of the said Table[5] as may be specified by the Central Government by notification in the Official Gazette.

	Description of goods	Rate of additional duty
	1	2
1.	[6]Motor spirit....	Two hundred rupees per kilolitre at fifteen degree of Centigrade thermometer],
2.	[7]Kerosene......	One hundred and sixty rupees per kilolitre fifteen degrees of Centigrade thermometer]
3.	[1]Refined diesel oils and....	[2]Two thousand rupees per kilolitre vaporizing cil. at fifteen degrees of Centigrade thermometer]
4.	Diesel oil, not otherwise....	One hundred and twenty-nine rupees specified. and forty-five paise per kilolitre at fifteen degrees of Centigrate thermometer.
5.	Furnace oil....	Fifty-six rupees and sixty paise per kilolitre at fifteen degrees of Centigrate thermometer.
6.	[3]Asphalt and Bitumen....	One hundred rupees per metric tonne] as described in item No. 11 (1) of the First Schedule to the Central Excises and Salt Act, 1944 (1 of 1944)
7.	[4]All products as described	[2]Two thousand rupees per metric in item No. 11A of the First Schedule to the Central Excises and Salt Act, 1944. (1 of 1944)

[5](1A) The provisions of sub-section (1) shall be deemed to have had effect in respect of the period commencing on the 1st day of April, 1959, and ending on the 31st day of October, 1959, as if from the words "at such rates" occurring in that sub-section up to the end thereof, the following had been substituted, namely: "at the rates specified in relation thereto in column 2 of the said Table -

	Description of goods	Rate of additional duty
	1	2
1.	Kerosene.	Twelve naye paise per imperial gallon.
2.	Motor spirit.	Fourteen naye paise per imperial gallon.
3.	Refined diesel oil.	Twelve naye paise per imperial gallon.
4.	Vaporizing oil.	Five naye paise per imperial gallon.
5.	Diesel oil, not other	Rupees twenty per ton. specified.
6.	Furnace oil.	Rupees twenty per ton."

(2) The duties of excise referred to in 6 this section in respect of the goods specified therein shall be in addition to the duties of excise chargeable on such goods under the Central Excises and Salt Act, 1944, (1 of 1944) or any other law for the time being in force.

(3) The provisions of the Central Excises and Salt Act, 1944, (1 of 1944) and the rules thereunder, including those relating to refunds and exemptions from duty, shall, so far as may be, apply in relation to the levy and collection of the additional duties of excise referred to in this section as they apply in relation to the levy and collection of the duties of excise in respect of the goods specified in this section.

(4) Notwithstanding anything contained in this section, the Central Government may, having regard to the administrative or other difficulties, if any, which may arise in relation to the levy and collection of all or any of the additional duties of excise under this Act for any period commencing on the 20th day of May, 1958, and ending on the 29th day of June, 1958 or commencing on the 1st day of April, 1959, and ending on the 31st day of October, 1959, as the case, may be, assess the additional duties of excise payable by any person under this Act to be such sum as to the Central Government appears proper in the circumstances.

4. Amendment of Act 32 of 1934.

5. Additional duties of excise and customs not to be added to price of goods for sale. Notwithstanding anything contained in Section 64A of the Indian Sale of Goods Act, 1930, (3 of 1930) or in any other law for the time being in force, or in any contract or agreement, no purchaser purchasing any of the goods referred to in Section 3, shall be liable to pay or be sued for, or in respect of -

(a) the whole or any part of the additional duties of excise leviable under this Act, or

(b) the whole or any part of the additional duties of excise leviable under the Indian Tariff Act, 1934, (32 of 1934) to the extent to which such duties have become leviable by reason of this Act, as on addition to the contract price payable by him in respect of the goods so purchased.

EXPLANATION. In this section, "purchaser" shall not include any person in principal charge of the distribution in India of any of the goods referred to in Section 3.

6. Repeal. *Rep. by the Repealing and Amending Act, 1960 (58 of 1960), s. 2 and Sch. I.*

❑❑❑

1. This Act has been extended to Goa, Daman and Diu by Reg. 12 of 1962 s. 3 and Sch., to Dadra and Nagar Haveli by Reg. 6 of 1963, s. 2 and Sch. I and to Pondicherry by Reg. 7 of 1963, s. 3 and Sch 1.
2. Subs. by Act 41 of 1964, s. 2, for "certain mineral oils".
3. Subs. by s. 3, ibid., for "Mineral Oils".
4. Subs. by Act 38 of 1960, s. 4, for s. 2 (w. e. f. 1- 10- 1960).
5. Subs. by Act 41 of 1964, s. 4, for the former Table.
6. Subs. by Act 19 of 1968, s. 41, for item 1 and the entry relating thereto.
7. Subs. by Act 11 of 1967, s. 2, for items 2, 3 and 4 and the entries relating thereto.

34

The Municipal Taxation Act, 1881

ACT NO. 11 OF 1881 [AS ON 1955] [25TH FEBRUARY, 1881]

AN ACT to give power to prohibit the levy of municipal taxes in certain cases.

WHEREAS it is expedient to empower Government to prohibit, in certain cases, the levy of municipal taxes payable by persons in the military, naval or air-force service or by the State Government; It is hereby enacted as follows :

1. Short title and local extent. This Act may be called the Municipal Taxation Act, 1881.It extends to the whole of India except the territories which, immediately before the 1st November, 1956, were comprised in Part B States.

2. "Municipal Committee" defined. In this Act "Municipal Committee" includes a Municipal Corporation or a body of Municipal Commissioners constituted by or under the provisions of any enactment for the time being in force.

3. Power to prohibit levy of tax. Notwithstanding anything contained in any enactment for the time being in force, the Central Government may, by an order in writing, prohibit the levy by a Municipal Committee of any specified tax payable by any person subject to the Army Act, 1950 (46 of 1950), the Navy Act, 1957 (62 of 1957), or the Air Force Act, 1950 (45 of 1950) who is compelled by the exigencies of military, naval or air-force duty to reside within the limits of a municipality.

The Central Government may, by a like order, rescind any such prohibition.

A. Power of State Government to prohibit levy of taxes on it. Notwithstanding anything in any enactment for the time being in force, the State Government may by an order in writing prohibit the levy by a Municipal Committee of any specified tax payable by the State Government and may by a like order rescind any such prohibition.

4. Central Government to pay taxes referred to in section 3. So long as any order made under Section 3, prohibiting the levy of a tax on any person mentioned in that section remains in force, the Central Government] shall be liable to pay to the Municipal Committee mentioned in the order the amount which otherwise would have been payable to such committee by such person ;

PROVIDED that Central Government shall not be liable to pay any sum in respect of any horse which such person is bound, by the regulations of the service to which he belongs, to keep.

5. Payments to be made in lieu of taxes referred to in section 3A. So long as any order made under Section 3A prohibiting the levy of any tax payable by the State Government, remains in force.

The said State Government shall be liable to pay to the Municipal Committee, in lieu of such tax, such sums (if any) as an officer from time to time appointed in this behalf by the State Government may, having regard to all the circumstances of the case, from time to time determine to be fair and reasonable.

6. Decision of questions arising under this Act. If any question arises whether any duty is military, naval or air-force duty within the meaning of this Act, the decision of the Central Government thereon shall be conclusive.

If any question arises whether any person is compelled as aforesaid to reside within the limits of a municipality or is bound as aforesaid to keep any horse, the decision thereon of such authority as the Central Government may, from time to time, appoint in this behalf shall be conclusive.

❑❑❑

35

The National Tax Tribunal (Amendment) Act, 2007

ACT NO. 18 OF 2007 [3RD APRIL, 2007]

AN ACT to amend the National Tax Tribunal Act, 2005.

Be it enacted by Parliament in the Fifty-eighth Year of the Republic of India as follows:

1. Short title and commencement.

(1) This Act may be called the National Tax Tribunal (Amendment) Act, 2007.

(2) It shall be deemed to have come into force on the 29th day of January, 2007.

2. Amendment of Section 5. In Section 5 of the National Tax Tribunal Act, 2005 (hereinafter referred to as the principal Act), in sub-section (5) -

(i) the words "in consultation with the Chairperson" shall be omitted;

(ii) the following proviso shall be inserted, namely :

"PROVIDED that no Member shall be transferred without the concurrence of the Chairperson".

3. Amendment of Section 6. In Section 6 of the principal Act, in sub-section (2), in clause (b), for the words "seven years", the words "five years" shall be substituted.

4. Amendment of Section 13. In Section 13 of the principal Act, in sub-section (1), the words "or any person duly authorised by him or it" shall be omitted.

5. Repeal and saving.

(1) The National Tax Tribunal (Amendment) Ordinance, 2007 is hereby repealed.

(2) Notwithstanding the repeal of the National Tax Tribunal (Amendment) Ordinance, 2007, anything done or any action taken under the principal Act, as amended by the said Ordinance, shall be deemed to have been done or taken under the corresponding provisions of the principal Act, as amended by this Act.

❑❑❑

36

The Opium and Revenue Laws (Extension of Application) Act, 1950

ACT NO. 33 OF 1950 [18TH APRIL, 1950]

AN ACT to provide for the extension of certain opium and revenue laws to certain parts of India.

1. Short title. This Act may be called the Opium and Revenue Laws (Extension of Application) Act, 1950.

2. Extension of certain opium and revenue laws to certain parts of India.

(1) The following Acts, namely —

(i) the Opium Act, 1857 (13 of 1857),

(ii) the Opium Act, 1878 (1 of 1878),

(iii) the Revenue Recovery Act, 1890 (1 of 1890),

(iv) the Government Trading Taxation Act, 1926 (3 of 1926),

(v) the Dangerous Drugs Act, 1930 (2 of 1930),

(vi) the Taxation on Income (Investigation Commission) Act, 1947 (30 of 1947), and

(vii) the Payment of Taxes (Transfer of Property) Act, 1949 (22 of 1949), and all rules and orders made thereunder, which are in force immediately before the commencement of this Act in certain parts of India, are hereby extended to and shall be in force in, the rest of India except the State of Jammu and Kashmir.

(2) The amendments specified in the Schedule shall be made in the aforesaid Acts.

3. Modifications in State laws relating to income-tax investigation. If immediately before the commencement of this Act there is in force in any Part B State other than Jammu and Kashmir any law (hereinafter in this Section referred to as "the State law") corresponding to the Taxation on Income (Investigation Commission) Act, 1947 (30 of 1947), that law shall continue to remain in force with the following modifications, namely :

(a) all cases referred to or pending before the State Commission (by whatever name called) in respect of matters relating to taxation on income other than agricultural income shall stand transferred to the Central Commission for disposal:

PROVIDED that the Central Commission shall not, by reason merely of the transfer of any case under the provisions of this Section, be bound to recall or rehear any witness who has given evidence in the case, and may act on the evidence already recorded by or produced before the Commission which was originally investigating into the case;

(b) in the disposal of cases transferred to the Central Commission under clause (a), it shall have and exercise the same powers as it has and exercises in the investigation of cases referred to it under the Taxation on Income (Investigation Commission) Act, 1947 (30 of 1947), and shall be entitled to act for the same term as under sub-section (3) of Section 4 of that Act;

(bb) any decision given, whether before or after the commencement of this Act, by the Chief Revenue Authority of Travancore or of Travancore-Cochin in the exercise or purported exercise of any powers conferred on it by any law for the time being in force in the State shall be deemed to be a decision given by the Income-tax authority for the purposes of sub-section (2) of Section 8 of the Travancore Taxation on Income (Investigation Commission) Act, 1124 (Travancore Act XIV of 1124);

(c) any reference in the State Law, by whatever form of words, to the State Government or the State Commission shall, in relation to income other than agricultural income, be construed as a reference to the Central Government or the Central Commission, as the case may be;

(d) the report of the Central Commission shall be submitted to the Central Government, and the Central Government may, by order in writing, direct that such proceedings as it thinks fit under the law in force in the State relating to income-tax, super-tax or excess profits tax or any other law, shall be taken against the person to whose case the report relates in respect of his income other than agricultural income, and upon such a direction being given, all such proceedings may be taken and completed under the appropriate law applicable in the State, as if the direction had been given and the proceedings had been instituted thereunder;

(e) where under any law in force in the State the agricultural income of an assessee is to be included in his total income for the purpose of determining the tax payable by him, the tax payable in respect of his income other than agricultural income shall be an amount bearing to the total amount of tax which would have been payable under the appropriate law in force in the State if a combined assessment had been made, the same proportion as such income bears to the total income including the agricultural income:

PROVIDED that for this purpose any reduction of tax allowed on the agricultural income by the appropriate law in force in the State shall not be taken into account.

EXPLANATION: In this Section, "Central Commission" means the Income-tax Investigation Commission constituted under the Taxation on Income (Investigation Commission) Act, 1947 (30 of 1947).

4. Repeals and savings. If immediately before the commencement of this Act there is in force in any Part B State, other than Jammu and Kashmir, or in the merged territory of Cooch Behar any law corresponding to any of the Acts specified in Section 2, other than the Taxation on Income (Investigation Commission) Act, 1947 (30 of 1947), that law shall, upon the commencement of this Act, stand repealed:

PROVIDED that such repeal shall not affect—

(a) the previous operation of that law, or

(b) any penalty, forfeiture or punishment incurred in respect of any offence committed against that law, or

(c) any investigation, legal proceeding or remedy in respect of any such penalty, forfeiture or punishment; and any such investigation, legal proceeding or remedy may be instituted, continued or enforced, and any such penalty, forfeiture or punishment may be imposed as if this Act had not been passed:

PROVIDED FURTHER that anything done or any action taken under any provision of that law shall be deemed to have been done or taken under the corresponding provision of the Central Act as now extended to the State and shall continue in force accordingly.

5. Removal of difficulties. If any difficulty arises in giving effect to the provisions of any of the Acts, rules or orders now extended to any part of India in which they were not in force before the commencement of this Act, the Central Government may, by order published in the Official Gazette, make such provision or give such direction as appears to it to be necessary for removing the difficulty.

❑❑❑

37

The Prevention of Terrorism (Repeal) Act, 2004

Act No. 26 of 2004 [21st December, 2004]

AN ACT to repeal the Prevention of Terrorism Act, 2002.

Be it enacted by Parliament in the Fifty-fifth Year of the Republic of India as follows:

1. Short title and commencement.

(1) This Act may be called the Prevention of Terrorism (Repeal) Act, 2004.

(2) It shall be deemed to have come into force on the 21st day of September, 2004.

2. Repeal of Act 15 of 2002 and saving.

(1) The Prevention of Terrorism Act, 2002 (hereinafter referred to as the principal Act) is hereby repealed.

(2) The repeal of the principal Act shall not affect-

(a) the previous operation of, or anything duly done or suffered under the principal Act, or

(b) any right, privilege or obligation or liability acquired, accrued or incurred under the principal Act, or

(c) any penalty, forfeiture or punishment incurred in respect of any offence under the principal Act, or

(d) any investigation, legal proceeding or remedy in respect of any such right, privilege, obligation, liability, penalty, forfeiture or punishment as aforesaid, and, any such investigation, legal proceeding or remedy may be instituted, continued or enforced and any such penalty, forfeiture or punishment may be imposed as if the principal Act had not been repealed:

PROVIDED that notwithstanding anything contained in this sub-section or in any other law for the time being in force, no court shall take cognizance of an offence under the principal Act after the expiry of the period of one year from the commencement of this Act.

(3) Notwithstanding the repeal of Section 60 of the principal Act, the Review Committee constituted by the Central Government under sub-section (1) of that Section, whether or not an application under sub-section (4) of that Section has been made, shall review all cases registered under the principal Act as to whether there is a *prima facie* case for proceeding against the accused thereunder and such review shall be completed within a period of one year from the commencement of this Act and where the Review Committee is of the opinion that there is no *prima facie* case for proceeding against the accused, then,-

(a) in cases in which cognizance has been taken by the Court, the cases shall be deemed to have been withdrawn; and

(b) in cases in which investigations are pending, the investigations shall be closed forthwith, with effect from the date of issuance of the direction by such Review Committee in this regard.

(4) The Review Committee constituted by the Central Government under sub-section (1) of Section 60 of the principal Act shall, while reviewing cases, have powers of a civil court under the Code of Civil Procedure, 1908 (5 of 1908) in respect of the following matters, namely:-

(a) discovery and production of any document;

(b) requisitioning any public record or copy thereof from any court or office.

(5) The Central Government may constitute more Review Committees, as it may consider necessary, for completing the review within the period specified in sub-section (3).

3. Repeal and saving.

(1) The Prevention of Terrorism (Repeal) Ordinance, 2004 (Ord. 1 of 2004) is hereby repealed.

(2) Notwithstanding such repeal, anything done or any action taken under the said Ordinance shall be deemed to have been done or taken under the corresponding provisions of this Act.

❑❑❑

38

The Produce Cess Act, 1966

ACT NO. 15 OF 1966 [21ST MAY, 1966]

AN ACT to provide for the imposition of cess on certain produce for the improvement and development of the methods of cultivation and marketing of such produce and for matters connected therewith.

Be it enacted by Parliament in the Seventeenth Year of the Republic of India as follows:-

1. Short title and extent.

(1) This Act may be called the Produce Cess Act, 1966.

(2) It extends to the whole of India.

2. Definitions. In this Act, unless the context otherwise requires,—

(a) "Collector" means the officer appointed by the Central Government to perform in any specified area the duties of a Collector under the provisions of this Act and the rules made thereunder, and includes any officer subordinate to that officer whom he may, by order in writing, authorise to perform his duties under those provisions;

(c) "customs airport", "customs port" and "customs station" have the meanings respectively assigned to them in the Customs Act, 1962 (52 of 1962);

(d) "Indian Council of Agricultural Research" means the body registered in that name under the Societies Registration Act, 1860 (21 of 1860);

(e) "lac" includes any form of manufactured or unmanufactured lac other than refuse lac;

(f) "managing agent" has the meaning assigned to it in the Companies Act, 1956 (1 of 1956);

(j) "prescribed" means prescribed by rules made under this Act;

(k) "produce" means any goods specified in the First Schedule.

3. Imposition of cess.

(1) There shall be levied and collected as a cess, for the purposes of this Act, on every produce specified in column 2 of the First Schedule, which is exported from any [3][customs station to any place] beyond the limits of India, a duty of customs at such rate, not exceeding the rate specified in the corresponding entry in column 3 thereof, as the Central Government may, by notification in the Official Gazette, specify:

PROVIDED that until such rate is specified by the Central Government, the duty of customs shall be levied and collected at the rate specified in the corresponding entry in column 4 of the said Schedule.

4. Persons who shall be liable to pay duty. Every duty of customs leviable under this Act on any produce shall be payable by the person by whom such produce is exported from India [1][xxx

5. Application of proceeds of cess.

(1) An amount equivalent to the proceeds of the duty levied and collected under this Act, reduced by the cost of collection as determined by the Central Government, together with any moneys received by the Central Government for the purposes of this Act, shall, after due appropriation made by Parliament by law, be utilized by the Central Government to meet the expenditure incurred in connection with measures which, in the opinion of that Government, are necessary or expedient to promote the improvement, development and marketing of produce.

(2) In particular, and without prejudice to the generality of the provisions of sub-section (1), the proceeds of the duty levied and collected under this Act may be utilized by the Central Government for all or any of the following purposes, namely:—

(a) undertaking, assisting or encouraging, agricultural, industrial, technological and economic research, including research on the utilization of the products obtained from any produce;

(b) supplying technical advice to cultivators, growers and millers;

(c) encouraging the adoption of improved methods of cultivation and storage of crops;

(d) producing, testing and distributing improved varieties of crops or assisting such work;

(e) assisting in the control of insects and other pests and diseases of the crops, both in the field and in storage;

(f) promoting the improvement of the marketing of produce and the products obtained therefrom in India and abroad including the setting up and adoption of grade standards for the produce and the products obtained therefrom;

(g) collecting statistics from cultivators, growers, dealers and occupiers of mills on all relevant matters and promoting improvement in the forecasting of crops and the preparation of all relevant statistics relating to the crops and the products obtained therefrom;

(h) maintaining, and assisting in the maintenance of, such institutes, farms and stations as the Central Government may consider necessary;

(i) advising and providing assistance on all matters connected with the improvement of the cultivation of crops (including advising on the best and most suitable varieties of the crops to be cultivated) and the improvement of the industries using the crops and the products obtained therefrom;

(j) promoting and encouraging the co-operative movement in any connected industry;

(k) adopting such measures as may be practicable for ensuring remunerative returns to the growers;

(l) organising the establishment of cultivators', growers', millers' and consumers' organisations;

(m) aiding and encouraging the establishment of exhibitions for demonstrating the uses of the produce and the products obtained therefrom;

(n) adopting any other measures which the Central Government may deem to be necessary or advisable to carry out the purposes of this Act.

(3) In this section, "crops" means crops or plants from which any produce is obtained[and "produce" includes cotton.

11. Collection of cess on any produce specified in First Schedule.

(1) The Collector shall in respect of any produce specified in the First Schedule which is exported by sea or air assess and collect the duty of customs at the customs port or customs airport] of export.

(2) Where any produce specified in the First Schedule is exported by land or inland water, the duty of customs leviable under this Act on such produce shall be assessed and collected by such authority and in such manner as may be prescribed, and, until so prescribed, such duty of customs shall be levied and collected in accordance with the law in force immediately before the commencement of this Act.

(3) The Central Board of Excise and Customs constituted under the Central Boards of Revenue Act, 1963 (54 of 1963), may, be rules, specify the conditions and restrictions subject to which—

(a) refund may be made of the duty of customs levied on any produce specified in the First Schedule which is exported by land or inland water, where such produce is subsequently imported into India,

(b) export may be made by land or inland water, without payment of any duty of customs, of any produce specified in the First Schedule which is intended to be brought back to India.

12. Recovery of sums due to Government. Where any duty of customs demanded from any persons or any penalty payable by any person under this Act is not paid—

(a) the Collector may deduct the amount so payable from any money owing to such person which may be under the control of the Collector or any other officer; or

(b) the Collector may recover the amount so payable by detaining and selling any goods belonging to such person which are under the control of the Collector or any other officer; or

(c) if the amount cannot be recovered from such person in the manner provided in clause (a) or clause (b), the Collector may prepare a certificate signed by him specifying the amount due from such person and send it to the Collector of the district in which such person owns any property or resides or carries on his business and the said Collector shall, on receipt of such certificate, proceed to recover from the said person the amount specified therein as if it were an arrear of land revenue.

15. Provisions of certain Acts to apply.

(1) The provisions of the Customs Act, 1962 (52 of 1962), and the rules and regulations made thereunder, including those relating to refunds and exemptions from duty, shall, so far as may be, apply in relation to the levy and collection of duties of customs on any produce specified in the First Schedule as they apply in relation to the levy and collection of duty payable to the Central Government under that Act.

16. Offences.

(1) Whoever—

(a) evades the payment of any duty of customs payable under this Act, or

(b) fails to furnish any return or information which it is his duty to furnish under this Act or furnishes a return or information which is false in material particulars or which he does not believe to be true, or

(c) obstructs the Collector or any other officer in the performance of his duties under this Act or any rules made thereunder shall be punishable with imprisonment for a term which may extend to six months, or with fine which may extend to two thousand rupees, or with both.

(2) Any court trying an offence under this Act may direct that any produce in respect of which it is satisfied that an offence punishable under this Act has been committed shall be forfeited to Government and may also direct that all packages, coverings or receptacles in which such produce is contained and every animal, vehicle, vessel or other conveyance used in carrying such produce shall be forfeited to Government.

17. Limitation of prosecution. No prosecution for any offence punishable under this Act shall be instituted against any person except by, or with the consent of, the Collector.

18. Composition of offences. Any offence punishable under this Act may, either before or after the institution of the prosecution, be compounded by the Collector or any other officer authorised by him in this behalf on payment to the Central Government, for the purposes of this Act, of such sum as the Collector or such officer, as the case may be, thinks fit.

19. Protection of action taken in good faith.

(1) No suit, prosecution or other legal proceeding shall lie against the Central Government or any person authorized by the Central Government for anything which is in good faith done or intended to be done in pursuance of this Act or any rule or order made thereunder.

(2) No suit or other legal proceeding shall lie against the Central Government or any person authorized by the Central Government for any damage caused or likely to be caused by anything which is in good faith done or intended to be done in pursuance of any of the provisions of this Act or any rule or order made thereunder.

20. Power to make rules.

(1) The Central Government may, by notification in the Official Gazette, make rules to carry out the purposes of this Act.

(2) In particular, and without prejudice to the generality of the foregoing power, such rules may provide for all or any of the following matters, namely : (e) the authority by which and the manner in which the duties of customs leviable under this Act shall be collected on any produce specified in the First Schedule which is exported [2][by land or inland water]; and (f) any other matter which is required to be, or may be, prescribed.

21. Power to remove difficulties. If any difficulty arises in giving effect to the provisions of this Act, the Central Government may be order, make such directions, not inconsistent with the provisions of this Act, as appear to it to be necessary or expedient for the removal of the difficulty:

PROVIDED that no such directions shall be made after the expiry of a period of three years from the date of commencement of this Act.

22. Rules of be laid before Parliament. Every rule made under this Act shall be laid as soon as may be after it is made, before each House of Parliament while it is in session for a total period of thirty days which may be comprised in one session or in two or more successive sessions, and if, before the expiry of the session immediately following the session or the successive sessions aforesaid, both Houses agree in making any modification in the rule or both Houses agree that the rule should not be made, the rule shall thereafter have effect only in such modified form or be of no effect, as the case may be; so, however, that any such modification or annulment shall be without prejudice to the validity of anything previously done under the rule.

❑❑❑

39

The Railways (Local Authorities Taxation) Act, 1941

[ACT NO. 25 OF 1941] [26TH NOVEMBER, 1941]

AN ACT to regulate the extent to which railway property shall be liable to taxation imposed by an authority within a State.

WHEREAS it is expedient to regulate the extent to which property vested in [2]the Central Government, being property of a railway, shall be liable to taxation imposed by an authority within a State; It is hereby enacted as follows:

2. Definitions. In this Act -

(a) "local authority" means a local authority as defined in the General Clauses Act, 1897, and includes any authority legally entitled to or entrusted with the control or management of any fund for the maintenance of watchmen or for the conservancy of a river;

(b) "railway administration" has the meaning assigned to the expression in clause (6) of Section 3 of the Indian Railways Act, 1890.

3. Liability of railways to taxation by local authorities.

(1) In respect of property vested in 1 the Central Government, being property of a railway, a railway administration shall be liable to pay any tax in aid of the funds of any local authority, if the Central Government, by notification in the Official Gazette, declares it to be so liable.

(2) While a notification under sub-section (1) is in force, the railway administration shall be liable to pay to the local authority either the tax mentioned in the notification or in lieu thereof such sum, if any, as a person appointed in this

behalf by the Central Government may, having regard to the services rendered to the railway and all the relevant circumstances of the case, from time to time determine to be fair and reasonable.The person so appointed shall be a person who is or has been a Judge of a High Court or a District Judge.

4. Modification of existing liability to taxation. The Central Government may, by notification in the Official Gazette, revoke or vary any notification issued under clause (1) of Section 135 of the Indian Railways Act, 1830; and where a notification is so revoked any liability arising out of the notification to pay any tax to any local authority shall cease, and where a notification is so varied the liability arising out of the notification shall be varied accordingly.

5. Saving. Nothing in this Act shall be construed as debarring any railway administration administering a railway from entering into a contract with any local authority for the supply of water or light or for the scavenging of railway premises, or for any other service which the local authority may be rendering or be prepared to render within any part of the local area under its control.

❑❑❑

40

The Revenue Recovery Act, 1890

ACT NO. 1 OF 1890 [14TH FEBRUARY, 1890]

AN ACT to make better provision for recovering certain public demands.

1. Title and extent.

(1) This Act may be called the Revenue Recovery Act, 1890.

(2) It extends to the whole of India except the State of Jammu and Kashmir;

2. Definitions. In this Act, unless there is something repugnant in the subject or context,—

(1) "district" includes a presidency-town;

(2) "collector" means the chief officer in charge of the land-revenue administration of a district; and

(3) "defaulter" means a person from whom an arrear of land-revenue, or a sum recoverable as an arrear of land-revenue, is due, and includes a person who is responsible as surety for the payment of any such arrear or sum.

3. Recovery of public demands by enforcement of process in other districts than those in which they become payable.

(1) Where an arrear of land-revenue, or a sum recoverable as an arrear of land-revenue, is payable to a Collector by a defaulter being or having property in a district other than that in which the arrear accrued or the sum is payable, the Collector may send to the Collector of that other district a certificate in the form as nearly as may be of the Schedule, stating—

(a) the name of the defaulter and such other particulars as may be necessary for his identification; and

(b) the amount payable by him and the account on which it is due. Amended in Assam by Assam Act 16 of 1971.

(2) The certificate shall be signed by the Collector making it or by any officer to whom such Collector may, by order in writing, delegate this duty, and, save as otherwise provided by this Act, shall be conclusive proof of the matters therein stated.

(3) The Collector of the other district shall, on receiving the certificate, proceed to recover the amount stated therein as if it were an arrear of land-revenue which had accrued in his own district.

4. Remedy available to person denying liability to pay amount recovered under last foregoing section.

(1) When proceedings are taken against a person under the last foregoing section for the recovery of an amount stated in a certificate, that person may, if he denies his liability to pay the amount or any part thereof and pays the same under protest made in writing at the time of payment and signed by him or his agent, institute a suit for the repayment of the amount or the part thereof so paid.

(2) A suit under sub-section (1) must be instituted in a Civil Court having jurisdiction in the local area in which the office of the Collector who made the certificate is situate, and the suit shall be determined in accordance with the law in force at the place where the arrear accrued or the liability for the payment of the sum arose.

(3) In the suit the plaintiff may, notwithstanding anything in the last foregoing section, but subject to the law in force at the place aforesaid, give evidence with respect to any matter stated in the certificate.

(4) This section shall apply if under this Act as in force as part of the law of Pakistan or Burma, or under any other similar Act forming part of the law of Pakistan or Burma, proceedings are taken against a person in Pakistan or Burma, as the case may be, for the recovery of an amount stated in a certificate made by a Collector in any State to which this Act extends.

5. Recovery by Collectors of sums recoverable as arrears of revenue by other public officers or by local authorities. Where any sum is recoverable as an arrear of land-revenue by any public officer other than a Collector or by any local authority, the Collector of the district in which the office of that officer or authority is situate shall, on the request of the officer or authority, proceed to recover the sum as if it were an arrear of land-revenue which had accrued in his own district, and may send a certificate of the amount to be recovered to the Collector of another district under the foregoing provisions of this Act, as if the sum were payable to himself.

6. Property liable to sale under this Act.

(1) When the Collector of a district receives a certificate under this Act, he may issue a proclamation prohibiting the transfer or charging of any immovable property belonging to the defaulter in the district.

(2) The Collector may at any time, by order in writing, withdraw the proclamation, and it shall be deemed to be withdrawn when either the amount stated in the certificate has been recovered or the property has been sold for the recovery of that amount.

(3) Any private alienation of the property or of any interest of the defaulter therein, whether by sale, gift, mortgage or otherwise, made after the issue of the proclamation and before the withdrawal thereof, shall be void as against the Government and any person who may purchase the property at a sale held for the recovery of the amount stated in the certificate.

(4) Subject to the foregoing provisions of this section, when proceedings are taken against any immovable property under this Act for the recovery of an amount stated in a certificate, the interests of the defaulter alone therein shall be so proceeded against, and no incumbrances created, grants made or contracts entered into by him in good faith shall be rendered invalid by reason only of proceedings being taken against those interests.

(5) A proclamation under this section shall be made by beat of drum or other customary method and by the posting of a copy thereof on a conspicuous place in or near the property to which it relates.

7. Saving of local laws relating to revenue. Nothing in the foregoing sections shall be construed—

(a) to impair any security provided by, or affect the provisions of, any other enactment for the time being in force for the recovery of land-revenue or of sums recoverable as arrears of land-revenue, or

(b) to authorise the arrest of any person for the recovery of any tax payable to the corporation, commissioner, committee, board, council or person having authority over a municipality under any enactment for the time being in force.

8. Recovery in India of certain public demands arising beyond India. When this Act has been applied to any local area which is under the administration of the Central Government but which is not part of India, an arrear of land-revenue accruing in that local area, or a sum recoverable as an arrear of land-revenue and payable to a Collector or other public officer or to a local authority in that local area, may be recovered under this Act in India.

9. Recovery in India of land revenues, etc., accruing in Burma.

(1) The Central Government may direct that an arrear of land-revenue accruing in Burma or a sum recoverable in Burma as an arrear of land-revenue and payable to a Collector or other public officer or to a local authority in Burma may be recovered under this Act in India and thereupon such arrear or sum shall be so recoverable:

PROVIDED that the Central Government shall not give any such direction unless it is satisfied that the remedy available under Section 4 of this Act in India to a person paying under protest in India an arrear accruing in India is available under Burma law in Burma to a person paying under protest in India an arrear accruing in Burma.

(2) For recovering by virtue of this section any arrears of tax or penalty due under the enactments relating to income-tax or supertax in force in Burma, the Collector shall have such additional powers as he has in the case of Indian income-tax and super-tax under the proviso to Section 46 (2) of the Income-tax Act, 1922 (11 of 1922).

(3) Sub-sections (1) and (2) shall apply in relation to Pakistan as they apply in relation to Burma.

10. Duty of Collectors to remit moneys collected in certain cases. Where a Collector receives a certificate under this Act from a Collector of another State or a Collector in Pakistan or Burma, he shall remit any sum recovered by him by virtue of that certificate to that Collector, after deducting his expenses in connection with the matter.

❑❑❑

41

The Sales-Tax Laws Validation Act, 1956

ACT NO. 7 OF 1956 [21ST MARCH, 1956]

AN ACT to validate laws of States imposing, or authorising the imposition of, taxes on the sale or purchase of goods in the course of inter-State trade or commerce.

1. Short title. This Act may be called the Sales-Tax Laws validation Act, 1956.

2. Validation of State laws imposing, or authorising the imposition of, taxes on sale or purchase of goods in the course of inter-State trade or commerce. Notwithstanding any judgment, decree or order of any court, no law of a State imposing, or authorising the imposition of, a tax on the sale or purchase of any goods where such sale or purchase took place in the course of inter-State trade or commerce during the period between the 1st day of April, 1951 and the 6th day of September, 1955, shall be deemed to be invalid or ever to have been invalid merely by reason of the fact that such sale or purchase took place in the course of inter-State trade or commerce; and all such taxes levied or collected or purporting to have been levied or collected during the aforesaid period shall be deemed always to have been validly levied or collected in accordance with law.

EXPLANATION: In this section, "law of a State" in relation to a State specified in Part C of the First Schedule to the Constitution, means any law made by the Legislative Assembly, if any, of that State or extended to that State by a notification issued under Section 2 of the Part C States (Laws) Act, 1950 (30 of 1950).

3. Repeal of Ordinance 3 of 1956.

❑❑❑

42

The Salt Cess Act, 1953

ACT NO. 49 OF 1953 [26TH DECEMBER, 1953]

AN ACT to provide for the levy and collection of a cess on salt for the purpose of raising funds to meet the expenses incurred on the salt organisation maintained by Government and on the measures taken by Government in connection with the manufacture, supply and distribution of salt.

1. Short title, extent and commencement.

(1) This Act may be called the Salt Cess Act, 1953.

(2) It extends to the whole of India.

(3) It shall come into force on such date as the Central Government may, by notification in the Official Gazette, appoint.

2. Definitions. In this Act, unless the context otherwise requires,—

(a) "manufacture" in relation to salt includes collection, removal, preparation, steeping, evaporation, boiling or any one or more of these processes, the separation or purification of salt obtained in the manufacture of saltpetre, the separation of salt from earth or other substance so as to produce alimentary salt, and the excavation or removal of natural saline deposits or efflorescence; and the word manufacturer' shall be construed accordingly and shall include not only a person who employs hired labour in the production or manufacture of a salt but also any person who engages in its production or manufacture on his own account if the salt is intended for sale.

EXPLANATION: In this clause, saltpetre includes rasi sajji, and all other substances manufactured from saline earth, and kharinun and every form of sulphate or carbonate of soda;

(b) "salt" includes swamp salt, spontaneous salt, and salt or saline solutions made or produced from any saline substances or from salt earth; The Act comes into force in Pondicherry on 1.10.

(c) "salt factory" includes—

(i) a place used or intended to be used in the manufacture of salt and all embankments, reservoirs, condensing and evaporating pans, buildings, and waste places situated within the limits of such place, as defined from time to time for the purposes of the Central Excises and Salt Act, 1944 ; (1 of 1944)

(ii) all drying grounds and storage platforms and storehouses appurtaining to any such place;

(iii) land on which salt is spontaneously produced;

(e) "prescribed" means prescribed by rules made under this Act.

3. Levy and collection of cess on salt. There shall be levied and collected in such manner as may be prescribed, a cess in the nature of an excise duty at the rate of fourteen naye paise per forty kilograms on all salt manufactured in India in any salt factory, whether owned by Government or not.

4. Application of proceeds of cess. The proceeds of the duty levied under this Act, reduced by the cost of collection as determined by the Central Government, shall, if Parliament by appropriation made by law in this behalf so provides, be utilised on all or any of the following objects, namely:—

(a) meeting the expenditue incurred in connection with the salt organisation maintained by the Central Government;

(b) meeting the cost of measures taken in connection with the manufacture, supply and distribution of salt by Union agencies and the regulation and control of the manufacture, supply and distribution of salt by other agencies; and in particular, measures for—

(i) the establishment and maintenance of research stations and model salt farms;

(ii) the establishment, maintenance and expansion of salt factories;

(iii) fixing the grades of salt;

(iv) promoting and encouraging co-operative effort among manufacturers of salt; and

(v) promoting the welfare of labour employed in the salt industry.

5. Validation of charges levied on salt before the commencement of this Act. The charge in respect of the manufacture or production of salt imposed by the rule made by the Central Government under Section 37 of the Central Excises and Salt Act, 1944 (1 of 1944) and published with the notification of the former Finance Department (Revenue Division) No. 3 dated the 29th March, 1944, shall be deemed to have been levied under this Act as if this Act was in force on the day on which the charge was so imposed and accordingly —

(a) any sum paid or payable by way of such charge shall be deemed to heve been paid or payable in accordance with the law; and

(b) no claim shall lie in any Court for the refund of any such so paid.

6. Power to make rules.

(1) The Central Government may, by notification in the Official Gazette, make rules for carrying out the purposes of this Act.

(2) In particular and without prejudice to the generality of the foregoing power, such rules may provide for—

(a) the assessment and collection of the cess levied under this Act;

(b) the determination of the cost of collection of the cess;

(c) the manner in which accounts relating to the proceeds of the cess shall be maintained;

(d) the manner in which the proceeds of the cess may be applied on the object specified in Section 4;

(e) the exemption from the whole or any part of the cess levied under this Act—

(i) in respect of salt exported from India;

(ii) in respect of salt manufactured by any specified categories of small manufacturers; and

(iii) in respect of salt utilised in the manufacture of any other product of industry.

(3) Every rule made by the Central Government under this section shall be laid as soon as may be after it is made before each House of Parliament while it is in session for a total period of thirty days which may be comprised in one session or in two or more successive sessions, and if, before the expiry of the session immediately following the session or the successive sessions aforesaid both Houses agree in making any modification in the rule or both Houses agree that the rule should not be made, the rule shall thereafter have effect only in such modified form or be no effect, as the case may be; so, however, that any such modification or annulment shall be without prejudice to the validity of anything previously done under that rule.

❑❑❑

43

The Sea Customs Act, 1878

Act No. 8 of 1878

This Act has been repealed by the Customs Act, 1962 (52 of 1962), s.160 and the Sch. (w.e.f. Ist February, 1963).

□□□

44

The Sugar Cess Act, 1982

Act No. 3 of 1982 [19th March, 1982]

AN ACT to provide for the imposition of a cess on sugar for the development of sugar industry and for matters connected therewith.

Be it enacted by Parliament in the Thirty-third Year of the Republic of India as follows:—

1. Short title, extent and commencement.

(1) This Act may be called the Sugar Cess Act, 1982.

(2) It extends to the whole of India.

(3) It shall come into force on such date as the Central Government may, by notification in the Official Gazette, appoint.

2. Definitions. In this Act, unless the context otherwise requires,—

(a) "occupier", in relation to any sugar factory, means the person who has ultimate control over the affairs of the sugar factory or the owner of the sugar factory in case he is not the occupier;

(b) "prescribed" means prescribed by rules made under this Act;

(c) "sugar factory" means any premises (including the precincts thereof) in any part of which sugar is manufactured by vacuum pan process;

(d) "sugar" means any form of sugar including crushed sugar or sugar in crystalised or powder form, containing ninety per cent, or more of sucrose and produced by the vacuum pan process and includes raw sugar produced by the said process.

3. Imposition of cess.

(1) There shall be levied and collected as a cess, for the purposes of the Sugar Development Fund Act, 1982, a duty of excise on all sugar produced by any

sugar factory in India, at such rate not exceeding fifteen rupees per quintal of sugar, as the Central Government may, by notification in the Official Gazette, specify from time to time:

PROVIDED that until such rate is specified by the Central Government, the duty of excise shall be levied and collected at the rate of fourteen rupees per quintal of sugar.

(2) The duty of excise levied under sub-section (1) shall be in addition to the duty of excise leviable on sugar under the Central Excises and Salt Act, 1944 (1 of 1944) or any other law for the time being in force.

(3) The duty of excise levied under sub-section (1) shall be payable by the occupier of the sugar factory in which sugar is produced.

(4) The provisions of the Central Excises and Salt Act, 1944 (1 of 1944) and the rules made thereunder, including those relating to refunds and exemptions from duty, shall, so far as may be, apply in relation to the levy and collection of the said duty of excise as they apply in relation to the levy and collection of the duty of excise on sugar under that Act.

4. Crediting proceeds of duty to Consolidated Fund of India. The proceeds of the duty of excise levied under Section 3 shall be credited to the Consolidated Fund of India.

5. Power to call for reports and returns. The Central Government may require an occupier of a sugar factory to furnish, for the purposes of this Act, such statistical and other information in such form and within such period as may be prescribed.

6. Power to make rules.

(1) The Central Government may, by notification in the Official Gazette, make rules for carrying out the provisions of this Act.

(2) In particular and without prejudice to the generality of the foregoing power, such rules may provide for the form in which and the period within which statistical and other information may be furnished under Section 5.

(3) Every rule made under this Section shall be laid, as soon as may be after it is made, before each House of Parliament, while it is in session, for a total period of thirty days which may be comprised in one session or in two or more successive sessions, and if, before the expiry of the session immediately following the session or the successive sessions aforesaid, both Houses agree in making any modification in the rule or both Houses agree that the rule should not be made, the rule shall thereafter have effect only in such modified form or be of no effect, as the case may be; so, however, that any such modification or annulment shall be without prejudice to the validity of anything previously done under that rule.

❑❑❑

45

The Sugarcane Cess (Validation) Act, 1961

Act No. 38 of 1961 [11th September, 1961]

AN ACT to validate the imposition and collection of cesses on sugarcane under certain State Acts and to amend the U.P. Sugarcane Cess (Validation) Act, 1961.

Be it enacted by Parliament in the Twelfth Year of the Republic of India as follows:-

1. Short title and commencement.

(1) This Act may be called the Sugarcane Cess (Validation) Act, 1961.

(2) Section 5 shall come into force at once, and the remaining provisions of this Act, insofar as they relate to any State, shall come into force in that State or such date' as the Central Government may, by notification in the Official Gazette, appoint and different dates may be appointed for different States.

2. Definition. In this Act -

(a) "cess" means the cess payable under any State Act and includes any sum recoverable under any such Act by way of interest or penalty;

(b) "State Act" means any of the following Acts as in force in any State from time to time, by way of amendment or adaptation, namely -

(i) The Andhra Pradesh (Andhra Area) Sugar Factories Control Act, 1949 (Act XX of 1949). The Act (except S. 5) has been brought into force in different States as under - Date State Notification 1-10-1961 Mysore G.S.R. 1190, dated 23-9-1961, Gazette of India, Pt. II, Sec. 3;

(ii) The Andhra Pradesh (Telengana Area) Sugarcane Cess Act, 1953 (Act IX of 1953);

(iii) The Bihar Sugar Factories Control Act, 1937 (Bihar Act VII of 1937);

(iv) The Bombay Sugarcane Cess Act, 1948 (Bombay Act LXXXII of 1948);

(v) The Bombay Sugarcane Cess (Extension) Act, 1958 (Bombay Act LIV of 1958);

(vi) The Hyderabad Sugarcane Cess Act, 1953 (Hyderabad Act IX of 1953);

(vii) The Madhya Pradesh Sugarcane (Regulation of Supply and Purchase) Act, 1958 (Madhya Pradesh Act 1 of 1959);

(viii) the Madras Sugar Factories Control Act, 1949 (Madras Act XX of 1949);

(ix) The Madras Sugar Factories Control (Mysore Amendment and Validation of Levy of Cess) Act, 1959 (Mysore Act 19 of 1959);

(x) The Mysore Sugarcane Cess Act, 1958 (Mysore Act 27 of 1958).

3. Validation of imposition and collection of cesses under State Acts.

(1) Notwithstanding any judgment, decree or order of any court, all cesses imposed, assessed or collected or purporting to have been imposed, assessed or collected under any State Act before the commencement of this Act shall be deemed to have been validly imposed, assessed or collected in accordance with law, as if the provisions of the State Acts and of all notifications, orders and rules issued or made thereunder, insofar as such provisions relate to the imposition, assessment and collection of such cess had been included in and formed part of this section and this section had been in force at all material times when such cess was imposed, assessed or col- lected; and accordingly,-

(a) no suit or other proceeding shall be maintained or continued in any court for the refund of any cess paid under any State Act;

(b) no court shall enforce a decree or order directing the refund of any cess paid under any State Act; and

(c) any cess imposed or assessed under any State Act before the commencement of this Act but not collected before such commencement may be recovered (after assessment of the cess, where necessary) in the manner provided under that Act.

(2) For the removal of doubts it is hereby declared that nothing in sub-section (1) shall be construed as preventing any person-

(a) from questioning in accordance with the provisions of any State Act and rules made thereunder the assessment of any cess for any period; or

(b) from claiming refund of any cess paid by him in excess of the amount due from him under any State Act and the rules made thereunder.

4. Omission of Section 11 of the Bombay Sugarcane Cess Act, 1948. Nothing in this Act shall be construed as validating Section 11 of the Bombay Sugarcane Cess Act, 1948 and accordingly the said section shall be omitted.

5. Amendment of U. P Sugarcane Cess (Validation) Act, 1961. In sub-section (1) of Section 3 of the U. P. Sugarcane Cess (Validation) Act, 1961, (4 of 1961) for the words, "figures and letters" during the period beginning with the 26th day of January, 1950 and ending on the 3rd day of February, 1961, the words, "figures and letters" before the 3rd day of February, 1961 shall be substituted and shall be deemed always to have been substituted.

❑❑❑

46

The Sugarcane Cess (Validation) Repeal Act, 2001

ACT NO. 35 OF 2001 [3RD SEPTEMBER, 2001]

AN ACT to repeal the Sugarcane Cess (Validation) Act, 1961.

Be it enacted by Parliament in the Fifty-second Year of the Republic of India as follows:

1. Short title. This Act may be called the Sugarcane Cess (Validation) Repeal Act, 2001.

2. Repeal of Act 38 of 1961. The Sugarcane Cess (Validation) Act, 1961 is hereby repealed.

❑❑❑

47

The Super Profits Tax Act, 1963

ACT NO. 14 OF 1963

This Act has been repealed by the Finance Act, 1966 (13 of 1966), S. 42 (*w.e.f.* 1-4-1966).

❑❑❑

48

The Taxation Laws (Amendment and Miscellaneous Provisions) Act, 1965

ACT NO. 41 OF 1965 [4TH DECEMBER, 1965]

AN ACT further to amend the Income-tax Act, 1961, the Estate Duty Act, 1953, the Wealth-tax Act, 1957, the Gift-tax Act, 1958 and to provide for exemption from tax in certain cases of undisclosed income invested in National Defence Gold Bonds, 1980.

Be it enacted by Parliament in the Sixteenth Year of the Republic of India as follows:

1. Short title. This Act may be called the Taxation Laws (Amendment and Miscellaneous Provisions) Act, 1965.

2. Exemption from tax in certain cases of undisclosed income invested in National Defence Gold Bonds, 1980.

(1) Where a person who hag acquired any gold out of his income which has not been disclosed by him, for the purposes of the 1922. Indian income-tax Act, 1922, (11 of 1922) or the Income-tax Act, 1961, (43 of 1961) or the Excess Profits Tax Act, 1940, (15 of 1940) or the Business Profits Tax Act, 1947, (21 of 1947) or the Super Profits Tax Act, 1963, (14 of 1963) or the Companies (Profits) Surtax 193 Act, 1964, (7 of 1964) tenders such gold as subscription for the National Defence Gold Bonds, 1980, prior to the detection of such income by the Income-tax Officer or the seizure of such gold under any law for the time being in force, such income shall, notwithstanding anything contained in the said Acts, not be included in his income, profits or gains Chargeable to tax under the said Acts in an assessment or reassessment for any assessment. year made under the said Acts on or after the 20th day of October, 1965.

(2) In computing the net wealth of a person under the Wealth-tax Act, 1957, (27 of 1957) the value of the assets represented by the income, which, under sub-section (1) is not includible in his income, profits or gains, shall, notwithstanding anything contained in the said Act, not be taken into account in an assessment or re-assessment for any assessment year made under the said Act on or after the 20th day of October, 1965.

(3) (a) The name of the person subscribing to the National defence Gold Bonds, 1980, and any particulars relating to the Bonds subscribed to by him, shall be treated as confidential, and, notwith standing anything contained in any law for the time being in force, no court shall be entitled to require any public servant to disclose the name of such person or any such particulars or to give any evidence in respect thereof.

(b) No public servant shall disclose the name of the person subscribing to the National Defence Gold Bonds, 1980 or any particulars relating to the Bonds subscribed to by him, except to an officer employed in the execution of any of the Acts mentioned in sub-section (1) or the Wealth-tax Act, 1957 (27 of 1957) or to any officer appointed by the Comptroller and Auditor-General of India or the Central Board of Direct Taxes (constituted under the Central Boards of Revenue Act, 1963) (54 of 1963) to audit income-tax receipts or refunds.

(4) In this section-

(a) "gold" means sold, including its alloy, whether virgin, melted, re-melted, wrought or unwrought, in any shape or form, and includes any gold coin (whether legal tender or not), any ornament and any other article of gold;

(b) "public servant" includes an officer or other employee of the Reserve Bank of India, the State Bank of India or any subsidiary bank of the State Bank of India.

3. Repeal and saving.

(1) The Taxation Laws (Amendment and Miscellaneous Provisions) Ordinance, 1965 (5 of 1965) is, hereby repealed.

(2) Notwithstanding such repeal, anything done or any action taken under the said Ordinance shall be deemed to have been done or taken under this Act as if this Act had commenced on the 19th day of October, 1965.

□□□

49

The Taxation Laws (Amendment) Act, 2000

Act No. 1 of 2001 [4th January, 2001]

AN ACT further to amend the Finance Act, 2000 and the Income-tax Act, 1961.

Be it enacted by Parliament in the Fifty-first Year of the Republic of India as follows -

1. Short title. This Act may be called the Taxation Laws (Amendment) Act, 2000.

2. Amendment of section 2. In Section 2 of the Finance Act, 2000 (10.of 2000) (hereinafter referred to as the principal Act),-

(a) in sub-section (4), in clause (b), for the words "ten per cent", the words "eleven per cent" shall be substituted;

(b) in sub-section (6), in clause (b), for the words "ten per cent", the words "eleven per cent" shall be substituted;

(c) in sub-section (7), in clause (b) for the words "ten per cent", the words "eleven per cent" shall be substituted;

(d) in sub-section (8), in the third proviso, in clause (b), for the words "ten per cent", the words "eleven per cent" shall be substituted.

3. Amendment of First Schedule. In the First Schedule to the principal Act,-

(a) in Part II, under the heading "Surcharge on income-tax", in clause (b), for the words "ten per cent", the words "eleven per cent" shall be substituted;

(b) in Part III, in Paragraph E, under the heading "Surcharge on income-tax", for the words "ten per cent", the words "eleven per cent" shall be substituted.

4. Amendment of Section 234C. In section 234C of the Income-tax Act, 1961 (43 of 1961) (hereinafter referred to as the Income-tax Act), in sub-section (1), in clause (b), after the first proviso and before the Explanation, the following proviso shall be nserted, namely:

"PROVIDED FURTHER that nothing contained in this sub-section shall apply to any shortfall in the payment of the tax due on the returned income where such shortfall is on account of increase in the rate of surcharge under section 2 of the Finance Act, 200 (10 of 2000), as amended by the Taxation Laws (Amendment) Act, 2000, and the assessee has paid the amount of shortfall, on or before the 15th day of March, 2001 in respect of the instalment of advance tax due on the 15th day of June, 2000, the 15th day of September, 2000 and the 15th day of December, 2000."

5. Payment of surcharge. Notwithstanding anything contained in the Income-tax Act, the surcharge payable under section 2 of, and Part III of the First Schedule to, the principal Act, as amended by this Act -

(i) in the case of an assessee being a domestic company shall, in respect of the instalment of "advance tax" paid or payable on or before the 15th day of June, 2000, the 15th day of September, 2000 and the 15th day of December, 2000, be payable on or before the 15th day of March, 2001;

(ii) in any case in which income-tax has to be charged under section 175 or sub-section (2) of Section 176 of the said Act, shall be payable, in the case of an assessee being a domestic company, only where such income-tax is so charged after the date on hich this Act receives the assent of the President.

❒❒❒

50

The Taxation Laws (Amendment) Act, 2001

Act No. 4 of 2001 [20th March, 2001]

AN ACT further to amend the Finance Act, 2000 and the Income-tax Act, 1961.

Be it enacted by Parliament in the Fifty-second Year of the Republic of India as follows:-

1. Short title and commencement.

(1) This Act may be called the Taxation Laws (Amendment) Act, 2001.

(2) It shall be deemed to have come into force on the 3rd day of February, 2001.

2. Amendment of Section 2. In Section 2 of the Finance Act, 2000 (10 of 2000) (hereinafter referred to as the principal Act),-

(a) in sub-section (4),-

(i) in clause (a), for the words "ten per cent", the words "twelve per cent" shall be substituted;

(ii) in clause (b), for the words "eleven per cent", the words "thirteen per cent" shall be substituted;

(b) in sub-section (6),-

(i) in clause (a), for the words "ten per cent", the words "twelve per cent" shall be substituted;

(ii) in clause (b), for the words "eleven per cent", the words "thirteen per cent" shall be substituted;

(c) in sub-section (7),-

(i) in clause (a), for the words "ten per cent", the words "twelve per cent" shall be substituted;

(ii) in clause (b), for the words "eleven per cent", the words "thirteen per cent" shall be substituted;

(d) in sub-section (8), in the third proviso, in clause (a),-
  (i) in sub-clause (i), for the words "ten per cent", the words "twelve per cent" shall be substituted;
  (ii) in sub-clause (ii),-
    (A) in item (A), for the words "ten per cent", the words "twelve per cent" shall be substituted;
    (B) in item (B), for the words "fifteen per cent", the words "seventeen per cent" shall be substituted;

(e) in sub-section (8), in the third proviso, in clause (b), for the words "eleven per cent", the words "thirteen per cent" shall be substituted;

(f) in sub-section (9), in the proviso,-
  (i) in clause (a),-
    (A) in sub-clause (i), for the words "ten per cent", the words "twelve per cent" shall be substituted;
    (B) in sub-clause (ii), for the words "fifteen per cent", the words "seventeen per cent" shall be substituted;
  (ii) in clause (b), for the words "ten per cent", the words "twelve per cent" shall be substituted.

3. Amendment of the First Schedule. In the First Schedule to the principal Act,-

(a) in Part II, under the heading Surcharge on income-tax,-
  (i) in item (a), for the words "ten per cent", the words" twelve per cent" shall be substituted;
  (ii) in item (b), for the words "eleven per cent", the words" thirteen per cent" shall be substituted;

(b) in Part III, in Paragraph A, under the heading Surcharge on income-tax,-
  (i) in item (i),-
    (A) in sub-item (A), for the words "ten per cent", the words "twelve per cent" shall be substituted;
    (B) in sub-item (B), for the words "fifteen per cent", the words "seventeen per cent" shall be substituted;
  (ii) in item (ii), for the words "ten per cent", the words "twelve per cent" shall be substituted;

(c) in Part III, in Paragraph B, under the heading Surcharge on income-tax, for the words "ten per cent", the words "twelve per cent" shall be substituted;

(d) in Part III, in Paragraph C, under the heading Surcharge on income-tax, for the words "ten per cent", the words "twelve per cent" shall be substituted;

(e) in Part III, in Paragraph D, under the heading Surcharge on income-tax, for the words "ten per cent", the words "twelve per cent" shall be substituted;

(f) in Part III, in Paragraph E, under the heading Surcharge on income-tax, for the words "eleven per cent", the words "thirteen per cent" shall be substituted.

4. Amendment of Section 10. In Section 10 of the Income-tax Act, 1961 (43 of 1961) (hereinafter referred to as the Income-tax Act), in clause (23C), after the eighth proviso, the following proviso shall be inserted, namely:-

> *"PROVIDED ALSO that any amount of donation received by the fund or institution in terms of clause (d) of sub-section (2) of Section 80G which has been utilised for purposes other than providing relief to the victims of earthquake in Gujarat or which rema ns unutilised in terms of sub-section (5C) of Section 80G and not transferred to the Prime Minister' s National Relief Fund on or before the 31st day of March, 2002 shall be deemed to be the income of the previous year and shall accordingly be charged to tax".*

5. Amendment of Section 12. In Section 12 of the Income-tax Act, after sub-section (2) and the Explanation thereto, the following sub-section shall be inserted, namely:- "(3) Notwithstanding anything contained in Section 11, any amount of donation received by the trust or institution in terms of clause (d) of sub-section (2) of Section 80G which has been utilised for purposes other than providing relief to the victims of earthquake in Gujarat or which remains unutilised in terms of sub-section (5C) of Section 80G and not transferred to the Prime Minister's National Relief Fund on or before the 31st day of March, 2002 shall be deemed to be the income of the previous year and shall accordingly be charged to tax".

6. Amendment of Section 80G. In Section 80G of the Income-tax Act -

(a) in sub-section (1), in clause (i) -

  (i) after the words, brackets, figures and letter "or in sub-clause (iiig)", the words, brackets, figures and letters "or in sub-clause (iiiga)" shall be inserted;

  (ii) after the words, brackets and letter "or in clause (c)", the words, brackets and letter "or in clause (d)" shall be inserted;

(b) in sub-section (2) -

  (i) in clause (a), after sub-clause (iiig), the following sub-clause shall be inserted, namely:

  "(iiiga) any fund set up by the State Government of Gujarat exclusively for providing relief to the victims of earthquake in Gujarat";

  (ii) after clause (c), the following clause shall be inserted, namely:

  "(d) any sums paid by the assessee, during the period beginning on the 26th day of January, 2001 and ending on the 30th day of September, 2001, to any trust, institution or fund to which this Section applies for providing relief to the victims of earthq ake in Gujarat";

(c) after sub-section (5B), the following sub-section shall be inserted, namely: "(5C) This sub-section applies in relation to amounts referred to in clause (d) of sub-section (2) only if the trust or institution or fund is established in India for a charitable purpose and it fulfills the following conditions, namely:

  (i) it is approved in terms of clause (vi) of sub-section (5);

  (ii) it maintains separate accounts of income and expenditure for providing relief to the victims of earthquake in Gujarat;

(iii) the donations made to the trust or institution or fund are applied only for providing relief to the earthquake victims of Gujarat on or before the 31st day of March, 2002 ;

(iv) the amount of donation remaining unutilised on the 31st day of March, 2002 is transferred to the Prime Minister' s National Relief Fund on or before the 31st day of March, 2002 ;

(v) it renders accounts of income and expenditure to such authority and in such manner as may be prescribed, on or before the 30th day of June, 2002."

7. Amendment of Section 234C. In Section 234C of the Income-tax Act, in sub-section 1, after the second proviso, the following proviso shall be inserted, namely:

"PROVIDED ALSO that nothing contained in this sub-section shall apply to any shortfall in the payment of the tax due on the returned income where such shortfall is on account of increase in the rate of surcharge under Section 2 of the Finance Act, 2000 (10 of 2000) as amended by the Taxation Laws (Amendment) Act, 2001 and the assessee has paid the amount of shortfall on or before the 15th day of March, 2001 in respect of the instalment of advance tax due on the 15th day of June, 2000, the 15th day of September, 2000 and 15th day of December, 2000".

8. Instalment of advance tax in case of additional surcharge, payable on 15th March, 2001. Notwithstanding anything contained in the Income-tax Act, the surcharge payable under Section 2 of, and Part III of the First Schedule to, the principal Act, as ammended by this Act -

(i) in the case of an assessee, in respect of the instalment of "advance tax" paid or payable on or before the 15th day of June, 2000, the 15th day of September, 2000 and the 15th day of December, 2000, shall be payable on or before the 15th day of March 2001;

(ii) in any case in which income-tax has to be charged under sub-section (4) of Section 172 or sub-section (2) of Section 174 or Section 175 or sub-section (2) of Section 176 of the Income-tax Act, shall be payable, only where such income-tax is so charg d after the date on which this Act comes into force.

9. Repeal and saving.

(1) The Taxation Laws (Amendment) Ordinance, 2001 (Ord. 2 of 2001) is hereby repealed.

(2) Notwithstanding such repeal, anything done or any action taken under the said Ordinance shall be deemed to have been done or taken under the corresponding provisions of this Act.

❑❑❑

51

The Taxation Laws (Amendment) Act, 2003

ACT NO. 54 OF 2003 [30TH DECEMBER, 2003]

AN ACT further to amend the Income-tax Act, 1961, the Wealth-tax Act, 1957 and the Expenditure-tax Act, 1987.

Be it enacted by Parliament in the Fifty-fourth Year of the Republic of India as follows:

CHAPTER - I : PRELIMINARY

1. Short title and commencement.

(1) This Act may be called the Taxation Laws (Amendment) Act, 2003.

(2) Save as otherwise provided in this Act, it shall be deemed to have come into force on the 8th day of September, 2003.

CHAPTER - II : AMENDMENTS TO THE INCOME-TAX ACT, 1961

2. Amendment of Section 10. In Section 10 of the Income-tax Act, 1961 (43 of 1961) (hereafter in this Chapter referred to as the Income-tax Act), in clause (15),-

(A) after sub-clause (iiia), the following sub-clause shall be inserted and shall be deemed to have been inserted with effect from the 1st day of April, 2001, namely:-

"(iiib) interest payable to the Nordic Investment Bank, being a multilateral financial institution constituted by the Governments of Denmark, Finland, Iceland, Norway and Sweden, on a loan advanced by it to a project approved by the Central Government in terms of the Memorandum of Understanding entered into by the Central Government with that Bank on the 25th day of November, 1986 ";

(B) in sub-clause (iv) -

(a) in item (c), the existing Explanation shall be numbered as Explanation 1 thereof and after Explanation 1 as so numbered, the following Explanation shall be inserted and shall be deemed to have been inserted with effect from the 1st day of April, 1962, namely:

"*EXPLANATION 2* - For the removal of doubts, it is hereby declared that the usance interest payable outside India by an undertaking engaged in the business of ship-breaking in respect of purchase of a ship from outside India shall be deemed to be the interest payable on a debt incurred in a foreign country in respect of the purchase outside India";

(b) in the Explanation 1 occurring below item (i), after clause (d), the following clause shall be inserted and shall be deemed to have been inserted with effect from the 1st day of April, 1991, namely:

"(da) the business of ship-breaking".

3. Insertion of new Section 10BA. After Section 10B of the Income-tax Act, the following Section shall be inserted with effect from the 1st day of April, 2004, namely:-

Special provisions in respect of export of certain articles or things -

(1) Subject to the provisions of this Section, a deduction of such profits and gains as are derived by an undertaking from the export out of India of eligible articles or things, shall be allowed from the total income of the assessee:

PROVIDED that where in computing the total income of the undertaking for any assessment year, deduction under Section 10A or Section 10B has been claimed, the undertaking shall not be entitled to the deduction under this Section:

PROVIDED FURTHER that no deduction under this Section shall be allowed to any undertaking for the assessment year beginning on the 1st day of April, 2010 and subsequent years.

(2) This Section applies to any undertaking which fulfils the following conditions, namely:-

(a) it manufactures or produces the eligible articles or things without the use of imported raw materials;

(b) it is not formed by the splitting up, or the reconstruction, of a business already in existence: Provided that this condition shall not apply in respect of any undertaking which is formed as a result of the re-establishment, reconstruction or revival by the assessee of the business of any such undertaking as is referred to in Section 33B, in the circumstances and within the period specified in that Section;

(c) it is not formed by the transfer to a new business of machinery or plant previously used for any purpose.

EXPLANATION. The provisions of Explanation 1 and Explanation 2 to sub-section (2) of Section 80-I shall apply for the purposes of this clause as they apply for the purposes of clause (ii) of sub-section (2) of that Section;

(d) ninety percent or more of its sales during the previous year relevant to the assessment year are by way of exports of the eligible articles or things;

(e) it employs twenty or more workers during the previous year in the process of manufacture or production.

(3) This Section applies to the undertaking, if the sale proceeds of the eligible articles or things exported out of India are received in or brought into, India by the assessee in convertible foreign exchange, within a period of six months from the end of the previous year or, within such further period as the competent authority may allow in this behalf.

EXPLANATION. For the purposes of this sub-section, the expression" competent authority" means the Reserve Bank of India or such other authority as is authorised under any law for the time being in force for regulating payments and dealings in foreign exchange.

(4) For the purposes of sub-section (1), the profits derived from export out of India of the eligible articles or things shall be the amount which bears to the profits of the business of the undertaking, the same proportion as the export turnover in respect of such articles or things bears to the total turnover of the business carried on by the undertaking.

(5) The deduction under sub-section (1) shall not be admissible, unless the assessee furnishes in the prescribed form, along with the return of income, the report of an accountant, as defined in the Explanation below sub-section (2) of Section 288, certifying that the deduction has been correctly claimed in accordance with the provisions of this Section.

(6) Notwithstanding anything contained in any other provision of this Act, where a deduction is allowed under this Section in computing the total income of the assessee, no deduction shall be allowed under any other Section in respect of its export profits.

(7) The provisions of sub-section (8) and sub-section (10) of Section 80-IA shall, so far as may be, apply in relation to the undertaking referred to in this Section as they apply for the purposes of the undertaking referred to in Section 80-IA.

EXPLANATION. For the purposes of this Section -

(a) "convertible foreign exchange" means foreign exchange which is for the time being treated by the Reserve Bank of India as convertible foreign exchange for the purposes of the Foreign Exchange Management Act, 1999 (42 of 1999), and any rules made thereunder or any other corresponding law for the time being in force;

(b) "eligible articles or things" means all hand-made articles or things, which are of artistic value and which requires the use of wood as the main raw material;

(c) "export turnover" means the consideration in respect of export by the undertaking of eligible articles or things received in, or brought into, India by the assessee in convertible foreign exchange in accordance with sub-section (3), but does not include freight, telecommunication charges or insurance attributable to the delivery of the articles or things outside India;

(d) "export out of India" shall not include any transaction by way of sale or otherwise, in a shop, emporium or any other establishment situate in India, not involving clearance of any customs station as defined in the Customs Act, 1962 (52 of 1962).'.

4. Amendment of Section 115P. In Section 115P of the Income-tax Act, for the words "one and one-fourth percent", the words "one percent" shall be substituted.

5. Amendment of Section 115S. In Section 115S of the Income-tax Act, for the words "one and one-fourth percent", the words "one percent" shall be substituted.

6. Amendment of Section 132B. In Section 132B of the Income-tax Act, in sub-section (4), in clause (a), for the words "eight percent", the words "six percent" shall be substituted.

7. Amendment of Section 158BFA. In Section 158BFA of the Income-tax Act, in sub-section 1, for the words "one and one-fourth percent", the words "one percent" shall be substituted.

8. Amendment of Section 201. In Section 201 of the Income-tax Act, in sub-section (1A), for the words "fifteen percent", the words "twelve percent" shall be substituted.

9. Amendment of Section 206C. In Section 206C of the Income-tax Act,-

(a) in sub-section (1),-

(i) for the Table, the following Table shall be substituted, namely:-

"TABLE Sl. No. Nature of goods Percentage (i) Alcoholic liquor for human consumption One percent (ii) Tendu leaves Five percent (iii) Timber obtained under a forest lease Two and one-half percent (iv) Timber obtained by any mode other than Two and one-half percent under a forest lease (v) Any other forest produce not being timber Two and one-half percent or tendu leaves (vi) Scrap One percent:";

(ii) for the proviso below the Table, the following proviso shall be substituted, namely:-

"PROVIDED that every person, being a seller shall at the time, during the period beginning on the 1st day of June, 2003 and ending on the day immediately preceding the date on which the Taxation Laws (Amendment) Act, 2003 comes into force, of debiting of the amount payable by the buyer to the account of the buyer or of receipt of such amount from the said buyer in cash or by the issue of a cheque or draft or by any other mode, whichever is earlier, collect from the buyer of any goods of the nature specified in column (2) of the Table as it stood immediately before the 1st day of June, 2003, a sum equal to the percentage, specified in the corresponding entry in column (3) of the said Table, of such amount as income-tax in accordance with the provisions of this Section as they stood immediately before the 1st day of June, 2003";

(b) after sub-section (1), the following sub-sections shall be inserted, namely :

"(1A) Notwithstanding anything contained in sub-section (1), no collection of tax shall be made in the case of a buyer, who is resident in India, if such buyer furnishes to the person responsible for collecting tax, a declaration in writing in duplicate in the prescribed form and verified in the prescribed manner to the effect that the goods referred to in column (2) of the aforesaid Table are to be utilised for the purposes of manufacturing, processing or producing articles or things and not for trading purposes.

(1B) The person responsible for collecting tax under this Section shall deliver or cause to be delivered to the Chief Commissioner or Commissioner one copy of the declaration referred to in sub-section (1A) on or before the seventh day of the month next following the month in which the declaration is furnished to him";

(c) in sub-section (3), for the words "seven days", the words "the prescribed time" shall be substituted;

(d) in sub-section (5), for the words "ten days from the date of debit", the words "such period as may be prescribed from the time of debit" shall be substituted;

(e) in sub-section (7), for the words "one and one-fourth percent", the words "one percent" shall be substituted;

(f) in the Explanation occurring at the end, in clause (a), for sub-clauses (i) and (ii), the following sub-clauses shall be substituted, namely:-"(i) a public sector company, the Central Government, a State Government, and an embassy, a high commission, legation, commission, consulate and the trade representation, of a foreign State and a club; or (ii) a buyer in the retail sale of such goods purchased by him for personal consumption".

10. Amendment of Section 220. In Section 220 of the Income-tax Act, in sub-section (2), for the words "one and one-fourth percent", the words "one percent" shall be substituted.

11. Amendment of Section 230. In Section 230 of the Income-tax Act, in sub-section (2), after the word, brackets and figure" sub-section 1", the words, brackets, figure and letter" or the first proviso to sub-section (1A)" shall be inserted and shall be deemed to have been inserted with effect from the 1st day of June, 2003.

12. Amendment of Section 234A. In Section 234A of the Income-tax Act, in sub-sections (1) and (3), for the words "one and one-fourth percent", the words "one percent" shall be substituted.

13. Amendment of Section 234B. In Section 234B of the Income-tax Act, in sub-sections (1) and (3), for the words "one and one-fourth percent", the words "one percent" shall be substituted.

14. Amendment of Section 234C. In Section 234C of the Income-tax Act, in sub-section 1 -

(i) in clause (a), in sub-clauses (i) and (ii), for the words "one and one-fourth percent", the words "one percent" shall be substituted;

(ii) in clause (b), in sub-clauses (i) and (ii), for the words "one and one-fourth percent", the words "one percent" shall be substituted.

15. Amendment of Section 234D. In Section 234D of the Income-tax Act, in sub-section 1, for the words "two-third percent", the words "one-half percent" shall be substituted.

16. Amendment of Section 244A. In Section 244A of the Income-tax Act, in sub-section 1, in clauses (a) and (b), for the words "two-third percent", the words "one-half percent" shall be substituted.

17. Amendment of Section 272A. In Section 272A of the Income-tax Act, in sub-section (2), after clause (i), the following clause shall be inserted, namely :

"(j) to deliver or cause to be delivered in due time a copy of the declaration referred to in sub-section (1A) of Section 206C".

18. Amendment of Second Schedule. In the Second Schedule to the Income-tax Act, in Rule 68A, in sub-rule (3), for the words "eight percent", the words "six percent" shall be substituted.

CHAPTER - III : AMENDMENTS TO THE WEALTH-TAX ACT, 1957

19. Amendment of Section 17B. In Section 17B of the Wealth-tax Act, 1957 (27 of 1957) (hereafter in this Chapter referred to as the Wealth-tax Act), in sub-sections (1) and (3), for the words "one and one-fourth percent", the words "one percent" shall be substituted.

20. Amendment of Section 31. In Section 31 of the Wealth-tax Act, in sub-section (2)-

(a) for the words "one and one-fourth percent", the words "one percent" shall be substituted;

(b) in the second proviso, for the words "one and one-fourth percent", the words "one percent" shall be substituted.

21. Amendment of Section 34A. In Section 34A of the Wealth-tax Act -

(a) in sub-section (3), for the words "eight percent", the words "six percent" shall be substituted;

(b) in sub-section (4B), in clause (a), for the words "two-third percent", the words "one-half percent" shall be substituted.

CHAPTER - IV : AMENDMENT TO THE EXPENDITURE-TAX ACT, 1987

22. Amendment of Section 14 of Act 35 of 1987. In Section 14 of the Expenditure-tax Act, 1987 (35 of 1987), for the words "one and one-fourth percent", the words "one percent" shall be substituted.

23. Repeal and saving.

(1) The Taxation Laws (Amendment) Ordinance, 2003 is hereby repealed.

(2) Notwithstanding such repeal, anything done or any action taken under the Income-tax Act, 1961 (43 of 1961), the Wealth-tax Act, 1957 (27 of 1957) and

the Expenditure-tax Act, 1987 (35 of 1987), as amended by the said Ordinance shall be deemed to have been done or taken under the corresponding provisions of those Acts, as amended by this Act.

❑❑❑

52

The Taxation Laws (Amendment) Act, 2006

ACT NO. 29 OF 2006 [13TH JULY, 2006]

AN ACT further to amend the Income-tax Act, 1961, the Customs Act, 1962, the Customs Tariff Act, 1975 and the Central Excise Act, 1944.

Be it enacted by Parliament in the Fifty-seventh Year of the Republic of India as follows:

CHAPTER - I : PRELIMINARY

1. Short title. This Act may be called the Taxation Laws (Amendment) Act, 2006.

CHAPTER - II : DIRECT TAXES INCOME-TAX

2. Amendment of Section 2. In Section 2 of the Income-tax Act, 1961 (hereafter in this Chapter referred to as the Income-tax Act), in clause (44), after the words "powers of a Tax Recovery Officer", the following shall be inserted, namely:-

"and also to exercise or perform such powers and functions which are conferred on, or assigned to, an Assessing Officer under this Act and which may be prescribed".

3. Amendment of Section 2. In Section 10 of the Income-tax Act, with effect from the 1st day of April, 2006 -

(a) after clause (23BBE), the following clause shall be inserted, namely :

"(23BBF) any income of the North-Eastern Development Finance Corporation Limited, being a company formed and registered under the Companies Act, 1956:Provided that in computing the total income of the North-Eastern Development Finance Corporation Limited, the amount to the extent of-

(i) twenty percent of the total income for assessment year beginning on the 1st day of April, 2006;

(ii) forty percent of the total income for assessment year beginning on the 1st day of April, 2007;

(iii) sixty percent of the total income for assessment year beginning on the 1st day of April, 2008;

(iv) eighty percent of the total income for assessment year beginning on the 1st day of April, 2009;

(v) one hundred percent of the total income for assessment year beginning on the 1st day of April, 2010 and any subsequent assessment year or years,shall be included in such total income;";

(b) in clause (23C),-

(i) in the eighth proviso, for the words, brackets and letters "notification issued by the Central Government under sub-clause (iv) or sub-clause (v) shall, at any one time, have effect for such assessment year or years, not exceeding three assessment years", the words, brackets, figures and letters "notification issued by the Central Government under sub-clause (iv) or sub-clause (v), before the date on which the Taxation Laws (Amendment) Bill, 2006 receives the assent of the President, shall, at any one time, have effect for such assessment year or years, not exceeding three assessment years" shall be substituted;

(ii) after the eighth proviso, the following provisos shall be inserted, namely:-

"PROVIDED ALSO that where an application under the first proviso is made on or after the date on which the Taxation Laws (Amendment) Bill, 2006 receives the assent of the President, every notification under sub-clause (iv) or sub-clause (v) shall be issued or approval under sub-clause (vi) or sub-clause (via) shall be granted or an order rejecting the application shall be passed within the period of twelve months from the end of the month in which such application was received:

PROVIDED ALSO that where the total income, of the fund or trust or institution or any university or other educational institution or any hospital or other medical institution referred to in sub-clause (iv) or sub-clause (v) or sub-clause (vi) or sub-clause (via), without giving effect to the provisions of the said sub-clauses, exceeds the maximum amount which is not chargeable to tax in any previous year, such trust or institution or any university or other educational institution or any hospital or other medical institution shall get its accounts audited in respect of that year by an accountant as defined in the Explanation below sub-section (2) of Section 288 and furnish along with the return of income for the relevant assessment year, the report of such audit in the prescribed form duly signed and verified by such accountant and setting forth such particulars as may be prescribed."

❑❑❑

53

The Taxation Laws (Amendment) Act, 2007

ACT NO. 16 OF 2007 [26TH MARCH, 2007]

AN ACT further to amend the Central Sales Tax Act, 1956 and the Additional Duties of Excise (Goods of Special Importance) Act, 1957.

Be it enacted by Parliament in the Fifty-eighth Year of the Republic of India as follows:-

CHAPTER -I : PRELIMINARY

1. Short title and commencement.

(1) This Act may be called the Taxation Laws (Amendment) Act, 2007.

(2) It shall come into force on such date as the Central Government may, by notification in the Official Gazette, appoint.

CHAPTER - II : CENTRAL SALES TAX

2. Amendment of Section 6. In the Central Sales Tax Act, 1956 (hereinafter in this Chapter referred to as the principal Act), in Section 6, for sub-section (2), the following sub-section shall be substituted, namely :

"(2) Notwithstanding anything contained in sub-section (1) or sub-section (1A), where a sale of any goods in the course of inter-State trade or commerce has either occasioned the movement of such goods from one State to another or has been effected by a transfer of documents of title to such goods during their movement from one State to another, any subsequent sale during such movement effected by a transfer of documents of title to such goods to a registered dealer, if the goods are of the description referred to in sub-section (3) of Section 8, shall be exempt from tax under this Act:

PROVIDED that no such subsequent sale shall be exempt from tax under this sub-section unless the dealer effecting the sale furnishes to the prescribed authority in the prescribed manner and within the prescribed time or within such further time as that authority may, for sufficient cause, permit -

(a) *a certificate duly filled and signed by the registered dealer from whom the goods were purchased containing the prescribed particulars in a prescribed form obtained from the prescribed authority; and*

(b) *if the subsequent sale is made to a registered dealer, a declaration referred to in sub-section (4) of Section 8:*

PROVIDED FURTHER that it shall not be necessary to furnish the declaration referred to in clause (b) of the preceding proviso in respect of a subsequent sale of goods if -

(a) *the sale or purchase of such goods is, under the sales tax law of the appropriate State exempt from tax generally or is subject to tax generally at a rate which is lower than three percent or such reduced rate as may be notified by the Central Government, by notification in the Official Gazette, under sub-section (1) of Section 8 (whether called a tax or fee or by any other name); and*

(b) *the dealer effecting such subsequent sale proves to the satisfaction of the authority referred to in the preceding proviso that such sale is of the nature referred to in this sub-section".*

3. Amendment of Section 7. In Section 7 of the principal Act, in sub-section (2A), for the words, brackets, letter and figures "clause (a) of sub-section (4) of Section 8", the words, brackets and figures "sub-section (4) of Section 8" shall be substituted.

4. Amendment of Section 8. In Section 8 of the principal Act,-

(a) for sub-sections (1) and (2), the following sub-sections shall be substituted, namely:-

"(1) Every dealer, who in the course of inter-State trade or commerce, sells to a registered dealer goods of the description referred to in sub-section (3), shall be liable to pay tax under this Act, which shall be three percent of his turnover or at the rate applicable to the sale or purchase of such goods inside the appropriate State under the sales tax law of that State, whichever is lower:

PROVIDED that the Central Government may, by notification in the Official Gazette, reduce the rate of tax under this sub-section.

(2) The tax payable by any dealer on his turnover in so far as the turnover or any part thereof relates to the sale of goods in the course of inter-State trade or commerce not falling within sub-section (1), shall be at the rate applicable to the sale or purchase of such goods inside the appropriate State under the sales tax law of that State.

EXPLANATION: For the purposes of this sub-section, a dealer shall be deemed to be a dealer liable to pay tax under the sales tax law of the appropriate State, notwithstanding that he, in fact, may not be so liable under that law";

(b) in sub-section (3), in the opening portion, for the words, brackets, figure and letter "The goods referred to in clause (b) of sub-section (1)", the following shall be substituted, namely :

"The goods referred to in sub-section (1)";

(c) for sub-section (4), the following shall be substituted, namely :

"(4) The provisions of sub-section (1) shall not apply to any sale in the course of inter-State trade or commerce unless the dealer selling the goods furnishes to the prescribed authority in the prescribed manner a declaration duly filled and signed by the registered dealer to whom the goods are sold containing the prescribed particulars in a prescribed form obtained from the prescribed authority:

PROVIDED that the declaration is furnished within the prescribed time or within such further time as that authority may, for sufficient cause, permit.";

(d) in sub-section (5), in clauses (a) and (b), the words "or the Government" and the words, brackets and figure "or sub-section (2)", wherever they occur, shall be omitted.

5. Amendment of Section 9. In Section 9 of the principal Act, in sub-section (1), in the proviso, in clause (a), for the words, letter, brackets and figures "clause (a) of sub-section (4) of Section 8", the words, brackets and figures "sub-section (4) of Section 8" shall be substituted.

6. Amendment of Section 10. In Section 10 of the principal Act, in clause (a), the words "certificate or" shall be omitted.

7. Amendment of Section 10A. In Section 10A of the principal Act, in sub-section (2), in clause (a), for the words, letter, brackets and figures "clause (a) of sub-section (4) of Section 8", the words, brackets and figures "sub-section (4) of Section 8" shall be substituted.

8. Amendment of Section 14. In Section 14 of the principal Act, clause (ix) shall be omitted.

CHAPTER -III : ADDITIONAL DUTIES OF EXCISE

9. Omission of Section 4. In the Additional Duties of Excise (Goods of Special Importance) Act, 1957 (hereinafter referred to as the Additional Duties of Excise Act), Section 4 shall be omitted.

10. Amendment of First Schedule. In the Additional Duties of Excise Act, in the First Schedule, headings 2401, 2402 and 2403, and sub-headings and tariff items thereunder, and the entries relating thereto shall be omitted.

11. Omission of Second Schedule. In the Additional Duties of Excise Act, the Second Schedule shall be omitted.

❏❏❏

54

The Taxation Laws (Continuation and Validation of Recovery Proceedings) Act, 1964

AN ACT to provide for the continuation and Validation of proceedings in relation to Government dues and for matters connected therewith.

Be it enacted by Parliament in the Fifteenth Year of the Republic of India as follows:-

1. Short title. This Act may be called the Taxation Laws (Continuation. and Validation of Recovery Proceedings) Act, 1964.

2. Definitions. In this Act, unless the context otherwise requires,-

(a) "assessee:, in relation to-

(i) the Excess Profits Tax Act, 1940, (15 of 1940) or the Business Profits Tax Act, 1947, (21 of 1947) means a person by whom the tax or any other sum is payable under that Act;

(ii) the Estate Duty Act, 1953, (34 of 1953) means a person accountable or an accountable person as defined in that Act;

(iii) any other scheduled Act, means an assessee as defined in that Act;

(b) "Government dues", in relation to any scheduled Act, means any tax, duty, penalty, fine, interest, annuity deposit or any other sum payable to the Government by an assessee under that Act;

(c) "scheduled, Act" means an Act specified in the Schedule;

(d) "Taxing Authority" in relation to any scheduled Act, means an officer (by whatever name called) empowered to serve upon an assessee a notice of demand in respect of any Government dues under that Act;

(e) "Tax Recovery Officer", in relation to any scheduled Act, means a Tax Recovery-Officer as defined in that Act and where there is no such definition, means an officer (by whatever name called) to whom a certificate for the recovery of arrears of Government dues may be issued under that Act.

3. Continuation and validation of certain proceedings.

(1) Where any notice of demand in respect of any Government dues is served upon an assessee by a Taxing Authority under any scheduled Act, and any appeal or other proceeding is filed or taken in respect of such Government dues, then -

(a) where such Government dues are enhanced in such appeal or proceeding, the Taxing Authority shall serve upon the assessee another notice of demand only in respect of the amount by which such Government dues are enhanced and any proceedings in relation to such Government dues as are covered by the notice or notices of demand served upon him before the disposal of such appeal or proceeding may, without the service of any fresh notice of demand, be continued from the stage at which such proceedings stood immediately before such disposal;

(b) where such Government dues are reduced in such appeal or proceeding -

(i) it shall not be necessary for the Taxing Authority to serve upon the assessee a fresh notice of demand ;

(ii) the Taxing Authority shall give intimation of the fact of such reduction to the assessee, and where a certificate has been issued to the Tax Recovery Officer for the recovery of such amount, also to that officer;

(iii) any proceedings initiated on the basis of the notice or notices of demand served upon the assessee before the disposal of such appeal or proceeding may be continued in relation to the amount so reduced from the stage at which such proceedings stood immediately before such disposal ;

(c) no proceedings in relation to such Government dues (including the imposition of penalty or charging of interest) shall be invalid by reason only that no fresh notice of demand was served upon the assessee after the disposal of such appeal or proceeding or that such Government dues have been enhanced or reduced in such appeal or proceeding:

PROVIDED that if as a result of any final order such Government dues (other than annuity deposit) have been reduced and the penalty imposed on the assessee for default in payment thereof exceeds the amount so reduced, the excess shall not be recovered and if it has already been recovered, it shall be refunded to the assessee on an application made by him to the Taxing Authority Within such time and in such manner as may be prescribed by rules made under this Act:

PROVIDED FURTHER that if the amount of penalty imposed on the assessee for failure to make any annuity deposit exceeds one-half of the amount of the annuity deposit required to be made as a result of such order, the excess shall not be recovered, and if it has already been recovered, shall be refunded to the assessee on an application made by him to the Taxing Authority within such time and in such manner as may be prescribed by rules made under this Act ;

PROVIDED FURTHER that where any Government dues are reduced in such appeal or proceeding and the assessee is entitled to any refund thereof, such refund shall be made in accordance with the provisions of that Act,

(2) For the removal of doubts, it is hereby declared that no fresh notice of demand shall be necessary in any case where the amount of Government dues is not varied as a result of any order passed in any appeal or other proceeding under any scheduled Act.

(3) The provisions of this section shall have effect notwithstandIng any judgment, decree or order of any court, tribunal or other authority.

4. Power to amend the Schedule. The Central Government may, by notification in the Official Gazette, add the name of any Central Act providing for the imposition or levy of an tax or duty in the Schedule and on the issue of any such notification, the Act so added shall be deemed to be an Act specified in the Schedule within the meaning of clause (c) of Section 2.

5. Act to have retrospective effect. The provisions of this Act shall apply and shall be deemed always to have applied, in relation. to every notice of demand served upon an assessee by any Taxing Authority under any scheduled Act whether such notice was or is served before or after the commencement of this Act.

6. Power to remove difficulties. If any difficulty arises in giving effect to the provisions of this Act, the Central Government may, by order published in the Official Gazette, make such provisions not inconsistent with the purposes of this Act, as appear to it to be necessary or expedient for removing the difficulty.

7. Power to make rules.

(1) The Central Government may by notification in the Official Gazette make rules for carrying out the purposes of this Act.

(2) Every rule made under this Act shall be laid as soon as may be after it is made, before each House of Parliament while it is in session for a total period of thirty days which may be comprised in one session or 1[in two or more successive sessions, and if, before the expiry of the session immediately following the session or the successive sessions aforesaid" both Houses agree in making any modification in the rule or both Houses agree that the rule should not be made, that rule shall thereafter have effect, only in such modified form or be of no effect, as the case. may be, so however that any such modification or annulment shall be without prejudice to the validity of anything previously done under that rule.

THE SCHEDULE
[*See* Section 2(c)]

1. The Indian Income-tax Act, 1922 (11 of 1922).
2. The Excess Profits Tax Act, 1940 (15 of 1940).
3. The Business Profits Tax Act, 1947 (21 of 1947).
4. The Estate Duty Act, 1953 (34 of 1953).
5. The Wealth-tax Act, 1957 (27 of 1957).
6. The Expenditure-tax Act, 1957 (29 of 1957).
7. The Gift-tax Act, 1958 (18 of 1958).
8. The Income-tax Act, 1961 (43 of 1961).
9. The Super Profits Tax Act, 1963 (14 of 1963).
10. The Companies (Profits) Surtax Act, 1964 (7 of 1964).

❑❑❑

55

The Tobacco Cess Act, 1975

ACT NO. 26 OF 1975 [12TH MAY, 1975]

AN ACT to provide for the Levy and collection, by way of cess, of a duty of excise on virginia tobacco and a duty of customs on tobacco, for the development of tobacco industry and for matters connected therewith.

Be it enacted by Parliament in the Twenty-sixth Year of the Republic of India as follows :

2. Definitions.

(1) In this Act, unless the context otherwise requires -

(a) "Board" means the Tobacco Board established under Section 4 of the Tobacco Board Act, 1975 (4 of 1975);

(b) "Prescribed" means prescribed by rules made under this Act;

(c) "Registered auction platform" means an auction platform registered with the Board in accordance with the rules made under the Tobacco Board Act, 1975 (4 of 1975).

(2) All words and expressions used in this Act and not defined, but defined in the Tobacco Board Act, 1975 (4 of 1975), shall have the meanings respectively assigned to them in that Act.

3. Duties of excise on virginia tobacco.

(1) There shall be levied and collected, by way of a cess for the purposes of the Tobacco Board Act, 1975 (4 of 1975), a duty of excise at the rate of one paisa per kilogram on virginia tobacco which is produced in India and sold at a registered auction platform.

(2) The duty of excise levied under sub-section (1) shall be in addition to any cess or duty leviable on virginia tobacco under any other law for the time being in force.

(3) The duty of excise payable under sub-section (1) in respect of any virginia tobacco sold at a registered auction platform shall be payable by the seller thereof to the person or authority prescribed in respect of such platform.

(4) The person or authority prescribed in respect of a registered auction platform shall collect the duty of excise payable on virginia tobacco sold at such platform and pay the amount so collected to the Central Government in such manner and within such time as may be prescribed.

(5) If any duty of excise payable under this Section, or if any amount collected under this Section by way of such duty, has not been paid to the Central Government within the period prescribed under sub-section (4), the Central Government may recover such duty or amount in the same manner as an arrear of land revenue.

4. Duties of customs on tobacco.

(1) There shall be levied and collected, by way of a cess for the purposes of the Tobacco Board Act, 1975 (4 of 1975), a duty of customs at such rate not exceeding one per cent, *ad valorem*, as the Central Government may specify, by notification in the Official Gazette, on all tobacco, which is exported.

EXPLANATION: "Exported" means taken out of the India by land, sea or air.

(2) The duties of customs levied under Sub-section (1) shall be in addition to any cess or duty leviable on tobacco under any other law for the time being in force.

(3) The provisions of the Customs Act, 1962 (52 of 1962) and the rules and regulations made thereunder, including those relating to refunds and exemptions, from duty, shall, as far as may be, apply in relation to the levy and collection of the duty of customs leviable under sub-section (1) as they apply in relation to the levy and collection of duties of customs under that Act or those rules and regulations.

5. Crediting proceeds of duties to Consolidated Fund of India: The proceeds of the duties of excise and customs levied under Sections 3 and 4 respectively shall first be credited to the Consolidated Fund of India and the Central Government may, if Parliament, by appropriation made by law in this behalf, so provides, pay to the Board, from time to time, from out of proceeds, after deducting the expenses on collection, such sums of money as it may think fit for being utilised for the purposes of the Tobacco Board Act, 1975 (4 of 1975).

6. Penalty for evasion of duty of excise payable under Section 3: Whoever wilfully or intentionally evades or attempts to evade the payment of any duty of excise payable by him under Section 3, or the payment of any amount collected by way of duty under that Section shall be punishable with imprisonment for a term which may extend to six months, or with fine which may extend to one thousand rupees, or with both.

7. Offences by companies.

(1) Where an offence under this Act has been committed by a company, every person who, at the time the offence was committed, was in charge of, and was responsible to, the company for the conduct of the business of the company as

well as the company shall be deemed to be guilty of the offence and shall be liable to be proceeded against and punished accordingly:

PROVIDED that nothing contained in this sub-section shall render any such person liable to any punishment, if he proves that the offence was committed without his knowledge or that he exercised all due diligence to prevent the commission of such offence.

(2) Notwithstanding anything contained in sub-section (1),where an offence under this Act has been committed by a company and it is proved that the offence has been committed with the consent or connivance of, or is attributable to any neglect on the part of any, director, manager, secretary or other officer of the company, such director, manager, secretary or other officer shall also be deemed to be guilty of that offence and shall be liable to be proceeded against and punished accordingly.

EXPLANATION: For the purposes of this Section -

(a) "Company" means any body corporate and includes a firm or other association of individuals; and

(b) "Director", in relation to a firm, means a partner in the firm.

8. Jurisdiction of court. No court inferior to that of a Metropolitan Magistrate or a Magistrate of the first class shall try any offence punishable under this Act.

9. Previous sanction of Central Government. No prosecution for any offence punishable under this Act shall be instituted except with the previous sanction of the Central Government.

10. Protection of action taken in good faith. No, suit, prosecution or other legal proceeding shall lie against the Central Government or any officer or other employee of the Central Government or against the Board or any officer or employee of the Board for anything which is in good faith done or intended to be done under this Act or the rules made thereunder.

11. Power of Central Government to make rules.

(1) The Central Government may, by notification in the Official Gazette, make rules for carrying out the purposes of this Act.

(2) In particular and without prejudice to the generally of the foregoing power, such rules may provide for all or any of the following matters, namely :

(a) The assessment and collection of the duties of excise levied under Section 3 and the functions and powers which may be exercised and the duties which may be discharged in connection therewith by the Board or any officers or other employees of the Board;

(b) The persons or authorities who may collect of exercise under sub-sections (3) and (4) of Section 3, the time within which and the manner in which the proceeds of such duties of exercises shall be paid to the Central Government;

(c) The returns which the persons or authorities referred to in clause (b) shall furnish to the Central Government and the form and the manner in which and the intervals at which such returns shall be furnished;

(d) Any other matter which has to be, or may be, prescribed by, or provided for, by rules, under this Act.

(3) In making any rule under this Section, the Central Government may direct that a contravention thereof shall be punishable with imprisonment for a term which may extend to six months, or with fine which may extend to one thousand rupees, or with both, and in the case of a continuing contravention, with an additional fine which may extend to fifty rupees for every day during which such contravention after conviction for the first such contravention.

(4) Every rule made under this Section shall, be laid, as soon as may be after it is made, before each House of Parliament, while it is in session, for a total period of thirty days which may be comprised in one session or in two or more successive sessions, and if, before the expiry of the session immediately following the session or the successive sessions aforesaid, both Houses agree in making any modification in the rule, or both Houses agree that the rule should not be made, the rule shall thereafter have effect only in such modified form or be of no effect, as the case may be; so, however, that any such modification or annulment shall be without prejudice to the validity of anything previously done under that rule.

❑❑❑

56

The U.P. Sugarcane Cess (Validation) Act, 1961

ACT NO. 4 OF 1961 [21ST MARCH, 1961]

AN ACT to validate the imposition and collection of cesses on sugarcane under certain Acts of Uttar Pradesh.

Be it enacted by Parliament in the Twelfth Year of the Republic of India as follows:

1. Short title and commencement.

(1) This Act may be called the U.P. Sugarcane Cess (Validation) Act, 1961.

(2) It shall be deemed to have come into force on the 3rd day of February, 1961.

2. Definitions. In this Act,—

(a) "cess" means the cess payable under any State Act and includes any sum recoverable under any such Act by way of interest or penalty;

(b) "State Act" means any of the following Acts, namely:-

(i) The United Provinces Sugar Factories Control Act, 1938 (U.P. Act 1 of 1938).

(ii) The U.P. Sugarcane (Regulation of Supply and Pur-chase) Act, 1953 ; (U.P. Act XXIV of 1953) and

(iii) The U.P. Sugarcane Cess Act, 1956. (U. P. Act XXII of 1956.)

3. Validation of imposition and collection of cesses under State Acts during a period.

(1) Notwithstanding any judgment, decree or order of any court, all cesses imposed, assessed or collected or purporting to have been imposed, assessed or collected under any State Act before the 3rd day of February, 1961 shall be deemed to

have been validly imposed, assessed or collected in accordance with law, as if the provisions of the State Acts and of all notifications, orders and rules issued or made thereunder, insofar as such provisions relate to the imposition, assessment and collection of such cess had been included in and formed part of this Section and this Section had been in force at all material times when such cess was imposed, assessed or collected; and accordingly -

(a) no suit or other proceeding shall be maintained or continued in any court for the refund of any cess paid under any State Act;

(b) no court shall enforce a decree or order directing the refund of any cess paid under any State Act; and

(c) any cess imposed or assessed under any State Act before the 3rd day of February, 1961 but not collected before that date, may be recovered (after assessment of the cess, where necessary) in the manner provided under that Act.

(2) For the removal of doubts it is hereby declared that nothing in sub-section (1) shall be construed as preventing any person,-

(a) from questioning in accordance with the provisions of any State Act and rules made thereunder the assessment of any cess for any period, or

(b) from claiming refund of any cess paid by him in excess of the amount due from him under any State Act and the rules made thereunder.

4. Repeal. The U.P. Sugarcane Cess (Validation) Ordinance, 1961, (1 of 1961) is here by repealed.

❑❑❑

57

The U. P. Sugarcane Cess (Validation) Repeal Act, 2001

ACT NO. 17 OF 2001 [3RD AUGUST, 2001]

AN ACT to repeal the U.P. Sugarcane Cess (Validation) Act, 1961.

Be it enacted by Parliament in the Fifty-second Year of the Republic of India as follows:

1. Short title. This Act may be called the U.P. Sugarcane Cess (Validation) Repeal Act, 2001.

2. Repeal of Act 4 of 1961. The U.P. Sugarcane Cess (Validation) Act, 1961 is hereby repealed.

❐❐❐

58

The Union Duties of Excise (Distribution) Act, 1957

ACT NO. 55 OF 1957

This Act has been repealed by the Union Duties of Excise (Distribution) Act, 1962 (3 of 1962), s. 6 (w.e.f. Ist April, 1962).

59

The Union Duties of Excise (Electricity) Distribution Repeal Act, 2006

ACT NO. 30 OF 2006 [13TH JULY, 2006]

AN ACT to repeal the Union Duties of Excise (Electricity) Distribution Act, 1980.

Be it enacted by Parliament in the Fifty-seventh Year of the Republic of India as follows:

1. Short title. This Act may be called the Union Duties of Excise (Electricity) Distribution Repeal Act, 2006.

2. Repeal of Act 14 of 1980. The Union Duties of Excise (Electricity) Distribution Act, 1980 is hereby repealed.

3. Savings.

(1) The repeal by this Act of the repealed enactment shall not affect any other enactment in which the repealed enactment has been applied, incorporated or referred to; and this Act shall not affect the validity, invalidity, effect or consequences of anything already done or suffered, or any right, title, obligation or liability already acquired, accrued or incurred, or any remedy or proceedings in respect thereof, or any release or discharge of or from any debt, penalty, obligation, liability, claim or demand, or any indemnity already granted, or the proof of any past act or thing; nor shall this Act affect any principle or rule of law, or established jurisdiction, form or course of pleading, practice or procedure, or existing usage, custom, privilege, restriction, exemption, office or appointment, notwithstanding that the same respectively may have been in any manner affirmed or recognized or derived by, in or from the enactment hereby repealed; nor shall the repeal by this Act of the enactment revive or restore any

jurisdiction, office, custom, liability, right, title, privilege, restriction, exemption, usage, practice, procedure or other matter or thing not now existing or in force.

(2) ***10 of 1897.*** Sub-section (1) shall not be held to prejudice or affect the general application of Section 6 of the General Clauses Act, 1897 with regard to the effect of repeal of this Act.

❑❑❑

60

The Union Territories Taxation Laws (Amendment) Act, 1971

AN ACT further to amend certain taxation laws in the Union territories.

Be it enacted by Parliament in the Twenty- second Year of the Republic of India as follows:-

1. Short title, extent and commencement.

(1) This Act may be called the Union Territories Taxation Laws (Amendment) Act, 1971.

(2) It extends to all the Union Territories;

(3) It shall come into force on such date 1 as the Central Government may, by notification in the Official Gazette, appoint.

2. Amendment of certain taxation laws. The taxation laws as in force in each of the Union Territories mentioned in the Schedule, shall have effect subject to the amendments specified therein:

PROVIDED that any such Amendment of a taxation law relating to the imposition of tax on the sale or purchase of goods declared to be of special importance under section 14 of the Central Sales Tax Act, 1956, (74 of 1956) shall be subject to the condition that in no case the amount of tax together with surcharge payable in respect thereof under the said taxation law shall exceed the tax calculated at the maximum rate prescribed under clause (a) of Section 15 of the said Act.

3. Levy and collection of additional duty, tax or surcharge. Save as otherwise Provided, the additional duty or tax or surcharge leviable or chargeable under the relevant taxation law, amended as aforesaid, shall be levied and collected in the same manner as the duty or tax is levied and collected under the said taxation law and the provisions, of that taxation law and the rules thereunder, as far as may be applicable in this behalf, shall apply accordingly.

❏❏❏

61

The Voluntary Surrender of Salaries (Exemption from Taxation) Act 1950

ACT NO. 61 OF 1950

This Act has been repealed by the Voluntary Surrender of Salaries (Exemption from Taxation) Act, 1961 (46 of 1961), s. 5.

62

The Voluntary Surrender of Salaries (Exemption From Taxation) Act 1961

ACT NO. 46 OF 1961 [6TH DECEMBER, 1961]

AN ACT to provide for exempting from taxes on income a portion of the salary or allowances payable to any person who has in the public interest volunteered to forego it.

Be it enacted by Parliament in the Twelfth year of the Republic of India as follows:—

1. Short title. This Act may be called the Voluntary Surrender of Salaries (Exemption from Taxation) Act, 1961.

2. Exemption from taxes on income in respect of salaries surrendered in favour of Government. Notwithstanding anything contained in the Indian Income-tax Act, 1922 , (11 of 1922.) or in any other law for the time being in force relating to taxation on income, no income-tax or super-tax shall be payable by any person—

(a) where his salary is paid out of the Consolidated Fund of India or of the Consolidated Fund of a State, in respect of that part of the salary due to him for any period after the 31st day of March, 1961 which he has, by a declaration in writing, volunteered to forego in the public interest;

(b) in any other case, in respect of that part of the salary which is due to him for any period after the 31st day of March, 1961 which has been, in the public interest surrendered in favour of, and paid to, the Central Government in accordance with the rules made in this behalf by that Government; and such part of the salary shall not be included in his total income for the purposes of any law relating to taxation on income.

3. Provisions of Section 2 apply to allowances. The provision of Section 2 shall apply in relation to any allowances due to any such person as is referred to therein for any period after the 31st day of March, 1961 as they apply in relation to his salary.

4. Power to make rules.

(1) The Central Government may, by notification in the Official Gazette, make rules to carry out the purposes of this Act.

(2) Every rule made under this Section shall be laid as soon as may be after it is made before each House of Parliament while it is in session for a total period of thirty days which may be comprised in one session or [1][in two or more successive sessions, and if, before the expiry of the session immediately following the session or the successive sessions aforesaid] both Houses agree in making any modification in the rule or both Houses agree that the rule should not be made, the rule shall thereafter have effect only in such modified from or be of no effect, as the case may be; so however that any such modification or annulment shall be without prejudice to the validity of anything previously done under that rule.

5. (1) **Repeal.** The Voluntary Surrender of Salaries (Exemption from Taxation) Act, 1950 , (61 of 1950) is hereby repealed.

(2) Notwithstanding such repeal any declaration made under the said Act shall be deemed to be a declaration made for the purposes of this Act.

❑❑❑

63

The Wealth-Tax Act, 1957

Act No. 27 of 1957 [12th September, 1957]

AN ACT to provide for the levy of wealth-tax.

Be it enacted by Parliament in the Eighth Year of the Republic of India as follows:

CHAPTER - I : PRELIMINARY

1. Short title, extent and commencement.

(1) This Act may be called the Wealth-tax Act, 1957.

(2) It extends to the whole of India.

(3) It shall be deemed to have come into force on the 1st day of April, 1957.

2. Definitions. In this Act, unless the context otherwise requires,—

(a) "Appellate Assistant Commissioner"means a person empowered to exercise the functions of an Appellate Assistant Commissioner of Wealth-tax under Section 9;

(b) "Appellate Tribunal"means the Appellate Tribunal constituted under Section 252 of the Income-tax Act;

(c) "assessee"means a person by whom wealth-tax or any other sum of money is payable under this Act, and includes—

(i) every person in respect of whom any proceeding under this Act has been taken for the determination of wealth-tax payable by him or by any other person or the amount of refund due to him or such other person;

(ii) every person who is deemed to be an assessee under this Act;

(iii) every person who is deemed to be an assessee in default under this Act;

(ca) "assessment"includes re-assessment;

(d) "assessment year" means the period of twelve months commencing on the 1st day of April every year;

(e) "assets" includes property of every description, movable or immovable, but does not include,—

(1) in relation to the assessment year commencing on the 1st day of April, 1969 or any earlier assessment year—

(i) agricultural land and growing crops, grass or standing trees on such land;

(ii) any building owned or occupied by a cultivation of, or receiver of rent or revenue out of, agricultural land:

PROVIDED that the building is on or in the immediate vicinity of the land and is a building which the cultivator or the receiver of rent or revenue by reason of his connection with the land requires as a dwelling-house or a store-house or an outhouse;

(iii) animals;

(iv) a right to any annuity in any case where the terms and conditions relating thereto preclude the commutation of any portion thereof into a lump sum grant;

(v) any interest in property where the interest is available to an assessee for a period not exceeding six years from the date the interest vests in the assessee;

(2) in relation to the assessment year commencing on the 1st day of April, 1970 or any subsequent assessment year—

(i) animals;

(ii) a right to any annuity in any case where the terms and conditions relating thereto preclude the commutation of any portion thereof into a lump sum grant;

(iii) any interest in property where the interest is available to an assessee for a period not exceeding six years from the date the interest vests in the assesse:

PROVIDED that, in relation to the State of Jammu and Kashmir, this sub-clause shall have effect subject to the modification that for the assets specified in items (i) to (v);

(iii) of this sub-clause, the assets specified in items (i) to (v) of sub-clause (1) shall be substituted and the other provisions of this Act shall be construed accordingly;

(f) "Board" means the Central Board of Direct Taxes constituted under the Central Boards of Revenue Act 1963 (54 of 1963);

(g) "Commissioner" means a person empowered to exercise the functions of a Commissioner of Wealth-tax under Section 10;

(h) "company" means a company as defined in Section 3 of the Companies Act, 1956, (1 of 1956) and includes (i) a company within the meaning of any law in force in the State of Jammu and Kashmir relating to companies; (ii) a company incorporated outside India which has a place of business in India; and

(i) "executor" means an executor or administrator of the estate of a deceased person;

(j) "Income-tax Act" means the Income-tax Act, 1961 (43 of 1961);

(ha) "co-operative society" means a co-operative society registered under the Co-operative Societies Act, 1912 (2 of 1912) or under any other law for the time being in force in any State for the registration of co-operative societies;

(hb) "Director of Inspection" includes an Additional Director of Inspection, a Deputy Director of Inspection and an Assistant Director of Inspection;

(k) "Income-tax Officer" means a person appointed to be an Income-tax Officer under the Income-tax Act;

(l) "Inspecting Assistant Commissioner of Wealth-tax" means a person empowered to exercise the functions of an Inspecting Assistant Commissioner of Wealth-tax under Section 11;

(la) "Inspector of Wealth-tax" means an Inspector of Income-tax empowered to work as an Inspector of Wealth-tax under Section 11A;

(lb) "legal representative" has the meaning assigned to it in clause (11) of Section 2 of the Code of Civil Procedure, 1908 (5 of 1908);

(m) "net wealth" means the amount by which the aggregate value computed in accordance with the provisions of this Act of all the assets, wherever located, belonging to the assessee on the valuation date, including assets required to be included in his net wealth as on that date under this Act, is in excess of the aggregate value of all the debts owed by the assessee on the valuation date other than —

(i) debts which under Section 6 are not to be taken into account;

(ii) debts which are secured on, or which have been incurred in relation to, any property in respect of which wealth-tax is not chargeable] under this Act; and

(iii) the amount of the tax, penalty or interest payable in consequence of any order passed under or in pursuance of this Act or any law relating to taxation of income or profits, or the Estate Duty Act, 1953, (34 of 1953) the Expenditure-tax Act, 1957, (29 of 1957) or the Gift-tax Act, 1958, (18 of 1958) -

(a) which is outstanding on the valuation date and is claimed by the assessee in appeal, revision or other proceeding as not being payable by him, or

(b) which, although not claimed by the assessee as not being payable by him, is nevertheless outstanding for a period of more than twelve months on the valuation date;

(n) "prescribed" means prescribed by rules made under this Act;

(o) "principal officer", used with reference to a company, means the secretary, manager, managing agent or managing director of the company, and includes any person connected with the management of the affairs of the company upon whom the Wealth-tax Officer has served a notice of his intention of treating him as the principal officer thereof;

(oa) "public servant" has the same meaning as in Section 21 of the Indian Penal Code; (45 of 1860);

(ob) "regular assessment" means the assessment made under Section 16;

(p) "Ruler" means a Ruler as defined in clause (22) of article 366 of the Constitution;

(q) "valuation date", in relation to any year for which an assessment is to be made under this Act, means the last day of the previous year as defined in Section 3 of the Income-tax Act if an assessment were to be made under that Act for that year:

PROVIDED that —

(i) where in the case of an assessee there are different previous years under the Income-tax Act for different sources of income, the valuation date for the purposes of this Act shall be the last day of the last of the previous years aforesaid;

(ii) in the case of a person who is not an assessee within the meaning of the Income-tax Act, the valuation date for the purposes of this Act shall be the 31st day of March immediately preceding the assessment year;

(iii) where an assessment is made in pursuance of Section 19A, the valuation date shall be the same valuation date as would have been adopted in respect of the net wealth of the deceased if he were alive;

(r) "valuer" means a valuer appointed under Section 4 of the Estate Duty Act, 1953 (34 of 1953);

(s) "Wealth-tax Officer" means the Income-tax Officer authorised to perform the functions of a Wealth-tax Officer under this Act.

CHAPTER - II : CHARGE OF WEALTH-TAX AND ASSETS SUBJECT TO SUCH CHARGE

3. Charge of wealth tax. Subject to the other provisions contained in this Act, there shall be charged for every assessment year commencing on and from the first day of April, 1957, a tax (hereinafter referred to as wealth-tax) in respect of the net wealth on the corresponding valuation date of every individual, Hindu undivided family and company at the rate or rates specified in the Schedule.

4. Net wealth to include certain assets.

(1) In computing the net wealth of an individual, there shall be included, as belonging to that individual—

(a) the value of assets which on the valuation date are held—

(i) by the spouse of such individual to whom such assets have been transferred by the individual, directly or indirectly, otherwise than for adequate consideration or in connection with an agreement to live apart, or

(ii) by a minor child, not being a married daughter, of such individual, to whom such assets have been transferred by the individual, directly or indirectly, otherwise than for adequate consideration, or

(iii) by a person or association of persons to whom such assets have been transferred by the individual otherwise than for adequate consideration for the immediate or deferred benefit of the individual, his or her spouse or minor child (not being a married daughter) or both, or]

(iv) by a person or association of persons to whom such assets have been transferred by the individual otherwise than under an irrevocable transfer, whether the assets referred to in any of the sub-clauses aforesaid are held in the form in which they were transferred or otherwise:

PROVIDED that where the transfer of such assets or any part thereof is either chargeable to gift-tax under the Gift-taxt Act, 1958 (18 of 1958) or is not chargeable under Section 5 of that Act, for any assessment year commencing after the 31st day of March, 1964, but before the 1st day of April, 1972, the value of such assets or part thereof, as the case may be, shall not be included in computing the net wealth of the individual;

(b) where the assessee is a partner in a firm or a member of an association of persons (not being a co-operative housing society)] the value of his interest in the firm or association determined in the prescribed manner.

(1A) Where, in the case of an individual being a member of a Hindu undivided family, any property having been the separate property of the individual has, at any time after the 31st day of December, 1969, been converted by the individual into property belonging to the family through the act of impressing such separate property with the character of property belonging to the family or throwing it into the common stock of the family (such property being hereinafter referred to as the converted property), then, notwithstanding anything contained in any other provision of this Act or in any other law for the time being in force, for the purpose of computing the net wealth of the individual under this Act for any assessment year commencing on or after the 1st day of April, 1972,

(a) the individual shall be deemed to have transferred the converted property, through the family, to the members of the family for being held by them jointly;

(b) the converted property or any part thereof, insofar as it is attributable to the interest of the individual in the property of the family, shall be deemed to be assets belonging to the individual and not to the family;

(c) any part of the converted property insofar as it is attributable to the interest of the spouse or any minor child of the individual in the property of the family and where there is a partition (partial or total) amongst the members of the family, the converted property or any part thereof which is received by the spouse or minor child on such partition shall be deemed to be assets transferred indirectly by the individual to the spouse or minor child and the provisions of sub-section (1) shall, so far as may be, apply accordingly:

PROVIDED that the property referred to in clause (b) or clause (c) shall, on being included in the net wealth of the individual, be excluded from the net wealth of the family or, as the case may be, the spouse or minor child of the individual.

(2) In making any rules with reference to the valuation of the interest referred to in clause (b) of sub-section (1), the Board shall have regard to the law for the time being in force relating to the manner in which accounts are to be settled between partners of a firm and members of an association on the dissolution of a firm or association, as the case may be.

(3) Where the value of any assets is to be included in the net wealth of an assessee in accordance with clause (a) of sub-section (1), there shall be deducted from such value any debts owing on the valuation date by the transferee mentioned in that sub-section in so far as such debts are referable to the assets.

(4) Nothing contained in clause (a) of sub-section (1) shall apply to any such transfer as is referred to therein made by an individual before the 1st day of April, 1956, and the value of any assets so transferred shall not be included in the computation of his net wealth.

(5) The value of any assets transferred under an irrevocable transfer shall be liable to be included in computing the net wealth of the transferor as and when the power to revoke arises to him.

(6) For the purposes of this Act, the holder of an impartible estate shall be deemed to be the individual owner of all the properties comprised in the estate.

(7) Where the assessee is a member of an association of persons, being a co-operative housing society, and a building or part thereof is allotted or leased to him under a house building scheme of the society, the assessee shall, notwithstanding anything contained in this Act or any other law for the time being in force, be deemed to be the owner of such building or part and the value of such building or part shall be included in computing the net wealth of the assessee; and, in determining the value of such building or part, the value of any outstanding instalments of the amount payable under such scheme by the assessee to the society towards the cost of such building or part and the land appurtenant thereto shall, whether the amount so payable is described as such or in any other manner in such scheme, be deducted as a debt owned by him in relation to such building or part.

EXPLANATION. For the purposes of this Section,—

(a) the expression "transfer" includes any disposition, settlement, trust, covenant, agreement or arrangement,

(b) the expression "irrevocable transfer"includes a transfer of assets which, by the terms of the instrument effecting it, is not revocable for a period exceeding six years or during the life-time of the transferee, and under which the transferor derives no direct or indirect benefit, but does not include a transfer of assets if such instrument—

(i) contains any provision for the re-transfer, directly or indirectly, of the whole or any part of the assets or income therefrom to the transferor, or

(ii) in any way gives the transferor a right to reassume power, directly or indirectly, over the whole or any part of the assets or income therefrom.

(c) the expression "property"includes any interest in property, movable or immovable, the proceeds of sale thereof and any money or investment for the time being representing the proceeds of sale thereof and where the property is converted into any other property by any method, such other property; and

(d) the expressions "interest of the individual in the property of the family" and "interest of the spouse or any minor child of the individual in the property of the family" mean, respectively, the proportion in which the individual or, as the case may be, the spouse or minor child would be entitled to share the property of the family if there had been a total partition in the family as on the valuation date of the family relevant to the assessment year for which the individual is to be assessed under sub-section (1A).

5. Exemptions in respect, of certain assets.

(1) Subject to the provisions of sub-section (1A), wealth-tax shall not be payable by an assessee in respect of the following assets] and such assets shall not be included in the net wealth of the assessee—

(i) any property held by him under trust or other legal obligation for any public purpose of a charitable or religious nature in India;

(ii) the interest of the assessee in the occupation property of any Hindu undivided family of which he is a member;

(iii) any one building in the occupation of a Ruler declared by the Central Government as his official residence under paragraph 13 of the Merged States (Taxation Concessions) Order, 1949, or paragraph 15 of the Part B States (Taxation Concessions) Order, 1950 ;

(iv) one house or part of a house belonging to the assessee.

PROVIDED that, where the value of such house or part exceeds one hundred thousand rupees, the amount that shall not be included in the net wealth of the assessee under this clause shall be one hundred thousand rupees;

(iva) agricultural land belonging to the assessee subject to a maximum of one hundred and fifty thousand rupees in value:

PROVIDED that where the assessee owns any house or part of a house situate in a place with a population exceeding ten thousand and to which the provisions of clause (iv) apply and the value of such house or part of a house together with the value of the agricultural land exceeds one hundred and fifty thousand rupees, then the amount that shall not be included in the net wealth of the assessee under this clause shall be one hundred and fifty thousand rupees as reduced by so much of the value of such house or part of house as is not to be included in the net wealth of the assessee under clause (iv):

(ivb) one building or one group of buildings owned by a cultivator of, or receiver of rent or revenue out of, agricultural land:

PROVIDED that such building or group of buildings is on or in the immediate vicinity of the land and is required by the cultivator or the receiver of rent or revenue, by reason of his connection with the land, as dwelling house, store-house or outhouse;

(v) the rights under any patent or copyright belonging to the assessee:

PROVIDED that they are not held by him as assets of a business, profession or vocation and no income or benefit accrues to him therefrom;

(vi) the right or interest of the assessee in any policy of insurance before the moneys covered by the policies become due and payable to the assessee;

(via) the right of the assessee to receive any annuity payable by the Central Government under the provisions of Section 280D of the Income-tax Act;

(vii) the right of the assessee to receive a pension or other life annuity in respect of past services under an employer;

(viii) furniture, household utensils, wearing apparel, provisions and other articles intended for the personal or household use of the assessee but not including jewellery:

PROVIDED that the furniture, utensils or other articles are neither made wholly or partly of, nor contain (whether by way of embedding, covering or otherwise), gold, silver, platinum or any other precious metal or any alloy containing one or more of such precious metals:

PROVIDED FURTHER that nothing in this clause shall operate to exclude from the net wealth of the assessee any conveyance or conveyances to the extent the value or the aggregate value thereof exceeds the sum of twentyfive thousand rupees.

EXPLANATION 1: For the purposes of this clause and clause (viii), "jewellery" includes -

(a) ornaments made of gold, silver, platinum or any other precious metal or any alloy containing one or more of such precious metals, whether or not containing any precious or semi-precious stone, and whether or not worked or sewn into any wearing apparel;

(b) precious or semi-precious stones, whether or not set in any furniture, utensil or other article or worked or sewn into any wearing apparel.

EXPLANATION 2: For the purposes of this clause, "conveyance" means any motor car or other mechanically propelled vehicle, aircraft or boat;

(viiia) growing crops (including fruits on trees) on agricultural land and grass on such land;

(ix) the tools, implements and equipment used by the assessee for the cultivation, conservation, improvement or maintenance of agricultural land, or for the raising or harvesting of any agricultural or horticultural produce on such land.

EXPLANATION. For the purposes of this clause, tools, implements and equipment do not include any plant or machinery used in any tea or other plantation in connection with the processing of any agricultural produce or in the manufacture of any article from such produce;

(x) the tools and instruments necessary to enable the assessee to carry on his profession or vocation, subject to a maximum of twenty thousand rupees in value;

(xi) instruments and other apparatus used by the assessee for purposes of scientific research;

(xii) any works of art, archaeological, scientific or art collections, books or manuscripts belonging to the assessee and not intended for sale;

(xiii) any drawings, paintings, photographs, prints and any other heirloom not falling within clause (xii) and not intended for sale, but not including jewellery;

(xiv) jewellery in the possession of any Ruler, not being his personal property, which has been recognised before the commencement of this Act by the Central Government as his heirloom or, where no such recognition exists, which the Board may, subject to any rules that may be made by the Central Government in this behalf, recognise as his heirloom at the time of his first assessment to wealth-tax under this Act;

(xv) deposits under any scheme framed by the Central Government and notified by it in this behalf in the Official Gazette, to the extent to which the amounts of such deposits do not exceed the maximum amount permitted to be deposited therein;

(xvi) ten year treasury savings deposit certificates, fifteen year annuity certificates, deposits in post office savings banks, post office cash certificates, post office national savings certificates (with retrospective effect) certificates, post office national plan certificates and twelve year national plan savings certificates, ten year defence deposit certificates and twelve year national defence certificates, to the extent to which the amount of such certificates or deposits do not exceed in each case the maximum amount permitted to be invested or deposited therein;

(xvia) 612 per cent Gold Bonds, 1977, 7 per cent Gold Bonds, 1980 and National Defence Gold Bonds, 1980;

(xvii) the amount standing to the credit of an assessee, being a salaried employee, in any provident fund maintained by his employer to which the Provident Funds Act, 1925 (19 of 1925), applies or which is a recognised provident fund within the meaning of clause (38) of Section of the Income-tax Act;

(xviia) the amount standing to the credit of an individual in any provident fund set up by the Central Government and notified by it in this behalf in the Official Gazette;

(xviii) the property received by an assessee from Government in pursuance of any gallantry or merit award instituted or approved by the Central Government;

(xix) the value of any shares held by the assessee in any other company in any case where the assessee is a company;

(xx) the value of any equity shares held by the assessee in any company of the type referred to in clause (d) of Section 45, where such shares form part of the initial issue of equity share capital made by the company after the 31st day of March 1964, but before the 1st day of June, 1971, for a period of five successive assessment years commencing with the assessment year next;

(xxi) that portion of the net wealth of a company established with the object of carrying on an industrial undertaking in India within the meaning of the Explanation to clause (d) of Section 45, as is employed by it in a new and separate unit set up after the commencement of this Act by way of substantial expansion of its undertaking:

PROVIDED that—

(a) separate accounts are maintained in respect of such unit; and

(b) the conditions specified in clause (d) of Section 45 are complied with in relation to the establishment of such unit:

PROVIDED FURTHER that this exemption shall apply of any such company only for a period of five successive assessment years commencing with the assessment year next following the date on which the company commences operations for the establishment of such unit;

(xxii) any security of the Central Government or a State Government[not being a security referred to in clause (xvi) or clause (xvia);

(xxiii) any shares not being shares referred to in clause (xx) held by the assessee in any Indian company where the assessee is an individual or a Hindu undivided family;

(xxiv) such debentures, issued by any co-operative society (including a co-operative land mortgage bank or a co-operative land development bank) or any other institution or authority, as the Central Government may, by notification in the Official Gazette, specify in this behalf;

(xxv) units in the Unit Trust of India established under the Unit Trust of India Act, 1963 (52 of 1963);

(xxvi) any deposits with a banking company to which the Banking Regulation Act, 1949, (10 of 1949) applies (including any bank or banking institution referred to in Section 51 of that Act), or with a co-operative society engaged in carrying on the business of banking (including a co-operative land mortgage bank or a co-operative land development bank);

(xxvii) any deposits with a financial corporation which is engaged in providing long-term finance for industrial development in India and which is approved by the Central Government for the purposes of clause (viii) of sub-section (1) of Section 36 of the Income-tax Act;

(xxviii) any shares held by the assessee in any co-operative society;

(xxix) any deposits with a co-operative society, not being deposits referred to in clause (xxvi) or clause (xxx), made by a member of the society;

(xxx) any deposits with a co-operative housing society made by a member of the society to whom a building or part thereof is allotted or leased under a house building scheme of the society, where such deposits have been made under such scheme.

(1A) Nothing contained in sub-section (1) shall operate to exclude from the net wealth of the assessee any assets referred to in clauses (xv), (xvi), (xxii), (xxiii), (xxiv), (xxv), (xxvi), (xxvii), (xxviii), and (xxix)] not being deposits under the Post Office Savings bank (Cumulative Time Deposits) Rules, 1959], to the extent the value thereof exceeds in the aggregate, a sum of one hundred and fifty thousand rupees: Provided that where the assets include any assets referred to in clause (xv) or clause (xvi)[not being deposits under the Post Office Savings Bank (Cumulative Time Deposits) Rules, 1959 which have been held by the assessee continuously from a date prior to the 1st day of March, 1970 and the value of the assets so included exceeds the limit of one hundred and fifty thousand rupees by any amount, such limit shall be raised by the said amount.

(2) Wealth-tax shall not be payable by an assessee in respect of any deposit made by the assessee with the Government or in any security of the Government or of a local authority not specified in clause (xv) or clause (xvi) or clause (xvia) of sub-section (1) which the Central Government may, by notification in the Official Gazette, exempt from wealth-tax; but the value of any deposit or security so exempted shall be included in computing the net wealth of the assessee.

(3) Notwithstanding anything contained in sub-section (1), wealth-tax shall be payable by an assessee in respect of the assets referred to in clauses (xv), (xvi), (xix), (xxii), (xxiii), (xxiv), (xxv), (xxvi), (xxvii), (xxviii), and (xxix) of sub-section (1) or in sub-section (2) for any assessment year unless the assets are held by him —

(a) in the case of shares in a company, from the date on which the shares were first issued by the company, or for a period of at least six months ending with the relevant valuation date, whichever is shorter; and

(b) in the case of other assets, for a period of at least six months ending with the relevant valuation date:

PROVIDED that for the purpose of making any assessment for the assessment year commencing on the 1st day of April, 1963, the provisions of clause (b) shall not apply to ten year defence deposit certificates and twelve year national defence certificates held by the assessee on the relevant valuation date.

EXPLANATION: For the purposes of clause (a) or clause (b) of this sub-section, in computing the period of six months in relation to any asset (not being any share or security held as stock-in-trade for the purposes of the business of the assessee) in a case where such asset (hereafter in this Explanation referred to as the relevant asset) was acquired by the assessee by conversion of, or in exchange for, or with the proceeds of, or with the money constituting, any other asset exempt from wealth-tax under sub-section (1) or sub-section (2), there shall be included, if the assessee acquired the relevant asset within thirty days after he ceased to own such other asset, so much of the period for which the assessee has owned such other asset as falls within the period of twelve months ending with the relevant valuation date.

6. Exclusion of assets and debts outside India. In computing the net wealth of an individual who is not a citizen of India or of an individual or a Hindu undivided family not president in India or resident but not ordinarily resident in India, or of a company not resident in India during the year ending on the valuation date —

(i) the value of the assets and debts located outside India; and

(ii) the value of the assets in India represented by any loans or debts owing to the assessee in any case where the interest, if any, payable on such loans or debts is not to be included in the total income of the assessee under Section 10 of the Income-tax Act; shall not be taken into account.

EXPLANATION 1: An individual or a Hindu undivided family shall be deemed to be not resident in India or resident but not ordinarily resident in India during the year ending on the valuation date if in respect of that year the individual or the Hindu undivided family, as the case may be, is not resident in India or resident but not ordinarily resident in India within the meaning of the Income-tax Act.

EXPLANATION 2: A company shall be deemed to be resident in India during the year ending on the valuation date, if—

(a) it is a company formed and registered under the Companies Act, 1956, (1 of 1956) or is an existing company within the meaning of that Act; or

(b) during that year the control and management of its affairs is situated wholly in India.

7. Value of assets how to be determined.

(1) Subject to any rules made in this behalf, the value] of any asset, other than cash, for the purposes of this Act, shall be estimated to be the price which in

the opinion of the Wealth-tax Officer it would fetch if sold in the open market on the valuation date.

(2) Notwithstanding anything contained in sub-section (1),—

(a) where the assessee is carrying on a business for which accounts are maintained by him regularly, the Wealth-tax Officer may, instead of determining separately the value of each asset held by the assessee in such business, determine the net value of the assets of the business as a whole having regard to the balance-sheet of such business as on the valuation date and making such adjustments therein as may be prescribed;

(b) where the assessee carrying on the business, is a company not resident in India and a computation in accordance with clause (a) cannot be made by reason of the absence of any separate balance-sheet drawn up for the affairs of such business in India, the Wealth-tax Officer may take the net value of the assets of the business in India to be that proportion of the net value of the assets of the business as a whole wherever carried on determined as aforesaid as the income arising from the business in India during the year ending with the valuation date bears to the aggregate income from the business wherever arising during that year.

(3) Notwithstanding anything contained in sub-section (1), where the valuation of any asset is referred by the Wealth-tax officer to the Valuation Officer under Section 16A, the value of such asset shall be estimated to be the price which, in the opinion of the Valuation Officer, it would fetch if sold in the open market on the valuation date, or, in the case of an asset being a house referred to in sub-section (4), the valuation date referred to in that sub-section.

(4) Notwithstanding anything contained in sub-section (1), the value of a house belonging to the assessee and exclusively used by him for residential purposes throughout the period of twelve months immediately preceding the valuation date may, at the option of the assessee, be taken to be the price which, in the opinion of the Wealth-tax Officer, it would fetch if sold in the open market on the valuation date next following the date on which he became the owner of the house, or on the valuation date relevant to the assessment year commencing on the 1st day of April, 1971, whichever valuation date is later: Provided that where more than one house belonging to the assessee is exclusively used by him for residential purposes, the provisions of this sub-section shall apply only in respect of one of such houses which the assessee may, at his option, specify in this behalf in the return of net wealth.

EXPLANATION: For the purposes of this sub-section —

(i) where the house has been constructed by the assessee, he shall be deemed to have become the owner thereof on the date on which the construction of such house was completed;

(ii) "house"includes a part of a house, being an independent residential unit.

CHAPTER - III : WEALTH-TAX AUTHORITIES

8. Wealth-tax Officers. Every Income-tax Officer having jurisdiction or exercising powers as such under the Income-tax Act in respect of any individual, Hindu undivided family or company shall perform the functions of a Wealth-tax Officer under this Act in respect of such individual, Hindu undivided family or company:

> [3][*PROVIDED that where two or more Income-tax Officers have jurisdiction or exercise powers under the Income-tax Act in respect of any individual, Hindu undivided family or company, they shall have concurrent jurisdiction* [2]*[and shall perform their functions in respect of such individual, Hindu undivided family or company, as the case may be, in accordance with such general or special orders in writing as the Commissioner or the Inspecting Assistant Commissioner authorised by the Commissioner in this behalf may make for the purpose of facilitating the performance of such functions.*

EXPLANATION: For the purposes of this Section, the Income-tax Officer or the Income-tax Officers having jurisdiction in relation to a person who is not an assessee within the meaning of the Income tax Act, shall be the Income tax Officer or Income tax Officers in respect of the area in which that person resides.

8A. Power of Commissioner respecting specified areas, cases or persons.

(1) The Commissioner may, by general or special order in writing, direct that such of the functions assigned to the Wealth-tax Officer by or under this Act as are specified in any such order may, in respect of any specified area or specified cases or classes of cases or specified persons or classes of persons, be performed by an Inspector of Wealth-tax or any member of the ministerial staff, appointed to work under the Commissioner or any other Wealth-tax authority subordinate to him, and specified in such order, subject to such conditions, restrictions or limitations as may be specified therein:

> *PROVIDED that the Commissioner shall not, unless he is authorised in this behalf by the Board by general or special order in writing, make an order under this sub-section in relation to the functions of a Wealth-tax Officer mentioned in the following provisions of this Act, namely, Sections 15B, 16, 17, 18, 20, 22, 24, 32, 37 and 37A.*

(2) For the purposes of any case or person or proceeding under this Act in respect of which or whom any order under sub-section (1) applies, references in this Act or in any rule made hereunder to the Wealth-tax Officer shall be deemed to include references to the Inspector of Wealth-tax or the member of the ministerial staff specified in such order.

8AA. Concurrent jurisdiction of Inspecting Assistant.

(1) The Commissioner may, by general or special order in writing, direct that all or any of the powers or functions conferred on or assigned to the Wealth-tax Officer or Wealth-tax Officers by or under this Act in respect of any area, or cases or classes of cases, or persons or classes of persons shall be exercised or performed concurrently by the Inspecting Assistant Commissioner. Commissioner and Wealth-tax Officer.

(2) Where under sub-section (1), an Inspecting Assistant Commissioner exercises concurrent jurisdiction with one or more Wealth-tax Officers in respect of any area, cases or classes of cases, or persons or classes of persons, the Wealth-tax Officer or Wealth-tax Officers shall exercise the powers and perform the functions under this Act in relation thereto as the Inspecting Assistant Commissioner may direct.

(3) Without prejudice to the generality of the provisions contained in sub-section (2) of Section 13, every Wealth-tax Officer shall also observe and follow such instructions as may be issued to him for his guidance by the Inspecting Assistant Commissioner within whose jurisdiction he performs his functions in relation to any particular proceeding or the initiation of any proceeding under this Act. Provided that no instructions which are prejudicial to the assesee shall be issued before an opportunity is given by the Inspecting Assistant Commissioner to the assessee to be heard.

EXPLANATION: For the purposes of this sub-section, no instruction as to the lines on which an investigation connected with the assesment should be made shall be deemed to be an instruction prejudcial to the assessee.

(4) Where an order is made under sub-section (1) and the Inspecting Assistant Commissioner exercises the powers or performs the functions of a Wealth-tax Officer in respect of any case or person or proceeding, references in this Act or in any rule made thereunder to the Wealth-tax Officer and the Appellate Assistant Commissioner shall be construed as references to the Inspecting Assistant Commissioner and the Commissioner respectively and, accordingly,—

(i) any provision of this Act requiring approval or sanction of the Inspecting Assistant Commissioner shall not apply;

(ii) any appeal which would otherwise have lain to the Appellate Assistant Commissioner shall lie to the Commissioner;

(iii) any appeal which would have lain from an order of the Appellate Assistant Commissioner to the Appellate Tribunal shall lie from the order of the Commissioner.

8B. Power to transfer cases.

(1) The Commissioner may, after giving the assessee a reasonable opportunity of being heard in the matter, wherever it is possible to do so, and after recording his reasons for doing so, transfer any case from one or more of the following officers subordinate to him, namely :

(a) any Wealth-tax Officer or Wealth-tax Officers;

(b) any Wealth-tax Officer or Wealth-tax Officers having concurrent jurisidiction with the Inspecting Assistant Commissioner, to any other Wealth-tax Officer or Wealth-tax Officers (whether with or without concurrent jurisdiction with the Inspecting Assistant Commissioner) also subordinate to him and the Board any similarly transfer any case from -

(i) any Wealth-tax Officer or Wealth-tax Officers, or

(ii) any Wealth-tax Officer or Wealth-tax Officers having concurrent jurisdiction with the Inspecting Assistant Commissioner, to any other Wealth-tax Officer or Wealth-tax Officers (whether with or without concurrent jurisdiction with the Inspecting Assistant Commissioner):

PROVIDED that nothing in this sub-section shall be deemed to require any such opportunity to be given where a transfer is from any Wealth-tax Officer or Wealth-tax Officers (whether with or without concurrent jurisdiction with the Inspecting Assistant Commissioner) to any other Wealth-tax Officer or Wealth-tax Officers (whether with or without concurrent jurisdiction with the Inspecting Assistant Commissioner) and the offices of all such officers are situated in the same city, locality or place:

PROVIDED FURTHER that—

(a) where any case has been transferred from any Wealth-tax Officer or Wealth-tax Officers to two or more Wealth-tax Officers to whom the case is so transferred shall have concurrent jurisdiction over such case and shall perform their functions in accordance with such general or special orders in writing as the Board or the Commissioner or the Inspecting Assistant Commissioner authorised by the Commissioner in this behalf, may make for the purpose of facilitating the performance of such functions;

(b) where any case has been transferred from any Wealth-tax Officer or Wealth-tax Officers (whether with or without concurrent jurisdiction with the Inspecting Assistant Commissioner) to two or more Wealth-tax Officers with concurrent jurisdiction with the Inspecting Assistant Commissioner, the officers (including the Inspecting Assistant Commissioner) to whom the case is so transferred shall have concurrent jurisdiction over such case and shall perform their functions in accordance with such general or special orders in writing as the Board or the Commissioner may make for the purpose of facilitating the performance of such functions and the Wealth-tax Officers shall perform their functions also in accordance with such orders or directions as the Inspecting Assistant Commissioner may make under Section 8 or, as the case may be, under sub-section (2) of Section 8AA.

(2) The transfer of a case under sub-section (1) may be made at any stage of the proceedings, and shall not render necessary the reissue of any notice already issued by the Wealth-tax Officer or Wealth-tax Officers from whom the case is transferred.

EXPLANATION: In this Section and in Section 8A, the word "case", in relation to any person whose name is specified in any order made thereunder, means all proceedings under this Act in respect of any year which may be pending on the date of such order, or which may have been completed on or before such date, and includes also all proceedings under this Act which may be commenced after the date of such order in respect of any year.

9. Appellate Assistant Commissioners of Wealth-tax. The Board may empower as many persons as it thinks fit to exercise under this Act the functions of an Appellate Assistant Commissioner of Wealth-tax, and on being so empowered the Appellate Assistant Commissioners shall perform their functions in respect of such areas or such persons or such classes of persons as the Board may direct, and where such directions have assigned to two or more Appellate Assistant Commissioners the same area or the same persons or the same classes of persons they shall perform their functions in accordance with such orders as the Board may make for the distribution and allocation of the work to be performed.

10. Commissioners of Wealth-tax. The Board may empower as many persons as it thinks fit to exercise under this Act the functions of a Commissioner of Wealth-tax, and on being so empowered the Commissioners of Wealth-tax shall perform their functions in respect of such areas or such persons or such classes of persons as the Board may direct and where such directions have assigned to two or more Commissioners the same area or the same persons or the same classes of persons they shall have concurrent jurisdiction and shall perform such functions in relation to the said area or persons or classes of persons as the Board may, by general or special order in writing, specify, for the distribution and allocation of the work to be performed.

10A. Directors of Inspection.

(1) The Board may empower as many persons as it thinks fit to exercise under this Act the functions of a Director of Inspection.

(2) A Director of Inspection shall perform such functions of any other Wealth-tax authority as may be assigned to him by the Board.

11. Inspecting Assistant Commissioners of Wealth-tax. The Commissioner of Wealth-tax may empower as many persons as he thinks fit to exercise under this Act the functions of an Inspecting Assistant Commissioner of Wealth-tax, and on being so empowered the Inspecting Assistant Commissioners of Wealth-tax shall perform their functions in respect of such areas or such persons or such classes of persons as the Commissioner may direct, and where such directions have assigned to two or more Inspecting Assistant Commissioners the same area or the same persons or the same classes of persons they shall have concurrent jurisdiction and shall perform such functions in respect of the said areas or persons or classes of persons as the Commissioner may, by general or special order in writing, specify, for the distribution and allocation of the work to be performed.

11B. [2][Wealth-tax Officer competent to perform any function or functions. In respect of any function to be performed by a Wealth-tax Officer under any provision of this Act, in relation to any assessee, the Wealth-tax Officer referred to therein shall —

(a) in a case where only one Wealth-tax Officer has jurisdiction over such assessee, be such Wealth-tax Officer;

(b) in a case where two or more Wealth-tax Officers have concurrent jurisdiction over such assessee, be the Wealth-tax Officer empowered to perform such function by the Board, or, as the case may be, the Wealth-tax Officer to whom such function has been assigned by an order of the Commissioner or of the Inspecting Assistant Commissioner of Wealth-tax authorised by the Commissioner in this behalf.

12. Control of Wealth-tax authorities.

(1) Inspecting Assistant Commissioners shall be subordinate to the Commissioner within whose jurisdiction they perform their functions and also to the Director of Inspection.

(2) Wealth-tax Officers shall be subordinate to the Commissioner and the Inspecting Assistant Commissioner within whose jurisdiction they perform their functions and also to the Director of Inspection.

(3) Inspectors of Wealth-tax shall be subordinate to the Wealth-tax Officer or other Wealth-tax authority under whom they are empowered to work and to any other Wealth-tax authority to whom the said officer or other authority is subordinate.

EXPLANATION. For the purposes of sub-section (1), "Director of Inspection" does not include a Deputy Director of Inspection or an Assistant Director of Inspection; and for the purposes of sub-section (2) of this Section and sub-section (2) of Section 13, "Director of Inspection" does not include an Assistant Director of Inspection.

13. Wealth-tax authorities to follow orders, etc., of the Board.

(1) All officers and other persons employed in the execution of this Act shall observe and follow the orders, instructions and directions of the Board:

PROVIDED that no orders, instructions or directions shall be given by the Board so as to interfere with the discretion of the Appellate Assistant Commissioner of Wealth-tax in the exercise of his appellate function.

(2) Every Wealth-tax Officer employed in the execution of this Act shall observe and follow such instructions as may be issued to him for his guidance by the Director of Inspection or by the Commissioner or by the Inspecting Assistant Commissioner within whose jurisdiction he performs his functions.

13A. Powers of Director of Inspection, Commissioner and Inspecting Assistant Commissioner to make enquiries. The Director of Inspection, the Commissioner of Wealth-tax and the Inspecting Assistant Commissioner of Wealth-tax shall be competent to make any enquiry under this Act, and for this purpose shall have all the powers that a Wealth-tax Officer has under this Act in relation to the making of enquiries.

CHAPTER - IV : ASSESSMENT

14. Return of wealth.

(1) Every person, if his net wealth or the net wealth of any other person in respect of which he is assessable under this Act on the valuation date was of such an amount as to render him liable to wealth-tax under this Act, shall, before the 30th day of June of the corresponding assessment year, furnish to the Wealth-tax Officer a return in the prescribed form and verified in the prescribed manner setting forth the net wealth as on that valuation date.

PROVIDED that in the case of a person whose net wealth or the net wealth of any other person in respect of which he is assessable under this Act includes the value of any assets held in a business or profession and the time (whether fixed originally or on extension) for furnishing the return of his total income or, as the case may be, of the total income of the other person aforesaid for the said assessment year under sub-section (1) or sub-section (2) or sub-section (3) of Section 139 of the Income-tax Act, expires on or after the 30th day of June aforesaid, the return in respect of such net wealth for the assessment year may be furnished before the expiry of the time for furnishing such return of income.

(2) If the Wealth-tax Officer is of the opinion that any person is assessable under this Act, whether in respect of his net wealth or the net wealth of any other person, then, notwithstanding anything contained in sub-section (1), he may serve a notice upon such person requiring him to furnish within such period, not being less than thirty days, as may be specified in the notice, a return in the prescribed form and verified in the prescribed manner, setting forth (along with such other particulars as may be required by the notice)], the net wealth of such person as on the valuation date mentioned in the notice.

(3) The Wealth-tax Officer may, if he is satisfied that it is necessary so to do, extend the date for the delivery of the return under this Section.

15. Return after due date and amendment of return. If any person has not furnished a return within the time allowed under Section 14, or having furnished a return under that Section discovers any omission or a wrong statement therein, he may furnish a return or a revised return, as the case may be, at any time before the assessment is made.

15A. Return by whom to be signed. The return made under Section 14 or Section 15 shall be signed and verified—

(a) in the case of an individual, by the individual himself; where the individual is absent from India, by the individual concerned or by some person duly authorised by him in this behalf; where the individual is mentally incapacitated from attending to his affairs, by his guardian or any other person competent to act on his behalf; and where for any other reason it is impossible for the individual to sign the return, by any person competent to act on his behalf;

(b) in the case of a Hindu undivided family, by the karta, and, where the karta is absent from India or is mentally incapacitated from attending to his affairs, by any other adult member of such family; and

(c) in the case of a company, by the principal officer thereof.

15B. Self assessment.

(1) Where a return has been furnished under Section 14 or Section 15 and the tax payable on the basis of that return exceeds five hundred rupees, the assessee shall pay the tax so payable within thirty days of furnishing the return.

(2) After a provisional assessment under Section 15C or a regular assessment under Section 16 has been made, any amount paid under sub-section (1) shall be deemed to have been paid towards the provisional assessment or regular assessment, as the case may be.

(3) If any assessee fails to pay the tax or any part thereof in accordance with the provisions of sub-section (1), he shall, unless a provisional assessment under

Section 15C or a regular assessment under Section 16 has been made before the expiry of thirty days referred to in that sub-section, be liable, by way of penalty, to pay such amount as the Wealth-tax Officer may direct, and in the case of a continuing failure, such further amount or amounts as the Wealth-tax Officer may from time to time direct, so, however, that the total amount of penalty does not exceed fifty per cent. of the amount of such tax or part, as the case may be:

PROVIDED that before levying any such penalty, the assessee shall be given a reasonable opportunity of being heard.

15C. Provisional assessment.

(1) The Wealth-tax Officer may, at any time after the receipt of a return made under Section 14 or Section 15, proceed to make, in a summary manner, a provisional assessment of the tax payable by the assessee, on the basis of his return and the accounts and documents, if any, accompanying it.

(2) After a regular assessment has been made, any amount paid towards the provisional assessment made under sub-section (1), shall be deemed to have been paid towards the regular assessment; and where the amount paid towards the provisional assessment exceeds the amount payable under the regular assessment, the excess shall be refunded to the assessee.

(3) Nothing done or suffered by reason or in consequence of any provisional assessment made under this Section shall prejudice the determination, on the merits, of any issue which may arise in the course of the regular assessment.

(4) There shall be no right of appeal against a provisional assessment made under sub-section (1).

(5) For the removal of doubts, it is hereby declared that the provisions of Section 31 excepting sub-section (6) thereof, and Section 32 shall apply in relation to any tax payable in pursuance of a provisional assessment made under this Section as if it were a regular assessment under Section 16.

16. Assessment.

(1) If the Wealth-tax Officer is satisfied without requiring the presence of the assessee or production by him of any evidence that a return made under Section 14 or Section 15 is correct and complete, he shall assess the net wealth of the assessee and determine the amount of wealth-tax payable by him or the amount refundable to him on the basis of such return.

(2) If the Wealth-tax Officer is not so satisfied, he shall serve a notice on the assessee either to attend in person at his office on a date to be specified in the notice or to produce or cause to be produced on that date any evidence on which the assessee may rely in support of his return.

(3) The Wealth-tax Officer, after hearing such evidence as the person may produce and such other evidence as he may require on any specified points and after

taking into account all relevant material which the Wealth-tax Officer has gathered, shall, by order in writing, assess the net wealth of the assessee and determine the amount of wealth-tax payable by him or the amount refundable to him on the basis of such assessment.

(4) For the purpose of making an assessment under this Act the Wealth-tax Officer may serve, on any person who has made a return under sub-section (1) of Section 14 or upon whom a notice has been served under sub-section (2) of that Section 1[or who has made a return under Section 15, a notice requiring him to produce or cause to be produced on a date specified in the notice such accounts, records or other documents as the Wealth-tax Officer may require.

(5) If any person fails to make a return in response to any notice under sub-section (2) of Section 14, or fails to comply with the terms of any notice issued under sub-section (2) or sub-section (4), the Wealth-tax Officer after taking into account all relevant material which he has gathered, shall estimate the net wealth to the best of his judgment and determine the amount of wealth-tax payable by the person or the amount refundable to him on the basis of such assessment.

17. Wealth escaping assessment.

(1) If the Wealth-tax Officer—

(a) has reason to believe that by reason of the omission or failure on the part of any person to make a return under Section 14 of his net wealth or the net wealth of any other person in respect of which he is assessable under this Act for any assessment year or to disclose fully and truly all material facts necessary for assessment of his net wealth or the net wealth of such other person for that year, the net wealth chargeable to tax has escaped assessment for that year, whether by reason of under-assessment or assessment at too low a rate or otherwise; or

(b) has, in consequence of any information in his possession, reason to believe, notwithstanding that there has been no such omission or failure as is referred to in clause (a), that the net wealth chargeable to tax has escaped assessment for any year, whether by reason of under-assessment or assessment at too low a rate or otherwise; he may, in cases falling under clause (a) at any time within eight years and in cases falling under clause (b) at any time within four years of the end of that assessment year, 1[serve on such person] a notice containing all or any of the requirements which may be included in a notice under sub-section (2) of Section 14, and may proceed to assess or re-assess such net wealth, and the provisions of this Act shall, so far as may be, apply as if the notice had issued under that sub-section.

(2) Nothing contained in this Section limiting the time within which any proceeding for assessment or re-assessment may be commenced, shall apply to an assessment or re-assessment to be made on such person in consequence of or to give effect to any finding or direction contained in an order under Section 23, 24, 25, 27 or 29:

PROVIDED that the provisions of this sub-section shall not apply in any case where any such assessment or re-assessment relates to an assessment year in respect of which an assessment or re-assessment could not have been made at the time the order which was the subject matter of the appeal, reference or revision, as the case may be, was made by reason of any provision limiting the time within which any action for assessment or re-assessment may be taken.

18. Penalty for failure to furnish returns, to comply with notices and concealment of assets, etc.

(1) If the Wealth-tax Officer, Appellate Assistant Commissioner, Commissioner or Appellate Tribunal in the course of any proceedings under this Act is satisfied that any person—

(a) has without reasonable cause failed to furnish the return which he is required to furnish under sub-section (1) of Section 14 or by notice given under sub-section (2) of Section 14 or Section 17, or has without reasonable cause failed to furnish it within the time allowed and in the manner required by sub-section (1) of Section 14 or by such notice, as the case may be; or

(b) has without reasonable cause failed to comply with a notice under sub-section (2) or sub-section (4) of Section 16; or

(c) has concealed the particulars of any assets or furnished inaccurate particulars of any assets or debts; he or it may, by order in writing, direct that such person shall pay by way of penalty—

(i) in the cases referred to in clause (a), in addition to the amount of wealth-tax, if any, payable by him, a sum, for every month during which the default continued, equal to one-half per cent. of—

(A) the net wealth assessed under Section 16 as reduced by the amount specified in sub-section (1A), or

(B) the net wealth assessed under Section 17, where assessment has been made under that Section, as reduced by—

(1) the net wealth, if any, assessed previously under Section 16 or Section 17, or

(2) the amount specified in sub-section (1A), whichever is greater, but not exceeding, in the aggregate, an amount equal to the net wealth assessed under Section 16, or, as the case may be, the net wealth assessed under Section 17, as reduced in either case in the manner aforesaid;

(ii) in the cases referred to in clause (b), in addition to the amount of wealth-tax payable by him, a sum which shall not be less than one per cent. of the assessed net wealth but which shall not exceed the amount of the assessed net wealth.

EXPLANATION: For the purposes of clause (ii),"assessed net wealth"shall be taken to be the net wealth assessed under Section 16 as reduced by the net wealth declared in the return, if any, furnished by such person, or, as the case may be, the net wealth assessed under Section 17 as reduced by—

(i) the net wealth, if any, assessed previously under Section 16 or Section 17, or

(ii) the net wealth declared in the return, if any, furnished by such person under Section 17, whichever is greater;

(iii) in the cases referred to in clause (c), in addition to any wealth-tax payable by him, a sum which shall not be less than, but which shall not exceed twice, the amount representing the value of any assets in respect of which the particulars have been concealed or any assets or debts in respect of which inaccurate particulars have been furnished.

EXPLANATION 1: Where,—

(i) the value of any asset returned by any person is less than seventy-five per cent. of the value of such asset as determined in an assessment under Section 16 or Section 17 (the value so assessed being referred to hereafter in this Explanation as the correct value of the asset), or

(ii) the value of any debt returned by any person exceeds the value of such debt as determined in an assessment under Section 16 or Section 17 by more than twenty-five per cent. of the value so assessed (the value so assessed being referred to hereafter in this Explanation as the correct value of the debt), or

(iii) the net wealth returned by any person is less than seventy-five per cent. of the net wealth as assessed under Section 16 or Section 17 (the net wealth so assessed being referred to hereafter in this Explanation as the correct net wealth), then, such person shall, unless he proves that the failure to return the correct value of the asset or, as the case may be, the correct value of the debt or the correct net wealth did not arise from any fraud or any gross or wilful neglect on his part, be deemed to have concealed the particulars of assets or furnished inaccurate particulars of assets or debts for the purposes of clause (c) of this sub-section.

EXPLANATION 2: For the purposes of clause (iii),—

(a) the amount representing the value of any assets in respect of which the particulars have been concealed or any assets in respect of which inaccurate particulars have been furnished, shall be the value of such assets determined for the purposes of this Act as reduced by the value thereof, if any, declared in the return made under Section 14 or Section 15;

(b) the amount representing the value of any debts in respect of which inaccurate particulars have been furnished, shall be the amount by which the value of such debts declared in the return made under Section 14 or Section 15 exceeds the value thereof determined for the purposes of this Act.

(1A) The amount referred to in sub-clause (A) and sub-clause (B) (2) of clause (i) of sub-section (1) shall be,—

(a) in the cause of an individual, Rs. 1,00,000;

(b) in the case of a Hindu undivided family, Rs. 2,00,000; and

(c) in the case of a company, Rs. 5,00,000.

(2) No order shall be made under sub-section (1) unless the person concerned has been given a reasonable opportunity of being heard.

(2A) Notwithstanding anything contained in clause (i) or clause (iii) of sub-section (1), the Commissioner may, in his discretion,—

(i) reduce or waive the amount of minimum penalty imposable on a person under clause (i) of sub-section (1) for failure, without reasonable cause, to furnish the return of net wealth which such person was required to furnish under sub-section (1) of Section 14, or

(ii) reduce or waive the amount of minimum penalty imposable on a person under clause (iii) of sub-section (1), if he is satisfied that such person—

(a) in the case referred to in clause (i) of this sub-section has, prior to the issue of notice to him under sub-section (2) of Section 14, voluntarily and in good faith, made full disclosure of his net wealth; and in the case referred to in clause (ii) of this sub-section has, prior to the detection by the Wealth-tax Officer of the concealment of particulars of assets or of the inaccuracy of particulars furnished in respect of the assets or debts in respect of which the penalty is imposable, voluntarily and in good faith, made full and true disclosure of such particulars;

(b) has co-operated in any enquiry relating to the assessment of the wealth represented by such assets; and

(c) has either paid or made satisfactory arrangements for payment of any tax or interest payable in consequence of an order passed under this Act in respect of the relevant assessment year:

PROVIDED that if in a case falling under clause (c) of sub-section (1) the amount in respect of which penalty is imposable for the relevant assessment year, or where such disclosure relates to more than one assessment year, such amount for any one of the relevant assessment years, exceeds five hundred thousand rupees, no order reducing or waiving the penalty shall be made by the Commissioner unless the previous approval of the Board has been obtained.

(2B) An order under sub-section (2A) shall be final and shall not be called in question before any court of law or any other authority.

(3) Notwithstanding anything contained in clause (iii) of sub-section (1), if in a case falling under clause (c) of that sub-section, the amount (as determined by the Wealth-tax Officer on assessment) in respect of which penalty is imposable under clause (c) of sub-section (1) exceeds a sum of twenty-five thousand rupees, the Wealth-tax Officer shall refer the case to the Inspecting Assistant Commissioner who shall, for the purpose, have all the powers conferred under this Section for the imposition of penalty.

(4) An Appellate Assistant Commissioner, a Commissioner or the Appellate Tribunal on making an order under this Section imposing a penalty, shall forthwith send a copy of the same to the Wealth-tax Officer.

(5) No order imposing a penalty under this Section shall be passed—

(a) in a case where the assessment to which the proceedings for imposition of penalty relate is the subject-matter of an appeal to the Appellate Assistant Commissioner under Section 23 or an appeal to the Appellate Tribunal under sub-section (2) of Section 24, after the expiration of a period of—

(i) two years from the end of the financial year in which the proceedings, in the course of which action for imposition of penalty has been initiated, are completed, or

(ii) six months from the end of the month in which the order of the Appellate Assistant Commissioner or, as the case may be, the Appellate Tribunal is received by the Commissioner, whichever period expires later;

(b) in any other case, after the expiration of two years from the end of the financial year in which the proceedings, in the course of which action for imposition of penalty has been initiated, are completed.

EXPLANATION: In computing the period of limitation for the purposes of this Section, the time taken in giving an opportunity to the assessee to be reheard under the proviso to Section 39 and any period during which a proceeding under this Section for the levy of penalty is stayed by an order or injunction of any court shall be excluded.

CHAPTER -V : LIABILITY TO ASSESSMENT IN SPECIAL CASES

19. Tax of deceased person payable by legal representative.

(1) Where a person dies, his executor, administrator or other legal representative shall be liable to pay out of the estate of the deceased person, to the extent to which the estate is capable of meeting the charge, the wealth-tax assessed as payable by such person, or any sum, which would have been payable by him under this Act if he had not died.

(2) Where a person dies without having furnished a return under the provisions of Section 14 or after having furnished a return which the Wealth-tax Officer has reason to believe to be incorrect or incomplete, the Wealth-tax Officer may make an assessment of the net wealth of such person and determine the wealth-tax payable by the person on the basis of such assessment, and for this purpose may, by the issue of the appropriate notice which would have had to be served upon the deceased person if he had survived, require from the executor, administrator or other legal representative of the deceased person any accounts, documents or other evidence which might under the provisions of Section 16 have been required from the deceased person.

(3) The provisions of Sections 14, 15 and 17 shall apply to an executor, administrator or other legal representative as they apply to any person referred to in those Sections.

19A. Assessment in the case of executors.

(1) Subject as hereinafter provided, the net wealth of the estate of a deceased person shall be chargeable to tax in the hands of the executor or executors.

(2) The executor or executors shall for the purposes of this Act be treated as an individual.

(3) The status of the executor or executors shall for the purposes of this Act as regards residence and citizenship be the same as that of the deceased on the valuation date immediately preceding his death.

(4) The assessment of an executor under this Section shall be made separately from any assessment that may be made on him in respect of his own net wealth or on the net wealth of the deceased under Section 19.

(5) Separate assessments shall be made under this Section in respect of the net wealth as on each valuation date as is included in the period from the date of the death of the deceased to the date of complete distribution to the beneficiaries of the estate according to their several interests.

(6) In computing the net wealth on any valuation date under this Section, any assets of the estate distributed to, or applied to the benefit of, any specific legatee of the estate prior to that valuation date shall be excluded, but the assets so excluded shall, to the extent such asset are held by the legatee on any valuation date, be included in the net wealth of such specific legatee on that valuation date.

EXPLANATION: In this Section,"executor"includes an administrator or other person administering the estate of a deceased person.

20. Assessment after partition of a Hindu undivided family.

(1) Where, at the time of making an assessment, it is brought to the notice of the Wealth-tax Officer that a partition has taken place among the members of a Hindu undivided family, and the Wealth-tax Officer, after inquiry, is satisfied that the joint family property has been partitioned as a whole among the various members or groups of members in definite portions, he shall record an order to that effect and shall make assessments on the net wealth of the undivided

family as such for the assessment year or years, including the year relevant to the previous year in which the partition has taken place, if the partition has taken place on the last day of the previous year and each member or group of members shall be liable jointly and severally for the tax assessed on the net wealth of the joint family as such.

(2) Where the Wealth-tax Officer is not so satisfied, he may, by order, declare that such family shall be deemed for the purposes of this Act to continue to be a Hindu undivided family liable to be assessed as such.

21. Assessment when assets are held by courts of wards, administrators-general, etc.

(1) In the case of assets chargeable to tax under this Act which are held by a court of wards or an administrator-general or an official trustee or any receiver or manager or any other person, by whatever name called, appointed under any order of a court to manage property on behalf of another, or any trustee appointed under a trust declared by a duly executed instrument in writing, whether testamentary or otherwise, the wealth-tax shall be levied upon and recoverable from the court of wards, administrator-general, official trustee, receiver, manager or trustee, as the case may be, in the like manner and to the same extent as it would be leviable upon and recoverable from the person on whose behalf or for whose benefit the assets are held, and the provisions of this Act shall apply accordingly.

(2) Nothing contained in sub-section (1) shall prevent either the direct assessment of the person on whose behalf or for whose benefit the assets above referred to are held, or the recovery from such person of the tax payable in respect of such assets.

(3) Where the guardian or trustee of any person being a minor, lunatic or idiot holds any assets on behalf or for the benefit of such beneficiary,] the tax under this Act shall be levied upon and recoverable from such guardian or trustee, as the case may be, in the like manner and to the same extent as it would be leviable upon and recoverable from any such beneficiary if of full age or sound mind and in direct ownership of such assets.

(4) Notwithstanding anything contained in this Section, where the shares of the persons on whose behalf or for whose benefit any such assets are held are indeterminate or unknown, the wealth-tax shall be levied upon and recovered from the court of wards, administrator-general, official trustee, receiver, manager, or other person aforesaid as if the persons on whose behalf or for whose benefit the assets are held were an individual who is a citizen of India and resident in India for the purposes of this Act, and—

- (a) at the rates specified in Part I of the Schedule 5; or
- (b) at the rate of one and one-half per cent., whichever course would be more beneficial to the revenue: Provided that in a case where—
  - (i) such assets are held under a trust declared by will; or

(ii) such assets are held under a trust created before the 1st day of March, 1970, by a non-testamentary instrument and the Wealth-tax Officer is satisfied, having regard to all the circumstances existing at the relevant time, that the trust was created bona fide exclusively for the benefit of the relatives of the settlor or where the settlor is a Hindu undivided family, exclusively for the benefit of the members of such family, in circumstances where such relatives or members were mainly dependent on the settlor for their support and maintenance; or

(iii) such assets are held by the trustees on behalf of a provident fund, superannuation fund, gratuity fund, pension fund or any other fund created bona fide by a person carrying on a business or profession exclusively for the benefit of persons employed in such business or profession. wealth-tax shall be charged at the rates specified in Part I of the Schedule.

EXPLANATION: Notwithstanding anything contained in Section 5, in computing the net wealth for the purposes of this sub-section in any case, not being a case referred to in the proviso, any assets referred to in clauses (xv), (xvi), (xxii), (xxiii), (xxiv), (xxv), (xxvi), (xxvii), (xxviii) and (xxix) of sub-section (1) of that Section shall not be excluded.

(5) Any person who pays any sum by virtue of the provisions of this Section in respect of the net wealth of any beneficiary, shall be entitled to recover the sum so paid from such beneficiary, and may retain out of any assets that he may hold on behalf or for the benefit of such beneficiary, an amount equal to the sum so paid.

EXPLANATION: In this Section, the term"beneficiary"means any person including a minor, lunatic or idiot on whose behalf or for whose benefit assets are held by any other person.

22. Assessment of persons residing Outside India.

(1) Where the person liable to tax under this Act resides outside India, the tax may be levied upon and recovered from his agent, and the agent shall be deemed to be, for all the purposes of this Act, the assessee in respect of such tax.

(2) Any person employed by or on behalf of a person referred to in sub-section (1) or through whom such person is in the receipt of any income, profits or gains, or who is in possession or has custody of any asset of such person and upon whom the Wealth-tax Officer has caused a notice to be served of his intention of treating him as the agent of such person shall, for the purposes of sub-section (1), be deemed to be the agent of such person.

(3) No person shall be deemed to be the agent of any person residing outside India unless he has had an opportunity of being heard by the Wealth-tax Officer as to his being treated as such.

(4) Any agent, who, as such, pays any sum under this Act, shall be entitled to recover the sum so paid from the person on whose behalf it is paid or to retain out of any moneys that may be in his possession or may come to him in his capacity as such agent, an amount equal to the sum so paid.

(5) Any agent, or any person who apprehends that he may be assessed as an agent, may retain out of any money payable by him to the person residing outside India on whose behalf he is liable to pay tax (hereinafter in this Section referred to as the principal), a sum equal to his estimated liability under this Section, and in the event of any disagreement between the principal and such agent or person, as to the amount to be so retained, such agent or person may secure from the Wealth-tax Officer a certificate stating the amount to be so retained pending final settlement of the liability, and the certificate so obtained shall be his warrant for retaining that amount.

(6) The amount recoverable from such agent or person at the time of final settlement shall not exceed the amount specified in such certificate, except to the extent to which such agent or person may at such time have in his hands additional assets of the principal.

(7) Notwithstanding anything contained in this Section, any arrears of tax due from a person residing outside India may be recovered also in accordance with the provisions of this Act from any assets of such person which are or may at any time come within India.

CHAPTER -VI : APPEALS, REVISIONS AND REFERENCES

23. Appeal to the Appellate Assistant Commissioner from orders of Wealth-tax Officers.

(1) Any person,—

(a) objecting to the amount of [1][net wealth] determined under this Act; or

(b) objecting to the amount of wealth-tax determined as payable by him under this Act; or

(c) denying his liability to be assessed under this Act; or

(d) objecting to any penalty imposed by the Wealth-tax Officer under Section 15B or Section 18; or

(e) objecting to any order of the Wealth-tax Officer under sub-section (2) of Section 20; or

(f) objecting to any penalty imposed by the Wealth-tax Officer under the provisions of Section 221 of the Income-tax Act as applied under Section 32 for the purposes of wealth-tax;

(g) objecting to any order made by the Wealth-tax Officer under Section 22 treating him as the agent of a person residing outside India; or

(h) objecting to any order of the Wealth-tax Officer under Section 35 having the effect of enhancing the assessment or reducing a refund or refusing to allow the claim made by the assessee under the said Section; or

(ha) objecting to any order of the Valuation Officer under Section 35 having the effect of enhancing the valuation of any asset or refusing to allow the claim made by the assessee under the said Section; or

(i) objecting to an order of the Wealth-tax Officer or Valuation Officer imposing a fine under sub-section (2) of Section 37; may appeal to the Appellate Assistant Commissioner against the assessment or order, as the case may be, in the prescribed form and verified in the prescribed manner.

(2) An appeal shall be presented within thirty days of the receipt of the notice of demand relating to the assessment or penalty objected to, or the date on which any order objected to, is communicated to him, but the Appellate Assistant Commissioner may admit an appeal after the expiration of the period aforesaid if he is satisfied that the appellant had sufficient cause for not presenting the appeal within that period.

(2A) Where a return has been filed by an assessee, no appeal under this Section shall be admitted unless at the time of filing of the appeal he has paid the tax due on the net wealth returned by him:

PROVIDED that, on an application made by the appellant in this behalf, the Appellate Assistant Commissioner may, for any good and sufficient reason to be recorded in writing, exempt him from the operation of the provision of this sub-section.

(3) The Appellate Assistant Commissioner shall fix a day and place for the hearing of the appeal and may, from time to time, adjourn the hearing.

(3A) If the valuation of any asset is objected to in an appeal under clause (a) of sub-section (1), the Appellate Assistant Commissioner shall,—

(a) in a case where such valuation has been made by a Valuation Officer under Section 16A, give such Valuation Officer an opportunity of being heard;

(b) in any other case, on a request being made in this behalf by the Wealth-tax Officer, give an opportunity of being heard to any Valuation Officer nominated for the purpose by the Wealth-tax Officer.

(4) The Appellate Assistant Commissioner may—

(a) at the hearing of an appeal, allow an appellant to go into any ground of appeal not specified in the grounds of appeal;

(b) before disposing of an appeal, make such further inquiry as he thinks fit or cause further inquiry to be made by the Wealth-tax Officer or, as the case may be, the Valuation Officer.

(5) In disposing of an appeal, the Appellate Assistant Commissioner may pass such order as he thinks fit which may include an order enhancing the assessment or penalty:

PROVIDED that no order enhancing the assessment or penalty shall be made unless the person affected thereby has been given a reasonable opportunity of showing cause against such enhancement.

(5A) In disposing of an appeal, the Appellate Assistant Commissioner may consider and decide any matter arising out of the proceedings in which the order appealed against was passed, notwithstanding that such matter was not raised before the Appellate Assistant Commissioner by the appellant.

(5B) The order of the Appellate Assistant Commissioner disposing of the appeal shall be in writing and shall state the points for determination, the decision thereon and the reasons for the decision.

(6) A copy of every order passed by the Appellate Assistant Commissioner under this Section shall be forwarded to the appellant and the Commissioner.

24. Appeal to the Appellate Tribunal from orders of the Appellate Assistant Commissioners.

(1) An assessee objecting to an order passed by the Appellate Assistant Commissioner under Section 18 or Section 18A or Section 23 or sub-section (2) of Section 37, or to an order passed by the Inspecting Assistant Commissioner under Section 18A, may appeal to the Appellate Tribunal within sixty days of the date on which the order is communicated to him.

(2) The Commissioner may, if he is not satisfied as to the correctness of any order passed by an Appellate Assistant Commissioner under Section 23, direct the Wealth-tax Officer to appeal to the Appellate Tribunal against such order, and such appeal may be made at any time before the expiry of sixty days of the date on which the order is communicated to the Commissioner.

(2A) The Wealth-tax Officer or the assessee, as the case may be, on receipt of notice that an appeal against the order of the Appellate Assistant Commissioner has been preferred under sub-section (1) or sub-section (2) by the other party, may, notwithstanding that he may not have appealed against such order or any part thereof, within thirty days of the receipt of the notice, file a memorandum of cross objections, verified in the prescribed manner, against any part of the order of the Appellate Assistant Commissioner and such memorandum shall be disposed of by the Appellate Tribunal as if it were an appeal presented within the time specified in sub-section (1) or sub-section (2).

(3) The Appellate Tribunal may admit an appeal or permit the filing of a memorandum of cross objections after the expiry of the relevant period referred to in sub-section (1) or sub-section (2) or sub-section (2A), if it is satisfied that there was sufficient cause for not presenting it within that period.

(4) An appeal to the Appellate Tribunal shall be in the prescribed form and shall be verified in the prescribed manner and shall, except in the case of an appeal referred to in sub-section (2), be accompanied by [3][a fee of one hundred and twenty-five rupees.

(5) The Appellate Tribunal may, after giving both parties to the appeal an opportunity of being heard, pass such orders thereon as it thinks fit, and any such orders may include an order enhancing the assessment or penalty:

PROVIDED that no order enhancing an assessment or penalty shall be made unless the person affected thereby has been given a reasonable opportunity of showing cause against such enhancement.

(6) (a) Where the appellant object to the valuation of any property, the Appellate Tribunal may, and if the appellant so requires, shall, refer the question of the disputed value to the arbitration of two valuers, one of whom shall be nominated by the appellant and the other by the respondent, and the Tribunal shall, so far as that question is concerned, pass its orders under sub-section (5) conformably to the decision of the valuers:

PROVIDED that—

(i) where the appellant or the respondent does not nominate any valuer within the time specified by the Appellate Tribunal or within such further time as the Appellate Tribunal may allow, the Appellate Tribunal may nominate a valuer on his behalf;

(ii) if there is a difference of opinion between the two valuers, the matter shall be referred to a third valuer nominated by agreement, or failing agreement, by the Appellate Tribunal, and the decision of that valuer on the question of valuation shall be final;

(iii) where any person has at any time expressed any opinion on the valuation of any property to which the provisions of this clause apply, such person shall not be nominated as a valuer in relation to that property.

(b) The valuers to whom a reference under clause (a) has been made by the Appellate Tribunal shall communicate their decision to the Appellate Tribunal within six months of the date of such reference or within such further time as the Tribunal may allow:

PROVIDED that if the decision of the valuers is not communicated within the period aforesaid, the Appellate Tribunal may order that the reference made under this sub-section shall be deemed to be withdrawn and proceed to dispose of the case on the evidence before it, including the report of either of the valuers if any such report has been submitted.

(7) The extent to which the costs of arbitration proceedings (including a case where a reference is deemed to be withdrawn) under sub-section (6) shall be borne by the appellant or the respondent shall be at the discretion of the Appellate Tribunal.

(8) The valuers may, in disposing of any matter referred to them for arbitration under this Section, hold or cause to be held such enquiry as they think fit and after giving the appellant and the respondent an opportunity of being heard, make such decision as they think fit and shall communicate such decision in writing to the Appellate Tribunal.

(8A) The valuers appointed under this Section, while acting as such, shall have all powers of a Civil Court while trying a suit under the Code of

Civil Procedure, 1908 (5 of 1908) in respect of the following matters, namely:—

(i) summoning and enforcing the attendance of any person and examining him on oath;

(9) A copy of every order passed by the Appellate Tribunal under this Section shall be forwarded to the assessee and the Commissioner.

(10) Save as provided in Section 27, any order passed by the Appellate Tribunal on appeal shall be final.

(11) The provisions of [1][sub-sections (1), (4) and (5) of Section 255] of the Income-tax Act shall apply to the Appellate Tribunal in the discharge of its functions under this Act as they apply to it in the discharge of its functions under the Income-tax Act.

25. Powers of Commissioner to revise orders of subordinate authorities.

(1) The Commissioner may, either of his own motion or on application made by an assessee in this behalf, call for the record of any proceeding under this Act in which an order has been passed by any authority subordinate to him, and may make such inquiry, or cause such inquiry to be made, and, subject to the provisions of this Act, pass such order thereon, not being an order prejudicial to the assessee, as the Commissioner thinks fit:

PROVIDED that the Commissioner shall not revise any order under this sub-section in any case —

(a) where an appeal against the order lies to the Appellate Assistant Commissioner or to the Appellate Tribunal, the time within which such appeal can be made has not expired or in the case of an appeal to the Appellate Tribunal the assessee has not waived his right of appeal;

(b) where the order is the subject of an appeal before the Appellate Assistant Commissioner or the Appellate Tribunal;

(c) where the application is made by the assessee for such revision, unless—

(i) the application is accompanied by a fee of twenty-five rupees; and

(ii) the application is made within one year from the date of the order sought to be revised or within such further period as the Commissioner may think fit to allow on being satisfied that the assessee was prevented by sufficient cause from making the application within that period; and

(d) where the order is sought to be revised by the Commissioner of his own motion, if such order is made more than one year previously.

EXPLANATION: For the purposes of this sub-section,—

(a) the Appellate Assistant Commissioner shall be deemed to be an authority subordinate to the Commissioner; and

(b) an order by the Commissioner declining to interfere shall be deemed not to be an order prejudicial to the assessee.

(2) Without prejudice to the provisions contained in sub-section (1), the Commissioner may call for and examine the record of any proceeding under this Act, and if he considers that any order passed therein by a Wealth-tax Officer is erroneous in so far as it is prejudicial to the interests of revenue, he may, after giving the assessee an opportunity of being heard, and after making or causing to be made such inquiry as he deems necessary pass such order thereon as the circumstances of the case justify, including an order enhancing or modifying the assessment or cancelling it and directing a fresh assessment.

(3) No order shall be made under sub-section (2) after the expiry of two years from the date of the order sought to be revised.

(4) Notwithstanding anything contained in sub-section (3), an order in revision under sub-section (2) may be passed at any time in the case of an order which has been passed in consequence of, or to give effect to, any finding or direction contained in an order of the Appellate Tribunal, the High Court or the Supreme Court.

EXPLANATION: In computing the period of limitation for the purposes of sub-section (3), the time taken in giving an opportunity to the assessee to be re-heard under the proviso to Section 39 and any period during which any proceeding under this Section is stayed by an order or injunction of any court shall be excluded.

26. Appeal to the Appellate Tribunal from orders of enhancement by Commissioners.

(1) Any assessee objecting to an order passed by the Commissioner under Section 18 or sub-section (2) of Section 25] may appeal to the Appellate Tribunal within sixty days of the date on which the order is communicated to him.

(2) An appeal to the Appellate Tribunal under sub-section (1) shall be in the prescribed form and shall be verified in the prescribed manner and shall be accompanied by a fee of one hundred and twenty-five rupees.

(3) The provisions of sub-sections (3) and (5) to (10) inclusive of Section 24 shall apply in relation to any appeal under this Section as they apply in relation to any appeal under that Section.

27. Reference to High Court.

(1) The assessee or the Commissioner may, within sixty days of the date upon which he is served with notice of an order under Section 24 or Section 26, by application in the prescribed form, accompanied, where the application is made by the assessee, by a fee of one hundred and twenty-five rupees], require the Appellate Tribunal to refer to the High Court any question of law arising out of such order and, subject to the other provisions contained in this Section, the Appellate Tribunal shall, within one hundred and twenty days of the receipt of such application, draw up a statement of the case and refer it to the High Court.

(2) The Appellate Tribunal may, if it is satisfied that the applicant was prevented by sufficient cause from presenting the application within the period specified

in sub-section (1), allow it to be presented within a further period not exceeding thirty days.

(3) If, on an application made under sub-section (1), the Appellate Tribunal,—

(a) refuses to state a case on the ground that no question of law arises; or

(b) rejects it on the ground that it is time barred; the applicant may, within ninety days from the date on which he is served with a notice of refusal or rejection, as the case may be, apply to the High Court, and the High Court may, if it is not satisfied with the correctness of the decision of the Appellate Tribunal, require the Appellate Tribunal to state the case to the High Court, and on receipt of such requisition the Appellate Tribunal shall state the case:

PROVIDED that, if in any case where the Appellate Tribunal has been required by an assessee to state a case the Appellate Tribunal refuses to do so on the ground that no question of law arises, the assessee may, within thirty days from the date on which he receives notice of refusal to state the case, withdraw his application, and if he does so, the fee paid by him under sub-section (1) shall be refunded to him.

(3A) If, on an application made under this Section the Appellate Tribunal is of the opinion that, on account of a conflict in the decisions of the High Courts in respect of any particular question of law, it is expedient that a reference should be made direct to the Supreme Court, the Appellate Tribunal may draw up a statement of the case and refer it through its President direct to the Supreme Court.

(4) The statement to the High Court or the Supreme Court shall set forth the facts, the determination of the Appellate Tribunal and the question of law which arises out of the case.

(5) If the High Court or the Supreme Court is not satisfied that the case as stated is sufficient to enable it to determine the question of law raised thereby, it may require the Appellate Tribunal to make such modifications therein as it may direct.

(6) The High Court or the Supreme Court, upon hearing any such case, shall decide the question of law raised therein, and in doing so, may, if it thinks fit, alter the form of the question of law and shall deliver judgment thereon containing the ground on which such decision is founded and shall send a copy of the judgment under the seal of the Court and the signature of the Registrar to the Appellate Tribunal and the Appellate Tribunal shall pass such orders as are necessary to dispose of the case conformably to such judgment.

(7) The costs of any reference to the High Court or the Supreme Court which shall not include the fee for making the reference, shall be in the discretion of the Court.

28. Hearing by High Court. When a case has been stated to the High Court under Section 27, it shall be heard by a Bench of not less than two Judges of the High Court and shall be decided in accordance with the opinion of such Judges or of the majority of such Judges, if any:

PROVIDED that where there is no such majority, the Judges shall state the point of law upon which they differ and the case shall then be heard upon that point only by one or more of the Judges of the High Court, and such point shall be decided according to the opinion of the majority of the Judges who have heard the case, including those who first heard it.

29. Appeal to Supreme Court.

(1) An appeal shall lie to the Supreme Court from any judgment of the High Court delivered on a case stated under Section 27 in any case which the High Court certifies as a fit case for appeal to the Supreme Court.

(2) Where the judgment of the High Court is varied or reversed on appeal under this Section, effect shall be given to the order of the Supreme Court in the manner provided in sub-section (6) of Section 27.

(3) The High Court may, on application made to it for the execution of any order of the Supreme Court in respect of any costs awarded by it, transmit the order for execution to any court subordinate to the High Court.

29A. Tax to be paid not withstanding reference, etc. Notwithstanding that a reference has been made to the High Court or the Supreme Court, or an appeal has been preferred to the Supreme Court, wealth-tax shall be payable in accordance with the assessment made in the case.

29B. Definition of High Court. In this Chapter, "High Court"means—

(i) in relation to any State, the High Court of that State;

(ii) in relation to the Union territory of Delhi, the High Court of Delhi;

(iii) in relation to the Union territories of Arunachal Pradesh and Mizoram, the Gauhati High Court (the High Court of Assam, Nagaland, Meghalaya, Manipur and Tripura);

(iv) in relation to the Union territory of Andaman and Nicobar Islands, the High Court at Calcutta;

(v) in relation to the Union territory of Lakshadeep the High Court of Kerala;

(vi) in relation to the Union territories of Dadra and Nagar Haveli and Goa, Daman and Diu, the High Court at Bombay;

(vii) in relation to the Union territory of Pondicherry, the High Court at Madras;

(viii) in relation to the Union territory of Chandigarh, the High Court of Punjab and Haryana.

CHAPTER -VII : PAYMENT AND RECOVERY OF WEALTH-TAX

30. Notice of demand. When any tax, interest, penalty, fine or any other sum is payable in consequence of any order passed under this Act, the Wealth-tax Officer shall serve upon the assessee a notice of demand in the prescribed form specifying the sum so payable.

31. When tax, etc., payable and when assessee deemed in default.

(1) Any amount specified as payable in a notice of demand under Section 30 shall be paid within thirty-five days of the service of the notice at the place and to the person mentioned in the notice:

PROVIDED that, where the Wealth-tax Officer has any reason to believe that it will be detrimental to revenue if the full period of thirty-five days aforesaid is allowed, he may, with the previous approval of the Inspecting Assistant Commissioner, direct that the sum specified in the notice of demand shall be paid within such period being a period less than the period of thirty-five days aforesaid, as may be specified by him in the notice of demand.

(2) If the amount specified in any notice of demand under Section 30 is not paid within the period limited under sub-section (1), the assessee shall be liable to pay simple interest at twelve per cent. per annum from the day commencing after the end of the period mentioned in sub-section (1):

PROVIDED that where as a result of an order under Section 23, or Section 24, or Section 25, or Section 26, or Section 27, or Section 29, or Section 35, the amount on which interest was payable under this Section had been reduced, the interest shall be reduced accordingly and the excess interest paid, if any, shall be refunded.

(3) Without prejudice to the provisions contained in sub-section (2), on an application made by the assessee before the expiry of the due date under sub-section (1), the Wealth-tax Officer may extend the time for payment or allow payment by instalments, subject to such conditions as he may think fit to impose in the circumstances of the case.

(4) If the amount is not paid within the time limited under sub-section (1) or extended under sub-section (3), as the case may be, at the place and to the person mentioned in the said notice, the assessee shall be deemed to be in default.

(5) If in a case where payment by instalments is allowed under sub-section (3), the assessee commits default in paying any one of the instalments within the time fixed under that sub-section, the assessee shall be deemed to be in default as to the whole of the amount then outstanding, and the other instalment or instalments shall be deemed to have been due on the same date as the instalment actually in default.

(6) Where an assessee has presented an appeal under Section 23, the Wealth-tax Officer may, in his discretion, and subject to such conditions, as he may think fit to impose in the circumstances of the case, treat the assessee as not being in default in respect of the amount in dispute in the appeal, even though the time for payment has expired, as long as such appeal remains undisposed of.

(7) Where an assessee has been assessed in respect of assets located in a country outside India, the laws of which prohibit or restrict the remittance of money to India, the Wealth-tax Officer shall not treat the assessee as in default in respect of that part of the tax which is attributable to those assets, and shall continue to treat the assessee as not in default in respect of that part of the tax until the prohibition or restriction of remittance is removed.

32. Mode of recovery. The provisions contained in Sections 221 to 227, 229, 231 and 232 of the Income-tax Act and the Second and Third Schedules to that Act and any rules made thereunder shall, so far as may be, apply as if the said provisions were provisions of this Act and referred to wealth-tax and sums imposed by way of penalty, fine and interest under this Act instead of to Income-tax and sums imposed by way of penalty, fine and interest under that Act and to Wealth-tax Officer and Commissioner of Wealth-tax instead of to Income-tax Officer and Commissioner of Income-tax.

EXPLANATION I: Any reference to Section 173 and sub-section (2) or sub-section (6) or sub-section (7) of Section 220 of the Income-tax Act in the said provisions of that Act or the rules made thereunder shall be construed as references to sub-section (7) of Section 22 and sub-section (2) or sub-section (6) or sub-section (7) of Section 31 of this Act respectively.

EXPLANATION II: The Tax Recovery Commissioner and the Tax Recovery Officer referred to in the Income-tax Act shall be deemed to be the Tax Recovery Commissioner and the Tax Recovery Officer] for the purposes of recovery of wealth-tax and sums imposed by way of penalty, fine and interest under this Act.

33. Liability of transferees of properties in certain cases.

(1) Where by reason of the provisions contained in Section 4, the value of any assets transferred to any of the persons mentioned in that Section have to be included in the net wealth of an individual, the person in whose name such assets stand shall, notwithstanding anything contained in any law to the contrary, be liable, on the service of a notice of demand by the Wealth-tax Officer in this behalf, to pay that portion of the tax assessed on the assessee as is attributable to the value of the asset standing in his name as aforesaid: Provided that where any such asset is held jointly by more than one person, they shall be jointly and severally liable to pay the tax as is attributable to the value of the asset so jointly held.

(2) Where any such person as is referred to in sub-section (1) defaults in making payment of any tax demanded from him, he shall be deemed to be an assessee in default in respect of such sum, and all the provisions of this Act relating to recovery shall apply accordingly.

34. Restrictions on registration of transfers of immovable property in certain cases.

CHAPTER -VIIA : REFUNDS

34A. Refunds.

(1) Where, as a result of any order passed in appeal or other proceeding (including a rectification proceeding) under this Act, refund of any amount becomes due to the assessee, the Wealth-tax Officer shall, except as otherwise provided in this Act, refund the amount to the assessee without his having to make any claim in that behalf.

(2) Where an order giving rise to a refund is the subject matter of an appeal or further proceeding or where any other proceeding under this Act is pending and the Wealth-tax Officer is of the opinion that the grant of the refund is likely to adversely affect the revenue, the Wealth-tax Officer may, with the previous approval of the Commissioner, withhold the refund till such time as the Commissioner may determine.

(3) Where a refund is due to the assessee in pursuance of an order referred to in sub-section (1) and the Wealth-tax Officer does not grant the refund within a period of six months from the date of such order, the Central Government shall pay to the assessee simple interest at twelve percent per annum on the amount of refund due from the date immediately following the expiry of the period of six months aforesaid to the date on which the refund is granted.

(3A) Where the whole or any part of the refund referred to in sub-section (3) is due to the assessee as a result of any amount having been paid by him after the 31st day of March, 1975 in pursuance of any order of assessment or penalty and such amount or any part thereof having been found in appeal or other proceeding under this Act to be in excess of the amount which such assessee is liable to pay as tax or penalty, as the case may be, under this Act, the Central Government shall pay to such assessee simple interest at the rate specified in sub-section (3) on the amount so found to be in excess from the date on which such amount was paid to the date on which the refund is granted:

PROVIDED that, where the amount so found to be in excess was paid in instalments, such interest shall be payable on the amount of each such instalment or any part of such instalment, which was in excess, from the date on which such instalment was paid to the date on which the refund is granted:

PROVIDED FURTHER that no interest under this sub-section shall be payable for a period of one month from the date of the passing of the order in appeal or other proceeding:

PROVIDED ALSO that, where any interest is payable to an assessee under this sub-section, no interest under sub-section (3) shall be payable to him in respect of the amount so found to be in excess.

(4) Where a refund is withheld under the provisions of sub-section (2), the Central Government shall pay interest at the aforesaid rate on the amount of refund ultimately determined to be due as a result of the appeal or further proceeding for the period commencing after the expiry of six months from the date of the order referred to in that sub-section to the date the refund is granted.

(5) Where under any of the provisions of this Act, a refund is found to be due to any person, the Wealth-tax Officer, Appellate Assistant Commissioner or Commissioner, as the case may be, may, in lieu of payment of the refund, set off the amount to be refunded or any part of that amount, against the sum, if any, remaining payable under this Act by the person to whom the refund is due, after giving an intimation in writing to such person of the action proposed to be taken under this Section.

CHAPTER -VIIB : REGISTERED VALUERS

34AA. Appearance by registered valuers. Notwithstanding anything contained in this Act, any assessee who is entitled to or required to attend before any wealth-tax authority or the Appellate Tribunal in connection with any matter relating to the valuation of any asset, except where he is required under this Act to attend in person, may attend by a registered valuer.

34AB. Registration of valuers.

(1) The Board shall maintain a register to be called the Register of Valuers in which shall be entered the names and addresses of persons registered under sub-section (2) as valuers.

(2) Any person who possesses the qualifications prescribed in this behalf may apply to the Board in the prescribed form for being registered as a valuer under this Section:

PROVIDED that different qualification may be prescribed for valuers of different classes of assets.

(3) Every application under sub-section (2) shall be verified in the prescribed manner, shall be accompanied by such fees as may be prescribed and shall contain a declaration to the effect that the applicant will—

(i) make an impartial and true valuation of any asset which he may be required to value;

(ii) furnish a report of such valuation in the prescribed form;

(iii) charge fees at a rate not exceeding the rate or rates prescribed in this behalf;

(iv) not undertake valuation of any asset in which he has a direct or indirect interest.

(4) The report of valuation of any asset by a registered valuer shall be in the prescribed form and be verified in the prescribed manner.

34AC. Restrictions on practice as registered valuer.

(1) No person, either alone or in partnership with any other person, shall practise, describe himself or hold himself out as registered valuer for the purposes of this Act or permit himself to be so described or held out, unless he is registered as a valuer or, as the case may be, unless he and all his partners are so registered under this Chapter.

(2) No company or other body corporate shall practise, describe itself or hold itself out as registered valuers for the purposes of this Act or permit itself to be so described or held out.

34AD. Removal from register of names of valuers and restoration.

(1) The Board may remove the name of any person from the register of valuers where it is satisfied, after giving that person a reasonable opportunity of being heard and after such further inquiry, if any, as it thinks fit to make —

(i) that his name has been entered in the register by error or on account of misrepresentation or suppression of a material fact;

(ii) that he has been convicted of any offence and sentenced to a term of imprisonment or has been guilty of misconduct in his professional capacity which, in the opinion of the Board, renders him unfit to be kept in the register.

(2) The Board may, on application and on sufficient cause being shown, restore to the register the name or any person removed therefrom.

CHAPTER -VIII : MISCELLANEOUS

34B. Transfers to defraud revenue to be void.

(1) Where, during the pendency of any proceeding under this Act or after the completion thereof, but before the service of notice under rule 2 of the Second Schedule to the Income-tax Act as made applicable to this Act by Section 32, any assessee creates a charge on, or parts with (by way of sale, mortgage, gift, exchange or any other mode of transfer whatsoever) the possession of, any of his assets in favour of any other person, such charge or transfer shall be void as against any other person, such charge or transfer shall be void as against any claim in respect of any tax or any other sum payable by the assessee as a result of the completion of the said proceeding or otherwise:

PROVIDED that such charge or transfer shall not be void, if it is made—

(i) for adequate consideration and without notice of the pendency of such proceeding or, as the case may be, without notice of such tax or other sum payable by the assessee; or

(ii) with the previous permission of the Wealth-tax Officer.

(2) This Section applies to cases where the amount of tax or other sum payable or likely to be payable exceeds five thousand rupees and the assets charged or transferred exceed ten thousand rupees in value.

EXPLANATION: In this Section, "assets"means land, building, machinery, plant, shares, securities and fixed deposits in banks to the extent to which any of the assets aforesaid does not form part of the stock in trade of the business of the assessee.

34C. Provisional attachment to protect revenue in certain cases.

(1) Where, during the pendency of any proceeding for the assessment of net wealth or for the assessment or re-assessment of net wealth which has escaped assessment, the Wealth-tax Officer is of the opinion that for the purpose of protecting the interests of the revenue it is necessary so to do, he may, with the previous approval of the Commissioner, by order in writing, attach provisionally any property belonging to the assessee in the manner provided in the Second Schedule to the Income-tax Act as made applicable to this Act by Section 32.

(2) Every such provisional attachment shall cease to have effect after the expiry of a period of six months from the date of the order made under sub-section (1):

PROVIDED that the Commissioner may, for reasons to be recorded in writing, extend the aforesaid period by such further period or periods as he thinks fit, so however, that the total period of extension shall not in any case exceed two years.

35. Rectification of mistakes.

(1) With a view to rectifying any mistake apparent from the record—

(a) the Wealth-tax Officer may amend any order of assessment or of refund or any other order passed by him;

(aa) the Valuation Officer may amend any order passed by him under Section 16A;

(b) the Appellate Assistant Commissioner may amend any order passed by him under Section 18 or under Section 23;

(c) the Commissioner may amend any order passed by him under Section 18 or under Section 25;

(d) the Appellate Tribunal may amend any order passed by it under Section 18 or under Section 24.

(2) Where the amount of tax, penalty or interest determined as a result of the first appeal or revision against the order referred to in sub-clause (iii)' of clause (m) of Section 2 is paid within six months of the date of the order passed in such appeal or revision, the Wealth-tax Officer may, notwithstanding anything to the contrary in this Act, rectify the assessment by allowing a deduction to the extent the tax, penalty or interest so paid stood disallowed therein as if such rectification were rectification of a mistake apparent from the record.

(3) Subject to the other provisions of this Section, the authority concerned—

(a) may make an amendment under sub-section (1) or sub-section (2) of its own motion; and

(b) shall make such amendment for rectifying any such mistake which has been brought to its notice by the assessee, and where the authority concerned is the Valuation Officer or the Appellate Assistant Commissioner or the Appellate Tribunal, by the Wealth-tax Officer also.

(4) An amendment, which has the effect of enhancing an assessment or reducing a refund or otherwise increasing the liability of the assessee, shall not be made under this Section unless the authority concerned has given notice to the assessee of its intention so to do and has allowed the assessee a reasonable opportunity of being heard.

(5) Where an amendment is made under this Section, an order shall be passed in writing by the Wealth-tax authority concerned or the Tribunal, as the case may be.

(6) Where any such amendment has the effect of enhancing the assessment or reducing a refund already made, the Wealth-tax Officer shall serve on the assessee a notice of demand in the prescribed form specifying the sum payable, and such notice of demand shall be deemed to be issued under Section 30 and the provisions of this Act shall apply accordingly.

(6A) Where any amendment made by the Valuation Officer under clause (aa) of sub-section (1) has the effect of enhancing the valuation of any asset, he shall send a copy of his order to the Wealth-tax Officer who shall thereafter proceed to amend the order of assessment in conformity with the order of the Valuation Officer and the provisions of sub-section (6) shall apply accordingly.

(7) No amendment under this Section shall be made after the expiry of four years—

(a) in the case of an amendment under sub-section (2), from the date of the order passed in the first appeal or revision referred to in that sub-section; and

(b) in any other case, from the date of the order sought to be amended.

(7A) Notwithstanding anything contained in sub-section (7), where the valuation of any asset has been enhanced by the Valuation Officer under this Section, the consequential amendment to the order of assessment may be made by the Wealth-tax Officer at any time before the expiry of one year from the date of the order of the Valuation Officer under this Section.

(8) Where any matter has been considered and decided in a profiling by way of an appeal or revision relating to an order referred to in sub-section (1), the authority passing such order may, notwithstanding anything contained in any other law for the time being in force, amend the order under this Section in relation to any matter other than the matter which has been so considered and decided.

35A. Wilful attempt to evade tax, etc.

(1) If a person wilfully attempts in any manner whatsoever to evade any tax, penalty or interest chargeable or imposable under this Act, he shall, without prejudice to any penalty that may be imposable on him under any other provision of this Act, be punishable,—

(i) in a case where the amount sought to be evaded exceeds one hundred thousand rupees, with rigorous imprisonment for a term which shall not be less than six months but which may extend to seven years and with fine;

(ii) in any other case, with rigorous imprisonment for a which shall not be less than three months but which may extend to three years and with fine.

(2) If a person wilfully attempts in any manner whatsoever to evade the payment of any tax, penalty or interest under this Act, he shall, without prejudice to any penalty that may be imposable on him under any other provision of this Act, be punishable with rigorous imprisonment for a term which shall not be less than three months but which may extend to three years and shall, in the discretion of the court, also be liable to fine.

EXPLANATION: For the purposes of this Section, a wilful attempt to evade any tax, penalty or interest chargeable or imposable under this Act or the payment thereof shall include a case where any person -

(a) has in his possession or control any books of account or other documents (being books of account or other documents relevant to any proceeding under this Act) containing a false entry or statement or

(b) makes, or causes to be made, any false entry or statement in such books of account or other documents, or

(c) wilfully omits, or causes to be omitted, any relevant entry or statement in such books of account or other documents, or

(d) causes any other circumstance to exist which will have the effect of enabling such person to evade any tax, penalty or interest chargeable or imposable under this Act or the payment thereof.

35B. Failure to furnish returns of net wealth. If a person wilfully fails to furnish in due time the return of his net wealth which he is required to furnish under sub-section (1) of Section 14 or by notice given under sub-section (2) of Section 14 or under sub-section (1) of Section 17, he shall be punishable —

(i) in a case where the amount of tax, which would have been evaded if the failure had not been discovered, exceeds one hundred thousand rupees, with rigorous imprisonment for a term which shall not be less than six months but which may extend to seven years and with fine;

(ii) in any other case, with rigorous imprisonment for a term which shall not be less than three months but which may extend to three years and with fine: Provided that a person shall not be proceeded against under this Section for failure to furnish in due time the return of net wealth under sub-section (1) of Section 14 —

(i) for any assessment year commencing prior to the 1st day of April, 1975 ; or

(ii) for any assessment year commencing on or after the 1st day of April, 1975, if —

(a) the return is furnished by him before the expiry of the assessment year; or

(b) the tax payable by him on his net wealth determined on regular assessment does not exceed three thousand rupees.

35C. Failure to produce accounts, records, etc. If a person wilfully fails to produce, or cause to be produced, on or before the date specified in any notice under sub-section (4) of Section 16, such accounts, records and documents as are referred to in the notice, he shall be punishable with rigorous imprisonment for a term which may extend to one year or with fine equal to a sum calculated at a rate which shall not be less than four rupees or more than ten rupees for every day during which the default continues, or with both.

35D. False statement in verification, etc. made under certain provisions of the Act. If a person makes a statement in any verification under this Act (other than under Section 34AB) or under any rule made thereunder, or delivers an account or statement which is false, and which he either knows or believes to be false, or does not believe to be true, he shall be punishable —

(i) in a case where the amount of tax which would have been evaded if the statement or account had been accepted as true, exceeds one hundred thousand rupees, with rigorous imprisonment for a term which shall not be less than six months but which may extend to seven years and with fine;

(ii) in any other case, with rigorous imprisonment for a term which shall not be less than three months but which may extend to three years and with fine.

35E. False statement in verification mentioned in Section 34AB. If a person makes a statement in a verification mentioned in Section 34AB which is false, and which he either knows or believes to be false, or does not believe to be true, he shall be punishable with imprisonment for a term which may extend to six months or with fine or with both.

35F. Abetment of false return, etc. If a person abets or induces in any manner another person to make and deliver an account, statement or declaration relating to any net wealth chargeable to tax which is false and which he either knows to be false or does not believe to be true or to commit an offence under sub-section (1) of Section 35A, he shall be punishable :

(i) in a case where the amount of tax, penalty or interest, which would have been evaded, if the declaration, account or statement had been accepted as true, or which is wilfully attempted to be evaded, exceeds one hundred thousand rupees, with rigorous imprisonment for a term which shall not be less than six months but which may extend to seven years and with fine;

(ii) in any other case, with rigorous imprisonment for a term which shall not be less than three months but which may extend to three years and with fine.

35G. Punishment for second and subsequent offences. If any person convicted of an offence under sub-section (1) of Section 35A or Section 35B or Section 35D or Section 35F is again convicted of an offence under any of the aforesaid provisions, he shall be punishable for the second and for every subsequent offence with rigorous imprisonment for a term which shall not be less than six months but which may extend to seven years and with fine.

35H. Offences by Hindu undivided families.

(1) Where an offence under this Act has been committed by a Hindu undivided family, the Karta thereof shall be deemed to be guilty of the offence and shall be liable to be proceeded against and punished accordingly:

PROVIDED that nothing contained in this sub-section shall render the Karta liable to any punishment if he proves that the offence was committed without his knowledge or that he had exercised all due diligence to prevent the commission of such offence.

(2) Notwithstanding anything contained in sub-section (1), where an offence under this Act has been committed by a Hindu undivided family and it is proved that the offence has been committed with the consent or connivance of, or is attributable to any neglect on the part of, any member thereof, such member shall also be deemed to be guilty of that offence and shall be liable to be proceeded against and punished accordingly.

35I. Prosecutions to be at the instance of Commissioner and power of Commissioner to compound offences.

(1) A person shall not be proceeded against for an offence under this Act except at the instance of the Commissioner.

(2) The Commissioner may, either before or after the institution of proceedings, compound any offence under this Act.

35J. Certain offences to be non-cognizable. Notwithstanding anything contained in the Code of Criminal Procedure, 1973, an offence punishable under Section 35A or Section 35B or Section 35D or Section 35F shall be deemed to be non-cognizable within the meaning of that Code.

35K. Bar on prosecutions and on inadmissibility of evidence in certain circumstances.

(1) A person shall not be proceeded against for an offence under Section 35A or Section 35D in relation to the assessment for an assessment year in respect of which the penalty imposed or imposable on him under clause (iii) of sub-section (1) of Section 18 has been reduced or waived by an order under Section 18B.

(2) Where any proceeding for prosecution has been taken against any person under this Act, any statement made or account or other document produced by such person before any of the wealth-tax authorities specified in Sections 8, 9, 10, 10A and 11 shall not be inadmissible as evidence for the purpose of such proceedings merely on the ground that such statement was made or such account or other document was produced in the belief that the penalty imposable would be reduced or waived under Section 18B or that the offence in respect of which such proceeding was taken would be compounded.

35L. Jurisdiction of courts. No court inferior to that of a Metropolitan Magistrate or a Magistrate of the first class shall try any offence under this Act.

35M. Section 360 of the Code of Criminal Procedure, 1973 and the Probation of Offenders Act, 1958, not to apply. Nothing contained in Section 360 of the Code of Criminal Procedure, 1973, or in the Probation of Offenders Act, 1958, shall apply to a person convicted of an offence under this Act unless that person is under eighteen years of age.

35N. Presumption as to books of account, etc., in certain cases.

(1) Where during the course of any search made under Section 37A, any books of account or other documents, articles or things including money have been found in the possession or control of any person and such books of account or other documents are tendered, or such articles or things including money are relied upon, by the prosecution in evidence against such person or against such person and the person referred to in Section 35F for an offence under this Act, the provisions of sub-section (5) of Section 37A shall, so far as may be, apply in relation to such books of account or other documents articles or things including money.

(2) Where—

- (i) any books of account or other documents taken into custody, from the possession or control of any person by any officer or authority under clause (a) or clause (b) of sub-section (1) of Section 37B, are delivered to the requisitioning officer under sub-section (2) of that Section; or
- (ii) any note or inventory of any articles or things including money taken into custody, from the possession of any person, by any officer or authority

under clause (c) of sub-section (1) of Section 37B, is furnished to the requisitioning officer under sub-section (2) of that Section, and such books of account or other documents are tendered, or such note or inventory is relied upon, by the prosecution in evidence against such person or against such person and the person referred to in Section 35F for an offence under this Act, the provisions of sub-section (5) of Section 37A shall, so far as may be, apply in relation to such books of account or other documents or, as the case may be, the articles or things including money, covered by such note or inventory.

36A. Power to tender immunity from prosecution.

(1) The Central Government may, if it is of opinion (the reasons for such opinion being recorded in writing) that with a view to obtaining the evidence of any person appearing to have been directly or indirectly concerned in or privy to the concealment of particulars of net wealth or the evasion of payment of tax on net wealth, it is necessary or expedient so to do, tender to such person immunity from prosecution for any offence under this Act or under the Indian Penal Code (45 of 1860) or under any other Central Act for the time being in force and also from the imposition of any penalty under this Act on condition of his making a full and true disclosure of the whole circumstances relating to the concealment of particulars of net wealth or evasion of payment of tax on net wealth.

(2) A tender of immunity made to, and accepted by, the person concerned shall, to the extent to which the immunity extends, render him immune from prosecution for any offence in respect of which the tender was made or from the imposition of any penalty under this Act.

(3) If it appears to the Central Government that any person to whom immunity has been tendered under this Section has not complied with the condition on which the tender was made or is wilfully concealing anything or is giving false evidence, the Central Government may record a finding to that effect, and thereupon the immunity shall be deemed to have been withdrawn, and any such person may be tried for the offence in respect of which the tender of immunity was made or for any other offence of which he appears to have been guilty in connection with the same matter and shall also become liable to the imposition of any penalty under this Act to which he would otherwise have been liable.

37. Power to take evidence on oath, etc.

(1) The Wealth-tax officer, Valuation Officer, Appellate Assistant Commissioner, Commissioner and the Appellate Tribunal shall, for the purposes of this Act, have the same powers as are vested in a court under the Code of Civil Procedure, 1908 (5 of 1908), when trying a suit in respect of the following matters, namely :

(a) discovery and inspection;

(b) enforcing the attendance of any person, including any officer of a banking company and examining him on oath;

(c) compelling the production of books of account and other documents; and

(d) issuing commissions.

(2) Without prejudice to the provisions of any other law for the time being in force, where a person to whom a summons is issued either to attend to give evidence or produce books of account or other documents at a certain place and time, intentionally omits to attend or produce the books of account or documents at the place or time, the authority empowered to issue such summons may impose upon him such fine not exceeding five hundred rupees, as it thinks fit, and the fine so levied may be recovered in the manner provided in Chapter VII of this Act.

(3) Subject to any rules made in this behalf, any authority referred to in sub-section (1) may impound and retain in its custody for such period as it thinks fit any books of account or other documents produced before it in any proceeding under this Act;

PROVIDED that a Wealth-tax Officer or a Valuation Officer shall not—

(a) impound any books of account or other documents without recording his reasons for so doing, or

(b) retain in his custody any such books or documents for a period exceeding fifteen days (exclusive of holidays) without obtaining the approval of the Commissioner therefor.

(4) Any proceeding under this Act before a wealth-tax authority or the Tribunal shall be deemed to be a judicial proceeding within the meaning of Sections 193 and 228, and for the purposes of Section 196, of the Indian Penal Code. (45 of 1860).

37A. Power of search and seizure.

(1) Where the Director of Inspection or the Commissioner or any such Deputy Director of Inspection or Inspecting Assistant Commissioner as may be empowered in this behalf by the Board, in consequence of information in his possession, has reason to believe that—

(a) any person to whom a notice under sub-section (4) of Section 16 or a summons under Section 37 was issued to produce, or cause to be produced, any books of account or other documents, has omitted or failed to produce, or cause to be produced, such books of account or other documents as required by such notice or summons, or

(b) any person to whom a notice or summons as aforesaid has been or might be issued will not, or would not, produce, or cause to be produced, any books of account or other documents which will be useful for, or relevant to, any proceeding under this Act, or

(c) any person is in possession of any articles or things including money disproportionate to his known assets, particulars of which will be useful for, or relevant to, any proceeding under this Act, then,—

(A) the Director of Inspection or the Commissioner, as the case may be, may authorise any Deputy Director of Inspection, Inspecting Assistant Commissioner, Assistant Director of Inspection or Wealth-tax Officer, or

(B) such Deputy Director of Inspection or Inspecting Assistant Commissioner may authorise any Assistant Director of Inspection or Wealth-tax Officer, (the officer so authorised in all cases being hereafter in this Section referred to as the authorised officer) to—

(i) enter and search any building, place, vessel, vehicle or aircraft where he has reason to suspect that such books of account or other documents, articles or things including money are kept;

(ii) search any person who has got out of, or is about to get into, or is in, the building, place, vessel, vehicle or aircraft, if the authorised officer has reason to suspect that such person has secreted about his person any such books of account or other documents, articles or things including money;

(iii) break open the lock of any door, box, locker, safe, almirah or other receptacle for exercising the powers conferred by clause (i) where the keys thereof are not available;

(iv) seize any such books of account or other documents;

(v) place marks of identification on any such books of account or other documents or make, or cause to be made, extracts or copies therefrom;

(vi) make a note or an inventory of any articles or things including money found which, in his opinion, will be useful for, or relevant to, any proceeding under this Act:

PROVIDED that where any building, place, vessel, vehicle or aircraft referred to in clause (i) is within the area of jurisdiction of any Commissioner but such Commissioner has no jurisdiction over the person referred to in clause (a) or clause (b) or clause (c) of this sub-section, then, notwithstanding anything contained in Section 10, it shall be competent for him to exercise the powers under this sub-section in all cases where he has reason to believe that any delay in getting the authorisation from the Commissioner having jurisdiction over such person may be prejudicial to the interests of the revenue.

(2) Where any Commissioner, in consequence of information in his possession, has reason to suspect that any books of account or other documents, articles or things including money in respect of which an officer has been authorised by the Director of Inspection or Inspecting Assistant Commissioner as may be empowered in this behalf by the Board to take action under clauses (i) to (vi) of sub-section (1) are kept in any building, place, vessel, vehicle or aircraft not mentioned in the authorisation under sub-section (1), such Commissioner

may, notwithstanding anything contained in Section 10, authorise the said officer to take action under any of the clauses aforesaid in respect of such building, place, vessel, vehicle or aircraft.

(3) The authorised officer may requisition the services of any police officer or of any officer of the Central Government, or of both to assist him for all or any of the purposes specified in sub-section (1) or sub-section (2) and it shall be the duty or every such officer to comply with such requisition.

(4) The authorised officer may, during the course of the search or seizure, examine on oath any person who is found to be in possession or control of any books of account or other documents, articles or things including money and any statement made by such person during such examination may thereafter be used in evidence in any proceeding under this Act.

(5) Where any books of account or other documents, articles or things including money are found in the possession or control of any person in the course of a search, it may be presumed that—

   (i) such books of account or other documents, articles or things including money belong to such person;

   (ii) the contents of such books of account or other documents are true; and

   (iii) the signature and every other part of such books of account or other documents which purport to be in the hand-writing of any particular person or which may reasonably be assumed to have been signed by, or to be in the handwriting of, any particular person, are in that person' s handwriting, and in the case of a document stamped, executed or attested, that it was duly stamped and executed or attested by the person by whom it purports to have been so executed or attested.

(6) The books of account or other documents seized under sub-section (1) or sub-section (2) shall not be retained by the authorised officer for a period exceeding one hundred and eighty days from the date of the seizure unless the reasons for retaining the same are recorded by him in writing and the approval of the Commissioner for such retention is obtained:

PROVIDED that the Commissioner shall not authorise the retention of the books of account or other documents for a period exceeding thirty days after all the proceedings under this Act in respect of the years for which the books of account or other documents are relevant are completed.

(7) The person from whose custody any books of account or other documents are seized under sub-section (1) or sub-section (2) may make copies thereof, or take extracts therefrom, in the presence of the authorised officer or any other person empowered by him in this behalf at such place and time as the authorised officer may appoint in this behalf.

(8) Where the authorised officer has no jurisdiction over the person referred to in clause (a) or clause (b) or clause (c) of sub-section (1), the books of account or other documents seized under that sub-section shall be handed over by the

authorised officer to the Wealth-tax Officer having jurisdiction over such person within a period of fifteen days of such seizure and thereupon the powers exercisable by the authorised officer under sub-section (6) or sub-section (7) shall be exercisable by such Wealth-tax Officer.

(9) If a person legally entitled to the books of account or other documents seized under sub-section (1) or sub-section (2) objects for any reason to the approval given by the Commissioner under sub-section (6), he may make an application to the Board stating therein the reasons for such objection and requesting for the return of the books of account or other documents.

(10) On receipt of the application under sub-section (9), the Board may, after giving the applicant an opportunity of being heard, pass such orders thereon as it thinks fit.

(11) The provisions of the Code of Criminal Procedure, 1973 relating to searches shall apply, so far as may be, to searches under this Section.

(12) The Board may make rules in relation to searches or seizure under this Section; and in particular and without prejudice to the generality of the foregoing power, such rules may provide for the procedure to be followed by the authorised officer—

(i) for obtaining ingress into any building, place, vessel, vehicle or aircraft to be searched where free ingress thereto is not available;

(ii) for ensuring the safe custody of any books of account or other documents seized.

37B. Power to requisition books of account, etc.

(1) Where the Director of Inspection or the Commissioner, in consequence of information in his possession, has reason to believe that—

(a) any person to whom a notice under sub-section (4) of Section 16 or a summons under Section 37 was issued to produce, or cause to be produced, any books of account or other documents has omitted or failed to produce, or cause to be produced, such books of account or other documents as required by such notice or summons and the said books of account or other documents have been taken into custody by any officer or authority under any other law for the time being in force, or

(b) any books of account or other documents will be useful for, or relevant to, any proceeding under this Act and any person to whom a notice or summons as aforesaid has been or might be issued will not, or would not, produce or cause to be produced such books of account or other documents on the return of such books of account or other documents by any officer or authority by whom or which such books of account or other documents have been taken into custody under any other law for the time being in force, or

(c) any articles or things including money disproportionate to the known assets of any person, particulars of which will be useful for, or relevant to, any proceeding under this Act, have been taken into custody by any officer or authority, under any other law for the time being in force, from the possession of such person, then, the Director of Inspection or the Commissioner may authorise any Deputy Director of Inspection, Inspecting Assistant Commissioner. Assistant Director of Inspection or Wealth-tax Officer (hereafter in this Section referred to as the requisitioning officer) to require such officer or authority —

(i) in a case falling under clause (a) or clause (b), to deliver such books of account or other documents to the requisitioning officer;

(ii) in a case falling under clause (c), to furnish a note or an inventory of such articles or things including money to the requisitioning officer.

(2) On a requisition being made under sub-section (1),—

(i) in a case falling under clause (a) or clause (b) of that sub-section, the officer or authority referred to therein shall deliver the books of account or other documents to the requisitioning officer either forthwith or when such officer or authority is of the opinion that it is no longer necessary to retain the same in his or its custody;

(ii) in a case falling under clause (c), the officer or authority referred to therein shall furnish the note or inventory to the requisitioning officer within a reasonable period.

(3) Where any books of account or other documents have been delivered to the requisitioning officer, the provisions of sub-sections (5) to (12) (both inclusive) of Section 37A shall, so far as may be, apply as if such books of account or other documents had been seized under sub-section (1) of that Section by the requisitioning officer from the custody of the person referred to in clause (a) or clause (b), as the case may be, of sub-section (1) of this Section and as if for the words "the authorised officer" occurring in any of the aforesaid sub-sections, the words "the requisitioning officer" were substituted.

38. Information, returns and statements. Where, for the purposes of determining the wealth-tax payable by any person, it appears necessary for the Wealth-tax Officer to obtain any statement or information from any, individual, company, firm, Hindu undivided family or other person, the Wealth-tax Officer may serve a notice requiring such individual, company, firm, Hindu undivided family or other person, on or before a date to be therein specified, to furnish such statement or information on the points specified in the notice, and the individual or the principal officer concerned or the manager of the Hindu undivided family, as the case may be, shall, notwithstanding anything in any law to the contrary, be bound to furnish such statement or information to the Wealth-tax Officer:

PROVIDED that no legal practitioner shall be bound to furnish any statement or information under this Section based on any professional communications made to him otherwise than as permitted by Section 126 of the Indian Evidence Act, 1872 (1 of 1872).

38A. Powers of Valuation Officer, etc.

(1) For the purposes of this Act, a Valuation Officer or any overseer, surveyor or assessor authorised by him in this behalf may, subject to any rules made in this behalf and at such reasonable times as may be prescribed —

(a) enter any land within the limits of the area assigned to the Valuation Officer, or

(b) enter any land, building or other place belonging to or occupied by any person in connection with whose assessment a reference has been made Section 16A to the Valuation Officer, or

(c) inspect any asset in respect of which a reference under Section 16A has been made to the Valuation Officer, and require any person in charge of, or in occupation or possession of, such land, building or other place or asset to afford him the necessary facility to survey or inspect such land, building or other place or asset or estimate its value or inspect any books of account, document or record which may be relevant for the valuation of such land, building or other place or asset and gather other particulars relating to such land, building or other place or asset:

PROVIDED that no Valuation Officer, overseer, surveyor or assessor shall enter any building or place referred to in clause (b) or inspect any asset referred to in clause (c) (unless with the consent of the person in charge of, or in occupation or possession of, such building, place or asset) without previously giving to such person at least two days' notice in writing of his intention to do so.

(2) If a person who, under sub-section (1), is required to afford any facility to the Valuation Officer or the overseer, surveyor or assessor, either refuses or evades to afford such facility, the Valuation Officer shall have all the powers under sub-sections (1) and (2) of Section 37 for enforcing compliance of the requirements made."

39. Effect to transfer of authorities on pending proceedings. Whenever in respect of any proceeding under this Act wealth-tax authority ceases to exercise jurisdiction and is successive by another who has and exercises such jurisdiction, the authority so succeeding may continue the proceeding from the stage at which the proceeding was left by his predecessor:

PROVIDED that the assessee concerned may demand that before the proceeding is so continued the previous proceeding or any part thereof be re-opened or that before any order of assessment is passed against him, he be re-heard.

40. Computation of periods of limitation. In computing the period of limitation prescribed for an appeal under this Act or for an application under Section 27, the day on which the order complained of was made and the time requisite for obtaining a copy of such order shall be excluded.

41. Service of notice.

(1) A notice or a requisition under this Act may be served on the person therein named either by post or as if it were a summons issued by a court under the Code of Civil Procedure, 1908 (5 of 1908).

(2) Any such notice or requisition may, in the case of a firm or a Hindu undivided family, be addressed to any member of the firm or to the manager or any adult

male member of the family, and in the case of any other association of persons be addressed to the principal officer thereof.

(3) After a finding of total partition has been recorded by the Wealth-tax Officer under Section 20 in respect of any Hindu family, notices under this Act in respect of the net wealth of the Hindu family shall be served on the person who was the last manager of the Hindu family, or, if such person is dead, then on all surviving adults who were members of the Hindu family immediately before the partition.

42. Prohibition of disclosure of information.

42A. Publication of information respecting assessees.

(1) If the Central Government is of opinion that it is necessary or expedient in the public interest to publish the names of any assessees and any other particulars relating to any proceedings or prosecutions under this Act in respect of such assessees, it may cause to be published such names and particulars in such manner as it thinks fit.

(2) No publication under this Section shall be made in relation to any penalty imposed under this Act until the time for presenting an appeal to the Appellate Assistant Commissioner has expired without an appeal having been presented or the appeal, if presented, has been disposed of."

42B. Disclosure of information respecting assessees. Where a person makes an application to the Commissioner in the prescribed from for any information relating to any assessee in respect of any assessment made under this Act, the Commissioner may, if he is satisfied that it is in the public interest so to do, furnish or cause to be furnished the information asked for in respect of that assessment only and his decision in this behalf shall be final and shall not be called in question in any court of law.

42C. Return of wealth, etc., not to be invalid on certain grounds. No return of wealth, assessment, notice, summons or other proceeding furnished or made or issued or taken or purported to have been furnished or made or issued or taken in pursuance of any of the provisions of this Act shall be invalid or shall be deemed to be invalid merely by reason of any mistake, defect or omission in such return of wealth, assessment, notice, summons or other proceeding if such return of wealth, assessment, notice, summons or other proceeding is in substance and effect in conformity with or according to the intent and purpose of this Act."

43. Bar of jurisdiction. No suit shall lie in any civil court to set aside or modify any assessment made under this Act, and no prosecution, suit or other legal proceeding shall lie against the Government or any officer of the Government for anything in good faith done or intended to be done under this Act.

44. Appearance before wealth-tax authorities by authorised representatives.

(1) Any assessee who is entitled to or required to attend before any Wealth-tax authority or the Appellate Tribunal in connection with any proceeding under this Act, except where he is required under this Act to attend in person, may attend by a person who would be entitled to represent him before any income-

tax authority or the Appellate Tribunal under Section 288 of the Income-tax Act.

(2) Notwithstanding anything in sub-section (1)—

(i) no person who has been convicted of an offence connected with any wealth-tax proceeding or on whom a penalty has been imposed under this Act other than a penalty imposed on him under clause (i) or clause (ii) of sub-section (1) of Section 18 shall be qualified to represent an assessee under sub-section (1) for such time as the Commissioner may be order determine;

(ii) if any person who is not a legal practitioner or a chartered accountant, if found guilty of misconduct in connection with any wealth-tax proceeding by the prescribed authority, the prescribed authority may direct that he shall thenceforth be disqualified to represent an assessee under sub-section (1);

(iii) no person not qualified to represent an assessee under the Indian Income-tax Act, 1922 (11 of 1922), the Estate Duty Act, 1953 (34 of 1953), the Expenditure-tax Act, 1957 (29 of 1957), or the Gift-tax Act, 1958 (18 of 1958), shall be entitled to appear on behalf of any assessee under this Act:

PROVIDED that any order or direction under clause (i) or clause (ii) shall be subject to the following conditions, namely:—

(a) no such order or direction shall be made in respect of any person unless he has been given a reasonable opportunity of being heard;

(b) any person against whom any such order or direction is made may, within one month of the making of the order or direction, appeal to the Board to have the order or direction cancelled; and

(c) no such order or direction shall take effect until the expiration of one month from the making thereof, or, where an appeal has been preferred, until the disposal of the appeal.

44A. Agreement for avoidance or relief of double taxation with respect to wealth-tax. The Central Government may enter into any agreement with the Government of any reciprocating country for the avoidance or relief of double taxation with respect to wealth-tax payable under this Act and under the corresponding law in force in the reciprocating country and may, by notification in the Official Gazette, make such provision as may be necessary for implementing the agreement.

EXPLANATION: The expression "reciprocating country" for the purposes of this Act means any country which the Central Government may, by notification in the Official Gazette, declare to be a reciprocating country.

44B. Countries with which no agreement exists. Where the net wealth of any assessee includes any foreign wealth and he proves that, in respect of such foreign wealth, he has paid in any country, with which there is no reciprocal arrangement under Section 44A for the relief or avoidance of double taxation, a tax in respect of wealth, under the law in force in that country, he shall be entitled to the deduction from the Indian wealth-tax payable by him of a sum calculated on such doubly taxed foreign wealth at the Indian rate of tax or the rate of tax of the said country, whichever is the lower, or at the Indian rate of tax if both the rates are equal.

EXPLANATION. In this Section—

(1) the expression "Indian wealth-tax" means wealth-tax charged in accordance with the provisions of this Act;

(2) the expression "Indian rate of tax" means the rate determined by dividing the amount of Indian wealth-tax after deduction of any relief due under the provisions of this Act but before the deduction of any relief due under this Section by the net wealth;

(3) the expression "rate of tax of the said country" means any tax in respect of wealth, actually paid in the said country, in accordance with the corresponding laws in force in the said country after deduction of all relief due, but before deduction of any relief due in the said country in respect of double taxation, divided by the whole amount of the wealth assessed in the said country;

(4) the expression "foreign wealth" in relation to any assessee means the value of all his assets located in any country outside India as reduced by the value of his debts in that country.

44C. Rounding off of net wealth. The amount of net wealth computed in accordance with the foregoing provisions of this Act shall be rounded off to the nearest multiple of one hundred rupees and, for this purpose, any part of a rupee consisting of paise shall be ignored and thereafter, if such amount contains a part of one hundred rupees, then, if such part is fifty rupees or more, the amount shall be increased to the next higher amount which is a multiple of one hundred and, if such part is less than fifty rupees, the amount shall be reduced to the next lower amount which is a multiple of one hundred; and the amount so rounded off shall be deemed to be the net wealth of the assessee for the purposes of this Act.

44D. Rounding off of tax, etc. The amount of wealth-tax, interest, penalty, fine or any other sum payable, and the amount of refund due, under the provisions of this Act, shall be rounded off to the nearest rupee and, for this purpose, where such amount contains a part of a rupee consisting of paise, then, if such part is fifty paise or more, it shall be increased to one rupee, and if such part is less than fifty paise, it shall be ignored.

45. Act not to apply in certain cases. The provisions of this Act shall not apply to—

(a) a banking company as defined in Section 5 of the Banking Companies Act, 1949 (10 of 1949);

(b) an insurer within the meaning of the Insurance Act, 1938 (4 of 1938);

(c) any company established with the object of financing, whether by way of making loans or advances to, or subscribing to the capital of, private industrial enterprises in India, in any case where the Central Government has made or agreed to make to the company a special advance for the purpose or has guaranteed or agreed to guarantee the payment of moneys borrowed by the company from any institution outside India;

(d) any company established with the object of carrying on an industrial undertaking in India in any case where the company is not formed by the splitting up, or the reconstruction of a business already in existence or by the transfer to a new business of any building, machinery or plant used in a business which was being previously carried on:

PROVIDED that the exemption granted by clause (d) shall apply to any such company as is referred to therein only for a period of five successive assessment years commencing with the assessment year next following the date on which the company is established, which period shall, in the case of a company established before the commencement of this Act, be computed in accordance with this Act from the date of its establishment as if this Act had been in force on and from the date of its establishment;

EXPLANATION. For the purposes of clause (d), "industrial undertaking" means an undertaking engaged in the manufacture, production or processing of goods or articles or in mining or in the generation or distribution of electricity or any other form of power;

(e) any company solely engaged in the business of transporting goods or passengers by ships:

(f) any company registered under Section 25 of the Companies Act, 1956 (1 of 1956).

46. Power to make rules.

(1) The Board may, by notification in the Official Gazette make rules for carrying out the purposes of this Act.

(2) In particular, and without prejudice to the generality of the foregoing power, rules made under this Section may provide for—

(a) the manner in which the market value of any asset may be determined;

(b) the form in which returns under this Act shall be made and the manner in which they shall be verified;

(c) the form in which appeals and applications under this Act may be made, and the manner in which they shall be verified;

(d) the form of any notice of demand under this Act;

(dd) the procedure to be followed in calculating interest payable by assessees or interest payable by the Government to assessees under any provision of this Act, including the rounding off of the period for which such interest is to be calculated in cases where such period includes a fraction of a month, and specifying the circumstances in which and the extent to which petty amounts of interest payable by assessees may be ignored;

(e) the areas for which lists of valuers may be drawn up;

(f) any other matter which has to be, or may be, prescribed for the purposes of this Act.

(3) The powers to make rules conferred by this Section shall on the first occasion of the exercise thereof include the power to give retrospective effect to the rules or any of them from a date not earlier than the date of commencement of this Act.

(4) The Central Government shall cause every rule made under this Act to be laid as soon as may be after it is made before each House of Parliament while it is in session for a total period of thirty days which may be comprised in one session or in two successive sessions, and if before the expiry of the session in which it is so laid or the session immediately following, both Houses agree in making any modification in the rule or both Houses agree that the rule should not be made, the rule shall thereafter have effect only in such modified form or be of no effect, as the case may be, so however, that any such modification or annulment shall be without prejudice to the validity of anything previously done under that rule.

❑❑❑

Bibliography

Acharya, Shankar, "Thirty Years of Tax Reform in India", *Economic and Political Weekly,* Vol. 40, No. 20, May 2005, pp. 2061-2069.

Aggarwal, B.R., "Corporate Taxes and Financial Management", *Indian Journal of Commerce,* Vol. 26, No. 90, 1971, pp. 227-233.

Aggarwal, Manju, *Tax Incentives and Investment Behaviour,* Unpublished Ph. D. Thesis submitted to Delhi School of Economics, Delhi University, 1987.

Ahluwalia, M.S., "Economic Reforms in India Since 1991: Has Gradualism Worked?" The *Journal of Economic Perspectives,* Vol. 16, No. 3, July 2002, pp. 67-88.

Ambiranjan, S., *Taxation of Corporate Income in India,* Asia Publishing House, Bombay, 1961.

American Economic Review, 61, 8-27 and 261-278.

Anand, R., "Prospective versus Retrospective Amendments", *Business Line,* August 2, 2008, p. 9.

Ansari, M.M., "Determinants of Tax Ratio: A Cross-Country Analysis", *Economic and Political weekly,* Vol. 17, No. 25, June 1982, pp. 1035-1042.

Arora, R.S. and Kumar, Rakesh, "Performance of Income Tax Department: An Appraisal", *Indian Management Studies Journal,* Vol. 9, 2005, pp. 133- 148.

Atkinson Anthony B. and Joseph E. Stiglitz. (1976), "The Design of Tax Structure: Direct versus Indirect Taxation." *Journal of Public Economics,* 6, 55-75.

Bagchi, Amaresh & Nicholas, Stern, *Tax Policy and Planning in Developing Countries,* Oxford University Press, Bombay, 1994.

Bagchi, Amaresh, "Inflation and Personal Income Tax", *Economic and Political Weekly,* Vol. 17, No. 17, May 1982, pp. 733-738.

Bagchi, Amaresh, "Recent Initiatives in Enforcement and Trends in Income Tax Revenues – An Appraisal", *Economic and Political Weekly,* Vol. 13, No. 3, January 1988, pp. 89-94.

Baweja D. and Baijal Nitin, "Salaried Need Tax Breather" *Business Line,* 4th July 2009, p. 9.

Becker, Gary S. (1964) *Human Capital.* New-York: National Bureau of Economic Research.

Bhattacharya, Sukumar , "Formalities for Availing Tax Benefits Under The Income Tax Act And Prima Facie Adjustments", *Indian Journal of Accounting,* Vol. 21, No. 4, December 1990, pp. 51-57.

Bird, R.M. and Zolt, E.M., "Technology and Taxation in Developing Countries: From Hand to Mouse", *National Tax Journal,* Vol. 61, No. 4, December 2008, pp. 791-817.

Bishnoi, Usha, *Union Taxes in India,* Chugh Publications, Allahabad, 1980.

Blundell, Richard and Thomas MaCurdy, "Labor Supply: A Review of Alternative Approaches", in O. Ashenfelter and D. Card, eds., *Handbook of Labor Economics,* Volume 3A, 1999.

Boskin, Michael. (1996), *Frontiers of Tax Reform,* Stanford: Hoover Institution Press.

Chakraborty, B., "The Corporate Income Tax - Its Trends and Elasticity", *The Indian Economic Journal,* Vol. 84, No. 4, January-March 1984, pp. 253-260.

Chander, Ramesh, "Issues on Taxation of Income Arising from Impartible Estates", *Taxman,* Vol. 163, No. 42, November 2007, pp. 181-188.

Chattopadhyay, Saumen and Das-Gupta, Arindham, *The Income Tax Compliance Cost of Indian Corporations, National Institute of Public Finance and Policy* , New Delhi, 2002.

Chelliah, R.J. and Rao, K.V., "Rational Ways of Increasing Tax Revenues in India", *Discussion Paper No. 4,* 2002, National Institute of Public Finance and Policy (NIPFP), New Delhi.

Chitale, M.P., "Rationalisation of Personal Income Taxation", *Economic and Political Weekly,* Vol. XIII, Nos. 4 & 5, February 1978, pp. 153-160.

Christiansen, Vidar A., (1984). "Which commodity taxes should supplement the income tax?", *Journal of Public Economics,* 24, 195-220.

Chythanya, K.K., "Special Economic Zone and Tax Incentives" *The Chartered Accountant,* Vol. 55, No. 5, November 2006, pp. 678-686.

Dadibhavi, R.V., "An Achievement of India Tax Reformt", *Yojna,* Vol. 44, No. 2, February 2000, pp. 13-16.

Das Gupta, Arindam and Mookherjee, Dilip, *Incentives and Institutional Reform in Tax Enforcement: An Analysis of Developing Country Experience,* Oxford University Press, New Delhi, 1978.

Das Gupta, Arindam, "Recent Individual Income Tax Reform", *Economic and Political Weekly,* Vol. 41, No. 14, April 2005, pp. 1397-1405.

Das, Geeta, "Penalty in Tax System", *Taxman,* Vol. 165, No. 45, December 2007, pp. 157-160.

Datar P. Arvind, "Why the Code must be shelved", *Business Line,* 8th May 2010, p. 9.

Dhar, Subrata, "Spreading and Deepening The Income Tax Net", *Yojna,* Vol. 45, No. 2, February 2001, pp. 19-26.

Diamond, Peter (1982), "Protection, Trade Adjustment Assistance, and Income Distribution." in Jagdish N. Bhagwati, ed., *Import Competition and Response*, Chicago: The University of Chicago Press.

Diamond, Peter and James Mirrlees (1971), "Optimal Taxation and Public Production."

Dipankor et al., "Relative Tax Performances- Analysis for Selected States in India", *Economic and Political Weekly*, Vol. 37, No. 40, October 2001, pp. 3869-71.

Dixit, Avinash and Victor Norman (1980), *Theory of International Trade*, Cambridge: Cambridge University Press.

Dixit, Avinash and Victor Norman (1986), "Gains from Trade without Lump-Sum Compensation." *Journal of International Economics*, 21, 111-122.

Duggal, Monica, *Corporate Tax Planning*, Published Ph. D. Thesis, RBSA Publishers, Jaipur, 2006.

Feldstein, Martin (1995), "The Effect of Marginal Tax Rates on Taxable Income: A Panel Study of the 1986 Tax Reform Act." *Journal of Political Economy*, 103(3), 551-572.

Foreast, A. and Sheffrin, M.S., "Complexity and Compliance: An Empirical Investigation", *National Tax Journal*, Vol. 40, No.1, March 2002, pp. 75-87.

Freeman, Richard. (1986), "Demand for Education" in O. Ashenfelter and R. Layard (eds.),

Frey, B.S. and Feld, L.P., "Deterrence and Morale in Taxation: An Empirical Analysis", *Cesifo Working Paper No. 760*, August 2002, http:/ssrn.com

Gaba, Tilak Raj, *Computer Usage, Extent, Effectiveness and Resistance in Income Tax Department*, Unpublished Ph. D. Thesis submitted to M. D. University, Rohtak, 1995.

Gandhi, V.P., "The Incidence of Company Tax in India- Suggested Hypothesis", *Artha Vijnana*, Vol. 10, No.1, March 1968, pp. 11-28.

Gandhi, V.P., *Some Aspects of India's Tax Structure- An Economic Analysis*, Vora & Co. Publishers, Bombay, 1970.

Garg, H.R., *Direct Tax Machinery in India – A Critical Evaluation*, Unpublished Ph. D. Thesis submitted to Punjabi University, Patiala, 1981.

Gaur, V.P. and Narang, D.B., *Income Tax Law & Practice*, Kalyani Publishers, New Delhi, 2010.

Godbole, Madhav, "Task Force Reports on Direct and Indirect Taxes: Some Issues", *Economic and Political Weekly*, Vol. 49, No. 49, December 2002, pp. 4884-4890.

Goenka, B.B., *Corporate Tax Planning- A Study of Selected Indian Companies*, Unpublished Thesis submitted to Delhi University, 1983.

Gokhale, Jayant, "Modifications in Provisions of FBT, TDS and Penalties", *The Chartered Accountant*, Vol. 55, No.10, April 2007, pp. 1519-1530. Gopal, M.H., "A realistic Tax Structure for India", *Indian Economic Journal*, Vol. 7, No. 3, January-March 1959, pp. 17-24.

Gruber, Jonathan and Emmanuel Saez, (2000) "The Elasticity of Taxable Income: Evidence and Implications.", NBER Working Paper No. 7512, forthcoming *Journal of Public Economics*.

Guesnerie, Roger (1998), "Peut-on Toujours Redistribuer les Gains `a la Sp´ecialisation et `a l'Echange? Un Retour en Pointill´e sur Ricardo et Heckscher-Ohlin.", *Revue Economique*, 49, 555-79.

Gupta, A.D., "Recent Individual Income Tax Reforms", *Economic and Political Weekly*, Vol. 40, No. 14, April 2005, pp. 1397-1405.

Gupta, S.P., *Statistical Methods*, Sultan Chand & Sons, New Delhi, 2005.

Handbook of Labor Economics, Amsterdam: North-Holland, 3-102.

Handbook of Labor Economics, Amsterdam: North-Holland, 357-386.

Har, Govind, "Minimum Alternate Tax in India", *Asia-Pacific Tax Bulletin*, Vol. 7, No. 3, March 2001, pp. 61-66.

Jain, A.K., "Tax Evasion, Economic Reforms and Corruption in India", *International Tax Review*, Vol. 25, No. 1, January 1997, pp. 18-22.

Jain, A.K., *Direct Taxation in India: Some Aspects*, RBSA Publishers, Jaipur, 2001.

Jha, S.M., *Taxation and Indian Economy*, Deep & Deep Publications, New Delhi, 1990.

Jha, Shikha, "Tax Evasion, Amnesty Schemes and Black Income: Theory, Evidence and Issues", in Parikh, K.S. (ed.), *India Development Report*, Oxford University Press, New Delhi, 1999.

Jhaveri, N.J., "Income Tax Concession and Choice of Financial Assets", *Economic and Political Weekly*, Vol. 7, No. 4, November 1972, pp. 2235-2250.

Joel, Slemrod, *Tax Policy in the Real World*, Cambridge University Press, New Delhi, 1999.

Kantawala, A.S., "Budgets in Post Liberalisation Era: Analysis of Some Provisions of I.T. Act , *Yojana*, Vol. 41, No. 12, December 1997, pp. 20-25.

Kaur, Harjeet, *Taxation and Development Finance in India*, Published Ph. D. Thesis, Classical Publishing Co., New Delhi, 1991.

Kennedy M.J. and Gnanaguru K., "Growth and Sensitivity Analysis of the Indian Tax System", *The ICFAI Journal of Public Finance*, Vol. 6, No. 2, May 2008, pp. 35-43.

Kothari, C.R., Research *Methodology- Methods and Techniques*, New Age International Publishers, New Delhi, 2009.

Krishniah, T., "Role of Taxation in a Developing Economy , *The Indian Economic Journal*, Vol. 23, No. 5, November 1975, pp. 129-134.

Kumar, Nitin, "A Frontier Approach to Income Tax Revenue Efficiency in Selected Indian States", *The ICFAI Journal of Public Finance*, Vol. IV, No. 4, November 2006, pp. 22-37.

Kumar, Vinay, *Tax System in India and Role of Income Tax*, Published Ph. D. Thesis, Deep and Deep Publications, New Delhi, 1988.

Kwatra, Gagan Kumar, "Taxation of Capital Gains: A Comparative Study", *Journal of the Indian Law Institute*, Vol. 30, No. 2, February 1988, pp. 138-164.

Lall, V.D., "Direct Taxes on Individual and Business Income: Economic Implications and Impact", *Economic and Political weekly*, Vol. 17, No. 12, March 1982, pp. 451-458.

Lall, V.D., *Fiscal Incentives and Corporate Tax Planning*, National Institute of Public Finance and Policy, New Delhi, 1983.

Maji, M.M. and Rakshit, D., "Basic Exemption of Taxable Income and Consumer Price Index: An Evaluation at Constant Rupee" *Management Accountant*, Vol. 37, No. 11, November 2002, pp. 829-832.

Maji, M.M. and Rakshit, D., "Taxation of Agricultural Income: Need of the Hour", *Management Accountant*, Vol. 36, No. 8, August 2001, pp. 631-635.

Maji, M.M., *Income Tax and Corporate Growth in India*, Unpublished Ph. D. Thesis submitted to University of Burdwan, West Bengal, 1990.

Manoharan, T.N., "Analysis of Proposals in Finance Bill 2008 Relating to Exemptions, Charitable Institutions and Deductions", *The Chartered Accountant*, Vol. 56, No. 10, April 2008, pp. 1646-1656.

Mehrotra, H.C. and Goyal, S.P., *Income Tax Law & Accounts*, Sahitya Bhawan Publications, Agra, 2009.

Meyer, Bruce and Daniel Rosenbaum (2001), "Welfare, the Earned Income Tax Credit, and the Labor Supply of Single Mothers," *Quarterly Journal of Economics*, 106, 1063-1114.

Mirrlees, James A. (1971), "An Exploration in the Theory of Optimal Income Taxation."

Mishra, B.; *Economics of Taxation- Theory and Application*, Akansha publishing House, New Delhi, 2006.

Mishra, Mayank, "Tax Matrix in Special Economic Zones", *Taxman*, Vol. 163, No. 41, November 2007, pp. 131-140.

Mitra, Sanjeev, "Direct Tax Code- Can It Deal with Corruption Which Ultimately Goes On to Abate Terrorism?" *Economic Times*, 12th December 2009, p. 9.

Mittal, Sujata, *The Impact of Corporate and Personal Income Tax Policy on Saving and Investment Behaviour in India*, Unpublished Ph. D. Thesis submitted to Delhi School of Economics, Delhi University, 1988.

Monsingh, Vasanthi et al., "Tax Policy in India", *Asian Journal of Public Administration*, Vol. 24, No.1, June 2002, pp. 111-138.

Murlidharan, S., "Give Youth A Tax Break", *Business Line*, 4th April 2009, p.9.

Murti, Padamni, *Some Aspects of Income Tax Administration*, Unpublished Ph. D. Thesis submitted to University of Bombay, 1982.

Nahar, Manak Chand, *Impact of Personal Income Tax on Household Savings with Special Reference to Salaried Class*, Unpublished Ph. D. Thesis submitted to Delhi School of Economics, Delhi University, 1994.

Naito, Hisahiro. (1996), "Tariffs and Production Subsidies as Devices to Relax the Incentive Problem of a Progressive Income Tax System.", Research Seminar in International Economics Discussion Paper No. 391, University of Michigan.

Naito, Hisahiro. (1999), "Re-Examination of Uniform Commodity Taxes under a Non- Linear Income Tax System and its Implication for Production Efficiency." *Journal of Public Economics*, 71, 165-188.

Pandey, T.N., "Misapplication of Surcharge and Cess", *Business Line*, 20th June 2009, p. 9.

Parmar, K.N., "Consequences of replacing Section 88 with Section 80C by Finance Act, 2005" *The Chartered Accountant*, Vol. 55, No. 4, October 2006, pp. 537-544.

Pencavel, John. (1986), "Labor Supply of Men." in O. Ashenfelter and R. Layard (eds.),

Piketty, Thomas. (1997), "La Redistribution Fiscale face au Choˆmage." *Revue Fran¸caise d'Economie*, 12(1), 157-201.

Poirson, H., "The Tax System in India: Could Reform Spur Growth?", *IMF Working Paper No. WP/06/93*, April 2006, www.imf.org.

Raikhy, Navjot and Om Prakash, "Tax Structure in India- Post Liberalization Scenario," *PSE Economic Analyst*, Vol. XX, No. 2, 2000, pp. 33-50.

Raj, Sukhwant, *Personal Income Tax in India*, Unpublished M. Phil. Dissertation submitted to Punjab School of Economics, Guru Nanak Dev University, Amritsar, 1990.

Rajaraman, Indira, "Presumption Direct Taxation: Lessons from Experience in Developing countries", *Economic and political Weekly*, Vol. 30, No. 15, May 1995, pp. 887-795.

Ramanujam, T.C.A., "Time to Revisit Dividend Taxation", 31st January 2009, *Business Line*, p. 9.

Ranka, N.M., "Taxation and Ethics", *Current Tax Reporter*, Vol. 21, No.1, January 2009, pp. 63- 65.

Rao, M. Govinda, "Fiscal Adjustment: Rhetoric and Reality", Economic *and Political Weekly*, Vol. 42, No. 13, April 2007, pp. 1252-1257.

Rao, M.G. and Rao, Kavita, "Direct Taxes Code: Need for Greater Reflection", *Economic and Political Weekly*, Vol. 44, No. 37, September 2009, pp. 35-38.

Rao, V.G., *The Responsiveness of Indian Tax System*, Allied Publishers Private Limited, New Delhi, 1979.

Review of Economic studies, 38, 175-208.

Roy, Ajit Kumar, *The Historical Evolution of Corporate Tax in India*, Unpublished Ph. D. Thesis submitted to University of Calcutta, Calcutta, 1977.

Sadka, Efraim (1976), "On Income Distribution, Incentive Effects and Optimal Income Taxation." *Review of Economic Studies*, 43(2), 261-8.

Saez, Emmanuel. (2000a), "Optimal Income Transfer Programs: Intensive Versus Extensive Labor Supply Responses." NBER Working Paper No. 7708, forthcoming *Quarterly Journal of Economics.*

Saez, Emmanuel. (2000b), "The Desirability of Commodity Taxation under Non-Linear Income Taxation and Heterogeneous Tastes." NBER Working Paper No. 8029, forthcoming *Journal of Public Economics.*

Saez, Emmanuel. (2001), "Using Elasticities to Derive Optimal Income Tax Rates.", *Review of Economic Studies*, 68, 205-229.

Sandhu, K.S., *Direct Taxation in India with Special Reference to Taxation of Income*, Dissertation submitted for Master of Science (Hons. School) in Economics to Punjab School of Economics, Guru Nanak Dev University, Amritsar, 1987.

Sarkar, Chitta Ranjan, *Tax Incentives and Economic Growth- an International Comparison*, New Century Publications, New Delhi, 2004.

Sarkar, Sandeep, "Corporate Income and Incidence of Corporate Taxation", *Economic and Political Weekly*, Vol. 32, No. 8, February 1997, pp. 413-416.

Saxena, V.B., *Taxation of Corporate Income in India*, Unpublished Ph. D. Thesis submitted to Rohilakhurd University, Bareilly, 1985.

Seade, Jesus K. (1977), "On the Shape of Optimal Tax Schedules." *Journal of Public Economics*, 7(2), 203-236.

Sen, Raj Kumar, "Taxation Principles during Kautilya s Age" *The Indian Economic Journal*, Vol. 37, No. 4, April-July 1988, pp. 133-138.

Shah, D.S., "Taxation of Dividends in India- A Perspective" *The Chartered Accountant*, Vol. 56, No.10, April 2008, pp. 1668-1672.

Shah, P. S. and Kadakia R. S., *Master Guide to Income Tax Act*, Taxmann Publications, New Delhi, 2010.

Sharma, K.C., "Corporate Tax Policy: Issues and Options", *Economic and Political Weekly*, Vol. 32, No. 8, February 1997, pp. 417-421.

Shome, P., Aggarwal, P.K., and Singh, Kanwaljit, *The System of Tax Deduction at Source: Coverage, Functioning and Suggestions for Reform*, National Institute of Public Finance and Policy, New Delhi, 1996.

Sidhu, A.S., "Direct Tax Reforms in India Post-Liberalisation Scenario", *The Indian Journal of Commerce*, Vol. 56, No. 2 & 3, September 2003, pp. 105-116.

Siegel, Sidney and Castellan, N. John Jr., *Non-Parametric Statistics for the Behavioural Sciences*, McGraw Hill Book Company, Singapore, 2002.

Singh, Jaspal & Sharma, Poonam, "Tax Professionals Perception of the Income Tax System of India an Empirical Evidence", *The ICFAI Journal of Public Finance*, Volume 5, No. 1, February 2007, pp. 45-56.

Singhania, V.K. and Singhania, Kapil, *Direct Taxes Laws & Practice*, Taxmann Publications, New Delhi, 2010.

Sinha, Ajit Kumar, "Individual Taxation and Inflation , *The Indian Economic Journal*, Vol. 42, No. 4, April- July 1994, pp. 24-31.

Spector, David. (1999), "Is it Possible to Redistribute the Gains from Trade Using Income Taxation?", MIT mimeograph.

Sreekantaradhya, B.S., *Structure and Reform of Taxation in India*, Deep and Deep Publication, New Delhi, 2000.

Srivastva, J.N., "Impact of Taxation on Savings in India- A Testing of Please s Hypothesis", *The Indian Economic Journal*, Vol. 41, No. 1, July - September 1993, pp. 18-30.

Stiglitz, Joseph E. (1982), "Self-Selection and Pareto Efficient Taxation." *Journal of Public Economics*, 17, 213-240.

Sudhaman, K.R., "Tax Reforms", *Yojna*, Vol. 50, No. 3, March 2006, pp. 35-37.

Suman, H.N.P.S., *Direct Taxation and Economic Growth*, Sterling Publishers Pvt. Ltd., New Delhi, 1974.

Sundram, K. and Pandit V., "Direct Tax Reform: Family as Tax Entity and other Issues", *Economic and Political Weekly*, Vol. 14, No. 17, April 1979, pp. 776-781.

Suri, M.M., *Taxation in India-1925 to 2007*, New Century Publications, New Delhi, 2007.

Thimmaiah, G., "Taxation and Savings in India: An Empirical Analysis"; *The Indian Economic Journal*, Vol. 23, No. 4, April-July 1975, pp. 51-66.

Torgler, Benno, "Compliance in India: An Empirical Analysis", *The ICFAI Journal of Public Finance*, Vol. 4, No. 2, May 2006, pp. 7-18.

Tuli, Arvind, *Conceptual Clarity on Income Tax & Central Sales Tax*, Kalayani Publishers, New Delhi, 2009.

Tyagi, B.P., *Public Finance*, Jai Parkash Nath & Co., Meerut, 2007.

Upender, M. (2002), "The Effectiveness of the Income Tax Laffer Curve in India", *The Indian Economic Journal*, Vol. 49, No.4, April-July 2002, pp. 74-84.

Verma, D.P.S. and Jain, Indu, "Income Tax A World Turned Upside Down", *Business Standard*, 22nd April 2002, p.10.

Vikas, Vasal, "Direct Tax Code: A Mixed Bag" *Chartered Financial Analyst*, Vol. XV, No. 11, November 2009, pp. 15-17.

Index

C

J

K

L

M

T

U

V

W

Z